DZIGA VERTOV
LIFE AND WORK

Film and Media Studies

Series Editors
ALEXANDER PROKHOROV AND ELENA PROKHOROVA
(College of William and Mary)

Editorial Board

NANCY CONDEE (University of Pittsburgh)

JOSHUA FIRST (University of Mississippi)

HELENA GOSCILO (Ohio State University)

DINA IORDANOVA (University of St. Andrews, Scotland)

MARK LIPOVETSKY (University of Colorado, Boulder)

RIMGAILA SALYS (University of Colorado, Boulder)

DZIGA VERTOV
LIFE AND WORK

Volume 1

1896–1921

JOHN
MACKAY

Library of Congress Cataloging-in-Publication Data

Names: MacKay, John, 1965 July 16-author.

Title: Dziga Vertov: life and work / John MacKay.

Description: Boston: Academic Studies Press, 2018. | Series: Film and media studies | Includes filmography. | Includes bibliographical references and index.

Identifiers: LCCN 2018018548 (print) | LCCN 2018018778 (ebook) | ISBN 9781618116031 (ebook) | ISBN 9781618117342 (hardcover: alk. paper)

Subjects: LCSH: Vertov, Dziga, 1896-1954—Criticism and interpretation.

Classification: LCC PN1998.3.V474 (ebook) | LCC PN1998.3.V474 M33 2018 (print) | DDC 791.4302/33092—dc23

LC record available at https://lccn.loc.gov/2018018548
© Academic Studies Press, 2018
All rights reserved.
ISBN 978-1-61811-734-2 (hardcover)
ISBN 978-1-61811-603-1 (electronic)
ISBN 978-1-64469-011-6 (paper)
Book design by Kryon Publishing Services (P) Ltd.
www.kryonpublishing.com
Published by Academic Studies Press in 2018.
28 Montfern Avenue
Brighton, MA 02135, USA
P: (617)782-6290
F: (857)241-3149
press@academicstudiespress.com
www.academicstudiespress.com

To
CHARLES MUSSER
and in memory of
GEOFFREY H. HARTMAN

Table of Contents

Note on Abbreviations, Transliteration, and Translations		viii
Introduction:	How Did It Begin?	xi
Chapter 1	Province of Universality: David Kaufman before the War (1896–1914)	1
	"The People's Benefit": A.K. Kaufman's Circulating Library in Bialystok	6
	Books, Films and Boisterous, Rich Bialystok	25
	"Be Reasonable!" Student and Worker Politics in Bialystok	36
	What was Adam's Nationality? The Bialystok Pogrom and its Aftermath	46
	David Abelevich Kaufman	58
Chapter 2	Social Immortality: David Kaufman at the Psychoneurological Institute (1914–16)	68
	War, Bekhterev, and the Psychoneurological Institute	70
	Beyond the Institute	84
	1. Connections, Connections	85
	2. A Rational Cinema	98
	3. Energy and Rhythm	106
Chapter 3	The Beating Pulse of Living Life: Musical, Futurist, Nonfiction, and Marxist Matrices (1916–18)	121
	Chuguev, Music, and Interval	125

	After the Revolution: Futurism Early and Late	139
	A Job in *"Khronika"*	157
	Democratic Nonfiction	163
Chapter 4	**Christ among the Herdsmen: From Refugee to Propagandist (1918–22)**	193
	Kino-Nedelia (1918–19): Author, Archive, Détournement, Censorship	193
	1. *Kino-Nedelia,* "*Khronika*," and Early Newsreel	198
	2. Newsreel Metamorphoses	210
	3. Newsreel Matrices	228
	Vertov's Theatrical Origins: The Agit-Trains	233
	1. Agitation and Propaganda	242
	2. An Enormous Front of Destruction	256
	3. A Lure to Gather Any Kind of Meeting	270

Acknowledgments	301
Archives Consulted	307
Filmography	310
Bibliography	319
Index	355

Note on Abbreviations, Transliteration, and Translations

ABBREVIATIONS

Of the names of frequently mentioned archives

GARF: Gosudarstvennyj Arkhiv Rossijskoj Federatsii (State Archive of the Russian Federation). Moscow, Russia.

NIAB: Natsional'nyj Istoricheskij Arkhiv Belarusi (National Historical Archive of Belarus). Grodno, Belarus.

RGAKFD: Rossijskij Gosudarstvennyj Arkhiv Kino-Foto Dokumentov (Russian State Archive of Film and Photo Documents). Krasnogorsk, Russia.

RGALI: Rossijskij Gosudarstvennyj Arkhiv Literatury i Iskusstva (Russian State Archive of Literature and Art). Moscow, Russia.

RGASPI: Rossijskij Gosudarstvennyj Arkhiv Sotsial'no-Politicheskoj Istorii (Russian State Archive of Social-Political History). Moscow, Russia.

TsGIASPb: Tsentral'nyj Gosudarstvennyj Istoricheskij Arkhiv Sankt-Peterburga (Central State Historical Archive of St. Petersburg). St. Petersburg, Russia.

References to materials in Russian archives use the standard abbreviations ("f." (*fond*, archive), "op." (*opis'*, list), "d." (*delo*, file), "l." or "ll." (*list/listy*, page/pages).

Of the titles of frequently cited books

DO: Dziga Vertov, *Dramaturgicheskie opyty* [Dramaturgical experiments], ed. A. S. Deriabin and introduction by V. S. Listov (Moscow: Ejzenshtejn-tsentr, 2004).

DVVS: E. I. Vertova-Svilova and A. L. Vinogradova, eds., *Dziga Vertov v vospominaniiakh sovremennikov* [Dziga Vertov in the recollections of his contemporaries] (Moscow: Iskusstvo, 1976).

KE: Dziga Vertov, *Kino-Eye: The Writings of Dziga Vertov*, ed. and introduction by Annette Michelson, trans. Kevin O'Brien (Berkeley: University of California Press, 1984).

LR: Yuri Tsivian, ed. and introduction, *Lines of Resistance: Dziga Vertov and the Twenties* (Sacile/Pordenone: Le Giornate del Cinema Muto, 2004).

LRK 1: V. Fomin et al., eds., *Letopis' Rossijskogo Kino 1863–1929* [Chronicle of Russian Cinema 1863-1929] (Moscow: Materik, 2004).

SDZ: S. Drobashenko, ed., *Dziga Vertov: Stat'i, dnevniki, zamysly* [Dziga Vertov: Articles, diaries, projects] (Moscow: Iskusstvo, 1966).

SV: Dziga Vertov, *Stat'i i vystupleniia* [Articles and speeches], eds., D. V. Kruzhkova and S. M. Ishevskaia (Moscow: Ejzenshtejn-Tsentr, 2008).

Of the names of Soviet institutions

VFKO: Vserossijskij Foto-Kino Otdel (All-Russia Film and Photo Division).

TRANSLITERATION

In this book, I use a slightly modified version of the GOST 2002 transliteration system for Cyrillic. I depart from the system in my spelling of certain very well-known names (e.g., Trotsky, Mayakovsky).

TRANSLATIONS

For translation help with Hebrew, my thanks to Zohar Rotem; with Italian, to Moira Fradinger; with Polish, to Krystyna Illakowicz and Małgorzata Rejniak; and with Ukrainian, to Constantine Rusanov. Unless otherwise indicated, all translations from foreign languages are my own.

Away with old romance!
Away with novels, plots and plays of foreign courts,
Away with love-verses sugar'd in rhyme, the intrigues,
    amours of idlers,
Fitted for only banquets of the night where dancers
    to late music slide,
The unhealthy pleasures, extravagant dissipations
    of the few,
With perfumes, heat and wine, beneath the dazzling
    chandeliers.
To you ye reverent sane sisters,
I raise a voice for far superber themes for poets and for art,
To exalt the present and the real,
To teach the average man the glory of his daily
    walk and trade,
To sing in songs how exercise and chemical life are never
    to be baffled,
To manual work for each and all, to plough, hoe, dig,
To plant and tend the tree, the berry, vegetables, flowers,
For every man to see to it that he really do something,
    for every woman too;
To use the hammer and the saw, (rip, or cross-cut,)
To cultivate a turn for carpentering, plastering, painting,
To work as a tailor, tailoress, nurse, hostler, porter,
To invent a little, something ingenious, to aid the
    washing, cooking, cleaning,
And hold it no disgrace to take a hand at them themselves.

              **—Walt Whitman, "Song of the
              Exposition" (1871)**

Introduction:
How Did It Begin?

Eleves, I salute you! come forward!
Continue your annotations, continue your questionings.

—Walt Whitman, *"Song of Myself"*

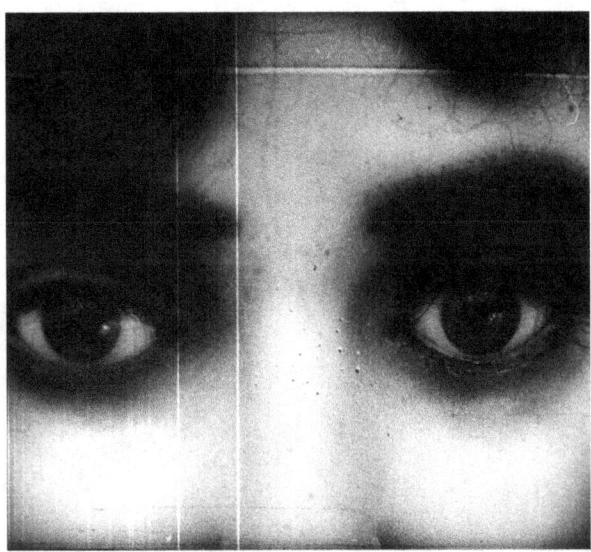

Image 1: From *Man with a Movie Camera* (Dziga Vertov, 1929). Source: Yale University Film Archive.

At first glance, it would seem that, if we were to provide a rigorously Vertovian response to the question of Soviet filmmaker Dziga Vertov's place within the history of cinema, that answer would have to be "virtually none whatsoever." After all, according to Vertov (born David Abelevich [later mutating into Denis Arkadievich] Kaufman in Bialystok, Russian Empire [now Poland], January 15, 1896; died in Moscow, February 12, 1954), what is conventionally designated the history of cinema would more properly be termed the history of cinema's suppression:

> Our eyes see very poorly and very little—and so men conceived of the microscope in order to see invisible phenomena; and they discovered the telescope in order to see and explore distant, unknown worlds. The movie camera was invented in order to penetrate deeper into the visible world, to explore and record visual phenomena, so that we do not forget what happens and what the future must take into account.
>
> But the camera experienced a misfortune. It was invented at a time when there was no single country in which capital was not in power. The bourgeoisie's hellish idea consisted of using the new toy to entertain the masses, or rather to divert the workers' attention from their basic aim: the struggle against their masters. Under the electric narcotic of the movie theaters, the more or less starving proletariat, the jobless, unclenched its iron fist and unwittingly submitted to the corrupting influence of the masters' cinema. The theater is expensive and seats are few. And so the masters force the camera to disseminate theatrical productions that show us how the bourgeoisie love, how they suffer, how they "care for" their workers, and how these higher beings, the aristocracy, differ from lower ones (workers, peasants, etc.)....
>
> The essential thing in theater is acting, and so *every motion picture constructed upon a [script] and acting is a theatrical presentation*, and that is why there are no differences between the productions by directors of different nuances.
>
> All of this, both in whole and in part, applies to theater [including acted films] regardless of its trend and direction, regardless of its relationship to theater as such. *All of this lies outside the genuine purpose of the movie camera—the exploration of the phenomena of life.*[1]

These "completely childlike words" (Vertov's phrase)[2] have been taken as adequate summaries of his basic theoretical position on a number of occasions,

---

1 Dziga Vertov, "Kino-Eye," in *Kino-Eye: The Writings of Dziga Vertov*, ed. and introduction by Annette Michelson, trans. Kevin O'Brien (Berkeley: University of California Press, 1984), 67–69); emphasis in original, translation slightly altered. Hereafter cited as *KE*.

2 The words were evidently addressed orally by Vertov to one of the earliest audiences of *Kino-Eye: Life Caught Unawares* (*Kino-Glaz: Zhizn' Vrasplokh*, 1924), his first major

and indeed they tell us quite a lot about him and his thinking, and not just on the level of content.³ Their deliberately condescending, faux-schoolmasterly tone is but one of the many polemical instruments, ranging from shrill denunciation to subtle, even cryptic onscreen critiques of contemporary film practice, that he used in his long and losing battle against fictional, acted cinema in the Soviet 1920s and 1930s. Even in a time and place of generalized and ferocious contestation over (among other things) what cinema should be, Vertov stood out. Who else, after all, would have openly described his old colleague Lev Kuleshov's more-or-less innocent comedy *The Extraordinary Adventures of Mr. West in the Land of the Bolsheviks* (1924) as "counterrevolutionary" at a meeting of members of the Left Front of the Arts (LEF) (and gotten shouted down for it)?⁴ No doubt, as one critic has noted understatedly, he "must have often alienated even potential allies by seeming intransigent."⁵

Seeming intransigent? Indeed, years later, director Grigorij Kozintsev wondered aloud whether Vertov's apparent injunction to "destroy fiction filmmaking [*khudozhestvennaia kinematografiia*] for its uselessness to the proletariat" was not also a form of "acting" (*igra*); and perhaps suspicions of posturing raised as many hackles back in the day as the injunction did.⁶ He was, as many have noticed, neither wholly consistent nor especially original

---

  feature-length film. "We are still being accused of using incomprehensible slogans. I think that is rather an unwillingness to understand—our program is so simple and clear. But, just in case, I shall repeat it for the thousandth time, in completely childlike words" (Dziga Vertov, "An Introductory Speech before a Showing of the First Part of *Kino-Eye* [13 October 1924]" in Vertov, "An Introductory Speech before a Showing of the First Part of *Kino-Eye*," in *Lines of Resistance: Dziga Vertov and the Twenties*, ed. and introduction by Yuri Tsivian (Sacile/Pordenone: Le Giornate del Cinema Muto, 2004), 99. Hereafter cited as *LR*.

3 For instance, in Guy Hennebelles's contribution to the debate "Pratique Artistique et Lutte Idéologique," *Cahiers du Cinéma* 248 (September 1973), 54; Hennebelle, review of Georges Sadoul's *Dziga Vertov* (1971) and of Vertov's *Articles, journaux, projets* (1972) in *Écran* 13 (1973): 45; and Stephen Crofts and Olivia Rose, "An Essay Towards Man with a Movie Camera," *Screen* 18, no. 1 (Spring 1977): 9.

4 The meeting of January 17, 1925 was convened by poet Vladimir Mayakovsky to bring LEF and various groups with kindred views together under a single organizational rubric (Russian State Archive of Literature and Art [hereafter RGALI] f. 2091, op. 2, d. 194, l. 3; RGALI f. 2852, op. 1, d. 115, l. 35); more about it to come in volume 2.

5 Ernest Larsen, "Kino Revolution [review of *KE*]," *The Independent* 9, no. 8 (October 1986): 12.

6 Kozintsev, *Sobranie sochinenij v piati tomakh*, vol. 4 (Leningrad: Iskusstvo, 1984), 196. Privately (in diary notes), Vertov himself raised the spectre that "Vertov" was a mere role, as we will see in volume 3.

in his anti-theatricalism.[7] Even on the personal level, Vertov befriended and esteemed various artists in the "enemy" fictional camp (like Vsevolod Pudovkin [1893–1953]),[8] while speaking or writing abusively about many others—critic, theorist, memoirist, and screenwriter Viktor Shklovsky (1893–1984), for instance; his own brother, cinematographer and director Mikhail Kaufman (1897–1980); or (perhaps most of all) his rival documentarian Esfir' Shub (1894–1959)—all of whom turned out to be, if not entirely on his side, nonetheless critical supporters and admirers of his nonfictional work.

Mikhail Kaufman noted in the 1970s that much of Vertov's invective and bluster reflected a desire to undo or invert documentary film's perennially secondary status within the cinema galaxy; and this desire, or its militant expression, just as surely congealed into a kind of public role-playing, as Vertov's contrastingly introspective diary notes suggest.[9] As far as antagonism to fiction goes, Kaufman thought (at least in retrospect) that even that apparently unshakable Vertovian principle required qualification as well:

> We had to show that we too were entitled to material resources—the struggle for a place in the sun. But I always felt that there was a certain hypocrisy in going to see feature [fiction] films with great pleasure, delighting in them, to go to the theater, let's say. . . . well, we didn't like anything but opera. That's the truth. And we wanted to reject art.[10]

Scripts might have been the nemesis for Vertov, but it's quite clear that he is constructing a scenario of his own in his fable about cinema's non-realization, one that conforms neatly to the fanciful (or even "childlike") conventions of romance.[11] He gives us the beginning of an adventure story, setting the stage for

---

7   His particular brand of which belongs to what we might call the Rousseau–Tolstoy tradition: see Jonas A. Barish, *The Anti-Theatrical Prejudice* (Berkeley: University of California Press, 1985), 256–74; and chapter 4 and volume 2 of the present work.
8   On Vertov's shock at the death of Pudovkin in 1953 (less than a year before his own), see E. Segal-Marshak, "To, chto sokhranilos' v pamiati," in *Dziga Vertov v vospominaniiakh sovremennikov* [hereafter *DVVS*] (Moscow: Iskusstvo, 1976), 258.
9   "Shy but impulsive" was Ernest Larsen's capsule impression of Vertov's character upon reading *KE* (Larsen, "Kino Revolution," 12).
10 "An Interview with Mikhail Kaufman [conducted by Annette Michelson]," *October* 11 (Winter 1979): 69–70.
11 For more on those conventions, see Northrop Frye, *The Secular Scripture: A Study of the Structure of Romance* (Cambridge, MA: Harvard University Press, 1978); Fredric Jameson, *The Political Unconscious: Narrative as a Socially Symbolic Act* (Ithaca: Cornell University Press, 1981), 89–136, esp. 96–106; and Barbara Fuchs, *Romance* (New York: Routledge, 2004).

the heroic rescue of the imprisoned princess (named "the camera," here surely a synecdoche for cinema as such) by those brash enough to storm the citadel. Cinema, having lost its autonomy and even identity from the get-go, would regain it through the efforts of the "masters of vision"—Vertov and the kinocs ("cinema-eyes," a neologism derived from the Russian *kino* [cinema] + *oco* [an old word for "eye"]), his friends and followers within (for the most part) the professional realm of Soviet nonfiction filmmaking—who would find their own identities, and much more besides, in the process.[12]

Vertov seems to stage something like this rescue operation (or its allegory) about ten minutes into his most famous film, *Man with a Movie Camera* (*Chelovek s kino-apparatom*, 1929).[13] We see two shots of a young woman (though not her face) sitting on, then standing next to a bed, pulling on stockings and stepping into shoes after waking up. Lodged between these two shots, in the kind of apparently unmotivated transition that has already become familiar by this point in the film, we see the eponymous "man with a movie camera" (Kaufman) standing erect with his tripod and camera in a chauffeured truck, rushing at great speed across and then alongside railroad tracks in some prairie-like setting. Here the filmmaker creates a hint, just a hint, of those back-and-forths between rescuer and rescuee (or "alternate syntagmas," as Christian Metz would call them) that D. W. Griffith, a significant influence on Vertov, made so famous. Classically, the heroine requiring melodramatic rescue would be right there, tied to the tracks; here, however, she will be rescued from the comfort of her own home—or so it would appear.

We return to the woman in dorsal view, now plainly standing inside some kind of domestic, apartment-type space—think of the apartment in Abram Room's *Bed and Sofa* (*Tret'ia Meshchanskaia*, 1927), one of the film's crucial intertexts—as she removes her nightgown and puts on her bra and slip. It is a peepshow, in other words, shot (and staged) in quite unobtrusive Hollywood continuity-editing style. A cut back to camera and cameraman shows us Kaufman, all hands and muscly arms and still out of doors, mounting a huge phallic lens on the camera—apparently (by association) energized and engorged by the striptease spectacle—then violently turning it ninety degrees to the right. Could this be a kino-rapist, and not the hero?

---

12 "Kinoks: A Revolution," *KE*, 20. Frye stresses romance's narrative function as radically oriented toward identity, a "self-creation and self-identity that passes beyond all the attached identifications, with society, or belief, or nature" (Frye, *The Secular Scripture*, 186).

13 Here I separate this sub-sequence from what surrounds it, as those who have seen the film will notice.

We might expect an even more detailed peepshow to follow, given this sort of equipment, but we get nothing of the kind. Instead, we find ourselves suddenly ogling from above a young homeless man, also in a state of semi-undress and scratching his armpits, who wakes up rather pleased to find himself being filmed, at least initially. (And he *is* being filmed: intercalated images of the lens and of Kaufman cranking the camera, quasi-reverse shots, keep reminding us of that.) Our vision is then carried, or drifts, to a woman sweeping streetcar tracks soon to be much traversed by traffic, with other homeless sleepers lying like bags in the background; to an older homeless man, one-legged and possibly a war veteran, waking up on a bench and trying to ignore the camera; to a nearly empty city intersection with a big banner hanging above it; and back to the woman in the apartment, now washing up just like (as we will see) the world outside her apartment is.

This sequence and (with it) the opening section of *Man with a Movie Camera* culminate in an allegorical subsequence clearly presaging the film's famous and more compact final emblem of an eye superimposed on a camera lens like the *Oculus Providentiae*. We see the woman's blinking eyes as she becomes accustomed to the morning light; venetian blinds flipping open and shut (or alternating with black) in a visual rhyme; and the camera lens as it brings a patch of lilacs into focus. Human eyes previously closed and contained are turned outwards, with and by the camera, beyond the confines of walls now become porous in any case. Only at this point, as *Man with a Movie Camera* shifts into its second movement, do we move more or less definitively out of the young woman's private space into the myriad, cinematically interconnected spaces of the film, just as the romance narrative also ends and its secret is silently revealed. We spectators, not (or not only) the young woman, were the ones rescued by the cameraman: rescued from another peepshow, or another melodrama, or another domestic comedy; and cinema was rescued along with us.[14]

---

14 My thoughts here have been influenced by Jean-Louis Comolli's great essay on *Man with a Movie Camera*, and particularly by this beautiful passage: "Dazzled by the morning light, the young woman blinks her eyes, her eyelids flicker; she is as though blinded, the world is blurry, overexposed ... [and] one assumes [she endures] some slight pain, a sort of discomfort.... But the eye of the young woman—decidedly human, all too human—perplexed by this bad awakening, receives unforeseen reinforcement. Between the still-dozing world and an eye slow to break into it, Vertov's montage interposes another eye, a mechanical one, the lens of the camera. The focus ring turns, and the eye (of the character [*personnage*], of the spectator, of the camera?) adapts itself to a bush with white blossoms. The blades of the iris open and close again; the eye measures the light. The gaze of the young woman, now inhabited by the machine, accedes to mastery of images. Finally we can see her eyes and even—identification— recognize in them the form of our own" (Jean-Louis Comolli,

Image 2: From *World Without Play* (Leonid Makhnach, 1966). Source: Russian State Archive of Film and Photo Documents (hereafter RGAKFD) 21650.

Or was it (and were we)? Vertov and his cocreators—the latter including, preeminently, his brother Mikhail and his wife, editor, and collaborator Elizaveta Svilova (1900–1975)—evidently did believe, at least through the 1920s, that the kind of experimental nonfiction practice they advocated amounted to nothing less radical than a Communism of film, on an analogy with that truly human history that would commence, according to Marx, once "the prehistory of human society" closed upon the disappearance of bourgeois capitalism.[15] Working in the immediate wake of the October Revolution,

---

"L'avenir de l'homme? Autour de *L'Homme à la caméra*," *Trafic* 15 (1994): 32–33. There may be a recollection in Comolli of a passage in Youri Tsyviane [Yuri Tsivian], "*L'Homme à la caméra* de Dziga Vertov en tant comme texte constructiviste," *La Revue du Cinéma/ Image et Son* 351 (June 1980): 125. See also Judith Mayne's remarks on the sequence in *Kino and the Woman Question: Feminism and Soviet Silent Film* (Columbus, OH: Ohio State University Press, 1989), 176.

15 See Marx's "Preface" to *A Contribution to the Critique of Political Economy* (accessed June 24, 2017 at https://www.marxists.org/archive/marx/works/1859/critique-pol-economy/preface.htm).

they, mainly via their helmsman Vertov, argued that such an approach to film would create new ways for a revolutionary people—which would comprise all people, ultimately—to represent itself to itself, by breaking away from the tropes, templates, types and canons of "art," and indeed from many of the prior limitations set by language and human subjectivity as such, while still generating ultimately legible (if initially obscure), endlessly novel, and sensuously captivating representations of the world in flux, and of changing perceptions of that world.

Noël Burch has noted that Vertov "[alone] among the Soviet masters [. . .] advocated an uncompromising tabula rasa," and that this position generated an array of internal ironies and paradoxes together with the predictable external opposition.[16] What Vertov saw as an opening up to hitherto unexplored possibilities was regarded by others, including many who admired his work, as stubborn asceticism, an unjustifiable jettisoning of slowly amassed formal and expressive resources, and an impoverishing of cinema rather than an enriching.[17] Has the past with all its undoubted squalor really left us with nothing—nothing—that we can use? This seems a burden at least as great as any "anxiety of influence," and evidently weighs much more heavily on our own era than it did on that of Vertov, who has become part of that past for us.[18]

At the same time, perhaps this insistence that everything is still out there to be discovered once the conventional "theatrical" obstructions are removed, and at relatively low cost, is what makes Vertov a perennial favorite of the young—I write as someone who teaches his work often to

---

16 Noël Burch, "Film's Institutional Mode of Representation and the Soviet Response," *October* 11 (Winter 1979): 93. See also Elisabeth Roudinesco and Henri Deluy, "Entretien avec Elisabeth Roudinesco: Dziga Vertov ou le regard interdit," *Action Poétique* 59 (1974): 310.

17 "After all, feature fiction filmmaking had amassed in its arsenal such tried-and-true tools in the struggle for the spectator as the story and plot [*fabula, siuzhet*], whose development the spectator would follow; and the play of actors, with whom the spectator might identify him or herself. Dziga Vertov consciously deprived himself of all of this, relying solely on the power of life itself and on the poetry loaded into the camera's film cassette" (director Sergej Iutkevich, "Pervoprokhodets," *DVVS*, 273).

18 "The new emancipatory politics will no longer be the act of a particular social agent, but an explosive combination of different agents. What unites us is that, in contrast to the classic image of proletarians who have 'nothing to lose but their chains,' we are in danger of losing everything" (Slavoj Žižek, "How to Begin from the Beginning," *New Left Review* [new series] 57 (May–June 2009): 55. See also Wolfgang Streeck, "The Post-Capitalist Interregnum," *Juncture* 23, no. 2 (2016): 68–77.

undergraduates—in the way he passes cinema on as something for *them* to create, endlessly. We know from an April 1953 issue of *Cahiers du Cinéma* that a rare screening of *Man with a Movie Camera* blew the minds of a crowd of young cine-club members at Paris's Cinémathèque Française on February 28 of that year, just five days before Joseph Stalin died. (Vertov, too, was still alive, unbeknownst to them apparently, and would miserably languish in Moscow for nearly another year.) The film seems to have elicited not only extraordinarily insightful remarks—after just one screening, and of *this* film!—but instances of devotion as well.[19] In a brief memoir of encounters and (mostly) missed encounters with *Man with a Movie Camera* between 1953 and 2001, the publisher, editor, and (like Mikhail Kaufman) ogler Ben Sonnenberg gave us evidence of this:

> *Paris, April 1953.* Flirted with a pretty French girl outside the Cinémathèque. Twenty or maybe twenty-one, three or four years older than me. Grey eyes, black brows, short skirt, good legs. She said, "Aimez-vous Dziga Vertov?" I answered truthfully, "Vertov? Connais pas." Exit pretty French girl. Drat. Should have said, "Vertov? Je l'*adore!*"[20]

Even then, Vertov, the "OG [Original Gangster] weirdo" as one contemporary enthusiast has called him, was cool.[21]

At the Cinémathèque Française, at least. Vertov and Svilova would have been surprised by the adoration, to put it mildly; or perhaps (in Vertov's case) too numbed by this time to even notice. Increasingly deprived of opportunities for creative work starting in the late 1930s, he had already told at least one

---

19 "Tribune de F.F.C.C.: le debat est ouvert sur 'L'Homme à la Caméra,'" *Cahiers du Cinéma* IV, no. 22 (April 1953): 36–40. From what I can tell, this is the sole transcript of a cine-club discussion to have appeared in *Cahiers*, at least during the 1950s. The transcript was translated in part by John Shepley as "*Cahiers Du Cinéma*: Open Debate" and included in the excellent program notes (preserved at Anthology Film Archives in New York) for the April–May 1984 "Dziga Vertov Revisited" retrospective at New York's Public Theater and Collective for Living Cinema. The discussion ought to be made available in English in full; I will refer to it later in these pages.
20 Ben Sonnenberg, "From the Diary of a Movie Buff," *Raritan* 21, no. 2 (2001): 1.
21 Nicole Disser, "Relive the Indie Film Forum That Brought Us *Heavy Metal Parking Lot* and *Penis Puppets*," *Bedford + Bowery* (June 24, 2016): accessed on September 12, 2016, http://bedfordandbowery.com/2016/06/relive-the-indie-film-forum-that-brought-us-heavy-metal-parking-lot-and-penis-puppets/.

interlocutor, probably around 1953 and "with a barely detectable touch of humor," that "Dziga Vertov was dead," no less.[22] Indeed, for many years, but especially post-1935, he had often referred to "Vertov" in the third person, like an ego-ideal who had done much in cinema but had to be projected outward, protected by personification. If "Vertov" was mainly the bearer of a roster of achievements by that time, it seems that in the 1920s—yes, the self-reflection began that early—"Vertov" or his equivalent had stood in for a kind of pure possibility.

In one of his first published articles (September 1922), for instance—entitled "He and I," and significantly not included in the widely disseminated Soviet collection of his articles from 1966[23]—Vertov described, with unusual public frankness, his frustrations with work at the All-Russia Photo-Film Division (where he was already embarked on the *Kino-Pravda* series) via the observations of one alter ego ("I") looking at another ("He"):

> Every day he shows up at work... intending to spend the day in unceasing, rhythmical labor.
>
> I see, regretfully, how his persistence resembles that of a sledgehammer swinging through the air, not noticing that the anvil's been taken away.
>
> The gear is turning.... But why should it, if it can't connect with other gears, if it can't turn the wheels of the machine?
>
> [....]
>
> ... He spoke to me about his impossible work conditions. No transport. No money.
>
> [.....]
>
> As far as shooting political [topics] is concerned, the situation is absurd. They [i.e., the authorities] demand it and forbid it at the same time. Which means: you have to film [political events], but we'll oppose the shooting with all our strength. You'll set up your lights, we'll take them away immediately; you'll catch up to us in corridors and on the street, and we'll wave you away with our hands and turn our backs to the camera. Dull incomprehension of the importance of film on political topics.

---

22 The interlocutor was Leonid Braslavskij, soon to become a prolific writer of scripts for documentaries (L. Braslavskij, "Istoriia odnogo zhurnala," *DVVS*, 236).

23 Dziga Vertov, *Stat'i, dnevniki, zamysly*, ed. S. Drobashenko (Moscow: Iskusstvo, 1966); henceforth *SDZ*. This edition is the basis for virtually all later translated collections of Vertov's writings; aspects of its circulation and presentation of the texts will be discussed below.

[.....]
Every day he returns home tired and in a bad mood, disgusted by the results of his work—yet the next day, somehow reassured, he goes off to pointlessly twirl his propeller in airless space.

"Air! Air!"

He envies me, of course, as I stride from factory to factory with physics and geometry in my hands, indifferent to the fate of *Kino-Pravda* and the All-Russia Photo and Film Division. He envies me, breathing heavily alongside a locomotive, enthusiast of driving belts, pressing a shuddering ampere-meter to my heart.

I've split in two.

It was the only solution. He wanted to work no matter what. Badly, absurdly, but still work. He couldn't just work on his own, with his own sensations and calculations, as I do.

I remained alone with my sensation of world movement, with eyes that serve as camera and film, fixing on my retina only the movements that I need.

I remained alone with pencil and paper, with my attempts to notate the film-études growing in the convolutions of my brain, alone, inebriated by my searches and somersaults into the souls of machines.[24]

In its reflexivity, the article almost reads like a script for a very different—more confessional, more pathos-laden—version of *Man with a Movie Camera*. One (or, at least, his biographer) wishes Vertov had appended names to the alter egos: do we have here the free radical "Dziga Vertov" observing the diligent, downtrodden "D. A. Vertov," the former the author of flamboyant kino-Futurist manifesta, the latter the morose signatory of innumerable bureaucratic documents? Probably most adults feel this way about their lives—a small oasis of dreams evaporating slowly or quickly in the midst of vast plains of dour scraping, scrounging, and scheduling—but it is notable that Vertov made such an

---

24 "On i ia," in Dziga Vertov, *Stat'i i vystupleniia* [hereafter *SV*], ed. D. V. Kruzhkova and S. M. Ishevskaia (Moscow: Ejzenshtejn-Tsentr, 2008), 18–20. The article first appeared in *Kino-Fot* 2 (September 8–15, 1922): 9–10, and was included (as "Er und ich") in the first large German collection of Vertov's writings, which incorporates a few pieces not in *SDZ* (Dsiga Wertow [Dziga Vertov], *Aufsätze, Tagebücher, Skizzen*, ed. and trans. Hermann Herlinghaus and Rolf Liebmann (East Berlin: Institut für Filmwissenschaft an der Deutschen Hochschule für Filmkunst, 1967), 60–65. A major absence from *SDZ* to which I will again refer, I expect to see it in what promises to be the most exciting edition of translated writings by Vertov in many years: *L'Oeil de la Révolution: Écrits sur le cinéma*, eds. François Albera, Antonio Somaini, and Irina Tcherneva (Paris: Les Presses du Réel, forthcoming).

early and conscious *internal* differentiation (he was only twenty-six) between a giddy longing for creative exploration on one hand, and entanglement in the viscous realities of money and regulations on the other. The contrast was analogous, to be sure, to his distinction between the "corrupting influence of the masters' cinema" and "the genuine purpose of the movie camera." We will see him making it again, over and over, particularly during his long post-1935 slide downwards.

Not the least problem with the tabula rasa is that it can't provide the material supports (film, cameras, labs, professionals, etc.) one needs in order to actually make films and not remain "alone with pencil and paper"; and with the ambiguous exception of a relatively brief but important period (from around mid-1924 through early 1925) to be discussed much later on, Vertov never really wanted to strip cinema clean of *authorship* as a value, either, even if it was a value he often seemed to ascribe to collective rather than individual practice. In his own lifetime, he constantly insisted on his own paternity vis-à-vis the entire later history of Soviet nonfiction film; was both profoundly flattered by the attention his films received and intensely anxious about others stealing his work or ideas; and would take all opportunities not only to promote his work but also to exaggerate his importance (as when he groundlessly claimed, as others did and do, that the "Camera Eye" and "Newsreel" sections of John Dos Passos's "USA Trilogy" were written under his influence).[25] Vertov's face accordingly became a famous

---

25 For some of his early (ca. January 1925) claims about the popularity of "Kino-Eye" as a slogan, see *SV*, 69. For his claims about Dos Passos, see RGALI f. 2091, op. 2, d. 241, l. 51 (from a 1932 notebook); *SV*, 322, 358, 363, 384, 442, 447 (all references from the 1940s). There is no even moderately persuasive evidence that Dos Passos so much as heard of Vertov or his work, although the novelist evidently met some filmmakers and saw some Soviet films when he visited the USSR in 1928, and was certainly interested in montage strategies of representation. "Newsreels" were standard fare in movie houses around the world during this time, of course, and "camera eye" (not "Kino-Eye" in any case) was an English-language commonplace in some variant or another at least since William Henry Fox Talbot in 1844 (e.g., the section "Plate VIII: A Scene in a Library," in Fox Talbot's *The Pencil of Nature*, introduction by Beaumont Newhall (New York: Da Capo Press, 1969); see also George Dawson's *Manual of Photography* (London: J & A Churchill, 1873), 90; "Canada Through the Camera's Eye," *American Amateur Photographer* 4 (1892): 135–41; and scores of other examples): the copresence of these rubrics in the novels proves nothing. Dos Passos's "Camera Eye" sections are, moreover, overwhelmingly subjective, stream-of-consciousness-type representations rather than anything readily derivable from Vertov's films or theories. In the original 1931 translation by Valentin Stenich of *The 42nd Parallel*, "Camera Eye" was in fact translated as "Camera Obscura," and "Newsreel" as "News of the Day" rather than the more Vertovian "*khronika*" (*42-ia parallel'*, trans.

Introduction: How Did It Begin? **xxiii**

one in the Soviet film press of the 1920s, and one glamor shot occupied a full page in *Soviet Screen*'s "gallery of film artists" series in 1926 (Hollywood star Norma Talmadge succeeded him in the next issue).[26] From a certain perspective, of course, his very retention of authorial identity and distinction—as the most "revolutionary" of post-1917 directors—constitutes Vertov's greatest counterrevolutionary betrayal, although it didn't really strike many people that way in the 1920s, it seems.

When he split himself into "He and I" in 1922, Vertov had no idea that he would be posing for that portrait four years later, and less idea of how much time he would end up spending "twirling his propeller in airless space." By the time he died of stomach cancer in February 1954 at age fifty-eight, he had not made a film (other than a few newsreels) that received even minimally significant distribution since the fraught *Lullaby* (*Kolybel'naia*, 1937), and arguably no creatively satisfying work since *Three Songs of Lenin* (*Tri Pesni o Lenine*, 1934) from two decades before. Indeed, he had made few films since 1934 at all, and bitter creative frustration alongside worsening health, probable but never publicly expressed grief over the deaths of his parents and other relatives in the Holocaust, and shock at being openly pilloried in 1949 during the anti-Semitic "anti-cosmopolitan" campaign of the late Stalin era, all combined to make his last years (in his words, often repeated) a "torment."

A significant and controversial figure in world cinema by around 1934 as well—though never nearly as prominent as his great rival Sergej Eisenstein (1898–1948)—Vertov was only dimly recalled by film writers and enthusiasts outside the USSR by the mid-1950s, making events like the February '53 Cinémathèque screening of *Man with a Movie Camera* most exceptional.[27]

V. Stenich (Leningrad: Khudozhestvennaia Literatura, 1931). This has not prevented scholars from repeating Vertov's claim of direct influence (though he doubtless got the idea from someone else): see among many others D. Mirskij, "Dos-Passos, sovetskaia literatura i zapad," *Literaturnyj Kritik* 1 (June 1933): 111–126, esp. 119; David Kadlec, "Early Soviet Cinema and American Poetry," *Modernism/modernity* 11, no. 2 (April 2004): 299–331, esp. 307–9 and 327; and Hans Günther, "Soviet Literary Criticism and the Formulation of the Aesthetics of Socialist Realism, 1932–1940," in *A History of Russian Literary Theory and Criticism: The Soviet Era and Beyond*, ed. Galin Tihanov and Evgeny Dobrenko (Pittsburgh: University of Pittsburgh Press, 2011), 90–108, esp. 98–99. To be sure, Dos Passos's work played an important role in discussions about realism/montage in the early 1930 relevant to Vertov's work as well; we will turn to those in volume 3.

26 "Dziga Vertov [photo]," *Sovetskij Ekran* 28 (July 13, 1926): 11. Roman Navarro was on the cover. For Talmadge, *Sovetskij Ekran* 29 (July 20, 1926): 11.
27 As those in attendance knew: one of the presenters that evening at the Cinémathèque described the film as "celebrated and almost never seen" ("Tribune de F.F.C.C.," *Cahiers*, 36).

His remaining family members, all in foreign lands except for Kaufman and Svilova, had no notion of his tribulations either. In New York, Vertov's youngest brother, the great cinematographer Boris Kaufman (1903–80), evidently heard nothing from him after November 1947 when they were still corresponding about the fate of their family during the war; in Israel, his much-loved aunt Masha Gal'pern (1883–1970) found out about his death in the April 1957 issue *Art of Cinema (Iskusstvo Kino)*, where the first Soviet-edited selection of his writings also appeared.[28] Those foreign family ties, best left unmentioned especially during the late Stalin years, demarcated yet another split in Vertov's identity: documentary filmmaker Semiramida (Seda) Pumpyanskaya (1916–2014), who knew Vertov well during the last twelve years of his life, told me he never said a word about any brother abroad.[29]

Obviously, many people suffered far more under the Soviet regime (and other regimes) than Dziga Vertov did. He certainly wanted and tried to fit in, above all because he wanted to make films. Still, it is difficult to disagree with Andrej Shcherbenok's general observation that with the exception of Vertov, "practically all notable Soviet directors of the 1920s continued to work [despite many frustrations] more or less fruitfully in the 1930s and '40s."[30] Indeed, incessant self-comparison with apparently more richly rewarded rivals constantly stoked the pyre of Vertov's sufferings, as we will see.

---

28 Dziga Vertov, "Iz rabochikh tetradej Dzigi Vertova," *Iskusstvo Kino* 4 (April 1957): 112–126; Boris Kaufman Papers, Beinecke Library, Yale University, GEN MSS 562.14.282. With the exception of a small script treatment published in a local newspaper, "Iz rabochikh tetradej" was the first piece of Vertov's writing to have appeared in the USSR since 1940. From Israel, Masha in July 1958 wrote to the editors of *Art of Cinema*—the oldest, most prestigious of Soviet film journals—looking for more details about her nephew; I do not know if they replied (RGALI f. 2912, op. 1, d. 63, l. 1). For Boris's part, he and his wife Lena read Nikolaj Abramov's 1962 study as well as (it seems) *SDZ* sometime before 1974, where they learned of Vertov's decline: "What a pity that his last years were so difficult and unproductive, through no fault of his own. My heart tightened when I read those extracts from his diary" (from a letter of June 1974 to Mikhail Kaufman; RGALI f. 2986, op. 1, d. 105, ll. 11–13).
29 Interview with Pumpyanskaya, November 20, 2006.
30 Andrej Shcherbenok, "Dziga Vertov: dialektika kinoveshchi," *Iskusstvo Kino* 1 (January 2012): 77. This would certainly go for Pudovkin, Abram Room, Iakov Protazanov, Boris Barnet, and indeed (relative to Vertov) Eisenstein. Shub and Kuleshov might be his nearest rivals in misfortune. Jay Leyda noted that "of all the original creators who had helped shape the modern Soviet film, the only ones not properly employed [in the immediate pre–World War II period]" were Kuleshov, who was busy teaching; Kozintsev and Leonid Trauberg, "bogged down in the commendable but tortuous task of a [never-produced] scenario about Karl Marx's life"; and "Vertov, whose later difficulties I have never understood" (*Kino: A History of the Russian and Soviet Film* [London: George Allen & Unwin, 1960], 355).

Introduction: How Did It Begin?   xxv

Documentary director and cinematographer Marina Goldovskaya, who grew up in the same special apartment building for "cinema workers" at Bol'shaia Polianka Street 28 in Moscow where Vertov and Svilova lived, recalled her encounters with his already spectral presence (she was but thirteen when he died):

> He used to sit on a bench near our entryway, always leaning on a walking stick, always gloomy and reserved. He seemed hopelessly ancient to me. . . . Seda Pumpyanskaya, who worked with him, told me that when they found out he had cancer (he wasn't told, although he knew he was very sick), he was given sick leave. He said, "No more than three months. Otherwise, I'll get fired."
>
> Exactly three months later, he came back to work, spent a few days, and went back to bed. But he had to work; otherwise he would starve.[31]

Perhaps the most striking thing about recollections of Vertov published during the Soviet period is their similar emphasis on the misery of Vertov's last years, setting a tone strikingly at odds with the official optimism typical of the time.[32] (Stalin-era studio bureaucrats are sometimes blamed, and we will discuss the wider implications of this censure later on.) In particular, the various drafts of Svilova's late memoir suggest, perhaps not surprisingly, that a great deal of bitterness lingered behind the sincere shows of sympathy and regret.

In its final, published version, Svilova—a woman from the working class, known for her bluntness, who began working as a film cutter before the age of fifteen—begins brightly and lyrically enough:

---

31 Marina Goldovskaya, *Woman with a Movie Camera: My Life as a Russian Filmmaker*, trans. Antonina W. Bouis, introduction by Robert Rosen (Austin: University of Texas Press, 2006), 24–25. Many other well-known names in Soviet cinema lived in the building, including Aleksandr Medvedkin, Roman Karmen, Mikhail Romm, Yuli Raizman, Grigorij Roshal', Efim Dzigan, Aleksandr Ptushko, Arsha Ovanesova, and Yakov Posel'skij. Posel'skij, a major nonfiction director, was pilloried alongside Vertov in March 1949. Goldovskaya's father Evsej (1903–71) was an important innovator in Soviet filmmaking technology who long taught at VGIK (the Higher State Institute of Cinema).

32 For instance, see (in *DVVS*) the memoirs of Mikhail Kaufman (77, 78); theater critic Natal'ia Arkina (234); writer and Vertov collaborator Elena Segal-Marshak (240–51, 261); writer and friend Evgeniia Dejch (242–44); and director and administrator Sergej Iutkevich (272). "Founder of a school of documentary cinema that has achieved world renown," wrote Lev Kuleshov, "that talented person saw little joy in his life" (cited in E. Gromov, *Lev Vladimirovich Kuleshov* (Moscow: Iskusstvo, 1984), 70). See also Esfir' Shub, *Krupnym planom* (Moscow: Iskusstvo, 1959), 81.

> My memory of Vertov is shot through ... not only with his films and manuscripts but also the corridors of the studios where we worked, the streets along which we walked, and even that Moscow morning air that was so easy to breathe after a sleepless night at the montage table.[33]

But her initial drafts of this reminiscence, far more accusatory in tone if also dotted with signs of incredulity at Vertov's fate (she frequently punctuates the text with "why?") commence with the words:

> It is difficult and painful for me to write about Dziga. . . .
>
> He was stern and forthright in everything. He was never hypocritical, never curried favor with anyone, and always spoke his mind directly. (Not everyone liked that.)

Vertov had consigned a great many of Vladimir Mayakovsky's poems to memory, and Svilova knew that these lines, written a year before the Futurist poet's suicide in 1930, became particular favorites as the years went by:

> One gets tired
> of having to answer abuse with abuse, blow with blow.
> Without you [Lenin], many
> Have gotten out of hand.
>
> All sorts of
> scoundrels
> wander our land
> and around it.[34]

In the drafts, Svilova's reproaches openly extended to other cinema workers, none of whom, when the fate of *Three Songs of Lenin*'s release was being decided in 1934, "encouraged him or said a single soothing word, which he very much needed; that would have given him strength." At the time Vertov gave Svilova some verses of his own, expressing how he was feeling:

> With images, songs,
> Music, verses,

---

33 E. I. Vertova-Svilova, "Pamiat' o Vertove," *DVVS*, 65.
34 From "Conversation with Comrade Lenin" (1929). RGALI f. 2091, op. 2, d. 486, l. 92.

> I heave from my throat
>> A lump of mold.³⁵

In the wake of *Lullaby*, she states flatly in the drafts, Vertov was "deprived of the right to fruitful work." She particularly recalled their awful experience with the elaborate *To You, Front!* (*Tebe, Front*, 1942), Vertov's last feature-length effort, which was subjected to a host of damaging alterations and refused broad release in the end anyway. Her explanation? "The nonentities did their work well [*melkie liudishki khorosho rabotali*]."³⁶

The earliest documentary film about Vertov's life and work, Leonid Makhnach's *World Without Play* (*Mir bez igry*, USSR 1966), was composed in a related, minor key.³⁷ The voiceover declares early on that Vertov's was a life marked by "bitterness, joy and chagrin," and despite many well-chosen extracts from Vertov's often ebullient works and a positive finale tacked on about thirty seconds before the fifty-three-minute film ends, bitterness and chagrin indeed provide the ground-tones.³⁸ Vertov himself is represented either as a shadow drifting along the Moscow River (image 2) or in shuffling point-of-view shots that coincidentally but uncannily recall the same technique as utilized in Samuel Beckett's and Alan Schneider's *Film* (shot by Boris Kaufman) from the previous year.³⁹ Walking past and glancing enviously at the work of a couple of women artists painting away on the embankment, the invisible Vertov mutters phrases culled and paraphrased from his diaries:

35　RGALI f. 2091, op. 2, d. 486, l. 103.
36　RGALI f. 2091, op. 2, d. 486, l. 104, 108–9.
37　The film was one of the first Soviet documentaries devoted to a filmmaker's life and work; earlier examples include V. Katanian's study of Eisenstein (1958), and films on Pudovkin (1960), the Vasiliev Brothers (1964) and Igor Savchenko (1965). "Play" here also can signify "acting," and indeed that double signification is perhaps intended: a world without acting (i.e., the world of Vertov's films, supposedly) and a world without play, that is, without joy (the world in which Vertov's career petered out).
38　The mood is powerfully reinforced by the strikingly dissonant and gloomy musical score by Vitalij Geviksman, a prolific and gifted composer for film better known for cheerful and sentimental melodies. Since 1948, Geviksman had been the musical director at the Central Documentary Film Studio (*Tsentral'naia studiia dokumental'nykh fil'mov* or TsSDF) where Vertov also worked in his last years (and which produced Makhnach's film), so they surely had crossed paths.
39　The voiceover was finely realized by actor Aleksej Konsovskij, who discussed the difficulties of incorporating acted scenes into nonfiction—and of playing the role of acted film's most militant detractor—in an intriguing interview published a year after the film's release (M. Kushnirov, "Akter i dokument," *Iskusstvo Kino* 8 (August 1967): 50–58).

> You can't preserve feelings like you do canned goods. They either develop, or they die... I am hungry. Unbelievably hungry. Hungry to create.[40]

No real explanation is given as to Vertov's hunger—something for which the film was criticized, as we will see—apart from ascribing it to the failure of his "terrible, irreconcilable struggle against cinematic routine, and against those who did not want to understand his revolutionary aspirations."

The director Leonid Makhnach (1933–2014) was himself no stranger, as it turns out, to the bitternesses (and, early on, the joys) of the Stalin period, leading me to wonder what resonances the film had for him, a non-fiction director of a much younger generation (and trained by Kuleshov, no less). Like Marina Goldovskaya's father Evsej, Makhnach's dad, the powerful head of Moscow's gas utilities concern, was one of many millions arrested by Stalin's brutal state security organs during the despot's rule (ca. 1929–53); unlike Evsej (who, though harshly treated, escaped long-term incarceration), Vladimir Makhnach spent fourteen years in the Taishet labor camp near Irkutsk, Siberia.[41] Plunged into poverty with the rest of his formerly privileged but newly suspect family after the 1941 arrest, Leonid had to lie about his father in order to get into VGIK (the Higher State Cinema Institute) in 1949—he told the admissions board that Makhnach Sr. had vanished during the war—and could never reconnect emotionally with the now irascible and insomniac Vladimir after his return from the camp in 1955.[42] Plenty of bitterness and chagrin to go around, in other words; and for us, this grim background brings a third, far greater non-realization, subtending those of both "Dziga Vertov" and "cinema," into stark relief: the non-realization of Communism, precisely. (Or perhaps it *was* realized, after a fashion?)

---

40 The script was written by Sergej Drobashenko, with Svilova as consultant. These lines derive from references found in *SDZ* (which appeared the same year as the film), 186–187, 250, and recurring in RGALI f. 2091, op. 2, d. 253, l. 17 (April 4, 1936); d. 269, l. 26 (September 16, 1944), among other sources.

41 Evsej was arrested during the Terror on March 13, 1938 and interrogated for five and a half months; Vladimir was detained in 1941 shortly after the Nazi invasion of June 22 (Goldovskaya, *Woman with a Movie Camera*, 7–12; Orlando Figes, *The Whisperers: Private Life in Stalin's Russia* (New York: Metropolitan Books), 164–65, 379–81).

42 Vladimir quickly regained much of his status in Moscow's Fuel and Energy Administration following his return to the city (Figes, *The Whisperers*, 474–75, 563–65).

Image 3: Elizaveta Svilova in the apartment on Bol'shaia Polianka, looking through the archive sometime in the late 1960s. Source: RGAKFD 22578.

Internationally, Dziga Vertov's reputation has never been higher, his fame never greater, than they are right now. To be sure, much of this acclaim is due to *Man with a Movie Camera* as both a critical and popular favorite: in 2012, the film reached eighth place in *Sight and Sound*'s celebrated decennial poll of "the 100 greatest films"—the first nonfiction film to make the top ten in the poll's sixty-year history—and my "Dziga Vertov" Google Alerts tell me of frequent showings at cinema clubs, summer arts festivals, museums, universities, and other venues, with laudatory publicity rhetoric invariably unfurled in advance of the screenings ("delirious," "exhilarating," and "decades ahead of its time" are familiar qualifiers).[43]

---

43 The poll aggregated top-ten lists offered by 846 critics and filmmakers from 73 countries. See Nick James, et al. "The Greatest Films of All Time 2012," accessed June 24, 2017, http://www.bfi.org.uk/sight-sound-magazine/greatest-films-all-time-2012-homepage.

Man with a Movie Camera's wide availability since around the year 2000 in digital formats has also been key to this dissemination, and a string of fine releases culminated recently with the appearance on Blu-ray of the legendary full-frame version of the film, as restored in 2014 by Amsterdam's EYE Film Institute and Lobster Films in Paris.[44] Musical scores of remarkable quality and variety have accompanied *Man with a Movie Camera* at screenings and sometimes on digital versions, playing a significant role in its popularization as well. Indeed, more scores have been composed for Vertov's intensely rhythmic and densely visually orchestrated masterwork than for any other silent film, from what I can tell; they are often sensitive and intelligent commentaries and/or homages in their own right.[45] Not less important has been the film's incorporation into introductory film courses in many countries, its pedagogical presence solidified by analyses and critical discussions in textbooks and other film-media books aimed at a broad readership.[46]

---

44 All previous digital versions were taken from 35mm films printed in "sound" rather than "silent" aperture, which resulted in a significantly cropped image; more on that in volume 2. The Blu-ray has been released by Flicker Alley (US), Eureka Entertainment (UK) and Lobster Films (France). The 2000 (laserdisc)/2002 (DVD) release by Image Entertainment included a superb and highly engaging commentary track by Yuri Tsivian, which has undoubtedly eased entry into this difficult film for many viewers.

45 Perhaps best known are the scores by the Alloy Orchestra (1995; based on Vertov's own musical indications [see L. M. Roshal', ed., "Chelovek s kinoapparatom: muzykal'nyj konspekt," *Kinovedcheskie Zapiski* 21 (1994): 188–97; Yuri Tsivian, "Vertov's Silent Music: Cue Sheets and a Music Scenario for *The Man with the Movie Camera*," *Griffithiana* 54 (October 1995): 92–121; "Chelovek s kinoapparatom [muzykal'nyj stsenarij]" and "Muzykal'nyj konspekt k kartine *Chelovek s kinoapparatom*," in Dziga Vertov, *Dramaturgicheskie opyty* (hereafter *DO*), ed. A. S. Deriabin, introduction by V. S. Listov (Moscow: Ejzenshtejn-tsentr, 2004), 126–34)]); and by British composer Michael Nyman (2002), which has also accompanied Nyman's own shot-for-shot remakes of the film (first screened in 2010, and to be discussed in later volumes). Other recorded scores include those by Un Drame Musical Instantané (1984), Pierre Henry (1993), Biosphere (1997), Tiziano Popoli (1998), In the Nursery (1999), Steve Jansen and Claudio Chianura (2001), The Cinematic Orchestra (2002), TVBC (2004), Werner Cee (2005), Steve Baun (for Perry Bard's crowdsourced *The Man with the Movie Camera: The Global Remake* [2008–, also to be discussed later]), Buscemi and the Michel Bisceglia Ensemble (2009), Art Zoyd (2011), James Whetzel (2014), and Pat Vollmer (2016). Many more unrecorded musical works, both improvised and scored, have accompanied the film, particularly in the last ten years or so. Most of the scores mix ambient with more abrasive electronic and electroacoustic elements, and perhaps it is not too early to speak of "the *Man with a Movie Camera* score" as a film-music subgenre. See also Stavros Alifragkis, "The Power of Musical Montage: Michael Nyman's soundtrack for Vertov's *Man with a Movie Camera* [interview with Nyman]," *Scroope* 19 (June 2009): 160–163.

46 For Anglo-American instances see, in particular, the various editions of David Bordwell and Kristin Thompson's *Film Art* (McGraw-Hill), but also references to the film in books

Introduction: How Did It Begin?   xxxi

Although they have been available (in some cases) in various formats for some decades now, and despite attracting significant scholarly attention, none of Vertov's other films have achieved anything like the notoriety of *Man with a Movie Camera*, though a gradual change might be in the offing due both to the recent bonanza of wonderful releases on DVD and Blu-ray, and to the appearance of other Vertov works, usually of unclear archival provenance, on the web.[47] Alongside his most famous film, the main anchors of Vertov's prominence have been his writings, which began to appear in piecemeal form in journals both inside and outside of the USSR starting in the late 1950s, and on a larger, book-length scale following the publication of his *Articles, Diaries, Projects* in Moscow in 1966.[48] These writings have become authoritative

---

like Timothy Corrigan and Patricia White's *The Film Experience* (Bedford/St. Martin's), Richard Barsam and Dave Monahan's *Looking at Movies* (W. W. Norton), and the excellent brief treatment in Michael Wood, *Film: A Very Short Introduction* (Oxford: Oxford University Press, 2012), 63–67. That *Man with a Movie Camera* is a fixture in film classes all over the world is something I've learned from colleagues; I know much less, alas, about the specific tools (textbooks, anthologies, etc.) used to present the film, although I presume that the existing translations of Vertov's writings (on which more below) play a crucial role, alongside resources newly available on the web. For one example, see Jean Breschand, *Le documentaire: l'autre face du cinéma* (Paris: Cahiers du Cinéma/SCÉRÉN-CNDP, 2002), 12–15.

47 *Kino-Eye: Life Caught Unawares* (*Kino-Glaz: Zhizn' Vrasplokh,* 1924), *One Sixth of the World* (*Shestaia Chast' Mira,* 1926), *Enthusiasm: Symphony of the Donbass* (*Entuziazm: Simfoniia Donbassa,* 1930), and *Three Songs of Lenin* were evidently available to varying degrees on 35mm and 16mm in Western Europe and the United States starting around the early 1970s. Low-quality VHS copies from Grapevine Video of *Enthusiasm* (unsubtitled) and of the Museum of Modern Art's compilation of scenes from early (1922) issues in the *Kino-Pravda* series (1922–25) appeared through the 1980s and 1990s in video stores and film libraries (many of my readers will recall that tape); Kino Video later produced superior subtitled copies of *Three Songs* (on VHS in Kino Video's "Red Silents" series in 1991), and of *Kino-Eye* (on VHS in 1999, and together with *Three Songs* on DVD in 2000). Besides the full-frame *Man with a Movie Camera,* the post-2004 cornucopia includes, from the Austrian Film Museum, a two-DVD release of *Enthusiasm* (2005), another twofer of *One Sixth of the World* and *The Eleventh Year* (*Odinnadtsatyj,* 1928) with music by Nyman (2009), and yet another of sound and silent versions of *Three Songs of Lenin* (2014); Flicker Alley's 2011 DVD release of *Stride, Soviet* (*Shagaj Sovet,* 1926) in their "Landmarks of Early Soviet Film" collection; and (in Lobster Films/Flicker Alley/Eureka Entertainments's 2015 Blu-ray/DVD releases) *Kino-Pravda 21, Kino-Eye, Enthusiasm,* and *Three Songs* alongside *Man with a Movie Camera.*

48 See footnote 23; I will discuss those earliest post-1954/pre-1966 publications/translations in more detail below. In the Anglophone context, the selections that appeared in 1962 in the Jonas Mekas-edited *Film Culture* ("The Writings of Dziga Vertov," *Film Culture* 25 (Summer 1962): 50–65) and later anthologized in Harry M. Geduld, ed., *Film Makers on Film Making: Statements on Their Art by Thirty Directors*

sources for critics, students, and scholars, and regularly find their way into anthologies and into courses on (among other topics) film and media history and theory, documentary, the avant-garde, twentieth-century art, sound studies, and Russian and Soviet culture.[49] (They could also, in the wake of

---

(Indianapolis: Indiana University Press, 1967 [and later editions]), 79–105); and in P. Adams Sitney, ed., *Film Culture Reader* (New York: Praeger, 1970 [and later editions]), 353–75), were evidently especially widely read. The *Film Culture* selections, apparently made on the basis of consultation with Svilova, included translations of "Kinoki. Perevorot [Kinocs: A Revolution]," *LEF* 3 (June–July 1923): 135–43; "Iz rabochikh tetradej" (cited above); and two "Lectures on Kino-Eye" given in Paris in 1929 and translated by Samuel Brody ("Dziga Vertov on Film Technique," *Filmfront* 3 [January 28, 1935]: 7–9). Translations of the 1966 collection include the 1967 East German edition mentioned above; *Articles, journaux, projets*, trans. Sylviane Mosse and Andrée Robel (Paris: Union générale de éditions/Cahiers du Cinéma, 1972); *Schriften zum Film*, ed. and afterword by Wolfgang Beilenhoff (Munich: Carl Hanser, 1973); *Cikkek, naplójegyzetek, gondolatok*, trans. Veress József and Misley Pál (Budapest: M. Filmtud. Int. és Filmarchívum, 1973); *El cine-ojo*, ed. and trans. Francisco Llinás (Madrid: Fundamentos, 1974); *Articulos, Proyectos y Diarios de Trabajo*, trans. Victor Goldstein, introduction by H. Alsina Thevenet (Buenos Aires: Ediciones de la Flor, 1974); *L'occhio della rivoluzione: Scritti dal 1922 al 1942*, ed. Pietro Montani (Milan: Mazzotta, 1975); *Człowiek z kamerą: wybór pism*, trans. Tadeusz Karpowski, introduction by Nikolaj Abramov (Warsaw: Wydawnictwa Artystyczne i Filmowe, 1976); our own, superbly translated English *Kino-Eye* from 1984; and *Sine-Göz*, trans. Ahmet Ergenc (Istanbul: Agora Kitapligi, 2007). A volume whose title translates as *Kinopravda and Kinoeye*, evidently also a version of *SDZ*, was published in Arabic by the Darel-Kuds editorial in Beirut around 1978, as translated by Jordanian critic and director Adnan Madanat (Iu. Danilychev et al., "Sinerama," *Iskusstvo Kino* 5 [May 1978]: 159). Not all remain in print, to be sure, although the internet has extended their longevity and reach in some cases. Other post-1966 volumes or journals containing Vertov's writings include Peter Konlechner and Peter Kubelka, eds., *Aus den Tagebüchern*, trans. Reinhard Urbach (Vienna: Österreichisches Filmmuseum, 1967 [a translation of the diary section from *SDZ*]); W. Klaue and M. Lichtenstein, eds., *Sowjetischer Dokumentarfilm* (East Berlin: Staatliches Film Archiv der DDR, 1967); Dziga Vertov, "The Vertov Papers" (a selection from *SDZ* including "*Man with a Movie Camera*," "From Kino-Eye to Radio-Eye," "Answers to Questions," and "On organizing a creative laboratory"), trans. Marco Carynnyk, *Film Comment* 8, no. 1 (Spring 1972): 46–51; Antonín Navrátil's monograph *Dziga Vertov, revolucionář dokumentárního filmu* (Prague: Český filmový ústav, 1973); Ulrich Gregor, ed., *Dokumentation zum Seminar Künstlerische Avantgarde im Sowjetischen Stummfilm* (Berlin: Freunden der Deutschen Kinemathek, 1974); Paolo Bertetto, ed., *Ejzenstejn, FEKS, Vertov: teoria del cinema del cinema rivoluzionario gli anni Venti in URSS* (Milan: Feltrinelli, 1975); and Vasco Granja, *Dziga Vertov* (Lisbon: Livros Horizonte, 1981).

49 For anthologized Vertov, see (among others) Richard Taylor and Ian Christie, eds., *The Film Factory: Russian and Soviet Cinema in Documents, 1896–1939* (London: Routledge, 1988), 69–72, 83–84, 89–94, 111–16, 129–31, 150–51, 200–203, 298–305, 340–43, 357–58, 377; Kevin Macdonald and Mark Cousins, eds., *Imagining Reality* (London: Faber & Faber, 2006), 48–55; Jonathan Kahana, ed., *The Documentary Film Reader: History, Theory, Criticism* (Oxford: Oxford University Press, 2016), 171–73. The Taylor/Christie volume

the new Russian editions of Vertov's written plans for film projects in 2004 and of his articles and talks in 2008, use some freshening up, as we will see soon enough.)[50] Finally, the internet has opened up a whole new ocean for Vertoviana to circulate and multiply within, just as it has for so much else.[51]

As the previous two sections have suggested, Vertov's current eminence—his first name has recently been claimed as the moniker for the top movie prizes (what we would call "Oscars") in Ukraine, where he made several of his greatest films—was in no way inevitable.[52] Major changes in political-economic orders, grand transformations of cinema and other media, profound shifts in intellectual climate, and (most of all) an enormous amount of hard creative, critical, historical, archival, and curatorial labor came together unevenly over the decades since 1954 to produce the Vertov we know (or are coming to know) today. The present work, a critical-biographical study of the filmmaker in three volumes, depends heavily on this history and on this wealth of fact, commentary, and controversy, and I shall devote the remainder of the introduction to a non-exhaustive overview of what I take to be the most important waves of Vertov reception since his death: 1954–61, a largely but not exclusively Soviet reception, during which time his recovery was both made possible and instrumentalized by political change; ca. 1962 through the end of the decade, marked both by the controversial dominance of "Kino-Pravda/cinéma-vérité" as a framework for thinking about Vertov's legacy, and (mainly in the USSR) the beginnings of the scholarly study of the filmmaker; the post-1968 period through the late 1980s, characterized at once by a shift to anti-mimetic readings of Vertov (and especially of *Man with a Movie Camera*) reflective of new, broadly antiauthoritarian tendencies in political thought and cultural theory, and by the full-scale emergence of film studies as an academic subject in various countries; and 1989–90 through the present, a heterogeneous period centrally conditioned by the implosion of most of the Communist world and renewed, archivally informed scrutiny of the history of Communist culture and its makers, including Vertov.[53] To be sure, these rough period designations are crisscrossed

---

contains many important Vertov-related pieces by others writing in the 1920s–1930s, and Kahana's includes classic articles on Vertov by Annette Michelson and Seth Feldman.

50 Something about to happen in French with *L'oeil de la révolution*; see footnote 24.

51 A favorite and immensely useful site is https://monoskop.org/Dziga_Vertov (accessed October 3, 2016).

52 Ulyana Dovgan, "The First Annual Golden Dziga," *Odessa Review* (May 5, 2017): accessed July 24, 2017, http://odessareview.com/first-annual-golden-dziga/. Commemorative postage stamps were issued in 2012 in Ukraine as well.

53 Apart from some necessary references in this introduction, I will reserve my discussion of Vertov's reception outside the USSR before 1954 for volumes 2 and 3. For a much more

by other phases as well—not least the intervals between major publications of Vertov's writings[54]—and swirl around a series of far-reaching historical vortices, perhaps most importantly 1956 (Nikita Khrushchev's denunciation of Stalin; the Suez Crisis; the Soviet invasion of Hungary), 1968 (major anti-systemic revolts around the globe; the Soviet invasion of Czechoslovakia; the midpoint of Mao's Cultural Revolution), and 1989–91 (the implosion mentioned above, accompanied by the Tiananmen Square massacre, the First Iraq War, the First Intifada, and the onset of the Yugoslav Wars).

The first thing to say about Vertov's reception from the mid-1950s onward is that he was posthumously very lucky: the exact opposite of Stalin, in this respect. The majority of his friends, colleagues and supporters in the Soviet film world—I have mentioned several already in the main text and footnotes—were still alive, could exert influence of various kinds, and in many cases would go on to live for another couple of decades or more. For a number of them, Svilova above all, the matter of Vertov's recovery was, as we say nowadays, personal. That his death was followed by the official anti-Stalin animus and institutional housecleaning of the Khrushchev "Thaw" (ca. 1954–64) gave those supporters an unanticipated opportunity rapidly to reinsert the filmmaker into the great narrative of Soviet and indeed world film—in part as an exemplary victim of a now-discredited despotism—though not without prudently editing the Vertov chapter of that narrative, as we will see. Finally and perhaps most importantly, his recovery was used in order to valorize new, more exploratory approaches to nonfiction filmmaking that drew on a carefully, gradually crafted picture of Vertov as an artist who, over the course of many years and via many errors and reconsiderations (including the error of rejecting "art"), had defended and developed documentary as an autonomous creative practice in ways that could and should be remobilized in the present.

---

concise account of Vertov's post-1954 reception than the one I offer here, see Seth Feldman, "Vertov after Manovich," *Canadian Journal of Film Studies* 16, no. 1 (Spring 2007): 39–50.

54 Indeed, those periods would be quite different: 1955–65 (the first post-Stalin appearance of discrete writings by and about Vertov, first in Russian and then in other languages); 1966–2004 (the publication of *SDZ* and its translation into various languages mainly over the succeeding ten years (see footnote 48), and the emergence of Vertov as a canonical film-theoretical presence); and 2004 to the present (that is, since the 2004 Vertov retrospective at the Giornate del Cinema Muto and the publication of *LR*, *DO*, and *SV*, the latter two of which are only now beginning to have a resonance outside of Russia). Like all periodizations, this one is schematic, and many other important publications will be mentioned in the chapters to follow.

Heartless though this may sound, the relative non-severity of Vertov's sufferings, despite their duration—he wasn't shot or physically tortured, though some of his patrons were; was never ejected from the Communist Party, to which he never belonged in any case; and was never incarcerated or (to my knowledge) even arrested or interrogated—also eased his recovery, which arguably began even before his death in 1954. Although he was indeed publicly and viciously humiliated in front of (and, in several cases, by) his documentary filmmaking colleagues at a meeting in March 1949, Vertov was not among the film professionals actively persecuted in the press during the loathsome "anti-cosmopolitan" campaign, a Stalin-driven crusade that targeted mainly Jewish members of the Soviet artistic, scientific, and academic elite for their supposed lack of patriotism and obsequious admiration of things Western between late 1948 and 1953.[55] His mortification was thus a more or less local affair, confined to the precincts of Moscow's Central Documentary Film Studio, and reverberated almost not at all in the pages of late Stalin-era periodicals, though lingeringly in the memories of those who had been in attendance.[56]

---

55 For the most important manifestations of the campaign in the cinema press (none of which mention Vertov), see "Za sovetskoe patrioticheskoe iskusstvo—protiv kosmopolitov!"; V. Shcherbina, "O gruppe estetstvuiushchikh kosmopolitov v kino"; Al. Abramov, "Rabolepstvuiushchie kosmopolity"; Gr. Grigor'ev, "Pravda zhizni i fal'shivye teorii"; and Vl. Kagarlitskij, "Dramaturgiia v dokumental'nykh fil'makh," all in *Iskusstvo Kino* 1 (February 1949): 1–3; 14–16; 17–19; 22–24; 28–30. See also the reminiscences of Sergej Iutkevich (another victim of the press campaign) in "My s uvlecheniem nachali s'emki," *Iskusstvo Kino* 2 (February 1988): 94–108, esp. 106–8. For an excellent recent overview of the campaign, see Sheila Fitzpatrick, *On Stalin's Team: The Years of Living Dangerously in Soviet Politics* (Princeton, NJ: Princeton University Press, 2015), 191–220. I will discuss the episode in much greater detail in volume 3.

56 Lev Roshal', "Protokol odnogo zasedaniia"; "Protokol N 11 otkrytogo partijnogo sobraniia Tsentral'noj studii dokumental'nykh fil'mov ot 14-15 marta 1949 goda," *Iskusstvo Kino* 12 (December 1997): 124–27; 128–33. Barring the 1950 remarks of Ilya Kopalin (discussed below), the only critical comment on Vertov I have found in the Soviet cinema press between March 1949 and 1954 is a denunciation of the "ugliness" and "formalism" of *Enthusiasm*'s depiction of industry by Gr. Grigor'ev, who had written an anti-cosmopolitan diatribe in February 1949 ("Vidy zemli sovetskoj," *Iskusstvo Kino* 3 [June 1949]: 34). Other mentions are basically positive: a reference to *Kino-Eye* as one of the first Soviet films to win acclaim outside the Soviet Union (Vas. Smirnov, "Sila sovetskoj pravdy," *Iskusstvo Kino* 3 (June 1949): 16–21); and his old nemesis Nikolaj Lebedev's praise of *Three Songs of Lenin* as a successful "first attempt to create a monumental image of the great leader using the methods of documentary cinema" (N. Lebedev, "Na podstupakh k 'Chapaevu,'" *Iskusstvo Kino* 2 (April 1951): 9–14, esp. 12, 13–14). Lebedev, who became inaugural head of film studies at VGIK when the department was formed in 1946, faced plenty of problems himself during these years: see this introductory chapter and volume 3, below.

Perhaps the relative obscurity of Vertov's name and the localized character of his disgrace were what emboldened Ilya Petrovich Kopalin (1900–1976)—an important protagonist in these pages, who had begun filmmaking under Vertov's tutelage in the mid-1920s, to become one of the grand old men of nonfiction by the post–World War II years—to offer an understated if still daring defense of his mentor both in a public lecture on Soviet documentary in Moscow in 1950, and in an important collection of articles marking the thirtieth anniversary of Soviet cinema published the same year.[57] Openly referring to Vertov as one of documentary's "old masters" (along with, among others, Svilova, Kaufman, Shub, and himself) and indeed as the "greatest documentarian of the early [Soviet] years," Kopalin succinctly laid out what would become some of the key features of the main Soviet line of Vertov reception. He located the center of Vertov's early work in the filmmaker's most unambiguously patriotic, intelligible, and populist films of the 1920s—*Kino-Pravda* 21 (the "Lenin" *Kino-Pravda* [1925]), *Kino-Pravda* 22 (subtitled "Lenin lives in the heart of the peasant" [1925]), and (perhaps more arguably) *One Sixth of the World*—but also identified a lamentable counter-tendency toward "formalist trickery" that reached its apogee in *Man with a Movie Camera*, a film that "received the most negative appraisal [despite being little seen] from the entire Soviet public." Not until *Three Songs of Lenin*, concludes Kopalin, did Vertov manage to shift decisively onto "the path of socialist realism" and thereby win general acclaim.[58]

Articulated by later writers with greater precision and sophistication and not without its affinities to earlier Stalin-era accounts, this implied master-narrative of Vertov's career as a dialectical struggle, resolved only in *Three Songs*, between a commitment to the representation of reality on one side (which could veer off into gross "naturalism" on occasion), and an irrepressible cinematic inventiveness on the other (which led him down the garden path of "formalism" rather more often), became the dominant framework for much later Soviet writing on Vertov, not least in the pioneering works of the very first

---

57 I.P. Kopalin, *Sovetskaia dokumental'naia kinematografiia* (Moscow: Vsesoiuznoe obshchestvo po rasprostraneniiu politicheskikh i nauchnykh znanij, 1950); I. Kopalin, "Sovetskaia dokumental'naia kinematografiia," *30 let sovetskoj kinematografii*, ed. D. Eremin (Moscow: Goskinoizdat, 1950), 98–117, esp. 99–100.

58 Kopalin, *Sovetskaia dokumental'naia kinematografiia*, 5–6, 11.

Vertov scholar, Nikolaj Abramov (1908–77).[59] Indeed, this stress on realism and communicability in tension with experimental ambition—a reading sometimes forced upon the Vertovian corpus in quite drastic ways—became, as we will see, one of the main vehicles by which his work could be ferried comfortably over into the Thaw epoch, during which time "socialist realism" remained the sole officially sanctioned program for Soviet art as a whole.

The most interesting moment in Kopalin's comments on Vertov is a terminological one, however. He describes Vertov's successful early silent films as "affirmations of a new form of cinematic art—the art of the publicistic [*publitsisticheskij*] documentary film."[60] *Publicistic* is one of the (blessedly) few Russian words that I propose retaining intact in my own text, for the simple but important reason that no English word really corresponds to it in a non-misleading way. A term coming from journalism and prominent in Soviet discussions of nonfiction film after World War II, and particularly after 1956, *publicistic* carried special weight due to Lenin's reported description of nonfiction/newsreel film as ideally "visual" or "image-based publicistics" (*obraznaia publitsistika*), a "broadly informative" kind of film that would take as its model the practices of "the best Soviet newspapers."[61] By the 1950s, *publicistic* on its own normally referred to journalistic writing that is at once synthetic (of discrete items of knowledge, and therefore usually long- or medium-form) and partisan (in regards to a specific position, which it claims to represent authoritatively).[62] A vague designation to be sure, but one that

---

59 See N. Abramov, "Dziga Vertov i iskusstvo dokumental'nogo fil'ma," *Voprosy Kinoiskusstva* 4 (1960): 276–308, esp. 289–90; Nikolaj Abramov, *Dziga Vertov* (Moscow: Akademiia Nauk, 1962); and the translations of the monograph into Italian (Nikolaj Abramov, *Dziga Vertov*, trans. Claudio Masetti, introduction by Mario Verdone [Rome: Bianco e Nero, 1963]) and French (N. P. Abramov, *Dziga Vertov* [Lyon: SERDOC, 1965]). My own references will be to the Russian original.

60 Kopalin, *Sovetskaia dokumental'naia kinematografiia*, 5; emphasis in original. In this, he was recycling his own published descriptions of Vertov as the pioneer documentary film-publicist: see I. Kopalin, "V sporakh o dokumental'nom fil'me," *Iskusstvo Kino* 5 (May 1940): 33–35, esp. 33; I. Kopalin, "Dokumental'noe kino za 30 let," *Iskusstvo Kino* 7 (December 1947): 22–25, esp. 22.

61 A. M. Zak, ed., *Samoe vazhnoe iz vsekh iskusstv: Lenin o kino* (Moscow: Iskusstvo, 1973), 166. An important and relatively early deployment of the term is to be found in R. Katsman, "Khronika — obraznaia publitsistika," *Iskusstvo Kino* 5 (May 1940): 4–10.

62 The widespread use of the term as a descriptor of the committed civic criticism of the Belinsky-Chernyshevsky type dates to the late nineteenth century at the latest, and the Soviet applications of "publicistic" allude to this venerated tradition as well. See Alexis Pogorelskin, "The Messenger of Europe," in Deborah A. Martinsen, ed., *Literary Journals in Imperial Russia* (Cambridge: Cambridge University Press, 1997), 129–49.

allowed later theorists/advocates of nonfiction to add their own content while borrowing the legitimacy and luster conferred upon the term by the USSR's founder.

Kopalin in his lecture briefly distinguished the "simple reflection of events and facts" typical of "ordinary non-fiction/newsreel [*khronika*]" from the publicistic proper, which involves a "generalization [from] facts and events."[63] This basic and not-entirely-rigorous distinction persisted as the basis for Kopalin's considerably more revealing elaboration of the publicistic in 1955, by which time his mentor (who never or hardly ever used the term) was already dead and the Thaw underway. What sets the best documentary films apart, argued Kopalin in the pages of *Art of Cinema*, is their "sharp publicistic gaze": that is, "the clearly expressed relationship of the artist (scriptwriter, director, cameraperson) to the event, phenomenon or fact imprinted [on film]," in contrast to some mere "enumeration of facts and events."[64] On the screen, the difference manifests itself in the contrast between "simple demonstration" of facts and their superior artistic condensation into coherent and affecting *images*, with "image" (*obraz*) clearly intended to allude at once to Lenin's desideratum for nonfiction and to a long tradition of reflection on image as a tool of *literary* representation stretching back through the 1930s deep into the nineteenth century.[65]

But such publicistic images, Kopalin stressed repeatedly, cannot be crafted without the subjective, creative and ideological engagement of those involved in making films; without the kind of "passion" sadly missing from the majority of nonfiction films produced in the previous few years (i.e., during the late Stalin period).[66] He offered, along with Joris Ivens's *Song of the Rivers* (1954), Vertov's *Three Songs of Lenin* as a signal example of precisely the sort of "image-based publicistics" that had gone into eclipse:

> After all, how powerful the impact of a fact once generalized! In D. Vertov's *Three Songs of Lenin*, the array of represented elements is very simple and

---

63 Kopalin, *Sovetskaia dokumental'naia kinematografiia*, 5.
64 I. Kopalin, "Sovershenstvovat' iskusstvo obraznoj publitsistiki," *Iskusstvo Kino* 6 (June 1955): 18.
65 Ibid., 25. On the literary "image," or what we would more likely call "imagery" in English, see Günther, "Soviet Literary Criticism"; and Katerina Clark and Galin Tihanov, "Soviet Literary Theory in the 1930s: Battles over Genre and the Boundaries of Modernity," in Tihanov and Dobrenko, *A History of Russian Literary Theory*, 137–38.
66 Kopalin, "Sovershenstvovat' iskusstvo," 23–24, 26. "Passion" and its cognates are very frequently attached to "publicistics," which often seems more about the affective than the conceptual or formal character of the work.

ordinary: school, factory, sovkhoz, kolkhoz. But the artist brings these everyday facts to the level of great and thrilling images.[67]

By deftly bending and shifting around various pieces of ideological boilerplate, in other words, Kopalin helped to move Vertov into the center of Soviet discussions of nonfiction in at least three important ways. First, Vertov-the-artist became exemplary of precisely the kind of individual creative investment and (relative) autonomy required in order for excellent and appealing nonfiction to be created. Second, Kopalin suggested that Vertov's works, hardly seen since the 1930s, become privileged objects of admiration, study, and even emulation as nearly forgotten but still vital instances of creative "publicistics."[68] Finally and very importantly, Vertov's fate became, still only by implication, a symptom of the kinds of institutional-administrative disfunctionality that now had to be corrected in order to free nonfiction of the dull clichés (*shtampy*) supposedly dominant during the late Stalin years and their immediate aftermath.

To elaborate on the last point first: as Raisa Sidenova has recently pointed out, Kopalin's 1955 article also fired arrows at the former administration of the Central Documentary Film Studio, and in particular at its previous chief, Nikolaj Kastelin, apparently an intensely and justly disliked man who (among other things) offered no aid whatsoever to Vertov during his miserable last months, despite the filmmaker's pleas.[69] Kopalin assigned a good deal of the blame for the current crisis on studio administrators, whose inability to think rigorously about nonfictional practice—Kopalin was particularly appalled by Kastelin's vocal advocacy of staging in documentary—and failure to organize

---

67 Ibid., 25.
68 See also I. P. Kopalin, "Blizhajshie zadachi sovetskogo dokumental'nogo kino," *Vsesoiuznaia tvorcheskaia konferentsiia rabotnikov kinematografii: stenograficheskij otchet* (Moscow: Iskusstvo, 1959), 320. Mentioned especially often were the sync sound interviews in *Three Songs of Lenin* and *Lullaby*, clearly (in Kopalin's case) in an effort to push for more use of and technical support for sync sound and "documentary portraiture" of individual subjects; and the remarkably mobile and dynamic cinematography achieved in the 1920s by kinocs like Kaufman, Ivan Beliakov and Aleksandr Lemberg, compared to which later (1950s) documentary footage appeared static and unimaginative (ibid., 329, 332).
69 Raisa Sidenova, "From Pravda to Verité: Soviet Documentary Film and Television, 1950–1985" (PhD diss., Yale University, 2016), 51–52, 79, 94–96. On the animosity towards Kastelin, see the excerpt from the memoirs of documentarian Vasilij Katanian, *Prikosnovenie k idolam* (Moscow: Zakharov-Vagrius, 2004) at http://www.nv.am/lica/35125—q (accessed October 20, 2016). For the pleas—mainly pleas to be allowed to do interesting work—see RGALI f. 2091, op. 2, d. 292, ll. 116–18; and volume 3.

the studio into an efficient and engaged creative collective had led to the mass production of boring and superficial films (he calls them "empiricist") without the slightest publicistic charge or distinction.[70]

With these remarks, Kopalin was participating in the widespread early Thaw-era denunciation of every variety of Stalin-era administration as inattentive to individual and local needs and abundant in despotic "mini-Stalins" across the institutions.[71] Allusions in the cinema journals of the 1950s to Vertov's entrapment in these conditions and to his "unrealized dreams" remained tacit if easily understood by former colleagues in the film world, and it was not until the publication of selections from his diary and working notes in *Articles, Diaries, Projects* in 1966—a selection made largely by Svilova, I believe, and an important work of documentary testimony in itself—that the magnitude of Vertov's frustration with administrators during his last two decades received full public expression.[72]

By the early 1960s, however, it had already become possible to explain Vertov's creative decline by pointing fingers at Stalin and the social order associated with him, as two review articles by the important film critic, historian, and educator Rostislav Iurenev (1912–2002) plainly reveal. In his largely positive response to Abramov's 1962 *Dziga Vertov*, Iurenev nonetheless criticized Abramov not only for smoothing over some of the more contradictory features of Vertov's aesthetic, but also for failing to give any account of what Iurenev took to be the devastating consequences of Stalin-era cultural and administrative practice on Vertov's career, consequences glaringly obvious in the Stalin-praising *Lullaby*:

> N. Abramov says nothing about the effect of the cult of Stalin's personality, vividly apparent in Vertov's final [sic] full-length film *Lullaby*.... N. Abramov

---

70 Kopalin, "Sovershenstvovat' iskusstvo," 20, 23.

71 See, among other sources, Josephine Woll, *Real Images: Soviet Cinema and the Thaw* (London: I. B. Tauris, 2000), 9–11; Polly Jones, "Introduction," in *The Dilemmas of De-Stalinization*, ed. Polly Jones (London: Routledge, 2006), 1–18, esp. 7–8.

72 "Unrealized dreams" comes from the editorial commentary to the first post-1954 publication of Vertov's writings ("Iz rabochikh tetradej Dzigi Vertova," 112). Those diary/notebook entries most important for narrating Vertov's institutional struggles stretch between 1934 and 1945 (*SDZ*, 186–265; *KE*, 185–268); they have not, alas, reappeared in the recent Russian editions of Vertov's work, and the German edition of the diaries/notebooks from 2000 is seriously marred by the complete absence of any reference to specific archival sources in RGALI (Dziga Vertov, *Tagebücher, Arbeitshefte*, ed. Thomas Tode and Alexandra Gramatke, trans. Alexandra Gramatke [Konstanz: UVK Medien, 2000]). Svilova evidently made the typescripts of those parts of the handwritten notebooks/diaries from which the *SDZ* selections were taken; see (inter alia) RGALI f. 2091, op. 2, d. 269.

is silent about the fact that *Lullaby*'s central protagonist was Stalin, extolled cloyingly and beyond all measure.

Having failed to mention this, it became impossible for N. Abramov to explain the profound artistic crisis that Vertov endured during his last 17 years. [Nor does he mention that] Vertov was deprived of the opportunity to make publicistic films after *Lullaby*, and condemned to editing short documentary sketches and newsreels.[73]

Four years later, in an evaluation of Makhnach's documentary, Iurenev similarly lamented the absence of any adequate explanation of Vertov's "hunger," so strikingly represented in the film, and proceeded to provide one:

> Broken by the incomprehension and indifference of the studio administration, paralyzed by the official ostentation and dogmatic templates [then] holding sway in our documentary cinema ... [Vertov] hadn't the strength to realize his projects, to bring them to the screen. ...
>
> [To the question of Vertov's decline after *Lullaby*] the film gives no answer, thus eliciting bewilderment and various, at times absurd conjectures on the part of the viewer...
>
> [Nor does it mention that in *Lullaby*] Stalin occupied inordinate space, and that Vertov in his unrestrained praise of a living political actor lost [all artistic] taste, and himself as well.
>
> At the same time, Vertov's attempts to make documentary film portraits of ordinary Soviet people went against the tendency toward official-ceremonial films about parades and holidays and informational overviews of the achievements of the Union's republics, which dominated our documentary cinema from the end of the 1930s to the middle of the 1950s. Finally, the film needed to say, with bitterness, that Vertov was never assigned work worthy of him even during the years of documentary's blossoming, those of the Great Patriotic War [the Nazi–Soviet War]. Here is the real Vertov tragedy![74]

There can be no doubt but that this kind of candor—which had its own limits, to be sure, even as explanation—was made possible by major changes in administrative personnel and practice that had occurred well before 1962,

---

73 R. Iurenev, "Dziga Vertov i kniga o nem," *Iskusstvo Kino* 9 (September 1963): 136.
74 R. Iurenev, "O Vertove," *Iskusstvo Kino* 6 (June 1967): 65, 67. Iurenev had scripted the above-mentioned documentaries about Eisenstein and Pudovkin.

and that touched not only the studios but the film journals (especially *Art of Cinema*) and film education (at VGIK) as well.[75]

Iurenev, like Kopalin, used the word "publicistic" to describe the kinds of film Vertov might have made during his last decade, in contrast to the undistinguished films he did make. It is important to stress once again that the use of "publicistic" always brought up the question of authorship, and specifically (and quite Romantically) the degree of affective and intellectual engagement evinced by a finished work, even in the case of collectively authored works like studio-produced documentary films. In this sense, the valorized notion of "image-based publicistics" participated in a broader valorization during the early Thaw period of authorial expression—and with it, individual professional identity—particularly in the literary arena.[76] And it was not by accident that the proceedings of an important 1957 round table discussion of the past, present and future of "cinema publicistics," focused overwhelmingly on the question of how best to organize nonfiction production in a way that might mobilize creative investment and (thereby) avoid cliché, appeared in the same April 1957 issue of *Art of Cinema* containing the first post-1954 publication of Vertov's writings.[77]

---

[75] This happened across the arts: for literature, see Evgeny Dobrenko and Ilya Kalinin, "Literary Criticism During the Thaw," in Tihanov and Dobrenko, *A History of Russian Literary Theory*, 184–206, here 186-187. On the changes at the Central Documentary Film Studio, see Sidenova, "From Pravda to Verité," 94. On the great Thaw-era editorial collective at *Iskusstvo Kino* that worked under Liudmila Pogozheva from 1956 to 1968 (when Pogozheva was dismissed), see Elena Paisova, "Armen Medvedev: 'Zhurnal ne daval sovetskomu kino rasslabit'sia' [interview with Medvedev]," *Iskusstvo Kino* 4 (April 2011): 106–12; and Liubov' Arkus et al., "Zhivoj zhurnal," *Seans* (13 August 2009), at http://seance.ru/blog/zhivoy-zhurnal/ (accessed October 20, 2016). On the changes in the film studies department at VGIK, which opened in 1946 but was in abeyance between 1951 and 1956, see M. Karaseva, "Nikolaj Lebedev," *Kinograf* 8 (2000): 77–89, esp. 84 (Lebedev's brief autobiographical account of the department's and his own troubles between 1949 and 1954, when he returned as its head); and "Istoriia kinovedcheskogo otdeleniia," at http://www.vgik.info/teaching/scenario/Kinoved/history.php (accessed June 24, 2017). The institutions overlapped in various ways, of course, and Kopalin, Iurenev and other VGIK pedagogues often wrote articles for *Iskusstvo Kino* and other publications.

[76] See in particular Dobrenko and Kalinin in *A History of Russian Literary Theory*, 188–89. Indeed, one by-product of this valorization was an upsurge of interest in incorporating literary writers in documentary film production: see "O masterstve kinopublitsistiki," *Iskusstvo Kino* 4 (April 1957): 1–14.

[77] Namely, "O masterstve kinopublitsistiki," in which Kopalin, Iurenev, Posel'skij, Katanian, and Ovanesova among others participated.

Around this time, another word rises to prominence in the Soviet nonfiction lexicon, a term seemingly very different from "publicistic" but which in fact was used in strikingly similar ways to describe at once a certain kind of film and a specific type of professional-authorial identity. That word is *poetic* (*poeticheskij*), a descriptor that Vertov did indeed use, starting in the mid-1930s, to describe his own films and vocation, and which others had also applied to him in a positive sense during the Stalin era.[78] The anonymous editorial comments accompanying the extracts from Vertov's "working notebooks" in *Art of Cinema* in 1957 stress the poetic character of the filmmaker's works almost ad nauseum, neither mentioning the "publicistic" nor providing even a minimally satisfying definition of "poetic," despite the distinguished history of Soviet film-theoretical treatments of the topic.[79]

It is clear enough, however, that like the publicistic mode, the poetic centrally involves a specific authorial gaze, a particular subjective engagement with themes, forms, and material that either brings hitherto unnoticed phenomena to the audience's attention, or typifies those phenomena in synthetic and emotionally affecting images.[80] One can imagine Kopalin's "publicistic" replacing Iurenev's "poetic" in these remarks by the latter without too much difficulty:

> ... the contemporary documentary film must be more poetic, must express more fully the relationship of the author to the phenomena of life. Remember how first D. Vertov, and later J. Ivens made their films. They were poets of documentary. They had their own way of seeing reality.[81]

---

78 See Nikolaj Otten, "Krasivyj mir [review of *Lullaby*]," *Iskusstvo Kino* 12 (December 1937): 36–38; and S. Ginzburg, "'Kino-Pravda,'" *Iskusstvo Kino* 1 (February 1940): 87–88. As far as the Thaw goes, "poetic" and its cognates are applied to Vertov's work no later than 1956: see A. P., "Kalendar' istorii kino [on *One Sixth of the World*]," *Iskusstvo Kino* 12 (December 1956): 117–18; S. Shuster et al., "Kalendar' istorii kino [on *Stride, Soviet*]," *Iskusstvo Kino* 12 (December 1961): 142–43.

79 Most famously in *Poetika kino*, ed. B. M. Ejkhenbaum, introduction by Kirill Shutko (Moscow and Leningrad: Kinopechat', 1927). On the importance of the "poetic" to Soviet cinema more generally, see James Steffen, *The Cinema of Sergei Parajanov* (Madison: University of Wisconsin Press, 2013), locations 573–618 [Kindle edition].

80 For the former, see "Iz rabochikh tetradej," 115; for the latter, see Abramov, *Dziga Vertov*, 145–46.

81 "O masterstve kinopublitsistiki," 7. Let it be said, however, that the question of "individual" creative autonomy remained a touchy one during the Thaw: see, for but one instance, *Iskusstvo Kino* editor Liudmila Pogozheva's 1959 attack on Polish directors Aleksander

Indeed, Abramov in his book veers back and forth between the two terms, as when he writes of the need for directorial intervention and involvement, on the levels of ideology and artistic creation both, in order to forge "poetic or publicistic images" out of filmed material.[82]

Although the awkward "image-based publicistics" never entirely disappears as a way of describing Vertov's practice—it sounds a little weird in Russian, too, or so my native-speaker friends tell me—"poetic" increasingly becomes the preferred qualifier, and eventually (as Sidenova has shown) is used to establish a lineage between Vertov's work and the most inventive Soviet nonfiction produced in the 1960s, primarily at the Latvian Film Studio and Kirghizfilm.[83] Iurenev among others had fretted about the distinction between news/informational and other, less utilitarian and more *artistic* kinds of nonfiction/documentary practice, both as types of film and as institutionalized sectors of nonfiction production; and certainly "poetic" would seem to draw this distinction much more firmly than (say) "publicistic" does.[84]

That said, one of the advantages of Kopalin's journalism-derived "publicistic" is that it seems to maintain a foothold in reportage, and thus in documentary as necessarily a form of discourse about actual history. Among the few critiques of Vertov from the 1920s to which Soviet film scholars from the late 1950s through the 1970s frequently referred was Shklovsky's 1926 "Where is Dziga Vertov Striding," where the great theorist argues that Vertov's relatively free manipulation of footage and avoidance of informational supplements (dates, times, places) deprives that footage of "its documentary quality."[85] The critique stuck, and (as we will see in volume 2) became very important about a year later during a major debate about documentary

---

Ford and Jerzy Kawalerowicz for their "bourgeois individualism" in "Sostoianie i zadachi kritiki i teorii sovetskogo kinoiskusstva," *Vsesoiuznaia tvorcheskaia konferentsiia rabotnikov kinematografii*, 355–56.

82 *Dziga Vertov*, 141–42.

83 Sidenova, "From Pravda to Verité," 11–20, 140–201. See also Verónica Jordana's entry on Herz Frank in *Encyclopedia of the Documentary Film*, volume 1, ed. Ian Aitken (London: Routledge, 2013), 445–46.

84 Iurenev, "Dziga Vertov i kniga o nem," 135. The distinction between "informational" and "artistic" or "poetic" kinds of documentary is a running sub-theme in Abramov's *Dziga Vertov* as well. Vertov's status as founder of Soviet poetic documentary would be a film-historical commonplace by the 1970s; see "Kto on dlia nas?" *Iskusstvo Kino* 2 (February 1971): 104–12.

85 In *LR*, 170. The piece was ostensibly a review of *Stride, Soviet*, but presented a more broadly applicable theoretical argument to Vertov.

conducted mainly in the pages of the Mayakovsky-helmed *Novyj LEF*.[86] Perhaps no one put the argument quite as pointedly as did veteran polemicist Ilya Trajnin (1887–1949), the studio chief who fired Vertov from Moscow's Sovkino at the beginning of 1927:

> ... there is no difference between the director of a fiction film who stages the scenes he needs in accordance with his plan for the film, and an editor who artificially attaches whatever shot selected from a film archive to whatever other shot selected from a film archive (the two shots having been taken at different times and for different reasons) simply to use them *to stage* some sequence of actions or ideas. In such cases, particular historical or everyday scenes are integrated, at the will of the editor, into a completely different plot that *he has staged*.[87]

The younger and some of the older critics of the late 1950s–early 1960s mounted a pitched battle against the Shklovsky position and in favor of Vertov's theory and practice, defending both a theoretical and an institutional space for authorial (artistic, poetic, publicistic) nonfiction practice untrammeled by "informational" imperatives.[88] That they were to a considerable extent victorious was both a symptom of and (in a small but significant way) a condition for the renaissance of documentary in the USSR from ca. 1960 onward.[89]

In my own view, however—and in this I differ from some other recent commentators on Vertov[90]—it was a victory that did not come without

---

86 For an overview of the debates, to which we will return in volume 2, see Valérie Pozner, "'Joué' versus 'non-joué': la notion de 'fait' dans les débats cinématographiques des années 20 en URSS," *Communications* 79 (2006): 91–104.

87 I. P. Trajnin, *Kino na kul'turnom fronte* (Moscow and Leningrad: Teakinopechat', 1928), 69; emphases in the original. Though Trajnin refrains from mentioning Vertov, it is quite clear who the target is.

88 See in particular Abramov, *Dziga Vertov*, 92–93; Drobashenko, "Teoreticheskie vzgliady Vertova," in *SDZ*, 3–42, esp. 32–35; and (for a reconsideration by an older critic, one also previously pilloried as a "cosmopolitan," incidentally) M. Blejman, "Istoriia odnoj mechty (Vmesto predisloviia)," in *DVVS*, 59–60. Those who sided with Shklovsky in the 1920s included Kuleshov and Osip Brik, and some continued to defend the Shklovskian critique after 1954 (e.g., Sergej Iutkevich, "Mirovoe znachenie *Bronenostsa Potemkina*," *Iskusstvo Kino* 1 (January 1956): 49–62, esp. 56–57; I am not certain that Shklovsky himself changed his mind. Much more on this to come in volume 2.

89 On this, see Sidenova, "From Pravda to Verité."

90 See in particular Jeremy Hicks, *Dziga Vertov: Defining Documentary Film* (London: I. B. Tauris, 2007), 42–43.

a price. Shklovsky's basic argument, that nonfiction footage must retain a distinct and legible historical inertia of its own if it is to remain nonfictional, is not in the end refutable by appeals to artistic autonomy alone; and it would return, without being named as such, at the end of the 1980s–beginning of the 1990s, when the question of Vertov's (and Soviet documentary's) *historical* participation in the creation of Communist culture came under renewed, already post-Communist scrutiny.

Vertov's name reappeared in Soviet periodicals in the 1950s much more quickly than did his films on Soviet screens; but gradually some of the films, too, were pulled from the vaults and exhibited, at first mainly in small-scale, educational, or memorial-tribute settings.[91] The great film scholar Naum Kleiman told me that he first saw Vertov's work at VGIK when Nikolaj Lebedev—former documentary filmmaker, sometime Vertov antagonist, major film historian and founder of VGIK's film studies department in 1946—starting showing it to students in 1956.[92] *Three Songs of Lenin* and *Lullaby* were shown, possibly only in part, at a Vertov-dedicated evening at the Central House of Cinema (the main official gathering place for people in the film industry) in Moscow on March 27, 1959, accompanied by an exhibit of documents, frame enlargements and posters that Svilova had put together.[93]

---

91 Other Soviet publications to discuss or present Vertov's films or writings between 1956 and 1967 include Vertov's own "O liubvi k zhivomu cheloveku," *Iskusstvo Kino* 6 (June 1958): 95–99; Boris Efimov (cartoonist brother of Vertov's mentor Mikhail Kol'tsov), "*Ocherki o mul'tiplikatsii* [review of S. Ginzburg's *Risovannyj i kukol'nyj fil'm*, which also mentions Vertov]," *Sovetskaia Kul'tura* (May 23, 1958): 3; Boris Agapov, "Poezdka v Briussel'," *Novyj Mir* 1 (1959); S. S. Ginzburg et al., eds., *Iz Istorii Kino* 2 (Moscow: Akademii Nauk SSSR, 1959), 22–155; and an appeal to rerelease, "as a fine gift to our youth, " *Three Songs of Lenin* in *Komsomol'skaia Pravda* (March 22, 1960) (RGALI f. 2091, op. 2, d. 274, l. 1037).

92 From a conversation with Kleiman in 2006. Kleiman particularly recalled the astonishment provoked by *Man with a Movie Camera*, which as far as I can tell had last been shown in the USSR at the Central Documentary Film Studio in March 1949, just prior to the infamous meeting: it was evidently selected as the strongest possible evidence of Vertov's formalism, and hence as justification of the humiliation to come. See the above-cited "Protokol N 11 otkrytogo partijnogo sobraniia," 132.

93 The occasion was probably the fifth anniversary of Vertov's death. RGALI f. 2091, op. 2, d. 274, ll. 838–40, 842, 845; "Vecher, posviashchennyj tvorchestvu Dzigi Vertova," *Soiuz Rabotnikov Kinematografii SSSR* [*SRK*] 8 (1959); "Pamiati Dzigi Vertova," *Moskovskaia Pravda* (March 29, 1959). Seda Pumpyanskaya informed me that Svilova paid for many of the reproductions, posters, and other display elements shown at Vertov exhibits post-1956 with money from her own quite meager pension.

Larger audiences got a chance to see Vertov's most multinational film, *One Sixth of the World*, alongside numerous other early Soviet films, for the first time in many years during the inaugural edition of the revived Moscow International Film Festival (MIFF) in August 1959.[94] French film historian and critic Georges Sadoul, soon to become a central figure in the Vertov revival, was in the audience for the screening of *One Sixth* (his first) on August 4, and wrote enthuastically in *Pravda* about what he deemed the film's prescience in regard to the spread of both anticolonial movements and (concomitantly) national cinemas across the globe.[95] (The association of *One Sixth* with contemporary political struggles would continue, as we will see, and the film was shown again the following April at the House of Friendship with Foreign Nations accompanied by a lecture by Abramov.)[96] By 1967, in time for the fiftieth anniversary of the Revolution and a year or so after what would have been Vertov's seventieth birthday, the mighty state film archive Gosfilmofond staged a Vertov retrospective in its new Illusion theater, a sure sign—like the raising of a monument above his grave in the famous Novodevichy Cemetery in Moscow, necropolis of the Russian cultural elite, in the summer of the same year—of his increasingly canonical status.[97] Posthumously lucky, as I have said.

---

94 RGALI f. 2091, op. 2, d. 274, ll. 848, 851, 854–58, 860, 864; "Fil'my 4-x kontinentov," *Vecherniaia Moskva* 180 (1 August 1959); "Fil'my, kotorye vy ne videli," *Vecherniaia Moskva* 182 (August 4, 1959); G. Kapralov and D. Zarapin, "Volnuiushchee nachalo smotra," *Pravda* 217 (August 5, 1959): 6. Among the many other (mainly silent) Soviet films shown, alongside a truly international lineup of contemporary work from Peru, Israel, Albania, Canada, the US, the UK, India, and Tunisia, among other places, were Shub's *Fall of the Romanov Dynasty* (1927), Mikhail Kalatozov's *Salt for Svanetia* (1930), and Sergej Iutkevich's *Lace* (1928).
95 RGALI f. 2091, op. 2, d. 274, l. 848; Zhorzh Sadul' [Georges Sadoul], "Zhivaia istoriia kino," *Pravda* 223 (August 11, 1959): 4.
96 RGALI f. 2091, op. 2, d. 274, l. 1042. The event took place on April 18, 1960.
97 The Illusion opened in 1966. V. Borovkov, *Dziga Vertov: Kratkaia letopis' tvorcheskoj zhizni Dzigi Vertova: Fakty. Zamysli. Fil'my. Publikatsii (k tsiklu prosmotrov v kinoteatre Gosfil'mofonda)* (Moscow: Iskusstvo, 1967); "Dzige Vertovu, khudozhniku revoliutsii," *Iskusstvo Kino* 10 (October 1967): 41–42. Vertov's remains had been brought to Novodevichy on June 29, 1965 (RGALI f. 2091, op. 2, d. 484, l. 11). This list of Soviet screenings between 1956 and 1967 is not complete, to be sure; I will reserve mention of later revivals, like the 1969–70 restoration/rerelease of *Three Songs of Lenin*, for chapters to come.

Image 4: From *Man with a Movie Camera* (1929). Source: Yale University Film Archive.

In the 1950s and 1960s, other countries were ahead of the USSR in publicly exhibiting Vertov's films, as it turns out: perhaps not surprisingly so, given both the "cosmopolitan" cloud that had formed over Vertov's head in his home country (and had first to be dispersed), and the grand flourishing of cinema and festival culture during those Cold War years in many countries, especially European ones.[98] The first real Vertov retrospective took place at the Third International Leipzig Documentary and Short Film Week that began on December 13, 1960. *Stride, Soviet, Three Songs of Lenin, One Sixth of the World,* and *Man with a Movie Camera* were shown, accompanied by a hefty booklet that contained some of the first significant foreign translations of the recent Vertov publications in the USSR.[99] In 1963, both *Kino-Pravda*

---

98   I will reserve my remarks on the circulation of Vertov prints outside the USSR—a very cloudy matter indeed—for the full filmography to come in volume 3.

99   See Barbara Wurm, "1960. Die erste Retrospektive," in *Bilder einer gespaltenen Welt: 50 Jahre Dokumentar- und Animationsfilmfestival Leipzig* [Leipziger Dok-Filmwochen], ed. Ralf Schenk (Berlin: Bertz + Fischer, 2007), 17–20. The title of the accompanying booklet

Introduction: How Did It Begin? **xlix**

21 (the "Lenin" *Kino-Pravda*) and *Man with a Movie Camera* were shown at the 25th Mostra Internationale d'arte cinematografica in Venice. The Festival dei Popoli in Florence staged a Vertov retrospective the same year, which occasion also served as the debut of the Italian translation of Abramov's *Dziga Vertov*, enriched by an introduction by Mario Verdone, a filmography by Svilova, and some writings by Vertov.[100] Peter Konlechner, film archivist and later cofounder (with filmmaker Peter Kubelka) of the Austrian Film Museum, showed *Man with a Movie Camera* at Vienna's Technical College on April 23, 1963, thus inaugurating a distinguished post-1954 Viennese tradition of Vertov reception and (later) acquisition, restoration, preservation and scholarship.[101] English-speaking countries took a bit more time to stage their

---

demonstrated the familiarity of its editor with current Soviet discourse about Vertov: *Dsiga Wertow: Publizist und Poet des Dokumentarfilms*, ed. Hermann Herlinghaus (East Berlin: VEB Progress Film-Vertrieb, 1960). See also the review of the retrospective by Erika Richter, "Dsiga Wertow: Publizist und Poet des Documentarfilms," *Filmwissenschaftliche Mitteilungen* 1 (March 1961): 24–25. Svilova was informed of the retrospective, and Herlinghaus presented *Man with a Movie Camera* in East Berlin's Möwe (Seagull) club in December 1960 as well, apparently just before the Leipzig retro began (RGALI f. 2091, op. 2, d. 274, ll. 1100, 1110). To my knowledge, the very first post-1954 foreign-language translations of Vertov's writings appeared in East Germany, near the end of 1957 ("Das Vermächtnis Dsiga Wertows" and "Tagebuchaufzeichnungen" [an incomplete translation of the Russian "Iz rabochikh tetradej" in *Iskusstvo Kino* from April of that year], *Deutsche Filmkunst* 10 (1957): 292–95).

100 Claudio Bertieri, "Taccuino della XXIV Mostra di Venezia," *Bianco e Nero* XXIV, nos. 9–10 (September-October 1963): i–vi. *Kino-Pravda* 21 was shown on August 29, and the "mythic and impossible to find" *Man with a Movie Camera* on September 5, as part of a twenty-film retrospective of Soviet film covering the years 1924 to 1939. Interestingly, it seems that actress Anna Karina and her then-spouse, future Groupe Dziga Vertov member Jean-Luc Godard, might have attended the Venice *Man with a Movie Camera* screening (vi). On the book launch at the Festival dei Popoli, which Iurenev attended, see "Vita del C.S.C. [Centro Sperimentale di Cinema]," *Bianco e Nero* XXV, no. 1 (January 1964): iii; R. Iurenev, "Zhizn' i ekran: zametki s florentijskogo kinofestivalia," *Sovetskaia Kul'tura* 22 (February 20, 1964): 4. *Stride, Soviet, The Eleventh Year, Enthusiasm*, and *Three Songs of Lenin* were screened at the Festival dei Popoli, as were Shub's *Fall of the Romanov Dynasty* (1927) and Viktor Turin's *Turksib* (1930). The Venice screenings in particular (which apparently attracted large audiences) elicited critical responses almost immediately: see Renato May's use of *Man with a Movie Camera* to critique cinéma-vérité's supposed pretentions to objectivity (in "Dal cinema al cinema-verità," *Bianco e Nero* XXV, nos. 4–5 [April–May 1964]: 1–15); and Leonardo Autera's evaluation of the same film as "artistically null" ("Retaggio teatrale e 'realismo socialista' del cinema sovietico [1924–1939]," *Bianco e Nero* XXIV, nos. 9–10 [September–October 1963]: 65).

101 Thomas Tode, "Vertov und Wien/Vertov and Vienna," in *Dziga Vertov: Die Vertov-Sammlung im Österreichischen Filmmuseum*, ed. Thomas Tode and Barbara Wurm (Vienna: SYNEMA, 2006): 33–50.

Vertov revivals, and Vertov was not screened at any of the famous Flaherty Seminars until 1962;[102] but by 1960 the British Film Institute was already circulating a print of *Man with a Movie Camera*, and Brandon Films in the US was distributing the same film no later than 1966.[103]

It was in cinema-mad Paris, however, where the earliest postwar screenings took place—we have already heard about one—and where the seeds of a particularly lively, complex, and influential later reception of Vertov were evidently planted.[104] A cluster of Soviet silent films, including at least one by Vertov, was shown in spring 1955 at the Musée National d'Art Moderne as part of a big celebration of cinema's first sixty years.[105] Some of the Soviet holdings in the Cinémathèque Française had apparently been destroyed during the Nazi occupation, including a print of *Three Songs of Lenin*, but Cinémathèque cofounder Henri Langlois managed to put together a "25 Years of Soviet Cinema" retrospective in 1955–56 that included work by Mikhail Kaufman alongside (probably) *Man with a Movie Camera*, a film that Langlois esteemed highly

---

102 Eight years, that is, after the famous documentary festival/seminar began (in 1955). *Kino-Pravda*, almost certainly the MoMA compilation, was shown at the Flaherty in 1962 and 1970, *Man with a Movie Camera* in 1966 and 1978: see "Films Screened," http://flaherty-seminar.org/the-flaherty-seminar/films-screened/ (accessed October 27, 2016; my thanks to Patricia Zimmermann for this reference).

103 Dai Vaughan, "The Man with the Movie Camera," *Films and Filming* (November 1960): 18; Herman J. Weinberg, "The Man with the Movie Camera," *Film Comment* 4, no. 1 (Fall 1966): 40.

104 Though I will focus here on screenings for which I have firm documentation, credible reports point to Vertov screenings at the Cinémathèque in the immediate postwar years as well as (later) at the Royal Belgian Film Archive in Brussels (correspondence with Bernard Eisenschitz [April 2009] and with Chris Marker [November 2011]).

105 I suspect the Vertov work was *Man with a Movie Camera*; films by Eisenstein, Pudovkin, Dovzhenko, and Room were also shown (Sergej Iutkevich, "Kinoiskusstvo Frantsii: zametki kinorezhissera," *Izvestiia* 249 [October 20, 1955]: 3; RGALI f. 2091, op. 2, d. 274, l. 823). No Vertov film was among the seven works shown during Paris's "Soviet Film Week" in December 1955 (which followed the "French Film Week" in Moscow in October of that year), but his work (specifically *The Eleventh Year*) was certainly recalled during that festival in a public lecture by Léon Moussinac who, along with René Marchand and Pierre Weinstein, pioneered the study of Soviet film in France: M. Shalashnikov, "Nedeli sovetskogo fil'ma vo Frantsii: vecher v Zale Plejel'"; and "Iz rechi L. Mussinaka," *Sovetskaia Kul'tura* 149 (December 4, 1955): 4. See Pauline Gallinari, "Les Semaines du cinéma de 1955. Nouveau enjeu culturel des relations franco-soviétiques," *Bulletin de l'Institut Pierre Renouvin* 24 (Fall 2006): accessed October 27, 2016, https://www.univ-paris1.fr/autres-structures-de-recherche/ipr/les-revues/bulletin/tous-les-bulletins/bulletin-n-24-art-et-relations-internationales/pauline-gallinari-les-semaines-du-cinema-de-1955-nouvel-enjeu-culturel-des-relations-franco-sovietiques/.

and which was evidently part of the Cinémathèque's holdings by that time.[106] Langlois was keenly aware of how Vertov had become "nearly invisible" by the postwar period, and made a point of including references to Vertov's work in program notes written for retrospectives of other Soviet directors, of German cinema (specifically the work of Walter Ruttmann, Vertov's German double in certain ways), and of the British G.P.O. (General Post Office) films.[107]

The tireless Langlois continued presenting Vertov in the 1960s—screenings of *Man with a Movie Camera* on May 6, 1960, and July 1, 1961; an homage to the filmmaker between November 4 to 17, 1963; a presentation of *One Sixth of the World* at the July 1968 Avignon festival (under the rubric "The Unknowns of Soviet Film") that apparently made an enormous impression[108]—and had been unofficially joined in the task of Vertov promotion by the aforementioned Georges Sadoul (1904–67), who probably did more to reinsert Vertov into both film history and discussions about contemporary film practice than anyone outside the USSR. Vertov was a late enthusiasm of Sadoul's: the historian had written about Vertov in his widely read 1949 *History of an Art: Cinema from its origins to our time*, but his evaluation of Vertov was then neither very positive nor (as we will see) especially well informed.[109] His belated interest in Vertov, which took up a good part of his final decade, might have been piqued in October 1955, when he went to Moscow as part of the French delegation during the first "French Film Week."[110] Sadoul had been friends and colleagues for years with poet and fellow Communist Louis Aragon and Aragon's wife, the writer Elsa Triolet; and this connection is probably what got him, along with the famous actor (and fellow Communist) Gérard

---

106 On the vanished Soviet films, see Henri Langlois, *Écrits de cinéma* (1931–77), ed. Bernard Benoliel and Bernard Eisenschitz (Paris: Flammarion, 2014), 698; and Laurent Mannoni, *Histoire de la Cinémathèque Française* (Paris: Gallimard, 2006), 106. Langlois was evidently a fan of *Three Songs*, too, and it was shown on a number of occasions between 1938 and 1940 (Langlois, *Écrits*, 700). He wrote program notes for *Man with a Movie Camera* in 1955. On the retrospective, see *Écrits*, 522–23, 697–705.

107 Ibid., 256, 561, 564, 625. In an interview from 1962, Langlois singled out the apparent disappearance of numerous Vertov films as a particularly serious gap in Soviet film history (ibid., 48).

108 Ibid., 705–715; Séverine Graff, *Le cinéma-vérité: Films et controverses*, introduction by François Albera (Rennes: Presses universitaires de Rennes, 2014), 59, 67. The 1963 homage presented only three films (*Man with a Movie Camera*, *Stride, Soviet*, *Three Songs*). Laurent Mannoni mentions a further homage in 1964, that honored Vertov alongside heterogeneous others, John Ford, George Cukor, and Greta Garbo among them (Mannoni, *Histoire*, 326).

109 Georges Sadoul, *Histoire d'un art: Le cinéma des origines à nos jours* (Paris: Flammarion, 1949), 170–75, 180–83, 193, 221, 300–301, 339. A Russian translation of Sadoul's one-volume history, based on a 1955 edition, appeared in 1958: "Novoe izdaniie 'Istorii kinoiskusstva' Zhorzha Sadulia," *Sovetskaia Kul'tura* 29 (March 8, 1958): 4.

110 See footnote 105.

Philipe, an invitation to the home of Lilya Brik, Triolet's sister and Mayakovsky's legendary muse and lover.[111] Either during that October 1955 gathering or sometime later (but before 1959), Brik and her husband, the Mayakovsky scholar Vasilij Katanian, gave Sadoul a copy of Vertov's article "Kinocs: A Revolution," published in 1923 in the Mayakovsky-edited *LEF*. Returning to Moscow in August 1959 for the inaugural MIFF, Sadoul together with his Russian-speaking wife Ruta stayed on into September to conduct interviews with Svilova and Kaufman and to gather more information about Vertov.[112] He would return to the Soviet capital at least three more times during the 1960s, and would write to Svilova at least eight times, mainly in pursuit of Vertov's writings and the filmographic and historical information that would end up in his 1971 monograph on Vertov, assembled by Bernard Eisenschitz after Sadoul's death in 1967.[113]

As Séverine Graff notes in her indispensable recent book on the early history (ca. 1960–70) of cinéma-vérité ("film-truth"), it has become almost de rigueur to designate Vertov, the main creator of the *Kino-Pravda* (*Film-Truth*) experimental newsreels (1922–25), one of the key predecessors and prophets of that immensely influential approach to documentary, as a simple Google search (say, "Vertov vérité") will confirm.[114] Sadoul was unquestionably the main fashioner and promoter of this lineage, although

---

111 *I, Maya Plisetskaya*, trans. Antonina W. Bouis, introduction by Tim Scholl (New Haven, CT: Yale University Press, 2001), location 3187 [Kindle edition]. Also present at the Brik-Katanian soirée were author Anne Philipe (the actor's wife), ballerina Maya Plisetskaya, and Plisetskaya's future husband, composer Rodion Shchedrin (they first met that evening). Sadoul had joined the French Communist Party in 1927 (Pierre Durteste, "Faut-il oublier Georges Sadoul? Georges Sadoul, une jeunesse nancéienne," *1895* 44 (2004): 30).

112 RGALI f. 2091, op. 2, d. 543, l. 1 (letter from Sadoul in Paris to Svilova in Moscow, dated December 19, 1959). Katanian was the father of the well-known documentary filmmaker who bore the same first name.

113 Georges Sadoul, *Dziga Vertov*, ed. Bernard Eisenschitz, introduction by Jean Rouch (Paris: Éditions Champ Libre, 1971). Sadoul was already talking about nearly completing the book in 1962, perhaps the earliest recorded instance of a finishability-syndrome not unknown among Vertov scholars (RGALI f. 2091, op. 2, d. 543, l. 6). He had been in Moscow in 1932 and 1952, and returned in the post-Stalin period in October 1955, October 1956 (briefly), August–September 1959, and (to attend MIFF) in July 1961, 1963 and 1965. He gave a talk about Vertov during the 1965 MIFF, and apparently used his time in Moscow to see as many Vertov works as he could. See the letters in RGALI f. 2091, op. 2, d. 543; Graff, *Le cinéma-vérité*, 65; and the transcribed documents at Georges Sadoul, et al., "Notes sur la famille Sadoul," http://sadoul.free.fr/Site_papa/HISTOIRE%20DE%20LA%20FAMILLE%20SADOUL.htm#Georges_bio (accessed June 24, 2017). The Sadoul-Svilova correspondence that I have seen stretches from December 19, 1959 to July 25, 1967.

114 Graff, *Le cinéma-vérité*, 53.

he can be counted (as Graff also shows) among the numerous skeptics who have doubted its validity. Those skeptics may be forgiven for wondering, as they surely did and do, what the filigree montage artifice of a film like *Man with a Movie Camera*—far and away the best known of Vertov's films even back in those days—has to do with the famous non-interventionism of the vérité or "direct cinema" approaches to documentary. (Direct cinema great Albert Maysles [1926–2015] told me that upon first watching *Man with a Movie Camera*, he was at once struck by how amazing it was, and by how little relation it had to anything he was trying to do in documentary.) Vertov wrote in 1936 that "showing the truth is far from easy," but that the truth itself "is simple."[115] As we will soon see, alas, the truth about "Kino-Pravda" is not simple at all.[116]

At least two different discourses, of distinct provenance, drew Vertov into discussions of "film-truth" as a topic and a desideratum around 1960, in France and beyond. The first is the ambiguous Thaw-era Soviet call for truth telling in the wake of the mythologizing, falsification and "varnishing" of reality characteristic of the Stalin period.[117] Important both in political rhetoric and in artistic theory/practice, the injunction to speak "truth" influenced the Soviet presentation of Vertov's writing already in 1957, as we can see on the first page of the selections, dated 1940, from his working notebooks:

> Implied in Kino-Eye were:
> all cinematic means,
> all cinematic inventions,
> all methods and means that might serve to reveal and show the truth.
> Not Kino-Eye for its own sake, but truth through the means and possibilities of the Kino-Eye, that is, *Kino-Pravda*.[118]

---

115 RGALI f. 2091, op. 2, d. 253, l. 1.
116 A shorter, less detailed version of the following reflections has already appeared as John MacKay, "The Truth about Kino-Pravda, or Censorship as a Productive Force," *Kino Kultura* 55 (2017), accessed June 22, 2017 at http://www.kinokultura.com/2017/55-mackay.shtml.
117 See Jones, *The Dilemmas of De-Stalinization*, 10–18; Katerina Clark, "'Wait for Me and I Shall Return': The Early Thaw as a Reprise of Late Thirties Culture?" in *The Thaw: Soviet Culture and Society during the 1950s and 1960s*, ed. Denis Kozlov and Eleonory Gilburd (Toronto: University of Toronto Press, 2013), 85–108, esp. 86–91 among other sources.
118 "Iz rabochikh tetradej," 113; citing here *KE*, 42.

These remarks were transmitted in early translations into German, English and French, and the centrality of "truth" to Vertov's project continued to be professed by Soviet scholars like Abramov and Drobashenko.[119] We will return to these affirmations later on in this section.

Secondly, the notion of Vertov as a truth seeker dovetailed with an established Western view of Vertov as a filmmaker preoccupied with *objectivity*, and with the kinds of supposedly objective knowledge the camera could be used to produce. Indeed, Vertov's reputation outside the Soviet Union between 1937 and 1960 was not simply that of a partisan defender of nonfiction against fiction, but of a dogmatic and often naive celebrant of the supposed "objectivity," and hence epistemological superiority, of the camera and what it registers. This view evidently derived from an identification, erroneous though understandable, of Vertov's term "Kino-Eye" with the movie camera or even just the camera's lens, whose name in both French and Russian—*objectif*—tempted a number of critics, especially but not only French ones, to designate Vertov a strict "objectivist."[120] In his 1949 history

---

119 "The Writings of Dziga Vertov," 54; A. Romanov, "Dzige Vertovu, khudozhniku revoliutsii," *Iskusstvo Kino* 10 (October 1967): 41–42; S. Drobashenko, "Teoreticheskoe nasledie Dzigi Vertova," *Iskusstvo Kino* 12 (December 1965): 74–83; and Drobashenko's introduction to *SDZ*, 3 and *passim*. *SDZ* was not translated into French until 1972, but the section cited above appeared in Georges Sadoul, "Actualité de Dziga Vertov," *Cahiers du Cinéma* XXIV, no. 144 (June 1963): 30. The translations of Abramov's book into French and Italian would have been important sources for the "truth" motif as well.

120 To be sure, textual support for such a position can be found in Vertov's writings, particularly those from around the beginning of 1925 through the end of the 1920s, even if he never openly espouses "objectivism" as a positive value—preferring, often frustratingly, to couch his own stance in largely negative terms ("*non*-played film," etc.); we will return to this problem in volume 2. Although Léon Moussinac stressed the filmmaker's "scientific" aspirations in his pioneering study, he properly sketched a more ambiguous portrait of Vertov by also noting his concern for the poetic and his incorporation of musical structuration (in *Le Cinéma Soviétique* [Paris: Gallimard, 1928], 173–79). The clearest source for the "objectivist" line is a brief summary of Vertovian theses published in 1937, entitled "Ciné-Oeil" ("Kino-Eye") and probably the remnant of program notes handed out by Vertov in France during his 1929 speaking tour—the piece derives from "Kino-Eye and *The Eleventh Year*" (written in January 1928; see *SV*, 135–37)—which indeed overwhelmingly presents "facts" and the "non-played" as the exclusive center of Vertov's notion of film: Dziga Vertov [spelled here "Vertof"], "Ciné-Oeil," *La Critique Cinématographique* 12 (April 15, 1937): 6. The summary was widely read as republished in 1946 ("Ciné-Oeil," in *Anthologie du Cinéma: Rétrospective par les textes de l'art muet qui devint parlant*, ed. Marcel Lapierre [Paris: La Nouvelle Édition, 1946], 207–9), and this last was probably Georges Sadoul's main source on Vertov's theories, along with Moussinac. See also Graff, *Le cinéma-vérité*, 60. A more nuanced view of Vertov that takes into account at once his reliance on "document,"

of cinema, Sadoul (who at this point thought that Vertov had begun his career as an "actuality cameraman") offered perhaps the clearest elaboration:

> [Vertov] was given charge of establishing and directing a newsreel, the *Kino-Pravda*, a supplement to the big daily *Pravda*. These words, which signify *cinéma vérité*, were taken by Vertov as a watchword... In their films and their manifestos, composed in a strange Futurist style, [Vertov and his Kino-Eye group] proclaimed that cinema must reject the actor, costumes, makeup, the studio, sets, lighting, in other words any *mise-en-scène*, and submit itself to the camera [alone], a more objective [*objectif*] eye than that of the human. For them, the impassiveness of the mechanical was the best guarantee of truth.[121]

Thus were connected, somewhat shakily, Vertov's "Kino-Eye" (the camera as an objective registrar of reality, a kind of extension and enhancement of the human eye and, later, ear), and "Kino-Pravda" (the capacity of cinema to help us know the world, in ways relatively untrammeled by the biases and limits of subjectivity), both terms assumed to be theorems critically and rigorously elaborated by the filmmaker. This influential take on Vertov—which had its

---

his experiments with visual rhythms and his sometime poetic romanticizations of nonfiction material appeared in Maurice Bardèche and Robert Brasillach, *The History of Motion Pictures*, trans. and ed. Iris Barry (New York: W. W. Norton and Museum of Modern Art, 1938 [translation of 1935 French edition]), 269–70.

121 Georges Sadoul, *Histoire d'un art*, 172. See also Jean Benoit-Lévy, *Les Grandes Missions du Cinéma* (Montréal: Lucien Parizeau, 1944), 139. The notion of "Kino-Eye" was sometimes applied, with reference to Vertov, to "objectivist" trends in literature and drama as well: see Edwin Jahiel's discussion of Claude Simon in "The New Theater: Paris 1962–63," *Symposium* 18, no. 4 (Winter 1964): 316. Whether these readings of Vertov had anything to do with André Bazin's formulation and development of his deeply influential "objectivity axiom" is a fascinating question I cannot broach here. See Dudley Andrew, "Ontology of the Photographic Image," in *The Routledge Encyclopedia of Film Theory*, ed. Edward Branigan and Warren Buckland (London: Routledge, 2015), 333–39). For varied non-French considerations of Vertov through the end of the 1960s plainly influenced by the "objectivist" idea, see Francisco Madrid, *Cincuenta Años de Cine: Cronica del Septimo Arte* (Buenos Aires: Ediciones del Tridente, 1946), 104–5; Ernest Lindgren, *The Art of the Film* (London: George Allen and Unwin, 1948), 80; Egon Larsen, *Spotlight on Films: A Primer for Film-lovers*, introduction by Sir Michael Balcon (London: Max Parrish & Co., 1950), 54; Guido Aristarco, *Storia delle storiche del film* (Turin: Giulio Einaudi, 1951), 58–59; Leyda, *Kino*, 176–79; Dai Vaughan, "*The Man with the Movie Camera*," 18–20, 43; Gianni Toti, "La 'produttività' dei materiali in Ejzenstejn e Vertov," *Cinema & Film* 3 (Summer 1967): 281–87.

own plausibility, to be sure, but also stood starkly at odds with the dominant Soviet emphasis upon publicistic or poetic *engagement,* as we will see—at once helped to connect Vertov to the vérité/direct cinema of the early 1960s, provided fodder for a critique of vérité and Vertov alike, and began to come under fire, as a characterization of Vertov's thought and work, by critics and historians inside and outside the USSR, starting in the mid-1960s.

One of the triggers that eventually and unintentionally catalyzed these two discourses was sociologist and filmmaker Edgar Morin's 1960 "For a new 'cinéma-vérité,'" which must count (especially when its influence is measured against its brevity) as one of the most important statements on nonfiction ever written.[122] The writing of the article was itself triggered by the new kinds of documentary creation recently made possible by lighter sync-sound camera equipment, as well as by postwar innovations in realist fiction filmmaking originating in Italian neorealism and extending into Morin's own moment of what was already being called the New Wave. Morin wrote the piece after serving as a judge, along with ethnographer and filmmaker Jean Rouch, at the first Festival of Ethnographic and Sociological Film (Festival dei Popoli) in Florence in December 1959. For Morin, already the author of two important books about film,[123] the "old" cinéma-vérité was nothing other than fiction film, of whose capacity to attain and express truths about human existence he had no doubt. (Here he began to swerve decisively away from Vertov, of course—and by extension from Sadoul, source of the phrase "cinéma-vérité"—and indeed he explicitly stated that Robert Flaherty far more than Vertov was the "father" of the new, nonfiction cinéma-vérité.)[124] But what fiction film, no matter how scrupulously crafted, cannot capture is "the authenticity of lived experience [*vécu*]." True, both early Soviet and Italian postwar cinema attempted to have people "act out their own lives," but they never attained what Morin called the

---

122   Edgar Morin, "Pour un nouveau 'cinéma-vérité,'" *France Observateur* 506 (1960): 23; very belatedly translated into English as "For a New Cinéma Vérité," trans. Steven Feld and Anny Ewing, *Visual Communication* 11, no. 1 (Winter 1985): 4–5.
123   *Le Cinéma ou l'Homme Imaginaire: Essai d'Anthropologie Sociologique* (Paris: Éditions de Minuit, 1956) and *Les Stars* (Paris: Éditions de Seuil, 1957). Morin's few mentions of Vertov in *Le Cinéma* (on 22–23, 52–53, 82–83) clearly derive from Moussinac (see footnote 120), with the partial exception of one passage offering one of the first articulations of what would later be thought of as "the Vertov paradox": "Dziga Vertov, in defining the Kino-Eye, recognized in his own way the double and irreducible polarity of cinema: the charm of the image and the metamorphosis of the universe; *photogenie and montage*" (82; emphasis in original).
124   Morin had almost certainly seen some Vertov by this time, at least *Man with a Movie Camera.* See Graff, *Le cinéma-vérité,* 61–62, on Morin's refusal to "pose [Vertov] as a model."

"irreducible je ne sais quoi found in [images] 'taken on the spot' ['pris sur le vif']." Earlier documentary filmmakers, largely because of the unwieldly equipment they had to lug around, were primarily capable of showing either large panoramas of mass activity or the movement of machines. Efforts like Vertov's to supposedly capture "life unawares" at a more intimate distance were, Morin implied, both ethically questionable and limited to catching occasional snapshot-like bits of "living behavior." By contrast, the new portable gear enabled the filmmaker to "plunge into a real milieu" and thereby to gain concrete social knowledge that might be shared to undo the social isolation so characteristic, in Morin's view, of modern life.[125]

---

125 See Graff, *Le cinéma-vérité*, 62–64. Graff also notes that Morin's notion of the camera seems to have as much or more to do with Alexandre Astruc's 1948 formulations about the "caméra-stylo [camera-pen]" (a phrase used by Morin in his article) as with Vertov's "Kino-Eye." In a way, the French reception of Vertov during this period could be said to have involved an unconscious fusion of the figures of "camera-eye" and "camera-pen," a figurative hybrid-machine that counts as an interesting media studies phenomenon in its own right. Without mentioning Vertov, Sadoul in 1957 had used the term "cinéma-oeil" to describe the coming "microcameras" capable of "wandering almost invisibly through the streets and in crowds. They will revolutionize mise-en-scène, and even more the documentary, reportage, and so on. New genres of films will be born, and the cinema will definitively supercede the printing press" (*Les Merveilles du Cinéma* [Paris: Éditeurs Français Réunis, 1957], 203; François Albera, "Le detour par Le Gray (en passant par Moussinac et Sadoul)," *1895* 58 (October 2009): 137–43, esp. 143). Sadoul would also employ the "stylo" metaphor to describe that somatically reconfigured camera—intimate with the photographer's body, but free of studio restrictions—in relation to Vertov, but with reference to Guillaume Apollinaire's "poèmes-convérsations" rather than Astruc (Sadoul, "Dziga Vertov: Poète du ciné oeil y prophète de la radio oreille," *Image et Son* 183 [April 1965]: 12). Morin's chief examples of "new" cinéma-vérité were Karel Reisz's *We Are the Lambeth Boys* (1959), Lionel Rogosin's *On the Bowery* (1956), John Marshall's *The Hunters* (1957), and the films of Rouch. The hope for a new documentary cinema that would "plunge" into life-as-it-happens was frequently reiterated in these years, and often associated with what were assumed to be Vertov's aspirations in the 1920s and 1930s. Wrote filmmaker Mario Ruspoli in 1963: "[The new light equipment is already] an avant-garde tool whose efficiency and manipulability are unique. . . . the cameraman, effortlessly carrying a well-balanced camera and becoming one with it, can penetrate into a new world. In the end it will become 'natural' to walk, to live with a camera, and to strip it of nearly all the old technological servitude, making it serve as a *continuous gaze* cast upon humans and things, as in Vertov's [Kino-Eye] conception from back in the silent period. More than that, as the technique becomes 'second nature,' the cameraman with ears on the alert can in a certain sense 'live' the filmed event and participate directly in it" (Mario Ruspoli, *Le Groupe Synchrone Cinématographique Léger* [report written by Ruspoli for UNESCO and presented at a round table in Beirut in October 1963] [Paris: UNESCO, 1963], 12; emphasis in original). Other references to Vertov as vérité pioneer—often juxtaposed with Flaherty—concerned to create a noninterventionist cinema "[revelatory] of human behavior" (2) appear on 3, 10, 13, 17–18, 31.

Morin and Sadoul were not friends—the former had angrily left the French Communist Party in 1951, while the latter remained in the PCF to the end of his days (and was, until 1956 rolled around, a Stalin apologist nonpareil)[126]—and the only thing Morin seems to have taken from Sadoul's *History* is the phrase "cinéma-vérité" itself, which he never links to "Kino-Pravda" in any case. Meanwhile Sadoul, who never directly engaged with Morin's text in print, began around May 1961 to use the terms "ciné-oeil" ("Kino-Eye") and "cinéma-vérité," invariably invoking the supposed Vertovian heritage, in reference to a variety of innovative films, fictional and nonfictional, that broke with cinematographic convention in pursuit of a more spontaneous, plunged-into-the-milieu style, such as John Cassavetes's *Shadows* (1959) or Shirley Clarke's *The Connection* (1961).[127]

---

126 As evidenced by (among other shameful remarks) his furious response to André Bazin's review of Mikhail Chiaureli's hyper-Stalinist *The Fall of Berlin* (1949–50): see Antoine de Baecque, *La cinéphilie: Invention de un regard, histoire de un culture 1944–1968* (Paris: Fayard, 2003), locations 1473–85, 1576–99 [Kindle edition]. Sadoul came close to denying Morin's coauthorship (with Rouch) of the great *Chronicle of a Summer* (1961) in his admiring review of the film, and all his mentions of the sociologist's impact on the film are negative ("Les Chevaux de Muybridge: *Chronique d'un été*, expérience de cinéma-vérité, par Jean Rouch," *Les Lettres Françaises* 898 [October 26, 1961]: 6). Morin completely ignored Sadoul's "cinéma-vérité" campaign as well (Graff, *Le cinéma-vérité*, 72–73).

127 See, among others, Georges Sadoul, "Ciné-Oeil et Film-Témoin: *Shadows*, film new-yorkais de Cassavetes," *Les Lettres Françaises* 873 (May 4, 1961): 6; "Cinéma-vérité ou Théâtre-vérité? *The Connection*, film américain de Shirley Clarke," *Les Lettres Françaises* 912 (1 February 1962): 6. Among his reviews of nonfiction films, see "Cinéastes et téléastes," *Les Lettres Françaises* 896 (October 12, 1961): 6; "Enfin le cinéma-oeil! [on Robert Drew and Richard Leacock's *Primary* (1960)]," *Les Lettres Françaises* 919 (March 22, 1962): 6; and others cited by Graff, *Le cinéma-vérité*, 65–66. Sadoul's "Dziga Vertov: Poète du ciné oeil y prophète de la radio oreille" appeared as one of the lead articles in an April 1965 issue of *Image et Son* dedicated to documentary ("Un Cinéma de la réalité" was the rubric) and including articles on Flaherty, Ivens, the British documentarists, and US direct cinema among other topics (see footnote 125). Sadoul's usage seems to have spread rapidly: in one installment of critic Marcel Martin's "Histoire du Cinéma en 120 Films" from the end of 1961, we read (in a brief account of *Three Songs of Lenin*) that "Vertov had a considerable influence abroad, especially among those directors who, like Vertov, were concerned to witness to the reality of their times. The work of Joris Ivens and of the British and New York documentary schools cannot be explained without taking into account the influence of [Vertov's] *cinéma-vérité*" (*Cinéma* [November–December 1961]: 43; emphasis in the original). See also Martin's installment in the same series from earlier in the year on *Stride, Soviet* ("En avant, Soviet," *Cinéma* [June 1961]: 62). In relation to contemporary French documentary, it seems hardly a coincidence that Sadoul's initial Vertov publications in *Cahiers* appeared alongside interviews/articles about Rouch (and on Chris Marker and Pierre Lhomme's *Le Joli Mai* (1963): Michel Delahaye, "La chasse à l'I"; Dziga Vertov, "Kinoks-Revolution II"; Sadoul, "Bio-filmographie de Dziga Vertov," *Cahiers du Cinéma* XXV, no. 146 (August 1963): 5–17, 18–20, 21–29).

Sadoul's discursive takeover of "cinéma-vérité" should not be regarded as mere opportunistic poaching upon Morin's reintroduction of the idea in his brief article or (even more) in *Chronique d'un été* (*Chronicle of a Summer*, 1961; in collaboration with Jean Rouch), a landmark documentary whose accompanying publicity materials sometimes foregrounded the term "cinéma-vérité" more than the title of the film itself.[128] As we have seen, Sadoul had become interested in Vertov well before Morin's essay or *Chronique* had appeared, though I suspect that Morin was felt by the prolific historian to have thrown down a film-historical gauntlet, not least through his demotion of Vertov. One cannot but wonder, too, whether Vertov—committed revolutionary filmmaker and victim of Stalin-era administrative caprice—did not function as a kind of de-Stalinizing tonic for Sadoul, who neither wrote about his doubtless fraught reaction to the revelations of 1956 nor, indeed, made any mention of Vertov's post-1938 marginalization.[129] Whatever the case may be, there is no doubt but that Sadoul, through his articles, talks, and the posthumous 1971 book, managed to insert Vertov into contemporary film culture—the New Waves in both documentary and fiction—very effectively.[130] The promotion campaign extended to the still-young academic discipline of film studies as well, beginning when Sadoul gave a series of eight lectures at the Sorbonne's Institute of Filmology on (as he told Svilova) "the life and work of Vertov and above all about his theories, so fecund and relevant in 1962."[131]

By March 8, 1963, even before his well-known Vertov publications appeared in *Cahiers du Cinéma*, Sadoul could exult in another letter to Svilova:

> I have just returned from Lyon where three days of academic lecturing and discussion were devoted to Cinéma-Vérité, with the best French,

---

128 Graff, *Le cinéma-vérité*, 63.
129 See de Baecque, *La cinéphilie*, locations 1688–1760 [Kindle edition]; Jean-Paul Fargier et al., "'Ne copiez pas sur les yeux,' disait Vertov," *Cinéthique* 15 (1973): 65. Oddly, de Baecque never mentions Sadoul's late work on Vertov in his excellent book.
130 The other crucial promoter was Rouch, who began to speak of "Dziga Vertov, [Robert] Flaherty and [Henri] Cartier-Bresson" as his "three masters" no later than June 1963 (in the same issue of *Cahiers du Cinéma* where Sadoul's selection from Vertov's "Kinocs: A Revolution" appeared: Eric Rohmer and Louis Marcorelles, "Entretien avec Jean Rouch," *Cahiers du Cinéma* XXIV, no. 114 [June 1963]: 15–16). Rouch appeared as a talking head in Makhnach's *World Without Play*, wrote the preface to Sadoul's posthumous book, and would in later years frequently testify to the inspiration he received from both Vertov and the Soviet director's presumed anti-type Flaherty (e.g., in Lucien Taylor, "A Conversation with Jean Rouch," *Visual Anthropology Review* 7, no. 1 [Spring 1991]: 92–102, esp. 100–101).
131 The lectures began on January 17, 1962. See RGALI f. 2091, op. 2, d. 543, l. 6 (letter from Sadoul to Svilova dated January 21, 1962).

English, American, and Italian documentarists present, along with our mutual friend Joris Ivens. The discussion opened with my report on the historical importance of Dziga Vertov, the veritable prophet of contemporary cinema.

In effect, there is now developing in the West a movement of Cinéma-Vérité, the term having been chosen with reference to Dziga Vertov and to his Kino-Pravda. I know, of course, that it would be more just to speak of Kino-Eye, but the word "Cinéma-Vérité" has become, in France, in Italy and in many other countries, a veritable keyword.[132]

The event in question is the March 2–4, 1963, MIPE-TV conference in Lyon, France,[133] a meeting convened by *musique concrète* composer and pioneering media researcher Pierre Schaeffer, and probably the most self-conscious manifestation of cinéma-vérité as a genuine film-historical conjuncture. Like Graff and unlike Sadoul, I would hesitate to call it the gathering-together of a *movement*, not least because of the major differences of opinion and practical approach that divided the participants, who included such luminaries as Rouch, Morin, Sadoul, Richard Leacock, Richard Drew, Albert Maysles, Morris Engel, Jacques Rozier, Joris Ivens, Michel Brault, Raoul Coutard, and many others.[134] While Soviet critics, looking upon the Lyon summit from afar, were appalled by the defenses of non-engaged, supposedly politically "neutral objectivity" and (even more) by the association of Vertov with such a position,[135] Sadoul in his remarks crafted

---

132 RGALI f. 2091, op. 2, d. 543, l. 11. Sadoul's remarks did not in fact open the conference, but they were among the most discussed; see Séverine Graff, "Réunions et désunions autour du 'cinéma-vérité': le MIPE-TV 1963 de Lyon," *1895* 64 (Fall 2011): 64–89.

133 Abbreviation for "Journées d'Études du Marché International des Programmes et Équipements du Service de la Recherche de la Télévision française" (Graff, "Réunions et désunions," 65).

134 Ibid. Some of the most important differences centered on the question of directorial intervention, with a major rift opening up between the anti-interventionist Leacock/Drew on one side and Jean Rouch on the other (ibid., 74).

135 Lack of "Party-mindedness" and ideological conviction were among the prime irritants. See "O reaktsionnykh kontseptsiiakh sovremennoj burzhuaznoj estetiki kino," *Iskusstvo Kino* 8 (August 1963): 120–28 [includes an attack on Leacock]; Sergej Iutkevich, "Razmyshleniia o kinopravde i kinolzhi," *Iskusstvo Kino* 1 (January 1964): 68–80 [includes attack on Morin and Rouch]; V. Basin, "Ob'ektivnost'?" *Iskusstvo Kino* 2 (February 1964): 97–98 [critique of Luc de Heusch's "objectivist" picture of Vertov in his *The cinema and social science: A survey of ethnographical and sociological films* (Paris: UNESCO, 1962); and S. V. Drobashenko, ed., *Pravda kino i "kinopravda": po stranitsam zarubezhnoj pressy* (Moscow: Iskusstvo, 1967), esp. 6–7. A more complex treatment of the relation between Vertov and vérité that takes into account the tensions within the Soviet director's conception of nonfiction (while still insisting on his "Party-mindedness") is to be found in T. F. Selezneva, "Nasledie Dzigi

a version of vérité capable of encompassing both the montage virtuoso Vertov and the patiently observational Flaherty—around whose names opposing nonfictional camps could and did form, as we will see—while couching his quite liberal account of vérité in expressly Vertovian terminology ("kino-eye," "radio-ear," "interval," etc.).[136]

Certain doubts about Vertov and vérité nagged away behind Sadoul's apparently confident rhetoric, however. We have already cited the passage from the *History* where he claimed that Vertov's "Kino-Pravda" was not merely the name, borrowed from the famous newspaper *Pravda*, for his experimental newsreel cycle of 1922–25, but rather a "watchword," a theoretical position, always rather vaguely defined, that the filmmaker developed over the course of his career. Just prior to the Lyon conference, however, and after carefully examining the texts he acquired from Svilova and others over the previous years, Sadoul began to doubt whether "Kino-Pravda" was indeed anything more than a label for the series. A scrupulous historian, he was gratified to discover, virtually on the eve of the MIPE-TV event, that Vertov had in fact used "Kino-Pravda" to describe a theoretical principle, at least late in his career:

> At the last minute, I found a late text by Dziga Vertov where, in 1940, he uses *Kino-Pravda* not as the title of a periodical, but as *Cinéma-vérité*, a logical consequence of his entire theory of *Kino-Eye* combined with *Radio-Ear* [which meant] knowing how to seize, as necessary, life as it is, in order to then capture it on film and later organize it into a work of art through montage.[137]

And that was that, it would seem. Still, persistent pockets of skepticism vis-à-vis the Kino-Pravda/cinéma-vérité nexus,[138] and (even more) the curious

---

Vertova i iskanniia 'cinéma-vérité,'" in *Razmyshleniia u ekrana*, ed. E. S. Dobin (Leningrad: Iskusstvo, 1966), 337–67.

136 "A Lyon les 'caméras vivantes' ont recontré le 'cinéma-vérité,'" *Les Lettres Françaises* 970 (March 14, 1963): 7; Graff, "Réunions et désunions," 73.

137 Graff, *Le cinéma-vérité*, 69. I omit here some of the fascinating details about the discovery that Graff discusses.

138 For but two skeptical remarks, see de Heusch, *The cinema and social science*, 29; William Rothman, *Documentary Film Classics* (Cambridge: Cambridge University Press, 1997), 92–94. For an account that both reflects the confusion that the vérité-Vertov nexus generated and attempts to introduce current Soviet views into the discussion (particularly the affirmation of Vertov's eventual arrival at "realism" after traversing the shoals of "formalism" and "naturalism"), see Louis Marcorelles [with Nicole Rouzet-Albagli], *Living Cinema: New Directions in Contemporary Film-making*, trans. Isabel Quigly (New York: Praeger, 1973 [original French edition published 1970]), 34–37.

frequency with which Sadoul told and retold the story of his last-minute discovery,[139] suggest the need for another look at the matter, which will entail our entering a small textual labyrinth.

The "late text" mentioned by Sadoul was undoubtedly "From the Working Notebooks of Dziga Vertov," the inaugural 1957 publication in *Art of Cinema*, which includes the following remarks on its second page (I have already quoted the first few lines):

> [I]mplied in Kino-Eye were:
> all cinematic means,
> all cinematic inventions,
> all methods and means that might serve to reveal and show the truth.
> Not Kino-Eye for its own sake, but truth through the means and possibilities of the Kino-Eye, that is, Kino-Pravda.
> Not "filming life unawares" for the sake of "filming life unawares," but in order to show people without masks, without makeup, to catch them through the eye of the camera in a moment when they are not acting, to read their thoughts, laid bare by the camera.
> Kino-Eye as the possibility of making the invisible visible, the unclear clear, the hidden manifest, the disguised overt, the acted nonacted.[140]

Already at this point, however, the textual complications begin. As Sadoul indicates, this section of the "Working Notebooks" is dated to February 1940 in the 1957 publication,[141] and evidently he never had a chance to acquaint himself with the version published in Vertov's *Articles, Diaries, Projects*, which appeared as we know it under the editorship of Sergej Drobashenko in 1966, less than a year before Sadoul's death. The same text is included in that edition, in an article entitled "The Birth of 'Kino-Eye,'" with the addition of a few lines:

> Kino-Eye as the possibility of making the invisible visible, the unclear clear, the hidden manifest, the disguised overt, the acted nonacted; making falsehood into truth.

---

139 In at least five different places: see "A Lyon les 'caméras vivantes,'" 7; "Dziga Vertov," *Artsept* 2 (April–June 1963): 18–19; "Cinémois," *Cinéma* (May 1963): 8; "Actualité de Dziga Vertov," 30; "Dziga Vertov: Prophète du ciné oeil," 10–11.
140 "Iz rabochikh tetradej," 113; as translated, with some modifications, in "The Birth of Kino-Eye," *KE*, 42.
141 "Iz rabochikh tetradej," 114.

Kino-Eye [as] the union of science with non-fiction/newsreel film in the struggle for the Communist decoding of reality, as an attempt to show truth on the screen: *film-truth* [*kinopravda*].¹⁴²

The date, however, has been drastically altered: from 1940 to 1924. This is the text and the date that has been disseminated around the world via translations of *Articles, Diaries, Projects*, and has stood for some years as the clearest evidence that "Kino-Pravda" was indeed a theoretical-practical watchword for Vertov from the early 1920s onward, and thus that he could be legitimately regarded as a predecessor of cinéma-vérité and related documentary movements of the late 1950s–early 1960s.¹⁴³

The 2008 Russian edition of Vertov's writings makes it clear, however, that "The Birth of Kino-Eye"—the name of the article's first draft, later changed to "How did it begin?"—dates neither to 1924 nor to 1940, but to 1934, obvious not least because the article makes references to *Three Songs of Lenin* (1934) and the major films that Vertov had made between 1924 and 1934.¹⁴⁴ "How did it begin?" went unpublished at the time, but was recycled in various ways for articles and talks written and delivered at the end of 1934 and beginning of 1935.¹⁴⁵ The editors of the 2008 edition suggest that "How did it begin?"—written sometime toward the end of August or the beginning of September 1934—was composed on the occasion of the fifteenth anniversary of Soviet cinema (August 27, 1934).¹⁴⁶ This might be

---

142 "The Birth of Kino-Eye," *KE*, 42, slightly altered based on the source in "Rozhdenie 'Kino-glaza,'" *SDZ*, 75. Emphasis in original.
143 See footnote 48 for the translations. The articles are all chronologically arranged in *SDZ*, and so there is virtually no possibility that "1924" was a typo.
144 The source is RGALI f. 2091, op. 1, d. 181, ll. 67–70. The editors of *SV* plausibly suggest that the misdating to 1940 (likely Svilova's decision, perhaps working with Nikolaj Abramov) was due to a confusion with another, quite different autobiographical talk from that later year (entitled "Ot Kino-Nedeli k Kolybel'noj"), delivered in connection with the celebrations of Soviet cinema's twentieth year (*SV*, 265–67, 320–23, 557, 569). See also Graff, *Le cinéma-vérité*, 70, footnote 56.
145 In particular "O Kino-Pravde" (*SV*, 267–74), dated September 2, 1934 and published in thoroughly edited form in *Sovetskoe Kino* 11–12 (1934), but also the April 5, 1935 talk "Kak rodilsia i razvivalsia Kino-Glaz" (*SV*, 289–95) and to a lesser extent "Moj raport" (*SV*, 281–82, published in much abbreviated form in *Izvestiia* on December 15, 1934).
146 Today known as "Russian Cinema Day," commemorating Lenin's nationalization of cinema on August 27, 1919.

true, but if so, the article was almost certainly doing a very special kind of double-duty.

As those knowledgeable in the history of Soviet culture may have already noticed, with eyebrows raised, the late August–early September composition date of "How did it begin?" means that it was written in the immediate wake of, or perhaps even during, one of the central cultural events of the entire Stalin era, namely the First Congress of Soviet Writers in Moscow (August 17–September 1, 1934). It was at this congress that an artistic dogma that had been taking on a shape and a name over the previous couple of years, specifically socialist realism, effectively came into its own as *the* artistic dogma of the USSR, along with the Writer's Union itself. As it would be during the Thaw, "truth" or (better) "truthfulness" (*pravdivost'*) was a key desideratum on the socialist realist wishlist (along with "realism in its revolutionary development," "revolutionary romanticism" and other ideologemes), as this well-known remark by the congress's organizer and convener Andrej Zhdanov reminds us:

> Soviet authors have already created not a few outstanding works, which correctly and truthfully depict the life of our Soviet country....
>
> Comrade Stalin has called our writers engineers of human souls. What does this mean? What duties does the title confer upon you?
>
> In the first place, it means knowing life so as to be able to depict it truthfully in works of art, not to depict it in a dead, scholastic way, not simply as "objective reality," but to depict reality in its revolutionary development.
>
> In addition to this, the truthfulness and historical concreteness of the artistic portrayal should be combined with the ideological remolding and education of the toiling people in the spirit of socialism. This method in belles lettres and literary criticism is what we call the method of socialist realism.[147]

Speaker after speaker invoked the importance of truthfulness-to-reality—considerably more often than they did the notion of "socialist realism" itself—while "formalism" (aka literary modernism or avant-gardism, especially the more anti-mimetic varieties) was correspondingly denounced.[148]

---

147 Zhdanov, "Soviet Literature—The Richest in Ideas, the Most Advanced Literature," in *Soviet Writers Congress 1934: The Debate on Socialist Realism and Modernism in the Soviet Union*, ed. Maxim Gorky et al. (London: Lawrence & Wishart, 1977), 15–26; accessed November 6, 2016, https://www.marxists.org/subject/art/lit_crit/sovietwritercongress/zhdanov.htm.

148 For but a few valorizations of "truthfulness," "truth," and related words at the congress, see in *Pervyj vsesoiuznyj s'ezd sovetskikh pisatelej 1934: stenograficheskij otchet* (Moscow:

Vertov could not but have been aware of the scope and tenor of the congress, and not only because it was covered extensively in the press and attended by several writers he knew well, in particular his patron and friend since childhood, journalist Mikhail Kol'tsov (1898–1940).[149] From the tribune of the congress, prose writer and screenwriter Boris Agapov and children's author Nikolaj Bogdanov praised Vertov's recently completed *Three Songs of Lenin* as a prime example of the way that film, too, had begun to satisfy the truthfulness-and-sincerity requirements of the new aesthetic ideology.[150] For Vertov, who had been criticized loudly and incessantly for his formalism among other sins by the "proletarian" critics of the Cultural Revolution period (especially between 1928 and 1933), these endorsements must have come as a major relief, and provided him with the opportunity to express his own agreement with the new general cultural line.[151]

And that, quite clearly, was what his remarks on "Kino-Eye" as but "the *means*" to "Kino-Pravda" were meant to do. Not merely, that is, to abjure formalism ("Kino-Eye for its own sake"), but to rearticulate those already historically

---

Sovetskij Pisatel', 1990 [reprint]) the remarks by Zhdanov (3, 4), writer Samuiil Marshak (30), novelist Leonid Leonov (150), veteran party ideologue and operative Karl Radek (306–7, 310–11), playwright and ideologue Vladimir Kirshon (403–11), and Maxim Gorky (676) among many others. Against formalism, see inter alia the comments by journalist and novelist Ilya Ehrenburg (185), novelist Vsevolod Ivanov (229), writer Boris Lavrenyov (432), and poet Nikolaj Aseev (567–69).

149 For Kol'tsov's remarks at the Congress, see ibid., 221, 350.

150 Agapov: "If you go watch *Three Songs of Lenin*, the new work by Dziga Vertov—that once implacable defender of raw facts [*faktovik*]—you'll see there the most authentic lyricism with nothing made-up." Bogdanov: "The young person of our epoch is not sentimental. Living through that epoch, he's received a large dose of good critical sense. [Nonetheless] tears roll out of his eyes when he sees the living [Feliks] Dzerzhinskij [first head of the secret police] standing by the coffin of Lenin in *Three Songs of Lenin*, that wonderful work by Dziga Vertov" (ibid., 605, 650). *Three Songs* had not yet been publicly released, but had been shown to a variety of audiences in closed screenings and had already been discussed positively in the press; see John MacKay, "Allegory and Accommodation: Vertov's *Three Songs of Lenin* (1934) as a Stalinist film," *Film History* 18 (2006): 376–91, esp. 376, 386–87.

151 As carried out by the organization ARRK (Association of Revolutionary Cinema Workers), the attacks on Vertov evidently extended past 1932, when the hub of Cultural Revolution militancy, the Russian Association of Revolutionary Writers (RAPP), was liquidated; indeed, Vertov most often used the acronym "RAPP" (not "ARRK") to refer to his antagonists. For more details on the period, see Peter Kenez, "The Cultural Revolution in Cinema," *Slavic Review* 47, no. 3 (Autumn 1988): 414–33, esp. 420–25; Evgeny Dobrenko, "Literary Criticism and the Transformations of the Literary Field during the Cultural Revolution, 1928–1932, " in Tihanov and Dobrenko, *A History of Russian Literary Theory and Criticism*, 43–63; *SV*, 531–34, 542–45, 549–56; V. Sutyrin, *Problemy sotsialisticheskoj rekonstrutsii sovetskoj kinopromyshlennosti* (Moscow: Khudozhestvennaia Literatura, 1932), 25–26, 60–61; RGALI f. 2091, op. 2, d. 212; and volume 3.

Vertovian terms and preoccupations—Kino-Eye, Kino-Pravda; "all cinematic inventions"—in a way that would retroactively pave a path connecting the early phase of Vertov's career (with the *Kino-Pravda* series and his early manifestos) to the present socialist-realist moment. As a discursive move, it has no precedent in Vertov before late August–early September 1934: his sole prior defense of "Truth" (the concept, not the newspaper or the newsreel series) dates to April 1926 and functions, characteristically for those years of belligerence, to mark the quite distinct difference between trashy "reddish" (*krasnovataia*) post-Revolutionary fiction films and his own nonfictional work, rather than the difference between formal means ("Kino-Eye") and revealed ends ("Kino-Pravda").[152] The latter distinction is made often post-1934, becoming almost a ritual formula, though its iteration didn't prevent him from being charged with formalism again, as we know.[153]

Thus, Vertov's valorization of "film-truth" pertains above all to his grappling with the socialist-realist conjuncture, not (as Sadoul and others have thought) to his more autonomous speculations about documentary. Somebody—probably either Drobashenko, or Svilova, or both—falsified "The Birth of Kino-Eye's" birthdate, although I think we can legitimately doubt whether Vertov, who after all came up with this re-historicization of "Kino-Pravda" in the first place and wanted to retain a significant place within Soviet film history, would have been opposed to the swap. So is the whole "Kino-Pravda/cinéma-vérité" episode a regrettable and not particularly funny farce, a red herring disturbing the waters of documentary history and theory for over fifty years for no good reason? Our story has one final twist that leads me to doubt whether even that by now apparently obvious truth is so obvious after all.

For whether he was prompted by the socialist-realist emphasis on individual heroes, by the official hostility to "montage," by new possibilities for documentary filming with synchronized sound, or by all of these factors, Vertov was in fact seized, in the mid-1930s and later, by the idea of a more observational kind of nonfictional cinema, which he pursued in a preliminary way via the pioneering sync-sound interviews in *Three Songs* and in *Lullaby*

---

152 In "Kino-Glaz i bor'ba za kinokhroniku: tri etapa bor'by," *SV*, 112. Terms apparently within the same semantic field as "truth"—"fact," above all—in fact work very differently in Vertov's (and others') discourse of the 1920s, and function above all to distinguish the raw materials of nonfiction film from the subjectively ("artistically") generated and staged building blocks of fiction film. More on this in volume 2.

153 See *SV*, 266, 271, 282, 295, 326, 376; RGALI f. 2091, op. 2, d. 212.

(1937), as well as in the unreleased *Three Heroines* (1938).[154] It seems certain that Drobashenko included several of Vertov's unrealized plans for documentary "portraits" of ordinary Soviet individuals in the 1966 *Articles, Diaries, Projects* not only because of the then-current importance of such film-portraiture in documentary worldwide—Drobashenko was concurrently editing an important collection of international essays on vérité[155]—but because Vertov did indeed intend to move in that more observational, subject-centered direction, as acute observers of his career knew and as the recent edition of his script ideas demonstrates.[156] Applications of any notion of "Kino-Pravda" to Vertov's work and thought before 1934 do, however, need to be fundamentally reconsidered—though not necessarily discarded, as we will see in volume 2.

All of this suggests that the boundaries between "socialist" and other kinds of realism—like cinéma-vérité—might on occasion be more porous, at least seen via a long historical view and considered in terms of representational *practice* rather than aesthetic ideology, than we might initially imagine. It might also suggest that we consider at least some acts of falsification, like the mis-dating of "The Birth of Kino-Eye," as examples of what Heather Hendershot has called "censorship as a productive force":[157] in this case, not only as a means of converting Dziga Vertov into always-already a socialist-realist (and thereby saving him as a Soviet artist), but also as a way of connecting a largely forgotten and indeed (post-1934) largely unrealized nonfictional corpus to some of the most vital, decidedly non-socialist-realist international cinematic currents of the 1960s and beyond. This, of course, is what Sadoul, Rouch and others succeeded in doing, errors notwithstanding.[158]

---

154 On the latter film and Vertov's intentions for it, see RGALI f. 2091, op. 2, d. 428, l. 13, and volume 3.

155 Drobashenko, ed., *Pravda kino i "kinopravda"* (1967).

156 See *SDZ*, 285–86, 303–506; as translated in *KE*, 296–97 ("She," "An Evening of Miniatures," "A Young Woman Composer"), 309–11 ("Letter from a Woman Tractor Driver"), 316–20 ("Gallery of Film Portraits," "Little Anya"); and many similar project sketches in *DO* (285–97, 439–40, 445–51, 454–74). On the vital importance of documentary portraiture in post-1954 Soviet documentary, see Sidenova, "From Pravda to Verité," 97, 174–78. For a recollection of Vertov's ambitions in portraiture, see Iurenev, "O Vertove," 65.

157 Heather Hendershot, *Saturday Morning Censors: Television Regulation before the V-Chip* (Durham, NC: Duke University Press, 1998), 2.

158 In this respect, the notion of "film-truth" is a good example of a term that requires historicization within multiple temporal frameworks: at once, that is, as a punctual "symbolic act" pertaining primarily to the Soviet 1930s, *and* as symptomatic of a larger "ideology of form" (centered on "documentary," in this case) with quite different historical range and

Image 5: Elizaveta Svilova in *Man with a Movie Camera* (1929). Source: Yale University Film Archive.

Despite being an old CP man, Georges Sadoul in no way followed the Soviet line in his own extended accounts of Dziga Vertov's work and artistic development.[159] We know that he linked the filmmaker to nonfiction practice both new (cinéma-vérité) and old (Flaherty, John Grierson); but Sadoul

---

implications. See Jameson, *The Political Unconscious*, 75–99; and my *Inscription and Modernity: From Wordsworth to Mandelstam* (Bloomington: Indiana University Press, 2006), 10–12.

159 Indeed, it is not clear to me how much he knew about the Soviet post-1954 reception of Vertov—"image-based publicistics" and all that—apart from what he might have inferred from the publications of Vertov's writings. Svilova was one of his major sources, as we have seen, just as she was for Abramov and Drobashenko, who produced very different portraits of Vertov. That even specialists in Soviet film had a very imperfect sense of Vertov's post-1954 Soviet

Introduction: How Did It Begin? **lxix**

also discussed him enthusiastically in relation to a full array of European avant-garde—or "formalist," in Sovietese—artistic practices and practitioners. Luigi Russolo's "noise music," Guillaume Apollinaire's poetic montages, Picasso and Braque's cubism, the Duchampian readymade, Dadaist and Surrealist poetry, Futurism of course: "driven by his avant-garde spirit," wrote Sadoul in a sentence that could never have appeared in a Soviet publication of the time, "Dziga Vertov oriented himself toward the investigations carried out in parallel by those Western innovators, whose names he surely did not even know."[160] (We should not forget that the original stimulus to inquire into Vertov came to Sadoul from Lilya Brik and Vasilij Katanian: like a radio signal from the Futurist solar system, heard decades later.) This meant that readers with French who were curious about the filmmaker were bequeathed not only a documentary Vertov, but also an avant-garde Vertov: less an attentive and engaged observer than a tireless experimenter with nonnarrative editing strategies, double-exposures, time reversals, noise and much more.

And not only those with French.[161] Vertov's writings reached US shores in summer 1962 between the covers of *Film Culture,* right around the time that journal was emerging as one of the key publications of the US avant-garde. Vertov, who indeed situated his own work within a broader international

---

reception is apparent in Jay Leyda, "*Dziga Vertov: A Guide to References and Resources* [review of Seth Feldman's indispensable 1979 book of that title]," *Cinéaste* 12, no. 1 (1982): 40–41.

160 Georges Sadoul, "Dziga Vertov: Poète du ciné oeil," 10. He writes of the "left" artistic groupings of the '20s, such as the Constructivists and LEF, as part of the "avant-garde" as well (ibid.). See also Sadoul, *Dziga Vertov,* 18–51.

161 I should mention here an outlier among writings on Vertov from the 1950s: the Armenian-Italian literary and film scholar Glauco Viazzi's remarkable "Dziga Vertov e la tendenza documentarista" (first part in *Ferrania* [August–September 1957]: 8–9), evidently the first significant article to appear anywhere on Vertov post-1954, with a distinct focus on Vertov's place in the Soviet artistic vanguard of the 1920s (Viazzi was a specialist in Italian Futurism and other experimental movements). The article was republished in Viazzi, *Scritti di cinema, 1940-1958* (Milan: Longanesi, 1979), 141–58. Viazzi had edited an important journal issue on Soviet cinema in 1949—"Il cinema sovietico (I)," *Sequenze* 3 (November 1949)—which contains extended mention of Vertov in an article on Soviet documentary by Tom Granich ("Cinema documentario sovietico," 24–26). Viazzi also corresponded with the great Soviet film historian Jay Leyda in 1955–56 (Jay Leyda Papers, Tamiment Library and Robert F. Wagner Labor Archive, New York University, series I, subseries B, box 8, folder 34). Regrettably, my poor Italian prevents me from studying how Vertov was read in that country, but my intuition is that Italy's experiences at once with Futurism, with Marxism and with authoritarian politics led to a quite distinct and complex reception early on. See also (for instance) Guido Aristarco, "Le fonti culturali de 'due novatori,' Dziga Vertov e Lev Kuleshov," *Cinema Nuovo* 8, no. 37 (1959): 31–37.

"avant-garde" (*avangardnyj*) conjuncture by the end of the 1920s,[162] shared that issue with articles by newer *vanguardistas* like Tuli Kupferberg, Ron Rice, Stan VanDerBeek, Stan Brakhage, Storm de Hirsch, and *Film Culture*'s editor Jonas Mekas—very different from the company he would keep in French film journals, not to mention Soviet ones.[163] As early as 1967, the US contemporary art journal *Artforum* became one of the founts of English-language writing on Vertov, and comparisons were made in its pages between Vertov and artists as different as Jean Vigo, Peter Kubelka, Nam June Paik, and, in one notable intervention, Ken Jacobs. Lois Mendelson and Bill Simon wrote in September 1971:

> Ken Jacobs' film *Tom, Tom, the Piper's Son* [1969], is, with Vertov's *Man with a Movie Camera* [1929], one of the two great works of a reflexive cinema whose primary subject is an esthetic definition of the nature of the medium.[164]

---

162   See especially Vertov's reports on his European trip of 1929 in RGALI f. 2091, op. 2, d. 412, l. 57 and elsewhere, where he names (among others) Germaine Dulac, Hans Richter, Walther Ruttmann, René Clair, Jean Renoir, Boris Kaufman and Jean Lods, Lotte Reiniger, Viking Eggeling, J. C. Mol, and Eugen Schüfftan as protagonists in that conjuncture. More to come in volumes 2 and 3.

163   Devoted primarily to European and American auteur cinema in its early years, *Film Culture* had published important articles on the contemporary avant-garde right from its inaugural year of 1955 (e.g., Jonas Mekas, "The Experimental Film in America," *Film Culture* 3 [May–June 1955]: 15–18; Parker Tyler, "Stan Brakhage," *Film Culture* 18 [April 1958]: 23–24; Tyler, "Sidney Peterson," *Film Culture* 19 [1959]: 38–43). The appearance of Vertov's articles was clearly part of the journal's shift toward experimental film that began notably with the double issue *Film Culture* 22–23 (Summer 1961), which included articles by Brakhage, Maya Deren, Len Lye, VanDerBeek, and Gregory Markopoulos. See "Discussion on the Legend of *Film Culture*," in *Film Culture Index*, ed. Adeline Coffinier, Victor Gresard, and Christian Lebrat (Paris: Paris Expérimental, 2012), 9–54. The journal had some connection to Soviet film journalism: Mekas had written on contemporary US cinema for the Soviet *Art of Cinema* in 1958 (Dzonas Mekas, "Kinematografiia SShA Segodnia," *Iskusstvo Kino* 12 [December 1958]: 136–140), and apparently *Film Culture* received some of the Vertov writings directly from Svilova.

164   Lois Mendelson and Bill Simon, "Tom, Tom, the Piper's Son," *Artforum* (September 1971): 47. Annette Michelson's "*The Man with a Movie Camera*: From Magician to Epistemologist," still probably the most important essay ever written on the filmmaker, appeared in the same March 1972 issue (on pages 60–72), as did the translation by Marco Carynnyk, "From the Notebooks of Dziga Vertov" (73–83); more on Michelson's essay below. See also Ronald Hunt, "The Constructivist Ethos, Part I," *Artforum* (September 1967): 23–30, esp. 28; Hunt, "The Constructivist Ethos, Part II," *Artforum* (October 1967): 26–32, esp. 32; Elena Pinto Simon, "The Films of Peter Kubelka," *Artforum* (April 1972): 33–39, esp. 35; Douglas Davis, "Video Obscura," ibid., 65–71; Paul S. Arthur, "A Retrospective of Anthropological Film," *Artforum* (September 1973): 69–73, esp. 70; Bill Simon, "Jean Vigo's *Taris* [shot, like

Between 1970 and 1975, eight of Vertov's films were integrated into the yearly "Essential Cinema" cycle at New York's Anthology Film Archives, then as now one of the hubs of the US avant-garde.[165] Anthology's European cousin, the Austrian Film Museum in Vienna—cofounded, as was Anthology, by materialist-structuralist film pioneer Peter Kubelka—staged major retrospectives of Vertov in 1967, 1970, and 1974, all informed by a reading of the filmmaker as an avant-gardist of materialist-structuralist bent.[166] By 1979 it did not seem at all odd to see Vertov's name in an ad in the British film journal *Screen* publicizing the "various strands of the historic and contemporary avant-garde ... represented in the [British Film Institute's] Distribution Library," alongside Germaine Dulac, Jean Epstein, Maya Deren, Gregory Markopoulos, Jon Jost, Peter Greenaway, Mark Rappaport, and Yvonne Rainer.[167]

In their preface to the 1972 French edition of Vertov's writings, the editors of *Cahiers du Cinéma*, then in its politically most radical, Maoist phase, could already identify two distinct post-1954 Vertov receptions—they ignored the Soviet one, which has remained largely out of view in the West, much as Soviet documentary has[168]—to which they would counterpoise another:

> Today Vertov has two official legacies. First, that which a historically erroneous interpretation of "Kino-Pravda" (Ciné-*Pravda*) has consecrated as

---

all Vigo's films, by Boris Kaufman]," *Artforum* (September 1974): 50–53, esp. 51. Stills from *Man with a Movie Camera* also appeared in *Artforum* (September 1971): 7, 32.

165 http://anthologyfilmarchives.org/about/essential-cinema (accessed November 10, 2016).

166 Tode, "Vertov und Wien/Vertov and Vienna," 40–46. Svilova attended the 1970 and 1974 retrospectives, her only trips abroad. Kubelka, as we will see in volume 3, was, with Edith Schlemmer, responsible for one of the most important of all restorations of a Vertov film, that of *Enthusiasm* in 1972 (ibid., 44). With regard to the West German reception, Wolfgang Beilenhoff's afterword to the 1973 *Schriften zum Film* put great stress on Vertov's avant-garde orientation, the similarity of his work to Constructivism, and his affinities to LEF (138–57).

167 Ad in the Winter 1979 issue of *Screen* (n.p.). There was, as we will see, a major Vertov reception within the British avant-garde of the 1960s and 1970s as well.

168 Most of the summaries from this period of the post-1954 Soviet reception (e.g., in the 1973 *Cinéthique* essay by Fargier et al., "'Ne copiez pas sur les yeux,' disait Vertov") are overwhelmingly tendentious, denouncing Soviet attempts to normalize and domesticate Vertov (not in itself an entirely incorrect observation, though grossly inadequate as a key to Vertov's effects on actual filmmaking practice in the USSR). There was a side of the French 1970s reception of Vertov that was more sympathetic to the requirements of socialist realism (and hence more impatient with Vertov's anti-mimetic side), perhaps best expressed in some of the writings of Guy Hennebelle and in the journal *La Revue du Cinéma: Image et Son*: for an example, see Jérôme Cornand, "Sur deux films de Dziga Vertov: *Kino Glaz* et *L'Homme à la Camera*," *La Revue du Cinéma: Image et Son* 297 bis (1975): 55–62.

> "cinéma-vérité": the fetishization of [direct] shooting, of the "revelatory" camera, Vertov as a link in the "beautiful continuity" of realists stretching from Lumière to Rouch. And on the other side, virtuoso montage, hysterical formalist manipulation, culminating in the optical mincemeat of the "underground."[169]
>
> These two directions, the only ones admissible by the bourgeois ideology of art (or of "anti-art"), suppress the specific contribution made by Vertov's practice. Despite their apparent antagonism, both of them aim to situate that practice within the continuum of a formal history of the avant-gardes, cut off from all political, ideological and economic determinations.
>
> Vertov's practice is *unthinkable* without those determinations: the October Revolution and the construction of socialism.[170]

Documentary (vérité in this case); the cinematic avant-garde; a left-wing critical and political filmmaking practice neither realist nor "underground": these were indeed the three dominant categorizations of Vertov's work that had become available outside the USSR by around 1972, readings that, despite *Cahiers*'s militant differentiation, could blur into one another at numerous points, as we will see.

Even more than in the case of vérité, and in part because of the notoriety that vérité brought to Vertov in France, the next cycle of Vertov reception (centrally, 1968 to the late 1970s, but resonating long past that period) was fundamentally conditioned by the French political and artistic-intellectual conjuncture on both the macro- and micro-scale. The big event was, of course, "May 1968" itself, which we should think of not only as a French occurrence—enormous as that was: "the largest mass movement in French history, the biggest strike in the history of the French workers' movement, and the only 'general' insurrection the overdeveloped world has known

---

169 The parenthesis "(Ciné-*Pravda*)" evidently points to the editors' own interpretation of the term as referring above all to the newspaper; "the underground" serves to denote the Euro-American film avant-gardes of the postwar period, as given notoriety in the titles of Sheldon Renan's *An Introduction to the American Underground Film* (New York: E. P. Dutton, 1967), and Parker Tyler's *Underground Film: A Critical History* (New York: Grove Press, 1969).

170 "Préface," *Articles, journaux, projets*, 7, emphasis in original. The preface is signed simply "Cahiers du Cinéma," but was largely the work of Jean Narboni; my thanks to David Fresko for pointing this out.

since World War II"[171]—but as involving revolts in various countries against US military involvement in Vietnam; in the US itself against that country's racist social order; against Soviet domination in Eastern Europe (especially in Czechoslovakia and Poland); against *franquismo* in Spain; and of students against the state in West Germany, Italy, Brazil, and Mexico.[172]

The time also saw an extraordinary, incandescent mingling of a wide variety of exploratory and even avant-garde forms of inquiry in France and some of its former colonies, emerging out of structural anthropology and linguistics, renewed investigation (much influenced by a rediscovered Russian Formalism) into the mechanisms of literary representation, new thinking about psychoanalysis and Marxism, radical approaches to history and historiography, and programmatically anti-authoritarian philosophical critique. To be sure, these novel modes of thought responded to diverse problems made newly visible by history: colonialism and Western imperialism above all, perhaps, but also the catastrophes of Nazism and Stalinism; the uneven postwar rise of consumer capitalism with its media instruments; and patriarchy and what would later be called heteronormativity.[173]

---

171 Kristin Ross, *May '68 and Its Afterlives* (Chicago: University of Chicago Press, 2002), 4. Its far larger twentieth century predecessor was the first Russian Revolution of 1905–6, which Vertov lived through as a child; see chapter 1.

172 Not without reason does world-systems theorist Immanuel Wallerstein write of "the world revolution of 1968" ("New Revolts Against the System," *New Left Review* II/18 [November–December 2002]: 33). See also Mark Kurlansky, *1968: The Year that Rocked the World* (New York: Ballantine, 2004).

173 This is not the place to go into greater depth about this astonishing and still-influential period in French intellectual life, which in my view stands for us as a great avant-garde Silver Age (after the historical avant-garde in the arts, of which Vertov was a part): Lévi-Strauss, Sartre, de Beauvoir, Fanon, Lacan, Benveniste, Barthes, Althusser, Foucault, Derrida, Deleuze, Kristeva, and Debord are but a few of the important participants. See among other sources Nick Browne's introduction to *Cahiers du Cinéma, Volume 3: 1969–1972 The Politics of Representation*, ed. Browne (London: Routledge, 1990), 1–20; Francesco Casetti, *Theories of Cinema 1945–1995* (Austin: University of Texas Press, 1999), 184–234; Denis Hollier and Jeffrey Mehlman, ed., *Literary Debate: Texts and Contexts* (New York: New Press, 2001); and Daniel Fairfax's introduction to Jean-Louis Comolli, *Cinema against Spectacle: Technique and Ideology Revisited*, ed. and trans. Daniel Fairfax (Amsterdam: Amsterdam University Press, 2015), 17–43. I do not want to sound utterly Francocentric: thinkers from many other places, perhaps above all the rediscovered Walter Benjamin (who wrote about Vertov), were/are of course central as well. The importance in this period of rediscovered (or simply *discovered*) early Russian-Soviet theory—one of whose major figures, Shklovsky, also published on Vertov—can hardly be exaggerated. See inter alia the pioneering presentation of the Formalists in T. Todorov, ed., *Théorie de la littérature: Textes des formalistes russes* (Paris: Seuil, 1965), published under the auspices of the key

If vérité arguably operated, in relatively precritical fashion, with the notion of a *subject* (with a camera) moving through a *world* (which he or she would explore, attentive to its boundaries and his or her own), the newer modes of thought would entirely undo the self-evidently autonomous status of both subject and world (and their "rationality"), reconceiving them as historical and contingent consequences of processes of representation. As representations, subjects and worlds (along with "ideas," "values," etc.) are *constructions*—with no one master builder identifiably responsible for them—comprised of diverse units, tropes, conventions and combinatory operations whose overlapping and conflicting paradigms and sub-paradigms, like "capitalism," "patriarchy" or "the unconscious," are to become the true objects of critical inquiry (along with what exceeds and disrupts them). And it is in relation to this project of critiquing representation and its social-historical effects that what we now think of as the *self-reflexivity* of Dziga Vertov's films, and of *Man with a Movie Camera* in particular, became an important object of theoretical reflection and argument at the beginning of the 1970s.

Neither Vertov nor his contemporaries overtly theorized the self-reflexivity of his work—thus leaving behind, from our perspective, a remarkable gap in his written corpus and early reception—and it took a while for post-1954 commentators to take notice of what to us now seems one of the most obvious features of Vertovian cinema. This eloquent 1960 statement by film editor and critic Dai Vaughan forecast numerous probings into Vertov's autoreferentiality—written in a very different idiom, to be sure—to come a full decade later:

> Persistently [in *Man with a Movie Camera*] we are shown the mechanics of what we are seeing . . . [which serves] to remind us that what is before us is merely an image, and that true reality lay in the subject of the shot. [*Man with a Movie Camera*] is, in fact, a study in film truth on an almost philosophical level (the levity of its treatment—the fact that it is argued in the mode of fun—does not disqualify this judgment). This film does deliberately what most others try hard to avoid: it destroys its own illusions.

---

avant-garde theoretical journal *Tel Quel*; Luda and Jean Schnitzer, *Le Cinéma soviétique par ceux qui l'ont fait* (Paris: Éditeurs français réunis, 1966); the writings by or about Soviet director-theorists, Eisenstein above all, that appeared in *Cahiers du Cinéma* mainly between January 1969 and January–February 1972; *Action Poétique* 59 (1974) (on Proletkult); (in English) *Russian Art of the Avant-Garde 1902–1934*, ed. and trans. John Bowlt (New York: Viking Press, 1976); and numerous issues of *October* right from that journal's inaugural year of 1976. See also the excellent overview of the French-Russian theoretical relationship during the 1960s and later in Christie and Taylor, eds., *The Film Factory*, 11–13, 412–14.

It refuses to allow us to accept the screen as a plane of reference for reality, and instead seeks to dissolve all such planes of reference, successively, as soon as they are formed, in the hope that reality will "emerge" from the process not as a creature of screen illusion but as a liberated spirit.[174]

The basic arguments surrounding Vertov's supposed dissolution of "all ... planes of reference" can be laid out economically by examining two important French statements on his work from the early 1970s, produced at the very moment that methodological anti-humanism was making its influential way into the study of cinema. As it turns out, an early reference to the self-referential/political Vertov inflects the conclusion of one of the five or six most discussed film-theoretical essays ever written: Jean-Louis Baudry's "Ideological Effects of the Basic Cinematographic Apparatus" (1970), which famously argues that all elements of cinema, from projection to theater architecture to standard narrative continuity, at once answer to, help construct, and reinforce the idealist illusion of a stable, autonomous perceiving subject.[175] Near the end of the essay, Baudry briefly contemplates how cinema might be used to counter these reifying representational effects, and produces what was perhaps the most important comment written on Vertov during these years. For the subject to become capable of "[accounting] for his own situation," writes Baudry,

> ... it was necessary to substitute secondary organs, grafted on to replace his own defective ones, instruments or ideological formations capable of

---

[174] Vaughan, *"The Man with the Movie Camera,"* 20. Here Vaughan seems to use "spirit" in a well-nigh Hegelian sense (*Geist*). I should note that Vaughan was at the time (late 1960) associated with various writers (including Stuart Hall and Paddy Whannel) for *Universities and Left Review*, whose editorial board had just merged in January 1960 with that of *The Reasoner* to form our familiar *New Left Review*. At the beginning of 1960, Vaughan had cofounded the short-lived but important and self-consciously political film journal *Definition* with Bolesław Sulik, a left-wing Polish émigré and who later became an important film director and (after the fall of Communism) the head of Polish TV. Considered together with these "politics of affiliation and allegiance" (Michael Denning), Vaughan's remark on *Man with a Movie Camera* provides an instance of an early British reception of Vertov that linked considerations of form with considerations of politics. That reception would not fully emerge until the 1970s in response to French thinking post-1968, as we will see. See John Gibbs, *The life of mise-en-scène: Visual style and British film criticism, 1946–1978* (Oxford: Oxford University Press, 2015), 96, 110–11.

[175] Jean-Louis Baudry, "Cinéma: effets idéologiques produits par le appareil du base," *Cinéthique* 7–8 (1970): 1–8; here as translated by Alan Williams as "Ideological Effects of the Basic Cinematographic Apparatus," *Film Quarterly* 28, no. 2 (Winter 1974–75): 39–47.

> filling his function as subject. In fact this substitution is only possible on the condition that the instrumentation itself be hidden or repressed. Thus disturbing cinematic elements—similar, precisely, to those elements indicating the return of the repressed—signify without fail the arrival of the instrument "in flesh and blood" [literally "in flesh and bone (*en chair et en os*)," but more idiomatically, "in person"], as in Vertov's *Man with a Movie Camera*. Both specular tranquility and the assurance of one's own identity collapse simultaneously with the revealing of the mechanism, that is, of the inscription of the film-work [*l'inscription du travail*].[176]

Baudry is of course referring not only to the continual appearance in *Man with a Movie Camera* of camera and cameraman, editing and editor, spectacle and spectator, but also to the way in which the film incessantly loops its representations of the world back into representations of the work of representation.

About a year later, in another widely influential essay, *Cahiers* editor Pascal Bonitzer questioned Baudry's muted optimism about the critical potential of Vertov's production-centered reflexivity, noting along the way (as we have) how the romance of *Man with a Movie Camera* sexualizes the agency of both "Man" and "Movie Camera":

> Baudry [appears to think] that the misrecognition inherent in representation could be dispelled by a representation, itself literally providential, of *the "flesh and blood" instrument* . . . The "instrument" (the camera, I assume), the originating repression of cinematographic representation, would accordingly, with reference to that representation, be situated in the place of the real. Hence the "effect of cognition" produced by its "unveiling". . . .
>
> It is clear that Baudry is here confusing camera, subject and work; if it is indeed the case, as he writes, that the camera, "central" to the process of film production, is the phantasmatic support of the "subject," then the "advent" in the film of this instrument . . . is at most the inscription of that support. In addition, would not this "inscription" be merely a fetishizing of the instrument (and this is certainly the case in *Man with a Movie Camera*, where the camera is invested with a sexual identity)? Baudry reinforces this fetishism: the notions of "unveiling" and of "flesh and blood" are the internal snares of the system of representation, metaphysical

---

176 "Ideological Effects," 46.

determinants of the *truth*, of *meaning*.... The fact that in *Man with a Movie Camera* there is a second camera, which represents the "first," a division of one into two, a process inseparable from the scenographic fragmentation and the metaphorical-metonymic substitution practiced in the montage, is the opposite of an unveiling. It is a surplus-text, a germination in which the instrument *as signifier* is declined in sexual terms (eye, penis, mouth, vagina ...) and the shooting process fetishized—[by contrast] it is the *montage* which, by way of the breaks and constant variations in level with which it marks the film process, transformationally inscribes and "analyzes" that fetishism; the montage is the productivity of the film.... [The] "inscription of the work" ... cannot be brought about by an irruption, a sudden wild *apparition* ("the advent of the instrument," magical, providential, miraculous, like many a Hollywood hero), but rather precisely through work—through a movement, excluding any immediacy, which displaces the ideological series.[177]

What the work of representation, cinematic or otherwise, generates is *coherence* (of narrative, of image, of protagonist, of the experience of viewing), inviting belief and affective investment. The "apparition" of cameras, camerapeople, filmstrips, editing, or editors does nothing to dispel this constructed coherence, and indeed adds another layer to it (a "surplus-text")—a layer to which garden-variety television news programming, with its endless display of media gadgetry and technological mastery, has accustomed us. If *Man with a Movie Camera* critiques representation, it does so (Bonitzer suggests) on the level of its often highly disjunctive montage, which thwarts efforts to follow or rationalize the transition from one shot to the next in terms of some coherent and autonomous represented whole (a scene, an

---

177 Pascal Bonitzer, "Hors-Champ (un espace en défaut)," *Cahiers du Cinéma* 234–35 (December 1971/January–February 1972): 15–26; translated by Lindley Hanlon as "Off-Screen Space," in *Cahiers*, ed. Browne, 299–300; emphases in original. Bonitzer, in my view, exaggerates the extent to which Baudry's "instrument" needs to be read as referring only or even mainly to the "camera," but his larger critique remains legible and compelling. For a related skeptical reading of self-reflexivity explicitly influenced by Bonitzer, see Christian Metz, *L'énonciation impersonnelle, ou le site du film* (Paris: Méridiens Klincksieck, 1991), 85–92. Rather like Bonitzer, P. Adams Sitney identifies *Man with a Movie Camera*'s "critique of visual illusionism" not in any representations of the act of filmmaking but rather in its "[playful] hyperbolizing of the power of shot-countershot and the authority of the visible (Vertov's 'Theory of the Interval')" (*Modernist Montage: The Obscurity of Vision in Cinema and Literature* [New York: Columbia University Press, 1990], 38).

action, an event).[178] Indeed, the refusal of *any* given film to cohere in this way becomes legible—and here Bonitzer's thinking becomes transparently allegorical, just as Vertov's often does—as symptomatic of the divisions fissuring capitalist class society, and the representational work (here, failed work) needed to obfuscate them.[179]

The Baudry-Bonitzer exchange left film critics and theorists, and us, with as many fascinating questions about self-reflexive formal-political strategies as it did answers, and helped set the terms for discussions of Vertov for the next twenty years or so, particularly in France, the UK and the US. Is Vertov in *Man with a Movie Camera* (and perhaps elsewhere) engaged in a critique of representation *avant le mot*? If so, where do we locate it? Does the self-reflexivity of the film serve this critique; exalt the power of cinematic representation and its technology "fetishistically," as it were; or somehow perform both of these apparently contradictory roles at the same time? (Given that it seems impossible to imagine a use of cinema to demystify cinematic representation that would not also affirm, at least tacitly, cinema's power to mount such a difficult critique, the last-named option might be less absurd than first appears.)[180]

As we will see again in volume 2, these questions, variously articulated, have produced a forbidding body of commentary worthy of *Man with a Movie Camera*'s own complexity. Perhaps the film's "subversion through consciousness . . . of cinematic illusionism" demonstrates how to convert cinema from mere spectacle into a self-conscious epistemological instrument;[181] or perhaps, in its

---

178 For a closer analysis of the film devoted to proving this point, see Alan Williams, "The Camera Eye and the Film: Notes on Vertov's 'Formalism,'" *Wide Angle* 3, no. 3 (1979): 12–17.

179 "Off-Screen Space," 303.

180 Thus, for Viennese avant-gardist Peter Weibel, *Man with a Movie Camera* at once exalts the material autonomy of film as a medium, and demonstrates the constructed or representational character of "every . . . reality" ("Eisenstein, Vertov and the Formal Film," in *Film as Film: Formal Experiment in Film 1910–1975*, by Phillip Drummond et al. [London: Arts Council of Great Britain, 1979], 50). Film scholar Robert Stam interprets the film as both affirmative and mimetic (when it shows cinema "as forming part of the collective life of societal production") and as a critical "assault on illusionism" (*Reflexivity in Film and Literature: From Don Quixote to Jean-Luc Godard* [New York: Columbia University Press, 1992], 80–82). For an early critical reflection on this awkward conjunction, see Judith Mayne, "Kino-Truth and Kino-Praxis: Vertov's *Man with a Movie Camera*," *Cine-Tracts* 1, no. 2 (Summer 1977): 81–89.

181 Annette Michelson, "*The Man with the Movie Camera*: From Magician to Epistemologist," *Artforum* 10, no. 7 (March 1972): 69. This essay was quickly translated into French ("*L'Homme à la Caméra*: de la magie à la épistémologie," *Revue de Esthétique* 26, nos. 2–4 [1973]: 295–310). For early testaments to the powerful effect of Michelson's argument, see Noël Burch and Jorge Dana, "Propositions," trans. Diana Matias and Christopher King,

denaturalizing of any principle of filmic organization, fictional or nonfictional, the film valorizes cinema as an ongoing work of representation and critique of representation, all in the service of the Revolution.[182] Maybe *Man with a Movie Camera* so boldly demonstrates cinema's powers of appropriating and redistributing perception in order to propose, in technocratic fashion, a new model for the perceiving human subject, "a new human being... a kind of organized nerve center, a reflection of the industrial era and of socialist society";[183] or maybe its

---

Afterimage 5 (Spring 1974): 41–66; esp. 44–45; and Malcolm Le Grice, *Abstract Film and Beyond* (Cambridge, MA: MIT Press, 1977), 53–62. (This edition of Le Grice's book has some frames from *Man with a Movie Camera* on its back cover.) Among the many excellent readings of *Man with a Movie Camera* influenced by Michelson's article is that of Jonathan L. Beller, who takes Vertov to be demonstrating how cinematic montage (recombination, sequencing, substitution) can both offer a paradigm for production and exchange relations under capitalism as such, and at the same time self-consciously make that paradigm visible, undoing the normally fetishized character of those relations (as mediated and obscured by money) ("Dziga Vertov and the Film of Money," *boundary 2* 26, no. 3 [1999]: 151–99; republished and revised as "Circulation: Dziga Vertov and the Film of Money," in Beller's *The Cinematic Mode of Production: Attention Economy and the Society of the Spectacle* [Lebanon, NH: Dartmouth College Press, 2006], 37–87).

182   This is effectively the argument—very close in spirit if not in idiom to some of the most radical Soviet Constructivist positions of the 1920s and (I believe) tacitly indebted to Eisenstein more than to Vertov—made in *Cahiers*'s 1972 "Préface" to *Articles, journaux, projets*, especially on 9 and 13. One of the most detailed essays ever written on *Man with a Movie Camera*, Stephen Crofts's and Olivia Rose's 1977 "An Essay toward *Man with a Movie Camera*," offers a strong defense of this position (in *Screen* 18, no. 1 [1977], 9–60). In its stress on Vertov's continual exposure of the *paradigmatic* categories and operations underlying any specific instance of montage sequencing, the Crofts/Rose article presages, in a much more political key, Lev Manovich's well known remarks on Vertov as a "database" filmmaker (in *The Language of New Media* [Cambridge, MA: MIT Press, 2001], 1–20).

183   Roudinesco, "Dziga Vertov" [1974], 311. For a hostile reading of Vertov that sees the filmmaker as emphatically technocratic and Taylorist and *Man with a Movie Camera* as devoted to "the conscious subsumption of social life under the ethic and imperative of production," see Stanley Aronowitz, "Film: The Art Form of Late Capitalism," *Social Text* 1 (Winter 1979): 119. Aronowitz's reading seems informed by Guy Debord's analysis of Soviet Communism in *La société du spectacle* (1967; in English as *The Society of the Spectacle* [Detroit: Black & Red, 1970], 73–124, esp. 99). For a more nuanced though still critical view of Vertov's techno-enthusiasm that better accounts for early Soviet preoccupations with underdevelopment and for the way that "scientific management" became (for the Bolsheviks) a way of sustaining and deepening the Revolution, see Robert Linhart, *Lénine, les Paysans, Taylor: Essai d'analyse matérial historique de la naissance du système productif soviétique* (Paris: Seuil, 1976 [2004 digital reprint]), 129–35. Linhart, one of the most important French radical intellectuals of the era, was a major influence on Jean-Luc Godard in the wake of the latter's "Groupe Dziga Vertov" period; more on that below.

dense visual rhyming of acts of filmmaking with other kinds of making affirms the "organic interdependency" of all parts of the Soviet "social whole."[184] In other words, how one reads Vertov's self-reflexivity has serious consequences for how one evaluates Vertov, and especially the political dimension of his work, more generally.

One question about all of this might be nagging at the back of my reader's mind: why was it so important at this time, and indeed later, to affirm that Vertov was a militant, critical, and intellectually sophisticated filmmaker of the left (even the *first* such filmmaker)? We shouldn't forget that French readers after 1954 were introduced to Vertov's writing not by the circumspect and even melancholy "From the Working Notebooks" (as Soviet readers were in 1957), but by Sadoul's excerpts from the fiery, experimentally typeset, take-no-hostages polemic "Kinocs: A Revolution" (first published in *LEF* in June 1923, in *Cahiers* in June and August 1963). It is not hard to see how the flamboyantly bellicose rhetoric of a man who claimed to have passed a "death sentence" on all hitherto existing film in 1919, made efforts to democratize (in a small way) access to media technology, and sought to create a "visual bond between the workers of the whole world,"[185] might find admirers in the post-May 1968 hothouse of cinema militancy.[186] (And, yet again, not only in France: students at the recently opened German Film and Television Academy in Berlin, eighteen of whom—including Harun Farocki, future master political film-essayist—occupied the office of the Academy's principal in November 1968, briefly renamed their school "the Dziga Vertov Academy" that year.)[187]

---

184 Noël Carroll, "Causation, the Ampliation of Movement and Avant-Garde Film," in *Theorizing the Moving Image* (Cambridge: Cambridge University Press, 1996), 175. Although materialist-structuralist filmmaker and theorist Peter Gidal insists that "a film is materialist if it does not cover its apparatus of illusionism [which is] never a matter of anti-illusionism pure and simple, uncovered truth, but rather, a constant procedural work against the attempts at producing an illusionist continuum's hegemony," he also notes the importance of "the sound/image montage of Vertov," whom he calls "the strictest Russian formalist," to post-war avant-garde attempts to make "all parts of the film inter-relate," in the manner of composer Anton von Webern's serialism (*Materialist Film* [New York: Routledge, 1989], 17, 171–73).
185 "Kinopravda and Radiopravda [1925]," in *KE*, 52.
186 "Kinoks-Révolution," *Cahiers du Cinéma* XXV, no. 146 (August 1963): 32.
187 The occupiers, including Farocki, were kicked out of the Academy (founded 1966) (Volker Pantenburg, *Farocki/Godard: Film as Theory*, trans. Michael Turnbull [Amsterdam: Amsterdam University Press, 2015], 22 [footnote 29]). For a reflection on Farocki's later use of Vertov, see Christa Blümlinger, "Mémoire du travail et travail de

In the fall of 1969 appeared the first mention in print of the "Groupe Dziga Vertov" (1969–72), the famous collaboration between Jean-Luc Godard and Jean-Pierre Gorin that effectively began with their editing work on the film *Vent d'Est* (1970).[188] Working outside of studios with little equipment and virtually no budget, and affirming a collective rather than individual-authorial identity, Godard and Gorin gave a number of reasons for naming their militant group after Vertov, all of which boil down to something like the following:

> Godard: ... The group name is to indicate a program, to raise a flag, not to just emphasize one person. Why Dziga Vertov? Because at the beginning of the century, he was really a Marxist moviemaker. He was a revolutionary working for the Russian revolution through the movies. He wasn't just an artist. He was a progressive artist who joined the revolution and became a revolutionary artist through struggle. He said that the task of the [kinocs] was not moviemaking ... but to produce films in the name of the World Proletarian Revolution. In that way, there was a big difference between him and those fellows Eisenstein and Pudovkin, who were not revolutionary.[189]

This is not the place to begin a comparison of Vertov's films with the formally sui generis, often overtly if somewhat perplexingly didactic, and always self-reflexive works of the Group, not least because fine-grained comparative analysis in this case is probably less useful than isolating general

---

memoire: Vertov/Farocki (À propos de l'installation *Contre-chant*)," *Intermédialités* 11 (2008): 53–68.

188 Antoine de Baecque, *Godard: biographie* (Paris: Grasset & Fasquelle, 2010), location 10839–12662 [Kindle edition]. The script for *British Sounds* (1969) appeared in *Cinéthique* 5 (September–October 1969), signed "for the Dziga Vertov Group" (de Baecque, *Godard*, location 11258). Filmmaker Jean-Henri Roger and several others were affiliated with the Group at various times.

189 Kent E. Carroll, "Film and Revolution: An Interview with Jean-Luc Godard [and Jean-Pierre Gorin]," *Evergreen* 14, no. 83 (October 1970): 47. "We," Vertov's very first manifesto, was published in the same issue under the title "We: A Manifesto by Film Worker Dziga Vertov" (50–51), with an introductory note mentioning a number of recent "Vertov festivals in Paris, Vienna, Brussels, Stockholm and other major cities." For other accounts of the Group's origins, see de Baecque, *Godard*, locations 11239–51; Richard Brody, *Everything Is Cinema: The Working Life of Jean-Luc Godard* (New York: Henry Holt, 2008), location 7850–55 [Kindle edition]; "Jean-Luc Godard, Mitglied der Gruppe 'Dsiga Wertow'" [interview with Georg Alexander and Wilfried Reichardt], *Süddeutsche Zeitung* 80, no. 3 (April 4, 1971): 4 [unpaginated supplement].

methodological affinities.[190] A controversial, complicated, and still imperfectly understood period in Godard's career, the Dziga Vertov moment yielded for the most part little-seen films that were often (though not always) met with dismay and/or incomprehension—another affinity with Vertov, to be sure—even in places where they were not screened at all.[191]

In the Soviet Union, for instance, veteran director Sergej Iutkevich was incensed by Godard wrapping himself in the Vertov banner, not least because of the French director's open disdain for the French Communist Party and equally open admiration for Mao's Cultural Revolution:

> I can only imagine how infuriated Dziga would be had he lived to see such perversions of his revolutionary theories, and with what fury he would go after these "followers" of his. . . . We must [denounce the Group] not only in defense of Vertov's memory in a purely academic sense, but to preserve the living practice of revolutionary cinema, and most of all to help the energetic youth who are setting out to struggle on behalf of such

---

190 The most important of these is arguably the Group films' intense focus on the very process of linking sounds and images to produce representations, presaging both the later *Cahiers* reading of Vertov as a filmmaker concerned with the making of representation, and Godard's own *Histoire(s) du Cinéma* (1988–98) among other works; see David Faroult, "Du vertovisme du Groupe Dziga Vertov," in *Jean-Luc Godard: Documents*, ed. Nicole Brenez et al. (Paris: Centre Pompidou, 2006), 134–38. Godard scholar Michael Witt offers a useful distillation of possible affinities: "[The] alignment with Vertov signaled an identification with a form of political cinema rooted in an engagement with the present and the everyday, and an engagement with some central strands of Vertovian theory, which continue to inform Godard's later practice. These include the dream of a quasi-scientific research laboratory in which to pursue audiovisual experiments; a deep-rooted mistrust of the application of a literary form of narrative to cinema, combined with contempt for the conventional written script, and a quest to develop an extra-linguistic visual symphonic-cinematic form; expansion of the idea and practice of montage to include every stage of the filmmaking process; the theorization and application of interval theory, whereby film poems are composed around the movements and transitions between the visual stimuli carried by individual shots; and an unshakable faith in the camera as a scientific scope through which to penetrate the surface of reality and reveal the invisible" (Michael Witt, *Jean-Luc Godard, Cinema Historian* [Bloomington: Indiana University Press, 2013], locations 2175–81 [Kindle edition]). The major works of the Group are usually thought to be *Un film comme les autres* (1968; retroactively labeled a Vertov Group film); *British Sounds* (1969), *Pravda* (1969; released 1970), *Vent d'Est* (1970), *Lotte in Italia* (1969; released 1971), *Jusqu'à la victoire* (1970; unfinished); *Vladimir et Rosa* (1971), *Tout va bien* (1972), and *Letter to Jane* (1972). See David Faroult, "Filmographie du Groupe Dziga Vertov," in *Jean-Luc Godard: Documents*, 132–33.

191 On the complicated reception of the Group films—considerably more positive, it would seem, in the US than in France—see Brody, *Everything Is Cinema*, 355–57. For some contemporary readings of the films, see the section on the Group in *Take One* 2, no. 11 (June 1971): 7–14.

a cinema, particularly in the developing nations on the African and Latin American continents.

Dziga Vertov's name must be cleansed of these layers of "Godardism."[192]

In the presentations they made during their trip to Austria, Sweden, and East and West Germany in February–May 1974, Svilova and Drobashenko attacked Godard's supposed anti-Soviet distortions of the revolutionary Vertovian legacy, dismissing at the same time the avant-garde's formalist appropriation of Vertov and the individualistic ideology of cinéma-vérité.[193] Back in the US, Boris Kaufman, a great veteran of French and American cinema and recently retired after an extraordinary career behind the camera, had apparently thought about suing Godard for his use/besmirching of the Vertov name—that the group was at that time (1970) engaged in the production of a film dedicated to "glorifying the [Palestinian] Fatah

---

192 Iutkevich, "Pervoprokhodets" [published 1976], 269–70. The year 1976 saw the fourth edition of the much-publicized Tashkent (Uzbek SSR) Festival of African and Asian Cinema, "expanded [that year] to include Latin America" (Rossen Djagalov and Masha Salazkina, "Tashkent'68: A Cinematic Contact Zone," *Slavic Review* 75, no. 2 [Summer 2016]: 279). See also S. Drobashenko, "Poet revoliutsionnogo kino: k 80-letiiu so dnia rozhdeniia Dzigi Vertova," *Sovetskaia Kul'tura* 44 (January 6, 1976): 5.

193 Or so they reported back to the Cinematographers' Union in any case. Drobashenko in 1976 (and at other times) would write positively about Rouch's enthusiasm for Vertov (see footnote 192). Svilova and Drobashenko's 1974 travels took them to East Berlin (February 4–13), Stockholm (February 26–March 5), Vienna (April 18–24), and Munich (May 14–20) (RGANI [Rossijskij Gosudarstvennyj Arkhiv Novejshej Istorii] f. 5, op. 67, d. 203, ll. 2–4, 16–19, 34–36, 72–76). My great thanks to Rossen Djagalov for sharing these archival gems with me. Interestingly, Godard had earlier (February 1968) requested from Svilova a letter of support for Henri Langlois during the notorious "Affair" of Langlois's dismissal from the Cinémathèque by French culture minister and novelist André Malraux (RGALI f. 2091, op. 2, d. 646); I do not know if she replied. Svilova and Drobashenko probably received some ideological coaching before and during their trip, but I wonder how necessary it was. Godard was definitely targeted during the visit to Stockholm, which had been the site of an important 1969 exhibition, curated by Ronald Hunt, that featured Vertov and later traveled to various cities in Canada. Wrote Hunt in the catalog, which linked the early Soviet avant-garde to the May '68 events, "*Man with a Movie Camera* is Utopian, but made with the elements of the present, as such it is also critique, critique of an actual monolithic state" ("Introduction," *Poetry must be made by all! Transform the world!* [Stockholm: Moderna Museet Stockholm, 1969], 8; see also Ron Hunt, "Icteric and Poetry must be made by all / Transform the World: A note on a lost and suppressed avant-garde and exhibition," accessed on November 20, 2016 at http://www.artandeducation.net/paper/icteric-and-poetry-must-be-made-by-all-transform-the-world-a-note-on-a-lost-and-suppressed-avant-garde-and-exhibition/).

organization" was especially provocative—but the lawsuit, like the film, was never realized.[194]

In any case, rather like cinéma-vérité had transported Vertov into the thick of contemporary documentary film practice, so the Dziga Vertov Group, far better known than other radical cinema collectives due to the fame of its most celebrated member, did a lot, together with Vertov's more pugnacious writings, to supply the Soviet filmmaker with his oft-invoked militant-political credentials.[195] As concerns Jean-Luc Godard, however, there is an important sense in which his most interesting engagement with Vertov came after the Group dissolved in 1972, during the early years of his work on video with Anne-Marie Miéville. That engagement was mediated by the activist, sociologist, and theorist Robert Linhart, who in his 1976 book *Lenin, the Peasants, Taylor* argued that Vertov's "ultra-Taylorist" interest in the cinematic microanalysis, through montage and slow motion, of working bodies was not intended for application to top-down practices of labor management, but instead was meant to offer a critical knowledge of labor processes and bodily discipline to workers themselves, or (in Linhart's words) "to deliver to each worker a vision of the ensemble," thereby rendering the "productive system" "transparent."[196] (The cover of

---

194 See Boris Kaufman Papers, Beinecke Library, GEN MSS 562.14.273 (correspondence with Paris-based producer and screenwriter Pierre Tarcali), especially a letter cited here from Tarcali to Kaufman of June 22, 1970. Tarcali was going to recruit the services of attorney Robert Badinter, future French justice minister and earlier Godard's own lawyer. The film in question was the never-to-be-finished and indeed disastrous *Jusqu'à la victoire*, footage from which was later reworked into Godard and Anne-Marie Miéville's *Ici et Ailleurs* (1976): see de Baecque, *Godard*, locations 5911, 11419–594, 12874–13048; Michael Witt, "On and Under Communication," in *A Companion to Jean-Luc Godard*, ed. Tom Conley and T. Jefferson Kline (New York: Wiley-Blackwell, 2014), 318–50, esp. 319–21.

195 For just two examples of Vertov's influence as a political filmmaker, see Thomas Tode's comments on the kinocs of Hamburg and Vienna (in "Vertov und Wien," 48–49); and Steve MacFarlane's "Interview with Jem Cohen" in *The White Review* (October 2014), accessed November 21, 2016 at http://www.thewhitereview.org/interviews/interview-with-jem-cohen/. By around 1980, juxtapositions of Vertov with Godard had become commonplace in film studies essays and anthologies: see (for instance) Antonio Bertini, ed., *Tecnica e ideologia* (Rome: Bulzoni, 1980), 51–64. For more on the militant film scene in the early 1970s, see Guy Hennebelle, "SLON: Working Class Cinema in France," trans. Catherine Ham and John Mathews, *Cinéaste* 5, no. 2 (Spring 1972): 15–17.

196 Linhart, *Lénine, les Paysans, Taylor*, 133. The managerial use of cinema for Taylorist purposes already had a significant history by the mid-1920s: see (on the Ford Motor

Linhart's book is an image from the last part of Vertov's *Enthusiasm*, which indeed presents Taylorist practices of body-training more explicitly than do any of his other films.) Godard at the end of the 1970s was hoping to make a television series entitled *Travail (Work)* with Linhart's participation; that project never got off the ground, but via conspicuous slow-motion techniques, Godard and Miéville applied Linhart's Vertov-inspired proposals for a "visual analysis" of work in their remarkable video series *Six fois deux: sur et sous la communication* (1976), *France tour détour deux enfants* (1979), and in the film *Sauve qui peut (la vie)* (1980). They also (in *Sauve qui peut*) quoted from Linhart's writing about the experience of assembly-line labor and (in *France tour détour*) included a fictional journalist named "Robert Linhart" who appears solely in voiceover (as spoken by Godard himself).[197] These experiments represent a major and precise response to Vertov's films and theories, and we will return to them during our discussions of *Man with a Movie Camera* and *Enthusiasm* in volumes 2 and 3.

Company) Lee Grieveson, "The Work of Film in the Age of Fordist Mechanization," *Cinema Journal* 51, no. 3 (Spring 2012): 25–51; and Mihaela Mihailova and John MacKay, "Frame Shot: Vertov's Ideologies of Animation," in *Animating Film Theory*, ed. Karen Beckman (Durham, NC: Duke University Press, 2014), 145–66. Linhart's highly original thesis intersects in intriguing ways with other production or economy-focused readings of Vertov, such as that of Jonathan Beller in *The Cinematic Mode of Production*; see footnote 181.

197 The passage quoted in *Sauve qui peut* is from Linhart's *L'Établi* (Paris: Éditions de Minuit, 1978), about Linhart's own experiences as a factory worker (which he became as part of a radical attempt to bridge the gap between workers and intellectuals). See Michael Witt, "Godard dans la presse d'extrême gauche," in *Jean-Luc Godard: Documents*, 165–73, esp. 167–68; Brody, *Everything Is Cinema*, 299–300, 328–33, 404–8, 425–27; de Baecque, *Godard*, locations 8668–73, 13537–43, 13606–19; Witt, "On and Under Communication," 334; Witt, "In Search of Godard's *Sauve la vie (qui peut)*," *NECSUS* (Spring 2015); accessed November 20, 2016 at http://www.necsus-ejms.org/in-search-of-godards-sauve-la-vie-qui-peut/; and Alberto Toscano, "Logistics and Opposition," in *Logistics, Circulation, Class Struggle and Communism*, accessed July 1, 2017 at https://advancethestruggle.files.wordpress.com/2014/08/logisticsreaderfinal1.pdf, 1–10, esp. 10. For more on Linhart, see Virginie Linhart, *Le jour où mon père s'est tu* (Paris: Seuil, 2008); Edouard Launet, "Rétabli," *Libération* (May 2010), accessed November 20, 2016, http://next.liberation.fr/culture/2010/05/17/retabli_626472.

Image 6: Young Pioneer Valia Shevchenko in Vertov's *Lullaby* (1937). The right fifth of the image was deliberately blacked-out. Source: RGAKFD 4078.

Meanwhile, the academic discipline of film studies emerged alongside of (and contributed to) all these exciting debates about Vertov, and proved vitally important in sealing his reputation. There has been a fairly steady flow of serious scholarly work on Vertov since around 1972 or so, coming primarily though not exclusively out of the USSR/Russia, France, Germany, Austria, Italy, the UK and the US.[198] With one exception, all the familiar arguments

---

198 I have mentioned a good number of these writings already, and will refer to many more over the course of this and the next two volumes. Some of them appeared in conjunction with major retrospectives, perhaps most importantly the release of *LR* in Sacile in 2004 at the Giornate del Cinema Muto. Pioneering studies of particular significance in the English-speaking context were David Bordwell's "Dziga Vertov: An Introduction," *Film Comment* 8, no. 1 (Spring 1972): 38–45; Masha Enzensberger's "Dziga Vertov," *Screen* 13, no. 4 (1972): 90–107; and Seth R. Feldman's *The Evolution of Style in the Early Work of Dziga Vertov* (New York: Arno Press, 1977) and *Dziga Vertov: A Guide to References and Resources* (Boston: G.K. Hall and Co., 1979). The year 1972, the publication date of Michelson's "From Magician to Epistemologist" and possibly the annus mirabilis of Vertov's international reception, also saw the prominent use of *Man with a*

about Vertov—How can his documentary aspirations be reconciled with his montage practice? Is his self-reflexivity really a political-critical tool? Is he best characterized as a documentarian, an avant-gardist, a political filmmaker, or in some other way? Does he really jettison the cinema of the past as he claimed he would? How does his work relate to that of other protagonists in the "historical avant-garde," inside or outside the USSR? and so on—still prompt serious discussion, theoretical innovation, and research. The exception, in my opinion, is the old view of Vertov (based primarily on an evaluation of *Man with a Movie Camera*) as a "disorderly" filmmaker, the undisciplined creator of a kind of visual chaos who just didn't know when to stop stuffing and overstuffing his films.[199] Detailed analytical work by (among others) Anna Lawton, Bertrand Sauzier, and above all Yuri Tsivian and Vlada Petric, long ago laid this opinion to rest;[200] and recent applications of digital technology to the analysis of Vertov's films have already revealed large and small formal patterns previously hard to see, and promise to reveal many more.[201]

Movie Camera and of Vertov's writings at the beginning of the first episode of John Berger's legendary and highly influential BBC TV series *Ways of Seeing*; my thanks to Joshua Sperling for this reference. On the cusp of the perestroika era appeared the second major Russian-language monograph on Vertov (Lev Roshal', *Dziga Vertov* [Moscow: Iskusstvo, 1984]).

199 Among the better known expressions of this view of Vertov are those of John Grierson ("[*Man with a Movie Camera*] is not a film at all [but] a snapshot album [with] no story, no dramatic structure...." [*Grierson on Documentary*, ed. Forsyth Hardy (New York and Washington: Praeger, 1971), 127]); A. Kraszna-Krausz ("[Vertov's] arabesques totally covered the ground plan, his fugues destroyed every melody" ("The First Russian Sound Films," *Close Up* 8, no. 4 [December 1931]: 301); and Walker Evans, who described *Man with a Movie Camera* as a "cacophony for the eye" ("Out of Anger and Artistic Passion" [review of Richard Griffiths's *The World of Robert Flaherty*], *New York Times* Book Review [May 3, 1953]: 3).

200 Anna Lawton, "Rhythmic Montage in the Films of Dziga Vertov: A Poetic Use of the Language of Cinema," *Pacific Coast Philology* 13 (October 1978): 44–50; Bertrand Sauzier, "An Interpretation of *Man with the Movie Camera*," *Visual Communication* 11, no. 4 (Fall 1985): 30–53; Tsivian, "L'Homme à la caméra de Dziga Vertov en tant comme texte constructiviste" and *Istoricheskaia retseptsiia kino: Kinematograf v Rossii 1896–1930* (Riga: Zinatne, 1991), 362–91; Vlada Petric, *Constructivism in Film: The Man with a Movie Camera, A Cinematic Analysis* (Cambridge: Cambridge University Press, 1987). The essays already mentioned by Alan Williams and Stephen Crofts and Olivia Rose could be added to this list, along with many others.

201 See especially Klemens Gruber, Barbara Wurm, and Vera Kropf, eds., "Digital Formalism: Die kalkulierten Bilder des Dziga Vertov," special issue of *Maske und Kothurn* 55, no. 3 (2009); Lev Manovich, "Visualizing Vertov" (2013), accessed November 21, 2016,

The 100th anniversary of Vertov's birth (1996) saw the publication of a couple of major essay collections,[202] and some of the pieces in these excellent volumes registered the impact of the last major historical shift to have significantly effected Vertov's reputation to date. This shift was, of course, the collapse of the Soviet-dominated Communist world between 1989 and 1991, which both compelled a rethinking of Vertov's work for and in relationship to the Soviet regime, and led to the opening of the Soviet archives that slowly made this rethinking possible. Vertov's activities as a Soviet propagandist and/or ideologue had not been entirely ignored before 1990—back in 1929 (for instance), the French Surrealist writer and actor Jacques Brunius, suggesting that the celebration of "Taylorism and [industrial] rationalization" in *The Eleventh Year* would have pleased Henry Ford himself, called the film "one of the most reactionary spectacles [he had] ever experienced"[203]—and had been more attentively discussed in Western scholarship since around the late 1970s.[204] But it wasn't until the late perestroika period and immediately after that Vertov as a filmmaker in the service of the Soviet state, and the relationship of his reputation to Soviet political and cultural history, came under close and critical scrutiny.[205]

As I hinted earlier, Vertov's now-established reputation as a truth-seeker and truth-teller became, at this point, something of a liability.[206] A Vertov

---

http://softwarestudies.com/cultural_analytics/Manovich.Visualizing_Vertov.2013.pdf; and Adelheid Heftberger, *Kollision der Kader: Dziga Vertovs Filme, die Visualisierung ihrer Strukturen und die Digital Humanities* (Munich: text+kritik, 2016).

202 Klemens Gruber, ed., "*Dziga Vertov zum 100. Geburtstag*," special issue of *Maske und Kothurn: International Beiträge zur Theaterwissenschaft* 42, no. 1 (1996); Jean-Pierre Esquenazi, ed., *Vertov: L'Invention du Rèel: Actes du Colloque de Metz, 1996* (Paris: L'Harmattan, 1997). 2000 saw the release of Natascha Drubek-Meyer and Jurij Murashov, eds., *Apparatur und Rhapsodie: Zu den Filmen des Dziga Vertov* (Frankfurt am Main: Peter Lang, 2000).

203 J. Bernard Brunius, "Le Ciné-Art et le Ciné-Oeil," *La Revue du Cinéma* 4 (October 15, 1929): 75–76.

204 One pioneering study: Richard Taylor, *Film Propaganda: Soviet Russia and Nazi Germany* (London: Croom Helm and Barnes and Noble, 1979).

205 A prescient early article that posed many of the questions that would be asked about Vertov after 1991—concerning, for instance, his place within Soviet debates over art in the 1920s, and his relation to/understanding of the developing Soviet regime—was Nataša Ďurovičová's "A Life Caught Unawares: Dziga Vertov's Collected Writings," *Quarterly Review of Film Studies* 10, no. 4 (April 1989): 325–33.

206 One of the earliest evidences of a new attitude in the Soviet film press was critic Elena Vinnichenko's late 1989 remark that despite all claims about Vertov's liberated camera moving and filming "everywhere," *Man with a Movie Camera* notably did not include footage of the notorious Shakhty show trial (underway while the film was being made) or of the execution

symposium in Moscow in the summer of 1992, during which the Stalin panegyric *Lullaby* was screened, drew out a new range of views, with one speaker inserting the film (without endorsing it politically) into the long artistic tradition of "great monuments to a tyrant" (scholar Viktor Listov). Another participant was surprised by its demonstration of Vertov's evident willingness to please the Stalin regime (ex-East German screenwriter and critic Rolf Richter); yet another took it as but one more example (alongside Vertov's positive representations of and participation in Soviet anti-religious campaigns) of just how thoroughly the filmmaker's ideology contaminated virtually his entire oeuvre (critic Neia Zorkaia); and still others were stunned into uncomfortable silence (Italian critic Gianni Toti, for instance).[207] The same year, one of the symposium's participants, the legendary filmmaker Chris Marker (1921–2012), released his *Le Tombeau d'Alexandre (The Last Bolshevik)*, a masterful documentary mainly dedicated to the life and work of director Aleksandr Medvedkin (1900–1989) but which also contains an unforgettable section on Vertov's erasure of individuals become "enemies of the people" from specific shots in *Lullaby* (made and released during the Great Terror, whose eightieth anniversary we mark this year; see image 6).[208]

Filmmakers, critics and scholars, not least in the soon-to-be-former and former Soviet Union, began to speak as often as not about Vertov as a virtuoso weaver of falsifications and mystifications, as in this typically forthright remark by the great director Aleksej German, Sr. (1938–2013):

> I am convinced that among the multitude of criminal organizations that existed in the Soviet Union, the most vicious system was that of the cinema—even though I love this art and revel in the artistry of a number of its masters.... Our documentary cinema, which perhaps served the regime even more zealously [than did fiction film], was also fake from the first to

---

of prisoners caught planning an escape at the Solovki concentration camp (which occurred in October 1929, well after the film was released) ("*Chelovek s kinoapparatom*," *Iskusstvo Kino* 12 (December 1989): 111–13, esp. 112). Vertov was briefly enlisted into the US culture wars around the same time in Jeremy Murray-Brown's hatchet job "False Cinema: Dziga Vertov and Early Soviet Film" (in the right-wing *New Criterion* 8, no. 3 [November 1989]: 21–33), which predictably concludes by linking Vertov, "fabricator of cinematic lies," to both the Nazis and to contemporary academia's "subversive political agenda" "designed for a rag-bag army of malcontents," which throng includes, on Murray-Brown's account, lesbian and gay people, the handicapped, immigrants, and the unemployed (32–33).

207 V. S. Listov, et al., "'Pryzhok' Vertova," *Iskusstvo Kino* 11 (November 1992): 96–108.
208 Filmmakers Fernando Birri, Artavazd Peleshian, and Herz Frank were also at the symposium (Listov, "'Pryzhok' Vertova," 96).

the last shot.... Once Dziga Vertov got the ball rolling, our entire lives were made up. Even people's characters were fabricated.... I hate Vertov as well [along with Eisenstein, Pudovkin, and Dovzhenko]. I understand that he's a great talent, but once again, he's from the ranks of the storytellers. What did he achieve? He covered all of that peasant groaning and industrial rasping in marvelous gilded bindings (so to speak).[209]

The celebrated direct cinema cameraman and director Richard Leacock (1921–2011), who had been central to all the 1960s discussions about vérité (and present at many of them), was not exactly thrilled when I told him that I was writing a study of Dziga Vertov. Vertov's films, Leacock insisted, should never have been associated with "film-truth" of any kind. He drew my attention to the apparently uncontroversial matter of Mikhail Kaufman and his Debrie Parvo camera and tripod, shown numerous times in *Man with a Movie Camera*. Those cameras, Leacock informed me (speaking from experience), were extremely heavy, and there was no way that Kaufman could have carried his as he appears to do in the film. What was depicted in *Man with a Movie Camera* (Leacock was certain) was nothing more than the hull of a Debrie, or perhaps even a mock-up of some kind; and this dummy camera encapsulated what needed to be said about Vertov as a documentary filmmaker. "Even *that*," said Leacock, looking me straight in the eye and pointing a finger in my direction, "was a lie."[210]

The end of the Soviet era also brought to the surface, for a while at least, major differences in opinion on Vertov and other Soviet matters that had developed in relative isolation on either side of the Cold War divide. Leacock's mentor Robert Flaherty shared the thematic stage with Vertov at the 1990 Flaherty Seminar in Riga, Latvia—one of several important meetings of Second and First

---

209 L. B. Shvarts, "Pozitsiia rezhissera: interv'iu s A. Iu. Germanom," in *Peterburgskoe "Novoe Kino": sbornik statej*, ed. M. L. Zhezhelenko (St. Petersburg: MOL, 1996), 124–25, 130.

210 I have not had the chance to hoist a Debrie myself, or secure independent verification of its weight. Leacock was the main speaker at the July 1965 UNESCO round-table meeting in Moscow on new methods of film-TV shooting (he first presented his well-known "Naissance de la Living Camera" there, in French) (Graff, *Le cinéma-vérité*, 450–53). His strongly anti-staging, anti-interventionist views were discussed seriously and quite respectfully in the Soviet cinema press of the time (e.g., G. Fradkin, "Prav li Richard Likok?" *Iskusstvo Kino* 11 [November 1965]: 24–25; S. Muratov, "Pristrastnaia kamera," *Iskusstvo Kino* 6 [June 1966]: 108–20, esp. 112–13).

World creators and critics during these heady perestroika years[211]—where it quickly became clear that Flaherty's focus on the independence and resilience of individual protagonists (like Nanook) was regarded by the Soviet participants as far more useful for their own struggle against "the rigidity of the [Soviet] state" than Vertov's apparent collectivism, which ultimately "propped up the goals of the 'regime.'"[212] Although Hungarian documentarian Péter Forgács was not at the Riga seminar, his remarks on it from almost a decade later (in conversation with film scholar Scott MacDonald in 1999) demarcate the fissure in outlook as well as anything else:

> *MacDonald*: . . . I was thinking of Vertov during those moments in *The Maelstrom* [1997] where you switch from motion to still images. They remind me of similar moments in [*Man with a Movie Camera*].
>
> *Forgács*: Yes, but Dziga Vertov, Kuleshov and Eisenstein were working to *destroy* the culture that I'm trying to *recover*. I don't see myself as an agent of the bourgeoisie, but *they* would see me that way.[213]
>
> *MacDonald*: I went to Riga in [1990], with the Flaherty Film Seminar. There were writers and filmmakers from the various Soviet states and various writers and filmmakers from the US. The seminar was called "Flaherty/Vertov." What was fascinating was that the American leftists at the seminar loved Vertov but were somewhat embarrassed about Flaherty (Flaherty's romanticizing of Eskimo life had come to seem a problem); and the representatives from the ex-Soviet states loved Flaherty and seemed to hold Vertov in contempt. Flaherty's focus on the individual was what *they* wanted.
>
> *Forgács*: Yes, very nice. Speaks for itself.
>
> *MacDonald*: We were surprised.

---

211 For a particularly detailed and arresting account of some of these exchanges (involving theorists and philosophers) between 1989 and 1991, see Susan Buck-Morss, *Dreamworld and Catastrophe: The Passing of Mass Utopia in East and West* (Cambridge, MA: MIT Press, 2000), 220–43.

212 Patricia R. Zimmermann, introduction to "Strange Bedfellows: The Legacy of Vertov and Flaherty," *Journal of Film and Video* 44, nos. 1–2 (Spring–Summer 1992): 5. "Regime" is in scare quotes in the original. For a defense of Vertov's practice as useful for the documentary representation of alternative collectivities (within the US context above all), see Zimmermann's essay in the same journal, "Reconstructing Vertov: Soviet Film Theory and American Radical Documentary," 80–90.

213 *The Maelstrom* recounts the fortunes of the Peerebooms, a Jewish family from the Netherlands, prior to and during World War II, primarily using home movie footage shot by Max Peereboom. The family was deported to Auschwitz in 1943.

Forgács: Well, before you went to Riga, you should have read Orwell. *Then* think of Dziga Vertov. If he hadn't died so early, he could have become one of the censors with the big scissors.

MacDonald: There's a depressing thought.

Forgács: ... [T]he Soviet regime was the most exploitative form of capitalism on earth. In twenty years of building up capitalism, it sacrificed millions of people. Soviet Communism was successful at industrializing, but at an incredible cost. Of course, Dziga Vertov and the avant-garde poets were not butchers, but they *were* blindly serving the devil. It might hurt some people's feelings to say it, but Vertov was Stalin's Leni Riefenstahl.

MacDonald: Stalin's, or Lenin's?

Forgács: Well, let's say Lenin, but Lenin for me is a butcher as well. I hate these little distinctions. Half a year after the revolution, Lenin executed his leftist friends because they said, "Now, what? *This* is not democracy." He just shot them.... So it may sound strange to you, but for me, Leni Riefenstahl and the Russian propaganda filmmakers are *exactly* the same.[214]

Kindred views on Vertov have entered into the history of his general reception, and still find fiercely denunciatory expression on occasion, even if they have settled into place with other major frameworks for interpreting the filmmaker ("poetic documentary," "vérité," "avant-garde," "political modernism") pretty much wherever he is discussed.[215] The arguments have flared up even in Vertov's native Bialystok, where some local city councilors recently advocated the removal of a memorial erected in 2009 to the filmmaker, on the grounds of his involvement in "Communist crimes."[216]

I will not tarry long in this already lengthy introduction on the post-perestroika academic reception of Vertov, given that the present work, primarily

---

214 Scott MacDonald, "Péter Forgács: An Interview," in *Cinema's Alchemist: The Films of Péter Forgács*, ed. Bill Nichols and Michael Renov (Minneapolis: University of Minnesota Press, 2011), 27–28.

215 For two fairly recent Russian excoriations, see Valentina Rogova, "Dziga Vertov: Zlodej ili genij? Ego predannost' vlastiam ne znala granits," *Vek* 38 (November 1, 2002): 10; Rogova, "Strannaia sud'ba Dzigi Vertova. VChK prosila vsevozmozhnoe sodejstvie," *Nezavisimaia Gazeta* 33 (February 18, 2005): 24.

216 Maciej Chołodowski, "Radni PiS: Wiertow zaangażowany w komunistyczne zbrodnie. Zniknie tablica filmowca?" *Wyborcza* (December 28, 2016), accessed May 30, 2017 at http://bialystok.wyborcza.pl/bialystok/1,35241,21174230,radni-pis-wiertow-zaangazowany-w-komunistyczne-zbrodnie-zniknie.html?disableRedirects=true. My thanks to Agata Pyzik for this reference. The memorial is in fact a highly effective installation by the artist Aleksandra Czerniawska that uses a famous image from *Man with a Movie Camera* as its basis.

devoted to examining Vertov in his historical and cultural context—that is, to representing Vertov as a *Soviet* artist (and sometime anti-artist)—is very much part of and dependent on that reception. As we will see, Vertov was definitely a propagandist and agitator (though we will have to inquire into the historical meaning of those vocations); he definitely made and exhibited militantly anti-religious films; he definitely worked for and within Soviet institutions his entire career; he definitely created films praising Soviet leaders like Lenin and Stalin; he definitely made films that endorsed major Soviet modernization projects, including those, like rapid industrialization and the collectivization of agriculture, that involved the massive application of state violence to large swathes of the population. But bullet points of this type, however handy they may prove for quick moral-evaluative purposes, are of little use if we seriously want to understand the trajectory of Vertov's cinematic and theoretical practice, the contexts in which it developed, the reasons for its early termination, and even what it might mean, or how it might be used, today.

Since so much has been done already, why write a big book about Dziga Vertov, now? A work in three volumes written in English about a Soviet experimental documentarian who died over sixty years ago might seem to require a full-scale apologia, rather than a mere preliminary summary. And a lot has been done, indeed; but very little has been written on Vertov that has made deep use not only of his archive—accessible to Western scholars for more than 20 years[217]—but also of other archival sources that have become available since the end of the Soviet era, some of them far from Russia. With these materials, it is possible to paint a more detailed and nuanced picture of Vertov's work on the films, his decisions and revisions, his relationship to studio administrators and coworkers, and much more. Similarly, the work of considering Vertov in light of (to quote the *Cahiers* editors) the "political, ideological and economic determinations" of his time has been eased by the flood of extraordinary work on Russian and Soviet history that has appeared since the perestroika period, more of which will be mined for insights in these pages than in any previous study of Vertov.

To be sure, the nonfictional character of Vertov's work necessitates this kind of historical precision: his were films that engaged directly with what was going on in the Soviet Union, and so a meticulous accounting of historical situation is simply unavoidable in his case. Indeed, historicization on multiple levels is as important for thinking about Vertov's effects outside the USSR as

---

217 Specifically, RGALI f. 2091.

within it, inasmuch as the now centenarian October Revolution, the central historical event of his life, was also (it is increasingly clear) the central political event of the twentieth century, creating the vortex around which everything post-1917—the rise of fascism; the various Popular Fronts; the Second World War; the Cold War; the Third World moment and decolonization; revolutions in China, Vietnam, Cuba and elsewhere; Communism's own fratricidal conflicts and ultimate global decline—swirled, at greater or lesser distance. And perhaps there is no need to cling to the past tense in this regard, given that the Soviet trauma, apparently residual, still seems capable in 2018 of sending spasms of phantom pain careening through the body of the global (or at least Euro-American) mediasphere.

This is not to say that previous ways of discussing Vertov, some of which I have just spent many pages summarizing, will be shunted aside here in favor of a kind of rigid archival empiricism: far from it. Indeed, as I discuss in volume 2, the archive can act to obscure major features of the "Vertov story," not least the role of his wife, cocreator and prime assembler of the archive, Svilova. And in the present volume I will cast lines of speculation forward to 1922 and beyond, in the hopes of sketching out major processes of determination—or better, overdetermination[218]—that unpredictably interacted to precipitate Vertov's life and work as I understand them.

While I keep Vertov at the book's focal center, I also expand or contract the field of vision in order to understand the historical milieux within and on which he acted, and which acted upon him (and many others as well). What kinds of "media experiences," as we might call them today, did Vertov and similarly situated contemporaries have, whether of film, print, spoken word, or other *dispositifs* long vanished (like agitational trains)? The Russian Empire into which he was born was socially striated not only by differences in "class" (in our sense) but in "estate" (*soslovie*) as well: what sort of class-estate formation did he have, and how might it have shaped, sharpened or limited his perceptions, values, and knowledge? Vertov became a certain kind of radical filmmaker of the left, but had he gone through some process of radicalization before 1922? What led to him to enter 1914 speaking, thinking, and feeling one way, and to exit on the other end (in 1921) speaking, thinking, and feeling quite differently? He was, as the anti-cosmopolitans reminded him (inexplicitly) in 1949, a Jew: what sort of Jew was he, and what did his Jewish identity mean to him and his work? What

---

218 See Louis Althusser, "Contradiction and Overdetermination," *New Left Review* [first series] 41 (January–February 1967): 15–35.

can we say in regard to his intellectual and artistic formation, about some aspects of which we already know a fair amount (Russian Futurism, for instance, or the advanced music of the day), and about others far less (e.g., his more specifically philosophical influences, considerably harder to divine)? Vertov certainly did not invent Russo-Soviet nonfiction film—but what kinds of nonfiction practice preceded him, and what did people say about it? And so on.

The present volume is dedicated for the most part to the period prior to 1922: that is, prior to Vertov's emergence as the filmmaker we recognize as "Vertov," who confidently appears only with the creation and release of the still very little-studied *Kino-Pravda* experimental newsreels and his first published writings. Chapter 1 investigates his home city of Bialystok, an industrial, largely Jewish, and explosively politicized city often badly mischaracterized as a "shtetl," to gain a sense of the kind of place it was, and what (in light of Vertov's later career) his experiences there imparted to him. Though not from a wealthy family, Vertov was born into the educated, Russian-speaking elite of the city, which gave him not only educational advantages (in Russian; in the study of literature and music) but a different kind of proximity to the cultural ferment occurring in the Russian Empire's metropolitan centers (St. Petersburg and Moscow), while not protecting him from encounters with the kinds of violence and discrimination to which Jews were subjected in the Empire and in early Soviet Russia between 1881 and 1921.

The second chapter delves into his time as a student and war refugee (1914–16) at the Petrograd Psychoneurological Institute, one of the crucibles of later revolutionary culture, where Vertov at once made contacts crucial to his later career, absorbed a variety of mainly materialist ideologies important at that time and later, and even had some kind of non-professional encounter with scientific filmmaking. Chapter 3 covers the period from the fall of 1916 (when Vertov was drafted into the Russian Army) through the spring of 1918 (when he was suddenly thrust into the new Soviet filmmaking institutions). While tracing out Vertov's biographical path in an environment of increasing violence and scarcity, this chapter provides detailed examinations of several practices and discourses—contemporary experiments in music and sound; Futurist poetry; pre-Revolutionary nonfiction film; and Marxist conceptions of collectivity and historical action—that would influence him decisively and permanently.

The final chapter moves directly into his early years as a filmmaker and administrator (1918–21), detailing his work in newsreel and other nonfiction modes, his involvement in propaganda and agitation on the legendary "agitational trains" that traversed the country during the Russian Civil War, and his training (so to speak) in socialist discourse and media practice, with which he had had little to no experience, lacking as he did any active revolutionary pedigree prior to 1918.

"The history of Cinema," wrote Annette Michelson in a great essay of 1966, "is, like that of Revolution in our time, a chronicle of hopes and expectations, aroused and suspended, tested and deceived."[219] If we could read chronicles backward—as Vertov himself proposes we do, in a famous, outrageous, luminous section of 1924's *Kino-Eye*—might we get a better look at those original germs of hope, now apparently so irredeemably squandered that we doubt, in our own age of paralyzed political imagination, whether they ever existed? Few filmmakers have created work that became central, even confusingly central, to more modalities of film practice—nonfiction, avant-garde, propaganda, film-poem, essay film, authorless "mass" film, no doubt more—than Dziga Vertov did; few filmmakers have held and roused so many hopes for cinema as a practice necessary to any transformative, utopian politics; and few have endured, and perhaps helped bring about, such shattering disappointments in that very regard. Maybe now is the time for another, hopefully closer look at the most revolutionary of early Soviet filmmakers, his achievements and aspirations and blunders and unrealized dreams, 100 years on from the event that turned him, he thought, into a revolutionary.

---

219 Annette Michelson, "Film and the Radical Aspiration," in *Film Culture Reader*, ed. and introduction by P. Adams Sitney (New York: Cooper Square Press, 2000), 404; originally published in *Film Culture* 42 (Fall 1966).

CHAPTER 1

Province of Universality: David Kaufman before the War (1896–1914)

> *Up just as much out of fathomless workings fermented and thrown,*
> *A limp blossom or two, torn, just as much over waves floating,*
> *Drifted at random....*
> —Walt Whitman, *"As I Ebb'd With the Ocean of Life"*

Legend has it that classics teachers in the old German gymnasia would always begin the school year by telling their students, "The first thing to know about the ancient Greeks is that they didn't know they were 'the ancient Greeks.'" This excellent lesson is notoriously difficult to absorb, partly because of what seems to be a near-natural human propensity to conceive of the past in narrative terms—complete with protagonists, acts, and scenes, and Aristotelian beginnings, middles, and ends—but also because fully accepting the classicist's advice would mean carrying its implications forward to our own time, thereby compromising in advance any effort we might make to understand who "we" (in our "historical era") are. Nor can the problem be solved through ironic resignation to time's peripeties, as if to inoculate ourselves against the notorious errors and fabulating hubris of those afflicted with an over-intense—in the Soviet case, a militantly intense—consciousness of history. For the old storyteller, endlessly sifting out past from present from future, reasserts his prerogatives the moment we rewrite those earlier imprudent narrators, not as "history's masters" (or "constructors," or "creators"), but as "history's fools."

In an insightful and witty essay, Philip Rosen has written about his efforts to identify "the Vertov we now know" in the ostensibly "pre-Vertovian" *Kino-Nedelia* (*Film-Week*) newsreels of 1918–19, on which Vertov worked in a variety of capacities, including as a sometime editor. Singling out a shot of a toy seller in *Kino-Nedelia* 1, where a hand holding a toy and "a figure in the background" are apparently deliberately (and, within the context of the *Kino-Nedelias*, atypically) arranged "in two planes of significance," Rosen asks, "Was this the emergence of the Vertov we now know?"

> This question reveals something about my own [i.e., Rosen's] personal fascination with the retrospective, but note also the peculiar temporal logic of that sentence. It includes two tenses, past and present, a then and a now. It also designates another temporal element, a punctual point in time at which something changes—that is, a transformation which is an emergence, a beginning of a historical object that will afterward continue. This means that there is an implicit future embedded *within* the past—call it the Vertov of the 1920s. For it was surely in the 1920s, not 1918, that Vertov can be first identified as the Vertov we now know.[1]

This problem, identified by Rosen as historiographic, can be cast more narrowly as a biographical one as well. That Vertov changed his name (from "David Abelevich Kaufman" to "Denis Arkadievich [Dziga] Vertov") in order to mark a narrative turning point says something (but *what*, exactly?) about his changing self-understanding over time; yet for a prospective biographer, the renaming (and *when* did it occur, exactly?) erects a signpost as potentially misleading as it is clarifying. For becoming (i.e., adopting the name) "Vertov"—which happened no later than 1918—is obviously different from becoming "the Vertov we now know," if not, perhaps, entirely unrelated to that later emergence. And how might the decision to become "Vertov" have emerged in turn out of the experiences of "David Kaufman"? The more intensively we reflect, the more rapidly the "beginnings of the historical object" called Vertov begin to slide away; and we are reminded of that infinitely backwards-running escalator of historical perspective described by Raymond Williams at the beginning of *The Country and the City*, where the quest to pinpoint the moment when the "timeless rhythms" of English rural life stopped pulsating commences in the post–World War I era only to terminate in—Eden.[2] Was there a Vertov "kernel" residing within the "shell" of David Kaufman?[3]

---

1 Philip Rosen, "Now and Then: Conceptual Problems in Historicizing Documentary Imaging," *Canadian Journal of Film Studies/Revue Canadienne d'Études Cinématographiques* 16, no. 1 (Spring 2007): 28; italics in the original. We will return to the issues raised by this essay in later chapters.
2 Raymond Williams, *The Country and the City* (New York: Oxford University Press, 1973), 9–12.
3 The answer to this only apparently rhetorical question is, of course, "no." For the "kernel-shell" metaphor, introduced in a discussion of Hegel's conception of history, see

For his part, Vertov had to edit his history together much like any biographer does—not that he can be counted as just "any biographer," of course—as here in this autobiographical fragment from mid-1934, written when he was thirty-eight years old:

> It began early in life. With the writing of fantastic novels (*The Iron Hand, Uprising in Mexico*). With short essays ("Whaling," "Fishing"). With long poems (*Masha*). With epigrams and satirical verse ("Purishkevich," "The Girl with Freckles"). It then turned into an enthusiasm for editing stenographic notations and gramophone recordings. Into a special interest in the possibility of documentary sound recording. Into experiments in recording, with words and letters, the noise of a waterfall, the sounds of a lumbermill, etc. And one day in the spring of 1918. . . .[4]

What was "it," exactly, that "began early in life"? Although Vertov purports to be discussing "the birth of Kino-Eye," his true topic seems to be his involvement in artistic practice as such, ranging from prose to poetry to sound collage (film would come later, though no later than "the spring of 1918"). We know that he studied music as well, at the Bialystok Music School, and so we can read Vertov's narrative as simple testimony to an early, wide-ranging (though not unbounded: the theatrical and visual arts go unmentioned) interest in art-making. And to be sure, the historical conjuncture during which Vertov's autobiographical excursus appeared—the Soviet mid-1930s, marked by a turn to the testimonial and the subjective, not least in Vertov's own films—provided the discursive occasion for fashioning this genealogical narrative.[5] Yet except for the sound collage—a peculiar enthusiasm to which we will return—we could say that the passage tells us little besides affirming that Kaufman/Vertov was a talented and energetic person: something we could figure out on our own by watching his films.

Marx's 1873 Afterword to *Capital*, vol. 1, accessed June 24, 2017 at https://www.marxists.org/archive/marx/works/download/pdf/Capital-Volume-I.pdf.

Louis Althusser's critical gloss on Hegel-Marx is also relevant here: "Great men [according to Hegel] are only clairvoyants who have a presentiment of but can never know the imminence of tomorrow's essence, the 'kernel in the shell,' the future in invisible gestation in the present, the coming essence being born in the alienation of the current essence" ("The Errors of Classical Economics: Outline of a Concept of Historical Time," in Louis Althusser and Étienne Balibar, *Reading Capital*, trans. Ben Brewster [London: Verso, 1997], 95).

4 Quoting here from "The Birth of Kino-Eye," in *KE*, 40 (translation altered); "Kak eto nachalos'?," in *SV*, 265. As I indicate in the introduction, the article was incorrectly (and very significantly) dated to 1924 (rather than 1934) in *SDZ*; see *SV*, 557.

5 See my discussion of *Three Songs of Lenin* (1934) in volume 3.

We know very little about David Kaufman before 1918; many things about what his home city of Bialystok was like during the time he lived there; and a great many things about the Russian Empire in the years leading up to the October Revolution. What I will try to do in this chapter is less to narrate, step by step, Vertov's early life—the verifiable details at our disposal hardly suffice for that—than to construct, on the basis of available documents and histories, the complex historical conjuncture out of which he emerged.[6] As will be seen, this conjuncture is less a bundle of causes than a field of forces, offering a variety of often conflicting emotional and conceptual vocabularies, and involving the agency of the state, the claims of "enlightenment," the circulation of written texts, the sometimes violent realities of ethnic, religious, and linguistic difference, the attractions of artistic creation, and the contradictions generated by capitalist modernization.[7]

---

6 In deploying the term "conjuncture," I intend to recall its specific use by Althusser in the section of *Reading Capital* already alluded to: "[I]t is only possible to give a content to the concept of historical time by defining historical time as the specific form of existence of the social totality under consideration, an existence in which different structural levels of temporality interfere, because of the peculiar relations of correspondence, non-correspondence, articulation, dislocation and torsion which obtain, between the different 'levels' of the whole in accordance with its general structure. It needs to be said that, just as there is no production in general, there is no history in general, but only specific structures of historicity, based in the last resort on the specific structures of the different modes of production, specific structures of historicity which, since they are merely the existence of determinate social formations (arising from specific modes of production), articulated as social wholes, have no meaning except as a function of the essence of those totalities, i.e., of the essence of their peculiar complexity.... [I]t is only in the specific unity of the complex structure of the whole that we can think ... so-called backwardnesses, forwardnesses, survivals and unevennesses of development which *co-exist* in the structure of the real historical present: the present of the *conjuncture*.... [T]he ultimate meaning of the metaphorical language of backwardness, forwardness, etc., must be sought in the structure of the whole, in the site peculiar to such and such an element of such and such a structural level in the complexity of the whole" (*Reading Capital*, 106, 108–9). For what I take to be a model of conjunctural reading, see Perry Anderson, "Modernity and Revolution," *New Left Review* I/144 (March–April 1984): 96–113.

7 I would distinguish my use of the term "modernization" from Cold War–era "modernization theory"—largely a matter of policy construction, formulated with an eye to synchronizing the world with the economic, social, and cultural norms of the "First World," though without compromising the wealth and hegemonic status of that "World"—and ally it to the description offered by Marshall Berman of "the new landscape in which modern experience takes place": "This is a landscape of steam engines, automatic factories, railroads, vast new industrial zones; of teeming cities that have grown overnight, often with dreadful human consequences; of daily newspapers, telegraphs, telephones and other mass media, communicating on an ever wider scale; of increasingly strong

Thus, I will provide something more like a map than a narrative, although stories large and small will certainly be told, and sometimes conjectured. A single thesis, as will be seen, is difficult to extract through such a procedure, which in some ways (to add another simile) is more akin to drawing a blueprint than to fashioning a syllogism. Yet if a central dynamic were to be identified, it would have to be that of the emergence of a horizon of (secular) *universality* that, I postulate, came to structure the experience of David Kaufman as a youth in provincial Bialystok. I use the term "universality" to point above all to the sensed reality of change touching all levels of existence, a reality that had (in the Hegelian sense) both "negative" and "positive" aspects.[8]

On the one hand, during the time and in the place Vertov was growing up, older identities and particularities were coming into novel forms of contact with one another, mutating, or vanishing altogether, tossed by forces of change whose apparently shapeless ubiquity gave the new sense of universality—and of connectedness, desired and undesired—its discomposing *basso continuo*. On the other, "universality" came to be ascribed to a new kind of subjectivity—secular, literate, mobile, politically engaged, *modern*—that would cohere with those forces of change, would be capable of managing them, and could be taught or cultivated: the universal as a kind of (positive) *content*, that is, rather than as a largely privative historical movement. (Mediating between these polarities is the negative-positive power of imagination, or the utopian impulse, made manifest when the shattering of "all fixed, fast-frozen relations"[9] becomes an occasion for conceiving of alternatives, whether radical, reactionary, liberal, or otherwise. We will return to this power and its effects in due course.)[10]

---

national states and multinational aggregations of capital; of mass social movements fighting these modernizations from above with their own modes of modernization from below; of an ever-expanding world market embracing all, capable of the most spectacular growth, capable of appalling waste and devastation, capable of everything except solidity and stability" (Marshall Berman, *All That Is Solid Melts into Air: The Experience of Modernity* [London; Verso, 1988], 18–19).

8 For an elaboration of the conception of "positive" and "negative" I am employing here, see G. W. F. Hegel, *The Encyclopedia Logic*, trans. T. F. Geraets, W. A. Suchting, and H. S. Harris (Indianapolis: Hackett Publishing, 1991), esp. 83–108, 173–74, 181–88.

9 Marx and Engels, *Manifesto of the Communist Party*, http://www.marxists.org/archive/marx/works/1848/communist-manifesto/ch01.htm.

10 The tripartite schema I offer here—the impositions of historical change; the power to shape and control; the capacity to rethink "power" in light of ongoing change—rewrites the fundamental dialectic outlined in Friedrich Schiller, *On the Aesthetic Education of Man*, ed. Elizabeth M. Wilkinson and L. A. Willoughby (Oxford: Oxford University Press, 1967).

Both of these universalities remain abstract as I have just articulated them, of course, and too much like staple formulae for describing the historical matrices and experiential textures of "the modern": it is now time to stock them with particulars.

"THE PEOPLE'S BENEFIT": A. K. KAUFMAN'S CIRCULATING LIBRARY IN BIALYSTOK

Bialystok, where Vertov was born as David Abelevich Kaufman on January 15, 1896, is a city of low hills, small, quietly flowing rivers (the Biała and the Dolistówka), and a deep and beautiful surrounding forest comprised of the large pine, oak, and spruce trees that proliferate in this part of northeastern Poland. Founded in the sixteenth century as a small settlement of tenant peasant farmers surrounding the estate of Mikołaj Michnowicz, a member of King Aleksander Jagiellonczyk's council, by 1697 Bialystok was the site of Count Jan Klemens Branicki's great palace and grounds, and had become a chartered city by 1749.[11] The partitioning of the Polish–Lithuanian Commonwealth between Prussia, Austria-Hungary and Russia in the late eighteenth–early nineteenth centuries brought the city first under Prussian control (1795–1807) and then, in accord with the Tilsit treaty signed by Napoleon Bonaparte and Tsar Alexander I, into the Russian Empire (1807–1918).[12] At first the center of its own administrative unit, the Bialystok region was incorporated in 1842 along with two other districts into a *guberniia* (roughly, "province") with its administrative center in the city of Grodno, now in western Belarus, about eighty kilometers northeast of Bialystok.

Home to 15,000 people in 1845, Bialystok could claim around 82,500 residents—a more than fivefold increase in population over the course of sixty-odd years—by 1910.[13] Jews made up approximately two thirds of Bialystok's citizenry by the late nineteenth century, having become the city's ethno-religious majority by no later than 1830, mainly because of

---

Much maligned and easily underestimated, Schiller's construct exerted an enormous if unconscious influence on later thinkers, such as (in my view) Jacques Lacan and his triad of "real-imaginary-symbolic."

11 The city with its palace was still impressive in 1805, according to the memoir of German traveler Georg Reinbeck; see his *Travels from St. Petersburgh through Moscow, Grodno, Warsaw, Breslaw &c to Germany in the Year 1805 in a Series of Letters* (London: Richard Phillips, 1807), 150.

12 The Bialystok-Grodno area also suffered considerable damage during the Napoleonic Wars.

13 Adam Dobronski, *Białystok: Historia Miasta*, 2nd ed. (Bialystok: Zarzad Miasta Białegostoku, 2001), 91. By 1913, the population had shot up to 98,170 (*Obzor Grodnenskoj gubernii za 1913 god* [Grodno: Gubernskaia Tipografiia, 1914], 33).

Province of Universality: David Kaufman before the War • CHAPTER 1   7

in-migration.[14] Jews had lived in the area since at least 1658, and a large Jewish community with synagogues, schools, a hospital and other facilities had been established there by the late 1760s.[15] Georg Reinbeck, a German traveler, academic and poet, wrote with distaste in 1806 that the Minsk and Grodno provinces

> may, in truth, be denominated the land of Jews, whose number is here incalculable. Every town, as it is called, every village, every public house and mill, is inhabited by Jews, who are, as it is said, daily repairing with their families to this part.[16]

Bialystok was located in the westernmost end of the Pale of Settlement, that large region (about the size of France) on the western side of the Russian Empire outside of which Jews were for the most part prohibited from settling within Russia between 1791 and 1917.[17] Like Grodno, Bialystok was

---

14   See Rebecca Kobrin, *Jewish Bialystok and Its Diaspora* (Bloomington: Indiana University Press, 2010), 26.
15   On the early history of Jewish settlement in what is now Poland, dating back to the twelfth century, see Bernard D. Weinryb, *The Jews of Poland: A Social and Economic History of the Jewish Community from 1100 to 1800* (Philadelphia, PA: Jewish Publication Society of America, 1973), 10–20; and Gershon David Hundert, *Jews in Poland-Lithuania in the Eighteenth Century: A Genealogy of Modernity* (Berkeley: University of California Press, 2004), 1–31.
16   Reinbeck, *Travels from St. Petersburgh*, 137. Reinbeck goes on to berate Jews as usurers and "leeches," while allowing that "although the spirit of Israel dwells in them, yet they do not appear to be abandoned characters, nor is it extraordinary to find among them a disinterested civility towards strangers" (140). Around half of the population of Grodno, where Vertov's father Abel Kaufman was born, was Jewish (48 percent in 1897, as opposed to 63 percent in Bialystok; see Ezra Mendelsohn, *Class Struggle in the Pale: The Formative Years of the Jewish Workers' Movement in Tsarist Russia* [Cambridge: Cambridge University Press, 1970], 5).
17   The boundaries of the Pale changed over time, but were basically set by an important statute of 1835. Historian John Doyle Klier provides a precise description of the Pale's classical contours: "Jews were permitted to settle freely in the provinces of Grodno, Vilna, Podolia, Minsk, Ekaterinoslav, and in the regions of Bessarabia and [Bialystok]. Residence in other provinces was somewhat circumscribed. Jews could live freely in Kiev province, with the exception of the city of Kiev itself (where they were confined to two districts); in Kherson province, except for the port of Nikolaev; in the Tauride, excluding the naval base at Sevastopol; in Mogilev and Vitebsk provinces, excepting peasant villages; in Chernigov and Poltava provinces except for Cossack villages; Kurland province was open only to Jews who had lived there before the last census, and a similar restriction applied to Riga and Shlok, the only areas in Lifland province where Jews were permitted to reside. An anti-smuggling initiative of 1843 produced a ban on new settlement of Jews in villages within 50 versts (33 miles) of the Empire's western frontier. [Congress Poland] was never considered part

effectively a border town, situated only a few kilometers from the line separating Russia proper from Congress Poland (in existence from 1815 to 1915), even if, in the largest political sense, the latter polity was only nominally independent of the Tsars.

Vertov's father, Abel Kushelevich Kaufman (born 1868—died sometime between 1941 and 1943 in the Holocaust), was born in Grodno but evidently left that city at some point in the late 1880s for Bialystok, where he found a job as a clerk in the library of the Bialystok city government.[18] On December 24, 1892, Kaufman petitioned the city with a request to open a bookstore "with a library and a special section with useful reading for children in Russian." Permission to open the bookstore with an adjunct "library for reading" was soon granted (on January 17, 1893), after the police had conducted a brief inquiry into Kaufman's loyalty and political reliability, which were deemed satisfactory. The bookstore was in operation by September 1893, near the center of Bialystok on Nikolaevskaia Street, and specialized in Russian, French, and German books, as well as writings for children. That September, Abel successfully petitioned the governor of the Grodno region for permission to sell books in Hebrew as well, "inasmuch as Jews," to quote the petition, "make up most of the population of the city of Bialystok."[19] By 1895, Kaufman's establishment contained nearly as many titles as the main public library in Grodno, and he was publishing thick catalogs of his holdings.[20] The business was in operation at least through 1929,[21] and probably well into the 1930s.

---

of the Pale" (Klier, *Imperial Russia's Jewish Question, 1855–1881* [Cambridge: Cambridge University Press, 1995], 9).

18 NIAB f. 1, op. 8, d. 2794, ll. 2, 7, 7ob. Kaufman's patronymic, Kushelevich, indicates that his father's name was Yekutiel (Kushel', in its Russianized form).
19 NIAB f. 1, op. 8, d. 2794, ll. 1, 2, 4, 5, 7, 7ob, 11–13, 15, 16.
20 See A[bel] Kaufman, *Katalog russkikh knig biblioteki dlia chteniia (pri knizhnom magazine) A. K. Kaufmana v g. Belostoke*, 1st ed. (Bialystok: Sh. Volobrinskij, 1895); located in the State Library of the Russian Federation, Moscow. In 1896, the public library in Grodno had 2,593 book titles and 105 journal titles (*Pamiatnaia knizhka Grodnenskoj gubernii na 1896 god* [Grodno: Grodnenskij Gubernskij Statisticheskij Komitet, 1897], 75). Russian law required circulating libraries to publish these catalogs.
21 See http://data.jewishgen.org/jri-pl/1929/1929top89.htm, at the website of the Jewish Business Project.

Province of Universality: David Kaufman before the War • CHAPTER 1   9

Image 1: Nikolaevskaia (today Sienkiewicz) Street in Bialystok in 1897, where the Kaufman bookstore was located. Source: Andrzej Lechowski, *Białystok: urok starych klisz* [*Bialystok: the charm of old photographic plates*] (Bialystok: Benkowski, 2005), 158.

Almost exactly a year after opening the bookstore, Abel Kaufman married Chaya-Ester Rakhmielievna Gal'pern (Halpern) (born 1873—died sometime between 1941 and 1943 during the Holocaust).[22] Chaya's family hailed from

---

22 These dates and names are derived from a comparison of the wedding registration of Abel and Chaya Kaufman of January 30, 1894 (in fund 155, book 3 in the Jewish marriage registries housed in the State Archive in Bialystok) with the only partially accurate records provided by Masha (Miriam) Halpern-Proginin, Chaya's sister, to the Yad Vashem Archive of Shoah Victims' Names on January 23, 1960. Grodno is indicated as Abel Kaufman's birthplace both in the marriage registration and in the birth registers of his sons; see registries for Jewish births (in the "Old Style" or Julian calendar) for January 3, 1896 (David Abelevich [Dziga]), August 24, 1897 (Mojsej Abelevich [Mikhail]), December 6, 1899 (Semyon Abelevich; died as an infant approximately six months later), and December 30, 1902 (Boris Abelevich), in the State Archive in Bialystok, Poland. See also NIAB f. 1, op. 9, d. 890, l. 85ob. Chaya Kaufman's parents were named Yerakhmiel and Hinda; she had at least one brother (Yaakov, dates of birth and death unknown) and three sisters (Masha [Rivka-Miriam] Halpern [Halperin]-Proginin (born 1883–died 1970), Dina Lipman (born 1884–died sometime between 1941–43 in the Holocaust), and Chana-Sora (dates of birth and death unknown); see entries under Chaja [*sic*] Kaufman, Abram [*sic*] Kaufman, and Dina Lipman for Bialystok in the Yad Vashem Archive of Holocaust Victims' Names (www.yadvashem.org).

Zabludovo, a small, relatively well-to-do town southeast of Bialystok.[23] By 1900, the couple had two sons—David (later Dziga/Denis Arkadievich Vertov: born January 15, 1896) and Mojsej (later Mikhail: born September 5, 1897)—and the bookstore had become one of the largest and best supplied in Bialystok. After a third son, Semyon (born June 25, 1899), died in infancy, the family was completed in 1903 with the arrival of Boris (born January 12 of that year).

What sort of business was a bookstore with a "library for reading"? Usually called "circulating libraries" in English,[24] these libraries were book-lending outlets with a fund of books that would be lent out for a subscription fee plus a deposit, the latter often equal to the cost of the book. Historian A. Rejtblat, in his study of Russian reading practices in the nineteenth and early twentieth centuries, describes this system of acquisition, accumulation and distribution of books as a kind of "collective purchase of the books by subscribers ... none of whom individually was able to buy all the books that interested him."[25] In Russia at the end of the 1850s, there were only about fifteen to twenty such libraries, with between five and seven thousand registered readers. As with so much else in Russia, they began to really flourish only in the decades following the Great Reforms of the 1860s, during which time they became an established part of urban life.[26]

---

23 NIAB f. 1, op. 8, d. 2794, l. 20. It has been suggested that Chaya was the daughter of a Bialystok chief rabbi (e.g., in Bela Gershgorin, "Chetyre izmereniia brat'ev Kaufman," *Russkij Bazar* 50/556 [December 14–20, 2006], accessed June 22, 2017, http://www.russian-bazaar.com/Article.aspx?ArticleID=9852; in Evgeny Tsymbal's 2002 film *Dziga and his Brothers*; and regrettably, in my own "Vertov before Vertov: Jewish Life in Bialystok," in *Dziga Vertov: The Vertov Collection at the Austrian Film Museum*, ed. Thomas Tode and Barbara Wurm [Vienna: Österreichisches Filmmuseum/SYNEMA, 2006], 9–12). There is, however, no documentary evidence to support this claim, and it is almost certainly false. Bialystok did have two chief rabbis with the last name Halperin (Yom Tov Lipman Halperin [d. 1882], and later Chaim Hersh Halperin), and Chaya had relatives with the last name Lipman, but these names were common and provide no proof of any direct connection. On Yom Tov Lipman Halperin, see Kobrin, *Jewish Bialystok and Its Diaspora*, 41–42.
24 The Russian "biblioteki dlia chteniia" is a calque from the French "bibliothèques de lecture," and indeed France seems to have been the place of origin of this form of library; the first German instance (founded by French immigrants) dates to 1704, with the earliest English and Russian examples appearing in 1725 (London) and 1770 (St. Petersburg) respectively (Rejtblat, *Ot Bovy k Bal'montu*, 51). Evidently, they were slowly replaced, starting in the 1880s, by growing numbers of city public libraries and free "libraries for the people," though they remained important well into the first decades of the twentieth century (ibid., 63–64).
25 Rejtblat, *Ot Bovy k Bal'montu*, 48–49.
26 By 1882, of the roughly 517 libraries in the empire, 286 (or 55 percent) were circulating libraries, most of which (66 percent) were, like Abel Kaufman's, affiliated with bookstores; about 100,000 people frequented them (Rejtblat, *Ot Bovy k Bal'montu*, 57–58, 62).

Image 2: Cover of Abel Kaufman's 1900 catalogue of Russian books and periodicals in his circulating library. At the top is the phrase: "Books are windows through which the soul looks at God's world." Source: State Library of the Russian Federation, Moscow.

Abel, at any rate, became confident enough about his business and his clientele to preface his 1900 catalogue with the following programmatic statement, one that evinces swagger and exasperation in equal measure:

> Over the course of our seven-year experience at the Library, we have very often heard:
>
> "Give us an interesting book to read!"
>
> "Give us something new!"
>
> As far as possible, we try to satisfy our readers by uniting for them the pleasant with the useful. On the one hand, [we avoid] cheap printed editions,[27] dominated as they are by a seductive title concealing a lack of content and absence of ideas. On the other hand, attending to the indications offered by criticism and the most intelligent of our readers, we have equipped the Library with the works of outstanding writers and the best journals.
>
> However, we do not believe that we succeeded in "making everyone happy," inasmuch as we try to satisfy only the best of our dear readers, those who seek in books not only nervous stimulation, leisure and pleasant somnolence, but food for the mind and the heart.
>
> We permit ourselves to observe, that our readers vainly persist in asking the librarians for the *best* or the *newest* books, because (as they explain it) they are too lazy to dig into catalogues.[28] But notwithstanding all his best intentions, the librarian cannot satisfy the requests of all subscribers for one simple reason: one person praises a given book, and another criticizes it severely... and so on, ad infinitum.
>
> It all depends on the level of development, the character, the abilities and the mood of the reader.
>
> In order that the reader might to some extent orient himself in this regard, we would suggest looking at the following: *How to Read Books* by

---

27 In Russian, *lubok*: here meaning not "folk woodcut illustrations," but rather cheaply printed and highly popular adventure stories about great heroes, robber barons, princes, and so on. For a fascinating edition of lubok narratives with an excellent introduction, see A.I. Rejtblat, ed. and introduction, *Lubochnaia povest': antologiia* (Moscow: O. G. I., 2005).

28 "The librarians" included, besides Abel Kaufman himself, his wife Chaya and her brother and sister, Naum-Iakov [Yaakov] and Chana-Sora Gal'pern; the latter two worked there both from September 1894 and then again for some time after July 1896, when Chaya, who frequently worked in the library, was busy taking care of the six-month-old Vertov (NIAB f. 1, op. 8, d. 2794, ll. 20–21).

Richardson (no. 2580 [in the catalogue])[29] and *The Opinions of Russian People About Which Books Are Best to Read* (no. 4089).

There is a proverb: "For the lazy and insensitive mind, a whole library can seem an infertile desert." Perhaps this serves to explain why "many" in the reading public so fervently pursue the newest (fashionable) novels, and almost never ask for the "dusty" classics on the shelves of the Library.[30]

What kind of person, living in Bialystok in 1900, would have written something like this? The first thing to note here is that although Bialystok was a multilingual (if predominantly Yiddish-speaking) city,[31] and although Kaufman sold books in a variety of languages[32] and even wrote pamphlets in Yiddish attacking alcohol and tobacco use,[33] his was clearly a *Russian*-language bookstore. By the time of the 1897 Russia-wide census, a significant percentage

---

29 Kaufman has in mind the Russian translation of Charles Richardson's 1881 *The Choice of Books* (Charl'z Richardson, *Kak chitat' knigi, chtoby oni prinosili nam pol'zu?* trans. A. P. Valueva-Munt [St. Petersburg: M. M. Lederle, 1893]).

30 *Katalog russkikh knig i periodicheskikh izdanij biblioteki (pri knizhnom magazine) A. K. Kaufmana v g. Belostoke*, 2nd ed. (Bialystok: Sh. M. Volobrinskij, 1900), V–VI. The scare quotes are all in the original.

31 Mainly Yiddish-speaking Jews comprised the majority of the city's population (around 65 percent in 1913, out of a total of 98,170), followed, in descending order, by Belorussians (26 percent) and various "others," primarily Germans (4 percent), Poles (3 percent), Lithuanians (1.5 percent) and ethnic Russians and Ukrainians (less than 1 percent). The best raw numbers I can find for 1913 are: 63,699 Jews, 25,343 Belorussians, 3,832 "others," 2,829 Poles, 1,477 Lithuanians, 874 Russians, and 116 Ukrainians. The Jewish population was heavily concentrated in the city, and represented a far lower percentage of the total in the surrounding area (less than 10 percent) (*Obzor Grodnenskoj gubernii za 1913 god*, 33, 81). By 1913, the proportion of Jews in Bialystok had fallen by 10 percent from 1896 levels, in spite of high birth rates, no doubt in large part due to emigration; the city's population had meanwhile risen by over 35,000, from 62,600 to 98,170. Grodno, Abel Kaufman's hometown, was likewise a mainly Jewish city by then (65 percent in 1896, out of a total of 37,579). Besides Judaism and Russian Orthodoxy, Catholicism was strongly represented in both Bialystok and Grodno; some Protestants and even a few Muslims lived there as well (*Pamiatnaia knizhka Grodnenskoj gubernii na 1898 god* [Grodno: Grodnenskij Gubernskij Statisticheskij Komitet, 1897], 4–5, 10–11, 14).

32 Except for some Ukrainian entries, no catalogues of Abel Kaufman's non-Russian-language holdings have survived, though we know from advertisements that he sold works in French, German, Yiddish, and Hebrew.

33 *Katalog russkikh knig* (1900), XIII. Kaufman was a vegetarian as well, and that fact together with his polemics against smoking and drinking make me wonder if he might have been a Tolstoyan; see below for some speculation in that regard.

(24 percent) of Jewish adults—slightly higher, indeed, than the percentage of ethnic Russians literate in the their own tongue (19.7 percent)—could read Russian.[34] Although only 29.2 percent of Jewish men and 16.6 percent of Jewish women in the entire Grodno guberniia in 1897 were literate in Russian, we can assume that the percentages were somewhat higher in an urban center like Bialystok.[35] Newspaper advertisements reveal that Kaufman stressed Russian-language texts and Russian-language learning when making his selections, and various guides and "companions" to Russian grammar and vocabulary were especially prominently featured in his newspaper and catalogue ads.[36] As Yiddish was almost certainly his first language—and the first language of his parents—under what circumstances did Abel Kaufman learn Russian, and develop his Russian bibliophilia (or bibliomania)?[37]

---

34 Russian rates were lower due both to the peasant character of much of the population and extremely low literacy levels among women. In 1897, around 96.9 percent of Jews in the Empire indicated that Yiddish was their native language, followed by Russian (1.28 percent), Polish (0.9 percent) and German (0.44 percent). 32 percent of all adult male Jews could read Russian, however, and 17 percent of adult female Jews could as well. Only the Germans among Russia's ethnic groups had higher levels of Russian literacy (O. V. Budnitskij, *Rossijskie evrei mezhdu krasnymi i belymi (1917–1920)* [Moscow: Rosspen, 2005], 42–43; B. D. Brutskus, *Statistika evreiskago naseleniia*, vyp. III [St. Petersburg: Sever, 1909], n.p. [diagram vi, indicating Jewish literacy in Russian as compared to that of Germans, Russians, Lithuanians, Latvians, and Poles]). Over 99 percent of Jews in the Grodno guberniia indicated that Yiddish was their native language in the 1897 census (Brutskus, *Statistika evreiskago*, n.p. [table 5, indicating self-ascribed native language among Jews in the Russian Northwest]).
35 I would estimate that around a third of the city's Jewish population was literate in Russian. In the northwest region of the Pale, where Bialystok was located, literacy rates among urban Jews in 1897 were 38.2 percent for men and 23.1 percent for women, as opposed to 26 percent for men and 13 percent for women outside the cities (Brutskus, *Statistika evreiskago*, n.p. [table 6, indicating Russian literacy among Jews in Russia]). Interestingly, however, on a comparative scale ranking Russian literacy rates among city-dwellers in the empire divided by ethnicity, Jews fared poorer than Germans, Russians, Balts, or Poles (ibid., n.p. [diagram vii]).
36 Kaufman was active in selling and promoting Russian grammars, with titles like *Companion* and *Comrade*, written by local Bialystok authors such as A. S. Vejsberg; see the extant catalogues.
37 With the small but fascinating exception of a script he wrote in the mid-1920s about Jewish agricultural colonization in the Crimea (to be discussed in volume 2), no evidence survives for any Yiddish-language knowledge Vertov might have had. It seems likely that he would have had some oral-aural grasp of Yiddish, though I doubt he could read or write it. As regards the russophone character of the Kaufman family, it is also worth noting that Abel and Chaya gave their last two sons (Semyon and Boris) Russian first names, both of which would have been unusual among Bialystok Jews. 3.29 percent of Jewish boys born between 1885 and 1905 in the city were named David, and 5.64 percent bore the name of Mojsej; by contrast, only 0.08 percent were named Boris, and a mere 0.04 percent had the name Semyon (as opposed to the much more common variant Shimon; see Zofia Abramowicz, *Imiona chrzestne białostoczan w aspeksie socjolingwistycznym (lata 1885–1985)* (Bialystok: Uniwersytet

Any answer to these questions is of necessity conjectural, as almost nothing is known about Kaufman's life before he petitioned to open the bookstore in 1892. To be sure, the Russifying of (some) Russian Jews, always an uneven and fragmentary process, did not occur because of attractions exerted by Russian culture, at least not until the end of the nineteenth century. Pragmatic goals such as personal advancement, conditioned by pressures to acculturate that sometimes (as I will discuss below) emanated from within the Jewish community itself, were of greater importance.[38] Yet by the close of the century, Russia could no longer be regarded as "a blank in the intellectual order," as the great philosophical provocateur Petr Chaadaev had put it in 1836.[39] Leo Tolstoy, alive until 1910, was possibly the most celebrated author in the world, and figures like (among many others) the writers Turgenev, Dostoevsky, and Chekhov, the chemist Mendeleev, the mathematician Lobachevsky, and the participants in the country's extraordinary musical culture (the violinists and pianists produced in the conservatories founded by the Rubinstein brothers; composers like Tchaikovsky and the members of the "Mighty Five") had all helped give Russia a global cultural prestige unprecedented in its history.[40]

Warszawski Filia w Białymstoku, 1993), 390, 394, 417, 426, 428. In this, the Kaufmans were following broader trends. In an essay on Marc Chagall's early years, Benjamin Harshav notes of the painter's family that, for them and many like them, "joining Russian culture seemed a natural act. The Chagall siblings are registered in the official Russian birth certificate by their Yiddish names only, but among themselves they used Russian names—the reverse of what one might expect" (Benjamin Harshav, with Barbara Harshav, *Marc Chagall and His Times: A Documentary Narrative* [Stanford: Stanford University Press, 2004], 50–51).

38 Historian Michael Stanislawski stresses a tenet "unanimously endorsed by all segments of the new [Jewish] intelligentsia: every Jew is obliged to learn at least one foreign language in order to be a civilized human being; while any pure tongue is permissible, including German, the most preferable language is that of the state in which one lives, hence Russian. This must be read, written, and spoken fluently, and taught to children in the schools" (Stanislawski, *Tsar Nicholas I and the Jews: The Transformation of Jewish Society in Russia: 1825–1855* [Philadelphia: Jewish Publication Society of America, 1983], 115).

39 See *The Major Works of Peter Chaadaev*, trans. Raymond T. McNally, introduction by Richard Pipes (Notre Dame, IN: University of Notre Dame Press, 1969), 23–51, esp. 39.

40 See Eric Hobsbawm's comments on Russia as a cultural "great power" (if an economically weak one, relative to the West) at the end of the nineteenth century in his *The Age of Empire: 1875–1914* (New York: Pantheon Books, 1987), 19. It should be added that Russian literature provided powerful models for Jewish secular literature as it was developing in the late nineteenth–early twentieth century in both Hebrew and Yiddish; on this, see Benjamin Harshav, *Language in Time of Revolution* (Berkeley: University of California Press, 1993), 37, 71; and Harshav, *Marc Chagall and His Times*, 49–55. For reflections on the relationship between Jewish education in the non-Jewish vernacular (Polish, in this case) and practical concerns with training and career in the interwar period, see Ezra Mendelsohn, *The Jews of East Central Europe between the World Wars* (Bloomington: Indiana University Press, 1983), 65–68.

And if the empire as a whole at the turn of the twentieth century might still be characterized, with qualifications, as a vast sea of rural "backwardness" studded with islets of "modernity," those islets—Moscow and especially St. Petersburg, but also smaller centers like Bialystok—were in many ways truly modern. Thus "Russia," thought of at once as cultural space, sometime career opportunity, and world-imperial power, with "Russian" as a common medium, swept the Jews of the Pale into its crowded, wayward and elliptical orbit.

Abel Kaufman's trade, his cultural aspirations, and his evident orientation towards Russian allow us to surmise a good deal about the milieu from which both he and Chaya, who worked alongside him in the library for years, emerged. This milieu, as I will describe it here, was a dynamic conjuncture involving at least three intricately interacting historical forces: the impact of Russia's Great Reforms of the 1860s; the continuing importance of the Jewish Enlightenment, which came to have a significant effect upon Jewish life in the first half of the nineteenth century; and the explosive development of commerce and transportation links in the western Russian Empire from the 1860s onward.

The Great Reforms, which took place in the 1860s and 1870s during the reign of Tsar Alexander II, changed Russian society in fundamental ways. The most significant reform was the 1861 emancipation of the twenty-three-million-strong serf peasantry, but others—of educational, judicial, political, military, and censorship-related institutions and organs—had their own far-reaching, and often unforeseen, results.[41] As historian Benjamin Nathans has shown, the reforms had mixed consequences for Russian Jewry. On the one hand, Jews were prohibited from buying land on an equitable basis with non-Jews after the emancipation of the serfs; they remained confined to the Pale of Settlement; Jews in the military did not enjoy the same opportunities for promotion as non-Jews; and the new local government bodies known as the *zemstvos* were not introduced into the far Western sections of the Empire, "for fear of electoral domination by Poles and Jews."[42] At the same time, however,

---

There may have been more secular knowledge available in book form in Yiddish than we realize, however: see Eli Maor's fascinating article "Science and Yiddish Don't Mix: Really?" *Journal of Scholarly Publishing* 44, no. 4 (July 2013): 340–54.

41 For an excellent overview of the reforms, see Ben Eklof, John Bushnell, and Larissa Zakharova, eds., *Russia's Great Reforms, 1855–1881* (Bloomington: Indiana University Press, 1994).

42 Benjamin Nathans, *Beyond the Pale: The Jewish Encounter with Late Imperial Russia* (Berkeley: University of California Press, 2002), 27–28, 71; see also 182.

the excitement over the prospect of reform in the early 1860s spread to sections of the Jewish community as it did to educated Russian society as a whole, and Jewish newspapers sprang up as venues for debate and discussion.[43]

Of equal importance was the November 1861 decision to give Jewish graduates from universities the same rights as non-Jewish graduates, "including unrestricted residence and choice of occupation."[44] Despite persisting barriers confronting Jews in search of employment in the Tsarist civil service, the reforms themselves created new institutional settings in which university-trained Jewish professionals, such as lawyers and engineers, could find work. The result was an upsurge in the number of Jews in universities and gymnasia (high schools) throughout the empire, such that by the 1870s, as Nathans notes, "Jews were flocking to educational institutions more enthusiastically than any other group."[45]

Although Judeophobic ideologues began to fret publicly about the proliferation of university-educated Jews from the mid-1860s onward, and severe *numerus clausus* quotas on Jewish admission into gymnasia and other institutions of higher education were established in 1887—partially as a reaction to perceived participation by Jewish students in demonstrations and other subversive political activities—young Jews continued to study in Russian universities in the late nineteenth and early twentieth centuries (though many sought education abroad as well).[46] Among them was Masha (Rivka-Miriam)

---

43 Ibid., 70.
44 Ibid., 215.
45 Ibid., 218. "By 1886, one in seven university students in the Russian Empire was Jewish, and at universities like Kharkov and Odessa, that figure was closer to one in four or even one in three" (ibid.). Historian Steven J. Zipperstein notes how the 1874 military reform, "which required universal military service but also drastically reduced the length of service required of those who held higher education degrees," also led many more Jewish families to send their children to Russian schools. "The number of Jewish students in gymnasiums more than doubled between 1870 and 1879 (from 2,045 to 4,913) and rose nearly eightfold between 1865 and 1887 (from 990 to 7,657). Jewish university enrollment rose thirteen times (from 129 to 1,739)" (Steven J. Zipperstein, *The Jews of Odessa: A Cultural History, 1794–1881* [Stanford: Stanford University Press, 1986], 19). See also Budnitskij, *Rossijskie evrei*, 26.
46 Nathans, *Beyond the Pale*, 257–307. "Quotas were set at 10 percent for institutions within the Pale (corresponding roughly to the Jewish population of the total population of the Pale), 5 percent outside the Pale (corresponding roughly to the Jewish proportion of the total population of the empire), and 3 percent in Moscow and St. Petersburg (where the most prestigious and arguably most 'Russian' universities were located, along with the most rebellious students)" (ibid., 267). See also Budnitskij, *Rossijskie evrei*, 47–48. As Nathans shows, the involvement of young Jews in both student groups (some of which were self-identified as Jewish) and in political movements, particularly in the wake of the 1905 revolution and the ensuing pogroms, was another major consequence of these restrictions; see below.

Gal'pern (June 1, 1883 in Zabludovo–June 5, 1970 in Acre, Israel), Chaya Kaufman's younger sister and Vertov's aunt, who studied at the prestigious Women's Medical Institute in St. Petersburg from 1903 to 1906 and again from 1908, receiving her medical license in 1912.[47] The family clearly took pride in Masha's academic success, and as we shall see, she provided a powerful motivating example to her young nephews, the Kaufman boys.

To be sure, this enthusiasm for secular education and even political participation was conditioned by long-term changes occurring within Russian Jewry itself, not least those introduced by the Haskalah or Jewish Enlightenment, whose adherents, the *maskilim*, promulgated a belief in the compatibility of Jewish life and secular modernity, including nonreligious learning and literacy in a given dominant national language.[48] Yet the influence of Haskalah was itself enabled by the ways in which the Russian state, from the late 1820s onward, interfered with traditional patterns of Jewish life. Two interventions, both complexly interacting, stand out.

The foundational one, and doubtless the most traumatic, was the 1827 Recruitment Statute of the Jews, which enforced the conscription of boys as young as eight into the Russian Army for twenty-five-year terms. Four out of every thousand subjects in any given social estate (*soslovie*) were to be recruited; in the case of Jews, conscription generally meant forced assimilation and the coerced abandonment of Jewish religious practice. As historian Michael Stanislawski has demonstrated, the conscription had a deeply fragmenting effect upon Russian Jewish communities: Jewish families used whatever resources they had to keep their sons out of the army, with the result that tensions developed between wealthier and more privileged sectors of the community and those less fortunate and therefore more vulnerable to conscription.[49]

---

47 TsGIASPb f. 436, op. 4, d. 906; op. 1, d. 2552; Boris Kaufman Papers, Beinecke Library, Yale University, GEN MSS 562.12.183. The institute was founded in 1897, and was one of only three (out of sixty-five) state institutions of higher education attended by women only (sixty-one were all male). The standards for admission were high and included proficiency in Latin; about half the students came from the upper (noble or civil-service) social estates (A. E. Ivanov, *Studenchestvo Rossii kontsa XIX-nachala XX veka: sotsial'no-istoricheskaia sud'ba* [Moscow: Rosspen, 1999], 102, 150, 193).

48 Steven J. Zipperstein provides an excellent summary of the main Haskalah tenets in his *The Jews of Odessa*, 11.

49 Stanislawski, *Tsar Nicholas I and the Jews*, 16ff., 106, 186. See also Nathans, *Beyond the Pale*, 27–28.

Clearly enough, the recruitment policy was part of a larger effort on the part of the Tsarist state under Nicholas I and later to manage what was perceived as an alien and (especially given the copresence in the Pale and to the immediate west of the unruly Poles) potentially disruptive mass.⁵⁰ The Jews' "antisocial tendency" and their "perspicacity, caution and cunning," surmised an army-produced statistical study of the Grodno guberniia from 1863, were unfortunate consequences of the dark centuries of persecution. In their place, a "civilized" spirit of belonging and hard work was to be promoted:

> It is strange to see [the Jews'] vain attachment to themselves and their blind, ignorant opposition to a people [i.e., the Russians] who have every right to their love and respect. Labor and enlightenment are the general and unavoidable tasks of today. Only through labor guided by enlightenment can our Jews free their land from oppression, self-interest and self-love ... Civilization alone, rational and expansive, will show the Jews their true field of action, which has up till now gone against the general good and paralyzed [their] finest powers....⁵¹

Indeed, in 1840, well before the reforms began, Count P. D. Kiselev, Tsar Nicholas I's minister of state domains, established a government "Jewish Committee" to develop policy in regard to the status of Jews, and a number of the officials on that committee helped preside over the Great Reforms as well.⁵² The committee's policy on Jews focused on undoing what Kiselev called "the estrangement of the Jews from the civil order,"⁵³ and effectively began

---

50 As historian Theodore Weeks has written, "the loyalty of the Jewish population was seen as an important weapon against the most dangerous foe in the region: the Poles." The Jews in the Western region "were seen as a problem sui generis.... They presented not so much an immediate threat to the government (unlike the Poles) as a feared foreign influence that was believed to have detrimental economic and moral ... effects on the surrounding population." At the same time, "Governors frequently pointed out the role of Jewish youth in socialist agitation, especially in the Bund [the General Jewish Labor Union of Lithuania, Poland and Russia]." (Theodore R. Weeks, *Nation and State in Late Imperial Russia: Nationalism and Russification on the Western Frontier, 1863–1914* [DeKalb, IL: Northern Illinois University Press, 1996], 64, 73–74). For more on socialist politics in Bialystok and its environs, see below.

51 N. Bobrovskij, ed., *Materialy dlia geografii i statistiki Rossii, sobrannye ofitserami general'nogo shtaba. Grodnenskaia guberniia. Chast' pervaia* (St. Petersburg: General'naia Shtaba, 1863), xxii, 849, 866. The book was apparently compiled on the basis of statistics gathered in the Grodno guberniia by the army's general staff between 1837 and 1854.

52 Nathans, *Beyond the Pale*, 69.

53 Ibid., 33.

by abolishing the kahals (local Jewish executive bodies) in 1844.[54] That the kahals did not in fact vanish—the local bodies were still needed to enforce state recruitment and taxation statutes—was but one of the symptoms of the overall incoherence of Tsarist policy regarding Jews. That policy writhed within a dialectic that bound innovation to conservation, assimilation to rigid separation, and the selective "modernization" of part of Russian society to restrictions on the kinds of social and geographic mobility that such modernization made imaginable and desirable.[55]

One of the committee's central proposals—and this is the second important intervention—involved the creation of specifically Jewish but state-run schools in the Pale of Settlement, through the agency of which, it was hoped, Jews would be integrated into Russian society. Although the long-term impact of these schools throughout the wider Jewish community was probably not large—and certainly less significant than those later reforms that led to high levels of Jewish university enrollment[56]—the school project did help create the myth, evidently believed by both modernizers and traditionalists, of a "royal alliance" between adherents of the Haskalah, hitherto entirely marginal within Jewry in the Russian lands and the Russian state. Entering into the breach opened up by the conscription, the "Haskalah-based Jewish schools," Stanislawski has argued, helped to exacerbate social and cultural distinctions, which had taken on a marked class tincture, within the Jewish community:

> A very common reaction to the abuses of the conscription system was a turning against the Jewish establishment, not an increase in alienation from the Russian government. As a result of the opening of the state schools, a significant segment of the poorer elements of Russian Jewry who had no voice in the communal decision-making process protested against their leaders by ignoring threats and prohibitions and enrolling their children in the "heretical" schools. In the last years of Nicholas's reign, Haskalah became the ideology not only of an intellectual or economic elite but also of a vocal portion of the destitute and dispossessed.[57]

---

54 Ibid., 34; Stanislawski, *Tsar Nicholas I and the Jews*, 47.

55 See Heinz-Dietrich Löwe, *The Tsars and the Jews: Reform, Reaction and Anti-Semitism in Imperial Russia 1772–1917* (Chur, Switzerland: Harwood Academic Publishers, 1993), 35, 410; and Budnitskij, *Rossijskie evrei*, 26.

56 Nathans, *Beyond the Pale*, 35–37; Eli Lederhendler, *The Road to Modern Jewish Politics: Political Tradition and Political Reconstruction in the Jewish Community in Tsarist Russia* (New York: Oxford University Press, 1989), 201n2.

57 Stanislawski, *Tsar Nicholas I and the Jews*, 97–98, 106. Stanislawski summarizes his argument as follows: "In the first decades of the nineteenth century, currents of Jewish enlightenment

Significantly, one of these schools was founded in Grodno, Abel Kaufman's home city, sometime between 1847 and 1853.[58] The strong initial resistance among local Jews to the Grodno school was apparently quite soon broken down:

> At the beginning, the wealthy and traditional Jews of Grodno refused to send their children to the school and enrolled only the poorest and least intelligent of the local children. After a short while, however, many of the [in the words of an official report] "reasonable and not-so-prejudiced" Jews noted that the unfortunates in the state school had achieved great progress in their studies and decided to send their own children to the school, raising the enrollment to 62 in 1853. Among the new students were children of prosperous families and even the son of the local rabbi.[59]

For its part, Bialystok also proved hospitable to the Haskalah, perhaps even earlier than Grodno. As historian Rebecca Kobrin notes, "more traditionally minded rabbis" denounced Bialystok "as a 'heretical city, filled with *haskalah* and *bildung*'" that "should be avoided at all costs."[60]

---

thought and practice had infiltrated into Russia. A few small pockets of maskilim [adherents of the Haskalah] appeared in the Pale; a larger number of Jews seem to have been attracted to the Haskalah but were unable or unwilling to join forces openly with the combative new movement. Soon, Nicholas's government—or rather, his minister of national enlightenment—began to support the purveyors and purposes of Haskalah. This alliance intensified the predisposition of Russian Jews to view the maskilim as powerful, well-connected friends of the authorities and hence a grave danger to traditional Jewish life. Although these fears quite probably were exaggerated, the intervention of the government was decisive. It led, on the one hand, to strengthen the Haskalah in Russia in size and in prestige and, on the other, to intensifying the opposition to enlightenment on the part of the bulk of Russian Jewry ... By the 1840s Russian Jewry was split into two new groups—the traditionalists and the enlightened ... Traditionalist Jewry in Russia began to transform itself into an Orthodoxy, united in a new militant defense against the danger it perceived from the outside ... The maskilim, on the other hand, were convinced that the march of history was on their side. And so they solidified their alliance with and dependence on the government, which they identified with the beneficent and progressive forces of modernity and civilization" (186–87). See also Stanislawski's "Russian Jewry, the Russian State, and the Dynamics of Jewish Emancipation," in *Paths of Emancipation: Jews, States, and Citizenship*, ed. Pierre Birnbaum and Ira Katznelson (Princeton, NJ: Princeton University Press, 1995), 262–83; esp. 272–73.
58 Stanislawski, *Tsar Nicholas I and the Jews*, 97–98.
59 Ibid., 105.
60 Kobrin, *Jewish Bialystok*, 25–26. Haskalah-inspired groups, such as the "Society for the Spread of Enlightenment among the Jews in Russia" (founded 1863), were active in Bialystok as well; in the 1870s, this organization created a "Society for the Promotion of

It is not unlikely that the Russophilic Abel Kaufman, born in 1868, attended some sort of Russian-language school in Grodno, whether this was a "state school" or (more likely) one of the later gymnasia. (It also appears probable—although I cannot prove this—that he was among those effectively barred from higher education by the *numerus clausus* of 1887, promulgated when he was nineteen years of age.) If we go further and examine Kaufman's circulating-library holdings, we find that they were at once overwhelmingly "secular" in character and typical of other Russian bookstore-libraries in the empire in terms of both range of subject matter and the relative dominance of Russian-language belles lettres and writing for children,[61] if also marked by a linguistic diversity (Russian, Yiddish, Hebrew, Polish, Ukrainian, German, and French) that reflected Bialystok's own.

Kaufman's circulating library was regularly replenished by new books and, especially, by new periodicals. All the classics and much new writing (Artsybashev, Gorky, Bunin, Leonid Andreev, Kuprin, Korolenko, Boris Zaitsev, great quantities of Chekhov) in Russian were well represented, alongside Russian translations of foreign works by writers both older (Homer, Dante, Shakespeare, Milton, Schiller, Scott, Hoffmann, Balzac, Cooper, Dumas), recent (Hugo, Dickens, Sand, Stowe, Flaubert, Louisa May Alcott) and contemporary (Twain, d'Annunzio, Ibsen, Bjørnson, Edward Bellamy, Wilde, Hardy, Gissing, Hamsun, Zola, Kipling, Maupassant, Strindberg, Schnitzler, Frank Norris, Bertha von Suttner). The relatively small "scientific section" was a mix of popular science, science-fantasy, nutrition, history, religion, philosophy, politics, and psychology, and included the writings of, among many others, astronomer and scientific popularizer Camille Flammarion, biologist Ernst Haeckel, psychologist Nikolaj Lange, Marxist political theorist Karl Kautsky (his early book on the origins of marriage), designer and utopian socialist thinker William Morris (*News from Nowhere* [1890]), and criminologist Cesare Lombroso, alongside Schopenhauer, Nietzsche, Max Nordau, Ernest Renan, Edward Tylor (*Anthropology* [1881]), Friedrich Engels (*The Origin of the Family, Private Property, and the State* [1884]), and large helpings of Darwin. Finally, all sections of the circulating library incorporated many books by Jewish writers and on Jewish themes, including the *Jewish Encyclopedia* and

---

Industry," intent on establishing "an exclusively Jewish craft school" in Bialystok (Klier, *Imperial Russia's Jewish Question*, 244–48, 260).

61 Focusing on library catalogues from the period 1879–81, historian A. Rejtblat has found that most of the circulating libraries had around two to three thousand titles, with belles lettres and children's literature making up 60–70 percent (Rejtblat, *Ot Bovy k Bal'montu*, 58).

works by authors like Lev Levanda (his attack on the infamous blood libel against Jews and much of his fiction), Sholem Asch (translations of some of his early work, such as "A Shtetl" [1904], into Russian), Theodor Herzl (*The Jewish State* [1896]), and historian Semyon Dubnov, among others.[62]

Although we should not be tempted to conclude too much about Kaufman's self-conception based on his choice of profession, we can entertain certain assumptions about him based on that choice and on a scrutiny of his catalogs and his way of presenting his business to the public. On the one hand, as Rejtblat argues,

> circulating libraries were pleasant and "proper" ways for people of the more privileged estates to earn money: the nobility, the bureaucracy, and the intelligentsia. They enabled a conjunction between earning one's livelihood and a sufficiently prestigious, "honest" and, often, educational function.[63]

To be sure, journalists in Moscow mocked the circulating libraries for the low quality of their offerings (popular literature instead of Karamzin, Pushkin, Gogol, and so on), and it is not surprising, given their commercial orientation, that these libraries aimed at immediately pleasing their clientele in ways that contrasted with the educational focus of the public libraries. Yet in cities with an adequate concentration of educated readers, the circulating libraries often did possess a good supply of scholarly and older, classic works, and Kaufman's was certainly one of those.[64]

Indeed, "educational function" seems to have been a major motive behind Kaufman's decision to open the circulating library. Though a common townsperson (*meshchanin*) and not a member of any elite, Abel Kaufman had earlier elected to serve in the city administration (specifically, in its library), rather than participating in the business world so overwhelmingly dominant in Bialystok, and about which I will have more to say in a moment. In the 1860s

---

[62] The library's holdings changed over the years, of course, though not the overall proportion of literature, children's literature, and "science" represented on its shelves. See the two already-mentioned catalogs, as well A.K. Kaufman, *Dobavochnyj katalog russkikh knig biblioteki A.K. Kaufmana v g. Belostoke* (Bialystok: Oppengejm, 1909); all in the State Library of the Russian Federation, Moscow.

[63] Rejtblat, *Ot Bovy k Bal'montu*, 58. In 1882, 50 percent of the proprietors of libraries were of the higher classes and professions (nobles, civil servants, military men, teachers, doctors etc.); 37 percent were merchants and townspeople, and 13 percent derived from other groups like peasants, the clergy, and foreigners. A high percentage (29 percent) were women, many of whom apparently opened their libraries with explicitly educational motives in mind (ibid., 56, 58).

[64] Ibid., 48–49, 54.

and '70s, there had been a Russia-wide surge in the number of libraries with a largely educational orientation,[65] and Kaufman's bookstore-library was also established with "enlightenment" rather than profit exclusively in mind; in 1896, the year of Vertov's birth, Abel petitioned to be allowed to call his library "The People's Benefit," a name selected to associate the library with popular uplift.[66] It is obviously impossible to infer any specific educational program out of the catalogues of the holdings in Kaufman's library, not least because those holdings answered to the diverse requests of his customers as well as to his own tastes and outlook. Clearly, however, he did regard his establishment as an instrument of public enlightenment, and must have selected many of the library's offerings in that light.

In sum, and based on what we can read out of Russian-Jewish history on the one hand, and the evidence we have about Kaufman's bookstore and its probable clientele on the other—particularly the bookstore's secular and Russian-language emphasis, but also the high proportion of books on Jewish controversies it contained—it seems safe to describe Kaufman as representative of what John Klier, Benjamin Nathans, Michael Stanislawski, and others have called the "Russian-Jewish intelligentsia," that public that began to form in the 1860s from the matrix that precipitated out of the reforms and the Haskalah, and which stressed at once participation in Russian society and concern for issues touching upon Russian Jewry specifically.[67] To be sure, this

---

65 Ibid., 56.
66 NIAB f. 1, op. 8, d. 2794, ll. 21, 22, 22ob. The request was dated July 31, 1896, and permission was granted October 23, 1896. I have not seen any advertisements billing the library under this name, although it is clear that circulating library and bookstore owners quite commonly gave their establishments such monikers. A St. Petersburg library and press that had existed since ca. 1860 was called "Society's Benefit" (*Katalog knizhnago magazina i biblioteki tovarishchestva "Obshchestvennaia Pol'za"* [St. Petersburg: Obshchestvennaia Pol'za, 1905].)
67 Klier's description of this intelligentsia is worth quoting at length: "They . . . were invariably the products of the state Jewish school system, and they often remained dependent upon the system created by Nicholas I for employment as teachers or Jewish experts. . . . they campaigned overtly for Jewish emancipation as a basic human right which did not need to be earned. They neglected significant features of the Haskalah schema, such as the civilizing power of the study of Biblical Hebrew. For them the customary Haskalah emphasis on the use of the vernacular became a virtual passion for Russia as an emblem and pledge of citizenship. While the maskilim . . . were inwardly directed in their efforts at reform—albeit willing to call upon the Russian state for support—members of the Russian Jewish intelligentsia considered themselves part of Russian society, entitled and obligated to participate in public debate, an attitude fostered by the atmosphere of the Reform Era." "The Russian Jewish intelligentsia," he adds, "early on confronted the challenge of defining a Jewish identity—and identifying a role for Judaism—in modern Russian society," but also stresses that the differentiations

was now a true intelligentsia that, however secular, took a determinedly (if not radically) critical attitude toward the Russian state's policies and prejudices, in contrast to their maskilim forbears.[68]

BOOKS, FILMS, AND BOISTEROUS, RICH BIALYSTOK

It is important to note, additionally, that the Bialystok-Grodno area was the site of a great deal of large-, middle-, and small-scale capital investment and exchange, which turned Bialystok into both a boomtown and (later) one of the cradles of the Russian labor movement. Although sometimes described as "out of the way," a backwards "shtetl," and so on—and may well have been perceived as provincial by many of its youngest, most restless inhabitants[69]—Bialystok was in fact the second-largest industrial city in the western Russian Empire (after Łodz), and thus roiling with all the activity, prosperity, inequality, and conflict that capitalism always generates. Already by 1862, the great Russian writer Nikolaj Leskov in his "From a Travel Diary" reported that Bialystok was known, at least locally, as "the Lithuanian Manchester."[70] In contrast to other provincial centers such as Grodno, wrote Leskov,

> The streets of Bialystok were filled with people. Jews were swarming everywhere. There was noise, chatter, quarreling, and barter: the whole city was like a marketplace.[71]

---

between various branches of what we might call the intellectual hegemons within Jewish society—traditionalists, maskilim, assimilationists, the intelligentsia—"cannot be considered hard and fast" (Klier, *Imperial Russia's Jewish Question*, 26–28).

68 Cf. Löwe, *The Tsars and the Jews*, 412.

69 The city is seriously mischaracterized in just this manner in Evgeny Tsymbal's 2002 *Dziga and His Brothers*, an otherwise informative documentary film. Viktor Listov's pioneering article on Vertov's early life and career does justice to the contrast between the impressions of memoirists (specifically, cartoonist Boris Efimov and polar explorer Ernst Krenkel') recalling the "boondocks" of Bialystok, and a social reality that only superficially appeared "quiet and stagnant" (Listov, "Molodost' Mastera," *DVVS*, 88–89).

70 Łodz, the greatest industrial city in the western Russian Empire, was well known as "the Polish Manchester."

71 Nikolaj Leskov, "Iz odnogo dorozhnago dnevnika," *Severnaia Pchela* 338 (December 14, 1862): 1335. According to the text, Leskov visited Bialystok on September 14, 1862. Although Leskov saw "no large buildings" in Bialystok, he noted that the hotel service was far superior to that offered in nearby cities. Just as English factories developed their own specializations, he added, Bialystok, where cloth manufacture had begun twenty years earlier, now had textile factories focusing just on the production of particular fabrics like tricot. Reflecting on the city's prospects, Leskov's host at the

Bialystok's location as a border town became important in 1831 when the Tsarist government increased duties from 1 to 15 percent on goods coming into Russia from Congress Poland, prompting entrepreneurs in Poland to set up shop across the frontier in the Bialystok-Grodno area, which was appealingly positioned relatively near to Prussia and on roads leading east.[72] The economic improvements that began in the wake of the serf emancipation, together with intensifying marketing for exports, led in turn to a general upsurge in trade and industrial growth in the 1860s and early 1870s. Bialystok became a major cloth producer—the Russian Army was the largest client—and its competitiveness in textiles was enhanced by the city's position at the junction of three important railway lines: the St. Petersburg-Warsaw line (built in 1862), the Odessa-Królewiec (built in 1873: the main conduit of Ukrainian grain to East Prussia), and the Bialystok-Baranowicze (built in 1886: offered access to Moscow and points east through Minsk and Smolensk). These tracks, main arteries within a web of ancillary rail, linked Bialystok to Congress Poland and beyond in the west, to the Baltic Coast and St. Petersburg in the northeast, to Crimea and Ukraine in the south, and to the Russian heartland in the east.[73]

As might be expected, the presence or absence of railway connections "significantly affected the degree to which a particular setting was influenced by modern currents, either economic or cultural."[74] A remarkable passage from Israel Weisbrem's Haskalah-inspired novel *Between the Times* celebrates the modernizing force of the train in terms that seem almost proto-Futurist:

> ... from the day the railway was laid down through [the] town, the spirit of Haskalah began to infect its youth ... The flutelike sounds of those chariots of fire were like manifestos for a nation walking until then in darkness, prompting it to come out and be enlightened, so that the glory of the Haskalah might shine upon it. ... [75]

Hotel Warszawsky complained only that Bialystok had no good rail connections (the St. Petersburg–Warsaw line had just been built), a situation that was to change over the next twenty years.

72 Dobronski, *Białystok: Historia Miasta*, 73.
73 Ibid., 74, 81–83. In 1914, between twenty-three and eighty-four trains passed a day through the city on the St. Petersburg–Warsaw line (ibid., 81).
74 Zipperstein, *The Jews of Odessa*, 16.
75 Quoted in Zipperstein, *The Jews of Odessa*, 16. Weisbrem's novel *Bein ha-zemanim* [*Between the Times*] was published in Warsaw in 1888.

To be sure, "Haskalah" is here a figure for modernization as such, which in Bialystok's case involved rail and much else besides. The colossal surge in the city's population in the sixty years after 1845 was largely due to an economic dynamism truly exceptional within the western Russian Empire.[76] Although only 260 of the Grodno guberniia's 3,565 factories and plants—many of them very small concerns, employing only a handful of people—were located in Bialystok in 1896, the city's industry produced a full 4,029,821 rubles out of the 14,041,854 rubles-worth produced by factories in the guberniia as a whole, by far the largest share generated by any municipality.[77] By 1913, Bialystok was home to 52 percent of the factory workers in the guberniia, and accounted for 54 percent of its textile production; 75 percent of workers involved in non-textile industry labored and resided there as well.[78]

A regional banking center by the 1890s, Bialystok's wealth was reflected in its many modern facilities and amenities, especially as compared with the surrounding area. In 1896, a third of the stone-built private homes in the entire guberniia were in Bialystok (977 out of a total of 2720).[79] Medical alumni from Vilna University and other prestigious schools began to appear in the city in the wake of the construction of important hospitals (a thirty-bed district hospital built in 1853; a forty-eight-bed Jewish hospital in 1862), and the influx of both

---

76 Home to fifteen textile factories in 1860, the city had thirty-six more ten years later (Dobronski, *Białystok: Historia Miasta*, 84), and the Russo-Turkish War of 1877 provided a major stimulus to production, ending the major recession of 1872–76 (Dobronski, *Białystok: Historia Miasta*, 84; Ezra Mendelsohn, *Class Struggle in the Pale*, 17). As Theodore Weeks writes, "Industry in the [Northwest Region of the Empire, comprising Kovno, Vitebsk, Vilna, Mogilev, Minsk and Grodno guberniias] was small and underdeveloped. In 1911–1912 the industrial production of the six provinces averaged 10.6 rubles per capita, much less than in the Kingdom of Poland where the figure was 60.8 rubles. The largest industry in the region was distilling; in this branch the Northwest outproduced even the Kingdom of Poland. Probably the sole 'industrial city' in the entire region was [Białystok], where a booming textile business had given rise to related trades such as the production of chemicals and dyes, and a well-developed credit and finance system. A visitor in the late 1880s wrote of 'boisterous, rich [Białystok].'" Weeks adds, "[Białystok] was a predominantly Jewish city, and much of the industry in all six Northwestern Provinces were in Jewish hands. Only in Vitebsk Province was the percentage of Jewish ownership of factories under 25 percent. To be sure, nearly all of the 'factories and plants' that figure in the statistic were small affairs indeed, more like artisanal workshops than industrial enterprises" (Weeks, *Nation and State*, 78).
77 In 1896, according to official records, Bialystok's 256 factories employed 3,012 male laborers (out of a total 13,930 in the guberniia), 1,600 females (out of 4,876), and 117 children (out of 838) (*Pamiatnaia knizhka Grodnenskoj gubernii na 1898 god*, 28–29).
78 Dobronski, *Białystok: Historia Miasta*, 86. Even as a textile center, however, Bialystok manufactured only eight percent of what Łodz produced in 1914 (ibid.).
79 *Pamiatnaia knizhka Grodnenskoj gubernii na 1898 god*, 16.

wealth and educated professionals meant the city was soon hosting performances by well-known musicians and theatrical troupes.[80] By 1913, the year before David Kaufman left to go off to St. Petersburg/Petrograd for university study, the city had seven pharmacies—the only ones in the district (*uezd*).[81] The physical, transport, and communications plants were all modernized between 1890 and 1910, which required a few preliminary feats of drainage to stabilize the city's marshy territory.[82] A water supply system was built in 1892 to the northeast of the city; an electric power plant rose on the banks of the Biała River in 1910; a local telephone network started operations in 1891; and by 1895, Białystok was transected by three lines of horse-drawn trams.[83] At the same time, the city's economic growth brought with it serious zoning problems—shops and warehouses proliferated in every backyard, on every riverbank, and even in the gaps between buildings—making daily life difficult for workers and nonworkers alike.[84]

Image 3: The *Modern* "electro-theater" (on the right, in the foreground) in Lipowa Street in Bialystok, ca. 1910. Source: Andrzej Lechowski, *Białystok: urok starych klisz* [*Bialystok: the charm of old photographic plates*] (Bialystok: Benkowski, 2005), 57.

---

80 Ibid., 76.
81 *Obzor Grodnenskoj gubernii za 1913 god*, 81.
82 Dobronski, *Białystok: Historia Miasta*, 100.
83 Ibid., 103.
84 Ibid., 101.

Cinema, born (arguably) in France just prior to Vertov's own birth in January 1896, naturally found its way to Bialystok as well.[85] Although it is not clear when the first cinema appeared in the city, in the years preceding World War I, there were apparently six movie theaters in operation there—*The Modern, The Whole World, Fantazia, Eden, The Bio Express,* and *The Palace*— with *The Modern* and *The Whole World* first in rank in terms of size, repertoire, and attendance.[86] In 1915, when *The Modern* decided to show films out of doors in an adjacent garden during the hot summer months, this exhibition novelty was reported in film journals published as far away as Riga:

> The garden is located next to the theatre and creates a very good impression due to its multitude of fruit trees, under which it is so pleasant to relax after the day's labors and listen to the theatre's neatly dressed orchestra.[87]

Film going was popular in Bialystok, and *The Palace* and *The Whole World* both expanded their premises in the pre–World War I years.[88] As far as repertoire is concerned, *The Modern* showed recent serials produced by Denmark's Nordisk studio, Max Linder comedies (*Le Chapeau de Max* [*Max's Hat*, 1913] was much publicized), and Pathé newsreels, while *Fantazia* exhibited the Italo-French actor Ferdinand Guillaume's "Polidor" comedies soon after their initial release, a fresh *World Journal* every week or so, and curiosities such as *Rhythmic Drawings from Nature*.[89] The theaters were well integrated into the town's central business district; for some years, Arkadij Pokhon'skij's *Eden* theater

---

85 The Lumière Brothers held the first public screenings of the "cinématographe" in Paris on December 28, 1895.
86 NIAB f. 15, op. 1, d. 155, ll. 59, 61, 63, 67, 67 ob; f. 8, op. 2, d. 1917, l. 1; f. 8, op. 2, d. 2190, ll. 1–16; f. 8, op. 2, d. 1971, l. 25; f. 103, op. 1, d. 106, l. 30a. See also V. Listov, "Molodost' Mastera," in *DVVS*, 89.
87 "Po gorodam (otdel Belostok)," *Kino* [Riga] 3–4 (1915): 4.
88 NIAB f. 8, op. 2, d. 1971, l. 25; f. 8, op. 2, d. 2190, ll. 1–16.
89 NIAB f. 15, op. 1, d. 155, ll. 59, 61, 61ob, 63, 67, 67ob. Guillaume's *Polidor ha caldo*, for instance, was released on August 4, 1913 and was playing in Bialystok no later than mid-October (see NIAB f. 15, d. 155, l. 59; and Elena Mosconi, ed., *L'Oro di Polidor: Ferdinand Guillaume alla Cineteca Italiana* [Milan: Il Castoro, 2000], 96). I have not seen evidence that any pre-Revolutionary newsreel was distributed in Russia under the title *World Journal*; perhaps this title came from the exhibitor, rather than the distributor. Listov indicates that *The Whole World* showed Pathé and Gaumont newsreels presenting everything from the Eiffel Tower and Cuban sugar plantations to conflicts in the Balkans and "the production of Cadbury cocoa" (Listov, "Molodost' Mastera," *DVVS*, 89).

evidently shared a building in Nikolaevskaia Street (the three-story Markus Building) with Abel Kaufman's bookstore.[90]

Finally, in 1895, Bialystok could boast five of the fifteen circulating libraries in the Grodno guberniia, more than twice as many as in any other city, alongside a number of smaller stores and photo/print related businesses.[91] Abel Kaufman's bookstore-library was not the only one in Bialystok—he had a number of big rivals even in the 1890s, and the bookstore was but one of twelve by 1929—but it was one of the most centrally located, best-stocked, and largest in the city, known broadly through word of mouth, connections with local schools, and through advertisements in papers in Russian, Yiddish and Polish.[92] By the 1880s, argues Rejtblat, the clientele of a circulating library like Kaufman's would be drawn from virtually the entire reading public of the city, with the likely exceptions of the very well to do and the utterly indigent:

> In the 19th century, especially during its second half, the number of readers of modest means, unable to buy the books they needed on their own, grew sharply. Libraries of other kinds (scientific, school- or club-based, and so on) were as a rule closed to the wider public, and indeed often did not contain the kinds of literature that interested that public. The basic readership of

---

90 NIAB f. 8, op. 2, d. 1917, l. 1. *The Bio Express* was in Nikolaevskaia Street as well (NIAB f. 103, op. 1, d. 106, l. 30a). Home to two library-bookstores and four bookbinderies, as well as the city's top hotels (the Warszawski and Hamburski), Nikolaevskaia Street was obviously one of Bialystok's more prestigious commercial arteries.

91 In 1898, the other four circulating libraries were owned by Mojsej Milanovskij, Iosel' Kagan, Sh. Lipshits, Kaplan, and Indirskij. There were, in addition, one bookstore without a library, two smaller bookshops (and numerous booksellers' stalls), a sheet music store, five photo studios (one dating from 1888), three lithographic shops, nine printing shops, and four printmakers (NIAB f. 1, op. 9, d. 890, ll. 85–87ob).

92 Kaufman's "library for reading" was one of five in the city in 1896—there had only been three when he set up shop in 1893—all of which were attached to bookstores (*Pamiatnaia knizhka Grodnenskoj gubernij na 1897 god* [Grodno: Grodnenskij Gubernskij Statisticheskij Komitet, 1896], 59 (section 4); *Pamiatnaia knizhka Grodnenskoj gubernii na 1898 god,* 74); for 1929, see footnote 21. He supplied books to the local Talmud-Tora, among other schools (Iu. Kaletskij, ed., *Otchet belostokskoj Talmud'-tory s remeslennym uchilishchem za 1901 i 1902 gg.* (Bialystok: Ts. Mishondzink, 1903), 9, 18, 21), and also purchased books from students "with a permission slip from the parents" (see, for instance, the Bialystok paper *Svobodnaia Mysl'* 8 [July 1–2, 1922]: 4). Judging from the newspapers I have seen, Kaufman advertised more than his competitors, at least in Russian-language papers: see his ads in *Belostokskaia Gazeta* (January 8, 1910): 4 (NIAB f. 103, op. 1, d. 106, l. 30a); *Golos Belostoka* 240, 242, 243 (October 20, 23–24, 1913), always on 4 (NIAB f. 15, op. 1, d. 155, ll. 66ob, 68ob, 70ob); *Svobodnaia Mysl'* 5 (June 10–11, 1922): 1; *Svobodnaia Mysl'* 18 (June 10–11, 1922): 1; *Svobodnaia Mysl'* 5 (February 17, 1923): 4; among others. (*Svobodnaia Mysl'* can be found in the library of the University of Warsaw.)

[circulating libraries] was made up of civil servants, students (university and high school), those involved in service in private enterprise or in stores, army officers, and members of the so-called "free professions."[93]

A given circulating library could have anywhere from 100 to 300, or even more, subscribers, and Rejtblat suggests that the heterogeneity of the public that made use of the libraries is reflected in the wide variety of their offerings, ranging typically (and certainly in Kaufman's case, as we have seen) from the Russian classics (Pushkin, Tolstoy, Turgenev, many others), foreign prose works (from Homer to Hamsun), children's literature (Jules Verne, Mayne Reid), adventure novels (often by forgotten favorites like Fortuné du Boisgobey and Xavier de Montépin) and works of mostly popularized science and scholarship (Camille Flammarion, Darwin, Henry Buckle, Samuel Smiles, J. S. Mill, Hyppolite Taine, even Proudhon were all mainstays Russia-wide).[94]

Rejtblat convincingly inserts the libraries for reading into the history of "media of mass communication, inasmuch as they sought to enable the widest possible circle of readers to become acquainted with a *new* journal or a *new* book," thus approximating the function both of bookstores—to which (as with Abel Kaufman's establishment) they were often attached in any case—and of periodicals as such, the latter being, unsurprisingly, among the libraries' most popular offerings. As a hybrid of library and bookstore, the circulating library emerged as a kind of "unification of autonomous readers [otherwise] unconnected with one another," and to whose desires the library's owner, motivated at least to a considerable degree by commercial goals, was bound to respond in some way.[95] At the same time, Kaufman's "address to his clientele" suggests that the bookstore's commercial identity—an identity shared, as we have seen, with many enterprises in Bialystok unconnected in such a direct way to knowledge—was to some extent at odds with its owner's evident concern with "uplift" and promotion of "the best books" rather than the "newest (fashionable) novels." Not only the circulation, but also the *management* of texts and their reception was the common concern of circulating library owners, publishers, booksellers, and, not least, the censorship, which sent out long lists of prohibited books every month to the libraries.[96]

---

93 Rejtblat, *Ot Bovy k Bal'montu*, 61.
94 Ibid., 58–60. For fascinating pages on the reading preferences of workers before and after 1917, see Mark D. Steinberg, *Proletarian Imagination: Self, Modernity, and the Sacred in Russia, 1910-1925* (Ithaca: Cornell University Press, 2002), 30–33, 124–26.
95 Rejtblat, *Ot Bovy k Bal'montu*, 50.
96 Tolstoy, Zola, Kautsky, Sidney and Beatrice Webb, and Bebel—but also Heine, Rimbaud and Mallarmé—were among the prominent names encountered on the lists of books

In Bialystok, to be sure, the constitution of a Russian-language reading public was complicated by the city's multilingual, multi-confessional, and (as we shall see) politically complex character. We shouldn't forget that the inventor of Esperanto, Ludwik (Eliezer) Zamenhof (1859–1917), was born and lived in Bialystok from 1859 to 1873, and reputedly was provoked to devise a universal language because of the disunity occasioned by the "Babel" of tongues in his hometown.[97] Besides Russian-oriented establishments like Kaufman's, there were other kinds of bookstores and circulating libraries in Bialystok, some of which catered primarily to Yiddish readers, or to minority groups.

On some occasions, as Rejtblat reports, the circulating libraries went beyond any relatively general "media" function to become more punctual countercultural (or "counterpublic") loci for the dispersal of radical, revolutionary writing, to the extent of offering space for circles of revolutionary youth to gather and discuss contemporary political problems.[98] As is well known, by the early twentieth century, Jews were participating in disproportionately large numbers in revolutionary parties Russia-wide (the Social Democrats, the Socialist Revolutionaries, above all the Bund); and Bialystok's Jewish population, unusually proletarian and radicalized in any case, was certainly no exception to this powerful critical and activist tendency.[99] Though I have no reason to believe that Abel Kaufman provided sanctuary for any subversive meetings, his bookstore-library surely was a popular spot among Bialystok's students—some of whom would soon become quite radical indeed—who would have encountered

---

censored within the Grodno guberniia (NIAB f. 1, op. 9, d. 890, ll. 10–28; f. 1, op. 9, d. 17, ll. 8–150). It is clear from these lists that publications in Polish and Ukrainian were scrutinized more assiduously, and banned more frequently, than those in Russian, at least in the Pale.

[97] Zamenhof lamented this disharmony in a well-known 1895 letter to his friend Nikolai Afrikanovich Borovko. In Bialystok, according to Zamenhof as paraphrased by his biographer, "there were only Jews, Russians, Poles, Germans . . . not people, but only races" ("ne homoj, sole gentoj"). Quarrels in the marketplace, strife on the street, and even pogroms (Zamenhof had in mind the 1906 massacre in Bialystok, discussed below) had a single cause: "Poles would hate Russians, Russians would want nothing to do with Germans, Germans wouldn't tolerate the French, the French wouldn't accept the English." Only a "neutral language" ("neutrala lingvo") could unite the peoples and bring about universal understanding (Edmond Privat, *Vivo de Zamenhof* [Leipzig: Ferdinand Hirt & Sohn/Esperanto Fako, 1923], 16–19). See also Kobrin, *Jewish Bialystok*, 52–55.

[98] Kobrin, *Jewish Bialystok*, 56. Rejtblat mentions "radical" libraries operating in St. Petersburg, Viatka, Perm′, and Irkutsk. Though the revolutionary character of these libraries was clearly exceptional, it is interesting to note that almost two-thirds of the libraries circulated (legally) copies of the first volume of Marx's *Capital* (ibid., 60); Engels and Kautsky, as I have already indicated, were on Kaufman's own shelves.

[99] See Budnitskij, *Rossijskie evrei*, 53–54; and below.

Province of Universality: David Kaufman before the War • CHAPTER 1   33

there not only diversion, but also much incitement to thought and critique. Indeed, as of 1898, the only circulating library in Bialystok that included a public reading room was Kaufman's, suggesting that his establishment might have been a gathering place unique in the city.[100] And an intriguing anecdote from a later era helps illustrate the attachments, sentimental as well as intellectual, which formed around a circulating library like Kaufman's.

Among the many small entrepreneurs in the city at the turn of the century was a merchant of the Second Guild named Chaim Movshov Fridliand, originally from a shtetl in the Minsk guberniia, and the owner of a footwear store in Kiev and a leather warehouse in Bialystok. Fridliand and his wife Rokhlia raised their two sons in Bialystok, and the boys became classmates of David and Mojsej Kaufman at the Modern School there. As it turns out, the younger Fridliand would become famous as Boris Efimov (1899/1900–2008), perhaps the most celebrated of all Soviet political caricaturists; the elder, originally named Mojsej, would grow up to be the even better known, globetrotting Soviet journalist Mikhail Kol'tsov (born June 12, 1898, in Kiev–executed February 2, 1940, in Moscow). Kol'tsov/Fridliand grew up with David Kaufman in Bialystok, studied in Petrograd with him at the Psychoneurological Institute (described in chapter 2), and would in spring 1918 give David his first job in film, at the beginning of eventful and peripatetic careers for them both.[101]

At any rate, sometime around 1930, Kol'tsov was evidently passing through Poland, and managed to make a brief stopover in his old hometown. In a postcard to Efimov, he indicates (adopting a female persona, curiously enough) that he paid Abel Kaufman's establishment a tributary visit:

> My dear sister!
> I'm walking along Nikolaevskaia and Lipovaia streets, recalling our school years. . . I dropped by Kaufman's bookstore (it still exists!), and by the women's gymnasium where we studied. Nothing's changed . . . A strange feeling—pleasant and sad.
> Kisses,
> Your M.[102]

---

100 See the 1898 police report on reading rooms in Bialystok in NIAB, f. 1, op. 9, d. 890, l. 85ob.
101 See Kol'tsov's student records from the Petrograd Psychoneurological Institute: TsGIASPb f. 115, op. 2, d. 9788, ll. 6, 12, 16, 21; and below. Although Kiev was not located (except for two districts) within the Pale, Jews played "a particularly visible role in the economic and social life" of the city (Budnitskij, *Rossijskie evrei*, 27).
102 From Boris Efimov's memoir in H. Z. Beliaev, B. E. Efimov, M. B. Efimov, ed., *Mikhail Kol'tsov, kakim on byl* (Moscow: Sovetskij Pisatel', 1989), 36. Kol'tsov, who was a famous

By the time this letter was written, of course, both Kol'tsov and Efimov were contributing to (Soviet) libraries and bookstores as authors in their own right, writing above all for periodicals in highly public forums. And it seems legitimate to speculate that the circulating library's role as a point of media exchange, as a site visited by a wide variety of people in order to find out what was new and interesting in the world, exerted a decisive effect upon the consciousnesses of Abel and Chaya Kaufman's three sons—all of them future workers in newsreel-documentary and/or fictional film—by making them aware of the heterogeneity of the local public, of the need to categorize and organize texts, and of the circulation of texts (or the suppression of that circulation) as constitutive of publics.[103]

At the same time, the library's prominence in the community would have given the family, if not wealth or power, then at least a certain social centrality and a reputation as one of the sustainers (and managers) of the city's cultural level, and thus might have impressed upon the Kaufman boys the importance of what we now call "cultural capital," and its relationship to other kinds of capital. (This would surely include inculcating them with that distinct intolerance of [to adapt Abel Kaufman's words] "seductive titles concealing a lack of content and absence of ideas" so evident in Vertov's later diatribes against fiction film.) If all this is true—and we will have other occasions to reflect on this question—it suggests that we might add the modest circulating library to the array of media forms—like museums, exhibitions, traveling lectures and the like—in relation to which emergent cinema, in its "public-building" role, ought to be considered.[104]

---

wit and lover of verbal play, probably adopted a female persona to disguise himself—he was already very famous—from the anti-Soviet Polish authorities (though possibly he wished to distract the Soviet ones, too).

103 For important extended reflections on the formation of publics in and through discourse, see Miriam Bratu Hansen, *Babel and Babylon: Spectatorship in American Silent Film* (Cambridge, MA: Harvard University Press, 1991); and especially Michael Warner, *Publics and Counterpublics* (New York: Zone Books, 2005), 65–124.

104 Certainly, the range, variability, and *organizability* of the library both as an archive and as a physical space for the (intellectual, affective) encounter with texts seems to relate, at least in an analogous way, to the formal and enunciative capacities of cinema as described in 1987 by Eric Hobsbawm: "The movement of the camera, the variability of its focus, the unlimited scope of trick photography and, above all, the ability to cut the strip of film which recorded it all into suitable pieces and to assemble or reassemble them at will, were immediately obvious and immediately exploited by filmmakers who rarely had any interest in or sympathies for the *avant garde* arts. Yet no art represents the requirements, the unintended triumph, of an utterly untraditional artistic modernism more dramatically than the cinema. ... There is no doubt that the revolutionary innovations of films as art, practically all of which had been developed in the USA by 1914, were due to its need to address a potentially

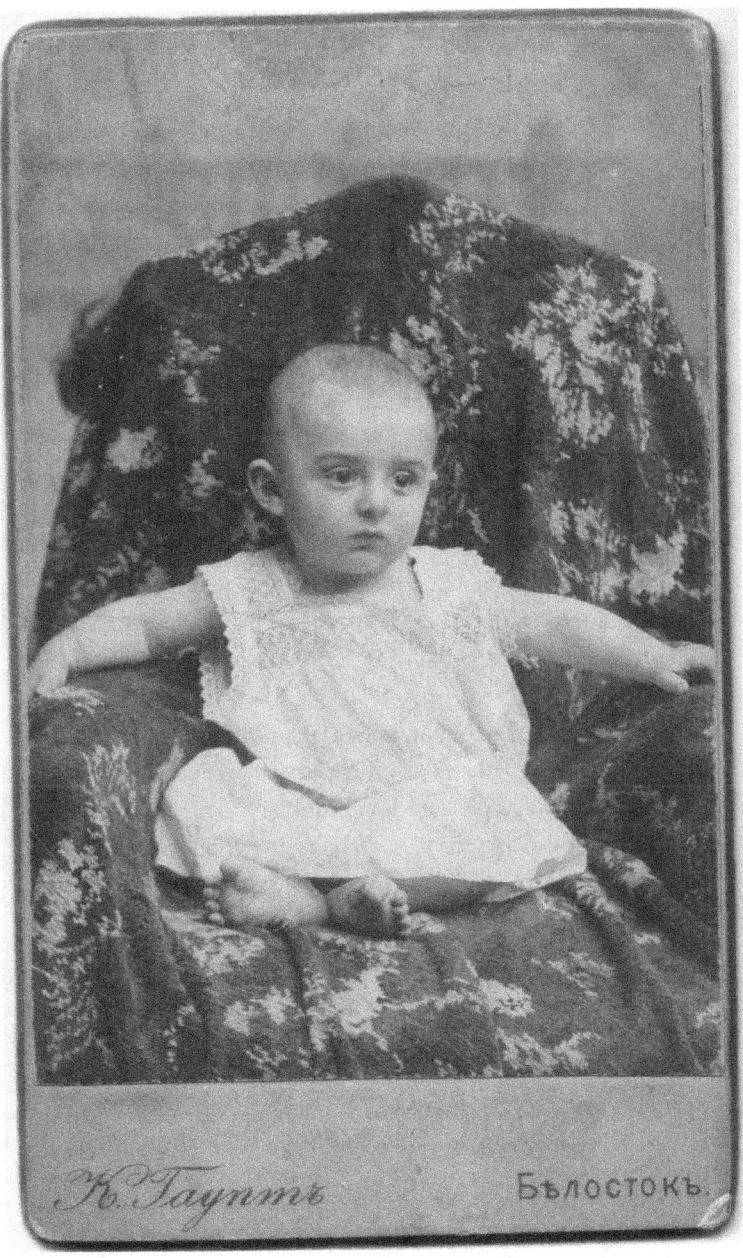

Image 4: Vertov as an infant. Image courtesy of Andre Kaufman.

"BE REASONABLE!" STUDENT AND WORKER POLITICS IN BIALYSTOK

David's arrival in the Kaufman household in 1896, followed by Mojsej's in 1897, took his mother Chaya away from her work in the bookstore for a few years,[105] though she and Abel probably sent the boys off to school when they reached five years of age. It is not clear where David studied between the ages of five and nine, though it seems unlikely, given the family's evident secularity, that he went to a traditional Jewish cheder, which the majority of Jewish boys in Bialystok would have attended starting from the age of five.[106] We do know that on September 2, 1905, the nine-year-old David became a student at the Bialystok Modern School (or Realschule: *real'noe uchilishche*), where he remained until graduating, after a supplementary year of pre-postsecondary work following the full eight years of regular study, in June 1914.[107] His school years thus began with the Russia-wide tumult of the years 1905 to 1907—the "First Russian Revolution," ignited by the Imperial Guard firing upon unarmed worker-demonstrators on "Bloody Sunday" (January 22, 1905) in St. Petersburg—and concluded a little more than a month before the beginning of World War I.

"Modern Schools" were junior high/high schools that stressed training in mathematics and the natural sciences, and whose graduates often went on to advanced study, mainly in engineering, agronomy, and medicine.[108] David took the regular course of study at the school, receiving good though not outstanding grades in all subjects (including Russian, German, French, science, and math) except drawing and drafting, where his performance was deemed only

---

universal public exclusively through the—technically manipulable—eye, but also that innovations which left the high-cultural *avant garde* far behind in their daring were readily accepted by the masses, because this was an art which transformed everything except its content" (*The Age of Empire: 1875–1914*, 238–39). For elaborations on this idea, see Hansen, *Babel and Babylon*, esp. 101–14; and "The Mass Production of the Senses: Classical Cinema as Vernacular Modernism," in Christine Gledhill and Linda Williams, ed., *Reinventing Film Studies* (London: Arnold, 2000), 332–50.

105   See note 28, above.
106   There was a four-grade "Bialystok Pushkin School," as well as a number of one- and two-grade Jewish elementary schools of a secular cast, that he might have attended (*Pamiatnaia knizhka Grodnenskoj gubernij na 1910 god* [Grodno: Grodnenskij Gubernskij Statisticheskij Komitet, 1909], 203–5).
107   TsGIASPb f. 115, op.2, d. 4048, ll. 5–6.
108   See A. E. Ivanov, *Studenchestvo Rossii*, 51–56.

Province of Universality: David Kaufman before the War • CHAPTER 1   37

Image 5: The Kaufman family, ca. 1906–7. Back row from left: Mojsej (Mikhail), Chaya, Abel, David (Dziga Vertov). Young Boris is holding his brother David's hand. This is the only photo I have seen of the entire family together. Photograph courtesy of Andre Kaufman.

satisfactory.[109] He evidently studied at the Bialystok Music School as well, a prestigious institute—bearing the imprimatur of the Imperial Russian Musical Society—that provided students with instruction in piano, violin, cello, singing, brass and woodwinds, certification as teachers of music, and even professional training in choir direction and accompaniment. David seems not only to have acquired musical performance skills there (including the ability to play the piano and violin) but also to have developed a lifelong interest, which we will discuss in more detail later, in musical structures and the organization of sound.[110]

The all-male Modern School on Alexandrovskaia Street was a well-established institution in Bialystok, having just celebrated its 100th anniversary in high official style in 1902.[111] A gymnasium until 1873, it became and remained a strictly Russian-language-only school following the January Uprising of 1863, after which all Poles teaching there were dismissed, surveillance of students was intensified, "Polish [faded] entirely from use," and even the teaching of religion to Roman Catholic students was conducted exclusively in Russian.[112] Around three-quarters of the student body, which comprised on average around 400 pupils in the early years of the twentieth century, was made up of Russian Orthodox and Roman Catholic students, with Jews and Lutherans more or less equally constituting the remainder: in other words, *not*

---

109 TsGIASPb f. 115, op.2, d. 4048, ll. 5–5ob. See also Valérie Pozner's "Vertov before Vertov: Psychoneurology in Petrograd," *Dziga Vertov*, ed. Tode and Wurm, 12–15.

110 See, among other sources, *DVVS*, 79; RGASPI f. 17, op. 125, d. 499, l. 49; and an advertisement for the Musical School in *Katalog russkikh knig* (1900), xiv. Vocal and instrumental training was offered at the Modern School as well (V. Angel'skij, *Otchet o sostoianii Belostokskago Real'nago Uchilishcha za 1901–2 uchebnyj god* [Belostok: Sh. M. Volobrinskij, 1902], 27–28).

111 The school was founded in 1802 as a gymnasium [i.e., a high school], on the basis of an earlier three-class institute created around 1770 by Countess Branicki. It became a "Modern School" in 1872–73 (*Opisanie prazdnovaniia 100-letniago iubileia Belostokskago Real'nago Uchilishcha* [Vilna: A. G. Syrkin, 1903], 3), and had been renovated and reconstructed over the years (V. Angel'skij, *Kratkie istoricheskie svedeniia o Belostokskom Real'nom Uchilishche* [Bialystok: Sh. M. Volobrinskij, 1902], 31–32). At the time David Kaufman was studying there, it was directed by one Aleksandr Efimovich Egorov, who oversaw the work of over thirty teachers (two of whom were women) and two instructors in singing and gymnastics (*Pamiatnaia knizhka Grodnenskoj gubernij na 1910 god*, 201–2; V. Angel'skij, *Otchet o sostoianii Belostokskago Real'nago Uchilishcha za 1901-2 uchebnyj god* [Belostok: Sh. M. Volobrinskij, 1902], 3).

112 V. Angel'skij, *Kratkie istoricheskie svedeniia*, 16–17. All school prayers were recited in Russian as well. Classes in Jewish religion were also offered at the school during the early twentieth century by one Perets Kliachko (V. Angel'skij, *Otchet o sostoianii*, 6), but David Kaufman apparently opted out of those classes (TsGIASPb f. 115, op.2, d. 4048, ll. 5–6).

a typical cross-section of the population of Bialystok as a whole.[113] Its student population had grown rapidly in the last years of the nineteenth century, an expansion due, according to the city council, to "the mounting significance of Bialystok as a center of light and heavy industry in our region."[114]

Indeed, the Modern School's technical emphasis early on led to the arrangement of field trips to local factories, including those owned by the school's patron, the Łodz-based manufacturer Adolf Buchholtz.[115] By the late nineteenth century it had developed a small trade school as well, training mainly Polish and Jewish turners and metal workers in drafting and sketching.[116] The school had become seriously overcrowded by the turn of the century and, according to the record of the anniversary celebrations, "unhygienic" by 1902; an additional wing was constructed sometime after 1903 to accommodate the crush of new pupils, who were soon to include Mojsej and Boris Fridliand (aka Mikhail Kol'tsov and Boris Efimov) and all three of the Kaufman brothers.

In an interview published in the 1980s, Boris Efimov indicated that both he and Mikhail Kol'tsov began their publishing career at the Bialystok Modern School, drawing and writing for satirical student-produced leaflets. The school, described by Efimov as "a panopticon of maniacs and sadists in blue uniforms,"[117] evidently provided rich fodder for caricature, although these student publications probably did not confine their attacks to unpopular teachers. Kol'tsov, for instance, who wrote satirical sketches under the pseudonym "Mikhail Syndeticonov"—the last name came from a well-known brand of glue, later used in Dadaist collage—also distributed illegal

---

113 Angel'skij, *Otchet o sostoianii*, 12. Around 40 percent of the students were from the noble and civil-service social estates, just under 35 percent from the urban estates (mainly petty townspeople or *meshchane*, like the Kaufmans), around 20 percent from the peasantry, and the rest either from the priestly estate or foreigners (ibid.).
114 *Opisanie prazdnovaniia 100-letniago iubileia*, 12–13. An adjoining Orthodox chapel was apparently also constructed (27).
115 Angel'skij, *Otchet o sostoianii*, 5.
116 Ibid., 40. This is not to say that the Modern School was an exclusively "tech" school by any means. Literature and language learning were taken seriously, and much effort was expended on celebratory evenings dedicated to major Russian writers like Nikolai Gogol' and Vasilij Zhukovskij (ibid., 49–59).
117 Not without tendentiousness, Efimov compared the atmosphere of the school to that of the Rovno gymnasium as described in Vladimir Korolenko's autobiographical *History of My Contemporary*, where the author depicts most of his teachers as cruel, strident and capricious, and the students as carrying out "an intriguing war with the bosses" (Beliaev et al., *Mikhail Kol'tsov, kakim on byl*, 30; V. G. Korolenko, *Istoriia moego sovremennika*, ed. A. V. Khrabrovitskij [Moscow: Khudozhestvennaia Literatura, 1965], 152).

pamphlets and, according to Efimov, attended banned discussion circles.[118] These activities continued even after a less stormy social climate had settled in the city (and in Russia) following the tumult of the years 1905–7, which in Bialystok as in many other places was marked by colossal strikes, firefights in the streets, police brutality, terrorism, and, on September 17, 1905, the imposition of martial law.[119] It is certain that the satirical papers, especially those emanating from Bialystok's student population during this period, would have included political commentary on their pages. Nine-year-old David Kaufman was obviously too young to participate in the student demonstrations and meetings that were also undoubtedly taking place in the Bialystok Modern School around the time he enrolled in 1905. Already at this early date, however, he was immersed in a student environment seething with political passion and debate.

Although I have not uncovered any examples of activist student publications from Bialystok in this period, I did find a few fascinating radical school brochures from the men's gymnasium in its rather less politicized sister-city of Grodno. One carbon-copied broadsheet simply entitled *School* (*Shkola*) featured caricatures of major state figures (like Tsar Nicholas II, who had made a royal visit with his family to Grodno and Bialystok in 1897)[120] and institutional enemies (like the police) alongside allegorical representations of the students' own political ideas and aspirations.

Another leaflet that appeared November 6, 1905[121]—sixteen days before the gymnasium students went on strike, and in the immediate wake of the vast October general strike—contained the following programmatic statement:

> We are living through a time of revolution. All levels of society have risen up in defense of the individual human being's profaned rights. All of Russia thirsts for a new life constructed on a new basis—on the basis of freedom. The struggle is at its very height. The proletariat, strong in organization, is carrying the entire burden using its own powers. Thousands of warriors have fallen victim to Tsarist despotism. In their ranks is included that part of the intelligentsia which has not yet been so suffused with the spirit of Mammon that it would reject the luminous ideals of the future in the name of satiety.

---

118 Beliaev et al., *Mikhail Kol'tsov, kakim on byl*, 30–32.
119 Dobronski, *Białystok: Historia Miasta*, 89.
120 Angel'skij, *Kratkie istoricheskie svedeniia*, 35.
121 *Shkola* 1 (November 22, 1905): 3.

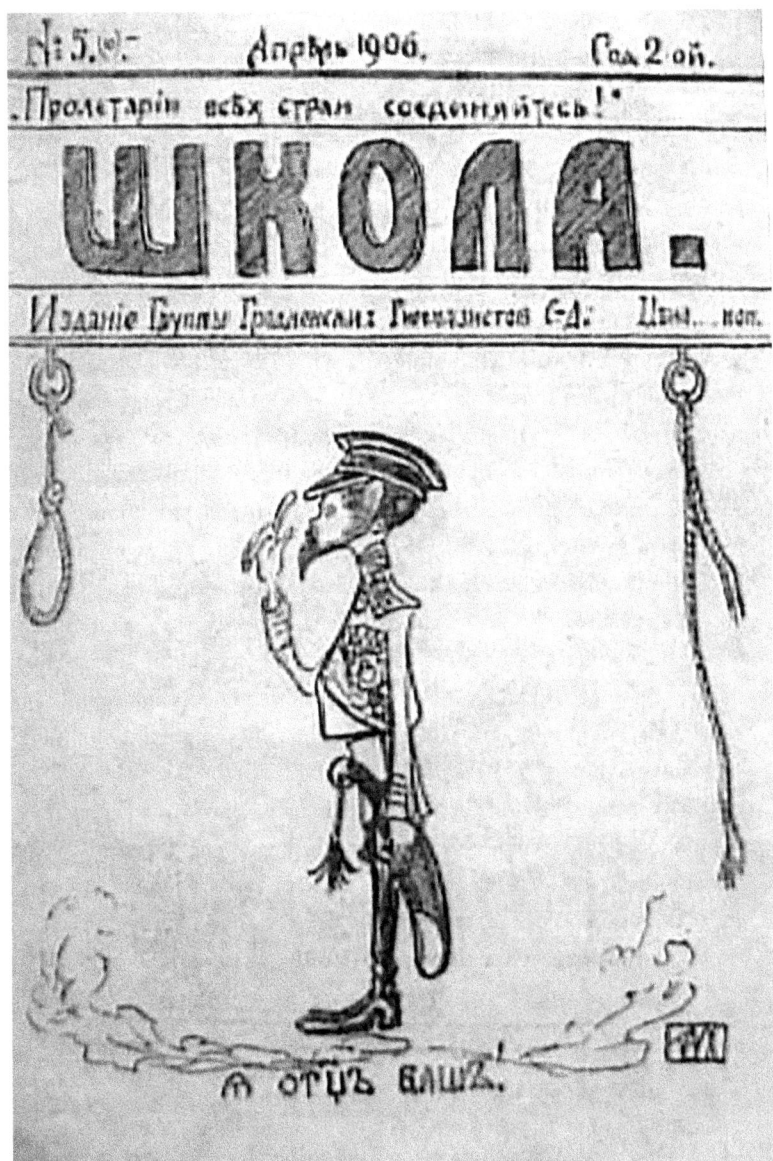

Image 6: Cover of *School (Shkola)*, issue no. 5 from April 1906. The paper was a carbon-copied "Publication of the Grodno Gymnasium Group of Social Democrats," and had as its slogan (above the name of the paper itself) "Proletarians of all countries unite!" Below the caricature of Tsar Nicholas II is the first phrase of the prayer "Our Father." Source: State Library of Poland, Warsaw.

Evidently, a teacher named Shimanovskij had forcefully exhorted the students to "be reasonable" rather than vocally express their displeasure with the regime. Shimanovskij's plea immediately came to stand for a kind of passivity that many if not most of the students rejected:

> "Be reasonable!" This means that we must above all "reasonably" close our eyes to everything now going on in Russia; that we must calmly and dispassionately watch (just as people have watched up to now) as the unarmed proletariat is fired upon on the streets of all the cities of Russia—that same proletariat that struggled and is struggling in the first ranks of the great revolutionary Russian army[122] for a better future, for universal happiness and freedom. It means that we must silently [watch with] anger involuntarily rising in our breasts... at how the barbaric government deals with peasants, workers, with our fathers and brothers, who openly conceive of announcing, in words and actions, that they are dissatisfied with the existing injustice and oppression, with the arbitrariness of the police and the rule of the billy club.
>
> "Be reasonable!" This means that we mustn't pay any attention to the bestial and foul acts of the "Black Hundreds"[123] who have been mobilized by the government, those faithfully mobilized thieves and conmen, scoundrels and pimps—in a word, we mustn't pay any attention to the "madness and horror"[124] now at large in Russia....
>
> We will study, but will not turn away from life. We will try to bring life into our dead gymnasium; we will try with the best of our powers to hold ourselves high in the struggle against the common foe, the current regime; and... having reduced to dust that entire edifice of falsity, we will build a new temple, a temple of science and knowledge, a temple of freedom and truth.[125]

---

122 That is, as part of the revolutionary movement (not as part of any official "army").

123 "*Chernaia sotnia*": movement formed in 1905 of ultrareactionary, monarchist, ferociously anti-Semitic politicians, intellectuals, nobles, clergy, merchants, and (in some cases) workers who organized, propagandized, and did physical battle against those whom they perceived to be the enemies of the Tsar, of Orthodoxy, and of the established order (revolutionaries, reformists, Jews). They were affiliated with such right-wing organizations as the Union of the Russian People and the Union of the Archangel Michael, and were certainly involved in pogrom violence, including the Bialystok pogrom of June 1906; see below.

124 "*Bezumie i uzhas*": a famous phrase from Leonid Andreev's antiwar story "Red Laughter" (1904), a horrifying depiction of wartime violence inspired by Russia's defeat in the Russo-Japanese War. Andreev (1871–1919) was arrested in 1905 for his involvement in anti-government agitation. He later opposed the Bolshevik regime and died in Finnish exile.

125 *Listok Grodnenskikh uchashchikhsia* 1 (November 6, 1905): 3–4. The leaflet, in carbon copy, is preserved in the State Library of Poland, Warsaw.

This rhetoric might seem breathless and naïve today, but the anonymous youthful authors were certainly right about theirs being a "time of revolution," and a time of oppression as well, from which students could hardly feel themselves to be detached. Despite their rarity, the surviving school leaflets neatly reveal the main preoccupations of this highly politicized student environment: national-ethnic rights (Polish and Jewish above all), the rights of students themselves, and (as in the excerpts just quoted) the rights and political prerogatives of the working class.

That students in the Grodno guberniia would be aware of workers' movements in 1905 is hardly surprising, given that Bialystok had been by this time a center of proletarian activism in the western Russian Empire for twenty-five or more years. Socialists had begun agitating in the city in the 1870s, but workers themselves started to organize there remarkably early, with the result that, by the 1880s, Bialystok had become (in the words of historian Ezra Mendelsohn)

> the chief center of agitation during the "prehistory" of the Jewish labor movement. Being the most industrialized city in Belorussia-Lithuania, Bialystok had a labor force of thousands of Germans, Poles and Jews who were among the first in Russia to conduct major strikes. "In those quiet, still times," a socialist journal boasted, "when Jewish workers throughout Russia were sound asleep, dreaming of the messiah and the world to come, we Bialystok workers were already waging economic battles, beating up the industrialists, breaking looms, striking, struggling." As early as 1882 Jewish weavers [in Bialystok] staged a strike which was exceptionally well organized for that period. Supported by funds collected both by other Jewish workers and by German weavers, the workers not only achieved their end, but, according to one expert, theirs was the first strike in Russia "that demonstrated the existence of a trade union organization among the workers."[126]

To be sure, terrible working conditions—long hours, meager wages, poor ventilation, lack of medical facilities, discourteous (and worse) treatment by managers and supervisors—were major incitements to indignation and collective action.[127]

---

126 Ezra Mendelsohn, *Class Struggle in the Pale*, 28. Mendelsohn mentions a host of other early meetings and struggles in Bialystok: an enormous strike (involving 8,500 Jewish and non-Jewish weavers) against factory administration in 1895; the first Russian conference of tanners in 1898; a successful boycott against the cigarette factory owner Janovsky ca. 1903; a strike of bakers in 1901 (ibid., 92, 78, 90–91, 89). In my account of the Bialystok workers' movement here, I rely heavily on Mendelsohn's remarkable work. On Bund activity in Bialystok, see Kobrin, *Jewish Bialystok*, 42–48.

127 Mendelsohn, *Class Struggle in the Pale*, 12, 18–19, 86, 88.

Beyond this, much of the work, particularly in the textile industry, was seasonal and comprised mainly of piece-work, placing laborers at the whims of employers and especially of middlemen known as *loynketniks* (*lonkietnicy* in Polish), who "received looms and raw materials from the factory owners and put the weavers to work in small shops," shops much less mechanized and more noisome than the larger industrial concerns.[128] Those larger factories were frequently off-limits to Jewish workers, who were regarded with particular suspicion and anxiety by employers due to their well-earned reputation for organized resistance.[129] With the large-scale economic downturns that began to ravage the local and global economy from the early 1870s, Bialystok workers' fortunes came to fluctuate even more drastically—despite net increases in production over the same period, both worldwide and in the western Russian Empire—with the result that many, particularly Jewish craftsmen and weavers whose livelihoods were threatened by the newer mechanized factories, decided to emigrate, primarily to the United States.[130]

Though I have no primary evidence of direct involvement by Modern School students in the workers' movement in Bialystok, it can be assumed, I think, that the more senior and radicalized students, particularly those sympathetic to the Social Democratic Party (like the Grodno students who produced *School*),[131] would have at the very least debated the possibility of association. As historian Samuel D. Kassow has shown, students across Russia were conflicted about activism, weighing as they did their desires for education and career against the more dangerous urge to participate in political movements, whether on behalf of students or of workers.[132] The student groups, though linked by a common antagonism to the regime and by specific demands for reform—including right of assembly, better funding structures, improved physical conditions at schools, and permission for students to attend

---

128 Ibid., 18–19. See also Dobronski, *Białystok: Historia Miasta*, 84, and Kobrin, *Jewish Bialystok and Its Diaspora*, 36–38.

129 Mendelsohn, *Class Struggle in the Pale*, 22; Löwe, *The Tsars and the Jews*, 92; Budnitskij, *Rossijskie evrei*, 35.

130 Hobsbawm, *The Age of Empire*, 35; Mendelsohn, *Class Struggle in the Pale*, 15, 113. Fierce competition from larger industrial centers, Łodz above all, also adversely affected Bialystok's economy; see Dobronski, *Białystok: Historia Miasta*, 84.

131 The Social Democratic Party was the party out of which emerged both the Bolsheviks and the Mensheviks (in 1903). It was evidently the preferred party of many university students in larger centers like St. Petersburg as well; see Samuel D. Kassow, *Students, Professors, and the State in Tsarist Russia* (Berkeley: University of California Press, 1989), 314.

132 Kassow, *Students, Professors, and the State*, 11, 238. Kassow argues that the student movement gave the majority of students a framework within which they could at once effectively protest, feel themselves part of an active and progressive collective, and avoid "making an extreme and dangerous commitment to the revolutionary movement," while still pursuing an education (11).

concerts, go to theaters and visit reading rooms[133]—were at once politically heterogeneous and deeply bound by a corporate student identity not always easily reconcilable with commitment to "external" causes like those of the workers.[134]

We know that students in Grodno, for instance, were well aware of the organizational, school-related resolutions taken by their peers in St. Petersburg, and that they published some of them in their own student brochures.[135] Workers, for their part, were often skeptical about the involvement of sympathetic, educated outsiders in proletarian struggles. Yet it also seems that many students saw the school and university-based demonstrations and strikes, which caused considerable disruption in their own right,[136] as part of

---

[133] In his study of the events of 1905, Abraham Ascher gives a précis of the main student demands: "In many localities of the empire, students submitted petitions for educational reform. Although there were variations among them, some themes appeared in almost all of them, and they can be summarized as follows: elimination of police surveillance; abolition of obligatory attendance at religious services; improvement of sanitary conditions; provision for parents to be allowed to select accommodations for their children; reduction of educational costs and fair distribution of stipends; permission for students to visit theaters, concert halls, libraries, and public reading rooms; access to all books authorized by the censorship; the granting to parents of the right to vote in pedagogical councils and to participate in the administration of schools; establishment of honor courts to settle disciplinary cases; and freedom for students to hold meetings in school buildings and to organize mutual-aid societies. In ethnically non-Russian regions of the empire, students and many of their parents wanted schools to be mindful of local cultural traditions. Thus, to cite just one example, a petition in Vilna and Kovno asked that students be permitted to speak Polish and Lithuanian at school and that the language of instruction be in those languages." On August 27, 1905, well after the protests began, the government "issued a decree restoring to universities and advanced institutes the autonomy they had been deprived of in 1884" (Abraham Ascher, *The Revolution of 1905: A Short History* [Palo Alto: Stanford University Press, 2004], 63).

[134] Kassow, *Students, Professors, and the State in Tsarist Russia*, 94, 118, 149, 184.

[135] Students in the Grodno gymnasium learned of the following resolution taken on October 27, 1905, by the three most senior classes in the Second St. Petersburg gymnasium only a week later: "In light of the fact that the political strike at the middle schools which has just ended very clearly showed the full insolvency of the organizations which have existed up to now, our complete fragmentation, and the lack of solidarity among individual students, we believe that the most urgent need at the present moment is for the complete unification of all educational institutions. Keeping all of this in mind, we students at the Second gymnasium [propose that] all high school students in St. Petersburg elect from each educational institution five delegates to the strike committee, both for the gathering-together and decision of issue concerning the high school [political] movement, and that they might lead this movement. Only through unification in a single elected center, and strengthened by that unification, can we be truly useful to that general movement which we have joined" (*Listok Grodnenskikh uchashchikhsia* 1 [November 6, 1905]: 7ob).

[136] Of the disruption—whose scale eclipsed that of any later European student movement, including May 1968—Ascher provides an incomparable account (Ascher, *The Revolution of 1905*, 49, 62, 64, 66).

a larger, relatively informal, coalition-based politics of protest of unified tendency if not party affiliation.[137]

WHAT WAS ADAM'S NATIONALITY? THE BIALYSTOK POGROM AND ITS AFTERMATH

The ethnically and religiously diverse character of the student body in the Modern School, and the students' lived proximity to the dominant political struggles of the time, contributed to an awareness of the multiple possibilities, resistances, and restrictions conditioning social life in Russia. As regards Jewish students, Bialystok's very "frontier" location and its consequent incorporation into various polities—now Poland, now Prussia, now Russia—may have enabled them to resist specifically Polonizing, Germanizing, or Russifying pressures, even as those pressures would have been exerted and registered in a plural, nonexclusive way.[138] Thus, the city's students were probably excellently positioned to perceive and even feel capable of mapping out the contours of Russia's complex political, socioeconomic, and multiethnic settings.

To be sure, the status of both Poles and Jews in the guberniia was an object of continual concern and indignation. The illegal *School*, for instance, published documents about arrests and even brief transcripts of overheard conversations to illustrate the authorities' contempt for national and language rights:

> Recently:
> Teacher [in Russian]: What is your last name?
> Student [in Polish]: Dziękuję panu. Mama i tato są zdrowi. [Polish for "Thank you, sir, my mother and father are healthy."][139]

---

137. In his excellent study, Kassow notes how the earlier hard-line "economists" of the workers' movement had "rejected the notions of establishing political coalitions between the workers and other social groups, allowing nonworkers to lead the labor movement, and, of course, attempting to forge an alliance between students and workers. The upsurge of the student movement between 1899 and 1902 played a major role in the decline of 'economism' and the concomitant rise of such new groups as *Iskra* and the Social Revolutionary party, groups that recognized the importance of political struggle against the autocracy based on coalitions of various social groups: the bourgeoisie, students, and workers" (Kassow, *Students, Professors, and the State in Tsarist Russia*, 94).
138. See Ezra Mendelsohn, "A Note on Jewish Assimilation in the Polish Lands," in *Jewish Assimilation in Modern Times*, ed. Bela Vago (Boulder, CO: Westview Press, 1981), 141–45; and Kobrin, *Jewish Bialystok*, 30.
139. The "joke" here is that the Polish student has misinterpreted the Russian word "familiia," which means not "family" but "last or family name." In the original, the Polish words are transcribed into Cyrillic.

> Teacher [in Russian]: Swine! Good for nothing! No speaking Polish!
> Student: Kiedy ja nie umiem mówić po rosyjsku! [Polish for "But I don't know how to speak Russian!"]
> Teacher [in Russian]: Then you'll have to stay here until six.[140]

Just as frequently, *School* and other illegal student publications in the guberniia ran articles and anecdotes, serious or satirical, about anti-Semitism and the realities of Jewish life in the Pale:

> Teacher: What was [the biblical] Adam's nationality?
> Student: Jewish. He was, after all, the first to lose his residence permit![141]

Jewish issues took on a particular urgency, and not only for students, after the June 1906 Bialystok pogrom, the major event in the city during the 1905–7 upheaval. The massacre was arguably the culmination of a series of incidents of anti-Jewish violence within the Pale, including the major pogroms that had occurred in Kishinev (1903), Odessa (1905), Ekaterinoslav (1905), Gomel (January 1906) and many other places in the preceding years and months.[142] Locally, Bialystok and environs had seen numerous acts of violence against Jewish workers between 1903 and 1905, capped by street fighting between soldiers and workers on July 30, 1903, that left thirteen dead and provoked a citywide strike on the following day.[143] On the eve of the pogrom itself, the May 1906 appointment of notorious anti-Semite S. D. Sheremetev as Bialystok's police chief was a further omen of impending trouble, one that elicited protest from the city's Jewish leadership; yet the scale of the June brutality—in a city where "[Jews] enjoyed demographic and economic dominance"—still came as an immense shock, as we will see in a moment.[144]

Students in the Grodno guberniia's major cities were of course aware of the pogrom wave, and commented upon it in their illegal publications, as in this mock "reportage" from *School* (1905):

> *Telegrams from the theatre of war*
> Odessa. The soldiers are bursting to go into action. The troops are in

---

140 *Shkola* 5 (April 1906): 8. My thanks to Krystyna Illakowicz for help with the Polish in this text.
141 *Shkola* 2 (1906): 8.
142 Six hundred fifty-seven pogroms occurred in the empire between October 1905 and January 1906 (Budnitskij, *Rossijskie evrei*, 57).
143 A. D. Kirzhnits and M. Rafes, eds., *1905: Evrejskoe rabochee dvizhenie* (Moscow and Leningrad: Gosudarstvennoe Izdatel'stvo, 1928), 62, 121–23.
144 Kobrin, *Jewish Bialystok*, 59.

excellent spirits....

Rostov-on-Don. Killed: Iakov Finkel'shtein, two years old, and Sora Kremer, three years old. No casualties on our side.[145]

As is well known, the last years of the nineteenth and first years of the twentieth centuries were marked by fierce anti-Jewish rhetoric, legislation, and violence in Russia, and concomitantly by the emigration of millions of Russian Jews, mainly to the United States.[146] A large number of anti-Semitic articles, some of them widely discussed, began to appear in the Russian press at the turn of the 1880s: that is, following the 1881 assassination of Alexander II, which popular rumor attributed to Jewish revolutionaries.[147] The first wave of pogroms—forecast by an 1871 massacre in Odessa, but largely taking place during 1881–82 in Elizavetgrad, Kiev, Odessa, and a host of other areas—led to soul-searching among many maskilim, who became more skeptical about the possibility or desirability of rapprochement with a Russian society characterized by such open and violent anti-Semitism.[148]

Jews, whose status within Russian society was indeed changing rapidly and in complex ways, became convenient scapegoats for those antagonistic to the social and economic mutations the country was undergoing—mutations in which the Tsarist state was deeply implicated, as we have seen. It might be said that Jews were structurally and even geographically positioned at the vulnerable and fraught juncture of a number of the contradictions driving historical motion in Russia at this time, that pit burgeoning capitalism (whether small or large scale, industrial or financial) against the old quasi-feudal landowning system, religious exclusivity against secularism and pluralism, revolutionary workers' egalitarianism against social and economic

---

145 *Shkola* 2 (1905): 4. The cover page of the issue depicted police trying to stop the distribution of *Shkola*.
146 See Budnitskij, *Rossijskie evrei*, 30.
147 Nathans, *Beyond the Pale*, 258; Löwe, *The Tsars and the Jews*, 59.
148 Zipperstein, *The Jews of Odessa*, 128, and (here) 20: "... the pogroms quickened the migratory process that had begun in the late 1860s and that by 1914 saw nearly one-half of Eastern European Jewry migrating within the region or beyond it. The flow of some Jewish youth into the revolutionary and Zionist movements created close ties, familial and otherwise, between sections of the Jewish masses generally unsympathetic to radical ideals and new political movements. By the first decade of the twentieth century, the heroism of Jewish radicals (especially the Bundists), their organization of Jewish self-defense, their participation in philanthropic activities throughout the Pale, even their conspiratorial form of internal organization, conferred on them an almost legendary aura. Mass migration, radically new political formulations, and chronic underemployment all challenged the foundations of traditional Jewish society before the 1917 revolution." See also Nathans, *Beyond the Pale*, 186.

oligarchy, and nationalism (sometimes of an imperialist variety) against cosmopolitanism. Add to this the tinder provided by centuries of accumulated prejudice, and many of the combustibles required for the appalling anti-Semitic wildfire of the years 1881 to 1921 were in place.[149]

Many Jews were provoked to emigrate by the notorious May Laws of 1882, which forbade "all new Jewish settlement outside of cities and towns,"[150] and led to demographic congestion in urban centers in the Pale, already reeling from the effects, noted above, of global economic recession. During this time, some of Abel Kaufman's relatives, bearing the last name Freeman, left for the States. One of them, a cousin named Nathan Freeman, founded a highly successful men's wear manufactory in Philadelphia in 1885. Many years later, Nathan's son Benjamin (1894–1973) would send money on a regular basis to Abel and Chaya in Poland, starting as early as the mid-1920s; he would also be instrumental in getting Boris Kaufman and his family out of Nazi-occupied Europe at the end of 1941, and in helping Boris find a job as a cameraman at the National Film Board in Ottawa in early 1942. Other relatives, apparently mainly on the Kaufman side of the family, emigrated around this time as well, in the first phase of what would be a classically tripartite migration for (some members of) the Kaufman-Gal'pern families out of the territories of the Pale of Settlement: to America, to Palestine, and, as in David Kaufman's case, to the Russian heartland and the Soviet Union.[151]

Bialystok, it turns out, had a special prominence in the anti-Semitic propaganda of the time—beyond its notoriety as a bustling industrial city with a Jewish majority—inasmuch as it was the seat of the legend, and for a time (after 1910) of the relics, of the Holy Martyred Infant Gavriil (Gabriel)

---

149 For more reflections on these dynamics, see Löwe, *The Tsars and the Jews*, 409–20; Budnitskij, *Rossijskie evrei*, 36–40. When I write "juncture" here, I mean to indicate that individual Jews could be located, in terms of both material and political interest, on either side of these intensely conflictual polarities, given locale within the empire, occupation, educational level, political or confessional commitment, and so on. Geographically, Bialystok was quite far from the epicenter of the violence, as "nearly 87 per cent (575) of all pogroms took place in the southern [Ukrainian] provinces of Chernigov, Poltava, Ekaterinoslav, Kherson, Podolia, Kiev and [outside Ukraine] Bessarabia" (Antony Polonsky, *The Jews in Poland and Russia*, vol. 2 [Oxford: Littman Library of Jewish Civilization, 2010], 57).

150 Stanislawski, *Tsar Nicholas I and the Jews*, 278–79.

151 See Boris Kaufman Papers, Beinecke Library, GEN MSS 562.12.205–206; "Benjamin Freeman, Tailor for Nixon and Eisenhower" [obituary], *New York Times* (February 21, 1973), 46. For the notion of a triple migration out of the Pale, see Yuri Slezkine, *The Jewish Century* (Princeton, NJ: Princeton University Press, 2006), 116, 212, and *passim*.

(d. 1690). According to an edition of saints' lives from 1875, the six-year-old Gavriil, son of pious Orthodox believers from a village near Chaya Kaufman's hometown of Zabludovo, was abducted by Jews and brought to Bialystok. There, on or around April 20, 1690, they tortured him, crucified him, punctured him through on one side, and drained him of all his blood. His corpse was then thrown onto a field, where dogs protected it from predatory birds until it was discovered three days later. Eventually, the body was found to be miraculously exempt from decay, and Gavriil's relics were transported to various monasteries in the area until they ended up in St. Nicholas Orthodox Cathedral in Bialystok in 1910.[152] Gavriil became the object of ritual pilgrimages and was memorialized as dedicatee of various chapels in the area, and so Bialystok Jews would certainly have known that the Orthodox Church was spinning this monstrous, absurd, and dangerous yarn, which made their city an important relay point in the circulation of the notorious "blood libel."[153]

On June 1, 1906, crowds were assembled on the streets of Bialystok awaiting two separate religious parades: an Orthodox procession honoring the founding of St. Nicholas Cathedral, and (a bit later in the day, though overlapping with the former) a Catholic one celebrating Corpus Christi. The disturbance started when a carter blindsided his team into the crowd just before the Corpus Christi march was to begin. Two shots suddenly rang out in Bazarnaia Square (near the Catholic cathedral), someone shouted "a bomb!"—though only four of fifty witnesses interviewed after the events said

---

152 The relics reposed in Moscow and in various "museums of atheism" during the Soviet period, and returned to Bialystok only in 1992. For the story of the "martyrdom," see *Zhitia sviatykh zemli rossijskoj: letopis' istorii otechestva X–XX vv.* (St. Petersburg: Pokrovskij Dar, 2004; based on an 1875 edition), 451; see also I. Bukharev, ed., *Zhitiia vsekh vviatykh prazdnuemykh pravoslavnoiu greko-rossijskoiu tserkoviiu* (Moscow: I. D. Sytin, 1896), 206. The legend of Gavriil was repeated not only in compilations of saints' lives but also in works of anti-Semitic propaganda like lexicographer V. I. Dal's *Investigation into the killing of Christian babies by Jews and the use made of their blood (printed by order of the Minster of the Interior)* (*Rozyskanie o ubienii evreiami khristianskikh mladentsev i utpotreblenii krovi ikh [napechateno po prikazaniiu g. Ministra Vnutrennikh Del]*) (1844). Dal's text was reprinted in 1995 as *Zapiska o ritual'nykh ubijstvakh* (Moscow: Vitiaz', 1995), a volume in the "Little Library of the Russian Patriot" series, which includes Dostoevsky on "The Jewish Question" and Henry Ford's "International Jewry"; the story of Gavriil is on page 45. For an instance of the story's unfortunate contemporary dissemination, see Ia. Kharkevich and V. N. Cherepitsa, "Gavriil," accessed June 24, 2017, http://www.pravenc.ru/text/161257.html.

153 For background on the libel itself—that is, the accusation that Jews incorporate the blood of freshly killed Christian infants into Passover matzos—see Marvin Perry and Frederick M. Schweitzer, *Antisemitism: Myth and Hate from Antiquity to the Present* (London: Palgrave Macmillan, 2005), 43–72; and the discussion of the Mendel Beilis case, below.

they heard anything like a bomb—and a large group began attacking Jews and pillaging Jewish stores, animated by their familiar chant of "Beat the Jews!" (*bej zhidov!*).

The shooting intensified on the central Alexandrovskaia Street, moving from there to Nikolaevskaia Street, where the Kaufman bookstore was situated and where many of the victims met their deaths.[154] The Jewish defense units began their desperate counterattack on Nikolaevskaia as well, eliciting return fire from army dragoons, who had been conspicuously absent up to that point in the melee: this, when Białystok was a major garrison town during the pre–World War I years, with an average of five thousand soldiers (infantry and cavalry) quartered there at any one time in various barracks scattered throughout the city.[155] Indeed, an attempt of March 25, 1907, to take the life of General Bogaevskij, the guberniia's chief army officer, which spared the general but killed his coachman, may have been in retaliation for the army's action and inaction during the pogrom.[156]

At any rate, around 200 people, including six non-Jews, were killed during the three days of the pogrom, around 700 were wounded, and at least 169 businesses were pillaged and wrecked.[157] Much of the damage occurred on Nemetskaia Street (including the destruction of the Kaplan bookstore) and Surazhskaia Street, populated by poorer Jews and long a center of working class, and especially anarchist, activism. Nikolaevskaia was among the six other streets devastated, and although I have no documentation regarding the fate of Abel Kaufman's store during those days, it stands to reason that a bookstore of secular orientation owned by a Jew might have proved an enticing target for the pogromists.[158] The pogrom was of extraordinary savagery even by the standards of such events, and in the extensive global newspaper coverage, outraged reports of people hurled from windows, tongues amputated, nails pounded into eyes, and legs sawed off gave added pungency to the by then familiar descriptions of beatings, rapes, and shootings.[159]

---

154 See V. Vladimirov, *Ocherki sovremennykh kaznej* (Moscow: A. P. Poplavskij, 1906), 42–47.
155 Dobronski, *Białystok: Historia Miasta*, 100–101; Ascher, *The Revolution of 1905*, 149.
156 Dobronski, *Białystok: Historia Miasta*, 89.
157 Ascher, *The Revolution of 1905*, 149; Kobrin, *Jewish Białystok*, 58; Polonsky, *Jews in Poland and Russia*, vol. 2, 62. For names, ages and descriptions of the dead, see Vladimirov, *Ocherki sovremennykh kaznej*, 42–47.
158 *Delo o pogrome v Belostoke 1–3 iiunia 1906 goda*, 2nd ed. (St. Petersburg: Trud, 1909), 40, 41, 46; Kobrin, *Jewish Białystok*, 58.
159 The coverage was truly global. See, for instance, "Russian Blood Bath," *Poverty Bay Herald* [Gisborne, New Zealand], XXXIII:10763 (August 4, 1906): 4; "Jews of Russian city are being massacred," *New York Times*, June 15, 1906, 1; among many others. The

The events in Bialystok prompted fierce arguments in the chambers of Russia's first State Duma (parliament), which had been formed only thirty-four days earlier.[160] Although an Internal Affairs investigation discovered that government administrators and soldiers had participated in the pogrom, the eventual prosecution of the case, which placed exculpatory stress upon the supposed revolutionary-terroristic proclivities of Jewish youth in Bialystok, was deeply disappointing to all concerned observers:

> The government . . . took two years before preferring charges against thirty-six rioters in Bialystok. Several of the accused failed to show up in court, and fifteen were acquitted. Of the rest, one received a jail sentence of three years, and thirteen were handed lighter jail sentences, ranging from six months to one year.[161]

Even if the imperial regime did not organize the violence, as many early commentators thought, those who committed the atrocities found sympathy from many high government and state officials, not least from Tsar Nicholas II himself, who "approved all petitions for pardon submitted by members convicted for participation in pogroms," whether in Bialystok or elsewhere.[162]

It is worth noting that Masha Gal'pern, already in St. Petersburg at the Women's Medical Institute for three years at the time of the pogrom, evidently took a break in her studies between 1906 and 1908. No reason is offered in the existing documentation for the hiatus, but it seems entirely possible, indeed

---

New York Times published a whole series of follow-up articles in June and July 1906. On the atrocities, see *Rechi po pogromnym delam*, introduction by I. V. Luchitskij (Kiev: S. G. Sliusarevskij, 1908), 121, 125; *Rechi po pogromnym delam*, ed. D. N. Tiagaj, introduction by V. G. Korolenko (Kiev: S. G. Sliusarevskij, 1908), 111; Vladimirov, *Ocherki sovremennykh kaznej*; and Kirzhnits and Rafes, *1905: Evrejskoe rabochee dvizhenie*, 316–17.

160 See *Rechi po pogromnym delam*, introduction by I. V. Luchitskij (Kiev: S. G. Sliusarevskij, 1908), 117, 119, 124.

161 Ascher, *The Revolution of 1905*, 151. See also *Rechi po pogromnym delam*, 119.

162 Richard S. Wortman, *Scenarios of Power: Myth and Ceremony in Russian Monarchy*, vol. 2 (Princeton, NJ: Princeton University Press, 2000), 400. "Nicholas remained convinced that the majority of the people remained personally loyal to him. He had written to his mother on October 25, 1905, defending the pogroms. He claimed that 'nine-tenths of the troublemakers are Jews' and that the people had turned against them violently for that reason. 'But not only the kikes suffered; so did the Russian agitators, engineers, lawyers, and all kinds of other bad people.' Because of his hatred of Jews and any group opposed to the monarchy, he regarded the pogroms as an expression of the unity of tsar and people and sympathized with the extreme right anti-Semitic organization, the Union of Russian People" (ibid., 399–400).

likely in my view, that she returned to Bialystok in the summer of 1906 to use her medical training to tend pogrom victims, as well as to be with her kinfolk. If so, it would have been at this time of crisis that she first became truly acquainted with her nephews—then ten (David), nine (Mojsej), and three (Boris) respectively—and formed that vital lifelong emotional bond with all of them.[163] As we will see in chapter 2, Masha was certainly involved in relief work among Jews during World War I; whether she actually returned to Bialystok after the pogrom or not, the violence must have enduringly impressed upon her the vulnerability of Jews within Russian society.

She would eventually emigrate to Palestine, in the 1930s, after the Pale of Settlement had vanished and Bialystok become part of newly independent Poland, and long after Zionism had emerged as a vital political force in the city. The Hibbat Zion (Love of Zion) movement took root in Bialystok in 1883 when its founder, Rabbi Samuel Mohilever, became the city's chief rabbi. Hibbat Zion took the resettling of Eastern European Jews in Palestine as its express goal—over fifteen years before the consolidation of "Zionism" proper in 1899—and drew an energetic minority of Bialystok Jews into its fundraising and promotional efforts.[164] To be sure, attacks on Russian anti-Semitism also came from left-wing, non-Zionist quarters in response to the pogrom wave; those critics blamed the violence and intolerance on widespread ignorance, and characterized it as an attempt to undermine the wider struggle for democracy.[165] But it is clear that even before June 1906, the violence gave new force to Zionist arguments in Bialystok and elsewhere in the Pale.

The pro-emigration *Jewish Voice*, for instance, began publication in Bialystok in January 1906, taking as its slogan "independence and land for the Jewish people!"

> [Our] skepticism [vis-à-vis the optimism of internationalist revolutionaries], despite all of its corrosive critical force, must lead only to the

---

163 See TsGIASPb f. 436, op. 4, d. 906, l. 2; op. 1, d. 2552, l. 1. Masha certainly returned to Bialystok during her holidays, as Mikhail Kaufman indicated in a major reminiscence (see below). Medical sanitariums for Jewish children in the Pale in the years after the pogrom wave treated children for "traumatic neurosis, brought about by the pogrom," along with tuberculosis and other maladies (*Otchet popetchitel'stva o evrejskoj detskoj kolonii v Druskenikakh (otdeleniia Vilensk[ogo] O[bshchest]va Evrejskikh Detsk[ikh] Kolonii) za 1910 god* [Bialystok: Dubner and El'ian, 1911], 4).
164 See Kobrin, *Jewish Bialystok*, 48–52.
165 See, for instance, *Evrei — nashi vragi! Tak li eto? Russkomu narodu na urazumenie i Soiuzu Russkago Naroda otvet* (Warsaw: Leppert and Co., 1907).

destruction of illusions, of the "exalted illusion," not to the destruction of hopes and ideals. Those ideals have been demonstrated to us through vast amounts of historical experience, which have brought to naught all attempts to resolve the Jewish question on the territories of "settlement"[166]—which would better be termed [territories of] "wandering"—and which have shown that attempting to "bind" the fate of our people *as a whole* with the fate of other peoples means to long (hopelessly, of course) for an act of historical violence. It means failing to reckon with Jewish reality, every manifestation of which demonstrates to us that we have remained "a people among other peoples."[167]

The paper's ideology is well summarized in this verse from the poem "Homeland" by M. Rivesman, which appeared in the second issue:

O, my poor people! Go and wander anew!
Seek out other fields, seek out another sky....
Do not await happiness from the old hearth and home,
And remember the bitter poison in a piece of *another's* bread....[168]

Though the paper's editors expressed serious doubts about the viability of Palestine as a homeland for Jews, they had only contempt for the Bund and other internationalist (or "cosmopolitan," in the terminology of the period) organizations for imagining that the non-Jewish "patriots" of the countries they live in "look upon the Jew as their brother." Even the offer of open higher education to Jews after October 1905 was dismissed by the paper as a "Mephistophelean" gift.[169] Eventually, 20,000 Bialystok Jews would emigrate to Palestine between 1920 and 1950: less than a third of the 65,000 who had already left for the Americas (mainly New York and Buenos Aires) after 1870, but a significant number all the same.[170]

In the years following the pogrom—only eight of them remained before David Kaufman would leave Bialystok for higher studies in Petrograd, and the world war would begin—the city would continue to bob along waves of social

---

166 I.e., in the Pale of Settlement.
167 *Evrejskij Golos* 1–2 (January 22, 1906): 5. This passage was possibly composed by the paper's editor, L. Paperin.
168 M. Rivesman, "Rodina," *Evrejskij Golos* 5 (February 12, 1906): 141–42.
169 *Evrejskij Golos* 6 (February 17, 1906): 184–88.
170 Kobrin, *Jewish Bialystok*, xvi.

and economic turbulence. The industrial downturn of the post-1907 period turned out to be relatively brief, and Bialystok factories modernized their production practices from 1908, in time to take advantage of the deluge of new orders (for military uniforms, especially) that arrived even before the summer of 1914.[171] At the same time, automation destroyed the livelihoods of growing numbers of hand weavers, even as many gains made by workers during the 1905 struggles, such as higher wages and a ten-hour workday, were retained.[172] Jewish migrant workers continued to move to Bialystok: astonishingly, despite emigration, the city's Jewish population increased by 20,000 (from 41,905 to 61,500) between 1906 and 1914.[173]

Yet as European interstate relations grew tenser, Russian national chauvinism increasingly infected public discourse and state policy, with both predictable and unpredictable consequences. Various ordinances, directed above all at Bialystok's Poles, forbade political organization, restricted fundraising efforts and the display of "national" flags, and cracked down on the establishment of bookstores and reading rooms.[174] Polish nationalists became increasingly restive in the city, and organized a boycott of Jewish businesses in response to perceived Jewish opposition to their national cause, presaging more economically damaging anti-Jewish boycotts to come in independent Poland, especially in the 1930s.[175] On the national level, right-wing, anti-Semitic politicians began to strut about more confidently on the floor of the Duma and in public forums, and more and more anti-Jewish legislation came into effect: voting rights for Jews were severely curtailed in 1911, Jews were removed from any role in the judiciary in 1912, and large numbers of Jews, including many in the Grodno guberniia, were expelled from villages now deemed technically outside the Pale of Settlement.[176]

---

171 *Obzor Grodnenskoj gubernii za 1908 god* (Grodno: Gubernskaia Tipografiia, 1909), 26–28; Dobronski, *Białystok: Historia Miasta*, 108. Already in the fall of 1913, Bialystok newspapers were writing in melancholy spirit about the "unavoidability of war between Austria and Russia" (*Novosti Belostoka* 18 [October 22, 1913]: 1).

172 *Obzor Grodnenskoj gubernii za 1908 god*, 27–28.

173 Kobrin, *Jewish Bialystok*, 62.

174 Dobronski, *Białystok: Historia Miasta*, 108; on surveillance of the reading rooms and libraries, see NIAB f. 103, op. 1, d. 106, ll. 28–56ob.

175 Dobronski, *Białystok: Historia Miasta*, 108; Kobrin, *Jewish Bialystok*, 138–40, 172.

176 For an extraordinary litany of anti-Jewish (and often illegal) ordinances promulgated during these years in Russia, see Löwe, *The Tsars and the Jews*, 290–93.

On the eve of David Kaufman's graduation from the Modern School, the most significant media event for Russian Jewry as a whole was certainly the notorious blood libel trial of Menahem Mendel Beilis, a Jewish clerk accused of murdering a Christian child for his blood in Kiev in 1911, and tried (and acquitted) in 1913. The details of the investigation and trial have been extensively researched, and need not be recapitulated here.[177] Suffice it to say that the Beilis case was indeed intended, by the extremist politicians, judicial officials, and journalists who promoted it, as a "media event," with an eye both to disseminating anti-Semitic sentiment and ideology and to publicly testing just how far their persecution and prosecution of the Jew Beilis—whom virtually all of them knew to be innocent—could go. The trial was clearly conducted with Tsar Nicholas's blessing and approval, and evidently the Tsar, who also believed Beilis to be innocent, took pains to ensure that those who prosecuted the case were duly rewarded with gold watches, promotions and so on.[178] The success of the enterprise was considerable, as measured by the number of officials (including the justice minister, Ivan Shcheglovitov) who helped pursue the case, the ambiguity of the verdict (which affirmed that a ritual murder had actually occurred, though not committed by Beilis), and the publicity the trial received, not all of it, alas, negative.[179]

It was reported on extensively in papers in Bialystok, with the famous writer S. An-sky providing much of the coverage printed in the Jewish Russian-language *Voice of Bialystok* (founded 1909).[180] The arguments of the prosecution were carefully recorded:

---

[177] The trial lasted thirty-four days, from September 25 to October 28, 1913. See *Delo Beilisa: stenograficheskij otchet*, 3 vols. (Kiev: Kievskaia Mysl', 1913); Vladimir Bonch-Bruevich, *Znamenie vremeni: ubijstvo Andreiia Iushchinskogo i delo Beilisa* (St. Petersburg: Zhizn' i Znanie, 1914); Mendel Beilis, *The Story of My Sufferings*, trans. Harrison Goldberg, introduction by Herman Bernstein and Arnold D. Margolin (New York: Mendel Beilis Publishing, 1926); A. S. Tager, *The Decay of Czarism: The Beiliss Trial* (Philadelphia: Jewish Publication Society of America, 1935); Maurice Samuel, *Blood Accusation: The Strange Story of the Beilis Case* (New York: Knopf, 1966). Beilis's autobiography furnished the basis for Bernard Malamud's 1966 Pulitzer Prize winning novel *The Fixer*. The murdered child, Andrej Iushchinskij, was in fact killed by a gang of criminals.

[178] Wortman, *Scenarios of Power*, 505–6.

[179] See Hans Rogger, *Jewish Policies and Right-Wing Politics in Imperial Russia* (Houndmills: Macmillan, 1986), 40–56; Löwe, *The Tsars and the Jews*, 284–96.

[180] See *Novosti Belostoka* 16 (October 19, 1913): 3; 18 (October 22, 1913): 3–4; 22 (October 26, 1913): 3; and *Golos Belostoka* 240 (October 20, 1913): 2–3; 242 (October 23, 1913): 3; 244 (October 25, 1913): 2–3. On *Golos Belostoka*, see Kobrin, *Jewish Bialystok*, 63. On

"We are standing," said [prosecutor A. S.] Shmakov, "before an international *kahal* with limitless resources. Jewry has always known how to use those weapons able to annihilate its enemies with the greatest force. Today, those weapons are machine-driven printing presses."[181]

Prominent among the Beilis-baiting reactionaries tracked and cited by Bialystok dailies during the trial was Vladimir Purishkevich, an anti-Semitic and monarchist Duma deputy (since 1906) from Bessarabia, landowner, poetaster, organizer of the pogromist Black Hundreds, and a scandal-mongering loudmouth and thug later implicated in the murder of Romanov family favorite Grigorij Rasputin.[182] For his antics—which included outbursts of colorful language in the Duma and provoking riots in movie theaters—Purishkevich had long been an object of derision among Russian progressives. Indeed, sometime after 1908, after the deputy had founded the extreme rightwing "Union of the Archangel Michael," none other than the young David Kaufman dedicated a verse epigram to him, one that almost made it to Bialystok's Russian-language readers:

> In school, from around the second grade, I was engaged in writing epigrams and satirical verses. I sent one such poem, "The Original Clown-Soloist Vladimir Mitrofanovich Purishkevich Makes an Appearance"... to the editor of the local paper. Without indicating the author's age, of course. I impatiently checked the paper every day. On the third day a note appeared on its pages, entitled "From the editors to someone or other": "With this note the editors declare that, unfortunately, they are not able to publish this satirical composition, for reasons beyond their control, although they find it interesting. They ask the author to drop by to chat with the editors." At the time, I was twelve years old. Not wanting to reveal my age and being very shy in any case, I didn't go visit the editors. I maintained my anonymity. A while later I wrote a short poem whose name I don't

---

An-sky and the Beilis trial, see Gabriella Safran and Steven J. Zipperstein, ed., *The Worlds of S. An-sky: A Russian Jewish Intellectual at the Turn of the Century* (Stanford, CA: Stanford University Press, 2006), xxv–xxvi, 17, 97–98.

181 *Golos Belostoka* 244 (October 25, 1913): 3.

182 See, for instance, *Novosti Belostoka* 22 (October 26, 1913): 3. Those in search of a contemporary (postmodern) Russian analogue to Purishkevich, at least on the level of ideology and comportment, might look to LDPR leader Vladimir Zhirinovskij. For an amusing account of Purishkevich's goonery and buffoonery, see S. B. Liubosh, *Russkij fashist Vladimir Purishkevich* (Leningrad: Byloe, 1925). For a sample of his verse, see Vladimir Purishkevich, *Soldatskie pesni* (Petrograd: K. A. Chetverikov, 1914).

recall. Once again, I sent it to the editors, but this time—there was nothing dangerous in the poem—I was surprised to find it published in the paper. They again asked the author to appear and drop his incognito....[183]

Judging from this passage—presented, we must remember, for public evaluation during the Soviet 1930s, and well after Vertov had been decisively radicalized during the Civil War—David Kaufman had not only absorbed the values and tropes typical of illegal student publications by around 1908 or so, but also aspired to participate, even if pseudonymously, in Bialystok's emergent public political culture. The Beilis case, despite its outrageously cynical motivations and naked squalor, offered a major occasion for the development of that culture: the famous neurologist Vladimir Bekhterev, one of the many experts who testified powerfully in Beilis's defense (and who were quoted extensively in Bialystok periodicals), insisted at the time that the trial was of "great historical significance" for Russia as a whole, in that it provided an arena for the "struggle between two ways of thinking about society."[184] Soon enough—in late summer 1914, to be precise—David would begin his studies at Bekhterev's Psychoneurological Institute in Petrograd, one of the most forward-looking educational institutions in Russia, where he would experience both a full immersion in the period's most vital modes of thinking about society, and the metamorphosis of that society as it began to change, under pressure of war and revolution, into something very different from the milieu in which he grew up.

DAVID ABELEVICH KAUFMAN

David Kaufman, about whom specifically we know so very little (before 1918), grew up in the midst of these events, these barriers, these pressures, and these

---

183 Vertov, "Kak rodilsia i razvivalsia Kino-Glaz" (1935), *SV*, 288. There is some doubt about whether the poem appeared in print or not: in a note written in 1928 to Pera Atasheva (when Atasheva was working as a secretary for the Union of Soviet Societies for Friendship and Cultural Relations [VOKS]), Vertov indicated that the Purishkevich satire had in fact been published (RGALI f. 2091, op. 2, d. 236, l. 104). See also RGALI f. 2852, op. 1, d. 537, l. 1.

184 V. A. Bekhterev, *Ubijstvo Iushchinskogo i psikhiatro-psikhologicheskaia ekspertiza* (St. Petersburg: Prakticheskaia Meditstina, 1913), 56. For his testimony, see *Golos Belostoka* 240 (October 20, 1913): 2; 242 (October 23, 1913): 3. For similar reflections on the public-building role of the trial, see G. M. Aleksandr, *Posle suda Beilisa* (Odessa: S. M. Tencher, 1913), 7.

possibilities. If they gave shape to the conceptual, ideological, and affective repertory available to him, that shape was a complex, topological one. At once relatively privileged (especially if evaluated according to a "modern" template of value), and a member of a dishonored, often terrorized, but singularly dynamic group (Jews) from whose traditional yet still vital beliefs, language, and practices he was sundered from the outset; at once born in a provincial city, and attached, by virtue of the occupations and aspirations of his relatives and the capitalist energies of "boisterous, rich Bialystok," to an increasingly global economy and culture; at once resident in an autocratic peasant empire, deeply furrowed by lines of class, estate, language, confession, and ethnicity, and surrounded by ideas for change (and forces of change) ranging from "enlightenment" and emigration to Esperanto and socialist revolution: David Kaufman received a complex social inheritance during his years in Bialystok, one that, while in no way generic, might have been expended in various ways, and funded all sorts of life-journeys. In what follows, in part, we will see how that inheritance came to be expended as it was.

Yet what of the things we *do* know about him, David Kaufman the person, before 1914? Allow me to give his brother Mikhail, unduly ignored up to now, the floor for a page or two. For one thing, Mikhail was the only person who really knew Vertov from childhood through youth into adulthood (despite rancorous hiatuses, about which more in later chapters). For another, what he had to say in 1976 about Vertov as a boy has never been translated into English:

> [Vertov] began composing poems in childhood. Usually they appeared in response to some strong emotional experience.
>
> When he was nine or ten years old, Dziga was really crazy about the works of Fenimore Cooper, Mayne Reid, Jack London and Conan Doyle. He read them avidly, often at the expense of his studies. So that no one would bother him about homework, he would disappear somewhere pretty much every day after dinner, and in the mornings on holidays. Attempts were made to find him, but without success. It never occurred to anyone that he'd withdrawn to one of the sheds in the backyard. This became clear only after Dziga caught a chill one cold autumn day while in his secluded corner and fell ill with lobar pneumonia. Dziga was bedridden for a long while during his recovery; he was very sad and wrote poems.
>
> By the time he graduated from the Modern School, Dziga had amassed a lot of poems. I recopied some of them and became their active

popularizer. Dziga was shy about reading his poems to outsiders (he didn't rate them very highly); so when Mother was eager to boast in front of guests, I was called upon to huff and puff. Obviously, that's why some of my brother's verses stuck in my mind for many years. The better part of [my] archival materials was destroyed in 1941, when my first-floor room was flooded.[185] Thus I am presenting my brother's poetic exercises partially by memory, partially on the basis of pages that were preserved.

I recall how once, when we were still little boys, we were strolling on the outskirts of the city, and wandered into a slaughterhouse where we saw how they kill cattle. We returned home dispirited. Neither Dziga nor I would touch meat for a long time. Mother was upset about this, as she thought that children wouldn't grow without eating meat. Father, however, was an adherent of vegetarianism, and was pleased. Thus it wasn't surprising that he was delighted to read what Dziga wrote after visiting the slaughterhouse:

> "Little cow, brown one,
> My good cow!
> Oh, my brown one,
> Oh, how I love you.
> > Little cow, you give us
> > Cheese, butter, milk.
> > You go to the nearby meadow
> > To feed on grass.
> Oh, brown one,
> How do I show my gratitude?
> I lead you to the slaughterhouse,
> And kill you there with a knife...."

My mother's sister, aunt Masha, played a big role in Dziga's and my development. When we were just beginning to go to school, she was already studying in St. Petersburg at the Women's Medical Institute. She was purposeful, energetic, strong and sociable, and liked by everyone who came in contact with her. Despite being very busy, she spent a lot of time with her nephews. Aunt Masha loved us, and we loved her back. She was our very own confidential agent, and gave every stimulus to her nephews' creative initiatives. Having noticed that I was mad about photography—I'd been

---

185 That is, in Moscow during World War II, probably after Kaufman had left during the evacuation.

experimenting with a homemade camera obscura—aunt Masha gave me a real brand-name camera. I still remember my boundless joy. I began to spend all my free time on photography, and aunt Masha was the main evaluator of my experiments.

For his part, Dziga shared his literary exercises above all with aunt Masha.

Of course, this all happened during her holidays. Young students surrounded her every time she visited from St. Petersburg, and I recall the meetings where they would discuss current political events. Naturally, we began to understand what they were about only later. Not without aunt Masha's participation did we formulate our first conceptions of revolutionary ideas, about the struggle with Tsarist oppression, and about the worker's movement.

Later, Dziga began composing verses on political themes. They were like pamphlets in which the conservatives who stood in defense of the Tsarist regime were mocked. One of the poems was written especially sharply. It was called "The Solo Performance of the Clown V. Purishkevich at a Session of the State Duma."

I can't repeat even one of the pamphlets Dziga wrote. I remember well, however, how they all got burned up in the stove, when we heard rumors about a general search being conducted [by the police] in the city.

Now a few words about the poem "Masha." Dziga Vertov recalled this composition in his diaries. It was a poem dedicated to aunt Masha on the occasion of her defense of her medical doctor's diploma.[186] In the poem, life was compared with the ocean, which accordingly would bring surprises in the form of storms and tempests. The poem's hero was a brave helmsman, expertly guiding his boat. It remains a shame that "Masha" wasn't preserved.[187]

Setting aside for the moment the question of Kaufman's own storytelling strategies, his reflexes, exclusions, and boldfacing—although what he writes is certainly credible on the whole—how should we assess and situate these reminiscences? David came from a book-and-education-oriented family, supportive of his (and his brothers') early artistic explorations, and possessing enough resources to be supportive of such interests. His father was an erudite and a moralist—perhaps

---

186 Masha received her diploma with distinction on November 13, 1912, when Vertov was sixteen (TsGIASpb f. 436, op. 4, d. 906, l. 1).
187 Mikhail Kaufman, "Poet neigrovogo," *DVVS*, 74–76.

a Tolstoyan?—who rejected drinking, smoking, meat-eating, and the reading of substandard literature; his mother, co-librarian of one of the city's (and the region's) largest circulating libraries. Masha was the family's exemplum and foremost success story, possessing charisma, intelligence, courage, drive, curiosity, personal warmth, and a distinguished record of study at one of the country's foremost medical institutes. That she was also politically somewhere on the left is unsurprising for someone in her structural position in Russian society, whether or not she really led political discussions, or returned to Bialystok to assist victims of the June 1906 pogrom (though I believe she did both). And David, of course, became an artist—despite "Dziga Vertov's" intricate chafing against that label, to be discussed in later chapters—and so it's not surprising that Mikhail stresses his brother's early creative impulses above all else, in this embryonic artist bio. Yet those impulses, as outlined in the memoir, have certain limitations and preconditions.

Some of these are fairly obvious. To be sure, what a later interviewer called the "division of labor" between Mikhail Kaufman and Vertov, with photography and direct visual "experiment" on one side and poetic articulation on the other, finds reflection (or retrospective anticipation) here.[188] The importance of Masha Gal'pern, not only as inspiration but also as evaluative authority and standard-setter, is at once immense and more difficult to account for in an non-reductive way. Her centrality to Vertov's imagination, rooted in both her academic and professional success and her personal charisma, is eventually revealed, I would postulate, in an aspect of his cinematic work that all serious commentators have noted, if not always with full comprehension or sympathy. I am thinking, of course, about Vertov's feminism, which distinguishes him sharply from most Soviet filmmakers (male or female) of the 1920s and

---

188 The interviewer was Annette Michelson:

> [*Kaufman*]: Ever since childhood Vertov had the ability to perceive things through images and to communicate them in poetic form. It's interesting, by the way, that even as a child I was attracted to different forms of representation than he. I studied photographs, I drew—and since we're discussing the early stages of our collaboration, we can say that it began when our beloved Aunt Masha graduated from medical school. Vertov wrote a poem for her, and I drew a sort of congratulation picture of a dove in flight. There was already a certain
> ...
>
> *October* [Michelson]: Division of labor.
> *Kaufman*: Division of labor, and a form of collaboration—even though I did not always feel that Vertov perceived the material I shot quite as I did, even when something was missing. (Mikhail Kaufman, "An Interview with Mikhail Kaufman," *October* 11 [Winter 1979]: 59.)

'30s, and which imposes itself as a theme with greater force the more often and more closely his films are scrutinized. For the mature Vertov—and here I am, no doubt, leaping ahead on paper wings of speculation, but also to analyses to follow in later chapters—women very often stand in as exemplary (Soviet) subjects, as those agents best able to build and live within the New; and Masha Gal'pern, along with Elizaveta Svilova and perhaps Chaya Kaufman as well, provided Vertov with a kind of prototype for such women as they appear in his films.

However, surely the most striking feature of Vertov's early artistic work as recalled by Mikhail is its *occasional* quality: that is, the way that it was prompted by relatively punctual events like an illness, the gory sight of an abattoir, Masha's graduation, or even the pogrom wave, figured by the absurd and sadistic Purishkevich (but perhaps by the slaughtered cattle as well). Neither artistic practice nor the materials of art—media, tropes, textures and so on—but rather the use of art to deal with, articulate, or memorialize *occurrences*, is what is stressed here. In a sense, of course, we notice this because Kaufman's recollections are doing what all artistic biography does: that is, they link specific events to specific works, binding the history of the artist's production along a single timeline with larger (family, national, international) history. And it is worth remembering that nearly all of Vertov's major films, with the exception of *Man with a Movie Camera*, were occasional themselves: that is, films made to order, in accord with some Soviet policy initiative, campaign, public ritual, or development project. However, in an intriguing 1935 talk that I have already cited, Vertov gives a suggestive hint as to the deeper motivations behind this responsive, or reactive, creative labor.

Although the lecture was entitled "How Kino-Eye Was Born and Developed," in it Vertov offers an account, not only of his early years in newsreel, but also of his childhood attempts at novel-writing and, more surprisingly, his strategies for learning what was assigned to him in school:

> [In school] I was never able to learn anything by heart. I found subjects like grammar—where you had to cram in all the exceptions—or history—where you have chronology—the most difficult, and in general, [had difficulty with] any academic assignment, where one had to not only grasp the idea, but also cram stuff in.
>
> I began looking for a way out of my difficulties. Let's say I had to immediately and quickly answer, without looking at the map, which are the cities and islands of Asia Minor? Normally one would go up to the map, find the cities and name them. But that was not an option.

Once, going through the names of those cities and islands, I had the idea of arranging them in a rhythmical series that could be memorized immediately. With the cities of Asia Minor, in particular, this is how I proceeded. I arranged their names and noticed that as soon as I read through them in a specific order, I immediately memorized the whole series—that is, I freed myself from the need to cram them into my head.

25 years have gone by, and although I haven't repeated them to myself once, I still remember the arrangement: Miletus, Phocaea, Smyrna, Halicarnassus, Samos, Ephesus, and Mytilene on the islands of Lesbos, Cyprus and Rhodes....

What did these experiments lead to? These experiments (that I was forced to carry out) led to my becoming interested in the organization of discrete elements of the visible and audible world.

The next phase involved my being occupied with stenographic records. Here it wasn't a matter only of the formal binding of these fragments, but of the interrelationships of the concepts [associated with] the discrete pieces of the stenograph record. The same can be said of my experiments with gramophone recordings, where a new composition was created out of discrete extracts, from recordings on gramophone records.

But I wasn't satisfied by experiments with already recorded sounds. Within the natural world I heard a significantly greater quantity of varied sounds ... I hit upon the idea that it was necessary to expand our capacities to hear in an organized way. Not to limit those capacities within the bounds of ordinary music. Within the concept "I hear," I included the entire audible world. To this period belongs my experiment in recording the sounds of a sawmill.[189]

An external imperative—to assimilate facts, to "cram stuff in"—leads to efforts to bind that raw "stuff" into a form, to master it. We can legitimately doubt that Vertov independently hit upon the idea of rhythmical organization of words (or sounds, or images), given the long history (to which we will allude later) of the use of rhythm and rhyme in practical mnemonics: perhaps the bookstore contained primers on memorization strategies, or perhaps his parents offered him some pointers.[190] It would seem, moreover, that the structural

---

189 Vertov, SV, 290–91. The article was first published in *Iskusstvo Kino* in 1986, and hence not included in SDZ or later translations of that volume ("Kak rodilsia i razvivalsia Kino-Glaz," *Iskusstvo Kino* 2 [February 1986]: 70–78).

190 It is worth recalling here that locations and place-names (like the cities of Asia Minor) are among the classic objects of mnemotechnic practice and speculation: see Jules Didier,

requirements of the school exercise long continued to shape Vertov's imagination, if we consider the tightly enumerated outline-form of some of his essays, or the report of Benno Reifenberg, Feuilletonchef of the *Frankfurter Zeitung*, on one of Vertov's 1929 German talks—irritatingly presented, according to Reifenberg,

> in the way one constructs high-school composition exercises—in chunks arranged according to roman numeral 1 and 2 with lots of a and b and d, and with that youthful optimism that wants to be at once entirely clear and as complete as possible.

(The talk's style was matched in naiveté, added Reifenberg, by the director's "Romantic" and old-fashioned belief in the possibility of "a stock taking of the entire world" through cinema.)[191] And was it by chance that Vertov the militant theorist rejected any reliance on familiar cognitive habits—or what he called "the human eye"—as the basis for cinematic structuration, and scoldingly compared such dependence to using a "cheat sheet" (*shpargal'ka*)?[192] In any event, a task that young David Kaufman "was forced to carry out," that threatened him with the possibility of significant failure and dishonor, is executed by fashioning a technical procedure of "formal binding": a procedure that, by virtue of both the anxiety informing it and its at least partial success, provokes experimental inquiry into a more general "expansion of capacities," into the "formal binding" of words, concepts, sounds ... everything.

Emerging out of both Vertov's and Kaufman's reminiscences is a conception of art as a way of dealing with change and with shock, to create new structures of cognition that would help one to coincide with that change and fend off that shock.[193] I will argue at various points in this book that such a

---

    Traité Complet de Mnémonique (Lille: Thomas Naudin, 1808), 164–98; *Mnemonik oder praktische Gedächtnisskunst zum Selbstunterricht nach den Vorlesungen des Herrn von Feinaigle* (Frankfurt am Main: Varrentrapp und Sohn, 1811), 78–108; and of course Frances Yates, *The Art of Memory* (Chicago: University of Chicago Press, 1966).

191 Benno Reifenberg, "Für wen sieht das 'Kino-Auge'? Zur Diskussion um den russischen Filmregisseur Dziga Vertov (Frankfurt, den 25 Juli)," *Frankfurter Zeitung* (July 25, 1929); RGALI f. 2091, op. 1, d. 96, l. 9. For good examples of Vertov's enumerations in prose, see "From Kino-Eye to Radio-Eye" and "Let's Discuss Ukrainfilm's First Sound Film: Symphony of the Donbas," in *KE*, 85–92, 106–12. Vertov wasn't the only one who practiced blunt enumeration in his speeches and articles: Stalin was famous for the same, as Stephen Kotkin has pointed out.

192 In the essay: "Kinocs: A Revolution," *SV*, 41; *KE*, 19 (translated there as "crib sheet").

193 Through this reference to "shock," I intend to recall Walter Benjamin's use of the term, especially in his essay "Some Motifs in Baudelaire" in *Charles Baudelaire: A Lyric Poet in the*

conception explains a considerable amount about Vertov's mature experimental documentary work, although it cannot account on its own (obviously enough) for the full subtlety and range of that work. Aficionados of Vertov, for instance, will have already recognized the affinities between Kaufman's slaughterhouse-story, Vertov's tribute to brown cows, and the great "beef-to-bull" backwards motion sequence in *Kino-Eye* (1924; to be discussed in volume 2), a sequence that, while bearing an expository function—a specifically economic one, that hopes to demonstrate the irrelevance of middlemen to the production of useful commodities—also aspires to fashion a secular and visible notion of resurrection, as grisly, lacerated slabs of meat are reanimated into a joyously corporeal and collective existence.

Such montage procedures signal the provisional character of our conceptions of reality—even in the face of the reality principle itself—and therefore our capacity to re-conceive.[194] To be sure, that capacity can never encompass the "entire . . . world," whose metamorphoses and resistances outstrip all subjective attempts at mastery (and the latter very much include, I would stress, today's familiar "ironic" and "play-centered" theoretical postures, as well as all the dialectically affiliated but more obviously reactionary and anti-intellectual appeals to timeless wisdom, or the newer scientismic fundamentalisms). And in this study, we will need to account for the "discrete elements" that elude such attempts, that find no place within the modern and universal memory palace, whether through censorship, self-censorship, the collision of conflicting models of "capacity," or sheer mutability and destruction.

I don't think we should doubt, for instance, that Masha Gal'pern—the family's spiritual helmswoman—spoke to the Kaufman boys about "the workers' movement": this was Bialystok, after all, in the early 1900s. But did she also talk to them about Zionism? About feminism?[195] Mikhail Kaufman, writing in the Soviet 1970s, in the wake of seven decades of de- and re-racination, probably wouldn't have even remembered; we'll probably never know.

Era of High Capitalism, trans. Harry Zohn (London: Verso, 1983), 155–200. See also my *Inscription and Modernity*, esp. 94–139.

194 On this, see also Rosen, "Now and Then," 36.

195 Given her medical education in St. Petersburg, she very well might have. See Richard Stites, *The Women's Liberation Movement in Russia: Feminism, Nihilism, and Bolshevism, 1860–1930* (Princeton, NJ: Princeton University Press, 1978), esp. 157–276.

Province of Universality: David Kaufman before the War • CHAPTER 1   67

Image 7: David Kaufman (Dziga Vertov) and Masha Gal'pern, ca. 1914. Image courtesy of Andre Kaufman.

CHAPTER 2

Social Immortality: David Kaufman at the Psychoneurological Institute (1914–16)

Have you guess'd you yourself would not continue?
Have you dreaded these earth-beetles?
Have you fear'd the future would be nothing to you?
—Walt Whitman, *"To Think of Time"*

The period 1914 through 1921, a formative one for Vertov, comprised years of uninterrupted crisis, and almost uninterrupted war, in Russia. Vertov was fortunate enough not to have been directly involved in combat,[1] but World War I (1914–17) and the Russian Civil War (1918–21) furrowed every dimension of his existence nonetheless, whether by virtue of the horizon of fear and despair they generated, the occasions they provided for revolt and commitment, or the opportunities for new forms of camaraderie and creativity that they afforded. War and its consequences, singularly dire in Russia during these years, thus must be regarded as among the determining instances in Vertov's biography. Those consequences blew through a whole array of other relatively independent life-variables—ranging from family and school to artistic and career aspirations—and slammed many doors shut along the way, blasting others off their hinges.

For these years and places, a naked listing of historical and biographical events is dramatic enough. Between 1914 and 1922, David Kaufman left

---

1 See Vertov's brief autobiography, written in 1947 as part of a petition to be awarded the title (which he received in June of that year) of Meritorious Artist of the Russian Soviet Federative Socialist Republic: RGASPI f. 17, op. 125, l. 48.

Bialystok; attended one of the most important and innovative institutions of higher learning in Russia; became one of many thousands of war refugees; was drafted and released from the draft; frequented avant-garde cafés in Moscow during the revolutionary year of 1917; conducted verbal and sound-transcription experiments in his "laboratory of hearing"; got a job in the new Soviet cultural administration working on (and sometimes restoring) newsreel and other nonfiction film; showed films on agitational trains that traversed the war-torn country; and married and divorced and changed his name. Still, we have very little precise documentation about Kaufman/Vertov's activities between 1914 and 1918, and the sketchy information we possess about the succeeding period (1918 through 1921) seems full and illuminating only by comparison with the relative blank of the earlier. Much can be said about his social and cultural surroundings, however, and at a high level of specificity. Perhaps a certain density of description, animated as much as possible by swift movement from one moment to the next, is the best strategy for re-creating the terrifying or exhilarating turbulence of this time, the time of Kaufman's transformation into Vertov.

The present chapter on David Kaufman's years at the Psychoneurological Institute and the two that follow are best thought of as a single long section dealing with this transformation. At the institute, as I hope to show, Kaufman acquired (without realizing it!) both some of the practical instruments and some of the ideologies and formal preoccupations that enabled him later on to construct "Vertov." Personal connections that he made (or might have made: the mood in this chapter will often be hypothetical) at the institute were the most important of the instruments, to be sure, especially as means of entering into Soviet cultural institutions as they were forming after 1917. His probable involvement in scientific filmmaking at the institute gave him both some concrete preparation for his later work and a stake in cinema itself as a means of exploring the world (rather than of staging fictions). And his likely exposure to then-current ideologies—specifically one that identified material energy as the universal substrate of existence and another that exalted rhythm as a medium that could bind the realms of intellectual (musical-artistic) and nonintellectual labor—furnished tropes and concepts that would, I will suggest, prove fertile for an artist who sought to make films that were scientific, proletarian, and symphonic-poetic all at once.

Again, a temporal or narrative paradox haunts my choice of these themes, insofar as they are identifiable as salient only in relation to Vertov's later work in cinema. If we were to confine ourselves to 1914–16, none of them could be isolated from among the infinitely tangled web of factors and influences through which

David Kaufman moved. But Kaufman did become Vertov, after all—that is, he didn't become anyone else, much as he might have wanted to at various points—and so we need to determine which of those pre-Vertovian experiences equipped Kaufman for that becoming. His years at the Psychoneurological Institute, largely ignored in the existing Vertov scholarship, are an important place to start.

WAR, BEKHTEREV, AND THE PSYCHONEUROLOGICAL INSTITUTE

After completing an extra, supplementary year of study at the Modern School—necessary for entry into an institute of higher learning—David Kaufman left Bialystok sometime late in the summer of 1914 to study at the Petrograd Psychoneurological Institute, where he remained through the spring of 1916. At least initially, he lived in Petrograd with Masha Gal'pern (by now a practicing MD), although he returned to Bialystok in the early summer 1915 to prepare for his Latin exam.[2] That city had been the target of intensive German bombing raids since late April 1915, however, and conflict terminated David's summer sojourn by early August at the latest. He and his family would have fled the city by that time, along with many if not most other Bialystokers, partially in anticipation of occupation by German forces (August 13, 1915) but mainly prompted by the scorched earth and anti-Semitic policies of the Russian Army itself.[3] Now among many hundreds of thousands of other war refugees, the

---

2   TsGIASPb f. 115, op. 2, d. 4048, ll. 2–5, 13–16.
3   Dobronski, *Białystok: Historia Miasta*, 112. These policies, as historian Peter Gatrell indicates, indeed had a distinct anti-Jewish coloration: "Within the extensive theater of operations, the Russian high command was accused of pursuing a scorched earth policy and driving civilians from their homes. Archival evidence supports this view.... The army went out of its way to target vulnerable minorities, in an attempt to find scapegoats for military failure. Jews suffered most acutely. The negative association between Jews and frontier security had been deeply ingrained in military consciousness ever since Nicholas I had decreed that they could not live within 50 kilometers of the western frontier. Russian generals confidently asserted that 'the complete hostility of the entire Jewish population toward the Russian army is well established'... Population displacement was ultimately caused by the advance of German and Austrian troops into Russian territory. But this explains little of the intensity and character of displacement. Although those who found an explanation in terms of 'spontaneity' deliberately or unwittingly camouflaged the active intervention of Russia's own armed forces, the part played by the Russian army in this dramatic upheaval was evident to any objective observer. Jews and Germans left involuntarily by order of Russian military commanders, who were acting out of a warped belief in the political unreliability of these ethnic minorities...." (Peter Gatrell, *A Whole Empire Walking: Refugees in Russia During World War I* [Bloomington: Indiana University Press, 1999], 16, 31). See also Eric Lohr, *Nationalizing the Russian Empire: The Campaign against Enemy Aliens during World War I* (Cambridge, MA: Harvard University Press, 2003), 137–50; and chapter 3, below.

Kaufman family went by train to Petrograd, where they were installed, no doubt in less-than-optimal living conditions, by the fall of 1915.[4]

After this point, the family began to split apart, never to be fully reunited: Mojsej (by now designated "Mikhail" in official documents) left in September for gymnasium study in Mogilev (now in Belarus, then the site of the headquarters of the Russian Imperial Army), which he completed on May 15, 1917.[5] The Kaufmans moved to Moscow sometime before the summer of 1917,[6] remaining there before returning to Bialystok, possibly as early as late 1917 and doubtless not beyond the fall of 1920, by which time the Poles had emerged victorious in their war against Soviet forces.[7] It seems that this Moscow sojourn was the last time Abel, Chaya, and all their sons—the two oldest were grownups now—lived in the same city. Meanwhile, Masha Gal'pern left Petrograd in January 1916 to carry out medical relief work in war-torn Minsk for the Society for the Protection of the Health of the Jews, where she remained until sometime in 1918.[8]

For his part, David was drafted in the fall of 1916—into the musical division of a military school in Chuguev, Ukraine, which I will mention again in the next chapter[9]—but not before completing the two-year "basic" course at the Petrograd Psychoneurological Institute, a remarkable school of higher learning that had a lasting impact upon him, both intellectually and with regard to the social connections he forged there. To be sure, the war and poor living conditions would have exerted their unsettling long- and short-range effects upon David at the institute as well. In this respect,

---

4   TsGIASPb f. 115, op. 2, d. 4048, l. 12.
5   RGALI f. 2896, op. 1, d. 112, ll. 1–2. It was evidently Mojsej who was the first of the older brothers to select a Russian first name.
6   It seems that the Kaufmans moved to Moscow sometime during the revolutionary year (see Simon Kagan's "Entretien avec Boris Kaufman," Boris Kaufman Papers, Beinecke Library, Yale University, Gen MSS 562.16.336.3); Mikhail Kaufman was certainly there by July 4, 1917, living near Sretenka Street (RGALI f. 2896, op. 1, d. 112, ll. 2–2ob).
7   German forces left the city in February 1919, but fighting in the area against the Bolsheviks under Marshal Tukhachevsky ended only at the end of August 1920; see Dobronski, *Białystok: Historia Miasta*, 118, 129–30.
8   Miriam Halperin-[Proginin] [Masha Gal'pern], "The Work of OZE in the Minsk District in the Years 1916–1918," *Minsk, 'ir va'em: korot, ma'asim, 'ishim, ha'vai*, ed. David Cohen and Shlomo Even-Shoshan (Tel-Aviv: Association of Immigrants from Minsk and Its Surroundings, 1975), 602–4. This article, about which more below, was originally published in *He'avar* (May–June 1968), and I am grateful to Zohar Rotem for translating it for me.
9   TsGIASPb f. 115, op. 2, d. 4048, ll. 8, 17–18; Mikhail Kaufman, "Poet neigrovogo," *DVVS*, 76. Kaufman's mention of Vertov's study at this military school has gone oddly unnoticed by nearly all writers on Vertov; his claims are plainly substantiated by external documentation. For more details, see chapter 3.

however, his situation would have been the same as that as virtually of all his fellows, and superior to that of many.

The institute had been formed in 1907 by the aforementioned Vladimir Mikhailovich Bekhterev (1857–1927), one of the founders of Russian neurology and a major figure in the history of education in Russia in the early twentieth century. A student of Wilhelm Wundt and Jean-Martin Charcot, Bekhterev was a world expert in brain anatomy whose articles frequently appeared in foreign journals, a prize-winning luminary in the Russian scientific world, a member of the prestigious Military Medical Academy in St. Petersburg, and an active teacher whose pupils included, among many others, Masha Gal'pern, who had studied "nervous illnesses" for two semesters in 1910 with Bekhterev at the Women's Higher Medical Institute in St. Petersburg.[10] Building on donations from well-to-do patrons, including a grant of crown lands, Bekhterev founded the institute on an exceptionally broad structural and intellectual basis that incorporated research and clinical treatment, humanistic, jurisprudential and scientific study, and a policy of "unrestricted admission to women and Jewish students."[11]

Students began their studies there with a two-year "basic" program that included courses in chemistry, physics, general biology, general and experimental psychology, geology, mathematics, modern languages, world history, history of philosophy, history of culture and art, history of political economy, literature, sociology, logic and epistemology, anatomy of the nervous system, and comparative and experimental psychology among many other topics; and it is this wide-ranging program that David Kaufman would have completed.[12] Three

---

10 TsGIASPb f. 436, op. 1 d. 2552, l. 5ob. On the Women's Medical Institute's ties to other medical institutes in St. Petersburg, see A. E. Ivanov, *Vysshaia shkola Rossii v kontse XIX-nachale XX veka* (Moscow: Akademiia Nauk, 1991), 109. On Bekhterev and the Psychoneurological Institute more generally, see David Joravsky, *Russian Psychology: A Critical History* (Oxford: Basil Blackwell, 1989), esp. 83–87, 107, 152; Ivanov, *Vysshaia shkola Rossii*, esp. 113–16, 202–3, 311–13; M. A. Akimenko, "Vladimir Mikhailovich Bekhterev," *Journal of the History of the Neurosciences* 16, no. 1 (2007): 100–109; David Wartenweiler, *Civil Society and Academic Debate in Russia 1905–1914* (Oxford: Clarendon Press, 1999), 200–203; and Valérie Pozner, "Vertov before Vertov: Psychoneurology in Petrograd," in *Dziga Vertov*, ed. Tode and Wurm, 12–15.

11 Joravsky, *Russian Psychology*, 83. Interestingly, the Psychoneurological Institute kept no statistics about the social estate (*soslovie*) of the students enrolled there (Ivanov, *Vysshaia shkola Rossii*, 279). The noble Alafusov family was the Institute's main financial patron (Wartenweiler, *Civil Society and Academic Debate*, 200).

12 See A. V. Gerver, ed., *Otchet o deiatel'nosti Psikho-Nevrologicheskago Instituta za 1912-j god* (St. Petersburg: Gramotnost', 1914), 176; Ivanov, *Vysshaia shkola Rossii*, 113; Pozner, "Vertov before Vertov."

Image 1: Portrait of Bekhterev by M. L. [Mojsej L'vovich] Majmon from *Vesenniaia vystavka v zalakh Imperatorskoj Akademii Khudozhestv 1916 g.* [Spring exhibition in the halls of the Imperial Academy of Arts, 1916] (Petrograd: Union, 1916). Source: RGALI f. 1951, op. 1, d. 10, l. 12.

higher-level divisions or "faculties"—pedagogical, juridical, and medical—each offered an additional three years of intensive study in those disciplines, while continuing to stress what we would now call "interdisciplinarity" through the inclusion of science courses (in psychology, especially) into the more humanities-oriented tracks.[13]

---

13 Wartenweiler, *Civil Society and Academic Debate*, 202.

The teaching faculty, which drew on a number of other universities in St. Petersburg, was one of the finest in Russia, and included (besides Bekhterev himself) the physiologist and psychologist Prince Aleksej Ukhtomskij, physiologist Nikolaj Vvedenskij, chemist Lev Pisarzhevskij, philosophers Semyon Frank and Nikolaj Losskij, linguist Jan Baudouin de Courtenay, lexicographer Max Fasmer, the left-wing scholar of government Mikhail Rejsner (father of Larisa Rejsner, herself a star student at the institute and soon to become one of the legends of early Soviet journalism), and the evolutionary biologist and animal psychologist Vladimir Vagner, about whom more below.[14] The diverse student body, extraordinary faculty, low cost of attendance, and (for Russia) uniquely wide-ranging curriculum made the institute a crucible of pre- and post-Revolutionary Russian culture and among the most remarkable sites of learning in the empire, one which enjoyed enormous popularity among young *intelligenty*, who would often audit courses there even when not officially enrolled.[15]

The institute's liberal-to-left-tending political culture was surely part of this appeal as well. A number of major figures in the institute, Bekhterev among them, had a history of taking independent, even antagonistic positions vis-à-vis the Tsar and his ministries. When the War Ministry threatened to close the Military Medical Academy in response to the student uprisings there during 1906, Bekhterev distinguished himself from his colleagues by his forceful insistence on the academy's autonomy.[16] His uncompromising exculpatory testimony during the Beilis trial in 1913—widely reported and discussed in newspapers across the Empire, including (as we know) in Bialystok[17]—was no doubt part of the reason that the conservative education minister L. A. Kasso refused that year to approve Bekhterev's re-appointment as the director of the Psychoneurological Institute.[18] Indeed, the following year, Kasso tried unsuccessfully to close the institute, still not an official "institute of higher education,"[19] on the grounds that its focus had shifted to education from scientific research, and that those pedagogical functions, now conducted

---

14 Gerver, ed., *Otchet o deiatel'nosti Psikho-Nevrologicheskago Instituta*, 176–77; Ivanov, *Vysshaia shkola Rossii*, 116.
15 Ivanov, *Vysshaia shkola Rossii*, 116.
16 Joravsky, *Russian Psychology*, 84.
17 *Novosti Belostoka* 16 (October 19, 1913): 3; and *Golos Belostoka* 240 (October 20, 1913): 2 (NIAB f. 15, op. 1, d. 155, ll. 62, 69ob).
18 Joravsky, *Russian Psychology*, 83–84. Joravsky notes that "[Bekhterev] continued to direct [the Institute] in fact, though another person took over the title" (84).
19 It would achieve that status only in 1916 (Ivanov, *Vysshaia shkola Rossii*, 114).

entirely outside the control of the Ministry of Education,[20] had helped spawn various student disorders, none of which had been opposed by the institute's "anti-government" professoriate.[21]

As David Joravsky has pointed out, Bekhterev's own position was of necessity ambivalent, inasmuch as he was at once a much-bemedaled beneficiary of state and private patronage and a critic of both autocracy and capitalism.[22] (The privilege, of course, provided the platform for the critique, in a fertile paradox familiar to academics still today.) Bekhterev was a scientist of positivist cast who evidently believed that the backwardness and obscurantism of the Tsarist regime worked together with the chaos and selfishness that came with incipient capitalism to prevent the emergence in Russia of rationally organized modern institutions (including scientific ones) and mature, mentally healthy, socially engaged individuals.[23] Thus his left-wing sympathies—he was to

---

20 The institute indeed conducted its internal affairs in remarkably autonomous fashion, as historian David Wartenweiler has pointed out. Apart from confirming the institute's director (who was "chosen [internally] by the Institute's council") and requiring a "list of its teaching staff" and the submission of "annual accounts," the Ministry of Education had little influence over the institute, whose "ruling body, the council (that is, the assembly of all full professors), was basically free to develop its activities within the framework of the statutes, according to its own judgment and plans" (Wartenweiler, *Civil Society and Academic Debate*, 201).
21 Ivanov, *Vysshaia shkola Rossii*, 114. Evidently, the ministry backed away from Kasso's proposal, fearing the outcry that the closure of this (mainly privately funded) institute would elicit (ibid., 115).
22 Joravsky, *Russian Psychology*, 85–87.
23 His most open polemics were, to be sure, directed against capitalism, as here in a speech delivered at the third Russian congress of psychiatrists and neurologists in 1909: "The basis of our civilization lies in the significance of capitalism in the life of contemporary society, which has led to [a] struggle for existence. The golden idol, that fearful enemy of humanity, paralyzes all strivings toward mutual aid . . . Thanks to it, [we find] the gravest exploitation of poor folk, leading to every sort of deprivation, to the rise of poverty and an extreme overexertion of the physical and moral powers of the population, especially among the working class . . . On the other hand, this struggle for existence, conditioned by the significance of capitalism in the life of contemporary society, leads the population into larger centers, [which in turn] leads to the sanitary conditions of the community becoming exceedingly unfavorable. . . The capitalist system: that is the basic evil of our time. We must in every way concern ourselves with achieving higher norms of social life; instead of capitalism, we must place labor and service to truth and goodness in the foreground" (V. Bekhterev, *Voprosy nervno-psikhicheskago zdorov'ia v russkom naselenii* [originally published in *Obozreniia Psikhiatrii*] [St. Petersburg: Pervoj Sankt-Peterburgskij Trudovoj Arteli, 1910], 16, 22; see also Joravsky, *Russian Psychology*, 87). At the same time, he was given to proposing bureaucratic measures for social improvement, such as (in the speech just quoted) forbidding epileptics, the "mentally ill," and even chronic alcoholics to marry (20). Other positions he took were securely in the mainstream of public opinion, as when he added his voice to the choir of patriots opposing "Germanism" during World War I, although he also strongly advocated the creation of an

endorse the Bolshevik government after the October Revolution, and retained his privileged status under the new regime until his death in 1927[24]—were prompted not merely by concerns for intellectual autonomy, but by a sense of his (in Joravsky's words) "professional mission to society at large," of a project realizable only if "state and society were completely transformed."[25]

Although never a member of a left-wing political party, Bekhterev stocked the institute's faculty with a number of affiliated radicals, including the aforementioned Mikhail Rejsner—a fellow traveler and (later) member of the Social Democratic Party who taught courses on law and state-church relations and led proseminars on utopian thought[26]—and historian Evgenij Tarle (1874–1955), a Social Democrat who lectured on modern history and conducted wide-ranging seminars on Rousseau's political philosophy and other topics.[27]

---

international parliament (or "a kind of United States of Europe," as he put it) upon the war's conclusion (V. M. Bekhterev, "Moral'nye itogi Velikoj Mirovoj Vojny," *Vestnik Znaniia* 10–11 (October–November 1915): 657–71; see esp. 670).

24 Claims that Bekhterev was done away with at Stalin's orders, after the neurologist supposedly diagnosed the dictator as clinically "paranoid" (see, for instance, Vladimir Lerner, Jacob Margolin, and Eliezer Witztum, "Vladimir Bekhterev: his life, his work and the mystery of his death," *History of Psychiatry* 16, no. 2 [2005]: 217–227), are, in my view, too feebly substantiated to be taken seriously.

25 Joravsky, *Russian Psychology*, 85–86.

26 See Gerver, ed., *Otchet o deiatel'nosti Psikho-Nevrologicheskago Instituta*, 44, 188; M. B. Kejrim-Markus, *Gosudarstvennoe rukovodstvo kul'turoj: stroitel'stvo Narkomprosa noiabria 1917-seredina 1918 gg.* (Moscow: Nauka, 1980), 160. Rejsner's major two-volume work on government (*Gosudarstvo* [Moscow: I. D. Sytin, 1911]) attempts to demonstrate how "humanity strives toward realizing the ideals of unity, justice and economic well-being," in a process that "is born out of social struggle and logical contradiction," and leads to "the creation of newer and newer forms [of social life]" and to "a new earth and a new sky" for human beings (*Gosudarstvo*, vol. 2, 290). Openly opposed to any participation in World War I from the outset of that conflict, Rejsner (1868–1928) was later to work as a publicist for the Soviet regime after 1917, producing defenses of "Soviet power" written in simple, stark language—*Chto Takoe Sovetskaia Vlast'?* (Moscow: Izdatel'stvo Narodnogo Komissariata Zemledeliia, 1918), atheistic propaganda pamphlets (*Nuzhno li nam verit' v Boga*, 2nd ed. [Kursk: Knigoizdatel'skoe tovarishchestvo pri Kurskom Gubkome RKP(b), 1922]), and a collection of short revolutionary plays (*Bog i Birzha: Sbornik Revoliutsionnykh P'es* [Moscow: Gosudarstvennoe Izdatel'stvo, 1921]), among other works. Larisa Rejsner was a participant in her father's seminars on comparative utopias, and one of her earliest works, the play *Atlantis* (1912), was clearly inspired by her utopian readings (Galina Prizhiborovskaia, *Larisa Rejsner* [Molodaia Gvardiia: Moscow, 2008], 100–101).

27 Tarle had first been arrested at a political meeting, along with the students in attendance, in April 1900 (Ivanov, *Vysshaia shkola Rossii*, 116, 240). Later a major historian of the 1812 and Crimean Wars, he suffered arrest and official censure a number of times during the 1930s and '40s; see B. S. Kaganovich, *Evgenij Viktorovich Tarle i peterburgskaia shkola istorikov* (St. Petersburg: Dmitrii Bulanin, 1995).

And there is good reason to believe that these and other freethinking professors had an impact upon the political viewpoints of their students, particularly during the lead-up to the February Revolution.[28]

The institute must have been an exciting place for young people to study, especially given its openness to auditors and breadth of field coverage, a range hardly smaller in the humanistic than in the scientific divisions. In addition to proseminars (at which students would present original work) on topics ranging from modern and ancient philosophy to the psychophysiology of sense organs to Pushkin, there were student-organized study circles (at which professors would often present their work as well) on epistemology, the study of religion and ethics, monism, Schopenhauer's philosophy, folktales from around the globe, Esperanto, physical education, and classical music, among other subjects.[29]

During the war years, regrettably, students would have had much on their minds besides study, particularly after the defeats of early 1915, which set in motion that colossal wave of refugees, mainly from the empire's western provinces,[30] of which many students and their families (including the Kaufmans, as we know) found themselves a part. Over six million people were made refugees in Russia during World War I, in a population displacement that "on this scale and at this intensity," as historian Peter Gatrell notes, "was unprecedented in Russia's recent history."[31] The historian and Moscow Duma deputy Sergej Bakhrushin— later known for his participation in Stalin-era debates about Ivan the Terrible, at this time active in the relief effort carried out by the Union of [Russian] Cities— succinctly captured the reality of the situation in a report from 1915:

> The conditions under which the migration of the refugees occurred are only too well known. Caught entirely unaware by the invasion, ... people

---

28 On this, see N. G. Zavadskij, *Ispytanie vojnoj: rossijskoe studenchestvo i politicheskie partii v 1914—fevral' 1917 gg.* (St. Petersburg: Nestor, 1999), 28.
29 Gerver, ed., *Otchet o deiatel'nosti Psikho-Nevrologicheskago Instituta*, 194–222.
30 Pskov, Smolensk, Vitebsk, Minsk, Mogilev, Kovno, Kurland, and Grodno provinces were among the worst afflicted, although there were considerable problems in the Caucasus (Yerevan and Tiflis provinces) as well ("Soiuz Gorodov v dele pomoshchi bezhentsam i vyselentsam," in *Bezhentsy i vyselentsy: otdel'nye ottiski iz no. 17 Izvestii Vserossijskago Soiuza Gorodov*, ed. S. Bakhrushin et al. [Moscow: Moskovskaia Gorodskaia Tipografiia, 1915], 17).
31 Gatrell, *A Whole Empire Walking*, 3. That figure of six million comprised "something like 5 percent of the total population." "In 1917, 'refugees' (*bezhentsy*) outnumbered the industrial proletariat... [The displacement] would be exceeded only by the Nazi invasion of 1941, which displaced around 10 million people" (ibid.). As we will see in volume 3, Vertov would be one of those ten million as well.

moved unconsciously forward like some giant, natural stream, moved in any direction and any which way, on foot and with supply trains, trampling down fields and crops as they went, drinking wells down to the bottom, hungry and ill-clothed, sowing the path [behind them] with corpses.[32]

The Kaufman family was relatively fortunate compared to the thousands seeking food in Dvinsk or Vitebsk,[33] or to those standing around in large, hungry crowds in cities as far away as Orenburg, Samara, and Cheliabinsk,[34] although their situation was hardly enviable. On the way to Petrograd from Bialystok—which had been made one of the three first isolation points in the Grodno guberniia for refugees sick with cholera in the summer of 1915[35]—the Kaufmans lost all of their luggage, which was traveling separately to the capital on a train destined to be captured by the Germans. Abel Kaufman, now living with Chaya and Boris (and possibly David as well) in the apartment of an engineer named Z. M. Begun, was compelled to petition the institute to cover David's tuition fees for fall 1915.

The institute obliged, and monies for the tuition were drawn from the "Jewish fund," one of the "mutual aid funds" (*kassy vzaimopomoshchi*) that had for some years existed at the institute but which began to operate on an entirely new scale during the war years.[36] Across Russia, student and external aid organizations came to the assistance of students, refugees, and victims of the war, all much burdened by severe inflation and a dire housing shortage,[37] while the institute

---

32 S. Bakhrushin, "Bezhentsy," in *Bezhentsy i vyselentsy*, 1. Bakhrushin (1882–1950), scion of a famous merchant family, would suffer arrest and exile in 1930 during the Cultural Revolution. Vertov encountered him much later at a sanatorium they both stayed at after World War II; see volume 3 of the present work. For powerful descriptive accounts of the refugee crisis and the state's attempts to respond, see Gatrell, *A Whole Empire Walking*; and W. Bruce Lincoln, *Passage through Armageddon: The Russians in War and Revolution, 1914–1918* (New York: Simon and Schuster, 1986), 156–58, 161, 177, 188, 218.

33 N. N. Polianskij, "Obsledovanie polozhenia bezhentsev i vyselentsev v vitebskoj i pskovskoj guberniiakh," *Bezhentsy i vyselentsy*, 62, 67.

34 "Sdvig bezhentsev s mest," in *Bezhentsy i vyselentsy*, 54.

35 "Soiuz Gorodov v dele pomoshchi bezhentsam i vyselentsam," *Bezhentsy i vyselentsy*, 12–13.

36 Kaufman wrote his petition in October 1915, when Mikhail was already in Mogilev (TsGIASPb f. 115, op.2, d. 4048, l. 12; Pozner, "Vertov before Vertov," 15). Before the war, the institute's mutual aid fund for Jewish students had received money from the Jewish Committee for the Spread of Higher Learning (Gerver, ed., *Otchet o deiatel'nosti Psikho-Nevrologicheskago Instituta*, 239).

37 Kassow, *Students, Professors, and the State*, 378–80; Lincoln, *Passage through Armageddon*, 373–74.

itself was partially converted into a military hospital with a neurosurgical unit.[38] Jewish organizations, whether in institutions of higher learning or not, were among the most active "national" organizations during the war, both because of ongoing discrimination in universities, the military, and in the wider society, and in response to the stark exposure of Jewish communities to the fighting, given that the Pale of Settlement largely overlapped with Russia's western front.

The Pale, to be sure, was in the end one of the conflict's more welcome casualties, when a decree of August 4, 1915, allowed Jews to settle outside of its bounds, thereby basically liquidating it under pressure of war and forced displacement.[39] Yet Jewish students (as a less than fully "suitable" social group, alongside Poles and those suspected of political radicalism) could not be recruited into the officer corps, and the regime never gave up attempting to impose quotas on the numbers of Jews allowed to attend university.[40] Those quotas, significantly alleviated in state universities and institutes during the war, were hardened in non-state institutions starting in March 1916: on March 8, the old 3 percent limit was reimposed, with the Tsar's blessing, for Jewish applicants to the Psychoneurological Institute, previously "one of the most democratic of the non-state institutes of higher learning."[41]

---

38 Akimenko, "Vladimir Mikhailovich Bekhterev," 104.
39 Anatolij Evgen'evich Ivanov, "Rossijskoe evrejskoe studenchestvo v period Pervoj Mirovoj Vojny," in *Mirovoj krizis 1914-1920 godov i sud'ba vostochnoevropejskogo evrejstva*, ed. O. V. Budnitskij et al. (Moscow: Rosspen, 2005), 145. Gatrell summarizes the change: "Nowhere was the reconfiguration of space more evident than with respect to the empire's Jewish population. So much has been written about the disabilities, indignities, and violence that Jews suffered at the hands of the tsarist state and the tsar's Russian subjects that it is easy to overlook the extraordinary change in their status that the war brought about. Unlike other refugees, Russia's Jews had previously enjoyed little scope to choose their place of residence. The war did not weaken the stereotype of the 'wandering' Jews, but it largely wrecked the capacity of the tsarist state to dictate where Jews should and should not settle. In distributing themselves across large parts of the empire, Russia's Jews broke the bounds of imperial Russia and walked toward a kind of freedom. . . . Government ministers, albeit reluctantly, conceded that the Pale of Settlement had disintegrated" (Gatrell, *A Whole Empire Walking*, 200).
40 Ivanov, "Rossijskoe evrejskoe studenchestvo," 144, 151. Those percentage limits were nonetheless the subject of considerable debate at the state level. On July 24, 1915, the restrictions were lessened for Jews who had served in the war, and a further decree of August 10, 1915, giving first preference to the children of veterans and war invalids "regardless of nationality and confession" led to a rapid surge in the number of Jewish students in many state institutions of higher learning (ibid., 151–53). See also A. E. Ivanov, *Evrejskoe studenchestvo v Rossijskoj Imperii nachala XX veka: kakim ono bylo?* (Moscow: Novyj Khronograf, 2007), 75–76.
41 Ivanov, "Rossijskoe evrejskoe studenchestvo," 154.

If the consolidation and growing self-consciousness of Jewish student organizations during these years did provoke a greater interest in Jewish culture—the Jewish history and literature study circle at the Psychoneurological Institute, active since 1910, became considerably more so during the war[42]—the basic concern of the groups, whether of majority "universalist" or minority Zionist cast, remained civilian relief. In this, of course, the Jewish organizations were like many others, and it seems that this aid work, carried out through a variety of state and non-state agencies and bringing together large numbers of people of differing backgrounds and political persuasions, helped to bring about that active, discursive sharpening of political consciousness that was emerging, as Gatrell argues, in part as a consequence of the refugee crisis itself.[43] Experience in providing organized aid, not to mention the experience of being a refugee, would have been personally and politically formative for many young people at the time.

Masha Gal'pern, for instance—thirty-two years old in 1916, but out of school for only four years[44]—left Petrograd, as I have indicated, in January 1916 to work for the Society for the Protection of the Health of the Jews (or OZE: *Obshchestvo Zdravookhraneniia Evreev*) as their representative in Minsk, then the main city of the war's northwestern front, organizing "medical assistance to the refugees and expellees who found their way to [that] region."[45] I have already suggested that she may have been engaged in medical relief work in Bialystok following the pogrom of 1906; ten years later, a far larger national calamity brought her into direct working contact with an array of important civic organizations.

In a 1968 article, Masha, by then long since resident in Israel, recalled how her first tasks in Minsk, after protecting the society's small apartment-headquarters from confiscation by the zemstvo, involved linking together all the various groups providing aid in the city (the Red Cross, the Union of Cities, the Association of Zemstvos, the Northern Aid Center, the OZE itself) into a single organized confederation. Only after this coalition of local

---

42 Ibid., 156.
43 "The constitution of ... 'refugeedom' helped not only to undermine established notions of social status and social control, but also to give shape to an emerging public sphere in Russia, whose spokesmen challenged established political, social, and cultural practices" (Gatrell, *A Whole Empire Walking*, 4).
44 She was awarded the general medical practitioner's diploma from the Women's Medical Institute on May 2, 1912 (TsGIASPb f. 436, op. 4, d. 906, l. 5).
45 Halperin-Pruginin, "The Work of OZE," 602.

governmental, private, and "national" (Jewish, Polish, Lithuanian) interests was realized, she wrote, could the urgent and immediate problems be adequately addressed:

> The entire refugee population (about 25,000) lived in synagogues and in other public facilities. These buildings did not provide even the most basic necessities for human habitation. Hundreds of families, including children and the elderly, were living together [in a single space] with no dividers.... The crowding and lack of sanitary conditions contributed to the accumulation of trash in these spaces and outside of them.
>
> The medical, nursing and sanitary staff working with this population came from all over Russia: both from the center and the provinces. Some of the nurses were from the Caucasus and Siberia. And everyone, everyone, including the physicians, the nurses, and the sanitation staff, worked loyally and devotedly for the public cause.[46]

To be sure, Masha regarded this work not only as an immediate task of relief, but as an opportunity permanently to establish better health and sanitary conditions for Minsk's Jewish community, even if under considerably straitened circumstances—that is, as a chance to act decisively in accord with a modernizing ethic of improvement:

> It was my honor to organize the maternity and pediatric stations in the Jewish settlements generally and in Minsk especially. Since I had no ready-made equipment I had to go to local artisans, who used drawings and sketches I showed them to produce the sterilizers, pasteurizers and the other equipment we needed for our work. For the first time, the Jewish mother was given the opportunity to receive medical advice on the correct feeding and care of her children from birth to the age of two. Those who needed additional food or artificial food were supplied bottles with pasteurized milk. Our sealed bottles shone in the dark corners of our refugees' dreary abodes like icons of hygiene and cleanliness.[47]

---

46 Ibid., 603.
47 Ibid., 604–5. For a discussion of the wider relation of "refugee relief," especially medical relief, to "self-improvement and eugenics," see Peter Gatrell, "Refugees in the Russian Empire, 1914–1917: Population Displacement and Social Identity," in *Critical Companion to the Russian Revolution 1914–1921*, ed. Edward Acton et al. (Bloomington: Indiana University Press, 1997), 554–64, esp. 559.

An intriguing anecdote near the end of her brief memoir finely captures the intertwining of individualist, corporatist-cooperative, and "national" idioms within the public that formed around the refugee crisis:

> The Jewish public organizations sent young people from the center [of Russia, i.e., from Petrograd and Moscow], with many women among them. Many of them lacked experience. The seriousness of the tasks and the great responsibilities helped in their development. It was here that they found the power of initiative, the might of execution, the deep gratitude and the joy of creation.... In the midst of the worries and tension our members would burst with an outpouring of joy and cheerfulness. They would show up in their best clothes, the tables were festively set, songs were sung and we would dance the Israeli *horah* with loud stamps of the feet. Stamping alongside us were the feet of our colleagues from the different Russian associations. They were caught up in the fiery *horah* and danced enthusiastically. Did these gentiles know that this was the dance of the free Jew in his homeland?

Masha wrote this, in Hebrew, fifty years after she had left Minsk behind; she had probably been in Palestine since sometime in the 1930s,[48] and so her description of the festive gathering is inflected by her knowledge of all that had occurred in the interim, by her relationship to her new country, and by the shading, fading, and highlighting wrought by memory itself. These qualifications should not prevent us from perceiving in her words some of the subtly differing registers of public awareness that seemed to coexist during the war years: a national-ethnic self-consciousness emerging out of an active enterprise linking Jews (men and

---

[48] Vertov apparently saw her during his last trip to Bialystok in mid-July 1931 (RGALI f. 2091, op. 1, d. 71, l. 1), and Boris Kaufman wrote to Masha in Palestine shortly after he arrived with his family in the US in January 1942 (Boris Kaufman Papers, Beinecke Library, Yale University, GEN MSS 562.12.214); Boris and Masha reconnected on a more consistent basis in the 1960s. The early 1930s saw a sharp jump in the rate of Jewish emigration from Europe (especially Poland and Germany) to Palestine, due above all to the rise of both popular and state-sponsored anti-Semitism. It seems likely that Masha made her passage between 1931 and 1936, during the immigration wave known as the fifth aliyah (1929–39), which "brought close to 200,000 new immigrants to Palestine—more than all the other aliyot combined" (James L. Gelvin, *The Israel-Palestine Conflict: One Hundred Years of War*, 2nd ed. [Cambridge: Cambridge University Press, 2007], 120; see also 103). The vast majority of emigrants left before 1936, when Great Britain imposed restrictions on Jewish migration to Palestine (Ezra Mendelsohn, *The Jews of East Central Europe Between the World Wars*, 78).

women) of varying classes and backgrounds ("the dance of the free Jew in his homeland"); the no less intense consciousness of participating in equality as a respected civic organization among others ("stamping alongside us . . . the feet of our colleagues from the different Russian associations . . . caught up in the fiery *horah*"); and a more generalized assertion of collectivity within the framework of a common project ("the power of initiative . . . the joy of creation").

All of this was elicited, for at least some young educated professionals and students, by the refugee crisis, which by no means ended with the conclusion of Russia's involvement in World War I in 1917. Much of Vertov's early work in cinema, and particular his work on the Civil War agit-trains (to be discussed in chapter 4), has clear affinities to these earlier relief projects, to their accompanying politics of modernization, and to the way they brought normally separated groups of activist professionals-intellectuals and non-intellectuals together in a unified mass, at least temporarily. It hardly seems incidental that Vertov's first relatively mature effort as a filmmaker—in *Kino-Pravda* 1 (June 5, 1922), to be discussed in volume 2—begins with a direct appeal for aid in response to yet another calamity, the 1921–22 famine in the Volga region.[49] That is, crisis—real or perceived—provided some of the occasions to which Vertov's creative practice responded, particularly in the late 'teens and early 1920s, and helped to push that practice in action-oriented and utilitarian directions (although these met with countervailing impulses, as we will see). Indeed, artists themselves were calling for their fellow creators to apply their work to famine relief in 1921–22; and considering early Soviet art more generally, we might speculate whether the famous Constructivist turn at the end of 1921, in the midst of the famine, to Productivism—that is, to "real, practical work in production," thoroughly aligned with then still embryonic state projects of modernization and industrialization, and involving such major figures

---

49 Indeed, as we will see, famine donations were collected in theaters during screenings of this and other famine-related films. For a study that touches on the dialectic between the "experience of administering welfare relief to refugees" and the training of "national elites in the conduct of politics and administration," see Nick Baron and Peter Gatrell, "Population Displacement, State-Building, and Social Identity in the Lands of the Former Russian Empire, 1917–23," *Kritika: Explorations in Russian and Eurasian History* 4, no. 1 (Winter 2003): 51–100, esp. 73. Food shortages and relief were major themes in some of the *Kino-Nedelia* newsreels as well, especially numbers 3, 5 and 22 (all 1918). On early Soviet efforts to deal with refugee problem during and after the Civil War, see N. V. Lazareva, "Gosudarstvennyj apparat Sovetskoj Rossii po evakuatsii naseleniia v 1918-1923 gg.," in *Gosudarstvennyj apparat Rossii v gody Revoliutsii i Grazhdanskoj Vojny*, ed. T. G. Arkhipova (Moscow: RGGU, 1998), 171–81.

as Aleksandr Rodchenko, Varvara Stepanova, and Karl Ioganson—might have been at least in part a direct reaction to the famine's harsh lessons.[50]

BEYOND THE INSTITUTE

The deepening crisis brought about by the war led to increasing restiveness among both students and the public at large, groups that had in the main—though not universally—supported the war effort when it began in the fall of 1914.[51] Although students, like the rest of Russian society, remained understandably concerned with national defense, their own worsening living conditions, the declining enrollments at the universities, and the antidemocratic and anti-Semitic policies of their own government and army began to provoke strikes, meetings, and the formulation of demands, the latter primarily of a liberal rather than radical character.[52] To be sure, radicals had been active among students for some time—the Socialist Revolutionary Party had a cell at the institute, and the Bolshevik wing of the Russian Social Democratic Labor Party organized speeches there during the war—but far-left parties had limited impact at the universities, not least because many of their agitators (Bolsheviks above all) were more engaged with organizing soldiers at the front.[53] The January 1916 decision to annul the exemption from military service that

---

50 See the early 1922 appeal of playwright and theater historian Mikhail Zagorskij, "Golod i rabotniki iskusstv," *Vestnik Iskusstv* 1 (1922): 5. On the shift to Productivism, see Maria Gough, *The Artist as Producer: Russian Constructivism in Revolution* (Berkeley: University of California Press, 2005), 102.

51 A student call-up on October 8, 1914, was met the next day with a large prowar rally in front of the Winter Palace. Antiwar activism among students dates to October 1914 as well (Zavadskij, *Ispytanie vojnoj*, 14). See also Kassow, *Students, Professors, and the State*, 378–79.

52 Historian N. G. Zavadskij has noted that November 1914 saw speeches and demonstrations at the Psychoneurological Institute and elsewhere to demand release of political prisoners, and suggests that the anti-government and early antiwar movements were linked. Due to the draft, bad living conditions, institutional speeding up of time-to-graduation to fulfill military needs, and the harsher attitude of the regime to student politics, the number of students in institutes of higher education dropped sharply between 1913 and 1916—from 2,276 to 1,053 in Petrograd's Technological Institute, for instance (Zavadskij, *Ispytanie vojnoj*, 5, 17). See also Kassow, *Students, Professors, and the State*, 379–81.

53 Zavadskij, *Ispytanie vojnoj*, 6, 18, 31. On the radicalization of soldiers at the front, see also Allan K. Wildman, *The End of the Russian Imperial Army*, vol. 1 (Princeton, NJ: Princeton University Press, 1980), xvii–xix and *passim*. Of course, the pre-1917 years did see increasing if localized student radicalism, including involvement in active party politics: at St. Petersburg University in December 1907, for instance, Social Democratic students elected as their representatives three Bolsheviks, three Mensheviks, and two Bundists (Ivanov, *Vysshaia shkola Rossii*, 311).

students in their early years of study had previously enjoyed provoked demonstrations at the Psychoneurological Institute and other schools; by February 13–14, 1917, students at the institute were resolving to stage a two-day strike, a mere two weeks prior to the Tsar's abdication—an event met with joy by students, faculty, and the public alike—and about six months after David Kaufman's studies had been cut short by the draft.[54]

We know nothing about David's relationship to these events and situations, apart from the fact that his studies took place in an atmosphere profoundly conditioned by them. Any attempt to describe what he took away from his years at the institute will necessarily involve a combination of "hermeneutic circularity"—that is, a reading of what we know was going on at the institute from 1914–16 in light of what we know Vertov did later on (and vice versa)—and sheer guesswork; indeed, the former may just be another, more fully articulated name for the latter. Still, it is necessary to hazard that guess, and I would therefore isolate three features of David Kaufman's time at the institute that, in decreasing order of importance and increasing order of presumptiveness, left their marks on him in a relatively permanent way, including in his work as that "kinoc" he was soon (unknowingly) to become.

1. CONNECTIONS, CONNECTIONS

First and most crucially, Kaufman/Vertov would have made contacts at the institute that were to be important for him later on. The most significant such link, with Mikhail Kol'tsov, had already taken shape in Bialystok, of course, but sustaining it over the war years in Petrograd was not without consequence for future filmmaker David Kaufman. Kol'tsov (still Mojsej Fridland, at least on official papers) entered the Psychoneurological Institute in the fall of 1915, a year later than Vertov did, and remained registered there until September 1918, by which time he was already much involved in journalistic and nonfiction/newsreel work for the fledgling Soviet regime.[55] Kol'tsov was apparently kicked out of the institute (briefly) in the summer of 1916, but in spite of this and his mediocre grades, he evidently finished the basic course and was preparing, at least in principle, to go on to medical study.[56]

---

54 Zavadskij, *Ispytanie vojnoj*, 4, 29, 35. See also Kassow, *Students, Professors, and the State*, 382–83. On David Kaufman's experience in the Chuguev Military School, see chapter 3, below.
55 TsGIASPb f. 115, op. 2, d. 9788, l. 10.
56 It is not clear why the institute dismissed Kol'tsov (on June 8, 1916): he requested certification of his student status in March 1916 for presentation to the police, but this could have

Kol'tsov in Petrograd was already writing, and even at this early stage exhibited remarkable acumen and the capacity, doubtless due in part to personal charm, to establish ties to important people. (Years later, Victor Serge would acidly describe him, already posthumously, as "a man as remarkable for his talent as for his pliant docility.")[57] During his time at the Institute, Kol'tsov wrote articles for the student paper *Put' Studenchestva* (*The students' path*), and demonstrated his journalistic ambition and savvy by conducting and publishing an interview sometime in 1915–16 with then-Duma deputy Aleksandr Kerensky, the future head of the post-February Provisional Government.[58] While back in Kiev in 1916 (where his parents moved in the summer of 1915), Kol'tsov made the acquaintance of poet and early cinema pedagogue Aleksandr Voznesenskij (whose wife, the famous actress Vera Iureneva, would leave Voznesenskij for Kol'tsov, over twenty years her junior, in 1918) and the important theater and literary critic and translator Aleksandr Dejch, who became a prominent and much-respected member of the Soviet cultural intelligentsia from the 1920s onward and (after World War II) a good friend of Vertov.[59] Kol'tsov was evidently based at the Psychoneurological Institute until at least the February Revolution, after which point he began moving between Kiev and Petrograd, eventually (after October) becoming acquainted with both Commissar of Enlightenment Anatoly Lunacharsky and Commissar of Foreign Affairs Georgij Chicherin, joining the Bolshevik Party, and finding journalistic work with the papers *Izvestiia* and *Vecherniaia Zvezda* (*Evening Star*).[60] In the early days of the Soviet regime—and later on as well—possessing affiliations of this order was no small matter; as I have already indicated, it was Kol'tsov's patronage that would bring Vertov into the film profession in the first place.

---

been for any number of banal reasons. His transcripts from the institute indicate that he took exams in inorganic chemistry, physics, general biology and medical zoology, and was transferred to the medical faculty on September 27, 1916 (TsGIASpb f. 115, op. 2, d. 9788, ll. 8, 11, 13).

57 Victor Serge, *Memoirs of a Revolutionary*, trans. Peter Sedgwick and George Paizis, ed. Richard Greeman, introduction by Adam Hochschild (New York: New York Review Books, 2012), 371. Serge's great memoir was first published in French in 1951.

58 Beliaev et al., *Mikhail Kol'tsov, kakim on byl*, 78; Viktor Fradkin, "Novoe o Mikhaile Kol'tsove," *Lekhaim* 8:100; accessed June 22, 2017, www.lechaim.ru/ARHIV/100/fradkin.htm.

59 Beliaev et al., op cit., 170; Fradkin, "Novoe o Mikhaile Kol'tsove"; E. Dejch, "Nezabyvaemoe," *DVVS*, 237–44.

60 TsGIASPb f. 115, op. 2, d. 9788, ll. 15, 22, 23, 39; A. Rubashkin, *Mikhail Kol'tsov: kritiko-biograficheskij ocherk* (Leningrad: Khudozhestvennaia Literatura, 1971), 8.

Image 2: Mikhail Kol'tsov, 1920s. Source: RGALI f. 2515, op. 1, d. 125, l. 9.

Image 3: Group portrait taken sometime around 1924. Back row from left: Aleksandr Rodchenko, Vladimir Mayakovsky, Anton Lavinskij, Mikhail Kol'tsov, Lev Grinkrug, Viktor Shklovsky (seated). Front row from left: A. Levin, Vasilij Katanian, Nikolai Aseev, B. Malkin. Source: RGALI f. 28, op. 2, d. 22, l. 63.

Other connections Vertov might have made at the institute are both harder to establish and less immediately significant, but still worthy of consideration. Already as a student, Larisa Rejsner (1895–1926) attracted the attention of painters (Vasilij Shukhaev crafted a memorable portrait), and poets (Sergei Kremkov, Nikolai Gumilev, Osip Mandelstam), and was acquainted with a whole range of writers and academics in Petrograd. Energetic, brilliant, argumentative, and magnetically attractive, Rejsner began her publishing career during her years at the institute with a pamphlet on *Shakespeare's Female Types* (1913) and the short-lived journal *Rudin* (1915–16), coproduced with her father Mikhail, in which Mandelstam, among others, published some early work. Shortly afterwards (1917) she began writing—about Rilke and children's theater, among other topics—for Maksim Gorky's journals *Novaia Zhizn'* (*New Life*) and *Letopis'* (*Chronicle*), where her associates would have included Kol'tsov, Isaak Babel', Mayakovsky, Viktor Shklovsky, and Lunacharsky.

Image 4: Larisa Rejsner, probably in Afghanistan. Source: RGALI f. 2563, op. 1, d. 151, l. 1.

In 1918, she both joined the Bolshevik Party and married the Bolshevik journalist and activist Fyodor Raskol'nikov (1892–1939), soon to become Trotsky's deputy in charge of the navy.[61] Raskol'nikov later participated in the famous Civil War battle for Tsaritsyn in 1918—the subject of Vertov's first (now lost) "experimental" film, *The Battle of Tsaritsyn*—on which Rejsner reported as an *Izvestiia* correspondent in her "Letters from the Front." Now a celebrated

---

61 Raskol'nikov and Rejsner can be seen together onboard a boat on the Volga in *Kino-Nedelia* 26 (December 3, 1918; shot by Eduard Tisse [RGALI f. 2091, op. 2, d. 5, l. 5]). The same shot was reused in *Kino-Nedelia* 31 (January 17, 1919) to announce that the British Royal Navy had taken Raskol'nikov prisoner; he was released on May 27.

correspondent, she traveled with Raskol'nikov in 1921 to Afghanistan after he took on diplomatic responsibilities for the Soviet government, still later (after she and Raskol'nikov drifted apart in 1923–24) traveling to Germany, where she became acquainted with Karl Radek, who was there helping to organize German communists. The books in which Rejsner recounted her travels and war experiences were among the most celebrated works of early Soviet journalistic literature, and her reputation took on a legendary glow after her premature death from typhus in 1926. Rejsner, whether she knew David Kaufman or not, was near the epicenter of that nimbus of high-level connections at whose perimeters Kaufman/Vertov, mainly through the intercession of Kol'tsov (who wrote an obituary for Larisa, his acquaintance and journalistic rival), would have hovered; thus, she can be thought of as belonging to his circle of connections, real or potential.[62]

Three other fellow students at the institute—Abram Room (1894–1976), Georgij Nikolaevich Tasin (Rozov) (1895–1956) and Grigorij Boltianskij (1885–1953)—were to become, like David Kaufman, significant figures in the history of Soviet cinema. Room apparently studied there between 1914 and around 1917, breaking off his studies briefly during the world war to assist Jewish refugees in his native Vilnius, later going on to further medical study in Saratov. After 1917, he served in the Red Army as a doctor on the Kazan' front, and worked extensively in revolutionary-experimental theater in Saratov before moving to Moscow and to filmmaking in 1924.[63] As a fiction filmmaker—and thus an artistic opponent, from Vertov's point of view, in the 1920s—Room would not have figured as a collaborator on any of Vertov's projects, to be sure. Yet the two were in significant institutional proximity in Leningrad in 1930, when Room was working on *The Plan of Great Works*—the earliest, and now lost Soviet sound film—and Vertov was fashioning the soundtrack for *Enthusiasm: Symphony of the Donbass*. More interestingly, the affinities between the "documentary" overture to Room's great *Bed and Sofa* (1927) and the "morning" sequence near the beginning of Vertov's *Man with a Movie Camera* (1929) are too striking to be ignored, Vertov's probable disdain

---

62 See Przhiborovskaia, *Larisa Rejsner*, esp. 92–143, 196–266, 415–32; and Larisa Rejsner, *Izbrannoe* (Moscow: Khudozhestvennaia Literatura, 1980).
63 See student records from the Psychoneurological Institute for Abram Mordkhelevich Rom [Room], TsGIASpb f. 115, op. 2, d. 366; Viktor Shklovsky [Shklovskij], *Room: zhizn' i rabota* (Moscow: Tea-Kino-Pechat', 1929), 3–6; I. Grashchenkova, *Abram Room* (Moscow: Iskusstvo, 1977), 231–44.

for Room's film notwithstanding; and we will reflect upon the relations between those films when we examine Vertov's masterpiece in volume 2.

Of the three figures mentioned here, Tasin is by far the least known. Born in the Mogilev guberniia, Tasin completed his studies at the institute in 1917, specializing in law. Like Kol'tsov, he began work in journalism and (later) photo and cinema journalism in Kiev in 1918, and became a major figure in the development of Ukrainian cinema in the early Soviet period, working in studios in Yalta, Khar'kov, and especially Odessa (where he made his best-known film, 1929's *The Night Cabman* [*Nochnoj Izvozchik*]). After World War II, Tasin worked (like Vertov) in newsreel, directing the series *Soviet Ukraine* (*Rad'ianska Ukraina*) and a number of documentary features. Vertov was based in Ukraine between 1927 and 1931, as we will see, and worked in Odessa and Khar'kov on a number of occasions; it seems likely that he would have crossed paths with Tasin at some point during those years, and perhaps later as well.[64]

It is not clear whether David Kaufman actually met Tasin, Room, or Grigorij Boltianskij at the institute; in the case of Boltianskij, however, we know that history and common interests would bring his trajectory into alignment with that of Kaufman soon enough. Boltianskij (1885–1953) is a crucial, understudied figure in the history of the development of Soviet nonfiction film, and himself one of the most important historians of Russo-Soviet film and photography. Born Iosif Berkov Boltianskij in 1885 in the Ukrainian village of Slavianka (located near the town of Pavlograd and the city of Ekaterinoslav [now Dnepropetrovsk] southeast of Kiev on the Dnepr)[65] into a Jewish family, Boltianskij was involved in education, socialist politics, and cinema from an early age. His mother was a schoolteacher, and Boltianskij himself was giving lessons in local villages to make extra money for the family from the age of sixteen.[66] Similar in background in many ways to Vertov, that he was eleven years older gave him time to become far more politicized prior to 1917.

---

64   See G. S. Kornienko, *Ukraine'ske radians'ke kinomistetsvo 1917–1929* (Kiev: Vidavnitstvo Akademii Nauk Ukrains'koi RSR, 1959), 122–26; Grashchenkova, *Abram Room*, 232.

65   TsGIASpb f. 115, op. 2, d. 965, l. 8. There is some doubt about both the name and the birth date, which I have derived from his student file from the Psychoneurological Institute, his own 1952 resume, and other biographical sources. His application to the institute indicates that he was born on February 7, 1889, but a police report from September 20, 1913, gives his real name as Girsh Abramov-Moiseev Boltianskij and his age as twenty-eight, putting his birth year back to 1885 (RGALI f. 2057, op. 1, d. 223, l. 1); similarly, the Central Documentary Studio in Moscow marked Boltianskij's sixtieth birthday in 1945, again making 1885 the true year of his birth (RGALI f. 2639, op. 1, d. 63, l. 6). He gives February 24, 1885 (NS), as his birth date in his 1952 account.

66   RGALI f. 2639, op. 1, d. 63, l. 17.

Image 5: Grigorij Boltianskij, ca. 1920. Source: RGALI f. 2057, op. 2, d. 26, l. IIa.

Even before entering the fifth year of private high school in Pavlograd in 1907, he was the organizer of a social-democratic discussion circle (*kruzhok*) that included both factory and office workers. Indeed, he was exiled for about three years (in 1905–6 and again perhaps from 1908–9) from the Ekaterinoslav province for his revolutionary activities.[67]

He continued his involvement in Russian Social Democratic Labor Party circles, almost certainly on its Menshevik wing, while working as a teacher in Pavlograd in Ukraine from 1911 until 1914,[68] when he successfully applied for

---

67 See the testimony of Boltianskij's old comrade A. Shved from March 25, 1930, on the occasion of one of Boltianskij's several unsuccessful attempts to join the Communist Party, in RGALI f. 2639, op. 1, d. 63, l. 2. Boltianskij was never admitted into the Bolshevik Party, I suspect, because of his known Menshevik background. For the 1913 police report on Boltianskij, see RGALI f. 2057, op. 1, d. 223, ll. 1–1ob; it indicates that Boltianskij completed eight years at the high school, and wrote for the radical papers *Krasnaia Zaria* and *Utro*. For his own autobiography, see RGALI f. 2639, op. 1, d. 63, l. 17. Part of his high school study may have taken place in Ekaterinograd (TsGIASPb f. 115, op. 2, d. 965, l. 15), where it seems he may have been involved in socialist activism as well.

68 RGALI f. 2639, op. 1, d. 63, l. 2; and f. 2057, op. 1, d. 223, l. 1ob. For more on the party's activities in Ukraine, see Ralph Carter Elwood, *Russian Social Democracy in the Underground: A Study of the RSDRP in the Ukraine, 1907–1914* (Assen: Van Gorcum, 1974).

admission to the Psychoneurological Institute in Petrograd, no doubt at least in part to avoid the draft. He studied at the institute through the fall of 1916—an older classmate of Kaufman and Kol'tsov—all the while continuing his underground political activities and sending information about the Zimmerwald Conference and other events of concern to socialists back to comrades in Ukraine.[69]

While all this was going on, Boltianskij was also actively involved in film in a variety of ways. In 1910, he began to work on the distribution and exhibition of educational cinema under the auspices of the zemstvo of the Pavlograd district.[70] This was by no means Boltianskij's personal project: as we will soon see, there was considerable interest in and use of scientific film in Russia before 1917, and the zemstvo of the Ekaterinoslav province was one of those councils particularly interested in promoting educational films in schools.[71]

At the same time, Boltianskij occupied himself writing both scripts and articles about cinema.[72] Always interested in the technology of film, Boltianskij in 1910 published a piece about a scientific lecture given by one S. Lifshits on "Photographing Sound," which discussed a method of using light rays to inscribe and then reproduce sound. Following a very technical account of the lecture, complete with diagrams, Boltianskij immediately and imaginatively applied the new ideas to cinema, managing both to show his fascination with cinema as a tool for assuring "realistic" representation (in a well-nigh Bazinian spirit) and to offer a foretaste of one of Vertov's best known slogans:

> If, to what has already been said about the new device, we add the great perspectives offered by simultaneously photographing movement and sound, and at the same time reproducing them via cinema and the photophone,[73] in order to achieve a complete illusion . . . this will then be the

---

69 TsGIASPb f. 115, op. 2, d. 965, l. 38; RGALI f. 2639, op. 1, d. 63, l. 2. Boltianskij's efforts to evade the draft were apparently aided by petitions from his cousin Aron Boltianskij, a decorated soldier who had received the Order of St. George (fourth level) (TsGIASPb f. 115, op. 2, d. 965, l. 37). As late as August 1917, Boltianskij seems to have been considering further medical study, probably in Ekaterinoslav, no doubt partially due to uncertainty about how long the war would continue (TsGIASPb f. 115, op. 2, d. 965, l. 38).

70 RGALI f. 2639, op. 1, d. 63, l. 17.

71 See S. Ginzburg's still-remarkable chapter on pre-Revolutionary educational film in Russia in his *Kinematografiia dorevoliutsionnoj Rossii* (Moscow: Iskusstvo, 1963), 67–98, esp. 83; and Lev Roshal', *Nachalo vsekh nachal: fakt na ekrane i kinomysl' "Serebrianogo Veka"* (Moscow: Materik, 2002), 43–55, 62–79; and below in the present chapter.

72 RGALI f. 2639, op. 1, d. 63, l. 17. I have not seen any of the scripts; apparently, they were never produced.

73 Evidently the name of the device described by Lifshits. Boltianskij's idea about simultaneous reproduction/transmission seems to point to television as well.

true triumph of photography in its reproduction of life as it is [*v vosproiz-vedenij zhizni, kak ona est'*].[74]

Boltianskij also contributed more general commentary on the educational function of cinema to journals, from a perspective typical of the socially conscious intelligentsia of the time. In the pages of the important film journal *Sine-Fono*, he wrote that those who denounced cinema in the name of preserving the theater—the theater vs. cinema debate was raging in Russia just as it was elsewhere[75]—would do better if they tried to make the theater a more open and democratic institution. Yet he acknowledged that radical criticisms of cinema, and of its potentially negative effect upon the theater and theater audiences, were justified, inasmuch as

> ... in relation to society, cinema is, in its present form, harmful, amoral and reactionary.... By virtue of its technical nature, cinema ... must strive to give the popular masses cultured and, in the social sense, healthy nourishment.
>
> Many note that among the people there is an attraction to authentic art—to the theatre, and not to its cinema-surrogate—and observe that attraction in the establishment of peasant and worker's theaters, and in the popular interest in music and declamation.
>
> And this is so. But ... [authentic] theatrical art is seen neither by the deprived masses, nor even by the middle class bourgeois public in all the tens of thousands of populated areas in the provinces....
>
> It's time for democratic thought to free itself from the bonds of tradition. A love for theater should not prevent us from seeing the enormous—but, as yet, potential—educational role that cinema is destined to play, one that goes well beyond the role to be played by theater.[76]

---

74 RGALI f. 2057, op. 1, d. 3, ll. 1–3ob. The article was published as "Fotografiia zvuka: po dokladu S. Ia. Lifshitsa v obshchem sobranie Russkogo Fotograficheskogo Obshchestva v Moskve 25 fevralia 1910 g.," in *Vestnik Fotografii* 4 (April 1910): 97. Sound cinema was an important topic in film journals during the 1910s in Russia as elsewhere: see, for instance, "Govoriashchiia kinematograficheskie lenty," *Vestnik Znaniia* 3 (March 1915): 204.

75 For a summary of the Russian discussions, see Roshal', *Nachalo vsekh nachal*, 99–109. For a brief account of German debates, see Helmut H. Diederichs's afterword to Béla Balázs, *Der sichtbare Mensch oder die Kultur des Films* (Frankfurt am Main: Suhrkamp, 2001 [originally published in 1924]), esp. 131–36.

76 RGALI f. 2057, op. 1, d. 3, l. 4. The article, entitled "Otkliki," was apparently in *Sine-Fono* 27; Boltianskij's archive does not indicate a precise date or issue number, but it was probably published sometime between 1911 and 1914.

Preoccupations typical of the formative years of Soviet cinema—an interest in advanced technology; a belief that working people thirsted after "culture," however defined; worries about the quality and "healthfulness" of that culture; an awareness of cinema's potential ubiquity and educational impact, transcending its attractions as "theater"—were thus directly of concern to Boltianskij well before 1917.

His more radical opinions on film, expressed in the pages of the left-wing press from 1913, offer explicit class-based analysis of the reasons behind the "harmfulness" of much cinema, and formulate proposals for alternatives, as here in "Cinema and the Proletariat":

> Thousands of workers dedicate an hour of their leisure time to the cinema, in order to satisfy their spiritual thirst for knowledge and for aesthetic pleasure.[77] The low cost and the convenience—that is, the possibility of attending a screening pretty much anytime—have essentially made the cinema into a democratic theatre.[78]
>
> But just as the boulevard, penny and other forms of the bourgeois press have poisoned and continue to poison the consciousness of workers, so the bourgeois cinema poisons it, falsifying life as it does.
>
> Cinema . . . depicts capitalists and the power of property holders as noble and wonderful, and workers as barbarians.
>
> Yet there are not a few films where the conflicts between workers and capitalists are directly represented. Here . . . the undisguised desire to inject "culture" into the working masses comes forward in all its nakedness through the representation of a strike breaker as a hero, and a striking worker as the devil incarnate.[79]

---

77 Boltianskij was no doubt right about this, although little research has been done on worker-peasant cinema attendance in the pre-Revolutionary years. For an exception, see V. S. Listov's discussion of a fascinating survey done in 1913 of workers in Kiev that showed that, once basic needs of food, shelter and clothing had been met, "theatre, spectacle, pleasure gardens, and cinema" occupied fifth place in an average proletarian budget, after (in this order) "tobacco and alcohol," "bodily hygiene," "money sent away [back to home villages, presumably]," and "the education of children," but before "medical treatment" and "cultural-educational needs" (*Rossiia, revoliutsiia, kinematograf: k 100-letiiu mirovogo kino* [Moscow: Materik, 1995], 14–16).

78 For an account of Louis Delluc's comparable celebration of cinema as a popular art in France in the post–World War I years, see *French Film Theory and Criticism*, Volume I: 1907–1929, ed. and introduction Richard Abel (Princeton, NJ: Princeton University Press, 1988), 101. Delluc's ideas were well known among film aficionados in early Soviet Russia, as we will see in volume 2.

79 It sounds like Boltianskij is writing about a specific film, but I have not determined its identity. Boltianskij acknowledges in the article that few films of this type are shown in Russia, due to the censorship.

"The consciousness of workers is poisoned by the hypocritical bourgeois morality of all these stupid and vulgar cinematic dramas," complains Boltianskij, and he insists that the only way workers can resist is with their own proletarian cinema practice. It will be difficult to mount such a challenge in Russia, he admits, and suggests that workers in Western Europe (Germany and Belgium especially), who are already involved in organizing theaters, sporting societies and other groups for workers, will have to take on this project.[80] Meanwhile, "for [politically] conscious Russian workers,"

> ... the issue is already awaiting them. The beginning of a solution is offered by the fact that culturally enlightened societies, taking into account the enormous educational role of cinema—[in the form of] travelogues, non-fiction [*khronika*], historical films accompanied by explanatory lectures...; [films on] geography, ethnography, medicine, and scientific film in general—will find ways to create at least a rational,[81] educational cinema, thereby deflecting workers from the bourgeois boulevard cinema, which clouds the class consciousness of workers.[82]

Already, we find not only that insistence on the need for a specifically "proletarian" cinema that became familiar in the 1920s, but a suggestion, clearly presaging and predating Vertov,[83] that it is precisely nonfiction film, as promoted by the zemstvos and philanthropic societies, that will best serve to undo the stupefying effect of "vulgar cinematic drama" upon proletarian subjectivity. Scientific film is evidently affiliated with the universal—with truth, with

---

80 As we have seen, workers' organizations in Russia during this period and earlier also organized cultural events of their own; however, Boltianskij seems to be intimating, perhaps rightly, that the greater intensity of state hostility to the workers' movement in Russia would preclude any thought of creating a proletarian cinema network there.

81 The phrase "rational cinema" [*razumnyj kinematograf*] was a common designation for "scientific-educational cinema" in the pre-Revolutionary years; see Ginzburg, *Kinematografiia dorevoliutsionnoj Rossii*, 84–95; and my discussion later in this chapter.

82 RGALI f. 2057, op. 1, d. 3, ll. 5–6. The article "Kinematograf i Proletariat" was first published under the pseudonym "Gam-Beta" in the Menshevik *Novaia Rabochaia Gazeta* [St. Petersburg] 91 (26/XI: 1913): 2.

83 Vertov acknowledged as much in a talk he gave on March 3, 1945, at a celebration in honor of Boltianskij's sixtieth birthday and thirty-five years of work in cinema: "[Boltianskij] divined before others did the significance of documentary cinema, *the significance of non-fiction/newsreel film* [*khronika*] *as a new form, previously unknown, of the history of humankind*, of history on film, history on the screen, leaving behind events for future generations in a living and exciting form" (RGALI f. 2639, op. 1, d. 63, ll. 7–14, here l. 8; emphasis in the original. See also *SV*, 349).

knowledge, and the undoing of convention, rather than with the class-bound tropes and mystifications of cinematic narratives—and as such belongs to the laboring multitudes as a symbolic authority in a way that fictions, largely inherited from the past, cannot.

Boltianskij, though he would soon cease to be a hardline opponent of fiction film, was serious about creating an alternative proletarian cinema, and in 1914 seems to have attempted to organize "the first international factory for newsreel about the life of workers" in Belgium.[84] But his true career as a filmmaker, and as a "revolutionary" filmmaker, began only after the February Revolution. His connection with the post-February Provisional Government, on which I will elaborate in chapter 3, seems to have been forged by virtue of the fact that he was a representative in the Petrograd Soviet of Workers' and Soldiers' Deputies, and was able to find administrative work in the Skobelev Committee, the sole state-run film enterprise in Russia and the kernel (as will be discussed in the next chapter) of what would later become Soviet newsreel/nonfiction filmmaking. Boltianskij headed up the Committee's new "Social Newsreel/Nonfiction [*khronika*]" section from the end of March 1917, and was one of those who shaped nonfiction filmmaking during this crucial period. Many of the cameramen with whom Boltianskij worked—such as A. Vinkler (from the Gaumont studio), Aleksandr Levitskij, Petr Novitskij and others—would end up working with Vertov on *Kino-Nedelia*, the first Soviet newsreel series, a year later.[85] Boltianskij, who was already celebrated as one of the grand old men of Soviet cinema by 1923, will appear again and again in these pages in various guises—not least as a frequent and vigorous critic and supporter of Vertov—and should be counted, along with Kol'tsov (who really did know anyone who was anyone), and far more demonstrably than either Room, Tasin, or Rejsner, as one of the most significant stars in the constellation linking "David Kaufman" to "Dziga Vertov."[86]

---

84 As Vertov indicated in the same 1945 tribute lecture ("O tvorcheskoi deiatel'nosti G. M. Boltianskogo": RGALI f. 2639, op. 1, d. 63, l. 7; *SV*, 348. I write "seems to have attempted" only because I have found no other affirmation that Boltianskij was involved in this remarkable project. He evidently did know French, and published translations from that language (RGALI f. 2639, op. 1, d. 63, l. 14).

85 Richard Taylor, *The Politics of the Soviet Cinema 1917–1929* (Cambridge: Cambridge University Press, 1979), 21–22; Ginzburg, *Kinematografiia dorevoliutsionnoj Rossii*, 338–47; V. M. Magidov, *Kinofotofonodokumenty v kontekste istoricheskogo znaniia* (Moscow: RGGU, 2005), 120; RGALI f. 2091, op. 2, d. 5, l. 7; d. 6, l. 3.

86 See the tribute to Boltianskij on the occasion of his tenth year in cinema, and fifth in Soviet cinema, by H. I. K., "G. M. Boltianskij: desiatiletie kino-deiatel'nosti," *Zrelishcha* 46

2. A RATIONAL CINEMA

In contrast to the left-wing cinephile Boltianskij, it might seem that David Kaufman had little relationship to or interest in cinema prior to the spring of 1918. There is some evidence to suggest, however, that his earliest work in film production might have taken place at the Psychoneurological Institute as well, under the supervision of important scientists working there at the time. The hints are few, but worth investigating all the same.

In an interview conducted by film scholar Donald Crafton in January 1978, Vertov's youngest brother, Boris Kaufman, gave an account of the origins of his elder sibling's work in cinema that contains an astonishing mention of Bekhterev's Institute:

> My earliest memory of my brother Dziga Vertov and myself was while we were still in Russia [in Petrograd] and he was just starting to become fascinated with cinematography. He took me twice to the Institute . . . I forget the name of it. We had some screening there and he showed me what could be done by this miraculous means. I still remember the time-lapse photography with plants growing out of the soil into full growth, and especially flowers opening before your eyes, in time-lapse photography. That is how early I was already aware of his early camera work.[87]

The period referred to here must be ca. 1915–16, when David/Dziga was around nineteen years of age and Boris was twelve or so and living with his refugee parents in Petrograd. The last sentence, which implies that this time-lapse photography was the product of Vertov's *own* "early camera work," is at the very least a tantalizing suggestion. What we can say with certainty is that, at this time, several major figures at the Psychoneurological Institute were writing about scientific-documentary cinema, and that at least one of them was involved in making scientific films.[88]

This was not in itself surprising, for as we have already indicated apropos of Boltianskij's early involvement in film, the development of educational-scientific cinema was of considerable concern to many writers and pedagogues in the

---

(1923): 9. The article describes Boltianskij as among the first to advocate a "workers' cinema."

87 Donald Crafton, "Boris Kaufman: Shooting Vigo's Films," in Boris Kaufman Papers, Beinecke Library, Yale University, GEN MSS 562.16.334.

88 None, to my knowledge, have survived.

prerevolutionary years. Film journals like *Sine-Fono* carried articles extolling the educational and scientific potential of film from their earliest issues (starting ca. 1907), with some writers already pitting the seriousness and utility of popular scientific cinema against the "mindless diversion" of fiction film, even arguing occasionally, as Vertov later would, for the need to give more proportional representation in commercial theaters to "scientific footage" and "footage from nature" (as against "comic films" and "dramas").[89] A large number of the articles, however, focused on school and university use of film, and many were responses to resolutions taken at teachers' congresses.[90] Other commentary of a more scientific (if still "popular") character speculated, as in other countries, about the capacity of film to generate new knowledge. An article by V. Verner in the Riga journal *Kino* from 1915 discussed the application of cinema to physical science in a proto-Vertovian spirit:

> By making the filmstrip move at this or that speed, forward or backward, it is possible to study all phases of movement with complete thoroughness... Theoretical mechanics received, in the cinema, a remarkable instrument for the analysis of movement, inasmuch as, in the words of the famous physicist Ernst Mach, "it gives us the capacity to change the magnitude and direction of movement at will."[91]

Still other authors reflected on the insights film might offer into the life of microorganisms and into the invisible stages comprising natural processes.[92] Even at this relatively early point, that is, the central epistemological insight generated by what we might call cinematic *montage* in the Muybridge-Marey-Vertov tradition—that is, that observable phenomena can be broken down into units

---

89 Roshal', *Nachalo vsekh nachal*, citing (on 51) articles by "Diadia Misha," "Sinematograf kak sredstvo vospitaniia," *Sine-Fono* 14 (1 June 1908): 4; and (on 65–66) by A. Shirman, "Kinematograf kak nauchno-obrazovatel'noe sredstvo," *Vestnik Kinematografii* 10/90 (1914): 12. See also 45, 66.
90 Roshal', *Nachalo vsekh nachal*, 63.
91 V. Verner, "Kinematograf i ego primenenie," *Kino* 2 (1915): n/p [3].
92 Roshal', *Nachalo vsekh nachal*, 72–73. The Pathé film *Makhaon*, depicting the emergence of a butterfly from the larva, made a strong impression in 1911. See also, among many other related writings, Zhorzh Vitu [Georges Vitoux], "Usovershenstvovannyj kinematograf" [on high-speed filming]," *Vestnik Znaniia* 10 (October 1910): 1056–60; "Kinematografirovanie podvodnykh glubin," *Vestnik Znaniia* 3 (March 1915): 127–29; and Evgenij Maurin's important book *Kinematograf v prakticheskoj zhizni* (Petrograd: N. Kuznetsov, 1916), esp. 285–86, 291–94. By no means were Russians the only ones thinking about scientific cinema in these years, of course: see, for example, Hugo Munsterberg, *The Photoplay: A Psychological Study* (New York: D. Appleton and Company, 1916), 21–28.

(stages, phases, particles) that might then be subjected to rearrangement and thereby made the object of precise intellectual inquiry—was already part of incipient film theory's conceptual arsenal.

But educational-scientific film was also a practical matter in Russia during these years, not only a theoretical one. As in other countries, traveling lecturers and organizers of public readings, whether local or from abroad—polar explorer Fridtjof Nansen enriched his Petersburg lectures on his travels with moving images in 1913—used films on a regular basis in Russia, both inside and outside the twin metropolises. One source indicates that hundreds of film-accompanied lectures (mainly at factories) took place in the Ekaterinburg region in 1910 alone.[93] Teachers' organizations discussed using films in classrooms as early as 1902—though only in 1913–14 did the use of film in primary and secondary schools begin to spread to the provinces—and philanthropic organizations (known as "people's universities") managed to establish "scientific cinemas" in Odessa (1908), Samara (1910), Nizhnii Novgorod (ca. 1912), and other centers, attended mainly by students.[94] In Moscow and St. Petersburg, some educational institutions like modern schools, gymnasiums, military academies and universities had scientific films and even projectors at their disposal; commercial cinemas were rented in smaller cities (like Riga, Tartu, Orel, and Kharkov) to present film-accompanied educational lectures to students.[95] In one of the most ambitious (and apparently never-realized) proposals, the Tsarist government apparently planned to set up mobile cinemas, based in trains decked out as full-scale agricultural institutes, to show educational films about agriculture to the peasantry—presaging in a more pacific key the agit-trains of the Civil War period to come.[96]

---

[93] Roshal', *Nachalo vsekh nachal*, 45–46; 50. For a pioneering discussion of the use of film and other visual aids in illustrated lectures in the United States, see Charles Musser, *The Emergence of Cinema: The American Screen to 1907* (New York: Charles Scribner's Sons, 1990), 38–42, 185–87, 221–23, 368–69.

[94] Ginzburg, *Kinematografiia dorevoliutsionnoj Rossii*, 71, 73–74; "Kinematograf i shkola," *Vestnik Kinematografii* 92/12 (June 21, 1914): 26; "Kinematograf i shkola," *Vestnik Kinematografii* 89/9 (May 7, 1914): 36; "Kinematograf i shkola," *Vestnik Kinematografii* 91/11 (June 7, 1914): 27; "Shkol'nyia zadachi i kinematograf" and "Razumnyj kinematograf," *Vestnik Kinematografii* 113/13–14 (July 1, 1915): 26–30. Small-scale efforts were made by individual enthusiasts to bring educational cinema to villages as well (Ginzburg, 81).

[95] Ginzburg, *Kinematografiia dorevoliutsionnoj Rossii*, 78. Practical applications of cinema to medicine were also frequently discussed in film journals; for one instance, see "Kinematograf na sluzhbe khirurgii," *Vestnik Kinematografii* 91/11 (June 7, 1914): 26.

[96] Roshal', *Nachalo vsekh nachal*, 54–55. Evidently, the Moscow Society for the Struggle against Alcoholism prepared a steamboat dedicated to itinerant propagandizing against

Doubtless, the efforts of film entrepreneurs were critical to the spread of educational-scientific cinema, or what in later Soviet parlance would be called "popular scientific" film, in the immediate pre-Revolutionary years. In 1912, Pathé began to sell its new "Coq" (later "Coq d'Or") 9.5mm projectors in Russia, along with acetate films made especially for this narrow gauge. A good proportion of the nonfiction films distributed in Russia for the "Coq" were educational films devoted to physics, zoology, botany, and especially various branches of agricultural science; provincial zemstvos and various philanthropic societies were among the main clients.[97] Yet commercial venues successfully exhibited science films as well. Pathé's series of "ultramicroscopic" films—offering startling views of microbes and blood cells—drew the praise of the Russian cinema press, as did Gaumont's science-and-hygiene film *The Plague* (1911).[98]

Nonetheless, the majority of commercial-theater films belonging to the rubric "rational cinema" (*razumnyj kinematograf*)—a peculiar locution of the period, perhaps a calque from another language—were geographic and ethnographic in focus. Most of these "scenic" (*vidovaia*) films were devoted to Europe, Asia, and Africa, and were purchased mainly from foreign firms like Pathé, Gaumont, Bioscope, and Edison, although domestic producers like Khanzhonkov and Drankov also made and collected them.[99] Short documentary subjects about various (mainly exotic) places—*Hunting Elephants, Catching Snails in France, From the Life of the Arabs* (all 1911)—were widely advertised and included in regular commercial cinema programs. Some of the Russian-made nonfiction short subjects, like the film made of Georgij Sedov's 1912 polar expedition and the wide-ranging travel footage shot by cameraman V. N. Bremer aboard the ship *Kolyma*, anticipated the popular Soviet "documentary-adventure" film of the 1920s and (especially) 1930s, as we will see.[100]

Pioneering producer Aleksandr Khanzhonkov took an additional step and established in 1911 a "scientific division" in his studio that made educational films until 1916. Khanzhonkov recruited important scientists as consultants along with skilled filmmakers, including animation pioneer Ladislas Starevich. The Khanzhonkov production of *Tuberculosis* (1914), a "frightful spectacle"

---

alcoholism, in part with the help of film, in 1914—"Bor'ba s p'ianstvom" (in section "Po Rossii"); *Vestnik Kinematografii* 92/12 (June 21, 1914): 32; "Parokhod-muzej," *Vestnik Kinematografii* 91/11 (June 7, 1914): 33. On the agit-trains, see chapter 4, below.
97 Ginzburg, *Kinematografiia dorevoliutsionnoj Rossii*, 87–88.
98 Roshal', *Nachalo vsekh nachal*, 57.
99 On the collections of geographical films, see Roshal', *Nachalo vsekh nachal*, 49–50.
100 Ginzburg, *Kinematografiia dorevoliutsionnoj Rossii*, 84–85, 89; Roshal', *Nachalo vsekh nachal*, 49, 52.

according to one account, was successfully exhibited at Moscow's Polytechnical Museum on April 17, 1914.[101] Another of the Khanzhonkov films, *Drunkenness and Its Consequences* (1913), starred Ivan Mozzhukhin and included a Starevich animation in which a tiny devil crawled out of a half-empty bottle of vodka—presaging a famous shot in *Man with a Movie Camera* by some fifteen years!—and then proceeded to tease and torment the drunkard (played by Mozzhukhin).[102]

Surely, this kind of fictionalizing and/or lyricizing of "science" was also enabled by the audience's familiarity with popular scientific writing, which often leavened otherwise dry and forbidding material with humor or sublime grandeur. I am thinking above all of the writing of the immensely popular Camille Flammarion (1842–1925), the Carl Sagan of his day, whose works were widely read all across Russia (including, to be sure, in Abel Kaufman's reading room).[103] Here is Flammarion rhapsodizing about the power of optical instruments, in a distinctly proto-Vertovian key:

> The sky's expanse is limitless, and you must not imagine that those 7000 stars that delight our vision and decorate the sky, and without which our nights would be sad and empty, contain all of the universe. They are but the threshold to the temple. There, where our vision stops, an eye more powerful, more all-encompassing, becoming greater with every century, directs its curious gaze into the infinite and reveals the light of numberless suns to the curiosity of scientists. This eye is the lens of optical instruments. With binoculars we can see stars of the seventh magnitude; a small telescope can reach the eighth. Stronger instruments bring us the ninth or even the tenth magnitude. All is expanded, the sky transmogrifies before the eyes of the astronomer.... Humans will continue to develop, the power of optics will increase, and one after another, stars of the 11th or 12th magnitude, four million in number, will be exposed to our eyes....[104]

---

101 Roshal', *Nachalo vsekh nachal*, 57; N. Prokof'ev, "V bor'be s tuberkulezom," *Vestnik Kinematografii* 89/9 (May 7, 1914): 14.

102 Ginzburg, *Kinematografiia dorevoliutsionnoj Rossii*, 96. See the description of the film (still shown in the late 1920s, evidently) in L. M. Sukharebskij, *Obzor sanprosvetitel'nykh kinofil'm za 10 let proletarskoj revoliutsii (1917–1927)* (Moscow: Moszdravotdel, 1928), 24–25; and Roshal', *Nachalo vsekh nachal*, 58. *Drunkenness and Its Consequences* was released for public exhibition only after a scene involving a rabbit and another displaying the beating heart of a live dog were excised ("Spisok kinematograficheskikh kartin, kotorye dopushcheny k publichnomu demonstrirovaniiu," *Vestnik Kinematografii* 87/7 [April 1, 1914]: 51).

103 See all extant catalogs (cited in chapter 1).

104 Kamill' Flammarion, *Populiarnye lektsii po astronomii*, trans. and ed. V. V. Bitner (St. Petersburg: Vestnik Znaniia, 1905), 24. In addition to his serious astronomical work

And to be sure, fantastical mixing, genre-bending and/or bricolage—whether of (animated) comedy with science film and medical propaganda, or of exposition with lyric description—was perceptible in films of a very straightforwardly "scientific" cast, as evidenced by this review of the widely screened *Wonders of the Plant World* (Timen and Reingadt, 1911):

> Not one detail slipped away from the vigilant and loving gaze of the cinema. Yes, loving! Hitherto, a certain unnecessary precision and dryness often harmed cinema.... But now the cinema takes on a new, unexpected role. It becomes a lyric poet. It would have been difficult to imagine such tenderness in the cinema. It would be most accurate to characterize this film as a poem without words.[105]

Thus, that union of science, fantasy, whimsy, and lyricism that, as we shall see, sometimes characterized Vertov's films and writing from 1922 onward, can be traced back in part to certain prerevolutionary educational films and pop-scientific discourses, some of which Vertov undoubtedly encountered, and which continued on into the Soviet period.[106]

A "scientific cinema," equipped with mobile projectors and about 150 films, appeared in Petrograd in 1915, but the city's educational institutions, including the Psychoneurological Institute, had been incorporating cinema into teaching for some time before that.[107] An article in the Petrograd film journal *Kinematograf* from early 1915 indicates that Professor Vladimir A. Vagner of the institute had "resolved to use cinema for scientific purposes," and to that end was having many zoological and natural-science samples filmed.[108] Vagner, the vice president of the Psychoneurological Institute and head of the Petrograd Imperial Commercial Training School, was one of the founders of "comparative psychology" and "animal psychology": what we would call today the study of animal behavior, though with a strong physiological inflection. He was also a major scientific popularizer who produced educational books for children on the scientific observation of nature well

---

and popular science writing, Flammarion wrote important pieces of science fiction. For similar passages in Flammarion, see his *V nebesakh i na zemle* (Moscow: I. D. Sytin, 1908), esp. 115–22.

105 Roshal', *Nachalo vsekh nachal*, 74, citing *Vestnik Kinematografii* 8 (1911): 17.
106 For a good example that mentions Flammarion several times, see P. A. Rymkevich, *Chudesa XX veka (trud i tekhnika)*, 3rd ed. (Leningrad, Priboj, 1925).
107 Ginzburg, *Kinematografiia dorevoliutsionnoj Rossii*, 80.
108 Fri-Dik, "Kinotrazhnia [sic]," *Kinematograf* 1 (1915): 12.

into the 1920s, and it was no doubt this public-directed aspect of his work that drew him into filmmaking, as his own major 1915 article on cinema ("The role of cinema in the area of phenomena in motion") suggests:

> The invention of cinema has been compared with the invention of the printing press. In this comparison lies the inarguable truth that both inventions have the capacity to serve both as a means of educating people, and as a means of vulgarizing or even bestializing them. In both respects cinema has the advantage inasmuch as it achieves its goal [of communication] more easily and more quickly than print.... Print is more subjective than cinema and in this respect has the same advantage over the latter that an artwork has over the most perfect ... photograph. On the other hand, cinema is not simply a device to represent events, but, ... directed by a researcher, can be turned from an instrument for the dissemination of existing knowledge into an instrument that facilitates the discovery of new knowledge which, without its help, would be inaccessible.[109]

"Cinema would lead to a revolution in science," Vagner insisted—right at the time David Kaufman was studying at the institute—"and would leave to future generations a large supply of scientific explanations."[110]

True, Vagner confessed, most science films have been dreadful; but a few promising ones have appeared, like the study of the spider *Sparassus viridissimus*, which revealed "the means by which the spider affixes his ... web to a spot from which he jumps onto another ... plant." As the title of his article suggests, he stresses the application of cinema to the study of movement, particularly extremely slow or rapid movement.[111] He mentions the Norwegian Carl Størmer's use of motion pictures to study the slow fluctuations of the northern lights; he discusses filming the growth of leaves, the development of eggs, and the rapid motion of the wings of insects. Indeed, the central power of the cinema, he asserts, lies in its ability to reveal otherwise invisible aspects of phenomena in motion: "*cinema literally opens up a new world of phenomena ... entirely new*

---

109 V. A. Vagner, "Rol' kinematografa v sfere iavleniia dvizheniia," *Kinematograf* 2 (1915): 1. Vagner's article appeared under the same title in *Vestnik Kinematografij* 111/9 (May 1, 1915): 10, and was reprinted as "Kinematograf, kak orudie izsledovanij" ("Cinema as a tool for research") in *Fotograficheskie Novosti* 6 (1915): 90–92.
110 Fri-Dik, "Kinotrazhnia," 12.
111 Vagner, "Rol' kinematografa v sfere iavleniia dvizheniia," 1–2.

points of view on these phenomena, and, in the end, new possibilities for grasping them."[112]

Vagner's colleague Bekhterev weighed in on "Cinema and Science" about a year later, though he noted that it was hardly new by then to observe how "cinema can be applied to the scientific study of various nervous disorders connected with motion." "Only the cinema," he affirmed, "can reproduce all the separate moments of a given movement, like an act of walking, derangement of gait, or gestural expression. . . ." Bekhterev discussed more directly pedagogical uses of scientific cinema as well, emphasizing the clarity with which cinema can show the details of "pathological phenomena . . . during scientific demonstrations in auditoriums."[113]

We cannot claim with certainty that David Kaufman was actually involved in scientific filmmaking at the Psychoneurological Institute, as much as Boris Kaufman's recollections might seem to warrant our doing so. We *can* claim, however, that David in Petrograd was studying in a place where scientific filmmaking was going on and was valued; that he was part of a milieu (including Masha Gal'pern, his parents, possibly Grigorij Boltianskij and other students) excited and activated by science and education as socially beneficial projects; and that he would have had the opportunity to view sophisticated educational and scientific films, including semi-fictional or "experimental" ones, in the years before the revolution. And of course, as we will see in more detail in volume 2, Dziga Vertov's writings a few years later would often claim a scientific, as well as a "revolutionary," vocation for cinema:

> The main and essential thing is:
>
> The sensory exploration of the world through film. . . .
>
> The kino-eye lives and moves in time and space; it gathers and records impressions in a manner wholly different from that of the human eye. . . .
>
> The mechanical eye . . . experiments, distending time, dissecting movement, or, in contrary fashion, absorbing time within itself, swallowing years, thus schematizing processes of long duration inaccessible to the normal eye.[114] . . .
>
> I advise you to make every effort, even in your first newsreel works, to create a slant toward the scientific illumination of reality.[115] . . .
>
> The kino-eye workers . . . are working in the area of newsreel . . . and in that of scientific film . . . or on the scientific part of a given film.[116] . . .

---

112 Ibid.; the emphasis is Vagner's.
113 V. M. Bekhterev, "Kinematograf i nauka," *Kinematograf* 3 (1916): 1.
114 "Kinoks: A Revolution," *KE*, 14, 15, 19.
115 "To the Kinoks of the South," *KE*, 51.
116 "Kinopravda and Radiopravda," *KE*, 52.

> Kino-Eye is understood as "that which the eye doesn't see,"
> As the microscope and telescope of time....[117]

3. ENERGY AND RHYTHM

We will have occasion to reflect on Vertov's "scientific" aspirations, and their consequences for the form and content of his films, a few times over the course of this study. In the meantime, however, it will be important finally to consider the scientific *ideas* that Kaufman/Vertov might have absorbed during his studies at the institute, and that might have had an effect upon his cinematic work. Those lurid "might haves" are, alas, unavoidable: we know virtually nothing about Vertov's specific reading during those years, beyond his completion of the "basic course" (for which I have no syllabi) and his extracurricular interest in poetry (to be discussed in the next chapter). Thus, the speculations I offer here are even-more-than-usually subject to amendment and augmentation, and do not pretend to outline a kind of *pensée sauvage* from which Vertov's later work might be deduced. Nonetheless, at least two currents of thought of importance at the institute during those years—a major ideology that saw "energy" as the universal substrate of the material and mental worlds, and a minor one that affirmed a close genetic relationship of labor processes to (musical) rhythm—are worth discussing at some length, both because of their suggestiveness vis-à-vis Vertov's later work, and because of their relative obscurity or obsolescence today.

One of the doctrines central to pedagogy and research at the institute was what the intellectual historian Anson Rabinbach has identified as "productivism," "transcendental materialism" or (my own preferred term) "energeticism." This was a nineteenth-century scientific ideology, grounded in the thermodynamic discoveries and models offered by Lord Kelvin, Rudolf Clausius, and above all Hermann von Helmholtz, which held that "human society and nature are linked" by virtue of that fact that underlying "all productive activity, whether of laborers, of machines, or of natural forces" is "a single, universal energy ... that cannot be either added to or destroyed."[118] In later physical and physiological research that took its premises from Helmholtz—particularly research into fatigue suffered by laboring bodies—energeticist monism was bound to the pessimistic implications of the Second Law of Thermodynamics, which adumbrates what we call "entropy," the notion that not only organic

---

117 "The Birth of Kino-Eye [1935]," *KE*, 41.
118 Anson Rabinbach, *The Human Motor: Energy, Fatigue, and the Origins of Modernity* (New York: Basic Books, 1990), 3.

being but the universe itself slowly but inevitably declines into "heat death."[119] Helmholtz, however, downplayed these grim prognoses, especially in his later work, stressing instead the capacity of the universe to "replenish itself";[120] and it seems that this optimistic reading of energeticism was the one bequeathed to Russian psychophysiology, at least in its Bekhterevian redaction.[121]

Whatever modifications he may have brought to the basic energetic theory through his neurological research and speculative ambition,[122] Bekhterev, whose views were dominant at the institute, was clearly always an orthodox Helmholtzian who regarded all phenomena as manifestations of a single, not-directly-representable energy, as he indicates in his 1902 essay on "The Psyche and Life":

> our entire inner world is . . . one of the manifestations of a general universal energy which serves, through the conversion of latent energy, as the origin for

---

119 Ibid., 62.
120 Ibid.
121 The centrality of Helmholtz in Russian writing on psychology at the turn of the twentieth century can hardly be exaggerated; he is crucial for the work of Ivan Pavlov, I. M. Sechenev, and Bekhterev among many others. As Rabinbach shows, Helmholtz should "be credited as a major contributor to social thought" for his "elaboration of the modern concept of labor power as the quantitative equivalent of work produced, regardless of the source of the energy transformed. Helmholtz was the first to demonstrate explicitly the equivalent between natural, inorganic, and social conceptions of labor power" (Rabinbach, *The Human Motor*, 57). For one important popular source, see Wilhelm Ostwald [V. Ostwal'd], *Energicheskij imperativ*, trans. V. M. Pozner, introduction by V. Verner (St. Petersburg: 1913 [supplement to the journal *Za 7 dnej*]). The movement's monism was matched by its secular internationalism and efforts to create a global language: see Ostwald's *O mezhdunarodnom iazyke* (Moscow: Esperanto, 1908). Popular energeticist works such as Ostwald's *The Mill of Life* continued to be published into the Soviet period (*Mel'nitsa zhizni*, trans. R. Kh. Makstys [Moscow: Latizdat, 1925]).
122 I have in mind here his late and not infrequently absurd theory of "collective reflexology," an effort to understand the totality of human behavior in terms of various displacements and conversions ("reflexes") of energy; see V. M. Bekhterev, *Collective Reflexology: The Complete Edition*, ed. Lloyd H. Strickland, trans. Eugenia Lockwood and Alisa Lockwood (New Brunswick, NJ: Transaction Publishers, 2001). I am dubious of any direct impact of collective reflexology on Vertov, both because it was formulated effectively in the post-Revolutionary period and because there seems to be little reason to believe that Vertov would have encountered Bekhterev's theories in any detailed way during his two years of general study at the institute. After the 1917 revolution Bekhterev worked on questions of labor efficiency, fatigue, and many other topics at the institute, now renamed the State University of Medical Science. "Bekhterevism" was officially disapproved following the so-called "reflexological discussion" of 1929, and Bekhterev's reputation revived in the USSR only very gradually after Stalin's death in 1953, although his hidden influence persisted in the intervening years through the work of his many students.

the self-determining activity of organisms with their particular goal-directed effects upon the external world; the whole variegated nature of the external and internal world is conditioned by many and varied conversions of a single, general, unified universal energy, the specific forms of which we call luminous, thermal, electrical and so on, including the latent energy of organisms.[123]

With "latent energy," Bekhterev is here referring to that energy, partially derived from the brain and partially from external stimuli, which within the conscious subject is actively converted into the two interlocked aspects of the psyche: the "nervous current" produced by the firing of neurons, and "psychic or subjective changes," associated with "material changes in the brain which occur in parallel with psychic processes."[124]

Clearly enough, Bekhterev's energetic conception is radically monistic: there is ultimately no difference, on his account, between mental entities and processes and physical ones. We find a particularly forceful articulation of this position in his lecture on "The Immortality of the Human Subject as a Scientific Problem," delivered at a ceremonial speech-day before the entire Psychoneurological Institute in February 1916, when David Kaufman was a student there. Bekhterev's chosen theme was a topical and painful one: he begins by noting how the question of immortality becomes particularly acute at times like the present, "when almost every day brings news of the deaths of many hundreds and thousands of people on the fields of battle."[125]

---

123 V. M. Bekhterev, "Psikhika i zhizn'," in *Psikhika i zhizn': izbrannye trudy po psikhologii lichnosti v dvukh tomakh*, ed. G. S. Nikiforov and L. A. Korostyleva (St. Petersburg: Aleteiia, 1999), vol. 1, 73. Helmholtz provides a constant fulcrum of authority for Bekhterev in his works on space perception (e.g., *Teoriia obrazovaniia nashikh predstavlenij o prostranstve*, 1884), neurology, and psychiatry. See especially the remarks in his 1902 *Die Energie des lebenden Organismus* on "latent energy" as the common basis for both psychic and physical phenomena in the body: "... with the designation 'energy' we are by no means linking it to the common notion of 'physical energy'.... According to our interpretation, energy or power [Kraft] is in its essence nothing less than an active ubiquitous principle within the nature of the universe itself." Bekhterev adds that we cannot perceive this energy in itself, but only its "expressions... in the constant transmutations of material things around us" (W. v. Bechterew, *Die Energie des lebenden Organismus* [number 16 in the series *Grenzfragen des Nerven- und Seelenlebens*, ed. L. Loewenfeld and H. Kurella] [Wiesbaden: J. F. Bergmann, 1902], 31).

124 Bekhterev, "Psikhika i zhizn'," 71.

125 "Bessmertie chelovecheskoj lichnosti kak nauchnaia problema," in Bekhterev, *Psikhika i Zhizn'*, 225. The lecture was first published as a special supplement to the important journal *Herald of Knowledge* (*Vestnik Znaniia*, otdel'nyj ottisk 2 [1916]: 1–23), and was reprinted several times. Bekhterev's arguments seem to derive in part from Wilhelm Ostwald's 1906

Part of the institute, as we know, had already been turned into a military hospital, and many in attendance at the lecture had been directly touched by the war, often by being made refugees: thus, the war's devastation would have been physically palpable in the auditorium as Bekhterev spoke. His goal, as it turns out, was to bring consolation to his audience within the terms of his own scientific outlook, and so he appeals to the law of conservation of energy—which states that the total amount of energy in a closed system, like the universe, remains constant, that energy considered within the bounds of such a system can neither be created nor destroyed—to fashion an idiosyncratic defense of the belief in immortality.

After reasserting that "all phenomena . . . including the internal processes of living creatures or the manifestations of 'spirit,' may and must be regarded as derivatives of a single universal energy,"[126] Bekhterev goes on to argue at once for the perishability of all things and for their paradoxical persistence as "traces" left by their activity within the total continuity of energy exchange in the universe:

> Everything in the world is in motion, everything is flowing; the world is an eternal movement, the unceasing conversion of one form of energy into another: thus declares science. There is nothing constant; one thing always succeeds another. People are born and die, kingdoms appear and are destroyed. Nothing stays the same even for a minute, and it only seems to the human being that upon death he decays and vanishes, turning into nothing. . . . But this is not so. The human being is an actor and participant in the overall universal process. It's obvious that any new step forward in science, technology, art and ethical life remains eternal. . . . But even the everyday activity of the person does not disappear without a trace.[127]

The reason for this persistence of "traces of activity" seems, again, to be the conservation of energy through its various conversions. (That energy might be indeed imperishable while its legible "traces" remain fully subject to decay seems not to occur to or concern Bekhterev.) What Bekhterev has in mind is a kind of grand cosmic developmental trajectory—he referred to his own outlook, tellingly, as an "evolutionary monism"[128]—in which each individual

---

Ingersoll Lecture at Harvard, *Individuality and Immortality* (Boston: Houghton Mifflin, 1906), esp. 53–74.
126 "Bessmertie chelovecheskoj lichnosti kak nauchnaia problema," 230.
127 Ibid., 242.
128 Ibid., 232. See also Rabinbach's remarks on the "unmitigated optimism of a synthesis between evolution and thermodynamics" among German energeticists (Rabinbach, *The Human Motor*, 68).

subject would participate actively, while recognizing both the contingency of her "individual" existence and its necessary consequentiality for the future. (Again, the problem of the absolute unpredictability and illegibility of those "consequences," given the complexity of the universe and the endlessness of the future, is not addressed.)

In profoundly utopian fashion, quotidian material existence is regarded through an optic that inflects it upward, in an immensely slow but still evolutionary arc:

> When a person dies, the organism decomposes and ceases to exist—that is a fact. Through the decomposition of complex protein and carbon-based substances the body breaks down into simpler substances. Thanks to this process, the energy is partially freed, partially again bound to serve as the basis for the growth of the vegetable kingdom, which in turn serves as nutritional material for life, and as a consequence as the condition for the development of energy in new organisms. In this way, that which is called the physical side of the organism, that which bears the name of the body, breaks down and decays, but this does not mean that it is destroyed. It is not lost, but is merely converted into other forms and serves the creation of new organisms and new creatures, which through the law of evolution are capable of endless metamorphoses and perfection. Thus, the cycle of energy does not end even after the death of the organism, and assists in the development of life on earth. . . . not one human act, not one step, not one idea, expressed in words or even with a simple look, gesture, or mimicry in general, disappears without a trace. This is because every act, word or gesture whatsoever or mimetic action is inevitably accompanied for the person himself by specific organic impressions, which in turn must have an effect on him as a subject, turning into new forms of activity in the succeeding period of time.[129]

Even if Bekhterev never uses the word "sacrifice," instead speaking of "disinterested service of . . . all of humanity to the point of forgetting oneself, to the point of annihilation of one's own personal interests,"[130] his evolutionary monism implies a continual sublating absorption of "individuals" into the evolving collective. In a passage whose general relevance to David Kaufman's later activities will be obvious, he clarifies that he is talking not about individual immortality but rather

---

129 "Bessmertie chelovecheskoj lichnosti kak nauchnaia problema," 233–34.
130 Ibid., 251.

social immortality, in view of the indestructibility of that psycho-nervous energy which constitutes the basis of the human subject. Or, to use the language of philosophy, we are speaking of the immortality of the soul, which in the course of its full individual life, through mutual interactions passes as it were into thousands of surrounding human subjects; through specifically cultural attainments (such as writing, the press, telegraph and wireless, telephone, gramophone, various works of art, tools of various kinds, and so on) as well, it spreads its influence far beyond the bounds of the immediate relation of one subject to another—this, not only if these subjects exist simultaneously, but also if they exist at various times, that is, in the relationship of the oldest generations to the newest.[131]

The question of the validity of Bekhterev's dubious defense of belief in immortality will not detain me here; more interesting by far is the demonstrable extent to which the influence of these notions can be recognized within Vertov's later creative and theoretical work.[132]

I strongly suspect that Vertov's preoccupation with movement and with labor, particularly obvious in early manifesta like "We: Variant of a Manifesto" (1922) and "Kinocs: A Revolution" (1923)—with their call for "the organization of movement," for "the ordered fantasy of movement," "the revelation of pure movement, the celebration of movement on the screen," for letting the camera "be drawn or repelled by movement" and so on[133]—derives in part from an immersion in energeticist materialism. Certainly, within the Helmholtzian framework dominant in Russian scientific thought during the early twentieth century, "movement" would invariably have been conceptualized in terms of energy flow.[134]

---

131 Ibid., 238.
132 To be sure, similar and indeed far more elaborate applications of energeticist thinking to ethical and political questions, often produced by distinguished scientists, preceded Bekhterev's. For perhaps the best example (which could be read as proto-environmentalist), see Ostwald's *Die Philosophie der Werte* (Leipzig: Alfred Kröner, 1913), esp. 263–344.
133 See *KE*, 9, 10, 19.
134 I have not come across Russian scientific writing from the period that radically dissents from the energeticist perspective on movement; even those who reject it (like O. D. Khvol'son in his *Znanie i vera v fizike* [Petrograd: F. R. Fetterlein, 1916], 14–15) criticize the materialist monism of the paradigm, its reductiveness and refusal to countenance nonmaterial realities, rather than its account of movement as such. Indeed, movement had been analyzed in terms of energy exchange and conservation in Russia since at least the 1870s; see *Istoriia mekhaniki v Rossii*, ed. I. Z. Shtokalo et al. (Kiev: Naukova Dumka, 1987), 223–58.

Yet by the time Vertov began to work in cinema, this "scientific" perspective had already had a major effect upon artistic practice and aesthetics as well, making both "art" and "science" reservoirs of energeticist ideology. As Charlotte Douglas has shown, energeticism exerted a profound influence upon both Russian experimental artists (from Malevich and Matiushin through the Stenberg Brothers and Konstantin Medunetskij) and theorists (especially Proletkult founder Aleksandr Bogdanov, but Nikolai Tarabukin, Nikolai Punin and Boris Arvatov as well) in the pre- and early post-October periods.[135] We will later affirm the importance of the Russian Futurist influence as well, while bearing in mind the centrality of Helmholtz disciple Étienne-Jules Marey to the Futurists (as well as to Duchamp) in their efforts to "represent the energy of the body in action."[136]

---

135   Charlotte Douglas, "Energetic Abstraction: Ostwald, Bogdanov, and Russian Post-Revolutionary Art," in *From Energy to Information: Representation in Science and Technology, Art, and Literature*, ed. Bruce Clarke and Linda Dalrymple Henderson (Stanford, CA: Stanford University Press, 2002), 76–94. "[These] artists and theorists," writes Douglas, "spoke of and attempted to represent energy itself, the energy of gases, of electromagnetic forces, and of the cosmic flux. The study of energetic systems, which was a major topic of discussion in Russia during much of the 1920s, led to paintings of graphs and painted diagrams of relationships, and to the presentation of organization paradigms as works of art. The primary visual element these artists had in common was an avoidance of depicted objects, objects in this view of the world being merely transitory webs or nodules of energy. In major part, this artistic trend was the product of the immediate ideological demands on artists created by the October Revolution, which required an art based on materialism, science, and analysis, rather than an idealist or essentialist abstraction" (76–77). I was regrettably unaware of Douglas's important work when writing an earlier version of the present discussion of energeticism (published as "Film Energy: Process and Metanarrative in Dziga Vertov's *The Eleventh Year* (1928)," *October* 121 [Summer 2007]: 41–78; esp. 49–56). See also the discussion of Malevich's anti-representational and energeticist account of Vertov's late-twenties films in volume 2.

136   Rabinbach, *The Human Motor*, 115. In addition to Duchamp (in the 1912 *Nude Descending a Staircase*), Rabinbach mentions Anton Giulio Bragaglia and Umberto Boccioni as among the artists directly influenced by Marey. "In rendering visible 'movements that the human eye cannot perceive' and in converging with Bergson, with cubism, and with Futurism, Marey entered the vocabulary of modern art" (ibid.). Marey had been known in Russia at least since 1875, when a translation of his 1873 *Machine Animale: Locomotion Terrestre et Aérienne* appeared (*Mekhanika zhivotnago organizma: peredvizhenie po zemle i po vozdukhu* (St. Petersburg: Znanie, 1875), and he was regularly recalled in pre-Revolutionary film journals (e.g., "Pamiatnik frantsuzskomu uchonomu Zhiuliu Marej — pervomu izobretateliu kinematografa," *Vestnik Kinematografii* 92/12 [June 21, 1914]: 13); a 1930 book on scientific uses of the movie camera mentions Marey as the first to use the camera in physics, singling out his work on "le mouvement des liquides étudié par la chronophotographie" (L. Sukharebskij and A. Ptushko, *Spetsial'nye sposoby kinos'emki* [Moscow: Khudozhestvennaia Literatura, 1930], 3). See also B. S. Likhachev, *Istoriia kino v Rossii* (Leningrad: Academia, 1927), 15–16.

If we leap ahead to Vertov's mature works, it is obvious enough that in at least three of them—*One Sixth of the World* (1926), *The Eleventh Year* (1928) and *Man with a Movie Camera* (1929)—processes of energy conversion, with human labor as a central relay point, provide crucial representational pretexts for the films' rhetoric, in whole or in part. As we will see in volume 2, it is in *The Eleventh Year*—a film about (hydroelectric) energy, the harnessing of energy, and the forms that energy takes, as registered across changing material surfaces—that an "energeticist" model, or myth, of cinematic signification finds fullest expression within Vertov's oeuvre.[137] But the shapes of other major Vertov works are also conditioned by energy exchange, in ways we will elaborate in later sections. In *One Sixth of the World*, which is essentially a cognitive map of the NEP economy's structural basis in state coordination of innumerable small productive enterprises as a means of slowly accumulating industrial capital and (thereby) of modernizing the USSR, the "evolutionary conversion" of energy is nothing less than the governing conceit of the entire film.[138] In a more anthropological spirit, the great "marriage-death-burial-birth" sequence in *Man with a Movie Camera* manages, without intertitles, to impart with extraordinary intensity a sense of the very cyclicality of life, inflected, to be sure, in the direction of birth and the New. In these works, as we will see, the task of documentary moving photography becomes to a significant extent one of registering as vividly as possible the traces of energy as manifested by human, animal or mechanical bodies; the job of montage, by extension, is to narrate the trajectory of that energy and the conversions it undergoes.

It should be stressed that energeticism was a strictly mechanical (rather than historical) materialism that had profound effects upon left-wing social thought, as

---

137 An initial discussion of energeticism in that film appears in "Film Energy." Malcolm Turvey has illuminatingly discussed the relevance of Rabinbach's work on "energeticism" to interpretations of Vertov in "Can the Camera See? Mimesis in *Man with a Movie Camera*," *October* 89 (Summer 1999): 25–50; esp. 35–37.

138 Cf. John MacKay and Charles Musser, "*Shestaia Chast Mira* / [*La Sesta Parte del Mundo/A Sixth Part of the World*]," in *23rd Pordenone Silent Film Festival Catalogue* (Pordenone: Giornate del Cinema Muto, 2004), 55–58. One of a number of "flow charts" Vertov drafted for *One Sixth* indicates the steps of energy conversion under NEP: the natural wealth of the USSR is converted by the labor of workers, peasants, and members of national minorities into useful products which are then processed and sold abroad in the foreign market by the State Trade Organization. The same organization then imports materials that go into developing Soviet industry, which in turn makes "perfected instruments of production" to be purchased and used by workers, peasants, and members of national minorities to increase their output (RGALI f. 2091, op. 1, d. 91, ll. 2–3). I will return to this and other charts in our discussion of *One Sixth* in volume 2.

well as upon physical and biological science, in the last quarter of the nineteenth century.[139] A more culturally grounded, if still "scientific" influence was exerted at the institute (and possibly upon David Kaufman) by the now largely forgotten theories about the relationship between the histories of economic production and of music developed in the work of Karl Wilhelm Bücher (1847–1930). Bücher was a German economist who, along with (but working independently of) the better-known Karl Polanyi, founded the discipline of non-market economics, a major branch of economic anthropology.[140] In the course of his historical study of "premodern" production practices, Bücher—continuing traditions begun in the eighteenth century by Herder and Bishop Percy—collected a large number of work songs from societies across the globe. Comparing these songs both chronologically and across national-linguistic borders, Bücher came to the

---

[139] The effect of materialistic ideologies on the "pre-October" generation of Marxist thinkers—Kautsky, Plekhanov, Bernstein, Lenin, etc.—has been usefully described by Lucio Colletti: "[The generation that came of age in the 1880s and '90s] had grown up into a world profoundly different from that of Marx. In Germany the star of Hegel and classical German philosophy had long since set. Kautsky and Bernstein were formed in a cultural milieu dominated by Darwinism, and by the Darwinism of Haeckel rather than that of Darwin himself. . . . Plekhanov too was at bottom rooted in positivism—think of the place he accords [Henry] Buckle in his *The Monist Conception of History*, for example. The cultural mentality common to this whole generation, behind its many differences, reposed upon a definite taste for great cosmic syntheses and world-views; the key to the latter was always a single unifying principle, one explanation embracing everything from the most elementary biological level right up to the level of human history ('Monism,' precisely!)" (Colletti, "Introduction" to Karl Marx, *Early Writings*, trans. Rodney Livingstone and Gregor Benton [London: Penguin, 1992], 8–9). The twin "worldviews" of historical and mechanical materialism can be seen as overlapping, to be sure, and materialist monism was in part politically motivated by a post-1848 struggle against obscurantism and superstition (see Rabinbach, *The Human Motor*, 49, 69–83; and Douglas, "Energetic Abstraction," 77); yet the fundamental Marxist categories of class conflict and mode of production seem irreducibly historical rather than transhistorically "physical," and the role they play in Vertov's work will have to be addressed in later chapters. On the contrast between historical and mechanical materialism—the latter of which (for the record) the author of the present work rejects as philosophically incoherent, in the face of its inexplicable current popularity—see Kenneth Burke, *A Grammar of Motives* (New York: Prentice-Hall, 1945), 200–210; Jameson, *The Political Unconscious*, 45–46; and "Pleasure: A Political Issue," in *The Ideologies of Theory: Essays 1971–1986*, vol. 2 (Minneapolis: University of Minnesota Press, 1988), 61–74, esp. 69–70.

[140] See Bücher's *Industrial Evolution* [*Entstehung der Volkswirtschaft*, 1893–1921], trans. S. Morley Wickett (New York: B. Franklin, 1967); and K. Bücher, J. Schumpeter, and [Friedrich] Freiherr von Wieser, eds., *Wirtschaft und Wirtschaftswissenschaft* (Tübingen: J. C. B. Mohr, 1914). Bücher is also a foundational figure in the history of the scholarly study of journalism; see *Unsere Sache und die Tagespresse* (Tübingen: J. C. B. Mohr, 1915).

conclusion, elaborated at length in his 1896 *Arbeit und Rhythmus* (*Labor and rhythm*), that rhythm as such—musical, poetic or otherwise—emerged out of the application of the human body to labor processes.[141]

In a very early instance of an argument for the reciprocal action of culture upon economics (or of "superstructure" upon the "base," to use the Marxist terminology), Bücher maintained that rhythm had to be considered an important historical factor in production and therefore within economics more generally. Musical sounds, percussive ones in particular, have their origin, according to Bücher, in the use of hand tools to process raw materials: pounding seed, scything wheat, hoeing gardens, and so on. Poetic meters, meanwhile, find their roots in the contraction and extension of muscles at work—codified, he argued, in the arsis and thesis of ancient prosody.[142]

Crucially, "rhythm" for Bücher emerges out of the need to labor collectively, to amass and apply the energy of a group. Rhythm, especially as reinforced by group singing, is a tool, a means of connecting my movements with everyone else's: it is a mode of corporeal communication, and thus possesses the power both to ease the burden of labor on individuals and to increase productivity. Finally, it also unites workers "organically," rather than through the imposition of some external disciplinary schema.[143]

---

141 Karl Bücher, *Arbeit und Rhythmus* (Leipzig: Hirzel, 1896). Later editions appeared in 1899, 1902, 1909, and 1919.

142 Karl Biukher [Bücher], *Rabota i ritm: rabochiia pesni, ikh proiskhozhdenie, esteticheskoe i ekonomicheskoe znachenie*, trans. I. Ivanov, ed. D. A. Koropchevskij (St. Petersburg: O. N. Popova, 1899), 65–87. Here I will cite throughout from the Russian translation that Vertov would most likely have encountered, rather than the German original.

143 Ibid., 12–20, 87–88. It is worth noting that Henri Bergson—highly influential in Russia during the pre-Revolutionary period—had made a related argument about the "communicative" powers of rhythm in his slightly earlier *Essai sur les données immédiates de la conscience* (1889), although he concerns himself not with labor but with the way rhythm can infect the relatively passive observer of a moving spectacle: "If curves are more graceful than broken lines, the reason is that, while a curved line changes its direction at every moment, every new direction is indicated in the preceding one. Thus the perception of ease in motion passes over into the pleasure of mastering the flow of time and of holding the future in the present. [Another] element comes in when the graceful movements submit to a rhythm and are accompanied by music. For the rhythm and measure, by allowing us to foresee to a still greater extent the movements of the dancer, make us believe that we now control them. As we guess almost the exact attitude which the dancer is going to take, he seems to obey us when he really takes it: the regularity of the rhythm establishes a kind of communication between him and us, and the periodic returns of the measure are like so many invisible threads by means of which we set in motion this imaginary puppet" (*Time and Free Will*, trans. F. L. Pogson [London: Macmillan, 1910], 12).

Yet the evolution of work rhythms, says Bücher, seems to have reached a terminal point in the contemporary period—that is, in Bücher's own epoch of industrial capitalism—even as productive capacities have increased exponentially:

> In their earliest phases, machines took over ... only specific motions of labor; it is remarkable that ... many of the oldest machines moved at a rhythmic pace because they ... simply imitated the movements made by the ... hand in previous labor processes.... But [the] new rhythms of labor differ greatly from the old ones. The working person is no longer master of his movements; the tool, [previously] his servant and supplement to the limbs of his body, now becomes his master. It dictates the measure of his motions.... In this lies the exhausting, oppressive effect of factory labor: the person becomes the servant of a never-relaxing, never-tiring instrument of labor, almost a piece of the machine... Along with these developments, the work song also disappeared. The human voice is powerless before the crash of flywheels, the rush of motorized belts, and all the indeterminate noises which fill ... factory spaces and which drive away any feeling of pleasure![144]...
>
> Art and technology are now moving along entirely different paths of professional development, and the mobile arts [dance, drama] in particular have almost no relationship to science and technological practice and play virtually no role in the lives of workers ... Thus, the life of each person has become duller, more boring; work for laborers has ceased to be accompanied by music and poetry ... Standardized commodities are what is required, and ... art itself goes to market for profit.[145]

Thus, economic production has developed into a distinct "sphere," sundered from other kinds of life-practice, and indeed from the human body as such. But after drawing these melancholy conclusions, Bücher ends his treatise with a qualification and a utopian aspiration:

> Technology and art, through the differentiation and division of labor, have achieved gigantic levels of productivity; labor has become more productive, and household goods more abundant. And we should not lose hope for some possibility of fusing technology and art in that higher rhythmic unity

---

144 *Rabota i ritm*, 99–100.
145 Ibid., 101.

that will again return good cheer to the soul and harmonious development to the body, in the way that distinguishes the best of the primitive peoples.[146]

Perhaps paradoxically, Bücher's writing stimulated psychophysiological inquiry, of a proto-Taylorist character, into the best, most efficient ways of rhythmically organizing labor processes and working bodies.[147] Yet it is at least as important to insert Bücher into the history of reflection on the differentiating, dialectically alienating capacities of modernity, a line that would include Marx, Rousseau, and perhaps above all the Schiller of the letters *On the Aesthetic Education of Mankind* (1794).[148] Indeed, the technocratic and the Romantic fascinations with rhythm sometimes overlapped, as in the occasional illustration, in Soviet textbooks devoted to the "scientific organization of labor" (or NOT: *nauchnaia organizatsiia truda*), of the importance of rhythmicized labor via the example of Konstantin Lyovin discovering the rhythmical secret of scything in a famous passage from Tolstoy's *Anna Karenina* (1877).[149]

Arbeit und Rhythmus is also a significant moment in the history of ideologies of folk music, which stretches back at least as far as those aforementioned pre-Romantic ancestors and extends to Bartók and Kodály, Alan Lomax, and indeed to Vertov's own folk song collecting during the production of *Three Songs of Lenin* (1934). As far as thinking about more recent art is concerned, at least one author, the Argentine critic and great defender of the avantgarde Jorge Romero Brest, applied Bücher to a fascinating study of cinematic rhythm (comparing it to the rhythms of athletic activities);[150] and eventually,

---

146 Ibid.
147 See Margaret Keiver Smith, *Rhythmus und Arbeit* (PhD diss., University of Zürich) (Leipzig: Wilhelm Engelmann, 1900) [available at the Open Source bibliobazaar.com]; Dobri Awramoff, "Arbeit und Rhythmus: Der Einfluß des Rhythmus auf die Quantität und Qualität geistiger und körperlicher Arbeit, mit besonderer Berücksichtigung des rhythmischen Schreibens," in *Philosophische Studien*, ed. Wilhelm Wundt, vol. 18 (Leipzig: Wilhelm Engelmann, 1903), 515–62; and Michael Cowan, *Cult of the Will: Nervousness and German Modernity* (University Park, PA: Pennsylvania State University Press, 2008), 188–98.
148 See especially the account of modern "fragmentation" in the Sixth Letter, in Friedrich Schiller, *On the Aesthetic Education of Man*, ed. Elizabeth M. Wilkinson and L. A. Willoughby (Oxford: Oxford University Press, 1967), 35.
149 For this Tolstoyan Taylorism, see V. Bekhterev et al., eds., *Voprosy organizatsii truda: sbornik statej* (Peterburg: Gosudarstvennoe Izdatel'stvo), 55.
150 Jorge A. Romero Brest, "El elemento ritmo en el cine y en el deporte," *Nosotros* 247 (December 1929): 352–67. Romero Brest mentions Dovzhenko (*Arsenal*), Eisenstein (*Potemkin*), Clair (*Entr'acte*), and Chaplin (*The Circus*), but not Vertov. Bücher, whose

Georg Lukács made considerable use of Bücher's work in his own writing on musical-poetic-rhythmic art in the late *Ästhetik*.[151]

It was precisely under the rubrics of aesthetics and the study of folk songs that Bücher's study was integrated into the curriculum at the Psychoneurological Institute. At least two proseminars on those topics, offered at the institute in and around the years David Kaufman was there, dealt regularly with Bücher's theories.[152] The book had been translated very early (in 1899) into Russian, and quickly became and long remained well known; indeed, Bücher's work kept its place in literary-encyclopedia entries and other works on folk poetry, work songs, and prosody for the rest of the Soviet period and even beyond.[153] Given Vertov's education, his bookstore upbringing, and his interests in music, in work processes, and especially in the relationship between musical and non-musical sound (to be discussed in detail in later sections), it seems likely that he would have encountered or osmotically absorbed Bücher, though he never mentions him anywhere, to my knowledge.

As for rhythm itself—initially sonic, then visual, then visual and sonic—Vertov's preoccupation with it, as we have already learned, emerged early and never flagged:

> We invite you... to flee... out into the open, into four-dimensions (three + time), in search of our own material, our meter and rhythm....
> *Kinochestvo is the art of organizing the necessary movements of objects in space as a rhythmical artistic whole, in harmony with the properties of the material and the internal rhythm of each object....*
> the poetry of machines, propelled and driving...[154]

---

     book had been translated into Spanish in 1914 (*Trabajo y ritmo* [Madrid: Daniel Jorro, 1914] appears on page 355).

151 See *Ästhetik* [Georg Lukács Werke 12–13] (Darmstadt and Neuwied: Luchterhand, 1962–63), I 254–273, esp. 256–58, 264–66; II 113, 339.

152 See Gerver, *Otchet o deiatel'nosti Psikho-Nevrologicheskago Instituta*, 203. The seminars on aesthetics at the Institute had a distinctly materialist cast: another topic discussed was "various interrelations between musical tempi and processes of breathing and blood circulation" (ibid.).

153 See for instance the encyclopedia article by V. Goffenshefer, "Karl Biukher," accessed June 24, 2017, http://feb-web.ru/FEB/LITENC/ENCYCLOP/le2/le2-0511.htm. *Arbeit und Rhythmus* was never translated into English, which probably accounts for its relative lack of resonance in the Anglo-American world. (But see Michael Golston, *Rhythm and Race in Modernist Poetry and Science* [New York: Columbia University Press, 2008], 23; and Michael Cowan's study, cited in footnote 147.) A second Russian translation of book appeared in the USSR in 1923 (*Rabota i ritm*, trans. S. S. Zaiaitskij [Moscow: Novaia Moskva, 1923]).

154 "We: Variant of a Manifesto," *KE*, 7–9; italics in the original.

We will have occasion to discuss Vertov's cinematic-rhythmic practice, and its affinities with Soviet "noise music" of the 1920s, in some detail later on, especially in the course of analyzing *Man with a Movie Camera* and *Enthusiasm: Symphony of the Donbass*.[155] Suffice it to say for the moment that Vertov in his mature work organized his footage with extraordinary metrical precision—at times taking single film frames, the quanta of the mechanical camera-eye, as his basic rhythmic units—and with his rhythmical cinema seemed to be aiming at a restoration of "that higher rhythmic unity" of technology and art that lies at the center of Bücher's own ideology of rhythm. The sound of industry is intolerable, and yet there is no going back (for Vertov and his peers, that is: we are, in this respect among others, no longer their contemporaries). How can the proletariat master its own surroundings, how can it survive, without entering into those inhuman vibrations? Or, to use Vertov's language from the early '20s, without bringing "the broad, gesticulating throng of workers...closer to the iron rhythm of advancing—crawling, driven, and flying—machines"?[156]

This "bringing closer" should also recall for us David Kaufman's early efforts to gain mnemonic control over his school assignments through rhythmic arrangements (the "cities of Asia Minor"). School administers trauma in a softer, perhaps more predictable and scheduled way than the industrial workplace does; accordingly, it affords more time and space for fashioning defenses, whether those involve collective organization or (as in the case of Kaufman's memorization strategies) technologies of management. Yet what the ideologies of energy and rhythm make imaginable is precisely a linkage between physical labor and intellectual "formal binding": energy, whose ubiquity can be traced in the passage of one movement into another, in the systole and diastole of what philosopher Gilles Deleuze termed "[Vertov's] material system in perpetual interaction," where everything is *work* in the strict physical sense ("Work = Force × Distance," as we all had to memorize in school); rhythm, the binding strategy itself, inseparable from labor, that can shape what Bücher

---

155 See B. Iurtsev's remarkable article on the Proletkult "Orchestra of Things"—an attempt to generate music out of mass-produced objects—in *Zrelishcha* 6 (1922): 22; and volume 2 of the present work. For a sweeping overview of French thinking about cinematic rhythm during the silent period, see Laurent Guido, *L'age du rythme: Cinéma, musicalité et culture du corps dans les theories françaises des années 1910–1930* (Lausanne: Editions Payot, 2007), esp. 19–300.
156 "The Fifth Issue of Kinopravda," *KE*, 11.

called "indeterminate noises" into perceptually graspable and even pleasurable cadences.[157]

It might even be said that energy and rhythm constitute the substance and the form, respectively, of the universal, now that "spiritual" entities have fled and the grounding of all social life in work—the formative and self-formative energy of the proletariat—has been revealed. Such, at any rate, will be Vertov's artistic gambit in his mature films with their rejection of character-centered narration: that is, after 1921, by which time a new, specifically Soviet and *historical* protagonist, the Party-State, will have come into being, and offer a temporary place for Vertov's experiments within the perimeters of its increasingly universal authority.

---

157 Deleuze's deeply perceptive comments on Vertov are worth citing here, though we will return to them later: "Whether there were machines, landscapes, buildings or men was of little consequence . . . They were catalysts, converters, transformers, which received and re-emitted movements, whose speed, direction, order, they changed, making matter evolve towards less 'probable' states, bringing about changes out of all proportion to their own dimensions . . . . [M]ontage itself constantly adapts the transformations of movements in the material universe to the interval of movement in the eye of the camera: rhythm" (Gilles Deleuze, *Cinema 1: The Movement-Image*, trans. Hugh Tomlinson and Barbara Habberjam [Minneapolis: University of Minnesota Press, 1986], 39–40).

CHAPTER 3

The Beating Pulse of Living Life: Musical, Futurist, Nonfiction, and Marxist Matrices (1916–18)

> *Just as any of you is one of a living crowd, I was one of a crowd,*
> *Just as you are refresh'd by the gladness of the river and the bright flow, I was refresh'd,*
> *Just as you stand and lean on the rail, yet hurry with the swift current, I stood yet was hurried,*
> *Just as you look on the numberless masts of ships and the thick-stemm'd pipes of steamboats, I look'd.*
>
> —**Walt Whitman**, *"Crossing Brooklyn Ferry"*

In a revisionary study of Western European culture after World War I, the historian Jay Winter has argued that the dominant responses to the war were not in that iconoclastic, critical, ironic mode that has come to be thought of (and canonized) as "modernist"—or as "modern memory," to use Paul Fussell's phrase, and which might characterize artists as different as George Grosz, Blaise Cendrars, and T. S. Eliot—but rather involved a turn to traditional vocabularies of representation, above all as a way of dealing with the unprecedented human losses (unprecedented for modern Europe, that is) brought about by the war:

> [T]he enduring appeal of many traditional motifs [during and after World War I]—defined as an eclectic set of classical, romantic, or religious images and ideas—is directly related to the universality of bereavement in the Europe of the Great War and its aftermath. The strength of what may be termed "traditional" forms in social and cultural life, in art, poetry and

ritual, lay in their power to mediate bereavement. The cutting edge of "modern memory," its multifaceted sense of dislocation, paradox, and the ironic, could express anger and despair, and did so in enduring ways; it was melancholic, but it could not heal ... There is considerable evidence of the power of traditional modes of commemoration within communities [after the war], from small groups of men and women in family circles, to séances, to those gathered in more conventional forms of religious worship, to universities, ex-servicemen's associations, widows' organizations, to communities unveiling war memorials, and finally, to the "imagined community" of the nation itself....

[T]he backward gaze of so many writers, artists, politicians, soldiers, and everyday families in this period reflected the universality of grief and mourning in Europe from 1914.... The "sites of memory," like [Walter] Benjamin's Angelus Novus, faced the past, not the future.[1]

Winter does not discuss Russia and its empire, but we might surmise, considering how war in those territories dilated from 1914 until 1921, that cultural conditions there would be especially ripe for the reemergence or persistence of traditional forms of memorialization.

The Russian Empire saw five million war casualties between 1914 and 1917 alone, more than any other combatant nation, and six million made refugees by war prior to February 1917. Soviet Russia saw another million dead either in combat or by falling victim to terror during the Civil War; millions more perishing during the same conflict due to disease or starvation; at least another million gone through flight or exile; five million dying in the famine of 1921; and millions of children made homeless or orphaned.[2] There was and would be much to mourn, though the scale and character of early Soviet commemoration, distinguished by (among other features) its official anti-religious animus, remain little investigated.[3] If we look even superficially at much of the

---

1   Jay Winter, *Sites of Memory, Sites of Mourning: The Great War in European Cultural History* (Cambridge: Cambridge University Press, 1995), 5–6, 223. The position against which Winter is arguing is that of Paul Fussell in *The Great War and Modern Memory* (Oxford: Oxford University Press, 1975).
2   Sheila Fitzpatrick, *The Russian Revolution*, 2nd ed. (Oxford: Oxford University Press, 1994), 37; Gatrell, *A Whole Empire Walking*, 3; Ronald Grigor Suny, *The Soviet Experiment: Russia, the USSR, and the Successor States* (New York: Oxford University Press, 1998), 93, 149. For a survey of recent scholarship on this topic and period, see Francesco Benvenuti, "Armageddon not Averted: Russia's War, 1914–21," *Kritika: Explorations in Russian and Eurasian History* 6, no. 3 (Summer 2005): 535–56.
3   See Nina Tumarkin, *Lenin Lives! The Lenin Cult in the Soviet Union*, enlarged edition (Cambridge, MA: Harvard University Press, 1997), esp. 141–43; Catherine Merridale,

most sophisticated Soviet filmmaking of the 1920s—Vertov's to be sure, but the work of Eisenstein, Pudovkin, Dovzhenko and many others as well—we find frequent corroboration of Winter's thesis in those decidedly un-"modernist" moments from which viewers often avert their eyes: all the parades, funeral processions, monuments, elegies to the dead Lenin and so on, like Gothic phantasms drifting spectrally and (for us) embarrassingly through those laboratories for advanced cinematic experimentation.

"For us," indeed. We might wonder how much contradiction Vertov and his contemporaries sensed, when we consider Vertov's famous film commemorations of Lenin (the 1925 *Lenin Kino-Pravda* and 1934's *Three Songs of Lenin*), or the cover of *Zrelishcha* (*Spectacles*) for January 27, 1925, titled "To Lenin's Grave," where arch-Constructivist Aleksej Gan affirmed, in a kind of prose pilgrimage, that Lenin, who wrote little about art but much about revolution and the need to industrialize, could be taken for that reason as defending Constructivism's anti-art stance.[4] (This does not mean that they sensed *no* contradiction: Vertov, speaking of himself in the third person in 1922, boasted of how, even in some of the earlier *Kino-Pravdas*, he managed at least partially to "inter the interments [*pokhoronil pokhorony*] and the parades of big-wigs.")[5]

Perhaps these bedfellows should not seem strange to us, given the now well-known affiliations that existed between Futurisms of nearly all stripes and various traditionalisms, primitivisms and even regressive authoritarianisms.[6] On the eve of the Russian war effort in 1914, Vertov's idol Vladimir Mayakovsky had, after all, embraced the conflict as virtually a Futurist project (he would change his mind soon enough):

> Now life has adopted us [the Futurists]. There is no fear. Now we will show you every day that under our yellow buffoons' jackets were the bodies of healthy, strong men, needed by you as warriors.[7]

"War, Death and Remembrance in Soviet Russia," in *War and Remembrance in the Twentieth Century*, ed. Jay Winter and Emmanuel Sivan (Cambridge: Cambridge University Press, 1999), 61–83, esp. 67–72; and above all Karen Petrone, *The Great War in Russian Memory* (Bloomington: Indiana University Press, 2011).

4 Gan, "Leninizm v iskusstve" [in the section "Na mogilu Lenina"], *Zrelishcha* (27 January 27, 1925): 1. A picture of Lenin appears on the page as well.
5 "On i ia" ["He and I"], *SV*, 20.
6 See Günter Berghaus's introduction to his edition of F. T. Marinetti, *Critical Writings*, trans. Doug Thompson (New York: Farrar, Straus and Giroux, 2006), xvii–xxix, esp. xxi–xxix.
7 "Teper' k Amerikam!" *Nov'* 115 (December 15, 1914): 6; cited in A. V. Krusanov, *Russkij avangard: 1907–1932*, vol. 1 (St. Petersburg: Novoe Literaturnoe Obozrenie, 1996), 252.

At the very least, these features of prerevolutionary and early Soviet experimental artistic ideology and practice should make us wonder whether a notion like "modernity"—whose range of applicability cannot be expanded indefinitely if it is to retain precision and salience—adequately describes this historical conjuncture. That is (and considering the films exclusively): are the ubiquitous ritual-memorial moments to be thought of as skillful absorptions of older mourning practices into a new, polymorphous "modernity" mediated by cinema, or (as Winter suggests) are they better characterized in terms of the persistence of traditional modes of commemoration into the present, indeed as their partial takeover of the "new" media?[8]

As I see it, a key difference between the Russian and West European postwar situations, at least from the perspective of early Soviet culture, lies not simply in the greater duration and magnitude of the suffering in Russia, but rather in the conjuncture of that suffering with the revolution of 1917 as a historical and ideological threshold. At almost the exact midpoint of the catastrophe, Russia became the site—at least for some of those, like Vertov, of revolutionary conviction—of a world-historical victory, the triumph of the proletariat. As we will see, Vertov seemed not to share that conviction in 1918; like many others, he did share it by 1922, and there can be no doubt but that it provided a fundamental support, when compounded with his existing enthusiasm for advanced contemporary art, for his attempts to imagine and create a cinema that at once would be of a piece with the new world augured by the revolution, and would help to bring that world into being. (The more prosaic fact

---

See also Hubertus F. Jahn, *Patriotic Culture in Russia during World War I* (Ithaca, NY: Cornell University Press, 1995), 14–16; and Stephen M. Norris, *A War of Images: Russian Popular Prints, Wartime Culture, and National Identity 1812–1945* (DeKalb: Northern Illinois University Press, 2006), 154–56, 167–69.

8 It should be clear that these two perspectives are not compatible, if cinematic "modernity" is to mean anything more than sheer crowding-together of different temporal or historical levels within a given medium-practice, or indeed to be distinguished from the most unhelpful truisms about the functions of "media" as such. The issue is a difficult one that raises numerous questions about periodization and the interrelating of levels of focus (historical, formal, biographical) within interpretation. For contrasting views, see Tom Gunning, "The Whole Town's Gawking: Early Cinema and the Visual Experience of Modernity," *Yale Journal of Criticism* 7, no. 2 (Fall 1994): 189–201; and David Bordwell, *Figures Traced in Light: On Cinematic Staging* (Berkeley: University of California Press, 2005), 244–49. For Winter's own superb discussion of Abel Gance's 1919 film *J'accuse*—"in which the dead arise and return home to see if their sacrifice has been in vain ... [using] the most 'modern' techniques ... to present ancient motifs and images about sacrifice, death and resurrection," see *Sites of Memory, Sites of Mourning*, 6–7.

that he ended up working *for* the Bolshevik regime, that it became the concrete framework for his own advancement, was no less significant, as we will see.) Yet his aspirations were conditioned through and through by the reality around him—apprehensible as either crippling poverty or a tabula rasa; as wracked by terrifying violence or as energized by revolutionary will—and by the efforts of the regime to "build socialism," and to build itself *as* a regime, in those conditions and in its own way.

Following Vertov's life trajectory, this chapter and the next chart the early stages of that building, from the months immediately prior to February 1917 through the beginning of 1922, by which time Dziga Vertov (rather than David Kaufman) had become a significant if not yet renowned participant in a still-embryonic Soviet cinema culture. It is a complex story, whose telling involves attending to the mutual actions and reactions of history, ideology, and creative personality, and whose leitmotif is the co-emergence, not nearly complete by 1922, of Soviet cinema with the Soviet state. The modes of writing found in these sections—veering from discussions of poems and music to film theory and analysis, history, biography, and political philosophy—may seem maddeningly heterogeneous. I can justify their diversity only by offering them as a way of being faithful to the wrenching confrontations of utopian possibility with violent closure, radical hope with radical fear, that characterized this historical juncture—a juncture crucial to much of the rest of the twentieth century, and not just in Russia.

CHUGUEV, MUSIC, AND INTERVAL

David Kaufman would become part of the Soviet story only in the spring of 1918, when he was hired by Mikhail Kol'tsov to work on the *Kino-Nedelia* newsreels. Between 1916 and that crucial moment, much would happen in Kaufman's life, though most of those happenings remain obscure; again, informed conjecture is required to illuminate them.

Of David Kaufman's time at the Chuguev Military School, there is, alas, little to say. We know that he began his studies there after being drafted sometime around September 1916, and had left for Moscow—his base city for the rest of his days[9]—by no later than around sometime in the late fall of

---

9 *DVVS*, 76. Even while working for the All-Ukraine Film and Photo Administration in Kiev from 1927–31, Vertov and Svilova kept a room in the same communal apartment where he had settled with the Lembergs in 1917. Oddly, a transit visa for traveling through Belgium in July 1931 indicates that he was residing in "Khorkoff" [Kharkov] (RGALI f. 2091, op. 1, d. 412, l. 29), and perhaps for a time, he was.

1917, although exactly when is unclear.[10] The school, located not far from Kharkov—later capital (until 1935) of the Ukrainian SSR, which Vertov would later visit on the agit-trains, and still later depict in a number of his films—had existed since 1865, first as an infantry school for junkers (officers-in-training) and later, after 1910, as a broadly based officer training institution. Entry into the school was dependent upon either prior education in a gymnasium or passing an exam or audition, and Kaufman evidently qualified on both counts.[11]

On the one hand, if the draft was unavoidable, one could have done worse than study music at this fairly out-of-the-way (if quite prestigious) military institute. On the other, of course, this was a time of war, and during the massive mobilization of July 1917, three months after the Provisional Government recommenced hostilities against Germany, the school sent a contingent of

---

[10] See TsGIASpb f. 115, op. 2, d. 4048, ll. 14, 17–18; and the discussion of Vertov's friendship with Aleksandr Lemberg, below. The head of the recruitment office in Bogorodsk (near Moscow) wrote to the director of the Psychoneurological Institute on September 12, 1916, that "David Abelevich Kaufman was fully able to serve" and would be sent into the army immediately; Vertov himself had requested copies of his documents from the Institute (on August 26, 1916), evidently in connection with the recruitment. Yet on July 18, 1917—after the Tsar's abdication, and a little over a month after War Minister Kerensky had ordered a massive Russian offensive against the Austro-Hungarians—a representative of the Student Commission of the Psychoneurological Institute wrote to the head of the Chuguev Military School asking that a document concerning David Abelevich Kaufman sent by the Institute be returned, in accord with some unknown agreement of June 9, 1917. I have been unable to sort out the full meaning of this correspondence, but it seems that perhaps some kind of amnesty had been granted to students at the institute (and perhaps elsewhere as well), and that the request had possibly been prompted by David Kaufman's intention to reregister (TsGIASPb, f. 115, op.2, d. 4048, ll. 8, 15, 18). On a form he filled out prior to being named an Honored Artist of the USSR by the Central Committee in June 1947, Vertov indicated that he had studied between 1916 and 1918 in the Physics and Mathematics Faculty of Petrograd University, but it seems as though these studies (of which I have found no other evidence) must have been very brief indeed, if they took place at all; perhaps Vertov in 1947 was loath to admit that he had studied in a well-known Tsarist military academy (RGASPI f. 17, op. 125, d. 499, l. 47). For his part, Boris Kaufman also indicated, in an interview with Simon Kagan in 1978, that Vertov was studying "somewhere in Ukraine" in and around 1917 (Boris Kaufman Papers, Beinecke Library, Yale University, GEN MSS 562.16.336). Lev Roshal' mentions Vertov attending the "military-musical school in Chuguev" as well, but implies that this recruitment and training preceded Vertov's study in the Psychoneurological Institute, contradicting the available documentation (*Dziga Vertov*, 12). I was unable to unearth any information about David Kaufman's time in Chuguev in the relevant archive, whose holdings on the Military School are spotty (RGVIA [Rossiiskij Gosudarstvennyj Voenno-Istoricheskij Arkhiv] f. 860, op. 1, dd. 1-2 [1915–16]).

[11] Boris Syrtsov, "Chuguevskoe voennoe uchilishche, 1916-1917 gg.," *Voennaia Byl'* 90 (1968): 36–38.

150 junkers to the front. I would surmise that David Kaufman had already left Chuguev by this time, released by what seems to have been an amnesty granted to university students in June 1917, although the evidence is admittedly very vague on this point.[12]

At any rate, David's experience in Chuguev would have been atypical, and not only because of its brevity. For one thing, discipline at the school eroded rapidly after February 1917, due to the increasing radicalization of trainees and even some of the teaching staff, who were visited regularly and openly by representatives of the Kharkov Soviet of Soldier's and Worker's Deputies.[13] It is more interesting, of course, to think about the kind of musical training Kaufman received there, although the frustrating dearth of documentary evidence condemns us largely to speculation. If the Chuguev School was not, from what I can tell, particularly well known among Russian military academies for its musical subdivision, the musical level achieved by those academies on the whole was very high, and we might expect that the Chuguev players strove to live up to those standards. Military orchestras in Moscow and St. Petersburg regularly performed elaborate arrangements of major works on the stages of both the Bolshoj and Mariinskij Theaters, often as benefits for war invalids; even in the provinces, various garrison orchestras would often unite to perform works by Wagner, Berlioz, Balakirev and Tchaikovsky (the *1812 Overture* was, predictably, a favorite). Thus, we can assume that the Chuguev School's music students, selected through audition and assembled from all over the empire, must have received a rigorous training in their craft.[14]

This musical thematic prompts me to insert a necessary parenthesis here about David Kaufman's early relationship to sound, in part because his Chuguev experience figured in his intensive early concern with music in the years 1916 through early 1918. We have already referred to his studies at the Bialystok Musical School, and to the possible influence of Bücher's *Arbeit und Rhythmus*. As we will see in future chapters, later critics and filmmaking colleagues would often point to music as providing a fundamental model for Vertov's nonnarrative

---

12 See footnote 10, above.
13 See Syrtsov, "Chuguevskoe voennoe uchilishche," 37–38. After the staff and students of the Aleksandrovskij Military School had risen up against the Bolsheviks in November 1917, the Chuguev School's director, General Ieremej Iakovlevich Vrasskij, called up a supporting brigade, but it was stopped in its tracks by the Kharkov Soviet, which soon afterwards took over the school itself by armed force.
14 See P. Voloshin, "Russkie voennye orkestry," *Voennaia Byl'* 56 (1962): 37–40.

formal practice, and not without reason.¹⁵ Though inchoate, the fragmentary evidence we possess suggests that the years immediately preceding his entry into cinema may have been his most music-centered period, as manifest in two ways: his reflections, mainly in poetic form, on the work of Aleksandr Scriabin (1872–1915); and his experimentation with the transcription and montage of sound in what he called a "laboratory of hearing."

In conversation with film scholar Vladimir Magidov in 1971, the pianist and journalist Olga Toom, Vertov's first wife and (as we will see later) one of his colleagues on the agit-trains, offered an astonishing anecdote about Vertov's intense love for and capacity to play the works of Scriabin, his favorite composer. Apparently, Vertov asked Toom to show him how to play one of Scriabin's fiendishly difficult etudes just by moving her fingers, without a piano. Toom obliged, Vertov observed her, and then (according to Toom) he proceeded to actually play the etude on a piano keyboard. Now, those of us who even feebly grasp the difficulty of Scriabin's music—not to mention the difficulty of translating finger gesticulations into actual music—may well have (envious?) suspicions about this story's veracity. Still, it no doubt affirms, from the standpoint of a professional pianist, Vertov's real musical gifts, and the depth of his interest in and understanding of one of the most exploratory composers of his day.¹⁶

This is not the place, of course, for an account of Scriabin's innovations in harmony or his virtuoso expansions of the resources of the piano: his "mystic chord," tritonal textures, galactically swelling and sweeping trills and glissandi, and so on.¹⁷ More important for thinking about Vertov, I believe, is some reference to the kinds of critical and ideological discourse that grew up in early twentieth-century Russia around Scriabin's harmonically unpredictable, emotionally hypercharged, bristlingly complex, formally unconventional compositions, the later works in particular. Russian music critics of the early twentieth century—who often punctuated their eulogies to the "genius" Scriabin with flashes of skepticism regarding his theories—offered numerous précis of Scriabin's musical ideology, linking his thought to that of the German Romantics and of Nietzsche, Schopenhauer and Vladimir Solovyov, describing it as a kind of mystical monism directed toward a historical endpoint at

---

15   For but one instance, see Mikhail Kaufman's remarks in *DVVS*, 71–72.
16   V. M. Magidov, *Zrimaia pamiat' istorii* (Moscow: Sovetskaia Rossiia, 1984), 122–23. Vertov's musical gifts were frequently mentioned by memoirists: for one instance, see Esfir' Shub, *Krupnym planom* (Moscow: Iskusstvo, 1959), 76.
17   For a musicological, historical, and ideological account of Scriabin's music, see Richard Taruskin, *Defining Russia Musically* (Princeton, NJ: Princeton University Press, 1997), 308–59.

which all difference would ultimately (and aesthetically) be subsumed in a cosmic "I": at once the self's unlimited expansion and its cancellation in Universal Consciousness.

Though much of Scriabin's music-theoretical writing seems to tend toward a solipsistic position wherein "the world is the result of my activity, my creativity, and my desire"—prompting the Marxist Georgij Plekhanov, upon meeting Scriabin in Geneva, to quip "so it's to you, Aleksandr Nikolaevich, that we owe this fine weather!"[18]—the fundamental movement of his thought, for the majority of critics, is toward constant self-transcendence, ultimately yielding a new collectivity:

> The stream of consciousness is a series of creative breakthroughs; the movement from one to the next is rhythmic, and together they make up a rhythmical figure. The creator strives always excelsior, excelsior; each of his breakthroughs present a passionate straining toward the overcoming of obstacles. . . . The transcendental *transformation of consciousness*, and with it the nature of all things, [amounts to] a mystic ekstasis, the flowing-together of all individual consciousnesses into a higher synthesis of Universal Consciousness.[19]

The practical upshot of this striving is a continual resistance to established form, decorum, and habit—although Scriabin did in fact write symphonies, mazurkas, sonatas, and so on, however unusually shaped—and a concomitant shedding of the accretions of convention, local or ethnic identity, political interest, even of language itself.[20]

The famous musicologist Aleksandr Petrovich Koptiaev went so far as to assert of Scriabin's work that, far from being "national," it returns music to its "primordial essence," to those Bacchic origins that lie beyond and beneath history.[21] And indeed, I believe that on some level, such notions about Scriabin's work (fortified with and complicated by inspiration offered by the poetry of the Futurists and Constructivism) provided Vertov with many of his standards for

---

18 I. Lapshin, *Zavetnye dumy Skriabina* (Petrograd: Mysl', 1922), 22.
19 Ibid., 17, 19; emphasis in the original.
20 A.P. Koptiaev (in his *A. N. Skriabin* [Moscow: I. Iurgenson, 1916], 38) discusses Scriabin's intense antagonism toward the incorporation of verbal texts into his work—an antagonism largely shared, as we will see, by Vertov.
21 A. Koptiaev, *Evterpe: vtoroj sbornik muzykal'no kriticheskikh statej* (St. Petersburg: Glavnoe Upravlenie Udelov, 1908), 102. For related reflections, see also Evgenij Gunst, *A. N. Skriabin i ego tvorchestvo* (Moscow: Mysl', 1915), esp. 8–13.

what art should be, even when he denied that he was producing "art": it should be complex, ecstatically emotional, *sui generis*, directed toward the Universal.[22]

Paradoxically, however, Koptiaev also directly relates Scriabin's Dionysian music to contemporary Russian social upheavals, which presumably also involve the dismantling of old traditions:

> Scriabin's art began to form in the period [around 1905] when revolutionary storms thickened across Russia. Sheer will came to the forefront, for law was absent. Scriabin gathered that revolutionary lightning in his crosier, like a true Jupiter. If it matters not at all, in terms of the world's movement, whether Russia has a constitution or not, the author of the "divine poem" was nonetheless an indubitable and involuntary singer of the howling of sheer movement. Movement as such, movement no matter what—that was what satisfied his musical outlook. . . . Is it not truly Scriabin who is the liberator of our souls?[23]

Two different conceptions of history overlap in Koptiaev's account of Scriabin's boundary-breaking music: on one side, history as a burden of tropes, values, and restrictions—those "[traditions] of all the dead generations [weighing] like a nightmare on the brains of the living"[24]—that must be shaken off; on the other, as the living, dynamic movement of a specific social totality now creating its own present and future. And it might be said that these "negative" and "positive" polarities shake hands in Scriabin's famous synesthetic project of linking colors to sounds, which would both undo the hardened opposition of aural and visual sensory modalities, and legislate a new set of correspondences.[25]

---

22 Indeed, Scriabin's influence is directly detectable in much early Soviet thinking about art, even in its most radical, past-denying varieties. An article by Iosif Iegis that surprisingly appeared in the pages of the Constructivist-leaning journal *Spectacles* (*Zrelishcha*) argued that Scriabin's search for an identity underlying gestures, color, and sound came from his interest in dreams, where such trans-sensory identities are supposedly experienced. The ultimate Scriabinian dream, according to Iegis, would amount to a unification (through the composer's *Mysterium*) of all the senses of all people—dream as utopian future, in other words—even if this apocalyptic performance could happen only when "the waking world disappears . . . at the end of this world and the beginning of the new, when the world is converted into a divine dream" ("O 'misterii' Skriabina," *Zrelishcha* 36 [1923]: 5).

23 Koptiaev, *Evterpe*, 108.

24 Marx, *Eighteenth Brumaire*.

25 On Scriabin's color-music projects, including his interest in constructing a one-octave color piano (a "tastiéra per luce"), see V. G. Karatygin, *Skriabin* (Petrograd: N. I. Butkovskaia, 1915), 65–66; and Konstantin Bal'mont, *Svetozvuk v prirode i svetovaia simfoniia Skriabina* (Moscow: Rossijskoe Muzykal'noe Izdatel'stvo, 1917). It seems that some of the "scientific"

On the face of it, this syncretic aspect of the composer's work would have met with disapproval from the fiercely purist Vertov of the early '20s, who protested

> ... against that mixing of the arts which many call synthesis. The mixture of bad colors, even those ideally selected from the spectrum, produces not white, but mud.
>
> Synthesis should come at the summit of each art's achievement and not before.[26]

Vertov's insistence on purity needs to be taken with a large grain of salt, however: certainly when measured against his own films, but also in light of Bruno Latour's chastening reminder that "moderns" of all sorts programmatically purify in order then to (consciously or unconsciously) hybridize and mix.[27] Indeed, in this respect, Scriabin's key affinity with Vertov's later work lies less in any attempts at cross-sensory or inter-art synthesis and more in the effort to divide up and recombine the phenomenal world in different ways, and to startle the senses themselves out of their reified inertia.[28] At the same time, as we know, Vertov's later explorations of pure movement had

---

impulse behind the Russian interest in synesthesia came from psychologist Alfred Binet, whose 1892 work on "colored hearing" ("La problème de l'audition colorée," *Revue des Deux Mondes* 113 [October 1892]: 586–614) was translated into Russian in 1894 (*Vopros o tsvetnom slukhe*, trans. D. N. [Moscow: I. N. Kushnerev, 1894]). From the 1960s onward, Scriabin's experiments were carried on in Kazan' by the "Prometheus" group, under the leadership of Bulat Galeev; see I. L. Vanechkina and B. M. Galeev, *Poema ognia: kontseptsiia svetomuzykal'nogo sinteza A. N. Skriabina* (Kazan': Izdatel'stvo Kazanskogo Universiteta, 1981).

26 "We: Variant of a Manifesto" [1922], in *KE*, 7.
27 Bruno Latour, *We Have Never Been Modern*, trans. Catherine Porter (Cambridge, MA: Harvard University Press, 1993). Insofar as purification impulses are the result of idealizations (of medium, of technology, and so on), however, it might be thought that postmodernism sublates this tension into an idealization of "impurity" itself (reified as "hybridity"), thereby becoming not a *post*modernism, but merely modernism's own final impasse. See the reflections in Emmanuel Renault, "L'idéologie comme légitimation et comme description," *Actuel Marx* 1, no. 48(2008): 80–95, esp. 84–92.
28 To be sure, as Juliet Koss's recent work on the *Gesamtkunstwerk* shows, the original Wagnerian notion of the "total work of art" cannot be reduced to a simple matter of "synthesis" either, inasmuch as the composer regarded such works as a space for the dialectical struggle of different arts for their own (ultimately limited) autonomy, almost a laboratory where the very boundaries between "media" might be investigated (Juliet Koss, *Modernism after Wagner* [Minneapolis: University of Minnesota Press, 2010], xii, 16–19).

norms and standards of their own, specifically provided by "the rhythm of machines, the delight of mechanical labor," with which his films would bring people into "closer kinship."[29] In his early encounter with Scriabin, however, Vertov, then a poet and schooled musician rather than a filmmaker, seems to have been more struck by the composer's relatively intuitive work upon the *material* of music—harmonies, scales, timbres—whose "primordial essence," and contingent relation to conventional tonal meaning, Scriabin's experiments helped to reveal.

Perhaps I can demonstrate this more easily through reference to a cluster of Vertov's Futurist-styled poems, composed as early as 1917 and probably no later than 1920, which he dedicated to Scriabin. It seems that these poems were examples of what Vertov later called "etudes" to be apprehended by listeners "simultaneously as music and as poetry." They appeared as part of a larger literary project that involved the composition of works that blurred the difference between prose and poetry as well:

> [These etudes] represented transitional steps from a poetic composition to a prosaic one. It turned out that alongside prose and poetry exist a whole series of transitional, intervening forms of a specific type [and between which there's no sense in setting boundaries].... Several of the [poetic-musical] compositions, which seemed to me more or less accessible to a wide audience, I attempted to declaim aloud. I wrote the more complex things [*veshchi*], which required long and attentive reading, on large yellow posters. I put up these announcements around the city, pasting them up myself [in both Moscow and the provinces].[30]

The passage implies that for Vertov—reflecting here on his own youthful work almost twenty years later, after a whole series of historical "intervening forms" had been traversed—the literary (prosaic and poetic), musical, and visual (in the form of the posters) ways of working upon form and material were conceived early on not in terms of atomized "arts" to be unified (or reunified) into a *Gesamtkunstwerk*, but rather as historically radically contingent in and of

---

29 "We: Variant of a Manifesto," in *Kino-Eye*, 9.
30 "Kak rodilsia i razvivalsia Kino-Glaz," *SV*, 291–92, 562. The English phrases inserted here in square brackets were included by Vertov in earlier drafts of the essay, but not in the final one.

themselves. The task, therefore, is less synthesis of different artistic modalities than the dissolution of those modalities as such.

One of the poetic-musical etudes, dated 1917 in one manuscript, was elaborately illustrated by N. Smolianinov with a decadent-symbolist (rather than Futurist) picture of severed hands and death's heads straining toward a huge, handsome visage emerging out of the sunrise:

> Otrazhalsia v ozere?
> Videl son li ia?
> V ognetomimoe nebo li nemo lez?

> Was he reflected in the lake?
> Was I dreaming?
> Did I climb silently toward the fire-parched sky?

> Ruki slomennye
> Tselymi grozd'iami
> Plyli neumolimomu LITSU naper[er]ez.

> Broken-off arms
> In whole clusters swam
> Heading off the implacable FACE.

> I zvuk ogromlennyi
> Otrazhalsia gulami
> Ukhodia bagrimomu nebu v grud'.

> And a sound grown enormous
> Was reflected in rumbles
> Departing into the incarnadined sky, to its breast.

> Obernulsia istomlennyj
> Pokazalis' grimami
> Zaria i grozdi ruk i zhut'.

> Exhausted, [I] turned around:
> The dawn, the clusters of hands, the terror
> Seemed like greasepaint.[31]

---

31 RGALI f. 2091, op. 2, d. 228, l. 4; the file contains several other poems dedicated to Scriabin, the latest dated February 1920 (ll. 4–7). The poem I have translated above is reproduced with Smolianinov's "music of pigments" (and presumably his calligraphy as well) in Tsivian, ed., *LR*, 37. The picture is inscribed with the phrase "Dziga Vertov sings-recites," and so it seems to be associated with a performance of the poem.

Image 1: Dziga Vertov, "Was he reflected in the lake?" Ca. 1917. Source: *LR*, 37.

A symbolic landscape of sorts emerges out of these verses—an apocalyptic dream-tableau of fiery skies, thunder, and a kind of "cult of personality" *avant le mot*—which, on the level of content, has a certain overtonal relationship of mood to Scriabin's darker, more writhing works (think, for instance, of the *Piano Sonata No. 9*, op. 68). Indeed, Vertov hints that the poem was written for recitation to the accompaniment of a specific, unknown Scriabin work.[32] Yet Yuri

---

32 In some 1929 notes, Vertov refers to his early work of "projecting musical fragments onto words" ("Vertov i kinoki," *SV*, 188), and "Was he reflected in the lake?" may well have been a musical ekphrasis of this sort. Another poem, dated 1920, is dedicated to Scriabin but subtitled "Prelude Op. 11" (RGALI f. 2091, op. 2, d. 228, l. 7).

Tsivian is certainly right to describe the poem as essentially untranslatable,[33] not least because the complex play of aural and visual echoing draws more attention to itself than to any meanings the words might convey.

This suggests, paradoxically, that readers without Russian could still discern the poem's corporeal textures, although the force of their prominence, of course, can only be adequately perceived in tension with the poem's semantics. All the same, non-Russian speakers (keeping in mind analogous practices in Hopkins and Joyce) might be able to appreciate how inter-resonating clusters like "otrazhalsia v ozere," "nebo li nemo," "ognetomimoe . . . neumolimomu," "ogromlennyj/Otrazhalsia gulami," "bagrimomu . . . grimami," and so on, pull the sonic and graphemic stuff of language, and thus the sense of poetry as a materially constructed thing, into view. Letters, phonemes, and the work of combining them, like chordal combinations for Scriabin, thus drift away into (partial) autonomy from the logic that normally and "self-evidently" governs them.

It is not clear whether Scriabin's recordings of his own music were among the works that Vertov subjected to recombination in his famous "laboratory of hearing," probably established sometime between 1916 and 1918, and far more likely in either Moscow or Petrograd than in Chuguev.[34] This "laboratory," invariably referred to in short bios of the filmmaker, is arguably the most poorly understood aspect of his early career, not least because Vertov offers only the vaguest hints as to what his "laboratory" work consisted in.[35] In the indispensable "How Kino-Eye Was Born and Developed" from 1935, he indicates that his work on the mnemonic montage of words—discussed in chapter 1—was succeeded by an interest in the "montage of stenographic recordings" and "experiments with gramophone recordings, where [he created] a new composition out of separate fragments [taken] from gramophone records."[36]

---

33 LR, 36.
34 All extant recordings of Scriabin playing his own music derive from piano rolls; however, he apparently made several wax cylinder recordings, now lost, in or around 1913. For more on his recordings, see Anatole Leikin, *The Performing Style of Alexander Scriabin* (New York: Routledge, 2016).
35 He refers to the "laboratory of hearing" in the 1929 notes cited above—a draft autobiography of sorts—under the heading "rhythmic montage of verbal and sound material," as the fourth and final entry preceded by "montage of words" ["Cities of Asia"], "montage of noises" ["sawmill"] and the "projection" of words onto music mentioned above ("Vertov i kinoki," SV, 188).
36 "Kak rodilsia i razvivalsia Kino-Glaz," SV, 289.

Whether the stenographic montages involved the juxtaposition of textual fragments written in some shorthand code or other is unknown, although the montage was certainly intended to be semantic as well as formal. It seems unlikely that these stenographic efforts were aural recordings, even if Vertov might have employed a Dictaphone (given that device's relative availability in cities globally after around 1910) or blank Pathé phonograph cylinders for work on a different project, his long lost "remixes" from existing recordings. It is almost impossible to determine, in truth, which recording apparatus Vertov actually used; that he employed some sort of homemade device, built or jerry-rigged perhaps with the assistance of his technically adept brother Mikhail, is not out of the question.[37]

In any event, Vertov's laboratory—which consisted of nothing more than "his work and the room in which he worked"[38]—was not a recording studio but rather a space for nonmechanical, manual inscription and transcription of various kinds, whether the medium be notes, words, or some other nomenclature.[39] Again, his experiments, which led him directly to an encounter with the problems of documenting "raw" reality, were provoked by a sense of the inadequacy of existing representational vocabularies to the complexities of experience.

> ... I wasn't satisfied by experiments with already recorded sounds. Within the natural world, I heard a significantly greater quantity of varied sounds, [beyond] singing or violin playing as heard in the repertoire of conventional gramophone records.
>
> I hit upon the idea that it was necessary to expand our capacities to hear in an organized way. Not to limit those capacities within the bounds of ordinary music. Within the concept "I hear," I included the entire audible world. To this period belongs my experiment in recording the sounds of a sawmill.

---

37 Gramophones, Zonophones, Lyrophones and many other record-playing devices were readily available in urban centers in Russia during these years; less has been written about home recording devices. For early recording, see P. N. Griunberg, *Istoriia nachala gramzapisi v Rossii* [in one volume with V. L. Ianin, *Katalog vokal'nykh zapisej rossijskogo otdeleniia kompanii "Grammofon"*] (Moscow: Iazyki Slavianskoj Kul'tury, 2002); and Anita Pesce, *La Sirena nel solco: Origini della riproduzione sonora* (Naples: Guida, 2005).

38 "Kak rodilsia i razvivalsia Kino-Glaz," *SV*, 292.

39 In other words, when Vertov writes of his "experiment in the recording of the sounds of the sawmill" [*moj opyt po zapisi zvukov lesopil'nogo zavoda*], it seems, judging from his text, that he has in mind written transcription rather than mechanical sound recording ("Kak rodilsia i razvivalsia Kino-Glaz," *SV*, 291); see below.

It happened while I still going to school,⁴⁰ during the holidays, not far from Lake Il'men'. There was a sawmill in the area that belonged to a wealthy landowner named Slavianinov.⁴¹ I had arranged with a girl I knew to meet at the sawmill. She was hard pressed to get there on time—she had to run out of the house without being noticed—and I ended up having to wait there for hours. I dedicated those hours to listening to the mill. I tried to describe this audible mill the way that a blind person might. At the beginning I jotted down words, and then made an attempt to record all the sounds with letters.

This system had the disadvantage, first, that the existing alphabet is inadequate for recording the sounds heard at a sawmill. Secondly, besides vowels and consonants, one heard various melodies and motifs. They also needed to be recorded with some kind of notational sign. But notes appropriate to the recording of natural sounds did not exist. I became convinced that, with the means I had at my disposal, I could achieve only the imitations of sounds, but could not analyze an audible mill or waterfall in the way that was necessary.

With my ear I distinguished not noises, as it's conventional to call natural sounds, but a whole series of highly complex combinations of specific sounds, sounds that often mutually destroyed or interfered with one another. The situation was difficult because there was no instrument I could use to record and analyze these sounds. So I gave up my attempts temporarily, and returned to working on the organization of words.⁴²

As we will see much later on, this passage develops notions that, within Vertov's textual corpus, are first clearly enunciated during his defenses of one of his most formally radical films, *Enthusiasm: Symphony of the Donbass* (1930), with its clamorous industrial soundtrack: the idea, specifically, that there is no such thing as noise, but only sounds (or other sense-data) that are either ignored or imperfectly comprehended. Yet as readers will have noted, the passage also continues the narrative ("How Kino-Eye was Born and Developed") that began

---

40   Vertov's diction here suggests that he might have still been at the Bialystok Modern School at this time.
41   Lake Il'men' is in the western part of the present-day Novgorod region, part of the basin of the Baltic Sea. A somewhat obscurely phrased Wikipedia entry indicates that a landowner named Slavianinov held land in this area, with mills and small factories built upon it (http://ru.wikipedia.org/wiki/Устъ-Волма, accessed October 25, 2016).
42   *SV*, 291.

with the account of the memorization strategies he used to gain conscious control over material assigned in school ("Miletus, Phocaea," etc.); and it is crucial that we see how Vertov, telling the story of his creative evolution, here drastically alters the meaning of those strategies.

For what originally seemed to be the *imposition* of an easy-to-remember rhythmical order upon a set of names ("a rhythmical series that could be memorized immediately")[43] now appears as the *discovery* "within the natural world" of infinite meaning, and the concomitant discovery of consciousness's capacity for discovery: as if (although Vertov doesn't say this) whatever "rhythmical series" David Kaufman had used to recall the names of Greek islands and cities had somehow inhered in the names themselves. An ad hoc mnemonic technique opens a passage toward an infinity of orders, all of them conceptual on some level ("not noises ... but ... highly complex combinations"), but in excess of any notational logic.

To be sure, we need to keep in mind Vertov's less visible motives for telling this story in the mid-1930s. Obviously (as the further unfolding of "How Kino-Eye was Born and Developed" makes clear), he is preparing a space for the heroic intervention of mechanical recording equipment, whether aural or optical, and therefore for his own vocation as experimental nonfiction filmmaker. The camera, for Vertov, will be the device that enables both capture and analysis: it grasps everything in the visible world—more, indeed, than the human eye does—but also produces records that can be enlarged, stopped, slowed down, reversed, and otherwise subjected to close scrutiny. The refusal to reduce and the need for order and understanding, impulses starkly opposed to one another, are reconciled in a cinematic technology appropriate both to the visible world's complexity and to a conscious articulation of that complexity. Vertov's early-1920s theory of the cinematic "interval"—which attempted to overcome what might be called the *Bergsonian* problem of the punctual, limited character of cinematic registrations (whether shots or film frames) by conceptualizing film's basic unit as a fluid *differential* between shots or frames, rather than shots or frames as such—is critical here as well, and we will bring that theory to bear upon Vertov's specifically filmic documentary practice in later chapters.[44]

---

43 See discussion at the end of chapter 1.
44 The privileged place occupied by sound in Vertov's theories may have something to do with this problematic as well, insofar as sound recording might be said to have a relatively continuous character, as compared with the object-units that comprise visual-cinematic "phenomena." See the discussion of *Enthusiasm* in volume 3.

It is more difficult but equally important to see how Vertov's 1935 tale links his apparently fanatically "formalist" concern with pattern and infinitesimal levels of detail to a utilitarian and even pedagogical impulse: the desire, that is, to liberate perception, or rather (to borrow from the rhetoric of the First Five-Year Plan) to push it to continual fulfillment and over-fulfillment of its own promise. Thus, a suspect formalism, much noted and denounced by Vertov's opponents, especially in the late 1920s–early 1930s, tries to clear its name by recalling its own origins as an eccentric form of sensory tutelage—thereby demonstrating its usefulness, presumably, in the modernizing Soviet Union of the 1930s.

I have again speculated on Vertov's formative period anachronistically, through the prism of his later career, and not for the last time. Certainly, and despite the probable impact of his poetic and musical interests, Vertov's later conception of cinema's unique perceptual vocation borrowed at least indirectly from contemporary pre-Revolutionary defenses of nonfiction and (as we have seen) scientific cinema as well. Some of those defenses, indeed, presage Vertov's shrillest formulations. "No one [*sic*] but the cinema," asserted critic S. Novodumskij in 1913,

> is able . . . to hurl harsh truth directly in the face—the unadorned truth, gray and monotone. The eye of cinema, if only freed from being led by the mendacious hand of the human being, bears the mystery of total impartiality and the possession of objective, unassailable truth.[45]

Yet that peculiar amalgam of science, music, poetry, and propaganda that is Vertovian "non-acted" cinema could only emerge in the post-Revolutionary world. That world would soon surround Vertov and his peers with sights and sounds different from anything they had previously encountered; as it turned out, it would also give Vertov the chance to capture and even "organize" those sights and sounds, on film.

AFTER THE REVOLUTION: FUTURISM EARLY AND LATE

In Moscow along with his family sometime after the Tsar's abdication in February 1917, David Kaufman seems to have largely ceased his studies and

---

45 *Vestnik Kinematografii* 1913 (13): 14; cited in Roshal', *Nachalo vsekh nachal*, 60. The *Vestnik Kinematografii* piece is a summary of an article by Novodumskij ("Vystavka uzhasa") that originally appeared in the journal *Den'*.

begun attending poetry readings and cafés frequented by the artistic *bohème*.[46] Mikhail Kaufman describes this as a period of hardship for his older brother, which implies that David was neither working nor studying at the time, and probably not living with his parents.[47] It was late in 1917 that David, already using "Dziga Vertov" as a pseudonym, apparently made his first major acquaintance with someone from the world of cinema, a man who was to work with him on a number of films, including some of the *Kino-Nedelias* and *One Sixth of the World*, the then-nineteen-year-old professional movie cameraman Aleksandr Lemberg (1898–1976). Lemberg, whose father Grigorij was also an important cameraman and (later) sometime newsreel director, had actually shot his first two fiction films at the end of 1915—*King with a Crown* and *Chess Game of Love*, both directed by M. Bonch-Tomashevskij and both starring the young Aleksandr Vertinskij—for the Perskij-Kogan firm.[48]

When Lemberg was drafted at the beginning of 1917, producer Robert Perskij paid him the then huge sum of 1,000 rubles a month to film the responses on the front to the February Revolution. After permission was received from the military authorities—the state monopoly on production of military newsreel had just been abolished[49]—Lemberg was stationed at the High Command of the Army in Mogilev (now in Belarus), from whence he filmed action on the front. When he met Kaufman/Vertov, evidently sometime late in the fall of 1917, he was an artillery reservist in Moscow, waiting to be called up.[50]

---

46 According to Boris Kaufman, the family was reunited in Moscow, after Vertov had returned there from Ukraine and Mikhail had finished his studies in the gymnasium (Boris Kaufman Archive, Beinecke Library, Gen MSS 562.16.335). Mikhail completed those studies in Mogilev (now in Belarus), the site of the headquarters of the Russian Imperial Army during World War I (RGALI f. 2986, op.1, d. 112), apparently between 1915 and the middle of 1917. It has been asserted that Vertov attended university, perhaps law school, in Moscow at some point between 1914 and 1918 (e.g., Abramov, *Dziga Vertov*, 8; Tsivian, ed., *LR*, 23); and in his "personal file" from 1947, Vertov indicates that he studied in the Physics and Mathematics Department at "Leningrad University" [sic] between 1916 and 1918 (RGASPI f. 17, op. 125, d. 499, l. 47). However, I have found no independent confirming evidence of study in either of these institutions. They took place, if at all, only between the very end of 1916/beginning of 1917 and May 1918.
47 *DVVS*, 76.
48 A. G. Lemberg, "Iz vospominanij starogo operatora," *Iz Istorii Kino: materialy i dokumenty* 2 (1959): 117–31; here 118–25.
49 See discussion of the Skobelev Committee, below.
50 A.G. Lemberg, "Iz vospominanij starogo operatora," 120. Lemberg is also famous for having filmed Lenin on May 1, 1917, in Petrograd. Interestingly, Mikhail Kaufman was still attending school in Mogilev when Lemberg was stationed there, though they surely never met during that time.

Our family lived in the same place I now live, in Kozitskij Lane.[51] I occasionally went to the "Poets' Café," located across from the Central Telegraph building, and there listened to poems and arguments about war, revolution, and art.

Once sitting next to me at the table was a young man who, as became clear during our conversation, was excited about the poetry of [Vladimir] Mayakovsky, which drew us together immediately. My new acquaintance became much interested when he found out that I was a cameraman. He asked me about the laws of cinematography, about the capacities of the nonfiction/newsreel camera, and finally about my most recent filming at the front.[52]

After that, we occasionally met at the "Poets' Café." I found out that my interlocutor was named Dziga Vertov, that he'd graduated from a music school, and afterwards studied at the Psychoneurological Institute in Petersburg. Arriving in Moscow, Vertov didn't have a permanent address, and was moving from one apartment to another. After we grew close and became friends, he began living with our family for a good long while.[53]

The "Poet's Café" was established by the Cubo-Futurist poets Mayakovsky, Vasilij Kamenskij, and David Burliuk in a former laundry on the corner of Tverskaia Street (Moscow's main central thoroughfare) and Nastas'inskij Lane in late November 1917, shortly after the Bolshevik takeover on October 25 (November 7 NS).[54] There they recommenced the Moscow readings that had been so popular in the prewar years. According to Lev Grinkrug, Mayakovsky's close friend and a frequent patron of the café,

---

51 This street is located near the center of Moscow, not far from Pushkin Square, and is where Vertov and Svilova also resided for many years (until December 1937: see RGALI f. 2091, op. 2, d. 254, ll. 78–78ob, and volume 3 of the present work), in the same communal apartment where Lemberg lived.

52 Lemberg was filming nonfiction/newsreel on the front for the Kogan-Perskij firm.

53 *DVVS*, 79. In another memoir, Lemberg claimed that Vertov actually worked as his camera assistant just before the October events—which they could not capture, not having their own camera or film—soon after which Lemberg was drafted by the Bolsheviks to serve as a watchman. Upon returning home, wrote Lemberg, he found that Vertov had drafted on paper a series of montage-like fragments, non-narrative but "very vivid," about the revolution. I am a bit dubious of these claims, not having found independent confirmation of them elsewhere (including in Lemberg's other writings), but perhaps they should be believed (A. Lemberg, "Dziga Vertov prikhodit v kino," *Iz Istorii Kino* 7 [1968]: 41).

54 See A. Iu. Galushkin et al., eds., *Literaturnaia zhizn' Rossii 1920-kh godov*, vol. 1, pt. 1 (Moscow: IMLI RAN, 2005), 63–64; Bengt Jangfeldt, *Majakovskij and Futurism: 1917–1921* (Stockholm: Almqvist & Wiksell International, 1976), 16. Kamenskij and V. Gol'tsshmidt were the main organizers of the venture.

> The most varied sort of public assembled [there] every day. Here were Red Army soldiers, sailors, and just plain philistines. Anarchists often came by, who at this time occupied the building next door... from time to time they created a scandal by firing shots, until they were liquidated entirely.
>
> The Futurists presented poems, agitational speeches, and attacked the philistines who, evidently, took great pleasure in this, for the public poured into the place in huge numbers.[55]

After the October Revolution, both poets and public lost interest in the café, as issues of politics and day-to-day survival began to take center stage, and it was closed on April 14, 1918.[56]

Prior to the closure, however, David Kaufman was a regular, and perhaps even read some of his own poems there. (Lemberg reported that David arrived at their apartment in Kozitskij Lane with nothing but "a rucksack half full of books.")[57] Boris Kaufman, then also in Moscow with his refugee parents, later spoke to Simon Kagan about the city's dynamic poetic culture:

> Intellectual life in Moscow was very intense. It was truly the intellectual center of Russia, [and] poets were the most popular people of the time. Mayakovsky, Anna Akhmatova, [Igor] Severianin... Poets read their own poems and the audience really participated in the reading. It was very intense... My brother Dziga, as you know, was a poet himself, and had a good relationship with the other poets.[58]

Boris, only fourteen or so at the time, might have exaggerated his oldest brother's closeness to those phenomenally popular "other poets"; but it was surely in Moscow in 1917–18 that David Kaufman drifted into the Futurist milieu, as an enthusiast of new poetry above all.[59]

---

55 Quoted in Jangfeldt, ibid.
56 Ibid., 17; and Krusanov, *Russkij avangard*, vol. 2, book 1 (Moscow: Novoe Literaturnoe Obozrenie, 2003), 321. There were other poetry cafés in Moscow as well, but judging from Krusanov's account (312–34), they had mostly ceased operation by the beginning of summer 1918, coinciding with the rapid sharpening of hostilities in the Civil War at the end of May.
57 *DVVS*, 79.
58 "Entrevue avec Boris Kaufman," Beinecke Library, Yale University, GEN MSS 562.16.336.3.
59 On the popularity that Futurism enjoyed in Moscow, see Krusanov, *Russkij avangard*, vol. 2, book 1, 324–25. For important accounts of Vertov's creative relationship to Futurism and Mayakovsky, see A. Fevral'skij, "Dziga Vertov i Maiakovskij," *Iskusstvo Kino* 10 (October 1973): 113–24; Petric, *Constructivism in Film*, 25–44.

We do not know when Kaufman first encountered the work of the Futurists, though it is not impossible that some of their writing might have trickled into his father's bookstore, starting in 1913. Mayakovsky, Burliuk, and Kamenskij may have made appearances in Bialystok and Grodno in March 1914, and it would have been possible for David Kaufman to have attended famous exhibits of experimental art like "Streetcar V" and "0.10" (in which Vladimir Tatlin and Kazimir Malevich both presented important work) in Petrograd during his years at the Psychoneurological Institute.[60] It seems, however, that Kaufman first saw Mayakovsky in the flesh only in 1917–18 in Moscow, in the auditorium of that city's Polytechnical Museum.[61] Judging from his own article drafts and diary reminiscences, all of which date from the 1930s, Vertov was a lifelong fan of Mayakovsky, the poet and political radical:

> [After the reading at the Polytechnical Museum] Mayakovsky noticed me in a group of excited young men. Evidently I was looking at him with enamored eyes. He came up to us. "We're looking forward to your next book," I said. "Get your friends together," Mayakovsky answered, "and demand that they publish it soon."
>
> My meetings with Mayakovsky were always brief. In the street, at a club, at a train station, a movie theater. He called me not Vertov, but Dziga. I liked that. "Well, Dziga, how's kino-eye doing?" he once asked me. That was in passing, at a train station somewhere. Our trains met. "Kino-eye is learning," I answered. I thought a moment and said it differently: "Kino-eye is a beacon [*mayak*] against the background of international film production's clichés." And when Mayakovsky shook my hand in parting (our trains were going in different directions), I added, stammering: "Not a beacon, but a Mayakovsky. Kino-eye is a Mayakovsky against the background of international film production's clichés." "A Mayakovsky?" The poet looked inquiringly at me. In answer I recited:

---

60 Krusanov, *Russkij avangard*, vol. 1, 252–72.
61 The Bialystok and Grodno readings were evidently planned, but it is not clear that they took place; see Krusanov, *Russkij avangard*, vol. 1, 220. Vertov mentioned in a 1935 talk he gave at a Mayakovsky memorial lecture that he first saw the poet at the Polytechnical Museum (*SV*, 296); the period in question was surely fall 1917 through spring 1918, when Mayakovsky made five appearances at the Museum (October 7, 1917, February 12 and 27, March 16, and May 23, 1918 [all NS]) (V. Katanian, *Maiakovskij: literaturnaia khronika*, 3rd ed. [Moscow: Khudozhestvennaia Literatura, 1956], 95, 100–105). Interestingly, this was also the period of Mayakovsky's initial major involvement with cinema, as actor and screenwriter.

> Where the people's dock-tailed eye stops short,
> at the head of hungry hordes,
> wearing the crown of thorns of revolution
> 1916 approaches.[62]

"You saw what the ordinary eye did not see. You saw how 'from the West red snow is falling in the juicy flakes of human flesh.' And the sad eyes of horses. And a mama, 'white, white as the brocade on a coffin.' And a violin that 'wore itself to pieces, entreating, and suddenly began howling like a child.' You are a kino-eye. You've seen 'that which travels across mountains of time, which no one sees.' And right now you're

> .... in the new,
>   future way of life,
>   multiplied
> by electricity
>   and communism."[63]

Certainly, Vertov's admiration for advanced work in poetry and visual art, and for that of Mayakovsky in particular, was intense, permanent, and often at odds with the values of his contemporaries. Cameraman Aleksandr Levitskij recalled the arguments he had with Vertov when they were working together on the agitational train *October Revolution* in 1920:

> Dziga Vertov headed up film exhibition on the train ... at the time [he] was still a young man about 22 years old, and was interested in left and ultra-left [i.e., avant-garde] tendencies in art. And it was precisely because of our conflicting views on art that we became friends.
>
> I was and always remained a supporter of the realist tendency, and never recognized ultra-left directions in either painting or literature.

---

62 Quotation from *A Cloud in Trousers*.
63 *KE*, 180–81; translation slightly modified. The provenance of this text, a translation from *SDZ*, is somewhat obscure (and in some cases converts statements *about* Mayakovsky into bits of dialogue *with* Mayakovsky), but it seems to be a reworking of drafts of a talk Vertov gave at a memorial for the poet on April 24, 1935, at the House of the Press, as well as some other, later notes (*SV*, 296–97, 433–37, 562–63, 590–91; RGALI f. 2091, op. 2, d. 253, ll. 14–16ob, 55ob–57). On Mayakovsky's youthful Social Democratic political activity, see Bengt Jangfeldt, *Mayakovsky: A Biography*, trans. Harry D. Watson (Chicago: University of Chicago Press, 2014), locations 119–220 [Kindle edition].

> Vertov, meanwhile, rejected the entire heritage of the art of the past, recited the poems of the Imaginists, and (in painting) reveled in Cubism. Because of these differences we had frequent [verbal] battles that, in truth, were completely pointless for both of us.[64]

At some point during these years, according to a well-known story told by Aleksandr Lemberg, Vertov attempted to act upon his Futurist enthusiasm for idiosyncratic mingling of the poetic and the visual, using the Lemberg family's apartment as his canvas. Lemberg returned home on one occasion to find that

> Vertov had covered the apartment—the walls and the ceiling—with a thick layer of soot. Imagine the parquet floor, and pitch-black darkness above it. The black walls were all covered with clocks painted in chalk, with their hands all showing different times. Each clock had a pendulum painted under its face, and these pendulums, too, were arrested in different positions, as if captured in swing. I did not like this at all. Vertov took pains to convince me that I just was not getting it, the room was his masterpiece. Can't you see how the black paint creates the effect of infinite space stretching in all four directions? he asked. And the clock faces are a poem! Poem, I asked? Recite it. All right, listen: tick-tock, tick-tock, tick-tock, tick-tock, tick-tock. . . .[65]

As Yuri Tsivian has suggested, "tick-tock" may well refer to a Vertov poem of that title—incomprehensible to everyone but Vertov himself, according to Lemberg—that dissolves the items in a room (table, chairs, lamp) in an swirl of figuration that links them to dogs, Zeppelins, and pool cues.[66] Lemberg later had the room repainted, to his family's probable relief and Vertov's temporary chagrin; and though Vertov's experiment had clearly perplexed him, Lemberg in old age paid homage to his friend's capacity "to feel the poetry both in the simple 'tick-tock' of a clock mechanism and in a complex sensation of limitless space."[67]

---

64 A. Levitskij, *Rasskazy o kinematografe* (Moscow: Iskusstvo, 1964), 204. The Imaginists were a group of poets—primarily Anatolij Mariengof, Sergej Esenin, and the former Futurist Vadim Shershenevich—who placed emphasis on the creation of verbal "image"; the group was in existence from 1918 to 1925.
65 DVVS, 85; as translated in LR, 4.
66 LR, 4, 34.
67 DVVS, 86.

Vertov's ties to Futurism and its main representatives were at once poetic, ideological-theoretical, and institutional, bound up with his identity even on the level of name: "Vertov," after all, is a Futurist neologism. Much of the poetry he wrote from around 1916 to 1920 is plainly indebted to the work produced by Mayakovsky during the same years, and particularly to the collection *Simple as Mooing* (1918), and the great long poem *A Cloud in Trousers* (1915; uncensored version published in early 1918), which Vertov claimed to have nearly committed to memory after a third reading.[68] It is almost impossible to convey a clear sense of this Futurist mode of poetic writing in translation, given the Futurists' programmatic emphasis upon the sonic and graphic materiality of verse, not to mention the sheer difficulty of their work. However, transcription and sensitive reworking can, with luck, give some impression of those features of Mayakovsky's verse that seized Vertov's imagination: thick internal rhyming that seems to loop every phoneme into every other phoneme; uninhibited play with roots and false cognates; high tension between the flow of syntactic periods and abrupt end-stops that splinter even single words into fragments, as here in the first lines of "From Street to Street" (1916):

U-
litsa.
Litsa
U
dogov
godov
rez-
che.
Che-
rez
zheleznykh konej
s okon begushchikh domov
prygnuli pervye kuby.[69]

The boule-
vard.
Bull-

---

68 *Prostoe kak mychanie* (Petrograd: Parus, 1916); KE, 180; SV, 296; *Literaturnaia zhizn' Rossii 1920-kh godov*, vol. 1, 110–11.
69 "Iz ulitsy v ulitsu," *Prostoe kak mychanie*, 32.

dogs
of years
your faces
grow steely.
Steel horses
steal the first cubes
jumping from the windows
of fleeting houses.⁷⁰

The poem develops a remarkable internal graphic mirroring effect ("U / -litsa. / Litsa / U"; "rez- / che. / Che- / Rez") alongside the more familiar rhyming entanglements ("dogov," "godov," "domov"; "rez," "zheleznykh"; "konej," "okon") that the translation cited here makes an honest attempt to suggest ("boule-," "Bull-"; "steely," "Steel," "steal"). Most importantly, by breaking up what would seem to be discrete units ("U-litsa" / "boule-vard"), and then integrating these word fragments into lines unpredictably bound together both phonetically and graphically, Mayakovsky at once abandons traditional prosodic syntagms (whether line- or stanza-length) and opens up his "material" to minutely conceived and novel sequencing. As we will see as early as the *Kino-Pravdas* (in volume 2), Vertov-the-filmmaker takes up this problematic of *radical sequencing* as his own, making it central to his pursuit of a cinema that resists the lure of narrative-fictional tropes.

Some of Vertov's Futurist efforts in poetry mimic both these crabbed, specular phonetic textures and perhaps even the famous Mayakovskian "egoism," as here in a poem entitled (what else?) "Dziga Vertov":

Zdes' ni zgi
Ver'te
Veki iga i
Grobov verigi
Prosto vetrov
Gibel'
Veki na vertep
No - dzin'! - vertet'
Diski
Gong v dver' aort

---

70 http://www.poemhunter.com/poem/from-street-to-street/, accessed October 15, 2016.

> I—ô go gò! Avtovizgi,
> Vertep rtov
> Dziga Vertov.[71]
>
> Pitch dark here
> Believe
> Centuries of the yoke and
> Fetters on coffins
> Simply the death
> Of winds
> But—dzin'!—to spin
> Disks
> A gong at the door of aortas
> And—oh ho ho! Yelps of cars,
> A den of mouths
> Dziga Vertov.

Vertov's poem, more than Mayakovsky's, seems almost like an extended anagram woven out of a delimited set of sounds ("ve," "ov," "rt / tr" and "zd / dz / zg" are especially prominent) that yields a cascade of inter-resonating clusters: "ver," "vek," "vet"; "zgi," "verigi," "diski," "avtovizgi," "Dziga"; "grobov," "vetrov," "rtov," "Vertov"; and so on. Indeed, the final appearance of "Dziga Vertov" might be thought of as an exposure of the poem's paradigm or underlying phonetic scale, rather than an authorial "name" of any kind: rather like *Man with the Movie Camera*'s famous revelation of its own paradigmatic categories—traffic, marketplace, factory and so on—in the editing room.

On the level of sense, what would become a classic Vertovian formal trope makes an early appearance here at the poem's exact midpoint ("But—dzin'!"), when the figuration suddenly shifts from bleak and mournful ("pitch dark," "centuries of the yoke," "death of winds") to rowdy and clamorous ("dzin'!", "spin / Disks," "yelps of cars"). This kind of passage from stasis, silence, darkness, and the Old to movement, sound, light, and the New will be repeated over and over in Vertov's films, at least from *Kino-Eye* onwards; and this poem, dated 1920, suggests that Vertov was concerned to convey the feel of radical transition even before his significant work in film began.

---

71 RGALI f. 2091, op. 2, d. 228, l. 20; the poem is dated September 1920. A different transcription of the same poem, along with a less literal, more "Futurist" translation by "T. S. Naivist" [Yuri Tsivian], appears in *LR*, 33.

The debt of Vertov's 1920s writing on film to Futurist theories and proclamations is plain. We will hold our detailed treatment of Vertov's writing in reserve until volume 2, but can note immediately how the imagery of his early manifestos—celebrating "the hurricanes of movement... the race of points, lines, planes, volumes... the poetry of machines... the blinding grimaces of red-hot streams," and so on[72]—derive to no small degree from Futurist rhetoric such as we find it in this 1914 lecture by Mayakovsky (as paraphrased by a journalist in attendance):

> The poetry of Futurism is the poetry of the city, of the contemporary city. The city replaces nature and the elements. The city itself is becoming nature, in whose bowels the new urban person is being born. Telephones, airplanes, express trains, elevators, rotating machines... factory chimneys ... these are the elements of beauty in the new, urban nature. We see the electric lamp more often than the old romantic moon. We city-dwellers do not know forests, fields, and flowers. We know the tunnels of streets with their movement, noise, banging, flashing, eternal rotation. Most importantly, the rhythm of life is changing. All has become lightning fast, fast flowing, like on a filmstrip. Even the peaceful, unhurried rhythms of the old poetry are not in accord with the psyche of the contemporary city-dweller. Feverishness—that's what symbolizes the speed of contemporary life. In the city there are no even, measured, rounded lines; angles, sharp bends, zigzags—that's what characterizes the image of the city. Poetry, according to the Futurists, must answer to the new elements of the psyche of the contemporary city.[73]

To be sure, even Vertov's very earliest manifestos (from 1922–23) not only move to replace the *urban* imagery of classical Futurism ("telephones ... elevators ... the tunnels of streets") with more strictly *industrial* topoi ("the delight of mechanical labor, the perception of the beauty of chemical processes ... film epics of electric power plants and flame"),[74] but also shy away from justifying "Kino-Eye" practice in terms of any modernized "psyche" already typical of contemporary life, instead giving primacy to technology as such—"electricity's unerring ways . . . the light, precise movements of

---

72 All from "We: Variant of a Manifesto" (1922), *KE*, 9.
73 From a lecture of January 24, 1914 in Nikolaev (today Mykolaiv, Ukraine), described in Flaner, "U futuristov," *Nikolaevskaia gazeta* 2391 (January 26, 1914): 3; cited in Krusanov, *Russkij avangard*, vol. 1, 214.
74 "We: Variant of a Manifesto" (1922), *KE*, 8.

machines"[75]—and its presumed capacity to generate entirely new, hitherto unknown modes of subjectivity in the future.[76] Indeed, it may be that the effect of classic prerevolutionary Futurism is perceptible above all not in Vertov's articles but in the iconography of his films—the "evening full of contrasts" sequence in *Stride, Soviet*, for instance (to be discussed in chapter 4), and of course the whole of *Man with a Movie Camera*—even if the early manifestos, rather than his poems, ultimately constitute Vertov's main contribution to the literature of late Futurism.[77]

In regard to questions of form and medium, the Futurist insistence on the "autonomy of the word" obviously had a decisive if complex impact on Vertov's thinking about art in general. Mayakovsky again, from the same 1914 lecture:

> The word must not describe, but express in and of itself. The word has its smell, color, spirit; the word is a living organism, and not only a badge for the determination of some meaning or other. The word is capable of endless cadences, like a musical scale.[78]

To be sure, this position helped to justify a project of radical experimentation that effectively bracketed the problem of communicable meaning, removing

---

75 Ibid., 7–8.
76 A full development of this notion would take up a good deal of space, and have to take account of countervailing assertions from within the Futurist camp. Viktor Shklovsky's 1919 attack in *Art of the Commune* on the Proletkult notion of the need for a new art to correspond to the new proletarian society and consciousness—when Futurism, insisted Shklovsky, had by contrast always proposed that "new forms [of art] would create new content [in art and life]"—would be one important counterexample ("Ob iskusstve i revoliutsii," *Iskusstvo Kommuny* 17 [March 30, 1919]: 2; cited in Krusanov, *Russkij avangard*, vol. 2, book 1, 197).
77 I would add here that Vertov's Futurist influences would appear to be exclusively Russian: there is effectively no good evidence that he was directly acquainted with the earlier Italian variant even in translation, and any influence was thoroughly mediated by Russian sources. On the influence of Italian Futurism upon the Russians, see Mario Verdone, "Dziga Vertov nell'avanguardia," in *Dziga Vertov*, ed. Nikolaj Abramov (Rome: Bianco e Nero, 1963), XXI–XXII; Anna Lawton, "Russian and Italian Futurist Manifestoes," *Slavic and East European Journal* 20, no. 4 (Winter 1976): 405–20. On relevant affinities between the movements, see Maria Elena Versari, "Futurist Machine Art, Constructivism and the Modernity of Mechanization," and Wanda Strauven, "Futurist Poetics and the Cinematic Imagination: Marinetti's Cinema without Films," in *Futurism and the Technological Imagination*, ed. Günter Berghaus (Amsterdam: Rodopi, 2009), 149–76, 201–28.
78 Krusanov, *Russkij avangard*, vol. 1, 214. See also the classic manifestos in Anna Lawton and Herbert Eagle, trans. and eds., *Words in Revolution: Russian Futurist Manifestoes 1912-1928* (Washington, DC: New Academic Publishing, 2004), 55–81.

conventional "sense" as a regulative principle for the construction of verse, while still reserving a necessary (if deferred) role for autonomous linguistic "expression." As we will see in later chapters, this attitude seems to have conditioned Vertov's artistic ideology on a number of levels and throughout his career: from his ambiguously purist insistence on separating artistic media to allow for their autonomous development; through his antagonism toward freighting images with the tropes of fiction, explanatory intertitles, or (later) voiceover; and on to his doctrine, perhaps best realized (as noted earlier) in *Enthusiasm*, that what was usually deemed mere sonic and visual raw material, or noise, in fact bore within itself expressive meaning whose actualization was cinema's true task. It might be thought that the Futurists operated with a far more counterintuitive set of presuppositions, insofar as their raw material, language itself, seems fatally petrified within well-nigh geological layers of sense that could hardly be chipped away by formal experiment. Vertov, as we have already suggested and will see again, would have the apparent advantage of working with less semantically burdened material— indexical/iconic image and sound—that could be reconfigured into "endless cadences" without ever losing its power immediately to refer.

Despite the frequent reliance of their poetry upon dense internal rhyming, the Futurists seem not to have consistently related this practice to any *mnemonic* function of the type that evidently interested Vertov from an early age. To be sure, they did acknowledge the formal affinities between their poetry and older, anonymous chants and incantations, and theorist Boris Arvatov in 1923 noted that the Futurist "coupling of words acquires an aural and a psychoassociative expressiveness" which is "easily memorized" after the fashion of "orally transmitted proverbs."[79] That Vertov's concern with mnemonic "formal binding" drew him toward this aspect of Futurist poetics seems plausible; we might wonder, too, whether he might also have accepted the paradoxical pressure that this binding could place upon conventional linguistic meaning and comprehensibility. After all, the more the material (phonetic, graphic) weight of words in combination is stressed in order to make them memorable, the more likely it is that those words might stray from "normal" significations.

Indeed, it is worth noting parenthetically that some traditional mnemonic practices involved the creation of extravagant, near-nonsense kinds of sentences as a consequence of the imposition of memorable patterns or even full-fledged codes upon language. A mnemonic technique commonly

---

79 B. Arvatov, "Language Creation (On 'Transrational' Poetry)," in *Words in Revolution*, 224. The essay was first published as "Rechetvorchestvo," *LEF* 2 (1923): 79–91.

described in nineteenth-century primers involved the systematic conversion of a sequence of numbers (or some other abstract order) that needed to be memorized into words that would then be linked together in phrases deemed more memorable than the original numerals. The results of this conversion—and I should stress that I am *not* trying to trivialize the work of experimental poets with this example—loosely recall, in their jingling inscrutability, avant-garde verse, as here in this typical late nineteenth-century instance:

> Shoot in a fury, ugly Sheriff. . . .
> Heave it off, my sooty deep robe.
> A tiny hoop of mamma shook a mummy.
> Asian warriors usually weigh each a share.[80]

(The first line cited here corresponds to "61284768," according to the primer's conversion table; the last three lines are presented in their original sequence.) The eccentricity here might seem to be my own more than the mnemotician's, but my point in mentioning these curios is simply to suggest how a mnemonic imperative, in asserting its formal dominance within the framework of a sentence or line, might exert radical pressure upon sense. We have already seen how Vertov's poetry illustrates this tension; we will see later how the photographic "fact" in Vertov's work of the 1920s will play the role of a "material unit" that can be subjected to well-nigh endless restructuring, while retaining a referential, that is, meaningful, function.

As is well known, the ramifications of the Futurist concern with work upon material, including photographic and other "facts," were worked through in the pages of the Futurist-led journals of the Left Front of the Arts in the 1920s, specifically *LEF* and *Novyj LEF*, both edited by Mayakovsky. It was in the pages of *LEF* that Vertov published what is arguably his single most important article, "Kinocs: A Revolution" (*LEF*, June 1923), and significant aspects of Vertov's thinking about film were presaged, as we will see in volume

---

80 This example is taken from Alphonse Loisette, *Physiological Memory: or, The instantaneous art of never forgetting; (which uses none of the "Localities," "Keys," "Pegs," "Links," "Tables" or "Associations" of "Mnemonics") by Prof. A. Loisette, sole originator, proprietor and teacher thereof*, 4th ed. (New York: Alphonse Loisette, 1886), 35, 40–41. Related techniques of translating orders or chronologies into sentences (or vice versa) are outlined in Anonymous [T. W. D.], *Mnemonics: or, the New Science of Artificial Memory* (New York: James Mowatt and Co., 1844), esp. 37–38; Aimé Paris, *Exposition et pratique des procédés de la Mnémotechnie* (Paris: Aimé Paris, C. Farcy, 1826), esp. VII and LXXXIII; and Lorenzo D. Johnson, *Memoria Technica*, 3rd ed. (Boston: Gould, Kendall and Lincoln, 1847). Mnemonics were certainly known in Russia, and by the time of Vertov's student years may have been distilled into relatively non-eccentric forms: see, for instance, P. A. Sokolov, *Pedagogicheskaia psikhologiia*, 5th edition (St. Petersburg: Ia. Bashmakov, 1913), esp. 90–106.

2, in the pages of the short-lived pre-*LEF komfut* (Communist-Futurist) paper *Art of the Commune* (December 1918 to March 1919). Other journals that published and discussed Vertov's work, especially Constructivist Aleksej Gan's *Kino-Fot* (1922), included writing, photos, and illustrations by artists like Mayakovsky, Rodchenko, and Varvara Stepanova, and helped to constitute that Futurist-Constructivist constellation so important for early Soviet experimental culture.[81] A controversial participant in the tumultuous meeting about the reorganization of *LEF* in January 1925,[82] Vertov was central enough to the loose *LEF* federation by 1927 for his face to be represented on an advertising leaflet for *Novyj LEF*, along with Mayakovsky, Brik, Eisenstein, Rodchenko, Stepanova, Pasternak, Sergei Tret′iakov, and other luminaries of the artistic left wing.[83] Thus Vertov's mature career as a publishing polemicist and theorist took place primarily within a Futurist-Constructivist milieu; indeed, he can be counted, with Eisenstein, Kuleshov, and Shub, as one of the favored filmmakers of that milieu.

The Futurist influence upon Vertov explicitly reasserted itself again in the 1930s, after Mayakovsky's suicide, when Vertov attempted to align his "ultra-left" and avant-gardist film practice with the new populism and emphasis on communication and clarity typical of emergent socialist realism. As we will see in volume 3, the striking and Stalin-affirmed popularity of Mayakovsky's poems, along with affinities that Vertov was able to draw between Mayakovsky's Futurist work and folk verse, enabled the filmmaker to assert that his own Futurist-inspired cinematic practice had been affined with the "popular" all along.[84] Indeed, it could be said that the strange intertwining of enthusiasm for technology and urbanism with archaism that many critics have noted in Russian Futurist poetry—the sense, that is, that their avant-garde practice amounted to a liberation of primordial linguistic and cultural (or national) possibilities long suppressed—found its most accessible and "classical" expression during the Stalin period, in that era's amalgams of industrial-technological

---

81 Work by Rodchenko and/or Stepanova appeared in every issue of *Kino-Fot*, and Mayakovsky made appearances in issues 4 and 6. The polemic between the Constructivist-leaning journal *Zrelishcha* [*Spectacles*, 1923–24] and *LEF* can be seen in retrospect to have taken place on a field of shared concerns, centering on the relationship between art and industrial production, the contemporary salience of the category "art" itself, and the status of the "fact."
82 See RGALI f. 2852, op. 1, d. 115.
83 The leaflet is reproduced in Leah Dickerman, "The Fact and the Photograph," *October* 118 (Fall 2006): 132.
84 *KE*, 180–87.

Image 2: From *Three Songs of Lenin* (1934): A woman in traditional Kazakh apparel starting a tractor. Source: Yale University Film Archive.

and folk-national iconographies, as in *Three Songs of Lenin*, a film made at what turned out to be the terminus of Vertov's years of peak productivity (1934).[85]

Finally, "Vertov," his name, a Futurist mintage, which he began to use both familiarly and as a professional nom de plume no later than 1917–18. It is derived from the Russian verb *vertét'* or (reflexive) *vertét'sia*, "to rotate or turn," and is cognate with other Russian words like *vértel* (a "spit" or "skewer"), *vertúshka* (a "whirligig," but also a "flirt"), the adjective *vertliávyj* ("restless" or "frivolous"), as well as some modern coinages, Futurist or Soviet, like *vertolyót* (the word for "helicopter," combining "revolve" with "fly" [*lyot-*]). It has many Indo-European kin, like the Latin *verto* ("to turn," but also "to flee," "to overthrow," and "to interpret"), from which derive our own "convert," "invert," "pervert," "revert," "vertigo," and so on.

---

85 See, among other sources, Vladimir Markov, *Russian Futurism: A History* (Berkeley: University of California Press, 1968), esp. 13 and 93; Roman Jakobson, "Novejshaia russkaia poeziia," in *Mir Velimira Khlebnikova: stat'i, issledovaniia 1911–1998*, ed. V. V. Ivanov et al. (Moscow: Iazyki Russkoj Kul'tury, 2000), esp. 56.

Although Mikhail Kaufman once suggested that "Dziga" was an onomatopoetic imitation of the "dz-z-z" sound made by the reel on an editing table (and that "Vertov" referred above all to the crank used to turn the reel), this is a less likely derivation than "(spinning, i.e., toy) top," which is what *dziga* means in Ukrainian.[86] Judging by the sound of it, *dziga* might already mimic the noise of a whirling gadget like a top or a reel. That the word is Ukrainian—not a language spoken in the Kaufman household, to my knowledge—makes me wonder whether it wasn't bestowed upon David Kaufman by his witty and eloquent friend from Kiev, Mojsej Fridliand (aka Mikhail Kol'tsov), though I have no proof that it was. In any event, we are probably not wrong to see the proliferation of spinning and turning things in Vertov's films (and especially in his most personal film, *Man with a Movie Camera*) as a kind of autobiographical signature, like Bach's B-A-C-H or Shostakovich's D-S-C-H. (On the other hand, of course, the motif of rotation inscribes a larger historical-political idea into an apparently personal name: "revolution," no less.)[87]

As far as the "*-ov*" in "Vertov" is concerned, that is of course a standard (genitive) ending characteristic of Russian family names, and perhaps "Vertov" could more accurately be termed a *Russo-Futurist* neologism. In my experience, it raises few eyebrows among native Russians, despite its artificial origins (though sometimes it is confused for the relatively common surname "Vetrov"). Indeed, like many other Futurist inventions, David Kaufman's postrevolutionary name fused elements of the Old with the New. "Dziga" is less easy to assimilate, perhaps because it sounds a bit like the Russian word for "gypsy" (*tsygan*), and more like a nickname than a "real" name.[88] Perhaps sensing the need for a "proper" proper name, Vertov at some point late in the fall of 1918 adopted "Denis Arkad'evich" as his first name and patronymic respectively.[89] These new monikers retain his original initials "D. A."—"Dziga," it will be noted, also begins with "D" and ends with "A"—and in the majority of later official documents he is indicated as either "D. A. Vertov" or "D. Vertov."

---

86 G.I. Kopalina, "Poslednee interv'iu Mikhaila Kaufmana," *Novyj Mir* 1 (1994); here cited from http://magazines.russ.ru/novyi_mi/1994/1/kaufman01.html.
87 A point also made by Erik Barnouw (in *Media Lost and Found*, introduction by Dean Duncan [New York: Fordham University Press, 2001], 164).
88 Indeed, I suspect that it *was* a childhood nickname, judging from the way it is used in the extant memoirs.
89 The earliest documented reference to "Denis Arkad'evich" I have seen is in Listov, *Istoriia smotrit v ob'ektiv* (171), and dates to the fall of 1918: later, evidently, than September 22 (see Magidov, "Iz arkhiva Vertova," 162). It is worth mentioning that, due to the patronymic character of Russian middle names, changing one's middle name virtually amounts to changing one's father's first name as well.

On one level, to be sure, this renaming was an instance of that self-russification embraced by so many young Jews of Vertov's class and educational background in those years, a token of their entry into what historian Yuri Slezkine has called "the Pushkin religion."[90] The transformation seems to have been at once a kind of flight response in the face of widespread anti-Semitism, a consequence of genuine attraction to Russian culture, and a way of asserting a distance (though not an absolute one, often) from Jewish beliefs and practices that, for this cohort, held little appeal. His younger brother Mojsej had already become "Mikhail" by 1917, and Boris, as indicated in chapter 1, always bore that Russian name. Vertov's siblings retained "Kaufman," although all of Dziga's and Mikhail's associates in Moscow in the '20s would have known that they were brothers. (We can safely assume that no one thought Mikhail had changed his name to "Kaufman" from "Vertov.")

Still, there are some interesting ambiguities to be teased out of "Denis Arkad'evich" as well. "Denis" comes to Russian from French, of course, and is the name of a famous eighteenth century Russian satirical playwright, Denis Fonvizin (1744/45–92), and of a well-known Russian Romantic poet-soldier (Denis Davydov, 1799–1837). "Arkadij" (from which "Arkad'evich" derives) was a name used almost exclusively by monks until the second half of the nineteenth century, and comes from the Greek *Arkadios*, meaning "Arcadia-dweller": that is, a shepherd or herdsman, but also (in the well-known literary applications of the toponym) a happy denizen of pastoral paradise, and/or celebrant of the feast of Demeter, goddess of the harvest. As happened with "Tatiana" after the appearance of Pushkin's *Eugene Onegin*, "Arkadij" was popularized by a literary prototype, Ivan Turgenev's eponymous character in *Fathers and Sons* (1862).[91] Thus, "Denis Arkad'evich" has a sophisticated, even literary ring to it, at least to my ear: the name of a fin-de-siècle aesthete, perhaps? In any case, most people who worked with or befriended Vertov in later years always referred to him as "Denis Arkad'evich." "Dziga" was primarily reserved for polemic and publicity on the one hand, and intimacy (especially with Liza Svilova and Misha and Borya Kaufman) on the other: even his parents called him "Dziga." Only Masha Gal'pern, now at a distance, evidently persisted in using "Dodia" (the familiar short form for "David").[92]

---

90 See Yuri Slezkine, *The Jewish Century* (Princeton, NJ: Princeton University Press, 2004), 127; and the discussion in chapter 1.
91 See A. V. Superanskaia, *Imia — cherez veka i strany* (Moscow: Nauka, 1990), 23, 153.
92 RGALI f. 2091, op. 1, d. 171, l. 1 (letter from Bialystok to Svilova in Moscow, dated July 14, 1931); Boris Kaufman Archive, Beinecke Library, Yale University, GEN MSS 562.12.214 (letter from Masha Gal'pern to Boris Kaufman of November 9, 1945).

A JOB IN "*KHRONIKA*"

It wasn't until the end of May 1918 that David Kaufman was offered a position, by his old friend and rapidly blossoming journalist Mikhail Kol'tsov, as an office manager and bookkeeper in the Moscow Film Committee.[93] As indicated earlier, Kol'tsov was traveling a good deal during 1917–18—despite never officially withdrawing from the medical faculty of the Psychoneurological Institute until September 13, 1918[94]—particularly between Petrograd and Kiev, where his parents and brother Boris Efimov were staying.[95] He witnessed Lenin's return to Russia at Petrograd's Finland Station in April 1917, and in 1918 published vivid descriptive feuilletons about both the February and October Revolutions in the Kiev paper *Evening* (*Vecher*).[96] His acquaintance with Lunacharsky and Chicherin led not only to coveted newspaper work, but also to his lifelong if irregular involvement with nonfiction (*khronika*) film. In February 1918, Kol'tsov was working with Boltianskij in the soon-to-be-dissolved Skobelev Committee's "social-film" division (discussed below), and traveled that month with cameraman Petr Novitskij to Finland to film the struggles between the Finnish Red and White Guards.[97] Shortly after this, he was made chair of the *khronika* division of the All-Russian Cinema Committee of the People's Commissariat of Enlightenment (Narkompros), the government ministry in charge of culture and education, famously headed by Lunacharsky.[98]

We have already suggested that David Kaufman may have developed an interest in cinema during his years at the Psychoneurological Institute; we can assume that Kol'tsov hired him for the film-administration position both on the basis of long friendship and because he thought Kaufman would do a good job. The job itself, no doubt, was the important thing for Kaufman. For a poor student in Moscow, and a refugee to boot, survival would have been the primary concern in the spring of 1918. Although the worst was yet to come, Moscow had already experienced famine during the years of the world

---

93 Magidov (in *Zrimaia pamiat' istorii*, 84) cites a form filled out by Vertov where he evidently indicates May 28 as his first day on the job (GARF f. 3524, op. 1, d. 30, l. 22); *Letopis' Rossijskogo Kino 1863–1929* (henceforth *LRK* 1) gives May 30 as Vertov's starting date (251), but I have seen no documentary confirmation of this. See also *KE*, 40, 119.
94 TsGIASPb f. 155, op. 2, d. 9788, l. 40.
95 Beliaev et al., *Mikhail Kol'tsov, kakim on byl*, 78.
96 Fradkin, "Novoe o Mikhaile Kol'tsove."
97 Magidov, *Zrimaia pamiat' istorii*, 64.
98 Boris Efimov indicates that Kol'tsov went with one D. Manuil'skij to Kiev with the nonfiction/newsreel unit in 1918 (probably after the Brest-Litovsk Treaty of March 3) (Beliaev et al., *Mikhail Kol'tsov, kakim on byl*, 79). See also Listov, *Istoriia smotrit v ob'ektiv*, 90–92.

war, and the transport and supply situation grew worse in 1917 and early 1918 with the ongoing breakdown of state institutions nationwide, the military catastrophes of the summer, the continuing threat from German forces, and the initial Civil War skirmishes in Ukraine and southern Russia.[99] Moscow's population had begun draining away after May 1917, and by September of that year, the city's population had dropped by almost 200,000, continuing to plummet through at least the middle of 1920, by which time a million people had left, mainly for the countryside.[100] As a Jew, however, and attached in some way or other to family members stuck in Moscow, David Kaufman would not likely have considered sitting out the hard times in a Russian village; indeed, it is not surprising that the Jewish populations in Russia's major cities evidently decreased far less than did the general population during the years of the Civil War.[101]

To be sure, the living situation in Moscow was dangerous as well as precarious. Boris Kaufman recalled that

> Moscow had been transformed into a military camp ... it was impossible to go out into the street because shots were being fired every second. We had to stuff pillows into the window frames....[102]

---

99 These disasters were of course a part of that "first demographic catastrophe" (1915–22) described in chapter 2; for a summary, see P. Polian et al., *Gorod i derevnia v evropejskoj Rossii: sto let peremen* (Moscow: OGI, 2001), 40–44.

100 Diane P. Koenker, "Urbanization and Deurbanization in the Russian Revolution and Civil War," in *Party, State and Society in the Russian Civil War: Explorations in Social History*, ed. William G. Rosenberg Koenker and Ronald Grigor Suny (Bloomington: Indiana University Press, 1989), 90. Most of the decline (of almost 700,000) took place between 1918 and 1920 (ibid., 91). Koenker summarizes: "Over the entire period from February 1917 to August 1920, Moscow's population dropped by almost one million, a loss of 520,000 males, and 470,000 females. During the same period, there were roughly 110,000 births and 200,000 deaths, a natural decrease of 90,000. Thus, about 900,000 people must have left the city by the summer of 1920" (ibid., 90). Petrograd's population "plummeted from 2.5 million in 1917 to 700,000 in 1920" (ibid., 81). See also S. G. Wheatcroft and R. W. Davies, "Population," in *The Economic Transformation of the Soviet Union, 1913–1945*, ed. R. W. Davies, Mark Harrison, and S. G. Wheatcroft (Cambridge: Cambridge University Press, 1994), esp. 62.

101 Budnitskij, *Rossijskie evrei*, 102. The diary of Grigorij Boltianskij's wife Olga, to which I will refer below, narrates her travels with their two children between Petrograd and a village called Vysokoe in the fall of 1918. An ethnic Russian, Olga still spent most of the war with her children in desperately hungry Petrograd (RGALI f. 2057, op. 2, d. 26, ll. 555–557). *Kino-Nedelia* 5 (1918) concludes with a vivid depiction of people crowded together around a Petrograd train station waiting to leave the city.

102 "Entrevue avec Boris Kaufman," Beinecke Library, Yale University, GEN MSS 562, box 16, folder 336, 3. Photographic evidence of the destruction in Moscow is offered in the third part of the Skobelev Committee's *October Revolution* (*Oktiabr'skij perevorot*, 1917

Yet procuring food was and would remain the major problem for residents of both Moscow and Petrograd for some time to come. The average daily ration of bread received by Muscovites declined from one pound to half a pound between early 1917 and the spring of 1919, shrinking at times to a mere eighth of a pound.[103] (We will see in chapter 4 and in volume 2 how Vertov makes precise historical reference to this "fractioning" of bread in a memorable animated sequence in *Stride, Soviet.*) People in the city were going hungry, and it is not surprising that Vertov on September 1, 1918—he was already "Vertov" by then, though he added "Kaufman" in parentheses—indicated on a questionnaire that the only "Soviet institution" he regularly made use of was "the First Soviet Cafeteria."[104]

In the same questionnaire, he rather saucily indicates that his main political sympathies—plainly a matter of affinity rather than party membership or even considered conviction—lay with the "anarcho-individualists."[105] It is difficult to know how seriously to take this acknowledgement. Anarchism had had a long and stormy history in Russia, of course, not least in Vertov's native Bialystok, one of the birthplaces of anarchist activism in the empire.[106] However,

---

[RGAKFD 12530]); in *October Socialist Revolution in Moscow and Petrograd* (1917 [RGAKFD 628]); and in *On the events in Moscow in November* (*K moskovskim noiabr'skim sobytiiam*, 1917 [RGAKFD 11905]), which prefaces—ironically?—its images of shot-up buildings with the title "Victory of the Bolsheviks and Red Guards. Brief overview."

103 Mauricio Borrero, *Hungry Moscow: Scarcity and Urban Society in the Russian Civil War 1917–1921* (New York: Peter Lang, 2003), 11, 75–79. On the high levels of famine and/or famine-related death in urban Russia between 1918 and 1920, see Nikolai M. Dronin and Edward G. Bellinger, *Climate Dependence and Food Problems in Russia, 1900–1990: The Interaction of Climate and Agricultural Policy and Their Effect on Food Problems* (Budapest: Central European University Press, 2005), 93.

104 V. M. Magidov, "Iz arkhiva Vertova," *Kinovedcheskie Zapiski* 18 (1993): 161–64; here 163; GARF f. 3524, op. 1, d. 30, l. 22. On the importance of the often unappealingly provisioned cafeterias, see Borrero, *Hungry Moscow*, 154–60. Vertov's entry into filmmaking in May 1918 coincided with the declaration of the regime's "food supply dictatorship" (involving requisitioning peasant grain, compulsory sale of food at fixed prices and much coercion) the same month (Lewis H. Siegelbaum, *Soviet State and Society between Revolutions, 1918–1929* [Cambridge: Cambridge University Press, 1992], 42).

105 Magidov, "Iz arkhiva Vertova," 163. Literally, the question read: "To which party do you belong, or do you belong to no party?" Vertov's response: "To no party. I sympathize with the anarchist-individualists."

106 On anarchism in Bialystok, see N. I. Rogdaev, "Kratkij ocherk anarkhicheskogo dvizheniia v Pol'she, Litve i Lifliandii," in *Anarkhisty: dokumenty i materialy*, ed. V.V. Shelokhaev et al. (Moscow: Rosspen, 1998),413–24, esp. 417–18; Iurij Glushakov, *"Revoliutsiia umerla! Da zdravstvuet revoliutsiia!" Anarkhizm v Belarusi (1902–1927)* (Moscow: ShSS, 2015); and Budnitskij, *Rossijskie evrei*, 46.

Moscow's anarchists, a disparate group by all accounts, had become targets of repression by the Cheka (the ruthless Communist state security organ) by no later than April 1918.[107] Vertov, it seems, gravitated toward the programmatically unsociable and therefore less dangerous "individualists," whose ideology derived from Max Stirner's egoistic anti-collectivism.[108] The offhand character of Vertov's response casts doubt on the intensity of his attraction to anarchism in any case; still, if Aleksandr Levitskij is to be believed, he seems to have persisted at least into the early 1920s in supporting and citing the poetic work of the Imaginists, whose openly if apolitically anarchist attitudes (and posturing) were well known.[109] What Vertov's response clearly *does* suggest, apart from his awareness of anarchism, is that in September 1918, he still felt comfortable proclaiming his personal ideological distance from the regime forming at the time, and for which he was already working: plainly, he did not take a job in the Film Committee because of a quasi-religious conversion to Bolshevism, or indeed because of any particular political commitments. As it turns out, he would never directly express political eccentricity again, at least not in any publicly available or unambiguous form. Meanwhile, the language and problematic of Marxism—channeled through Constructivism, official political rhetoric, personal reading, and perhaps other sources—would come to exert its effects upon his filmmaking and his thinking about cinema, powerfully if idiosyncratically.

Vertov was twenty-two years old when he began working for the Moscow Film Committee. In retrospect, he does not seem to have been easily categorizable in terms of any of the old or new rubrics of social classification on offer in Russia. He had not completed his university studies, and probably was not even a student by that time; he had been drafted, but had not served in the army as a soldier; he had not acquired a profession or professional identity; he had not been involved in the revolutionary movement, and was certainly not a worker or peasant; and, though a Jew, he clearly did not regard himself as an

---

107 Evan Mawdsley, *The Russian Civil War* (Edinburgh: Birlinn, 2000), 82. Some traces of anarchism remained for a while: the anarchist-communist leader Apollon Karelin (1863–1926) was a member of the All-Russian Central Executive Committee in 1918, and appears in Vertov's *Brain of Soviet Russia* from that year; he was later involved in memorials to Kropotkin in Moscow, and in anarchist journals published abroad. See Paul Avrich, *The Russian Anarchists* (Princeton, NJ: Princeton University Press, 1967).
108 On anarcho-individualism in Russia, see V. I. Federov-Zabrezhnev, "Propovedniki individualisticheskogo anarkhizma v Rossii," in *Anarkhisty*, ed. Shelokhaev et al., 429–43; and V. D. Ermakov and P. I. Talerov, eds., *Anarkhizm v istorii Rossii ot istokov k sovremennosti: bibliograficheskij slovar'-spravochnik* (St. Petersburg: Solart, 2007), 517–18.
109 Krusanov, *Russkij avangard*, vol. 2, part 1, 357–82; and footnote 64, above.

observant member of any confessional community. Nor, being a refugee, could he claim even the status of local *intelligent* that his father, past and future owner of a large, up-to-date bookstore in Bialystok, probably did claim.[110] Indeed, "refugee" was the only label that really fit him, although being a Bialystoker was perhaps also important in cementing the connection with his *zemliák* (local compatriot or *landsman*) Mikhail Kol'tsov. Peter Gatrell writes,

> To be a refugee ... was to stand outside established boundaries of society, to be waiting on the margins of social life in the hope that one's status would be resolved, and to become accustomed to new structures of space.[111]

To be sure, Vertov was a refugee with certain tools and advantages at his disposal, among them a solid if incomplete education and useful connections. As it turns out, for a refugee to find work in the Commissariat of Enlightenment in those early months was far from unusual, as historian M. B. Kejrim-Markus has shown. Many on staff in the Commissariat were refugees from the Baltics, Poland, and the western and later southern regions of Russia and its empire: young people, overwhelmingly, who had lost their opportunity to get a diploma before the revolution but found a way, Kejrim-Markus asserts, to acquire professional training and do interesting intellectual and cultural work, and eventually make a career, within the confines of the Commissariat.[112]

In the most general terms, it might be said that Vertov was part of an important cohort of participants in the formation of Soviet society who were too young to claim membership in any wing of the pre-Revolutionary intelligentsia—much less in the revolutionary underground[113]—and too old to be beneficiaries of the systematic educational and professional promotion of (mainly) workers and peasants that began in earnest in the late 1920s: the *vydvizhentsy* ("promotees") of the Stalin era, made famous by the work

---

110 His parents' "estate" identity (townsperson, *meshchanin*) had, of course, been abolished along with all the other estates on October 28, 1917.
111 Gatrell, "Refugees in the Russian Empire, 1914–1917," in Acton et al., eds., *Critical Companion to the Russian Revolution*, 562.
112 Kejrim-Markus, *Gosudarstvennoe rukovodstvo kul'turoj*, 182. On Jews entering state service at this early date, see Budnitskij, *Rossijskie evrei*, 97–98, 102–3.
113 Kejrim-Markus indicates that the overwhelming majority of workers in the lower ranks of the Commissariat—mainly clerical and office staff, like Vertov at the outset— were non-Party members; they made up 64 percent of the Commissariat's total labor force (*Gosudarstvennoe rukovodstvo kul'turoj*, 184).

of historian Sheila Fitzpatrick.[114] I have searched in vain through the existing historical and sociological literature on Russia during this period to find an established term for Vertov's cohort, despite the fact that many "cultural workers" of the 1920s, including many in the film industry, surely had similar backgrounds.[115] Think of Eisenstein (who never completed his engineering studies), Boris Barnet (who never finished art school), and Vertov's brother Mikhail, all of whom were born between 1896 and 1902 and ended up serving, in some capacity or other, in the Red Army before becoming art-workers. But for chronic pleurisy, Vertov would doubtless have served as well; his agit-train work would stand in for that experience, as we will see.[116]

It would seem that, if Vertov's case is in any way exemplary, entry into Soviet cultural institutions for this floating cohort was more a matter of luck and connections than of long-standing political conviction (as with the older radicals) or of state policy and practice (as with the *vydvizhentsy* to come). For Vertov, his luck consisted above all in his connection to Kol'tsov: as his later career would show, he was no master of the vital art of "schmoozing," and I believe that without Kol'tsov's intercession, he never would have made films.

---

114 Sheila Fitzpatrick, *Education and Social Mobility in the Soviet Union, 1921–1934* (Cambridge: Cambridge University Press, 1979); and *The Cultural Front: Power and Culture in Revolutionary Russia* (Ithaca, NY: Cornell University Press, 1992), esp. 11–15, 141–80.

115 Another possible category, the "lower-middle strata" studied by historian Daniel Orlovsky, does not seem to fit either, insofar as members of those important strata—"white-collar workers, statisticians . . . clerks, sales personnel . . . village school teachers, and middle and lower-level technical personnel"—seem to have already possessed some quasi-professional skills, if not identities, prior to the Bolshevik takeover. At the same time, members of these highly heterogeneous strata did, according to Orlovsky, sympathize with the democratic ideals of the February Revolution and ended up "graft[ing] themselves onto the workers' and peasants' revolution and indeed managed to infiltrate a wide range of revolutionary class institutions. The presence of large numbers of intelligentsia, specialists, protoprofessionals, and the like imparted stability, skills, and the promise and reality of an effective apparatus for the new soviet state" (Daniel T. Orlovsky, "State Building in the Civil War Era: The Role of the Lower-Middle Strata," in *Party, State and Society in the Russian Civil War*, ed. Koenker, Rosenberg and Suny, 181 and 202).

116 Again, we know of Vertov's malady—which had not been of concern to recruiters for the Imperial Army, apparently, or had been contracted later—from the same September 1918 questionnaire (Magidov, "Iz arkhiva Vertova," 163). Vertov was still subject to recruitment during the Civil War, however, and was spared service only by "serving in the Photo and Film Division of Narkompros" (RGALI f. 2091, op. 2, d. 384, l. 1; dated November 17, 1919). On Red Army service as means of asserting a kind of "proletarian" identity, see Sheila Fitzpatrick, "Class Identities in NEP Society," in *Tear Off the Masks! Identity and Imposture in Twentieth-Century Russia* (Princeton, NJ: Princeton University Press, 2005), 54.

We might usefully contrast Vertov's lack of institutional grounding prior to 1918 with Grigorij Boltianskij's various points of access into the new regime. Boltianskij, more than a decade older than Vertov, was at once a former schoolteacher (associated with the zemstvos), a political activist affiliated with the Social Democrats, a sometime journalist, an executive member of the Skobelev Committee's "social nonfiction (*khronika*)" division, and, at least through the early fall of 1918, a delegate from the Psychoneurological Institute (where he was still enrolled) at congresses devoted to the reform of higher education.[117] Boltianskij was surely unusual in being situated in multiple groups and institutions, but I draw the contrast simply in order to suggest how much more organic (in Gramsci's sense) his participation in the cultural commissariat was, in part because of his age and experience, than Vertov's considerably more fortuitous involvement. Certainly (and most importantly for us), Boltianskij was among those who had already worked prior to October 1917 to establish the framework within which nonfiction film would be produced in early Soviet Russia. This is the framework into which Vertov stepped in May 1918, and which would largely determine his professional and even artistic identity for the rest of his career—though not, as usual, in any straightforward way.

DEMOCRATIC NONFICTION

This is as much as to say that early Soviet newsreel (most often *zhurnál* or *kinozhurnál* in Russian, even in these early years) and what was then known as *khronika* and would later be called "unstaged" or "documentary" film[118] were not created ex nihilo, and certainly not by Dziga Vertov. Soviet nonfiction film was founded primarily on the basis of two pre-Revolutionary predecessors: the shorts and newsreels produced by private firms, particularly Pathé and Gaumont (to be discussed in a later section), and the resources offered by the sole partially state-financed film concern in pre-Revolutionary Russia, the still-understudied Skobelev Committee.

---

117 RGALI f. 2057, op. 2, d. 26, ll. 547, 555. *Kino-Nedelia* 7 (July 18, 1918) concluded with a subsection on one these congresses.
118 The latter terms did not exist at the time, of course. For a discussion of the terminological problems surrounding "documentary," see chapter 4 and volume 2. In the years 1915–17, the dominant distinction, not especially well developed in film journals or elsewhere, seems to have involved a contrast between *khronika* and "staging" (*instenirovka*): see Roshal', *Nachalo vsekh nachal*, 132; and some of Boltianskij's 1917 proposals to the Skobelev Committee (RGALI f. 2057, op. 1, d. 261, ll. 51–52; discussed below).

Princess Nadezhda Belosel'skaia-Belozerskaia, sister of the famous General Mikhail Skobelev, founded the latter institution after the 1905 Russo-Japanese War as a philanthropic organization to help wounded and crippled soldiers. The committee, part of the culture and education division of the War Ministry, enjoyed state patronage and some state funding, published postcards and photographic albums, released phonograph records, and from March 1914 operated a cinema division with offices in both Moscow and Petrograd that produced short films about the Russian combatant service and the conditions on the front. It had a monopoly over military nonfiction production from 1914 through the end of 1916, and briefly contracted private cinema entrepreneurs to make its films, until it bought its own equipment and began independent production.[119] During those two years, the committee produced fiction and educational films, a number of short, well-advertised nonfiction films, and at least two longer nonfiction films about the war.[120]

As indicated in chapter 2, the film branch of the Skobelev Committee, renamed the Social Nonfiction/Newsreel (*sotsial'naia khronika*) Section of the Skobelev Educational Committee, continued and intensified its work after the February Revolution under the direction of Grigorij Boltianskij. Boltianskij headed up the section from the end of March 1917, and on April 25 received an official mandate to represent the Petrograd Soviet on the committee, now operating under the auspices of the Education Ministry, from the well-known Lev

---

119 The best account of the Skobelev Committee's work in cinema is in V. M. Magidov, *Zrimaia pamiat' istorii* (Moscow: Sovetskaia Rossiia, 1984), 50–66. See also V. Rosolovskaia, *Russkaia kinematografiia v 1917 g.: materialy k istorii* (Moscow: Iskusstvo, 1937), 36–64; N. A. Lebedev, *Ocherk istorii kino SSSR I: nemoe kino* (Moscow: Goskinoizdat, 1947), 36; Leyda, *Kino*, 74; Richard Taylor, *The Politics of the Soviet Cinema, 1917–1918* (Cambridge: Cambridge University Press, 1979), 12, 21; Ginzburg, *Kinematografiia dorevoliutsionnoi Rossii*, 181, 335–36; Daniel T. Orlovsky, "The Provisional Government and its Cultural Work," in *Bolshevik Culture: Experiment and Order in the Russian Revolution*, ed. Abbott Gleason, Peter Kenez, and Richard Stites (Bloomington: Indiana University Press, 1985), 39–56, esp. 52. The monopoly on military nonfiction production was lifted December 8, 1916 (OS). Two of the earliest Skobelev cameramen, Petr Novitskij and Petr Ermolov, continued to work through 1917 and later with Vertov on *Kino-Nedelia* (Ginzburg, ibid., 181).

120 *Pod Russkim Znamenem* [*Under the Russian Banner*] (probably 1915) and *Vtoraia Otechestvennaia Voina 1914–1915 godov* [*The Second Patriotic War of 1914–1915*] (1916) (Ginzburg, *Kinematografiia dorevoliutsionnoi Rossii*, 183). Pathé and Gaumont news shorts covering the Western front were widely shown in Russia as well (ibid., 187). Production was complicated by the fact that the committee's studio was located in Moscow, while the film lab was in Petrograd (Magidov, *Zrimaia pamiat' istorii*, 59). For inventories of the Skobelev Committee's films made through the end of 1917, see RGALI f. 2057, op. 1, d. 256, ll. 22ob–30ob.

Karakhan, a future Soviet diplomat and victim of the Great Terror. Karakhan was at that time still affiliated with Menshevism and its strategy of cautious cooperation with bourgeois liberals, advocacy of parliamentary participation, and broad involvement with trade unionists and non-party activists.[121] Mensheviks and members of the Socialist Revolutionary Party (SRs) dominated the Petrograd Soviet at this point, and both its composition and other evidence suggest that Boltianskij was attached to the Menshevik rather than Bolshevik wing of the SD Party.[122] In any event, it was under the supervision of a politically motley group—left-tending former monarchist V. I. Dement'ev, previously in the War Ministry; the Menshevik V. K. Ikov; and one Marianov of the Socialist Revolutionary Party[123]—that Boltianskij directed the filming of longer works like *The National Funeral of the Heroes and Victims of the Great Russian Revolution*, and starting in June headed up the Provisional Government's popular newsreel series *Svobodnaia Rossiia* (Free Russia), to be discussed in more detail in the next chapter.[124]

As indicated in chapter 2, personnel from both the Skobelev Committee and private cinema firms, particularly cameramen, would go on to work on *Kino-Nedelia* in 1918;[125] but what sorts of practices and attitudes would they

---

121 Magidov, *Zrimaia pamiat' istorii*, 57; RGALI f. 2639, op. 1, d. 63, l. 8. Karakhan joined the Bolsheviks the following month.
122 Magidov, *Zrimaia pamiat' istorii*, 59; Alexander Rabinowitch, *The Bolsheviks Come to Power: The Revolution of 1917 in Petrograd* (New York: W. W. Norton, 1976), 76–77; Rabinowitch, *The Bolsheviks in Power: The First Year of Soviet Rule in Petrograd* (Bloomington: Indiana University Press, 2007), 226. A. Shved, a friend who supported Boltianskij's petition to join the Communist (Bolshevik) Party in 1930, indicated that Boltianskij had abjured Menshevism in 1912, but this seems unlikely, given that he was still writing for Menshevik papers in 1913 (RGALI f. 2639, op. 1, d. 63, l. 2; d. 3, ll. 5–6). Bolshevik representation in the Soviet increased sharply in the fall of 1917, and with it, the Soviet's intransigence.
123 Leyda, *Kino*, 98.
124 At the beginning of March, a large group of foreign and domestic private film companies together with the Skobelev Committee produced a long chronicle film of the February Revolution in Moscow, *Velikie Dni Revoliutsii v Moskve 28 fevralia-4 marta 1917 g.* [*The Great Days of the Revolution in Moscow, February 28–March 4, 1917*] (Magidov, *Zrimaia pamiat' istorii*, 57). The Skobelev Committee also produced a remarkable pseudo-documentary entitled *Tsar Nicholas II, Autocrat of All of Russia*, a scripted film which juxtaposed acted scenes and archival footage for satirical effect (Ginzburg, *Kinematografiia dorevoliutsionnoi Rossii*, 347.) Thirteen issues of *Svobodnaia Rossiia* appeared, covering events from June 5 to October 2, 1917 (Magidov, *Zrimaia pamiat' istorii*, 59); see chapter 4 for a more detailed discussion.
125 Magidov (in *Zrimaia pamiat' istorii*, 59) has shown that by July, the Skobelev Committee's cinema section was divided into several units in both Moscow and Petrograd, involving such important figures as (in Petrograd) Boltianskij and cameraman Petr Novitskij and (in Moscow) cameraman Aleksandr Levitskij and director Vladislav Starevich. Aleksandr Lemberg (of the Perskij firm), Ianis Dored (Pathé), Petr Ermolov (Gaumont), Eduard

bring to that earliest "Soviet" newsreel? Judging from the instructions received by the committee's Social Nonfiction/Newsreel workers, most of their time was spent on what seem like straightforward matters of organization and news-gathering. The newsreel supervisor (Boltianskij) was to formulate and give precise instructions to his staff, attend important shoots, secure permissions to film, compose intertitles, and identify usable footage already on hand. His assistant was to read over the morning and evening newspapers, making notes and extracts and getting a sense of what would be happening on a given day. The cameramen—usually two, with Petr Novitskij in charge—would provide technical advice, keep records of what was filmed and how much stock was used, while shooting "lively scenes that convey the [given] situation and mood, trying to incorporate a variety of cinematic techniques [*priemy*]." The entire working collective was to gather together twice a week to watch rushes and discuss problems and ways to improve the newsreel.[126]

Directives of this sort seem relatively neutral, practical, and unsurprising. However, more programmatic statements made by committee members make it clear that the Social Nonfiction/Newsreel was to be truly "social" in its political orientation as well. Analysis of these statements, involving a certain amount of theoretical as well as historical elaboration, will help us to tease out some of the fundamental ideological matrices, linking the activity of filmmakers and their public to interpretations of wider social and political dynamics, out of which Vertov's cinema emerged.[127]

One document, a kind of policy proposal written by Boltianskij in April 1917, is particularly illuminating in this respect and needs to be quoted at length:

> The political revolution ... has led to a fundamental break in [the trajectory of] cinema affairs. The ideological shift brought about by these enormous events has roused different subjective needs among filmgoers, and has led, as a consequence, to an entirely changed marketplace demand. Political and social-economic questions are now at the center of attention of ordinary people, and will remain so for some time due to the [future] convocation and work of the Constituent Assembly.

Tisse (Skobelev Committee), and Mark Izrail'son-Naletnyj (Khanzhonkov) were among the other experienced cameramen who shot extensive footage for *Kino-Nedelia* (see Listov, *Istoriia smotrit v ob'ektiv*, 78; and RGALI f. 2091, op. 2, d. 5, ll. 5–7; d. 6, l. 3).

126 RGALI f. 2057, op. 1, d. 260, ll. 1–2.

127 For a discussion of another important and related presentation by Boltianskij (at the Second All-Russian Conference of Cinema Workers, August 22–23, 1918), see Taylor, *Politics of the Soviet Cinema*, 24–25.

In formulating this necessary, new conception of cinema affairs, and in these changed conditions, it is also important to keep in mind that, over the course of these events, the democracy [*demokratiia*]—foremost, the working class as a cultural force, as well as the army and the peasantry—have been moved to the front of the stage.

All of this gives full opportunity to those who are closely associated with cinema and who are able correctly to find the beating pulse of living life [*b'iushchijsia pul's zhivoj zhizni*] to determine the nature of the work that now needs to be done.

It is necessary by the same token to remember that the data we have on hand indicate that up to around 70 percent of all spectators are comprised of members of the working class and urban townspeople [*meshchanstvo*], with the latter group comprised mainly of women.[128] A still larger part of both of these groups now has the opportunity to go to movie theaters ([due to] higher salaries and rations provided by the state).

This entire contingent belongs entirely to the democracy and has its own particular interests and needs, which ought to be satisfied. Moreover, as a consequence of the [new] role of the democracy, members of the other, less numerous classes of society are showing an intensified interest in its activities.

All of this points to the kind of material that the screen ought to reflect, and to what it must draw upon creatively.

First, political nonfiction/newsreel [*khronika*] about the life of the democracy, which swiftly and in timely fashion reflects and develops [nonfiction/newsreel] items about the most important political [events] of the day.

Second, concerning fiction film production (that relates to the liberated situation of the new Russia) . . . we need to develop a new cinematic form for scripts based on political pamphlets, as well as adaptations of colorful social novels relevant to a given moment, alongside representations of lively moments from revolutionary history.

All of this work must be concentrated in a single division, in order to ground [production] on a single administrative basis and thereby to win

---

128 Regrettably, I have no other information about the Committee's data on cinema audiences in 1917. For scholarship and reflection on cinema spectatorship in Russia in this period, see Listov, *Rossiia, revoliutsiia, kinematograf*, 14–16 (cited in chapter 2); and Yuri Tsivian, "Early Russian Cinema and its Public," *Historical Journal of Film, Radio and Television*, trans. Alan Bodger 11, no. 2 (1991): 105–20.

in the marketplace a solid brand-name reputation artistically, in terms of content, and in terms of political literacy [*v smysle politicheskoj gramotnosti*].

Today, organizing a special film division—*a worker's division and division of political propaganda*—might have enormous historical significance and bring great popularity to the first cinema concern that establishes such a division in the proper way. In this regard, it is worth remembering the enormous demand today for books of social-economic and political content; cinema, answering to the same burning questions of the day, will doubtless attract at least as much if not more attention than books. Many important [historical] moments have already been lost to preservation on film, and... negatives [of newsreel footage]... could well have enormous value for museum collections. One need only recall not only the first days of the revolution and the birth of a new order, but the meetings among various groups of [political] émigrés, the historic opening of the Sejm in free Finland, the congress of provincial soviets of workers' and soldiers' deputies (with speeches by Plekhanov and French and English socialist delegations), the women's, teachers', cooperative and railroad workers' congresses, and the enormous meetings.[129]

The first thing to notice here is that, in conceptualizing what he believes to be a new, emergent kind of spectator, Boltianskij employs the term "democracy" in a sense unfamiliar to us today, but common in Russia in 1917, when "democracy" was a true *ideologeme*: that is, an object of discursive-political struggle.[130] Rather than some minimal set of procedures available to a citizenry for the purposes of (usually rather limited) political decision-making—classically, periodically voting for "representatives" who are to constitute a given polity's governing body—"democracy" here refers to a specific constituency, to "*the* democracy," helpfully if not unambiguously identified by Boltianskij as "foremost, the working class as a cultural force, as well as the army and the peasantry." As historian Boris Kolonitskij has shown, socialists in particular frequently placed "democracy" in opposition

---

129 RGALI f. 2057, op. 1, d. 261, ll. 51–51ob.
130 My use of "ideologeme" is indebted to the discussion in Jameson, *The Political Unconscious*, 75–99. See also my gloss in *Inscription and Modernity*, 11. The major study of the vicissitudes of "democracy" is Jens Christophersen, *The Meaning of "Democracy" as used in European Ideologies from the French to the Russian Revolution* (Oslo: Universitets-forlaget, 1966).

not to "dictatorship" (*diktatura*), "police state" (*politsejskoe gosudarstvo*), and the like, but rather to "privileged elements" (*tsenzovye elementy*), "the ruling classes" (*praviashchie klassy*), and, quite often, "the bourgeoisie" (*burzhuaziia*).[131]

The democracy, in other words, was neither a structure nor a set of procedures but a relatively specific content, made up of "the aggregate of the working masses and the socialist intelligentsia supporting the Soviets."[132]

This usage seems peculiar to us primarily because of the near-total victory, in our age of "democratic states," of the procedural ideology of democracy most succinctly expressed in economist Joseph Schumpeter's notion of "the democratic method" as "free competition among would-be leaders for the vote of the electorate."[133] In fact, as classicist M. I. Finlay has shown, the vacillations of *democracy* ("rule by the *demos*, the people") go back to democratic Athens and the word *demos* itself, which meant among other things "'the people as a whole' (or the citizen-body to be more precise) *and* 'the common people' (the lower 13 classes)."[134] It is an inflection of this second

---

131 Boris Ivanovich Kolonitskij, "'Democracy' in the Political Consciousness of the February Revolution," *Slavic Review* 57, no. 1 (Spring 1998): 100. Kolonitskij adds, "The position of the socialists sometimes influenced even the language of liberal publications. Thus *Birzhevye vedomosti* [*Stock Exchange News*] called the Executive Committee of the Soviet of Workers' and Soldiers' Deputies 'the managing organ of democracy.' The equating of 'democracy' with the socialists could be found also in [Menshevik] I. G. Tsereteli's speeches to the Constituent Assembly. He said that 'the internecine civil war of democracy, which with the hands of one part destroys the achievements of all of democracy, even surrenders it trussed by the arms and legs of the bourgeoisie.' As we see, 'democracy' was contrasted to the 'bourgeoisie,' and even at this time and in this situation he unconditionally included the Bolsheviks in the camp with 'democracy'" (ibid., 101).

132 Ibid., 101. Again, it is crucial to keep in mind that democracy in 1917 could indeed also mean a "form of government," "universal suffrage," as it did, for instance, for the exiled SR Mark Vishniak. Socialists—including SR leader Chernov, Menshevik leader Martov, and even, as we will see below, Lenin—used the word "in protean fashion, referring sometimes to a class or a presumed constituency ... and sometimes to representative procedures"; see Jane Burbank, *Intelligentsia and Revolution: Russian Views of Bolshevism 1917–1922* (New York and Oxford: Oxford University Press, 1986), 63 and (here) 95.

133 Joseph A. Schumpeter, *Capitalism, Socialism and Democracy*, 3rd ed. (New York: Harper & Row, 1975 [originally published in 1942]), 285. For a powerful critique of this Schumpeterian ideology of purely political (rather than social) democracy, see Michael Denning, "Neither Capitalist nor American: The Democracy as Social Movement," in *Culture in the Age of Three Worlds* (London: Verso, 2004), 208–26, 266–68.

134 M. I. Finley, *Democracy Ancient and Modern* (New Brunswick, NJ: Rutgers University Press, 1985), 12; my emphasis. Finlay notes that Aristotle in the *Politics* defined democracy as

sense, of *demokratiia* as (most broadly) "the revolutionary lower classes,"[135] that socialists like Boltianskij employed most frequently during this period. That specific group has now "been moved," punctually, "to the front of the stage," and it is this that constitutes the "fundamental break" to which cinema must now presumably respond.

A closer reading of Boltianskij's statement, however, reveals ambiguities in his picture of the post-Revolutionary spectator that make that "break" more difficult to characterize. The constituency of *demokratiia* as described here seems inherently, and perhaps indefinitely, to enlarge, in a dynamic announced by that slippery "foremost" ("foremost, the working class..."). We learn, for instance, that the democracy includes not only "members of the working class" but also "urban townspeople" (*meshchanstvo*: that is, the estate to which David Kaufman and his family belonged), and particularly women residing in the city: in class terms, a broad category indeed. Later in his statement, when he comes to suggest specific kinds of film work, Boltianskij incorporates Russia's vast imperial horizon into *demokratiia* as well, when he proposes that the new "screen newspaper" depict events "from the life of the great multinational democracy of Russia."[136]

Similarly, what we might call the consciousness or ethos of *demokratiia* dilates or contracts unpredictably in Boltianskij's brief account, calling into question the degree to which with "those [professionals] ... closely associated with cinema" are truly "able correctly to find the beating pulse of living life" in a particular social locus. Boltianskij assumes a new, common interest in "social-economic and political content," linking that new interest to society's preparation for engagement with the Constituent Assembly to come. Indeed, at least three of the major productions of the post-February Skobelev Committee were pedagogical films instructing viewers in democratic (in *our* habitual sense) participation.

One such film, shot by Novitskij and probably supervised by Boltianskij, was entitled *Toward the Opening of the Constituent Assembly* (1917) and was devoted primarily to the demonstrations in support of the assembly that took place on

---

"where the poor rule" (ibid., 13). The relevant passage (book 3, chapter 8) is in Aristotle, *The Politics*, trans. and introduction by Carnes Lord (Chicago: University of Chicago Press, 1984), 96–97.

135 Suny, *The Soviet Experiment*, 39.

136 RGALI f. 2057, op. 1, d. 261, l. 51ob. There may be some ambiguity here—that is, some reference to procedural democracy—given that "the Provisional Government ... established voting rights for all—men and women, nationalities and classes—in one of its first proclamations" (Marianne Kamp, *The New Woman in Uzbekistan: Islam, Modernity and Unveiling under Communism* [Seattle: University of Washington Press, 2006], 13).

November 28 in Petrograd: the day the assembly was to have convened, about two weeks after the elections to the Assembly (which saw 40 percent of the votes going to the SRs, and 24 percent to the Bolsheviks), and almost a month after the Bolshevik insurrection.[137] The film (a fragment of which has survived) combined news footage of some of the main participants in the demonstrations—former Petrograd Duma chief Grigorij Shrejder, representatives from various Russian provinces, the massive crowds and their encounter at the Taurida Palace (seat of the Provisional Government and the Petrograd Soviet) with guards loyal to Soviet power, and even a final, self-referential image of the members of the Skobelev Committee's own "social section of fictional-feature film" [*sotsial'naia sektsiia khudozhestvennoj kinematografii*]—with more generically instructional footage of pre-election canvassing and agitation, the hanging of posters, and meetings.[138]

Another Skobelev production, *Elections to the Constituent Assembly* (1917), is a remarkable staged film devoted to explaining voting eligibility and registration procedures. A middle-aged woman clasps her hands after being told by officials sitting at a table that her mentally ill nephew is not permitted to vote; a young man is rejected because he's not yet twenty years old; a man Asian in appearance is turned away because he's a foreigner; an older man (clearly an actor, or at least a ham) has been deprived of the right to vote due to being a "fraudulent bankrupt"; and a smiling, youthful soldier turns out to enjoy full voting rights despite being younger than twenty, due to his military service. Another brief section, involving some unusually elaborate camera movement and cutting for the day, explains how to fill out a vote; it culminates in the bearded, very patriarchal-looking "Stepan Petrovich Kotov" learning from a woman official that he's not allowed to vote on behalf of his wife.[139] This was the sort of "political nonfiction/newsreel about the life of

---

137 Suny, *The Soviet Experiment*, 59.
138 RGALI f. 2057, op. 1, d. 261, l. 61; for the existing fragment, see RGAKFD 11502. *Svobodnaia Rossiia* also contained brief agitational segments showing the activities (speeches, distributing pamphlets) of political activists (see issue 5 from July 3, 1917 [RGAKFD 12377]).
139 *Vybory v Uchreditel'noe Sobranie*, 1917 (RGAKFD 12214); the director and release date of the film are unknown, but Boltianskij was likely somehow involved in its making. A version of it can be seen on YouTube (https://www.youtube.com/watch?v=i03h2l1azZo [accessed October 15, 2016]). The importance of women voters was stressed frequently in post-February political actualities: see, for instance, *Demonstratsiia v Petrograde za Uchreditel'noe Sobranie* [*Demonstration in Petrograd in support of the Constituent Assembly*] (1917 [RGAKFD 578]). The third film was entitled *Toward the Government of the People* (*K narodnoj vlasti*) (1917), which may have used some of the same footage as *Constituent Assembly*; see RGALI f. 2057, op. 1, d. 261, l. 47. I will return below to the *Constituent Assembly* film and the demonstration it portrays.

the democracy," alongside adaptations of "social novels" and works of political satire[140]—evidently replacing Tsarist-era newsreel, fictional melodrama, and screen comedy respectively—that Boltianskij was proposing as one of the main genre frameworks for the new post-February cinema.

However, he additionally argues not only that this new "material" reflects the life and interests of the democracy, but that it attracts "members of the other, less numerous classes of society" as well—thereby drawing them, on the level of consciousness and concern, within the circle of democracy (in Boltianskij's primary, non-procedural sense). At the same time, however, the fact that *demokratiia* makes up around 70 percent of film audiences *at present* blurs the boundaries from the other direction. After all, if so much of the film audience is of "democratic" background already, it would seem that the films answering to *current* "marketplace demand" (*rynochnyj spros*) must satisfy some of their "subjective needs" (*zaprosy*) as well. Can the ruptures Boltianskij identifies, whether temporal (before/after the February Revolution) or social (between *demokratiia* and all the "less numerous classes") be so easily demarcated?

I would argue that these boundaries are, in fact, purposefully—or better, necessarily—represented as porous. For Boltianskij and fellow socialists of whatever party, the working contingent comprising "the democracy" stands in a special, intimate proximity to the core of social life as such, namely, to production (of goods, of services, of families, of value tout court). The productive and self-organizing activity of that contingent, therefore, will have a special relationship to whatever shape the new revolutionary society will take, now that a dominant but unproductive minority has been pushed to the sidelines, allowing for a novel and newly conscious configuration of society by those who have been generating its fundamental content, and much of its form, all along.

Yet such replacement of one dominant group or class by another can hardly be taken as the terminus of an emancipatory socialist politics that would set the *dissolution* of class-based inequality, injustice and conflict—of class itself—as its goal. Thus, we can discern in Boltianskij the envisioning of a crucial double movement of convergence, within the confines of a reflection on film spectatorship, between the large but still limited *demokratiia* and a vaster, strictly boundless whole that would both eventually incorporate and be politically activated by *demokratiia* itself. Even the relatively undifferentiated film-going public of April 1917, drawn to any and all *current* (i.e., non-"revolutionary") film, carries the seeds of social transformation, insofar as "the democracy" vibrates within it; meanwhile, the interests and discourse

---

140   RGALI f. 2057, op. 1, d. 261, l. 52.

of the more organized and visible *demokratiia*, now a true social movement "at the front of the stage," pulls all the "less numerous" classes toward itself, as it changes the whole of society through its action, thereby fulfilling its function as an "avant-garde." Fully gauging the importance of this convergence, however—or what might be better called an oscillation, on the level of ideological focus, between specific class and larger multitude—requires a somewhat deeper inquiry into aspects of the Marxist tradition that informed socialist thought and practice in 1917–18 and beyond.

That tradition has another familiar term closely bound to "the democracy," namely "proletariat," which, since Marx and Engels, has drifted revealingly between the poles of this binary, though not, as philosopher Étienne Balibar has shown in a series of brilliant writings, without tension or contradiction. On the one hand, the proletariat is in fact simply humanity, the *mass* or multitude, which emerges—as a concept or a horizon, rather than as a representation—primarily through the "negative" action of capitalism, through capitalism's capacity endlessly to connect and disconnect, to dissolve old identities and endlessly to shape new ones; and this, Balibar maintains, is the primary meaning of "proletariat" for Marxism.[141] In 1844, Marx defined the proletariat as simply "an estate [that] is the dissolution of all estates";[142] and four years later, with Engels, he wrote in the *Manifesto*:

> The bourgeoisie cannot exist without continually revolutionizing the instruments of production, hence the relations of production, and therefore social relations *as a whole*. . . . The continual transformation of production, the uninterrupted convulsion of *all* social conditions, a perpetual uncertainty and motion distinguish the *epoch* of the bourgeoisie from *all* earlier ones. *All* the settled age-old relations are dissolved; *all* newly formed ones become outmoded before they can ossify. . . . [The bourgeoisie] must get a foothold *everywhere*, settle *everywhere*, establish connections *everywhere*.[143]

---

141 Étienne Balibar, *The Philosophy of Marx*, trans. Chris Turner (London: Verso, 2007), 51.
142 From the "Introduction" to *A Contribution to the Critique of Hegel's Philosophy of Right*, accessed June 24, 2017, http://www.marxists.org/archive/marx/works/1843/critique-hpr/intro.htm.
143 "Manifesto of the Communist Party," in Karl Marx, *Later Political Writings*, ed. Terrell Carver (Cambridge: Cambridge University Press, 1996), 4; emphases mine.

The human condition brought about by these dynamics, for the overwhelming majority at any rate, is one that should be called "proletarian" in the most general sense.[144]

On the other hand, and because this transformation does not happen evenly or all at once, the proletariat is a specific *class*—that is, the industrial working class—with particular interests, outlook, and culture, which can attain political power only through a concerted struggle against the property-owning classes. This is a group with a special relationship to the production and distribution of value, to capitalism, and therefore to history. The *Manifesto* again:

> With the development of industry the proletariat not only increases; it is forced together in greater masses, *its* power grows and it feels it more. The interests, the circumstances of life within the proletariat become ever more similar ... the confrontations between individual workers and individual bourgeois increasingly take on the character of confrontation between *two classes*.[145]

Thus, on the one hand, we have the elimination of existing social relations and the generation of a new "whole" or universal, a mass; on the other (but at the same time), the creation of two particular and antagonistic classes, whose political-economic struggle culminates either (quoting the *Manifesto* yet again) in "a revolutionary reconstitution of society at large, or in the common ruin of the contending classes."[146]

Those who know the *Manifesto* well will already have realized that I have teased apart strands within a text that weaves them together continually; thus,

> ... as we have seen, there are whole sections of the ruling class dumped into the proletariat as a result of the advance of industry, or at least threatened in their essential circumstances.... at the time when the class struggle comes to a head, the process of dissolution within the ruling class, within the whole of the old society, takes on such a violent and striking character that a part of the ruling class renounces its role and commits itself to the

---

144 For a historical and critical reflection on the vicissitudes of Marxist conceptions of the "proletarian condition," see Giovanni Arrighi, "Marxist Century, American Century: The Making and Remaking of the World Labor Movement," *New Left Review* [1st series] 179 (January–February 1990): 29–63, esp. 32–38, 54–61.
145 "Manifesto of the Communist Party," 9; emphases mine.
146 Ibid., 2.

> revolutionary class, the class that holds the future in its hands. As in the past when a part of the nobility went over to the bourgeoisie, so now a part of the bourgeoisie goes over to the proletariat, in particular, a part of the bourgeois ideologists who have worked out a theoretical understanding of the whole historical development....
>
> All previous movements were movements of minorities or in the interest of minorities. The proletarian movement is the independent movement of the vast majority in the interests of that vast majority.[147]

To be sure, this drift or "vacillation" characterizes Marx's thought on the historicity of social change from its beginnings, as Balibar has clearly demonstrated (I have drawn my examples mainly from the *Manifesto* for convenience's sake alone).[148] And although I am attempting here to identify a *general* matrix emerging from a tradition of radical thought, the problematic of the relationship between class particularity and "mass" universality was absolutely salient for the protagonists of 1917, as we can see in this passage from *The State and Revolution*, on which Lenin worked (but never finished) in that revolutionary year:

> Democracy means equality. The great significance of the proletariat's struggle for equality and of equality as a slogan will be clear if we correctly interpret it as meaning the abolition of classes. But democracy means only *formal* equality. And as soon as equality is achieved for all members of society in *relation* to ownership of the means of production, that is, equality of labor and wages, humanity will inevitably be confronted with the question of advancing farther, from formal equality to actual equality, i.e., to the operation of the rule "from each according to his ability, to each according to his needs." By what stages, by means of what practical measures humanity will proceed to this supreme aim we do not and cannot know. But it is

---

147 Ibid., 10–11.
148 See especially Balibar's "The Vacillation of Ideology in Marxism," "In Search of the Proletariat: The Notion of Class Politics in Marx," and "Politics and Truth: The Vacillation of Ideology, II," in *Masses, Classes, Ideas: Studies on Politics and Philosophy before and after Marx*, trans. James Swenson (New York: Routledge, 1994), 88–123, 125–49, 151–74, 233–40; esp. 92–100 and 142–49; and the discussion (drawing on texts from *Capital*) of the "negation of the negation" in *The Philosophy of Marx*, 81–83. Other Marxist texts shaped by this problematic include *The German Ideology* (1846; first published 1932) and the "Introduction" to *A Contribution to the Critique of Hegel's Philosophy of Right* (1844). On the latter text, see Balibar, *The Philosophy of Marx*, 51–54, and Peter Osborne, *How to Read Marx* (New York: W. W. Norton, 2006), 55–69.

> important to realize how infinitely mendacious is the ordinary bourgeois conception of socialism as something lifeless, rigid, fixed once and for all, whereas in reality *only* socialism will be the beginning of a rapid, genuine, truly mass forward movement, embracing first the *majority* and then the whole of the population, in all spheres of public and private life.[149]

Indeed, Lenin's formulation of the problem in *The State and Revolution*—where he offers a "phase" model of the transition to communism, in which the passage to the "higher phase" is made possible both by high levels of educational, technological and economic development, *and* by the prior, forcible undoing of capitalist economic relations, and their attendant inequality, by a "dictatorship of the proletariat"—draws a clear strategic line between the *class* agency of "armed workers" who will vanquish "capitalist habits," and the *mass* freedom ("embracing . . . the whole of the population") that will emerge once all state formations, democratic or otherwise, have been rendered obsolete through the masses' seizure of and mastery over the means of production.

All too clear, perhaps—inasmuch as the "phase" model seems to imply a rigorous if temporary isolation of the "dictatorship of the proletariat" from any exterior classes while it does its vital work.[150] Evidently, a mechanism for concentrating and focusing that class interest like a laser beam—an interest that, once acted upon, would have transformative consequences for the whole of society—would be required. That mechanism would emerge as a Party-State, which would eventually take upon itself the fundamentally economic task of defining and maintaining the lines separating "classes," whose identities were much disordered between 1918 and 1921, from one another.[151] (By no means has this problematic vanished from the

---

149 V. I. Lenin, "The State and Revolution," in Robert C. Tucker, ed., *The Lenin Anthology* (New York: 1975), 381–82.
150 Foreshadowing of this conception appears in Marx, to be sure: see, for instance, *The Class Struggles in France, 1848–1850*.
151 "[I]n the factory and soldiers' committees, the workers' militia units and above all the soviets of workers', soldiers' and peasants' deputies, Lenin discerned the seeds of the future socialist order and the corresponding state formation, 'which is *no longer* a state in the proper sense of the term, for . . . these contingents of armed men are *the masses themselves*, the entire people.' As for other public functions, the process of centralizing and therefore simplifying administration had proceeded so far under capitalism, that they could be performed by any literate person. Therefore it would be possible 'to cast "bossing" aside and to confine the whole matter to the organization of the proletarians (as the ruling class), which will hire "workers, foremen and bookkeepers" in the name of the whole of society.' . . . But, as suggested by the implicit contradiction between 'the proletarians' and the 'whole of society,' such qualifications as 'in the proper sense of the

contemporary political sphere, despite all appearances to the contrary. The order that we call "neoliberal," and know as our own, involves a different kind of systematic separation of the sphere of the economic—now conceived, by that order's ideologues, in largely technocratic-administrative rather than explicitly class terms—from popular control.)[152]

Translating into literary categories, we might say that the work of the Party-State involved, on this level, less the imposition of some "utopian" plan, and more specifically the construction-and-identification of narrative *protagonists*, whose purity and distinctiveness had to be implacably affirmed until (in Lenin's words) "actual equality" had been achieved. This was indeed one practical strategy for arresting the vacillations in the notion of the proletariat that we have discussed, but at the cost of simplifying that conception, and of creating another protagonist (or author) in the shape of the Party-State itself. The extent to which these protagonists could be seen

---

word' and the use of inverted commas, this model . . . was not without its own ambiguities. . . . The theorization of the proletarian dictatorship . . . . rested on both a profound sense of the proletariat's historic mission and an acute awareness of the limitations of that class. Rather than admitting their audaciousness, the Bolsheviks sought to compensate for the proletariat's weakness by assiduously building up what in their view all ruling classes required, namely, a powerful state" (Lewis H. Siegelbaum, *Soviet State and Society between Revolutions, 1918-1929* [Cambridge: Cambridge University Press, 1992], 9–10, 12). For an excellent account of the measures taken by the Bolsheviks during the Civil War (and sustained afterwards) to eliminate worker control over production, see Laura Engelstein, *Russia in Flames: War, Revolution, Civil War 1914–1921* (Oxford: Oxford University Press, 2017), esp. 585–605. See also Sheila Fitzpatrick, "The Bolshevik Invention of Class," in *Tear Off the Masks! Identity and Imposture in Twentieth-Century Russia*, 29–50; Christopher R. Browning and Lewis H. Siegelbaum, "Frameworks for Social Engineering: Stalinist Schema of Identification and the Nazi Volksgemeinschaft," in *Beyond Totalitarianism: Stalinism and Nazism Compared*, ed. Michael Geyer and Sheila Fitzpatrick (Cambridge: Cambridge University Press, 2009), 231–65; and Balibar, "In Search of the Proletariat," in *Masses, Classes, Ideas*, 147–48.

152 See Pierre Dardot and Christian Laval, *The New Way of the World: On Neo-Liberal Society*, trans. Gregory Elliott (London: Verso, 2013); William Davies, "The New Neoliberalism," *New Left Review* II/101 (September–October 2016): 121–34. For a brilliant historical reflection on the continuity between these apparently different forms of order across the Russian *longue durée*, see Catherine Owen, "A Genealogy of *Kontrol'* in Russia: From Leninist to Neoliberal Governance," *Slavic Review* 75, no. 2 (Summer 2016): 331–53. Whether the very emergence of the abstraction of "the economy" as a distinct sphere of praxis inaugurates this process is not a question I can address here. On the transformation of Marxists in power into "Weberians in substance," see Alasdair MacIntyre, *After Virtue: A Study in Moral Theory*, 2nd ed. (Notre Dame, IN: University of Notre Dame Press, 1984), 109.

primarily as agents or even forces or processes, rather than substantialized as "subjects," is an issue that will preoccupy us later in these pages, especially when we turn to the 1930s.[153]

Thus, behind Boltianskij's description of contemporary "cinema affairs" and filmgoers' new "subjective needs" lies an extremely tense ideological configuration, one that stresses radical class difference operating dynamically within and toward a horizon of absolute universality. For socialists committed to parliamentary politics, the Constituent Assembly, forcibly and unilaterally dissolved by the Bolsheviks in January 1918, was to have functioned as one of the major battlegrounds of struggle for the wider hegemony of "the democracy."[154] Boltianskij depicts cinema as another such battleground, where already-existing commercial concerns would presumably vie with "social" film production—whose appeal, Boltianskij thinks, can be attested—for the attention of spectators.

In other words, even if *demokratiia* drives "the beating pulse of living life," as Boltianskij clearly suggests it does, a "social" (or indeed, *socialist*) film practice cannot conceive of itself simply as an agent of *demokratiia* speaking to *demokratiia*, for at least three reasons. First, as we have seen, the ambit of a revolutionary socialist politics can never simply amount to a takeover of the state by a specific class—in accord, that is, with Aristotle's derisive notion of democracy as "where the poor rule"—but rather moves toward the elimination of class distinctions and the emergence of liberated conditions for "the whole of the population," a horizon of political aspiration at once utopian *and* (as history would show) ideological.[155] This is an aspiration, I should

---

153 Conversely, and in relation to the contemporary neoliberal situation, it may be that the now-familiar denunciations of "grand narratives"—a codeword for "Marxism," ninety-nine percent of the time—have as an additional effect an attenuation of the capacity for giving narrative form to a specific political-economic conjuncture, thereby rendering the crises of the current order insusceptible to effective public articulation. For what I take to be a strong appeal for the reassertion of this capacity, see Corey Robin, "Reclaiming the Politics of Freedom," *The Nation* (April 25, 2011): http://www.thenation.com/article/159748/reclaiming-politics-freedom, accessed October 15, 2016). The recent emergence in public discourse of the opposition between "99 and 1 percent" can clearly be read as part of such a reassertion.

154 See Rabinowitch, *The Bolsheviks in Power*, 92–95, 116–19.

155 In this connection, it is interesting to note that in November 1917, when Lenin and Trotsky were already threatening in all seriousness to employ "Jacobin"-style violence against their class enemies, one astute socialist critic went directly for the jugular and derided their "references to the French Revolution with the rejoinder that, for all their talk about a socialist revolution, the Bolsheviks were in fact 'entrapped in purely bourgeois

add, that found remarkable cinematic expression even under the Bolshevik regime, and not only in Vertov's work. Much of the great and lasting power of Eisenstein's *Battleship Potemkin* (1925), for instance, resides in its ecstatic representation of precisely this kind of *mass* convergence in the long central sequence on Odessa's waterfront, and of its fragility, as demonstrated in the legendary and terrifying "Steps" scene, in the face of organized brute force.[156]

Second, and keeping in mind restrictions on circulation on the one hand, and the barriers presented by literacy and linguistic difference on the other—the latter of which, in particular, Vertov would attempt to overcome by fashioning a wordless "universal language of cinema" in *Man with a Movie Camera*—the *signs* (visual, textual, aural) generated by social nonfiction/newsreel or any other film practice are in fact available to everyone, regardless of the intended direction of the filmmakers' address, and thus have to be thought of as discursively destined for some more undefined mass (or "public") as well.[157] Certainly, this last principle—a truism only on first glance, as I hope to show

---

forms of political revolution'" (Rabinowitch, *The Bolsheviks in Power*, 78). The critic was Left SR Sergej Mstislavskij, who later became Molotov's official biographer. It is also the case, however, that what would later be known as "White" forces had already occupied important regions of southern Russia and Ukraine by this time; see the discussion of the agit-trains in chapter 4.

156 Among many others, the aforementioned Trotsky offered strong assertions of the finitude of proletarian rule: "And what sort of culture will there be [under socialism]? Proletarian? No, it will be a socialist culture; for the proletariat, in contrast to the bourgeoisie, cannot and does not wish to remain forever the hegemonic class. On the contrary, it took power that it might more quickly cease to be the proletariat. Under socialism there is no proletariat, but instead a powerful, advanced and professional [*kul'turnaia*] cooperative working association [*artel'*], and thus a cooperative-associative—or socialist—culture" (L. Trotskij, *Voprosy kul'turnoj raboty* [Moscow: Gosudarstvennoe Izdatel'stvo, 1924], 70–71). See also his *Kul'tura i sotsializm* (Moscow: Gosudarstvennoe Izdatel'stvo, 1926), 182; and Lenin's famous and fateful remarks on socialism as the "annihilation of classes" in "Ekonomika i politika v epokhu diktatury proletariata," published in both *Pravda* (250) and *Izvestiia* (260) on November 7, 1919.

157 Just one example of how considerations of the "mass" character of cinematic reception inflected early Soviet thought on film: in some telling comments from 1925, Pudovkin insisted that cinema "by its very nature" is "organically linked" to the mass of spectators, for the simple reason that the film exists only by virtue of "the intense associative work of the spectator ... [who] completes the creative process begun by the director." If films are to have a proletarian *class* character, however, they must be created by—that is, *directed* by—individuals organically tied to the proletariat ("Proletarskij kinematograf," *Kino-Gazeta* 6 [1925]: 2). To be sure, films, like other texts, do *project* intended audiences; but their actual circulation can never be deduced from that projected public. See Michael Warner, *Publics and Counterpublics*, esp. 69–77 and 114–16; Jacques Rancière and Davide Panagia, "Dissenting Words: A Conversation

in later chapters—from the beginning informed the distribution practices of "social newsreel," which targeted audiences both within the Russian Empire (Kharkov, Kiev, Baku, and Riga, along with Russian cities like Irkutsk, Rostov and Samara) and beyond.[158] Prints of the first seven issues of *Svobodnaia Rossiia*, along with one print of *Funerals for the Victims of the Revolution* and (on Lenin's orders) five prints of the anti-Tsarist *Tsar Nicholas II, Autocrat of All of Russia* and ten of the film *October Revolution*, were sent by the Skobelev Committee to the United States in 1917–18; various Scandinavian cinema firms purchased and exhibited Skobelev productions as well.[159] Thus the films were viewed, in specific and undocumented acts of reception, by audiences well outside the bounds of any specifically Russian *demokratiia*, as well as in the Russian heartland (*Svobodnaia Rossiia* was exceptionally popular in Petrograd).[160] We will see later that "Soviet" film, too, could never be (and never was) "of and for the Soviets," but was multiply addressed, invariably and constitutively.[161]

Finally, the filmmakers, whether in 1917 or later, do not on the whole belong in any unproblematic *class* sense to "the democracy" themselves—except

---

with Jacques Rancière," *Diacritics* 30, no. 2 (Summer 2000): 113–26, esp. 113–16; and my *Inscription and Modernity*, 3–34.
158 RGALI f. 2057, op. 1, d. 261, ll. 108–9.
159 RGALI f. 2057, op. 1, d. 261, ll. 47, 104; d. 256, l. 6. I have not found more specific information about any US or Scandinavian screenings.
160 Between fifty and one hundred eighty copies of each *Svobodnaia Rossiia* installment were sold or distributed in the capital city (RGALI f. 2057, op. 1, d. 261, l. 104).
161 Such considerations link the problematic I am discussing to that of "the public sphere" that has generated so much interesting work in recent years. The difference, at least as regards the Russian revolutionary situation, can be illustrated by reference to Miriam Hansen's summary of the Negt-Kluge notion of a "proletarian public sphere": "[L]abor power contains and reproduces capacities and energies that exceed its realization in/as a commodity—resistance to separation, *Eigensinn* (stubbornness, self-will), self-regulation, fantasy, memory, curiosity, cooperation, feelings and skills in excess of capitalist valorization. Whether these energies can become effective depends on the organization of the public sphere: the extent to which experience is dis/organized from 'above'—by the exclusionary standards of high culture or in the interest of profit—or from 'below', by the experiencing subjects themselves, on the basis of their context of living" (Miriam Hansen, "Early Cinema, Late Cinema: Permutations of the Public Sphere," *Screen* 34, no. 3 (Autumn 1993): 204–5). The tension of class and mass, however—particularly in its "class" aspect, as it relates to political action—centrally involves making that "context of living" the object of radical, continual, and organized (even programmatic) contestation. It involves, in other words, maintaining social revolution as a continual horizon of possibility; and the disappearance of this horizon is surely part of what makes theories of "public sphere" appear more pertinent to current conditions.

as (to use Marx's and Engels's self-description in the *Manifesto*) "bourgeois ideologists who have worked out a theoretical understanding of the whole historical development"—and certainly not as the "working class," "army," and "peasantry" given in Boltianskij's definition. Red Army service, as we have indicated, would serve to render the democratic-proletarian pedigrees of some intellectual workers more "organic"; yet their relationship to *demokratiia* would remain oblique. To note this fact is in no way to argue for the illegitimacy of the political-cultural work of socialist intellectuals: as Balibar has written, "no 'working-class party' has ever existed except as the relative and conflictual fusion of a portion of the working class with a determinate group of intellectuals."[162]

It may not be obvious what all this has to do with Vertov, or with his films. I will argue throughout this book, sometimes only implicitly, that the problematic outlined here is profoundly embedded in Vertov's cinematic practice, as a kind of ideological matrix affecting their formal structure and their modes of addressing audiences, but can offer no more than a few anticipations of those arguments here. On the most general level, surely the fundamental and insoluble Vertovian antimony of "staged" versus "non-acted film"—that is, the sometimes embarrassing contradiction between his fierce rejection of staging and his apparent practice of it—can be recoded in terms of the tension between self-conscious class-based action and more multiply layered, less representable activities of the "mass." The films seem caught, in this regard, in an overlapping drift between a vision of social life and its protagonists as defined in some knowable way by class, alongside other social categories—with agents who do certain things and don't do others: an anxious epistemological concern that blurs into paranoia during the duplicity-obsessed late 1930s—and another vision that conceives of that life as something economically unified, like a "city symphony," but which (as Vertov remarked in some important notes for *Man with a Movie Camera* from March 20, 1927) "goes its own way," "never stops," and does not "obey [the camera]."[163]

But the oscillation between class and mass has more local effects as well. Sometimes it is transmuted into spatial terms, as when, in *One Sixth of the World* (1926), a caricatured foreign bourgeoisie, set brusquely apart from the Soviet world in the first part of the film, turns out eventually to be participating in the "building of socialism" anyway through its consumption of Soviet products. The Soviet economy, supposedly characterized by different class relations than its

---

162 Balibar, "Politics and Truth," in *Masses, Classes, Ideas*, 152; Sheila Fitzpatrick, "The Bolshevik's Dilemma: The Class Issue in Party Politics and Culture," in *The Cultural Front*, 16–36.
163 RGALI f. 2091, op. 2, d. 236, l. 36ob.

Western counterpart, thereby emerges, perhaps inadvertently, as part of some larger economy incorporating both socialist and capitalist "systems."

More complex examples involve shifts in ideological focus from specific class to larger multitude, sometimes within in a single sequence. In one crucial section in the second part of *One Sixth of the World* that directly addresses various members of the Soviet polity (as "you"), images of the industrial proletariat in factory workplaces ("you, who overturned the power of capital in October") are given momentary visual privilege, in part through a spectacular use of superimposition differentiating them from other addressees. They are then engulfed, however, in a long Walt Whitman–inspired syntagmatic chain that places the "proletarians" on one level with a woman "washing clothes with [her] feet," a baby "sucking [its] mother's breast," a boy "playing with a trapped Arctic fox," and even the audience "sitting in this movie theater," all represented as mutual "owners of the Soviet land" both on the basis of their engagement in these unremarkable actions, and by virtue of being addressed by the film.[164]

Most importantly, perhaps, the thematic of *production and construction* in Vertov's films—and especially in *Man with a Movie Camera* and *Enthusiasm*—leads on the one hand to a "class" iconography of specific proletarian motifs ("socialist construction") and a vision of harmony-within-labor, and on the other to an autoreferential stress upon process, contingency, and (above all) upon identity as a *product* of representation, in accord with the volatilizing "mass" dynamics of capital as conceptualized by Marxism. In a way, the problem boils down to an ambiguity at the heart of that array of constructive acts that we call *montage*, particularly as it forms part of a cinematic practice, like Vertov's, that attenuates or subtracts conventional narrative linkages. Those cuts, those splices: do they connect, or do they separate?

It is worth underscoring once again how the class-mass tension, or "aborted dialectics," to use Balibar's phrase, can be said to emerge from Marxism's representation of capitalism itself.[165] Capitalism at once dissolves

---

164 A "Soviet" ideological closure caps the sequence, to be sure, but mechanically, and almost as an afterthought; see the discussion in volume 2.
165 *Masses, Classes, Ideas*, xviii. It is crucial that the class-mass opposition not be reduced to any variant of what is arguably today's dominant and most intellectually debilitating ideological binary, that of the "open" versus the "closed," with its banal and reified ethical valences. Rather, the opposition pertains to the need to coordinate, as part of social analysis, multiple spatial, temporal and structural levels of focus with complex causal explanation. Balibar clarifies, crucially, that "far from concluding from these 'aporetic' inquiries that Marxist theory was, after all, collapsing due to its internal contradictions, [he suspects] that the difficulties in Marx are closely connected with problems that remain open in the present—particularly

(earlier social formations), creates (new formations), unifies (everyone into a single market economy, with the sale of labor power structurally at the center), and separates (people into different classes, depending on their fluctuating place within the relations of production). Each of these tendencies generates consequences with multiple valences: the creation of new possibilities *and* deracination, immiseration; interconnectedness *and* imperialism; new kinds of solidarity *and* new kinds of antagonism.[166] Most importantly, capitalism is also historically finite—it did not and will not always exist—but the causes of its finitude are to be found within capitalism's own dynamic, not exterior to it (if only because capitalism admits of no exterior: an important consideration in the far from classically capitalist space of the Russian Empire in 1917).[167] The vacillation between "class" and "mass," which will shape Vertov's modes of addressing spectators and of structuring his films, is a consequence of taking economic production under capitalism to be the *dominant* underlying the very constitution of societies *worldwide and in all their complexity*. It stems from the certainty that every person stands in some knowable and consequential relation, including some *subjective* relation, to that productive center; and from an equally strong conviction that those relations are, like capitalism itself, mutable and finite.[168] How else would Communism be possible, were they *not* mutable

---

with problems which concern the new forms and functions of racism in the 'world-economy,' 'world politics,' and 'world communications' of the late twentieth century" (ibid.). I would concur, and hope to demonstrate some of the ongoing salience of this problematic in later chapters and particularly in the conclusion. Certainly, the "class-mass" problematic has the double advantage of 1) being able to link considerations of economics, culture and identity, and 2) being applicable to both "Communist" and "capitalist" social formations, without reducing them to related-but-alternative forms of "modernity."

166 For a famous account of the importance of "the *traffic in commodities and news*" to the emergence of society or the "public sphere" in the eighteenth century, and of Marx's discovery of the nonequivalence, based in unequal property relations, between the classical bourgeois participant in civil society and the "abstract human being," see Jürgen Habermas, *The Structural Transformation of the Public Sphere: A Inquiry into a Category of Bourgeois Society*, trans. Thomas Burger and Frederick Lawrence (Cambridge, MA: MIT Press, 1991), 15 and 125.

167 An important and relevant critique of the very notion of "classically capitalist space," developed through an elaboration of Trotsky's notion of "combined and uneven development," is to be found in Justin Rosenberg, "Why Is There No International Historical Sociology?" *European Journal of International Relations* 12, no. 3 (2006): 307–40.

168 Belief in capitalism's global hegemony, or status as absolute political-economic horizon for the present, was an article of faith for Russian Social Democrats, as popular manuals on Communist thought perhaps reveal best: see, for instance, the accounts of capitalism given in the various editions of Platon Kerzhentsev's *Biblioteka kommunista* (Moscow: Gosudarstvennoe Izdatel'stvo, 1919), 7 (in the fourth edition). For a far more detailed theoretical elaboration of these ideas, see Balibar, *Masses, Classes, Ideas*, esp. 142–49, 162–74. On the

and finite? But how could Communism be realized, except through a struggle among the classes generated by capitalism?[169]

In any event (and to return at last to our narrative), it was precisely in the way that specific members of the Skobelev Committee conceptualized their relationship to *demokratiia* and its others that the committee's politics, and the political differences that apparently raged within it, were made manifest. Boltianskij, for instance, created a stir with a script he wrote entitled *Born out of Chaos* (*Iz khaosa rozhdennago*, 1917), whose production several members of the Moscow branch of the committee, in particular the great animator Ladislas Starevich, opposed, because that they deemed it liable to foment "class hatred" through its highly negative representation of the intelligentsia.[170] A letter of April 1917 from one of the Skobelev Committee's members—probably Boltianskij—to the Executive Committee of the Petrograd Soviet of Worker's and Soldier's Deputies indicates a desire to serve, "as an old SD Party worker," "the cause of the democracy by popularizing the slogans of the democracy, [and making known] the nature of its organization and its activities" by means of a "division of political propaganda"—in other words, through the Social Nonfiction/Newsreel division that the Skobelev Committee had just established. Among the ideas this member promised to pitch to the committee was an "imposing" film "about our proletarian May 1st," profits from which would go in part to the Soviet, and a propaganda film that would defend the introduction of an eight-hour workday by contrasting counter-arguments from the bourgeois press (i.e., that a workday of that duration would undermine industry; or [by contrast] would lead to intensified work during that span and therefore to rapid disablement of workers) with images of "work being carried out at full speed" under an eight-hour regime: "among the people, vivid, lively photography will dispel the slanders of the bourgeois press better than anything else."[171]

---

level of representation, the problem also relates to the paradoxical bond linking "symbolic" and "allegorical" thought as discussed in Paul de Man, "The Rhetoric of Temporality," in *Blindness and Insight: Essays in the Rhetoric of Contemporary Criticism*, 2nd ed., intro. Wlad Godzich (Minneapolis: University of Minnesota Press, 2003), 187–228. I will return to this theme in volumes 2 and 3.

169 I should note in passing that the tension I have outlined here has nothing directly to do with any claims as to Communism's historical "inevitability": it is compatible, as a problematic, with a variety of points of view as to the temporality of Communism's emergence or non-emergence.

170 RGALI f. 2057, op. 1, d. 256, l. 7. The film was never made, and I have been unable to find a copy of the script.

171 RGALI f. 2057, op. 1, d. 261, ll. 41–41ob. Three filmic tributes to May 1st, shot in Petrograd, Kronstadt, and on the front, were made by the Committee (RGALI f. 2057, op. 1, d.

Although Russia's complex and fluctuating leadership in 1917 was represented quite evenhandedly in the thirteen *Svobodnaia Rossiia* newsreels (which ran from April to October 2, 1917)—Socialist Revolutionary leader Chernov, Menshevik leader Tsereteli, Prime Minister Kerensky, Constitutional Democrat (abbreviated "Kadet") Miliukov, and (late in the series) Bolsheviks Trotsky, Lunacharsky, Kamenev, and Kollontai all made appearances, among many others—the Skobelev Committee also made more strictly "democratic" films that presage later Soviet nonfiction genres and themes.[172] One such film, *In the Petrograd Proletariat's Children's Colony* (*V kolonii detej Petrogradskogo proletariata*, 1917), depicted the activities at a large (nearly 1,000-strong) proto-Pioneer camp in Siverskaia Station near Petrograd, including food preparation, medical care, reading, girls sewing, swimming and games, and children taking a leadership role as medical orderlies and supervisors.[173] A distillation of the film was incorporated into the tenth installment of *Svobodnaia Rossiia*, wedged between images of Kerensky, Ekaterina Breshko-Breshkovskaia (the "Grandmother of the Russian Revolution," one of the founders of the SR Party), prowar sailor (and later White *and* Red agent) Fyodor Batkin, and the First All-Russian Congress of Worker's Cooperation on the one side, and of a priest blessing a battalion on the Riga Front on the other.[174] Such diversity in a single newsreel seems to reflect the Skobelev Committee's efforts to incorporate multiple political viewpoints in its productions, if not indeed the varied positions of the committee's own membership.[175]

261, ll. 7–7ob); I have found no evidence that any film endorsing the eight-hour day was produced.

172 RGALI f. 2057, op. 1, d. 261, ll. 10–16, 69, 71–72. I will discuss the *Svobodnaia Rossiia* newsreels in more detail in the next chapter.

173 RGALI f. 2057, op. 1, d. 261, l. 58. This short film presages important "children's camp" sequences in both *Kino-Eye* and Vertov's early *The Red Star Literary-Instructional Agit-Steamer of the All-Russia Central Executive Committee* (1919), both discussed in volume 2.

174 RGALI f. 2057, op. 1, d. 261, l. 13. This is one of the few *Svobodnaia Rossiias* that have (in part) survived (RGAKFD 12655), though without the image of Kerensky. The youngsters were evidently sons and daughters of tobacco factory workers.

175 In October, after being initially forbidden by the Petrograd Military-Revolutionary Committee from filming (October 30 [OS]), Boltianskij and two cameramen were allowed to shoot footage of the revolutionary events. As Listov has written, the Skobelev film *Oktiabr'skij Perevorot* [*October Turning Point*] (1917), made under Boltianskij's direction, refuses all evaluation of the event: using "cautious, neutral" intertitles, it gives equal weight to the funerals of Red Army soldiers and those of officers of the Provisional Government's forces—a neutrality adopted, no doubt, because of uncertainty as to what the future would hold (*Rossiia, revoliutsiia, kinematograf*, 31). Simply listing the items in *Svobodnaia Rossiia* 5 (July 7, 1917) reveals this diversity of perspective: a portrait of Left SR leader Maria Spiridonova; a

Within the socially polarized Russia of 1917, however, this relatively liberal approach to political representation was hardly a guarantee of the films' success, or even acceptability; and the Skobelev Committee encountered serious problems in distributing and exhibiting its most political productions. Although some committee members suspected in mid-1917 that distributors and theater owners were proving reluctant to show their films, the real difficulties did not emerge until the beginning of 1918 and the heightening of the tensions that preceded the opening and dispersal of the Constituent Assembly on January 5–6 (OS). Although Boltianskij claimed at the time that *Toward the Opening of the Constituent Assembly* had been shown successfully in Petrograd, his Moscow Skobelev colleagues were more skeptical about its chances in that city, and not without reason. At the Forum—one of five Moscow theaters that had, with trepidation, accepted the *Constituent Assembly* film—the first screening was broken off by wild commotion among spectators, culminating in fistfights and chairs being hurled through the air. At another theater, Casino-Roma, the large advertising poster describing the contents of the film was torn down by order of the Moscow Soviet of Workers' and Soldiers' Deputies; four Red Guards were then dispatched to stand in front of the theater, which was prohibited from exhibiting the film. Needless to say, the other three theaters cancelled their screenings, and Moscow Committee members were furious that Boltianskij's "worker's section" had produced a film that proved unmarketable even (or especially) to the workers' Soviets and their sympathizers.[176]

Today we know, through the work of historian Alexander Rabinowitch, that the demonstration depicted in *Toward the Opening of the Constituent Assembly* was anything but a manifestation of social and political harmony. Led primarily by socialists of moderate ideological cast but opposed to exclusive rule by the Bolshevik-dominated Soviets—including SRs, representatives of the now-persecuted executive committees of the workers', soldiers' and peasants' Soviets, and Menshevik-Defensists, though few workers or soldiers—the demonstration, involving anywhere from 10,000 to 100,000 people, instead "revealed the immense rift that divided the population of Petrograd after six weeks of Soviet power":

---

group portrait of some peasant deputies, possibly SRs as well; activists (party unidentified) working on the eve of elections to the Petrograd city duma; a demonstration in Petrograd of Ukrainians in support of Ukrainian independence; and another demonstration in favor of drafting those who had previously refused to serve and sending them to the front.

176 RGALI f. 2057, op. 1, d. 256, ll. 1, 1ob, 10. The information about the abortive Moscow screenings comes from a letter of January 15, 1918, from Konstantin Markovich Brenner of the Moscow Skobelev Commitee to V. I. Dement'ev. See also Magidov, *Zrimaia pamiat' istorii*, 63.

As the marchers turned north on Liteinyi Prospekt, they were greeted by a huge banner displayed above the street: "Make Way for the Electors chosen by the People!" Arriving at the Taurida Palace and finding the gates in the wrought iron fence surrounding it locked and heavily guarded, they clambered over it and stormed into the palace gardens. There they listened to fiery speeches calling for an immediate end to Soviet rule . . . Pushing past [Bolshevik leader and later Petrograd Cheka head Mojsej] Uritskij, the crowd forged into the palace . . . There, at 4:00 PM, a meeting was convened of some 60 of the estimated 127 Constituent Assembly delegates then in Petrograd. . . . On 29 November, they managed to reassemble in the Taurida Palace. However, their meeting was forcibly dispersed, and, from then on, they were barred from reentering the palace.[177]

Members of the Kadet (Constitutional Democratic) party—some of whose leaders were indeed implicated in "the counterrevolution on the Don led by Generals Kornilov, Alekseev, and Kaledin"—also joined in the demonstration, and Lenin and the Bolsheviks took their participation as sufficient reason to construe the march as an "armed uprising against Soviet rule" and to outlaw the Kadets. Meanwhile, critics of the Bolsheviks, including Commissar of Justice Isaac Shtejnberg (an SR), denounced their action as both motivated by unjustified paranoia about the Kadets' influence and as bound to reinforce suspicions that the Soviet regime, directed by the Bolsheviks, was attempting to undermine the Constituent Assembly even before it met (which it was).[178]

What ensued—to grossly simplify an impossibly complex story—was an increasing monopolization of power in the hands of the Bolsheviks, who proved incapable, because of a combination of ideological rigidity and seasoned mistrust, of working with either the "right-leaning" socialists (the Right SRs and Mensheviks, who believed that the Constituent Assembly needed to include bourgeois parties like the Kadets, given that the revolution's "bourgeois phase" had not yet terminated) or those closer to a "centrist-socialist" position, like the

---

177 Rabinowitch, *The Bolsheviks in Power*, 75–76. Indeed, the film *Toward the Opening of the Constituent Assembly* (RGAKFD 11502) clearly advocates (as does the crowd it depicts) endorsing those elected already to the city Duma, and mentions that troops were trying to keep them out of the palace (guns and bombs are shown). The crowd shown in the film is mainly made up of "townspeople," but representatives from the provinces and even one from the army are shown and named as well.
178 Ibid., 76–77. Shtejnberg was also (incidentally) the father of the famous art historian Leo Steinberg (1920–2011).

Left SRs and moderate Bolsheviks, who advocated a multiparty socialist assembly, in line with the wishes of nearly all workers and soldiers, at least in Petrograd. In retrospect, the situation, unfolding against a background of simmering counterrevolution, foreign hostility, economic collapse, and the distance though not the indifference of much of the population from the decisive goings-on in the major cities, had the locked-in, entropic quality of tragedy: proletarians desiring a strictly socialist government with multiple parties; Right SRs and their allies refusing a socialist-only government on the basis of what they believed to be rigorous theoretical principle; the Bolsheviks breaking the deadlock through a unilateral seizure of power "in the name of the Soviets" and the dissolution of the Constituent Assembly on January 5, thereby sidelining both the long-hoped-for Assembly and the aspirations of the workers in whose name they acted.[179]

As regards the Skobelev Committee's productions, or at least those like the *Constituent Assembly* film, we must conclude that they projected a collective addressee—a complex *demokratiia*, engaged by and in politics—that did not conform to the radically fragmented polity that was then emerging. A year later Vertov, now employed by the Moscow Film Committee and reworking some of the same Skobelev Committee footage for his *Anniversary of the Revolution* (1918), was able to misleadingly frame (through intertitles) all those images of mass meetings and marching as straightforward representations of "the people" (*narod*) united in opposition to the Old Regime and Provisional Government. "Social" nonfiction/newsreel that addressed an entire *society* was impossible, under conditions of incipient civil war; and the list of intertitles for the committee's *Opening and Dissolution of the Constituent Assembly* (1918) points to this emergent reality with woeful clarity:

1. 5 January 1918
   OPENING AND DISSOLUTION OF THE CONSTITUENT ASSEMBLY.
2. In the Taurida Palace.
3. General view of the Taurida Palace from the sidelines.
4. The meeting hall in the Taurida Palace prepared for the opening of the Constituent Assembly.

---

179 See Ronald Grigor Suny, "Toward a Social History of the October Revolution," *American Historical Review* 88, no. 1 (February 1983): 31–52; Suny, *The Soviet Experiment*, 58–60; Rabinowitch, *The Bolsheviks in Power*, 78–127; Steve Smith, "Year One in Petrograd" [review of *The Bolsheviks in Power*], *New Left Review* II/52 (July–August 2008): 151–60. It is worth noting that Skobelev Committee films made in 1917 post-October described the destruction in Moscow and Petrograd, and the funerals of victims of the violence, already as consequences of "civil war" (e.g., *Oktiabr'skij perevorot* [RGAKFD 12530]).

5. Uritskij, Commissar of the Constituent Assembly.
6. Taurida Palace Commandant Prigovorskij and Commissar Uritskij.
7. Guarding the Taurida Palace on 5 January.
8. Picket of Red Guards.
9. Three-inch field guns in the palace square.
10. Machine gun inside the building (in the room occupied by the Left SRs).
11. A crowd [*publika*] that broke through the fence surrounding the Taurida Palace.
12. SVERDLOV. Chairman of the Central Executive Committee of the Workers', Soldiers' and Peasants' Deputies, opens the Constituent Assembly.
13. CHERNOV. Elected chairman of the Constituent Assembly.
14. The meeting hall at the opening of the Constituent Assembly, during Sverdlov's speech.
15. During Chernov's speech.
16. After Sverdlov's speech, all deputies rise to sing the "International."
17. The Bolshevik deputies to the Constituent Assembly.
18. The Left SRs.
27. FORWARD.[180]
28. Shooting at demonstrators and panic.[181]

The Skobelev Committee continued to make films about political news of the day—including a short about the "nightmarish murder" of the Kadets Fyodor Kokoshkin and Aleksandr Shingarev in their hospital beds by drunken sailors

---

180 Items 19 through 26 are missing from the montage list.
181 RGALI f. 2057, op. 1, d. 261, ll. 80–80ob; see also RGALI f. 2057, op. 1, d. 256, l. 1ob. An incomplete Skobelev film bearing the same title (*Otkrytie i likvidatsiia Uchreditel'nogo Sobraniia* [RGAKFD 12521]) bears some resemblance to the description of the event offered in these intertitles; it is unclear whether it was part of that other film, an entirely separate film, or perhaps the only film actually made under this name. The film stresses the mass, broadly public character of the pro–Constituent Assembly demonstrations of January 5, the diverse make-up of the crowd (soldiers, officers, townspeople are all seen), and that soldiers and artillery were summoned—by whom it is not said—to remove the demonstrators from the Taurida palace square. Though no political actors or parties are named, the film is clearly on the side of the crowds, some members of which died (to quote an intertitle) as "fighters for popular government." Listov suggests that the Skobelev Committee began to make "anti-Bolshevik" films at this time; if so, this *Opening and Dissolution* film may well have been banned (*Rossiia, revoliutsiia, kinematograf*, 84). For an account of that historic day, see Rabinowitch, *The Bolsheviks in Power*, 104–27.

and Red Guards on January 7, another about negotiations on the front (in which a young Mikhail Kol'tsov appeared), and a new version of *Toward the Government of the People*, which was banned in August 1918[182]—but there was little left for it, in the changed circumstances, but to be nationalized and absorbed into the new system of commissariats, a process completed by the time Vertov arrived to work in the Moscow Film Committee in May 1918.[183]

To speak of nationalizing an institution like the film division of the Skobelev Committee, already the recipient of state subsidies from the Tsarist and the Provisional Governments, seems peculiar, but in fact accords entirely with the convoluted history of cinema's nationalization after October 1917, one of the crucial phases in the development of Soviet cinema, whose full retelling would take us well beyond the bounds of the present study.[184] The actual order from Narkompros to nationalize the Skobelev Committee's property—the first significant cinema-nationalization act of the new regime—did not come until March 19, 1918, but was preceded by a series of confusing signals, starting on November 22, 1917 (OS), with Lunacharsky's affirmation of the committee's autonomy, and a declaration on the 23rd that the soon to be defunct War Ministry's cultural-education division (including the Skobelev Committee) would be transferred to Narkompros.[185]

This was a time, as Viktor Listov has noted, when decrees were pronounced experimentally, virtually as a kind of agitation designed to get things moving rather than as carefully crafted legislation, and not only by the Bolsheviks.[186] The most important event immediately preceding the committee's absorption into

---

182 RGALI f. 2057, op. 1, d. 261, l. 33ob; V. S. Listov and E. S. Khokhlova, eds. *Istoriia otechestvennogo kino: dokumenty, memuary, pis'ma* (Moscow: Materik, 1996), 91–93; Rabinowitch, *The Bolsheviks in Power*, 118.

183 *LRK* 1, 244–45; 250; Taylor, *Politics of the Soviet Cinema*, 46.

184 For more on the early nationalization—which was anything but a unified, gracefully managed event—see Taylor, *Politics of the Soviet Cinema*, 43–51; Vance Kepley Jr., "Soviet Cinema and State Control: Lenin's Nationalization Decree Reconsidered," *Journal of Film and Video* 42, no. 2 (Summer 1990): 3–14; and Listov, *Rossiia, revoliutsiia, kinematograf*, 45–76.

185 *LRK* 1, 230. For the nationalization decree, signed by Lenin, see RGALI f. 2057, op. 1, d. 258, l. 3; for Lunacharsky's affirmation of November, RGALI f. 2057, op. 1, d. 258, l. 1. Some closed but apparently inconsequential discussion about cinema nationalization did occur within Narkompros in December 1917 (*LRK* 1, 233). Famously, Lunacharsky would affirm the regime's opposition to full nationalization of cinema in an interview of April 1918; see Listov, *Rossiia, revoliutsiia, kinematograf*, 50. To be sure, some prominent Bolshevik ideologues did press publicly for nationalization early on: see V. [Platon] Kerzhentsev, *Revoliutsiia i teatr* (Moscow: Dennitsa, 1918), 37.

186 *Rossiia, revoliutsiia, kinematograf*, 60.

Narkompros was the strange decree promulgated on February 12, 1918, by the newly formed "Legislative Soviet" of the Union of Workers in Artistic Cinema (or SRKhK: *Soiuz rabotnikov khudozhestvennoj kinematografii*), without sanction by either the central government or the union's membership, demanding that "all film factories, studios, distribution outlets, theaters and repositories" be placed under the control of the union.[187] The decree generated uproar, not least among members of the union, and evidently led to defensive reactions (stashing away film and other resources; plans to pull up stakes and move south or abroad) on the part of already panicked producers, film artists, and theater owners. The motives for the decree remain unclear, although it may have been intended as a provocation to Narkompros's Cinema Subsection (headed by Lenin's wife, Nadezhda Krupskaia, from January 1918) to take control of a rapidly deteriorating situation, on the levels of production, distribution and exhibition, due to the incipient flight of much of the film industry, the unpredictable confiscatory actions of local soviets, and the generally worsening economic situation in the cities.[188]

At any rate, it seems that Listov is mistaken to claim that the "Legislative Soviet" acted on behalf of less commercially viable film enterprises like the Skobelev Committee, which depended heavily on state funding and therefore may have sought to level the playing field through nationalization. Archival documents make it clear that the members of the Skobelev Committee, at least in Petrograd and probably in Moscow, in fact opposed even their own absorption into Narkompros and protested it, even while preparing inventories of their equipment, films, and other property for the inevitable transfer.[189] The protest of March 27, formulated with the aid of legal counsel, complained that the nationalization was simply declared without argued justification; that it left the fates of the committee's employees entirely uncertain; that it potentially compromised the future of the Petrograd Skobelev Committee's newly founded Studio of Screen Art, headed by Aleksandr Voznesenskij and already instructing more than 150 students; that the continuation of its new

---

187 Ibid., 47–48. The main figure in the five-person soviet was actor and director Vladimir Gardin, with whom Vertov would soon be working on *Kino-Nedelia*.
188 *LRK* 1, 237–41; Taylor, *Politics of the Soviet Cinema*, 43–46. That the various "instances" were acting independently was clear from the confusing variety of different nationalizing or "municipalizing" initiatives. In January 1918, for instance, the Petrograd Soviet affirmed the right of their counterpart in nearby Petropavlovsk to confiscate theaters (in response to complaints from one Nazarov, whose theater had already been confiscated by the Petropavlovsk Soviet) (*LRK* 1, 236).
189 Among those involved in the inventories was Elizaveta Svilova, already overseeing editing at the Skobelev Committee in Moscow (RGALI f. 2091, op. 2, d. 653, l. 4).

Scientific Division was likewise put in question; that it placed in jeopardy all sorts of commercial/contractual relationships with buyers and institutions at home and abroad; and that the committee could not be nationalized in any case, given that it had been under government auspices (the War Ministry) to begin with.[190]

Indeed, how is the nationalization of a state institution to be carried out? Even this nationalization evidently occurred in a context of uncertainty and perhaps disagreement on the highest levels. Lunarcharsky, for instance, gave an order eleven days after Lenin's decree (March 30, 1918) to "suspend the transfer" of the committee's inventory prior to getting clarification (from Lenin himself, presumably) about the import of the decree.[191] The main question for the committee's members concerned not its status as a "state" institution, but rather its autonomy within the array of other cultural divisions, commissariats, committees and so on forming at the time. (As we will see in later chapters, the issue of institutional autonomy would persist for Dziga Vertov, as he attempted to carve out a distinct place for his "kinocs," for the affiliations he began to establish with the incipient Young Pioneers organization, and his dream of a "creative laboratory," within the changing framework of the Soviet film industry and cultural organizations.) As it turns out, nonfiction/newsreel filmmaking would continue, involving many of the same people who had been working on it before, but now as part of a specifically Soviet and centralized cultural administration (Narkompros, until the end of 1922): that is, within a state apparatus, still very much in formation, that claimed to govern the whole Russian Republic, though now in the name of the Soviets. But what would "Soviet" nonfiction film look like?

---

190 *Rossiia, revoliutsiia, kinematograf*, 48–49, 56–58; RGALI f. 2057, op. 1, f. 257, ll. 11–12ob; f. 258, ll. 14–16. I have found no evidence in Skobelev Committee documents that any of its members advocated the nationalization of private cinema concerns. The committee's staff had already expressed much concern regarding their salaries, and sought guarantees of employment in the future (RGALI f. 2057, op. 1, f. 257, ll. 33–37; dated March 3, 1918); evidently, some attempt was made to separate the committee's "philanthropic" and "educational" sections, and to pass only the former to Narkompros (RGALI f. 2057, op. 1, f. 258, l. 10). The Studio of Screen Art would later continue under Narkompros auspices as the first Soviet film school.

191 RGALI f. 2057, op. 1, d. 258, l. 4. For an account of Lunacharsky's resistance to nationalizing all movie theaters under Narkompros in 1918 (advocating instead that they operate under the jurisdiction of local soviets), see Iu. N. Flakserman, *V ogne zhizni i bor'by: vospominaniia starogo kommunista* (Moscow: Izdatel'stvo politicheskoj literatury, 1987), 140–41.

CHAPTER 4

Christ among the Herdsmen: From Refugee to Propagandist (1918–22)

> *No bargainers' bargains by day—no brokers or speculators—*
> *would they continue?*
> *Would the talkers be talking? Would the singer attempt to sing?*
> *Would the lawyer rise in the court to state his case before the judge?*
> *Then rattle quicker, heavier drums—you bugles wilder blow.*
> —Walt Whitman, *"Beat! Beat! Drums!"*

KINO-NEDELIA (1918–19): AUTHOR, ARCHIVE, DÉTOURNEMENT, CENSORSHIP

There were other media forms in Vertov's time that worked to give the nation-state—its central authorities, its cosmopolitan centers, its symbolic landscape, its crises—representational coherence: newspapers and journals, of course, but also photographic compendia, public rituals, Civil War–era curiosities like agitational trains, certain kinds of novels, and no doubt much else besides. Considered both as form and as experience, however, newsreel film seems unique in the way it combined mass spectacle with the seriousness of a collective encounter with the day's great topics ("current events"). It was newspaper-like in its periodicity, its public character, its episodic, headlined structure and its sober, even scientific claims to index and articulate the real world, or what was vital to know about that world; and parade-like in the way it physically brought together masses of people largely unknown to one another to witness the Remarkable and the Important go floating by, to musical accompaniment and as a unified whole. At least potentially, newsreel seems to wind together epistemic sobriety and collective enthusiasm (or boredom, its dialectical counterpart) in a way that no still-existing media form quite does.[1] At the very least, we need to exert our imaginations if we are to gain an understanding of newsreel's now obsolescent forms and modes of appeal.

Kino-Nedelia (*Film-Week*; forty-three installments between May 1918 and June 1919) was the earliest Soviet newsreel—or "screen newspaper," to use Boltianskij's phrase—and although it usually leads off any Vertov filmography, it cannot be considered a Vertov work in the strictest sense. Initially employed as an office manager and bookkeeper for the Moscow Film Committee's Photo-Film Division, at that time (until July, 2 just prior to the onset of the major Civil War hostilities) under the direction of Mikhail Kol'tsov, Vertov did not become the acting chair of that division until September 1. It was only after that point, but no later than the end of October, that he got involved in editing and reediting: that is, certainly not before *Kino-Nedelia* 14 (released September 3) and probably not until around the time *Kino-Nedelia* 22 (released October 29) was produced.[2] In February 1919, moreover, the Film Division apparently sent Vertov to work on the Civil War's southern front (in Ukraine and the North Caucasus), where he may have coordinated nonfiction/newsreel filming.[3] If this is the case, he did not supervise the editing of installments 34 (February 7) and 35 (February 14), either. Besides Kol'tsov and Vertov,

---

1 The closest contemporary equivalent might be the collective watching of a major news event on television (in a bar, for instance), though this analogy seems very approximate. The "wholeness" of the newsreel contributes part of its ideological force as spectacle. Interrupting a newsreel screening—as happened in 1918, as we have seen—would be like stopping a parade in its tracks, at least as Louis Marin describes parades: "A parade is indeed an agent of social, political, or religious legitimation: even the popular 'demonstration' that might appear on the contrary to be a collective force of destabilization finds the legitimacy of political contestation in what is customarily called the 'success' of its march or cortège, even if none of its demands is satisfied by the actual occurrence of the demonstration" (Louis Marin, "Establishing a Signification for Social Space: Demonstration, Cortège, Parade, Procession [Semiotic Notes]," in *On Representation* [Stanford: Stanford University Press, 2001], 47).

2 Magidov, *Zrimaia pamiat' istorii*, 84; *KE*, 40, 119; Ajmermakher et al., *Instituty upravleniia kul'turoi*, 78; GARF f. A-2306, op. 36, d. 16, l. 11. Vertov indicates that he was still working as a "secretary" on a questionnaire of September 21 (Magidov, "Iz arkhiva Vertova," 162). Kol'tsov left the Film Committee at the beginning of July; between that time and August 1918, and again after February 1919, it seems that he spent a good deal of time in his native Kiev, working for the military press agency and on the first Ukrainian newsreel, *Zhivoj Zhurnal* (*Living Journal*, none of whose four known installments have survived; it is unclear what relation *Ukrainskaia Khronika* [1919 (RGAKFD 10695)] might have to those issues). He shifted his base to Petrograd for a time starting in 1921 (*LRK* 1, 256; Rubashkin, *Mikhail Kol'tsov*, 8–9; G. Zhurov, "Pervye shagi sovetskogo kino na Ukraine," *Voprosy Kinoiskusstva* 7 (1963): 187–209, esp. 190–91).

3 Listov, *Istoriia smotrit v ob'ektiv*, 150.

G. P. Novikov, M. Ia. Shnejder, director and actor Vladimir Gardin, and a host of cameramen all worked in the Film Committee on *Kino-Nedelia*. This is probably not a complete list of the cocreators, and the best scholarship on the series has no doubt correctly stressed that the newsreel was collectively authored. Given that a number of gifted and experienced people worked on the newsreel, including several who had made pre-Revolutionary films, there is no need to imagine that the virtues of *Kino-Nedelia*—of which there are many, as we will see—were all due to Dziga Vertov.[4]

At the same time, it is important not to underestimate Vertov's contributions to *Kino-Nedelia* or its importance to his development, either, despite the fact that we cannot confidently attribute even one sequence in the series to his editorial hand. In early 1919, he was charged by Gardin, then head of the Photo-Film Division, with directing the restoration of the first thirty-five installments of *Kino-Nedelia*, from which Vertov and his collaborators had taken much of the footage (primarily from issues 1–22) included in *Anniversary of the Revolution* and *Brain of Soviet Russia*. The former compilation film was prepared in time for the November 7 anniversary celebrations, while the latter was a gallery of film-portraits of regime leaders that actually comprised a section of *Anniversary* but was often shown independently.[5] By mid-March 1919, according to a VFKO bulletin, *Kino-Nedelia* was in "terrible condition," "a sauce of negatives, positives, intertitles, fragments of fiction films, and so on," which Vertov was assigned to bring back into proper order.[6] Thus Vertov was at least

---

[4] On *Kino-Nedelia*, see V. Listov, "Dve 'Kinonedeli,'" *Iskusstvo Kino* 5 (May 1968): 93–100; *Istoriia smotrit v ob'ektiv*, 129–53; and *Rossiia, revoliutsiia, kinematograf*, 78–94; Magidov, *Zrimaia pamiat' istorii*, 84–86. Although *Evolution of Style in the Early Work of Dziga Vertov* (esp. 32–51) ascribes too much editorial control over *Kino-Nedelia* to Vertov, no doubt due to the inaccessibility of the archival materials available to Listov and Magidov, Seth Feldman's book contains many useful reflections on and analyses of the films themselves.

[5] See GARF f. 2306, op. 27, d. 12, l. 46; Listov, *Istoriia smotrit v ob'ektiv*, 152; Magidov, *Zrimaia pamiat' istorii*, 85–86. *Brain* was cocreated with one Savel'ev, possibly the talented photographer A. Savel'ev. Many stills from *Brain* are reproduced on pages 240 and 241 of V. M. Magidov, *Kinofotodokumenty v kontekste istoricheskogo znaniia*; my thanks to Natalie Ryabchikova for this reference. Both chronology and Vertov's notes on the earliest surviving montage lists (RGALI f. 2091, op. 2, dd. 1–4) indicate that *Kino-Nedelia* 22 (dated October 29, 1918) was the last newsreel in the series from which images were drawn for inclusion in the *Anniversary* film, although footage from *Svobodnaia Rossiia* was also used. Vertov wrote down a detailed description of the "condition of *Kino-Nedelia*," still drastically incomplete, on May 5, 1919 (RGALI f. 2091, op. 2, d. 381, l. 3–8).

[6] Listov, *Istoriia smotrit v ob'ektiv*, 152. The phrase about the "sauce of negatives" may have come from Vertov's own report on the condition of *Kino-Nedelia*. According to the bulletin, five issues of the newsreel had been restored by March 24.

partially responsible for the shape later taken by the *Kino-Nedelias*, although that restored shape did not conform to their earlier (or "original") condition, as we will see. It is also worth noting that during the period Vertov was busy working on the restoration—from around mid-March through early May—no new installments of *Kino-Nedelia* appeared, which might suggest that he was either running the show by then, or at least central to its operation (although shortages of film stock were endemic at the time as well).[7]

---

7   Prints of most installments of *Kino-Nedelia*, not all complete by any means, exist in RGAKFD. At some point in the early 1920s, probably not earlier than 1923, 18 installments (including 1, 3–5, 21–26, and 31–35, and possibly 2 and 28–30 as well) were transported to Norway under the auspices of Aleksandra Kollontai, who served in the Soviet trade delegation there, most of the time as its head, from 1922–25. They later apparently ended up in the Soviet embassy in Sweden (where Kollontai was ambassador from 1930–45), were purchased by a Swedish TV station in the '50s, and were finally acquired by the Swedish Film Institute in 1968 (see Barbara Evans Clements, *Bolshevik Feminist: The Life of Aleksandra Kollontai* [Bloomington and London: Indiana University Press, 1979], 223–51; and Anna-Lena Wibom, "Der Fund der *Kinonedelja* in Schweden," *Maske und Kothurn* 50, no. 1 [2004]: 73–76). Copies of these prints, all of which definitely postdate the 1919 restoration, were later acquired by the Austrian Film Museum and by Gosfilmofond (Listov, *Istoriia smotrit v ob'ektiv*, 131). It is unclear why *Kino-Nedelia* was brought to Norway four years after the newsreel series had terminated, and when the events it depicted were no longer news. The Herman Axelbank Motion Picture Film Collection at Stanford University's Hoover Institution may also contain footage from *Kino-Nedelia*, although the way the collection is cataloged makes it almost impossible to tell without inspecting all the material. The most important surviving montage lists—mostly but not exclusively lists of intertitles, and including some indications as to which items were excised and used in other films (see below)—are to be found in Vertov's archive in RGALI (f. 2091, op. 2, dd. 1–5). The first thirty-five lists, however, also clearly date to no earlier than the restoration, as I will discuss below. A remarkable poster announcing *Kino-Nedelia* 4 (June 25, 1918), which includes a list of items in the newsreel, was reproduced in an important recent volume (V. P. Tolstoj, ed., *Agitmassovoe iskusstvo Sovetskoj Rossii: materialy i dokumenty*, vol. 1 [Moscow: Iskusstvo, 2002], 122); the announcement presumably dates to 1918 and is the earliest record of the contents of this particular installment, but I have seen no other *Kino-Nedelia* posters. In 1965, a censored/bowdlerized catalog of montage lists for Soviet newsreel produced between 1918 and 1925 was produced as a guide to archival holdings. In this catalog, no mention is made, for instance, of the many major early Soviet leaders who appeared in *Kino-Nedelia* (e.g., Kamenev, Zinoviev, Trotsky above all) but were later purged. Still, materials from both Vertov's and Boltianskij's archives (at that time still in private hands) were evidently used in creating this catalog, and it is worth consulting for that reason alone (*Sovetskaia kinokhronika 1918-1925 gg.: annotirovannyj katalog*, part 1, ed. Iu. A. Poliakov and S. V. Drobashenko [Moscow: Glavnoe Arkhivnoe Upravlenie pri SM SSSR, 1965], 9–38; on the use of the Svilova [Vertov] and Boltianskij archives, see page 5). Finally, there is the online catalog of the holdings in RGAKFD (http://www.rusarchives.ru/federal/rgakfd/catalog/catalog.htm), which contains brief descriptions of the films as they exist in the archive. See also *LR*, 403.

Although Vertov began to boast of his authorship of "the first Soviet newsreel" by the early 1940s[8]—as part of an increasingly desperate effort, I would postulate, to generate much-needed cultural capital, especially after losing a number of his patron-supporters (like Kol'tsov) during the Great Terror—for many years previously he had dismissed *Kino-Nedelia* as "primitive," as little more than prerevolutionary (i.e., Pathé, Gaumont, or Skobelev Committee) newsreel with "Soviet" intertitles and "post-revolutionary" content, even as he acknowledged the series as the beginning of his career in film.[9] And indeed, the images of demonstrations, meetings, and parades contained in Vertov's earliest coauthored work, the 1918 found-footage film *Anniversary of the Revolution*, are drawn largely from the Skobelev Committee's *Svobodnaia Rossiia* as well as from *Kino-Nedelia*, and would have no precise narrative or ideological charge independently of the often quite lengthy intertitles in which they are nested.

Still, if they do not allude to *Kino-Nedelia* explicitly, a number of Vertov's post-1922 works—several of the *Kino-Pravdas, Stride, Soviet*, and *Three Songs of Lenin*—make use of footage from the series, mainly images from the Civil War period (a famous shot of a soldier on guard during a blizzard, for instance, used by Vertov to signify the suffering wrought by cold during the war) and of Lenin (e.g., speaking from the balcony of the Moscow Soviet after the murders of Karl Liebknecht and Rosa Luxemburg).[10] And although we know little about the provenance of the footage used in Vertov's early compilation films, such as the largely lost *History of the Civil War* (1921), some of it, and probably much of it, came from *Kino-Nedelia*.[11]

---

8   See esp. *SV*, 320, 326, 359, 387.
9   Ibid., 49, 64, 133.
10 The image of Lenin appears in *Kino-Pravda* 21 and *Stride, Soviet*, among others; that of the cold-embattled soldier, in *Three Songs of Lenin* as well (see image 1). Both shots likely come from *Kino-Nedelia* 32 (January 24, 1919). Like the *Kino-Pravdas* to follow—though formally far less complex than most of those later, experimental works—*Kino-Nedelia* is extraordinarily packed with fascinating if time-bound representations, meriting detailed explication; I will deal with them only superficially here.
11 For example, shots taken by Eduard Tisse of military action on the Kama River (sunken ships, naval inspection) and included in *Kino-Nedelia* 27 (December 10, 1918) found their way into the second section of *History of the Civil War* (RGALI f. 2091, op. 2, d. 5, l. 5). Much of the footage in that film depicting forces under the command of Innokentij Serafimovich Kozhevnikov (1879–1931) comes from the newsreel as well (issues 32, 33, 34, 42); see below.

Image 1: Soldier in a blizzard, from *Three Songs of Lenin* (1934/38); probably taken from *Kino-Nedelia* 32 (January 24, 1919). Source: Yale University Film Archive.

1. *KINO-NEDELIA*, "*KHRONIKA*," AND EARLY NEWSREEL

Vertov's snubbing of *Kino-Nedelia* raises the question—never seriously posed or addressed, to my knowledge—of the concrete relationship of the series to other early newsreels in form and content, and its place within the early history of "film-journals" as such. That history has yet to be written; thus, my own tentative efforts to situate *Kino-Nedelia* are strictly confined to the framework provided by important recent research into the *Pathé Journal*, descriptions of surviving Skobelev Committee nonfiction films, and archival materials on the committee's post-February *Svobodnaia Rossiia*.

Before doing this, however, a major terminological/translation issue surrounding the very word "newsreel" needs to be cleared up. Readers may have noticed that I have frequently used the clumsy hybrid "nonfiction/newsreel" to describe the kind of filmmaking Vertov was or would be engaged in. This hybrid has functioned as my jerry-rigged translation of *khrónika* ("chronicle," literally), the elusive word used during these early years (particularly until 1927 or so, when "documentary" starts to appear) to name this sort of film practice, and whose accurate translation presents significant challenges.[12] Most often, *khronika* is rendered in English as *newsreel*, but a close look at the uses of *khronika* reveals that newsreel—that is, sequences of "items" devoted for the most part to events taken to be minimally publicly significant, often condensed from single-subject nonfiction reels, and arranged into short films numbered periodically (like newspapers) and typically exhibited prior to a theatrical feature—was but one of the word's referents, and then only imperfectly, in Russia from the late 'teens through the 1920s.[13] ("Minimally publicly significant" events could include anything from major disasters and political assemblies to holiday parades and sports.) Nor does the use of *khronika* within film discourse of the time map in any important way onto the then-current meaning of *khronika* as a category of newspaper item: that is, a brief digest of recent events taken to be important enough to mention, but not important enough to merit treatment in a separate article.

The majority of what we think of as nonfiction films, whether newsreels or not, were all referred to in Russian as *khronika* or (more rarely) *khronikal'nye fil'my*. "Journal" or "film-journal" was the readiest designator of newsreel, as we will see, but phrases like "chronicle of current events" (*khronika tekushchikh sobytij*, more often *tekushchaia khronika*), "chronicle-almanac" (*sbornaia khronika*), even "informational chronicle-almanacs of events" (*sbornye khroniki sobytij informatsionnogo tipa*) were also applied to this kind of filmmaking,[14] even if one of the key distinguishing features of newsreel at this time was simply that its issues were numbered chronologically and bore a single name, like a newspaper.[15]

---

12 The other major term within this discursive constellation, "non-acted" or "unplayed" (*neigrovoj*), will be discussed in volume 2.

13 The convention of translating *khronika* as "newsreel" is observed in nearly all English-language publications on Vertov, including in the collections KE and LR. In his *Dziga Vertov*, Jeremy Hicks briefly notes the problems of interpretation posed by *khronika* (51), but both persists in translating the term as "newsreel" and misreads the usages of *khronika* and other nonfiction-related vocabulary in the 1920s, in part by relying on anachronistic dictionary definitions as evidence. My thoughts in this section have been influenced by Maxim Pozdorovkin's "Khronika: Soviet newsreel at the dawn of the information age" (PhD diss., Slavic Languages and Literatures, Harvard University, 2012), although I come at the topic from a somewhat different angle.

14 For one of many usages of *tekushchaia khronika* to distinguish newsreel (in this case the *Goskinokalendar'* series) from other from other nonfictional types like the "thematic-political" or "scientific-domestic [*nauchno-bytovaia*]," see Vertov's plan for the film *Proizvodstvo Goskino na grani 1924 i 1925 goda* (RGALI f. 2091, op. 2, d. 30; *DO*, 89–91. For the other usages, see *SV*, 33–34, 43; G. Boltianskij, *Kino-khronika i kak ee snimat'* (Moscow: Kinopechat', 1926), 27, 35.

15 See Vertov's notations for *Kino-Nedelia* and the shorter films that it condensed and incorporated (RGALI f. 2091, op. 2, d. 381, ll. 9–10). Vertov would sometimes use *khronika* to refer

To a considerable extent, indeed, "newsreel" during the period was constructed and regarded in light of the newspaper analogue, in the USSR and elsewhere (as we will see soon enough). In his original 1922 pitch to Soviet authorities for what would eventually (under Vertov's supervision) become the *Kino-Pravda* series, director Fyodor Otsep praised *khronika* for its value as "the surest means of [disseminating] agitation, enlightenment and new ideas," but used the term "journal"—*zhurnal*; or "film journal" (*kinematograficheskij zhurnal, kinozhurnal*) or "screen journal" (*ekrannyj zhurnal*)—to name the multi-item periodical format he was proposing.[16] The important 1924 history of cinema by Nikolaj Lebedev (later to appear as a protagonist in these pages) defines *kino-khronika* both as "the filming not of staged but of actual events" *and* as "a film showing us the day's current events": the latter can in turn take the shape of *"periodical screen newspapers"*—of great use, Lebedev suggests, in a country where 70 percent of the citizens are illiterate—or of *"special screen almanacs [sborniki]"* on specific themes, into which staged agitational sequences might also be incorporated.[17] By 1925, the party's Agitprop division was distinguishing between "film-*khronika*" (*kino-khronika*) and "film-journals" (*fil'mo-zhurnaly*), while privileging them both for their presumed agitational effectiveness relative to other media forms.[18]

Was newsreel ("journal," "chronicle-almanac") then simply a subset of the more general category *khronika*? Vertov's own usage often seems to confirm this proposition: particularly at the series' outset, he usually referred to *Kino-Pravda* as a "screen newspaper," a "periodical film journal" or a "chronicle-almanac," while sometimes referring to it simply as *khronika*, though often in connection with specific issue numbers.[19] Similarly, judging from Boltianskij's usage in his 1926 book on the topic, *kino-khronika* could refer to both single-topic, event-focused nonfiction films *and* to newsreel more narrowly considered. Whereas the "screen newspaper," opines Boltianskij, has become the default form of "bourgeois *kino-khronika*" in the West—presumably in the wake of the early "actuality" period—many short nonfiction works of neither the "scenic" nor

---

to the *Kino-Pravdas* when discussing the individual films as numbered items as well; see *SV*, 32–33.
16 Listov and Khokhlova, eds., *Istoriia otechestvennogo kino*, 130–36. See volume 2 for more on Otsep's proposal.
17 Nikolaj Lebedev, *Kino: ego kratkaia istoriia, ego vozmozhnosti, ego stroitel'stvo v sovetskom gosudarstve* (Moscow: Gosudarstvennoe Izdatel'stvo, 1924), 119, 124–25; Lebedev's emphasis.
18 As quoted in Boltianskij, *Kino-khronika*, 4.
19 See for instance *SV*, 18, 24–25, 32.

"newsreel" type have continued to appear in the USSR, with the non-newsreels primarily "agitational" in function, and the newsreels (he names the "weekly almanac-chronicle *Sovkinozhurnal*") primarily "informational."[20] (The meanings of these two descriptors will also need to be unpacked in the pages that follow, needless to say.)

But a closer look at the term's functions in the early Soviet period reveals that *khronika* did not subsume "newsreel" in at least two highly important respects. First, as we have already indicated via Lebedev's remarks on the form, newsreel (*zhurnal, sbornik*) could and did incorporate staged sequences, and Otsep's 1922 proposal expressly made room for staged agitational numbers in his *zhurnal*.[21] Indeed, one can find all kinds of *explicitly* (not surreptitiously) staged material in Soviet and other newsreel during this period, at least through the early 1930s (when even elaborate stop-action animated sequences began to appear): just as newspapers could contain fictional sections, so could newsreels. Such sequences seem not to have raised many eyebrows among newsreel-goers, either: Boltianskij in 1926 grumbled that the Ukrainian newsreel *Makhovik* (*Flywheel*) relied almost completely on staged material—that is (in his words), it contained almost no "khronika," here clearly signifying unstaged/nonfictional footage.[22] Whatever else *khronika* meant—and we need to be careful not to ascribe to the term *too* much stability or coherence—it certainly meant "nonfiction" (that is, unstaged and unscripted), although what exactly constituted "staged/unstaged," for these filmmakers and these audiences, is far from obvious, as we will see. The important point to make for now is that Vertov's alliance with *khronika* (not newsreel) immediately and persistently raised the question of the fictiveness (or not) of his films: an old motif of Vertov studies, to be sure, but one that has not always been framed with due discursive/philological precision.

However, there is a second contrast to be drawn to *khronika*, this time *within* the sphere of "nonfiction," that has been largely ignored and which, in my view, is at least as consequential for an understanding of Vertov's films as the issue of fiction (to which it is related, in fact). Boltianskij in 1926 singles

---

20 Boltianskij, *Kino-khronika*, 10–12, 27. See also 19 for mention of the success won abroad by one of the non-newsreel *khronika* films produced by Mezhrabpom after 1922. Importantly, when offering an example for amateur workers in *khronika* to follow, Boltianskij explicitly discusses not an "almanac chronicle-journal [i.e., newsreel], but the more difficult-to-structure thematic-chronicle-picture" of the *Kino-Pravda* type (30, 35).
21 Listov and Khokhlova, eds., *Istoriia otechestvennogo kino*, 132.
22 Boltianskij, *Kino-khronika*, 33.

out *khronika* as "*the first form of filmmaking to have appeared*," but immediately draws a distinction between *khronika* as devoted to capturing *events* on screen ("a parade in honor of Queen Victoria," "the coronation of Nikolaj II"), and "other forms of filming outside the studio [*s'emki natury*]," specifically the kind of film known in Russia as the *vidováia*, coeval with *khronika* proper.[23] Perhaps a calque from the French "vue" or "scène" (the word "vid" means "view"), the closest silent-era English-language equivalent of this term is probably the "scenic," a nonfiction type which (as the name suggests) was devoted to representations of sights and places rather than narrated events—Moscow in winter, a marketplace, a sunny beach, mountain ranges, various "exotic" locales, and so on—and which persisted as an explicit genre marker in nonfiction films of the 1920s.[24] In a perceptive 1926 review of *One Sixth of the World* to which we shall return, critic and filmmaker Vitalij Zhemchuzhnyj clarifies the basic *khronika/vidovaia* distinction in passing, if not unproblematically:

> Events [in *One Sixth*] are linked not as they follow each other chronologically (as in [*khronika*]), or [in terms of their] territorial [proximity] (as in a "scenic film" [*kak v "vidovoj"*]), [but] are connected by thematic features.[25]

Along the status hierarchy of early Soviet nonfiction, the *vidovaia*, seemingly static photographically and merely contemplative, certainly occupied a lower rung than *khronika*—which in part explains, on the institutional level, Vertov's pact with the latter term—even if, as we will see, Soviet newsreel (including the *Kino-Pravdas*) contained plenty of "views," and Vertov's most complex film could be described without derisive intent by a *New York Times* writer in 1929 as a "scenic."[26]

---

23 Ibid., 6.
24 See for instance the "scenic [*vidovaia*] in two parts," *Dagestan* (1926) by (cameramen) Petr Zotov, Iakov Tolchan and (editor) Sergej Liamin (RGAKFD 22016). The *vidovaia* was close kin to the travelogue proper, but seemed not to require any travel-narrative structural backbone: see "Travel films" in Richard Abel, ed., *Encyclopedia of Early Cinema* (New York: Routledge, 2010), 642.
25 V. Zhemchuzhnyj, "*Shestaia chast' mira*," *Novyj Zritel'* 42, no. 145 (October 19, 1926): 16; RGALI f. 2091, op. 2, d. 271, l. 352. Translated in LR as "*A Sixth Part of the World*," 198, with *khronika* rendered as "newsreel." Translation modified.
26 "*Moscow Today* [*Man with a Movie Camera*] Hailed: Film Guild Cinema Audience Applauds Sovkino Scenic," *New York Times* (May 13, 1929): 32. I should qualify this point, however, by noting that the *vidovaia* could be defended for its potential scientific and educational value: that is (to use another important term in the nonfiction glossary of the time) as a "*kul'turfil'm*," or (roughly) educational nonfiction film (from the German *Kulturfilm*). See Al. Abramov, "Vspomnim o vidovoj," *Sovetskoe Kino* 4–5 (1926): 10–11; and especially

Chronology, *pace* Zhemchuzhnyj, was certainly no distinguishing marker of *khronika* form (the way it is of much *fictional* form). *Exposition* is clearly at least as important a discursive strategy for *khronika* as chronological narration; and as far as newsreel proper goes, I have seen virtually no multi-themed newsreels, Soviet or otherwise, that observe chronology across (in contrast to *within*) their various "subjects": periodicity, not chronology, is their dominant temporal frame. Possibly already thinking about Vertov in 1926, Boltianskij insists that *khronika* montage is in no way tied to any "dry, chronological and protocol-type" norms; can be inflected by a whole range of "epic, lyrical or dramatic" genre colorations; and (in a crucial observation to which we will return in volume 2) can be vastly freer and more formally varied than fiction-film montage, insofar as it is not required to represent any "logically developing action ... with specific characters."[27]

Yet Zhemchuzhnyj's more basic implication—that *khronika* means effectively *historicized* or *narrativized nonfiction*, of which chronological form would be but one structural variant—captures what I take to be the term's dominant meaning. *Khronika*, unlike the *vidovaia*, presents putatively real events as unfolding within some version of public, collective time: that of the nation-state, most often. Short films as minimally historicized as (say) single-shot depictions of military parades, or even sporting events (as part of the history of the teams and their sponsors and fans) would count as *khronika*; "mere" panoramas of the Caucasus or close-ups of nesting polar birds would not. Thinking about the appeal of *khronika* films, it is hard to decide whether they drew audiences primarily by virtue of their spectacular character (i.e., as "attractions"), or because of the interest they generated as moments in larger historical trajectories (like wars; elections; the building of socialism) in which spectators were somehow invested: perhaps for both reasons, inseparably.

All I would emphasize for the moment is the way that the distinction between the *vidovaia* and the *khronika*—between de-historicized presentation and historicized structuration—becomes absolutely critical for Vertov from the *Kino-Pravdas* onward, as a kind of line along which the films continually dance in their explorations of (in Philip Rosen's words) the "differentiation[s] between the temporalities of the object and the documentary/historiographic subject."[28] Everyday actions like washing clothes, sewing and even "playing

---

Oksana Sarkisova's *Screening Soviet Ethnicities: Kulturfilms from the Far North to Central Asia* (London: I. B. Tauris, 2016).
27 Boltianskij, *Kino-khronika*, 50–51.
28 Rosen, "Now and Then," 33.

with a trapped Arctic fox" turn out (in *One Sixth of the World*) not to be merely "scenic" but contributions to socialist construction itself; the rocky profile of the Dnieper River, initially offered very much as a "scenic," turns out (in *The Eleventh Year*) to be the site of an epochal collective harnessing of nature to human ends; and the exciting spectacle of intrepid filmmakers at work turns out (in *Man with a Movie Camera*) to be the event that makes the event of socialist construction visible in the first place. Generically shifting between "scenic" and *khronika*, in other words, enables the films to inquire into what counts as history: what is in, and what is out? To be sure, the line separating "scenic" and *khronika* runs parallel to that distinguishing fiction and nonfiction as they traverse a common ideological terrain, even if the former contrast concerns primarily spectator positioning through filmic structure (or "montage"), and the latter the difference between the "played" and the "unplayed" (*igrovoe/neigrovoe*), to name a binary that becomes important around 1926 or so.

So at the risk of irritating my readers, I propose mostly retaining the term *khronika* in untranslated form in these pages, in part because of the inelegance of any adequate English equivalent (like "historicized nonfiction"), and in part to push against the normative translation "newsreel," which plainly will not do and has led to serious mischaracterizations of Vertov's practice as primarily oriented around the purveying of "news," or what in Soviet parlance would more likely and precisely be termed "*informatsiia*."[29] Early on, *kino-khronika* already meant far more than that, and thus gave Vertov a more expansive range of theoretical and practical options than "newsreel" does, or did. To be sure, we will need to attend to the later vicissitudes of *khronika* and associated terms, as it is partially supplanted both as a generic marker and as a name for a certain film-industrial practice (by "documentary," above all), re-signified (to mean "historical footage," for instance), but never entirely superseded.

All of this does *not* go to say that newsreel as a practice and set of conventions is unimportant to an assessment of Vertov's work: on the contrary, as will

---

29 The mischaracterization is perhaps plainest in Hicks's *Dziga Vertov* (see 2, 17–18, and *passim*) but finds significant early expression in Erik Barnouw's designation of Vertov as "Reporter" in his *Documentary: A History of the Nonfiction Film*, 2nd rev. ed. (Oxford: Oxford University Press, 1993), 51. Perhaps the best alternative English translation of *khronika* might be thought to be "actuality," but my sense is that term, at least as currently understood, is on the one hand too restrictive (excluding newsreel or long-form documentary, for instance) and, perhaps more importantly, too inclusive, specifically of the "scenic," from which *khronika* seems to have been distinguished. I take my sense of the contemporary meanings of "actuality" largely from Philip Rosen, *Change Mummified: Cinema, Historicity, Theory* (Minneapolis: University of Minnesota Press, 2001).

be seen in volume 2, I conceptualize my own discussion of the *Kino-Pravdas* largely around that series' conformity with and departures from newsreel convention. And Vertov emphatically did *begin* with newsreel (to recover the thread with which this section began); and we now need to get a concrete sense of what newsreel practice proper would have meant by the time he got involved with it in 1918.

Although the notion of a photographic "living journal" goes back at least to 1882,[30] and single-themed nonfiction or "actuality" films had appeared as early as 1895, the newsreel or film-journal proper was a relatively recent invention, dating back only to 1909 and Charles Pathé's first *Journal*.[31] Actualities were the progenitors, to be sure: the primary innovation leading to the newsreel, as identified by film historians Jeannine Baj and Sabine Lenk, was simply the sequencing-together of several actualities in a row. Eager for more product to exhibit, Pathé began to market these sequences as discrete films, leading to the emergence of a daily newsreel journal in October 1913. The status of "journal" was later solidified by printing an eight- to sixteen-page brochure to accompany the screenings, which functioned both as program notes and as a bridge between the films and the prestigious informational dailies.[32] The success of the new form was considerable, and by 1912, Pathé's newsreels had attracted enough of a public to warrant opening a special newsreel-only cinema in the Rue Saint-Denis.[33]

Judging from examples preserved in Belgium and the Netherlands, the number of items in early Pathé newsreel averaged around eight in 1909–10 and around twelve in 1911, with approximately one minute given over to each

---

30 Jeannine Baj and Sabine Lenk, "'Le Premier Journal Vivant de l'Univers!' Le Pathé Journal, 1909–13," in *La Firme Pathé Frères 1896–1917*, ed. Michel Marie and Laurent Le Forestier (Paris: AFRHC, 2004), 263. Perhaps the earliest "informational" actuality is the one-shot Lumière film of the participants in the Congress of Photography disembarking from a boat (ibid.). I rely heavily here on Baj and Lenk's fascinating and informative essay.

31 French precedents to the *Pathé Journal*—a *Journal Lumineux* from 1901, Gabriel Kaiser's exhibition from 1906 of "always-new attractions, up-to-date" ("d'actualité") in his Gab-Ka cinema—are numerous but evidently do not display that essential newsreel characteristic of a sequence of terse and disparate "items" linked together like discrete columns in a single newspaper. The first *Pathé Journal*, entitled *Pathé Faits Divers*, appeared in March 1909 (ibid., 265).

32 Ibid. Indeed, an examination of Russian illustrated journals, such as Petersburg's *Niva* (1870–1917), makes it clear that they were a likely source of some of the popular topics—ranging from royal pageantry to scientific discoveries to sites of disasters—of newsreel and other nonfiction films.

33 Competitors Gaumont and Éclair began producing their own journals in 1910 and 1912 respectively, and German firms began producing newsreels around the same time (ibid., 264, 266). See also the extensive remarks on newsreel throughout Abel, ed., *Encyclopedia of Early Film*.

item. Each subject would open with an intertitle indicating the place of shooting, names of important figures, the occasion, and sometimes the date, thereby amplifying and situating the image. This basic newsreel format was carried over into *Svobodnaia Rossiia* (April–October 1917) as well, a typical installment of which included around fifteen items, each prefaced by an informative intertitle; evidently, this template was standard for other Russian newsreel of the time.[34] On average, *Pathé Journal* items incorporated around three or four shots—as few as one, as many as eight—filmed with a fixed camera and (at least in the early years) rarely panning.[35]

Generalizations about number of shots-per-item are not especially informative, however, as that number depended upon the content of the item itself, and especially on the prominence accorded it within the overall sequence. Indeed, perceived importance as well as the sheer size or scope of a given event or spectacle—aristocratic families and their celebrations, royal visits and marriages, the dedication of monuments to historical figures, military parades, events attracting large crowds, spectacular achievements (like balloon flights), whopping big disasters—evidently justified not only an item's inclusion in the newsreel, but also its placement near or at the beginning, greater length, and whether or not the person or persons onscreen were named in the intertitles. Predictably, reports on the war came to occupy more newsreel space starting in 1914, although the largest overall proportion of Pathé newsreel subjects was consistently taken up by sports (with horse racing a particular favorite) throughout these early years.[36]

---

34 RGALI f. 2057, op.1, d. 261, ll. 10–16, 69–72. Because so few installments of *Svobodnaia Rossiia* have survived, it is difficult to determine their average length or average number of shots per item; however, they evidently ranged from 114 to 210 meters in length. Average length for a typical *Kino-Nedelia* issue is hardly easier to figure out, for related reasons, although much more footage from the series has survived. Indications on montage lists for seventeen of the newsreels suggest an average of 161.3 meters (ranging from 118 to 195 meters), although that figure is probably slightly low; the lengths of the majority of the apparently more complete copies of *Kino-Nedelia* in RGAKFD fall within that range, although at least two are significantly longer (issues 20 [209.8 meters] and 38 [239.8 meters]). It is also worth noting that although an average *Kino-Nedelia* issue contained about thirteen to fifteen items, the number varied from a mere four (in *Kino-Nedelia* 11 [August 13, 1918]) to twenty-five in issue 43 (June 27, 1919)—a far greater range than we find, for instance, in *Svobodnaia Rossiia*.

35 I suspect that the number of pans increased over time; certainly, *Kino-Nedelia* included many pans from the beginning of the series.

36 Baj and Lenk, "'Le Premier Journal Vivant,'" 266–69. For some surviving *Pathé Journal* coverage of the war, see RGAKFD 11796 (French scenes) and 12240 (Russian front), among many other examples.

Pathé's Russian division was by far the largest distributor and producer of newsreel in the country prior to February 1917, distantly followed by the Skobelev Committee, Gaumont, and the Khanzhonkov and Drankov firms.[37] Although sporting events were sometimes depicted in Russian Pathé—boxing, bicycle racing, yachting and so on—alongside accidents and fires,[38] the overwhelming stress was on military, aristocratic, and imperial spectacle, mainly but not exclusively Russian.[39] The pre-1917 films of the Skobelev Committee shared this focus, although the committee, perhaps because of its solemn affiliation with the state, avoided straightforwardly entertaining items like sports sequences or slices of life, producing instead (among other films) elaborate, two- to five-reel films on battles and various military operations which contained, in Russia as elsewhere, plenty of staged sequences.[40]

---

37 Pathé newsreels began to appear in Russia already in 1909, soon after their Parisian debut; there was a noticeable falling-off of productivity after the peak reached in 1914 (V. N. Batalin, *Kinokhronika v Rossii 1896-1916 gg.: opis' kinos'emok khraniashchikhsia v RGAKFD* [Moscow: OLMA-PRESS, 2002], 469–76).

38 Ibid., 252. See RGAKFD 472 for a charming newsreel fragment depicting Boy Scouts guarding boxes of film saved from a warehouse fire.

39 See RGAKFD 12867 (on the celebration of the 300th year of the Romanov dynasty) and 12083 (on the funeral of Sergej Muromtsev [1850–1910], chair of the first imperial Duma) for two typical examples. The same themes were commonplace in illustrated journals like *Niva*.

40 See the two-reel *Padenie Trapezunda* (*Fall of Trebizond*, 1916; RGAKFD 11535); the two-reel *Padenie Peremyshlia* (*Fall of Przemysl*, 1915; RGAKFD 11504); the three-reel *Shturm i vziatie Erzeruma* (*Storm and Taking of Erzurum*, 1915; RGAKFD 13076); the five-reel *Galitsiia* (*Galicia*, 1914; RGAKFD 810); and the descriptions in Batalin, *Kinokhronika v Rossii*, 45, 163, 169, 392. The *Trebizond* film does depict military maneuvers and the firing of guns, but the "combat" narrative is entirely constructed with the help of lengthy intertitles. The proportion of staged to nonstaged sequences in these films is not easy to determine (and depends on what is meant by "staged"), although it is plain that "nonfiction" battle scenes filmed during these years certainly did incorporate frequent staging: see Batalin, *Kinokhronika v Rossii*, 192; Jahn, *Patriotic Culture in Russia during World War I*, 154–58. On ubiquitous fakery in early news film, see Raymond Fielding, *The American Newsreel: A Complete History, 1911–1967* (Jefferson, NC: McFarland and Company, 2006), 25–31 and especially (on World War I) 68–70. The practice seems to have originated with still photography: see, for example, the heavily retouched and often plainly staged photos in Francis Trevelyan Miller, ed., *Photographic History of the Great War* (New York: New York Tribune, 1914). Objectivity and truth were proclaimed goals nonetheless: "This monumental 'Photographic History of the Great War' is being produced to give the American people the first absolutely *unbiased record* of the epoch-making events that are destroying nations and remolding the geography of the world. . . . *It will be strictly neutral* in its viewpoint, according to the proclamation of President Wilson" (ibid., 39; italics in original).

Importantly for us, if the dynasts, their relatives, and great military men dilated across pre-1917 newsreel (Pathé or Skobelev), their parliamentary counterparts—above all, members of the State Duma, intermittently in operation between 1906-1917—almost never appeared. A couple of appearances by well-known figures like Purishkevich, Kadet leader Pavel Miliukov, or Octobrist Aleksandr Protopopov made up pretty much the sum of Duma representation in newsreel, judging from the existing films and descriptions; nor, evidently, was there any reporting on Duma activities and resolutions. Indeed, French prime minister Raymond Poincaré and British monarch George V appeared far more often than any Duma representatives.[41] Whether this was due to censorship, lack of access to Duma figures, or lack of public interest is not clear; what *is* clear is that the committee's post-February *Svobodnaia Rossiia* newsreels moved those new, "democratic" state authorities front and center.

In this and other ways, as indicated in chapter 3, *Svobodnaia Rossiia* and other pre-October nonfiction films provided crucial templates for the Soviet newsreels that succeeded them.[42] Although the second installment of *Svobodnaia Rossiia* (April 1918) contains footage of a visually spectacular "news event" (a fire), the bulk of the newsreel presents spectators with images and intertitle identifications of leaders of the new Provisional Government (I. G. Tsereteli, M. N. Skobelev, V. N. Chernov, and so on), alongside heads of the army and navy (such as General Brusilov and Admiral Kolchak), gatherings of various committees and political groups (the Petrograd Executive Committee of Soviet Workers and Soldier Deputies), and foreign dignitaries in Russia (representatives from the Italian consulate and various Italian socialists; British feminist Emmeline Pankhurst).[43] Such film-portraits of state luminaries, presented either

---

41 Batalin, *Kinokhronika v Rossii,* 167, 225, 341, 384, 439, 457. Footage apparently taken of the 1906 opening of the First Duma very much falls into the "spectacle" category: see https://www.youtube.com/watch?v=Kxe0gFgnjiY, accessed October 15, 2016; my thanks to Natalie Ryabchikova for pointing it out to me. More newsreel footage of Duma members was likely taken, though in miniscule proportion to dynastic/aristocratic items; some of it appears in Esfir Shub's *Fall of the Romanov Dynasty* (1927). It would be important to know how often "secular" state leaders appeared in, say, British and German newsreel of the day, but I have not been able to uncover sufficient information to make the comparison. My suspicion is that portraiture of "parliamentary/republican" leaders began to take up much more newsreel space Europe-wide after the Great War.

42 Neither *Svobodnaia Rossiia* nor the short nonfiction subjects produced by the Skobelev Committee after February 1917 have been much studied, in part because only a couple of the newsreel's thirteen installments, bits and pieces of other newsreels and short films, and montage lists (essentially lists of the items in the newsreels) have survived.

43 RGALI f. 2057, op. 1, d. 261, l. 69.

as individuals or in groups, persisted in *Svobodnaia Rossiia* and would become one of the mainstays of Soviet newsreel, beginning with *Kino-Nedelia*.[44]

Sometimes entire installments were devoted to a major political event, as in the case of *Svobodnaia Rossiia* 12 (September 21), which dealt exclusively with the "democratic assembly" of September 14–20 in Petrograd, thereby presaging, in its unity, such works as *Kino-Pravda* 14 (1922; on the Fourth Congress of the Comintern). Most strikingly, perhaps, the "trial film," which might be thought to have been a specifically post-October innovation—the Soviet examples include Vertov's early *Trial of [Colonel Filipp] Mironov* (1919); his coverage of the 1922 trial of the Right SRs (in both a single-subject film and in *Kino-Pravdas* 1–3 and 7–8, to be discussed at length in volume 2); Grigorij Lemberg's remarkable "Trial of the Provocateur Okladskij," which comprised the whole of *Goskinokalendar'* 46 (1925); and the filming of some of the notorious show trials of the 1930s, conducted in some cases by ex-kinocs[45]—in fact commenced no later than the account offered in *Svobodnaia Rossiia* 11 (September 18, 1917) of the August–September 1917 trial of General Vladimir Sukhomlinov and his wife on charges of treason and abuse of power. This newsreel, which treats the

---

44 See the discussion of early Soviet political film-portraits in Listov, *Rossiia, revoliutsiia, kinematograf*, 89; and (for further examples) the portrayal of Maria Spiridonova and the group portrait of peasant deputies in *Svobodnaia Rossiia* 5 (dated July 3, 1917 [RGAKFD 12377]). Vertov and Savel'ev's *Brain of Soviet Russia* (1918) is essentially a full-scale gallery of such portraits, although it also includes images of former commissars as well as nonpoliticians (like poet Demian Bednyj) who occupied important positions. One finds similar portrait series in White newsreel and actuality film: for one example, see the gallery (of General Vladimir Maj-Majevskij and his lieutenants and adjutants) offered in *Vziatie goroda Poltavy vojskami Generala Maj-Majevskogo* [*The taking of the city of Poltava by General Maj-Majevskij's forces*] (1919 [RGAKFD 12374]). Illustrated journals in the prerevolutionary period contained much photo-portraiture of well-known writers, soldiers, and royals; politicians were less frequently represented, at least in Russia.

45 [*Protsess*] *Mironova* (1919; RGAKFD 384); *Goskinokalendar'* 46 (1925, filming and montage by G. Lemberg; RGAKFD 228); I. Kopalin [cameraman I. Beliakov], *Prigovor suda — prigovor naroda* [*The court's verdict is the verdict of the people*] (1938; RGAKFD 4140). Filipp Mironov (1872–1921) was a celebrated Don Cossack military commander on the Red side who was sharply and publicly critical of the Bolsheviks' coercive measures against peasants and Cossacks. After initiating a march against General Denikin against Trotsky's orders in August 1919, he was arrested, sentenced to death, but soon pardoned and freed at the end of October. After returning to the battlefield and many successes against the Whites, Mironov was rearrested in late 1920 and shot in prison, doubtless on Cheka orders, on April 2, 1921 (see *DO*, 35–39, 480–81; V. Danilov and T. Shanin, eds., *Filipp Mironov: Tikhij Don v 1917–1921 gg.* [Moscow: Fond "Demokratiia," 1997]). Ivan Okladskij (1859–1925) was tried for his work as a police double agent and agent provocateur inside the People's Will party.

trial exclusively, included depictions of guards holding him and his wife under house arrest (and demonstrating the marks placed on the outside wall of the Sukhomlinov's apartment to distinguish it), shots of defense and prosecution council, and (in its first, now lost redaction) shots of travel to the Hall of Justice and repurposed archival images of the general from 1912 and 1915. (The "historical value" of the 1912 image was intriguingly stressed in an intertitle presenting it as a "rare photograph of SUKHOMLINOV... taken from the German newspaper *Berliner Tageblatt*.")[46] Topics such as these—heads of state, meetings, and trials, alongside brief surveys of state institutions and achievements, and the usual parades—remained central, as we have said, to Soviet newsreel from 1918 onward.

2. NEWSREEL METAMORPHOSES

Vertov likely felt ambivalent about claiming authorship of *Kino-Nedelia* after 1940, given that so many figures who appear prominently in the newsreel—Trotsky, Kamenev, Zinoviev, Fyodor Raskol'nikov, Karl Radek, no doubt literally scores of others—had been murdered by the regime, mainly during the Terror of 1937–38. All installments were securely shelved and inaccessible by that time, of course, and the very existence of copies in Scandinavia (brought over in the early 1920s by Aleksandra Kollontai) surely forgotten.[47] Although many items and almost the whole of certain installments of *Kino-Nedelia* have gone missing, there is no clear evidence of any Orwellian retroactive excision of "enemies of the people" from the newsreel. Issue 7, for instance (June 16, 1918)—dedicated to the Fifth All-Russian Congress of Worker's, Peasant, Red Army and Cossack Deputies—has largely disappeared, and it might be thought that the high number of prominent political figures in this newsreel (as indicated in the montage lists) made it a target of "revisionist" censorship during the Stalin years. It is clear from the archival records, however, that it was Vertov and his collaborator Savel'ev who ransacked issue 7 (among others) to make *Brain of Soviet Russia* back in 1918; indeed, as we will see shortly, one of the main forms of *Kino-Nedelia*'s posterity was its partial deployment in other films.[48]

---

46 RGALI f. 2057, op.1, d. 261, l. 14; RGAKFD 12741. See also Ginzburg, *Kinematografiia dorevoliutsionnoj Rossii*, 344.
47 See footnote 7.
48 RGALI f. 2091, op. 2, d. 381, l. 3; dated May 5, 1919. At this time, some footage was simply "missing" from the newsreels, according to Vertov's notes; this footage, however, ranged from

Given the complexity of the history of *Kino-Nedelia*, and the variety of uses to which it was put, we must speak of the newsreel as a set of processes—involving restoration, reuse, archiving, and so on—rather than as a set of finished film-artifacts. *Kino-Nedelia* is what happened *to Kino-Nedelia*, and following (or reconstructing) the trajectory of the newsreel helps bring to the fore a variety of conceivable practices of organizing footage, from fixing it in an authoritative place all the way to the possibility of near-infinite repositioning. My main argument in this section will be that these different practices, and the potential conflict among them, constitute a horizon (or another "matrix") for later montage work; but we need to recount the story of *Kino-Nedelia* and its reworking in some detail before that horizon becomes clear.

The first stage was the organization of filming and the actual shooting and gathering of dailies, procedures about which we know very little. Certainly, *Kino-Nedelia* was created in a far less rationalized way, at least outside of the biggest cities, than Boltianskij had advocated in his 1917 proposal for integrating technical advice (provided by cameramen), the mining of newspapers for notices of upcoming events, and overall coordination of personnel and shaping of the newsreel into a single newsreel-studio structure.[49] Instead, it seems that much of the *Kino-Nedelia* footage, especially after the summer of 1918, derived from the expeditions of specific Film Committee cameramen who had joined up with Red forces traveling mainly on trains along various fronts of the Civil War. Eduard Tisse, later famous for his work with Eisenstein, worked in Moscow, Pskov, and along the Volga and Kama rivers; Aleksandr Lemberg traveled with his camera from Tver', Nizhnii Novgorod, and Pskov to Astrakhan and the Caucasus; Petr Novitskij, on the *October Revolution* agit-train with Mikhail Kalinin (to be succeeded by Aleksandr Levitskij and Vertov himself); Petr Ermolov, from Moscow to the Southern (Ukrainian) front, accompanied on occasion by Vertov; and Ianis Dored (who would later shoot *Paramount News* for twenty years in the US), who filmed the graduation of Red officers in Tver'.[50]

---

images of political figures (including controversial ones, like [in *Kino-Nedelia* 7] heads of the Left SRs and anarcho-communists) to quite commonplace shots of parades and gatherings.

49 See discussion in chapter 3.
50 RGALI f. 2091, op. 2, d. 5, ll. 5–7; d. 6, l. 3; RGALI f. 2091, op. 2, d. 381, ll. 9–10; Listov, *Rossiia, revoliutsiia, kinematograf*, 78–79; *SV*, 283. Other cameramen (A. F. [Al'fons] Vinkler, Nikolaj Efremov, M. V. [Mark] Naletnyj, numerous others) also worked on the newsreel. See RGALI f. 2091, op. 2, d. 381, l. 11 for a list of the Committee's cameramen, their studio affiliations and the cameras they used, as well as V. M. Korotkij, *Operatory i rezhissery russkogo*

We have no records of communications between Vertov and these war correspondents, and it seems that it would have been difficult to direct them in any precise way from afar, even if certain personages and themes (major military figures; sites of destruction and construction; newly nationalized property) appear again and again and were obviously sought out systematically, as part of the cameramen's assignments.[51] At the same time, there seems to have been little coordination of the coverage in major Soviet newspapers like *Pravda* and *Izvestiia* with *Kino-Nedelia*, contrary to what has been suggested: if the leitmotif of most of the *Kino-Nedelias* (war and the drive for Red victory) certainly overlapped with the concerns and biases of the papers, there was little if any fine-grained, punctual binding of print journal with cine-journal either rhetorically or in terms of content.[52]

The footage taken by the cameramen was then organized into short actualities of greatly varying length, very much in the Pathé fashion, and integrated en bloc or (more often) in part into *Kino-Nedelia* or other nonfiction shorts. Thus ten meters (out of thirty-one) of "Tank transported from Odessa" and the full nineteen meters of "Comrade Kalinin, Chairman of the All-Russian Central Executive Committee" went into *Kino-Nedelia* 36; while 249 meters (from 376 total) of "Celebration of May 1" and 429 meters (of a total 694) of "The Journey of Comrade [cameraman Aleksandr] Lemberg on Comrade Mekhonoshin's train-convoy" were included in *Kino-Nedelia* 41.[53] The actualities were also incorporated into other nonfiction films—such as the now-lost *Cultural Work of Soviet Russia*, which included "Worker's Palace" (122 meters) and "Kindergartens" (70 meters)—or exhibited on their own, either without apparent augmentation (the 1,089 meters of *The Funeral of Comrade Sverdlov*), or with additional

---

    igrovogo kino, 1897-1921. Biofil'mograficheskij spravochnik (Moscow: NII kinoiskusstva, 2009); my thanks for Natalie Ryabchikova for the reference to this book.

51 Indeed, Vertov indicated in a 1940 talk that *Kino-Nedelia* had no "information division" mediating between the cameramen and the editors ("Ot *Kino-Nedeli* k *Kolybel'noj* [kak vse eto nachalos']," cited from RGALI f. 2091, op. 2, d. 214, l. 7). See also Listov, *Istoriia smotrit v ob'ektiv*, 135.

52 The link is suggested in Liliana Mal'kova, *Sovremennost' kak istoriia: realizatsiia mifa v dokumental'nom kino* (Moscow: Materik, 2001), 21. I would not exaggerate my point here, as events covered in *Kino-Nedelia* were sometimes written about more or less simultaneously in print journals (for examples, see Listov, *Istoriia smotrit v ob'ektiv*, 144, and below); but it would be very misleading to think of *Kino-Nedelia* as a set of illustrations to *Pravda*, *Izvestiia*, or other newspapers.

53 RGALI f. 2091, op. 2, d. 381, l. 9. The list of examples could be readily expanded, although I have no evidence about the integration of actualities into newsreel for any *Kino-Nedelia* issues prior to number 36. Konstantin Aleksandrovich Mekhonoshin (1889–1938) was a key member of the Revolutionary Military Soviet, active mainly on the eastern and southern fronts.

War	81% (35 newsreels)
Political figures, including non-Bolshevik leaders	63% (27 newsreels)
Public rituals, including parades; birthday celebrations; tearing down or raising of monuments	37% (16 newsreels)
State achievements, including services for children; construction; provision of aid; life on communes; artistic and technological work; education	44% (19 newsreels)
Natural and man-made disasters	26% (11 newsreels)
Slices of life	23% (10 newsreels)
Funerals (of soldiers, of various luminaries)	23% (10 newsreels)
Meetings and demonstrations	21% (9 newsreels)
News from abroad (including Ukraine)	19% (8 newsreels)
Sport	7% (3 newsreels)
Trials and criminal proceedings	9% (4 newsreels)
Cinema	9% (4 newsreels)
Agitational-propaganda activity (including agit-trains)	7% (3 newsreels)
Religion	2% (1 newsreel)

Chart 1: Showing a breakdown of the topics treated in the forty-three issues of *Kino-Nedelia*, with the approximate frequency of their occurrence (as a percentage of the total).

footage (the films of the exposures of the relics of Sergius of Radonezh and Tikhon of Zadonsk, discussed at the end of this chapter). Of course, actuality footage could be used to fashion newsreel *and* other *khronika* films as well, as with the 1,428 meters of "The Journey of Comrade [cameraman Petr] Ermolov on Comrade Antonov's train-convoy," parts of which went into *Kino-Nedelias* 36, 40, and 41, but 431 meters of which also made up a separate (now lost) release entitled *The Taking of Odessa*.[54] It may be that the severe shortage of raw film stock also occasioned these disparate uses of actuality footage, which could be made to serve multiple purposes: as material for an autonomous actuality; as incorporated into a larger nonfiction short; or as distilled to become a *Kino-Nedelia* item.[55]

---

54 RGALI f. 2091, op. 2, d. 381, ll. 9–10. "Antonov" likely refers to the well-known Bolshevik military leader Vladimir Antonov-Ovseenko (1883–1938). For other examples of actualities incorporated into *Kino-Nedelia*, see Listov, *Rossiia, revoliutsiia, kinematograf*, 88.
55 Listov suggests that cameramen may have received assignments to shoot material for specific *Kino-Nedelia* items starting in the fall of 1918 (*Rossiia, revoliutsiia, kinematograf*, 87). The extent to which workprints (positives) rather than negatives were used in fashioning these various actualities, and *Kino-Nedelia*, is unclear. Certainly, editing straight from a camera negative without

It is worth noting parenthetically that the frequent reference to cameramen—particularly in the provisional names of the actualities, but also on a number of the montage lists for *Kino-Nedelia*, though not in the intertitles or, indeed, in the titles under which they were exhibited—may quietly signal the beginning of the later Soviet celebration of newsreel cameramen, a highly masculinist kind of "star-making" that reached its apotheosis in the heady career of Roman Karmen (1906–78). Starting in the 1930s, cameramen, who were virtually always credited in discreet newsreel items, frequently won major awards and honors and contributed to film journals and other publications, many of which followed their exploits as they filmed in dangerous and exciting places like the Arctic, the Far East, in the air, and on vast construction sites.[56] As we will see later, the publicity for Vertov's films of the 1920s–early 1930s helped to establish this interest, especially in reports on the work of cameramen Mikhail Kaufman (during the shooting of *One Sixth of the World* and *The Eleventh Year*) and Boris Tsejtlin (*Enthusiasm*).

Indeed, perhaps Vertov's earliest nonfiction script is devoted to "The Mission of Comrade Vertov, Director [*Instruktor*] of Filming, under the command of Red Army Commander Comrade Kozhevnikov," which includes shots of a recaptured factory, speeches by various army heads, and a concluding, explicit, and apparently authentic depiction of the execution of a deserter. If the film was ever produced, it was made under a different title, and neither Vertov nor the cameraman (Ermolov) appeared onscreen; all the same, the motif of the filmmaker's or cameraman's journey seems to have been established very early, and finds its most extraordinary silent-era elaboration, of course, in *Man with a Movie Camera*, described sarcastically by Aleksandr Lemberg in 1960–61 as in part an "advertisement . . . for the work of cameraman Kaufman."[57]

No working notes survive from the period of *Kino-Nedelia*, and so we have no evidence on paper about the thought processes informing those

---

making a workprint, or cutting from negatives of already final-edited films, seems to have common practice at this time in Russia, and no doubt partially accounts for the seriously incomplete state of *Kino-Nedelia* today. See Aleksandr Deriabin, "Vremia sobirat': Otechestvennoe kino i sozdanie pervogo v mire kinoarkhiva," *Kinovedcheskie zapiski* 55 (2001), here (below) cited from http://www.kinozapiski.ru/ru/article/sendvalues/542/, accessed October 15, 2016; and D. Batalin, "Iz opyta RGAKFD po vosstanovleniiu kinematograficheskikh raritetov," unpublished paper (*ekovideofilm.ru/doccenter/doc/D_Batalin.doc)*; accessed October 15, 2016).

56   This practice may also be an extension/elaboration of illustrated magazine captioning, which also normally (in *Niva*, for instance) attributed specific gravures to particular artists.

57   RGALI f. 3017, op. 1, d. 20, l. 2. Descriptions of a lost film called *The March of the Red Partisans on Ukraine* (1919) are similar to Vertov's "mission," and material from the expeditions of Tisse and Ermolov with Kozhevnikov's troops appears in *Kino-Nedelias* 26, 29, 32–34, and 38 (*DO*, 478).

condensations of actuality into newsreel. Still, close examination of the newsreels, even in their current incomplete state, reveals that they were carefully constructed, if not with anything like the kind of imagination, even abandon, that marks Vertov's later *Kino-Pravdas*. Sometimes, entire sections of an issue were unified thematically, across several apparently disparate items, as in the first nine units of *Kino-Nedelia* 3 (June 15, 1918), all of which were devoted to the theme introduced in the first intertitle, "The struggle against hunger"—a struggle that would become much more desperate by year's end:

1. The struggle against hunger[58]
2. The People's Commissar for [Food] Provisions [Aleksandr] TSURIUPA
3. Commissar for Provisions in the SOUTHERN DISTRICTS, [Aleksandr] SHLIAPNIKOV
4. Main Commissar of the Provisions Army [i.e., military units involved in food requisitioning] [Grigorij] ZUSMANOVICH
5. Members of the intelligentsia working in gardens near the Butyrskaia Gate[59]
6. Planting cabbage
7. Citizens planted potatoes across a large expanse of land
8. Lunches for the unemployed at the labor exchange
9. Lunch costs one ruble, 10 kopecks (2 shots)[60]

The newsreel then moves on to a host of other topics, from the arrival of Russian wounded released from German captivity to the new Briansk train station in Moscow, but the thematic unity of the three broad subdivisions of this opening section—the Bolshevik leadership in charge of fighting hunger (intertitles 1–4), labor brigades at work planting vegetables (5–7), feeding the unemployed (8–9)—is quite plain. Indeed, I would go further and suggest that the sequence incorporates a causal logic as well, inasmuch as we move from the motif of requisitioning and the military approach to solving the hunger problem (intertitle 4) to a concrete example of compulsory labor in food

---

58 This intertitle, an important thematic framing device for the section, is missing from all prints of the newsreel I have seen, though not from the montage list.
59 The images that follow depict what is apparently gardening work made compulsory by the Provisions Commissariat and performed by nonworkers. Butyrskaia Gate is near a famous (and notorious) prison in Moscow.
60 RGALI f. 2091, op. 2, d. 1, l. 8.

production, to a final demonstration of the benefits brought about by the government's "struggle against hunger."[61]

Processes large and small were also expertly narrated in *Kino-Nedelia*. An especially well-constructed sequence in issue 33 (January 31, 1919) was devoted to snow removal on the front during that unusually hard winter. Across fourteen shots, the film recounts three basic phases indicated on the montage list: "A train derailed [because of snowdrifts]. Cleaning the track. The first train to pass through after the snow is cleared."[62] The first four shots, all in long or medium-long shot and sometimes involving pans rightward, offer a vista of trains sunk in snow with hordes of men digging into banks that rise to the wagon windows. These panoramas are followed by three more tightly framed shots that move from close-up to pan to reveal derailed wheel assemblies plugged with snow, thus showing how the snow not only covers the landscape, but penetrates machinery as well. A pair of static shots then briefly depicts the organization of snow removal, as men heave snow upward from the tracks to be cleared by others on the high banks above. Three further shots then move back and forth between images of men working on the now partially visible track and teams just beginning to dig into the massive pile; a penultimate high-angle view of mainly cleared rails is succeeded by the triumphant leftward passage of a smoking train down the track, flanked on either side by enormous walls of shoveled snow. Interestingly, similar but less suspenseful or artful sequences about snow removal appeared in the previous two issues of *Kino-Nedelia* as well (31 [January 17] and 32 [January 24]), which might suggest that the editors of the series were rapidly gaining expertise at shaping actuality material to give it greater narrative drive. At any rate, representations of process, not all as thoughtfully constructed as this one, are to be found throughout *Kino-Nedelia*, early and late.[63]

---

61   See also Listov, *Istoriia smotrit v ob'ektiv*, 134. Other examples of thematically highly unified sequences would include the section on the trial of Commander Pavel Dybenko in issue 1 (June 1, 1918) and an item on the difficulties of milk distribution in hungry Moscow in issue 22 (October 29, 1918). *Kino-Nedelia* 11 (August 13, 1918) included as its final item what appears to have been a short instructional film on "how to protect oneself from cholera" (RGALI f. 2091, op. 2, d. 2, l. 10). On the causal logic, see the discussion of propaganda/agitation, below.

62   RGALI f. 2091, op. 2, d. 6, l. 3. The sequence is prefaced by an intertitle: "Along the way, Comrade Kozhevnikov's train-convoy had to struggle stubbornly with snowdrifts along the tracks"; Ermolov provided the photography. The montage lists for issues 25 onward very occasionally include brief shot descriptions along with the texts of the intertitles.

63   Other examples might include the return of the Russian war invalids mentioned above (from issue 3), giving ID passes to refugees in issue 5 (July 2, 1918), and the demonstration of a

Finally, *Kino-Nedelia* incorporated excellently fashioned non-narrative "slice of life" sequences as well. A good example appears in the eighth item of issue 22 (October 29, 1918), where we see the bustling marketplace of Kazan' after the city was taken by the Reds and "life" (the intertitle tells us) "had settled back down to normal again." Five shots of men getting their hair and beards trimmed manage to give a vivid impression of the activity at the bazaar by rapidly capturing both the specific motions of shaving and the energy of the surrounding crowds. As so often throughout *Kino-Nedelia*, the people filmed often stare back at or even seem to play (or want to play) with the camera, giving this actuality footage a haunting immediacy. This effect is especially keenly felt in the next two shots, depicting the baking and rolling-out of *bliny* (pancakes) by merchants who seem to be doing their best to demonstrate their craft as requested by the cameraman. The editors even manage to insert a moment of self-reflexivity, in a penultimate shot showing a small crowd impatient to watch moving images through a kinetoscope-like device. The intentionality behind the sequence is perhaps best revealed in the last image, a god's-eye view of the entire marketplace, rhetorically summing up the scene as a whole ("life... back to normal") while suggesting that the images we have seen have indeed been mere views or "slices" of a complex social organism.[64] The key point is that the sequence is clearly edited to give the impression of both variety (of activities: grooming, food preparation and consumption, entertainment, sheer milling-about) and of unity, particularly enforced by that final summary shot.[65]

---

motorized hand cart in issue 21 (October 22, 1918). *History of the Civil War* (1921) presented quite elaborate sequences about specific battles, such as the narrative in the film's third part about the fight against Kolchak's forces in Ufa, which moves from reconnaissance to artillery barrages, funerals, fighting on the front, and finally (in some very early Soviet industrial shots) revived factories ("factories in those areas taken by the Red Army are immediately put into production"); much of this footage seems to have been taken from *Kino-Nedelia*.

64 My sense is that such god's-eye view shots became (or already were) a standard way of closing-off "slice of life" sequences like this one, particularly if the topic was a bazaar or bustling urban scene. For another example, see Boris Kaufman and André Galitzine, *Les Halles Centrales* (1927).

65 Another excellent "slice of life" sequence, set in Petrograd, is found in issue 5 (July 2, 1918), although its unity as a sequence is slightly compromised in the existing copies of the film because the opening title, "From the life of Petrograd," is missing (RGALI f. 2091, op. 2, d. 1, l. 13). Occasionally, sections of *Kino-Nedelia* were tinted in order to give them greater representational charge, as in some blue-tinted shots at the end of issue 26 of Kozhevnikov's flotilla on the moonlit Volga at night; this footage seems to have been drawn from another short film about Kozhevnikov fighting the Czechoslovak forces (RGALI f. 2091, op. 2, d. 5, l. 4).

Images 2 and 3: Reactions to the camera from (top) *Kino-Nedelia* 5 (July 2, 1918 [RGAKFD 549]) and *Kino-Nedelia* 27 (December 10, 1918 [RGAKFD 12644]).

To be sure, these depictions of coordinated state action (to combat hunger), of concrete efforts to secure victory (like snow removal), and of restored normalcy all worked together to produce an impression of the government's wide-ranging and efficient involvement in the war effort and, by extension, in the country as a whole. This representation of ubiquity and simultaneity—of some great "meanwhile" joining the agents onscreen with the audiences viewing them—is, of course, one of the crucial functions of periodicals as such, as Benedict Anderson has argued, and probably of greater ideological significance than any approbatory images of the state conveyed via newsreel.[66] Indeed, although the first item of the very first *Kino-Nedelia* was a tribute to Marx on his 100th birthday, the earliest issues contained relatively little of a tendentious, "Soviet" character: soldiers on the revolutionary side are even referred to as "Russian" (rather than "Red Army") in the first three issues, and only in issue 4 (June 22, 1918) does the term "socialist fatherland" appear.

As *Kino-Nedelia* progressed, however, specific issues did incorporate overtly agitational intertitle phrasing, sometimes as jolts delivered to the audience either at the beginning or end of the film.[67] Occasionally entirely apolitical (like "Citizens, watch out for trolley cars!": found in a Moscow slice-of-life sequence near the end of *Kino-Nedelia* 10 [August 6, 1918]), these phrases most often inflected specific news items in a pro-revolutionary direction, such as at the conclusion of *Kino-Nedelia* 24 (November 19, 1918), when "Soviet border patrols congratulate their German comrades on their liberation from monarchist slavery"; at the beginning of issue 34 (February 7, 1919), when shots of the funeral of three fallen soldiers is preceded by the lapidary slogan "THE REVOLUTION DEMANDS SACRIFICES"; or in the 12th and penultimate title of issue 36 (May 1, 1919), which greets the first

---

66 "We know that particular morning and evening editions will overwhelmingly be consumed between this hour and that, only on this day, not that.... The significance of this mass ceremony—Hegel observed that newspapers serve modern man as a substitute for morning prayers—is paradoxical. It is performed in silent privacy, in the lair of the skull. Yet each communicant is well aware that the ceremony he performs is being replicated simultaneously by thousands (or millions) of others of whose existence he is confident, yet of whose identity he has not the slightest notion. Furthermore, this ceremony is incessantly repeated at daily or half-daily intervals throughout the calendar. What more vivid figure for the secular, historically clocked, imagined community can be envisioned?" (Benedict Anderson, *Imagined Communities: Reflections on the Origins and Spread of Nationalism*, 2nd ed. [New York: Verso, 1991], 35).

67 "Agitation" here means terse, sharp slogans intended to provoke immediate response or action; I reserve a more detailed discussion of agitation and its relationship to "propaganda" for later in this chapter.

post-monarchy elections in Red Vienna with "Hail the Socialist Republic."[68] Similarly, an image of a detachment of the All-Russian Central Executive Committee of Soviets assembled to "do battle with [Admiral] Kolchak" is followed and framed by two concluding intertitles:

> Under the Red Flag—against the black flag of Kolchak, the generals, and capitalists, the landowners
>
> Hail the world union of Republics of Labor.[69]

A much more elaborate agitational sequence appears at the end of *Kino-Nedelia* 25 (November 26, 1918), which offers a kind of advertisement in intertitles—directly derived from a letter written by Lenin to attendees of an October 1918 meeting of various committees and soviets, published in *Pravda* and *Izvestiia*—for the newspaper *The Armed People*, the first issue of which was about to hit Moscow newsstands:

> We need an army of three million men
> We will have an army of 100 million men
> We will train the entire nation (shot: training workers on Strastnaia Square)
> Read *The Armed People*[70]

---

68 RGALI f. 2091, op. 2, d. 2, l. 7; d. 4, l. 13; d. 6, ll. 6, 9.
69 RGALI f. 2091, op. 2, d. 6, l. 15. By no means were such strategies found in *Kino-Nedelia* alone, of course. Perhaps their most consistent deployment is to be found a couple of years later in *History of the Civil War*, which juxtaposes not only images of orating revolutionary leaders like Trotsky with intertitles excerpted from speeches ("To White Terror we answer with Red Terror"), but intertitles with images of banners bearing the same messages ("Death to the bourgeoisie and their hangers-on"). Shots that had been framed in a quite neutral way in *Kino-Nedelia*, such as some images of the aftermath of a conflagration at the Kursk station in Moscow in issue 31, were inflected by accusatory intertitles ("They blew up sections of trains, railway stations, railway workshops") in the first section of *History of the Civil War* (a section called "White Terror," succeeded by "Organized revolts," "Partisans," "Czechoslovak Front," "Kolchak Front," "Denikin Front," and "Vrangel' Front"). See *DO*, 48–50. The larger, fascinating story of how Soviet newsreel/actuality film was made more polemical (or less "neutral") over the course of the first years of Soviet power has been little studied. As late as June 1918, however, it was possible for an actuality about an explosion at a gunpowder warehouse to be presented as a series of "views" of the catastrophe, without any assignment of blame (*Katastrofa v Kieve* [*Catastrophe in Kiev*; RGAKFD 12724]). How the film might have been presented during screenings, however, is a different matter.
70 RGALI f. 2091, op. 2, d. 5, l. 1; see also Feldman, *Evolution of Style*, 41. This newspaper may have simply been the renamed version of a venerable military periodical dating back to the post-Napoleonic period. For background on the unattributed citation from Lenin, see Listov, *Istoriia smotrit v ob'ektiv*, 137.

Kino-Nedelia 40 (May 13, 1919) develops an agitational technique that would be much used in later Soviet silent newsreel: interspersing shots of speakers with pointed excerpts from their speeches. The first item of this issue was dedicated to the opening of the First All-Russian Congress for Extracurricular Education, and concluded with an extract from a speech by Lenin (intertitles 4–7):

> N. Lenin in his speech of welcome said: "Only now that we have had done with external obstacles and broken the old institutions, does the first task of the proletarian revolution—
>
> "truly rise before us in its full scope and for the first time: the organization of 10s and 100s of millions of people.—
>
> "We must engage in a simple and essential task: the mobilization of the literate in a struggle against illiteracy.
>
> "We must create an organized network of libraries, to help the people make use of EVERY BOOK WE HAVE."[71]

Agitation, as we will see, was a permanent feature of Vertov's work from the early 1920s onward. On one level, his films of the 1920s became laboratories for experimentation with agitational strategies, involving intertitles (sometimes graphically dynamized in remarkable ways), cited speech, images of posters and shouting mouths, and much else besides. Indeed, it might be argued that the most politically tendentious features of Vertov's work—these explicit efforts to startle, to provoke, to motivate—were at times the most experimental or "formalist," in the way they drew attention to themselves and broke up the expected unity of the filmic text.[72]

In this regard, we might refer in passing to Vertov's earliest truly formally innovative work, the lost "experimental etude" *Battle for Tsaritsyn* (*Boj pod Tsaritsynom*, 1919 or 1920), an intertitle-less film which employed very short shot lengths, as brief as five frames, in what was evidently an effort to convey the intensity of the battle by a direct "agitation" of vision via extremely rapid montage. (Famously—or as legend would have it—the first editor to whom Vertov

---

71 RGALI f. 2091, op. 2, d. 6, l. 13. For other examples of political sloganeering in *Kino-Nedelia*, see Listov, *Istoriia smotrit v ob'ektiv*, 138.

72 That the need to "agitate" and exert emotional effect created an important opening into formal experimentation is a central (if inexplicit) point in Nikolaj Abramov's pioneering 1960 essay ("Dziga Vertov i iskusstvo dokumental'nogo fil'ma," esp. 280–81).

presented the footage for *Battle for Tsaritsyn* simply threw most of it out, thinking it was but random bits and pieces not intended for inclusion in a film. Vertov duly reestablished the shots and entrusted them to none other than Elizaveta Svilova, who in a couple of years time would become his life partner and editor of nearly all his important films.)[73] Though a minority of Vertov's colleagues, including Lev Kuleshov, praised the experiment, the Film Committee's Artistic Council and top brass reacted with hostility at its blasts of images unanchored by text; and Vertov wryly noted in a talk from February 1929 that although *Tsaritsyn* was a direct predecessor of the recently-completed *Man with a Movie Camera*, the response to the film at the time was such that he felt "unable to count on being able to [carry out any more] experiments."[74]

---

73 In 1919, Svilova (about whom much more in volumes 2 and 3) was heading up the editing section of the Moscow Film Committee. According to her memoir published in the 1970s, Vertov dropped by in dejected mood one day with a box of short pieces of film, complaining that the other editors had refused to put the pieces together. "Vertov had given the editor an unusual assignment. In this etude . . . pieces of footage of normal size—three or four meters in length—alternated with short, fast-moving responses [*repliki*] of 20, 10 or even five frames. It never occurred to the editor that such small blotches were needed for the film, and so she just threw them into the trash. All of Vertov's work went to naught." Feeling sorry for him, Svilova put the pieces together as he had wanted. From then on, she wrote, only she edited his work (*DVVS*, 66). The film was evidently shot by Aleksandr Lemberg (RGALI f. 2091, op. 2, d. 486, l. 84).

74 *SV*, 165. It is not exactly clear when *Battle for Tsaritsyn* was made—the struggle for the city dragged on from the summer of 1918 to January 1920—nor when nor why it disappeared. A brief and probably fragmentary film from 1919 (*Na Tsaritsynskom Fronte* [*On the Tsaritsyn Front*; RGAKFD 12399]) includes a small amount of near-analytic editing —a medium-long shot of an orator on a car, filmed from behind; orator gets out of the car, again in medium long shot; sudden close-up of a dead soldier and wreath in the car (which turns out to be a hearse)—but nothing resembling Vertov's description (especially as regards shot length) and nothing about the battle itself. Tsaritsyn, it should be noted, was renamed Stalingrad in 1925 in recognition of Stalin's role there during 1918 as a political commissar (see Geoffrey Roberts, *Stalin's Wars: From World War to Cold War, 1939–1953* [New Haven, CT: Yale University Press, 2006], 12–13). Although it was still possible in 1928 to write a history of the battle that barely made mention of Stalin's role (L. Kliuev, *Bor'ba za Tsaritsyn: 1918–1919* (Moscow and Leningrad: Gosudarstvennoe Izdatel'stvo, 1928), this was not the case by 1940, when an account was published that stressed his centrality on almost every page. See E. Genkina, *Bor'ba za Tsaritsyn v 1918 godu* (Moscow: Politizdat pri TsK VKP[b], 1940). Indeed, in 1937, Stalin's leadership during the Tsaritsyn battle and his successful organization there of grain requisitioning— all in the face of Trotsky's supposed incompetence and sabotage, of course—received semi-fictional treatment in Aleksej Tolstoj's novella *Khleb: Oborona Tsaritsyna* (Moscow: OGIZ, 1937): a literary precursor, I suspect, of the famous Stalin-films of the postwar period. The defense of the city therefore became an important feature of the official narrative of Stalin's greatness, and any approach to the topic of "Tsaritsyn" would have

Given the risk, no doubt still imperfectly conceptualized, of formal agitational strategy overwhelming message, cited political speech of the kind found in *Kino-Nedelia* 40 might have proven an especially effective and relatively unobtrusive agit-method, insofar as it could convey agitational content within the framework of "objective reportage" of a newsworthy event like a speech or conference.

In short, the *Kino-Nedelias* were no crude repositories of strung-together actuality material, but carefully fashioned works. Nonetheless, as we have already mentioned, they shared in the common newsreel fate by being mined—by Vertov, among others—as sources of footage for other films, including other *Kino-Nedelia* issues, and sometimes mingled with material from other sources like *Svobodnaia Rossiia*. Already by 1919, the relationships between *Kino-Nedelia*, the films made out of it, and the films out of which it was made, were very intricate indeed.[75] Given these complex borrowings and reshufflings, and

---

required exceptional ideological caution. Though we have no idea why the film vanished, it is at least worth entertaining the possibility that it represented Stalin's role in the battle somehow inadequately, and thus, at some later point, came to be thought to merit shelving or destruction, regardless of its formal brilliance or historical importance. For more detail on the Tsaritsyn debacle, see Stephen Kotkin, *Stalin, Volume 1: Paradoxes of Power* (New York: Penguin, 2014), 300–310.

75 As indicated above, the main destination of footage taken from *Kino-Nedelias* 1 through 22 was *Anniversary of the Revolution*, whose fourth reel was often exhibited independently as *Brain of Soviet Russia* (both 1918). The bulk of the footage used in *Anniversary* and *Brain* consisted of images of political figures and regime leaders—almost exclusively so, in the case of *Brain*, with the exception of three opening shots of the Kremlin and environs—although other material, like the above-mentioned shots of Russians returning from German captivity (from *Kino-Nedelia* 3), slices of Petrograd life (from *Kino-Nedelia* 5), and records of the taking of Kazan' (from *Kino-Nedelia* 17) also went into *Anniversary*. Two wholly or largely lost shorts from 1918–19 in whose making Vertov may not have participated, *Advance on Ufa* and *At the Rear with the Czecho-Slovaks*, used (in *Ufa*) footage from *Kino-Nedelia* 31 of firing on enemy positions and of captured White Guards and (in *At the Rear*) reused an image from the same issue of Fyodor Raskol'nikov (RGALI f. 2091, op. 2, d. 2, ll. 8, 13; d. 3, l. 10; d. 5, l. 12; d. 381, ll. 3–8; see also N. A. Lebedev, *Ocherk istorii kino SSSR*, vol. 1 (Moscow: Goskinoizdat, 1947), 76).

As if matters were not complicated enough: that shot of Raskol'nikov in issue 31 had in turn been recycled from issue 26; and indeed, *Kino-Nedelia* would both occasionally cannibalize its own earlier footage and (more often) borrow wholesale from earlier newsreel, *Svobodnaia Rossiia* in particular. For instance, the shot (mentioned in the previous chapter) of Fyodor Batkin from *Svobodnaia Rossiia* 10 was integrated as the thirteenth item in *Kino-Nedelia* 19, only now to indicate that Batkin had been executed "for his crimes against Soviet power." The same issue of *Kino-Nedelia* contains three more shots borrowed from Skobelev newsreel, including the image from (again) *Svobodnaia Rossiia* 10 of Ekaterina Breshko-Breshkovskaia, included as anachronistic and dubious proof that contrary to rumor, she was alive and well in Samara (RGALI f. 2091, op. 2, d.

the fact that the newsreels were largely comprised of distillations from prior actualities, we need to ask why the *Kino-Nedelias* were subjected to a restoration in the first place—although our answer, as so often, must remain on the level of conjecture.[76] Judging from the existing scholarship, little care was taken in these years to preserve newsreels over the long term, in any country; and restoration to the condition in which they had been released was then simply unheard of, from what I can tell.[77] No authoritative decree from the higher reaches of Narkompros seems to have prompted the restoration—Gardin's order to Vertov originated in the Moscow Film Committee itself, and is recorded only in a committee bulletin[78]—although concerns with both preservation and control over may have emanated from a variety of administrative levels, and even from concerned individuals. Certainly, simply asserting control over the committee's own stock of films must have been part of the motivation. With both inventory and censorship in mind, the committee had begun surveying its film holdings in

---

381, ll. 5–6; d. 3, l.16; Breshko-Breshkovskaia was indeed alive, and would emigrate the following year). The other shots evidently borrowed from Skobelev newsreel for *Kino-Nedelia* 19 were one of Hetman Skoropadskij (item 12), and a shot of Women's Battalion of Death leader Maria Bochkareva erroneously placed at the end of the newsreel (item 14) during the restoration. *Kino-Nedelia* 28 (December 17, 1918) contained a final, derisive image of Grand Duke Nikolaj Nikolaevich, whom some on the White side had apparently hoped to enlist as their leader, taken from an unknown Skobelev newsreel (RGALI f. 2091, op. 2, d. 5, l. 7ob).

Moreover, much of the (partially) surviving first and second parts of *Anniversary* are clearly made up of material taken from newsreel and nonfiction made by the Skobelev Committee and other concerns between February and October 1917. Developing a negative portrayal of the Provisional Government and making sure to offer visual reminders of its least attractive figures (Purishkevich; War Minister Guchkov), this second section also includes images of a cameraman near the Taurida Palace (possibly Novitskij) that may have been taken from *Toward the Opening of the Constituent Assembly*. See RGALI f. 2057, op. 1, d. 261, l. 61.

76 Reuse of newsreel *in* newsreel (or other nonfiction work) was, to be sure, far from unusual—it can already be found in *Svobodnaia Rossiia*, and no doubt earlier—although more unusual than simple discarding of the films. Surely the most remarkable aspect of *Kino-Nedelia*'s history was *not* the redeployment of its footage, but the decision to restore it. Evidently, the vast majority of newsreel films made before 1920 worldwide have been lost, although the productions of some countries (e.g., France) have been better preserved than that of others (e.g., the United States). See William T. Murphy, "The Preservation of Newsreels in the United States" and Michelle Aubert, "News before Newsreel," in *Newsreels in Film Archives: A Survey Based on the FIAF Newsreel Symposium*, ed. Roger Smither and Wolfgang Klaue (Wiltshire, UK: Flicks Books, 1996), 8–12, 22–25.

77 Indeed, the earliest clearly documented Soviet legislation on preserving film-documents of the Revolution dates only to 1925–26; see Deriabin, "Vremia sobirat'," and below.

78 Listov, *Istoriia smotrit v ob'ektiv*, 152; Magidov, *Zrimaia pamiat' istorii*, 85–86.

May 1918—420 films had been examined by mid-July, and forty-one of those withdrawn from exhibition—in advance of a decree of July 17, requiring the committee's permission for any releases of old or new films.[79]

A more widespread preoccupation among those heading up the cultural commissariats with preservation and archiving may also have exerted an influence. On October 11, 1918, the Petrograd Film Committee had issued a decree requiring the registration of all film and photographic records of the revolution, and we might conjecture that the intentions informing this edict extended to Civil War–related footage as well.[80] Central to the Petrograd Committee's operations was, of course, Grigorij Boltianskij, who argued for the need for preservation of historical footage when working for the Skobelev Committee in 1917, and conceivably intervened on behalf of a restoration (although there is no record of him doing so).[81] Boltianskij certainly knew of Polish cameraman Boleslas Matuszewski's pioneering articles "Une nouvelle source de l'histoire" and "La Photographie animée" ("A new historical source" and "Animated photography," both 1898), which pointed out the value of film as a form of historical documentation, and hence of film preservation and archiving. The arguments of this Lumière cameraman and former

---

79 LRK 1, 257. Natalie Ryabchikova has pointed out to me that the restoration coincided with the (unwilling) departure of Nikolaj Preobrazhenskij as head of the Film Committee in early 1919, and thus with a change in administration (though this does not explain the decision to restore as such, obviously enough): see V. M. Magidov, "Moskinokomitet i natsionalizatsiia kinopromyshlennosti," *Vestnik Moskovskogo Universiteta*, Seriia IX: Istoriia, vol. 5 (Moscow: Izdatel'stvo Moskovskogo Universiteta, 1972), 3–19, esp. 15–17.

80 LRK 1, 265; see also Deriabin, "Vremia sobirat'." Given the timing of the restoration (late winter–early spring 1919), one also wonders whether the Film Committee might have had the intention of exhibiting the *Kino-Nedelias* as part of some First of May celebration. *Brain of Soviet Russia* was certainly shown, along with a number of the very earliest (now mainly lost) Soviet films, on May 1, 1919 (*LRK* 1, 291).

81 In 1917, Boltianskij was already writing about how "[film] negatives" could be assembled to make up a "valuable collection" with "enormous value for museums" (RGALI f. 2057, op. 1, d. 261, l. 51ob). Boltianskij struggled for the creation of a museum of cinema in the USSR until the very end of his life, and willed all of his cinema-related materials to that still nonexistent film museum in a final statement made a month and half before his death on June 15, 1953 (RGALI f. 2639, op. 1, d. 63, l. 20; dated April 24, 1953). Viktor Listov has also persuasively speculated that Boltianskij might have resented the fact that much of the Skobelev Committee's film archive, and therefore the capacity to use it, had been transferred to Moscow, the new capital and institutional hegemon; indeed, Moscow Film Committee head Nikolaj Preobrazhenskij complained in late summer 1918 that Boltianskij was ignoring his orders to send the material. Given all of this, the manhandling that *Svobodnaia Rossiia* received at the hands of Vertov and others might have been especially provocative (*Istoriia smotrit v ob'ektiv*, 175–76).

photographer to the Tsar, eventually translated into Russian sometime around 1943 by Boltianskij after he was put in charge of the film-documentary records of the Great Patriotic War at Moscow's Central Documentary Film Studio, doubtless had some currency among the more historically aware Soviet film administrators in 1919.[82]

Slightly further afield, intense debates were occurring within the Visual Arts Section (IZO) of Narkompros at precisely this time (February–March 1919) about what Soviet art museums should look like, what should be collected, who should curate and so on; thus, preservation was on the minds of many cultural workers and authorities in early 1919.[83] What all this suggests is that *Kino-Nedelia* was regarded and valued from an early stage as a series of *historicizations*—as a sequence of (partial) definitions of that early Soviet "meanwhile," determinations not only of what might be called National Space-Time, but also of what contemporaries took to be the epochal world-historical turning point of the Revolution—rather than as a ephemeral platform for the dissemination of "news."[84] Still, this historicizing impulse would seem to be transected by a tension between (on the one hand) the desire to preserve as much footage as possible from a specified historical period, and (on the other) an interest in arranging the footage in order to give specific faces and names *to* that period ("the Civil War," "the Revolution") and its protagonists.

The restoration was in any case never completed, and probably could not have been completed. Although a significant amount of the footage that had

---

82 Boleslas Matuszewski, *Écrits cinématographiques*, ed. Magdalena Mazaraki (Paris: Association française de recherché sur l'histoire du cinéma and La Cinémathèque française, 2006); Boleslav Matushevskij, "Zhivaia fotografiia: chem ona iavliaetsia, i chem ona dolzhna stat'," trans. Grigorij Boltianskij, ed. Svetlana Ishevskaia and Denis Viren, *Kinovedcheskie Zapiski* 83 (2007): 127–61; V. Magidov, "Itogi kinematograficheskoj i nauchnoj deiatel'nosti B. Matushevskogo v Rossii," *Kinovedcheskie Zapiski* 43 (1999); online as http://www.kinozapiski.ru/ru/article/sendvalues/1075/, accessed October 15, 2016). The significance of film as a record of history was much discussed in Germany as well: see the remarkable cluster of essays from 1908–12, "The Cinematographic Archive: Selections from Early German Film Theory," ed. Anton Kaes, Nicholas Baer, and Michael Cowan, *October* 148 (Spring 2014): 27–38.

83 See the polemical articles by Nikolaj Punin and Kazimir Malevich (written in responses to a conference on the future of museums in mid-February 1919) in *Iskusstvo Kommuny* 12 (February 23, 1919): 1–2; and Krusanov, *Russkij avangard*, vol. 2, part 1, 228–41.

84 This may partially explain why those apparently stale issues of *Kino-Nedelia* were sent to Norway under Kollontai's auspices; see footnote 7, above. It seems critical that the *newsreels* were restored, rather than the actualities out of which they were (for the most part) made: these cine-journals were at once the most widely shown and prestigious of the committee's releases and the most capacious definitions of their historical moment among those releases.

been used in *Anniversary* and *Brain* was evidently tracked down and put back in place, other *Kino-Nedelia* material had simply gone missing by May 5, 1919, and, judging from the condition of some of the extant issues, was never found (or at least never reintegrated into the newsreels).[85] The absence of original montage lists or other documentation for issues 1–35 was an equally serious matter, and surely part of the reason for the mistakes that crept into both the "restored" newsreel and the working montage lists created at the time of the restoration.[86] Moreover, we know that Vertov (and probably others) continued

---

85 A blow-by-blow account of the restoration would take up numerous detail-laden pages and still contain a great many gaps. Suffice it say that many of the images of state and party leaders taken from *Kino-Nedelias* 3–5 and 8–12 for *Anniversary* and *Brain* were evidently restored, judging from extant copies. Missing footage would have been harder to track down, of course, and some issues—especially 7, 10, and 30—had lost a great deal of footage by May 5 (all eight items, in the case of number 30). I have not managed to see what remains of these particular issues of *Kino-Nedelia*, but the descriptions in RGAKFD suggest that little was restored. For unknown reasons, former Film Committee chair Nikolaj Preobrazhenskij had also requisitioned footage from issues 19 and 25, the second of which today seems relatively complete; see RGALI f. 2091, op. 2, d. 381, ll. 4–6.

86 Gauging the accuracy of the extant working montage lists (which date to no earlier than the spring of 1919) is difficult to be sure: that they were at least sometimes fairly accurate is suggested by the one surviving *Kino-Nedelia* poster from 1918 (for *Kino-Nedelia* 4), which contains a description of the film's contents conforming quite closely to both the working montage list and to existing prints (RGALI f. 2091, op. 2, d. 1, l. 10; Tolstoj, ed., *Agitmassovoe iskusstvo*, 122; the montage list actually gives more detail about the contents of a couple of the items, and contains one extra item at the end ["the grave of Plekhanov"], but otherwise is identical).

All the same, it is clear that the early lists cannot be relied upon as a guide to what *Kino-Nedelia*'s first thirty-five issues originally looked like. According to the lists, for instance, issue 3 contained a prerevolutionary newsreel image of Admiral Kolchak, indicating his new role as the "commander of the counterrevolutionary forces in Siberia"; and indeed, all extant prints of the film contain this shot. At the time of the release of *Kino-Nedelia* 3, however (June 15, 1918), Kolchak was domiciled at a resort in Japan (where he had been since May), having left Russia in the summer of 1917. He would arrive in Vladivostok only on September 8, 1918, and then not initially as a commander-in-chief (RGALI f. 2091, op. 2, d. 1, l. 8; Listov, *Istoriia smotrit v ob'ektiv*, 150–51; Jon Smele, *Civil War in Siberia: The Anti-Bolshevik Government of Admiral Kolchak, 1918–1920* [Cambridge: Cambridge University Press, 1996], 74, 76).

In the preceding item in the same issue, an image of a bearded man standing next to a car on a wintry day is labeled "Delegate of the Caucasian Government [Iraklij] Tsereteli." Not only is there no historical record of Tsereteli—then involved in the formation of the short-lived Menshevik government in his native Georgia—traveling to Moscow at this time (or a few months earlier, during the winter), but such a journey seems highly unlikely, given that he had left for Georgia after the murders of Kokoshkin and Shingarev in January 1918 on the advice of Lenin, who evidently feared for his safety (Rabinowitch, *The Bolsheviks in Power*, 119; the image in question is not clearly of Tsereteli in any case). In a sequence devoted to the graduation of Red Army officers in issue 24, Lev Kamenev is misidentified in the intertitles at least twice in the extant prints (he appears at other

to borrow footage from *Kino-Nedelia* for later films, the chronicle *History of the Civil War* (1921) in particular, and we have little evidence as to how much care was taken to preserve the source material in its "restored" order.[87]

3. NEWSREEL MATRICES

Thus, *Kino-Nedelia*'s history involves a complex set of processes and procedures wrought upon filmed footage, including selection, extraction, compression, rearrangement, restoration, reuse, and sometimes suppression. It is plain

---

points in the sequence, without identification), while a lengthy shot of Aleksej Rykov, then head of no less important a body than the Supreme Soviet of the National Economy (*Vesenkha*), improbably receives no identification in the film or on the montage lists.

There are, finally, occasional gross linguistic errors in the intertitles as well, all of which suggests that the restoration was hastily made (although the errors might have been carried over from the original). Just one example for readers of Russian: in issue 23, "miting nad rukovodstvom Torganova" (rather than "*pod* rukovodstvom") in item 6. The phrase was written correctly on the extant montage list (RGALI f. 2091, op. 2, d. 4, l. 10).

87 A difficult film to discuss because so much of it was lost, the originally thirteen-reel *History of the Civil War*, for which both Vertov and Boltianskij claimed authorship, is close kin to the many photographic, illustrated, and occasionally cinematic compendia produced during this period in Russia and elsewhere. Some of these were very general (like the century overview *XIX vek: illiustrirovannyj obzor minuvshago stoletiia*, eds. L. Z. Slonimskij et al. [supplement to *Niva* 52 (1901)]), but many were packaged as annals of war, such as Francis Trevelyan Miller, ed., *Photographic History of the [American] Civil War in ten volumes* (New York: Review of Reviews, 1911); Francis Trevelyan Miller, eds., *Photographic History of the Great War* (New York: New York Tribune, 1914); and Capt. Donald C. Thompson's remarkable *Blood Stained Russia* (New York: Leslie-Judge, 1918). Among the major film documents produced during the war, Geoffrey Malins's and John McDowell's *The Battle of the Somme* (UK, 1916) would be the preeminent point of comparison. In a somewhat enigmatic remark from the late 1970s, Mikhail Kaufman describes a civil war film made by Vertov that arranged its exclusively archival material "without regard for chronology, but for the expressiveness which lay within each frame" (Kaufman, "An Interview with Mikhail Kaufman," *October* 11 (Winter 1979): 61); it is not entirely clear that *History of the Civil War* is the film he is referring to, not least because he mentions *Stride, Soviet* (with its opening collage of archival footage) in the same paragraph. As regards *History*'s borrowings from *Kino-Nedelia*: shots of conflagrations at Simonovo station and the Kursk station in Moscow from *Kino-Nedelias* 6 and 31 respectively; of the funerals of Volodarskij and Uritskij from *Kino-Nedelias* 6 and 16; of the aftermath of the Iaroslavl' rebellion of June 1918 from *Kino-Nedelias* 10, 14 and 16; of Fyodor Raskol'nikov and Larisa Rejsner from *Kino-Nedelia* 26; of the recovering Lenin from *Kino-Nedelia* 22 (1918); and the animated map of the Eastern Front from *Kino-Nedelia* 20 were all included in *History*. Years later, Vertov indicated that it was put together (though not fully finished) in three weeks, in time for exhibition at the Third World Congress of the Comintern in June–July 1921. One can only wonder, and worry, about the consequences of such haste for *History*'s source material (*SV*, 165). The short film *Trial of Mironov* (*Protsess Mironova*, 1919) was also extensively recycled for use in the fourth and final section of *History*. See *DO*, 48–53, 480–84.

enough that these processes should also be regarded as decisions concerning whether or not, to whom, and in what context images will be *made visible*. These modes of working with and legislating upon images and their visibility are genuinely complex and interwoven, and it might be clarifying to roughly spatialize their interrelationships, with the help of the famous Greimasian "semiotic rectangle," in terms of a basic dynamic pitting the *moving* of filmed footage on one hand—from actualities to newsreels; from newsreels to other, longer films, and back again—against, on the other hand, its *stabilization*: in specific, meaningful sequences in newsreels; as a legitimate or "original" version; and so on. This elementary opposition yields a set of variants on montage practice that are useful for thinking about Vertov's work, early and late.[88]

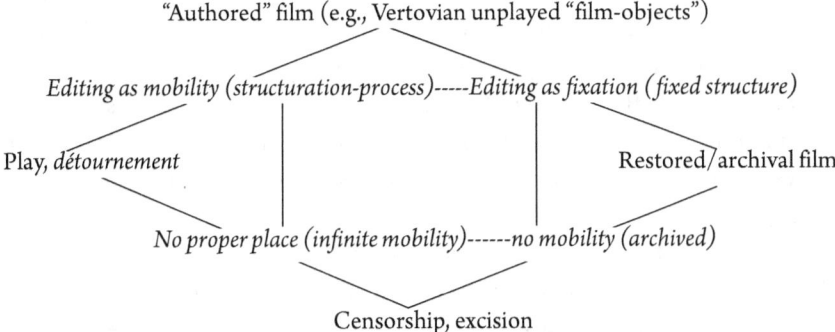

Chart 2: Dynamics entangling mobility and stability of film footage.

As an institutionalized practice, restoration determines what should or should not be visible (in a given "film") in accordance with a presumably

---

88 The rectangle has become well known in the English-speaking world mainly through its use by Fredric Jameson in a number of books and essays. Motivated by the desire to give conceptual shape to a complex discursive field without resorting to typological reifications, its basic principle can be summarized as follows: If one can identify, within a given discursive situation, a dominant two-term tension or binary structuring that situation (e.g., male/female), then those same two *contrary* terms, considered independently, also imply the existence of two additional terms that stand in a logical relation of *contradiction* to each of them (e.g., not-male/not-female). These four terms—an initial contrary and its derived contradiction, along with their tertiary implications (e.g., male/not-female = "hypermasculine," "macho"; female/not-male = "hyperfeminine")—articulate a field of discursive potentials emerging out of an apparently dominant "original" binary, demarcating thereby both the logical possibilities generated by the original binary that were left half- or un-thought, *and* the logical limits beyond which a field generated by that binary cannot go. The best and most detailed explication I have found of the semiotic rectangle (or square) is in Joseph Courtès, *La sémiotique narrative et discursive: méthodologie et application*, introduction by A. J. Greimas (Paris: Hachette, 1993), 53–86.

objective, impersonal standard (such as the shape of the film as it was originally exhibited or purchased for exhibition; or the intent of an author, as determined by historical evidence like montage lists, posters, reviews, correspondence, oral testimony, and so on), even if specific persons, normally legitimized by canons of expertise or otherwise credentialed, are plainly involved in fixing that standard. For the individual or collective agent creating an authored work, by contrast, their subjective or autonomous decisions as to what should be visible or invisible in that work are taken to be objective—that is, definitive of the work—whether the specific practices in question involve the stringing-together of a whole series of radically sui generis choices (as in Schoenberg's earliest atonal compositions, for instance) at one extreme, or the preliminary selection of some objective template on the other (as when, for example, a filmmaker settles on a fixed mathematical paradigm or algorithm in advance, which then determines how footage of unpredictable content is to be distributed; or in the very rare form of the shot-for-shot remake, such as in the different versions of Michael Nyman's *NYMan with a Movie Camera*; or the even rarer re-photographing of authored works *à la* Sherrie Levine; or the Duchampian readymade).

The two other categories generated by the square, however, are of a slightly different conceptual order, insofar as they concern less *how* (or to whom) principles of structuring footage might be attributed than the presence or absence of those principles as such. The possibility of complete mobility of footage—a possibility inherent in the well-known Situationist procedures of *détournement*, or free recontextualization—implies the absence of any standard for determining what should or should not be visible, except perhaps for the physical boundaries presented by the sheer mortality of image and sound on one side, and the limits of the human perceptual apparatus on the other. (Superimpositions and multiplication of screens cannot be infinitely dense or unlimited: we can't see everything at once, regardless of what Vertov sometimes seemed to think.)

On the other end of the spectrum, *censorship*, occupying a seemingly impossible fourth slot uniting non-mobility and non-stability, involves the power both to *change* the standards by which visibility/invisibility are determined, and to absolutize those standards by legislating not only upon the visibility of images (or audibility of sound), but upon their very existence: a filmic "zone of exception" that remains nonetheless parasitic upon its dialectical opposites, and compels creative responses. Censors might be regarded as the ultimate authors, except that they always need a work and an author to exploit, even if that work and author are produced in part by their own paranoia. At the same time, considerations of censorship almost always figure into creative decisions from the get-go—certainly so, in the Soviet setting we will be discussing—and thus have their own powerful formal effects.

Most importantly, the diagram must not be read as a *typology*, whether of filmed footage or of specific practices of signification. Rather, it outlines a dialectic coursing through these practices as socially apprehended, one that has the capacity to turn them into their putative counter-terms. Authored films, including Vertov's to be sure, can take from (or *détourne*) other authored works—as Vertov-the-author would learn in 1929, during his scandalous encounter with Albrecht Viktor Blum's *In the Shadow of Machines* (1928), a found-footage work that not only incorporates (without attribution) edited footage from *The Eleventh Year*, but inverts its meaning, celebratory in Vertov, into a critique of industry's soullessness and inhumanity.[89] The entanglement of authored film with censorship will be a leitmotif of Vertov's career, but is perhaps best illustrated by *Three Songs of Lenin*, whose successive versions (1934, 1938, 1970) all censor both the Lenin visual archive in general as well as their own previous iterations, in accord with changing political paradigms. Here, however, we will need to attend to censorship not simply (to use Heather Hendershot's words again) "as a reified, prohibitory force but as a dynamic, productive force"—an aspect of censorship largely ignored in existing scholarship on Soviet cinema, though not in film and media studies generally[90]—as when, in *Three Songs* for instance, the enforced authority of the Lenin myth generates a specifically Soviet kind of comic allegory, where history and present individual experience alike are hierarchized around and coordinated with a heroic center, in a grand monument "to a revolutionary change, from political chaos to political cosmos."[91]

In turn, authored film requires archival protection and validation to remain itself; and Vertov, as we will see, would often have good cause for anxiety about the fate of his own films (from the *Kino-Pravdas* onward), as they came under full control of the studios for which he worked (and which were highly mutable

---

89 See volume 2 and *LR*, 377–82.
90 See in particular Annette Kuhn's demonstration of the role of censorship in the emergence of the British propaganda film in her *Cinema, Censorship, and Sexuality, 1909–1925* (New York: Routledge, 1988); Lea Jacobs on the "fallen woman" film in *The Wages of Sin: Censorship and the Fallen Woman Film, 1928–1942* (Madison: University of Wisconsin Press, 1991); and Heather Hendershot's *Saturday Morning Censors*, here quoted from page 2.
91 Angus Fletcher, *Allegory: The Theory of a Symbolic Mode* (Ithaca, NY: Cornell University Press, 1964), 366.

institutions themselves) and of the censors, who could *détourne*, in a largely privative sense, as part of their professional duties. Of course, even partially or entirely lost, destroyed or unrealized films can become the object of research and restoration of a sort (as we will see), and thereby reabsorbed into circuits of valuation: what was the complete *Greed* like? Can we recover a sense of Vertov's original 1926 idea for *Man with a Movie Camera*? His never-produced *The Girl and the Giant*? And so on.[92]

To be sure, archives are also shelving facilities, and can and do function as repositories for suppressed material, and thus as instruments of censorship: out of sight, out of mind. And if archivists and preservationists are to function in part as guardians of authored films, their restoring function can require that they, too, ransack other "complete" films in order to finish a given restoration. (Such would certainly be the case, as we will see, for any restoration of a number of Vertov's films, as well as *Kino-Nedelia*, whose footage is scattered in who-knows-how-many different places.) Finally, the ordinances of the censor can act on occasion to preserve, through shelving, films or parts of films that otherwise have disappeared—as in the case of Vertov's *History of the Civil War* and *Anniversary of the Revolution*, the extant versions of which were withdrawn from exhibition in 1926[93]—even as the *détourneur* Blum turns out to have saved, through his pillage, the concluding section of Vertov's *Eleventh Year*, inexplicably missing from all prints of that film.

What both arrests and impels the motion through and across these various possibilities—and what stands outside of my diagram, and marks its conceptual limit—is of course *law* and the effective legitimation of certain practices, and de-legitimation of others. Indeed, on one level, the history of Vertov's films (and not only his) could be written in terms of the dialectic between these concrete, interwoven practices of moving or fixing images and sounds, and the various ordinances pertaining to them (about which we know far too little), chronologically arranged: the introduction of a new censorship structure after the Civil War;[94] the formation of the state documentary film archive in 1926; the October 8, 1928 law giving copyright to the studio producing a given film, and the director the right to the status of author; the revision of the same law at the beginning of 1939; and so on. To be sure, we will be tracking this dialectic,

---

92 See the writings collected in Thomas Beard, introduction and ed., *The Unfinished Film* (New York: Gladstone Gallery, 2011).

93 See Deriabin, "Vremia sobirat'." The first state film archive—today, the Russian State Archive of Film and Photo Documents (RGAKFD) in Krasnogorsk—was founded in 1926.

94 See Michael S. Fox, "Glavlit, Censorship and the Problem of Party Policy in Cultural Affairs, 1922–28," *Soviet Studies* 44, no. 6 (1992): 1045–68.

already operative in the *Kino-Nedelia* story, as it unfolds across the history of the increasingly despotic and repressive Soviet regime from the 1920s until Vertov's death, even as we take note of those moments—such as when Vertov and Svilova reused images from the *Enthusiasm* shoot for their own photomontages at the beginning of the 1930s—when creative decision-making was made at a greater distance from state or studio policy.

VERTOV'S THEATRICAL ORIGINS: THE AGIT-TRAINS

Image 4: Vertov (on the far right in fur cap) guiding children into the film car of the *October Revolution* agit-train, 1920. The cameraman was probably Aleksandr Levitskij. Source: RGAKFD 1145.

Obstacles of a concrete, material sort—the exigencies of war, severe shortage of film stock—put an end to *Kino-Nedelia*'s run after issue 43 (June 27, 1919). Although small numbers of nonfiction and fiction films continued to be produced in the capital cities, newsreel would not be revived until the emergence of *Kino-Pravda* in 1922, and of *Goskinokalendar'* in 1923. Soviet filmmakers, now (after Lenin's decree of August 27, 1919) working in an officially nationalized industry, were also working in conditions of severe deprivation.[95]

---

95 On August 27, Lenin signed the decree nationalizing all cinema enterprises; the process of nationalization was entrusted to the All-Russian Cinema Committee, soon to be reconfigured into the VFKO (Taylor, *The Politics of the Soviet Cinema*, 27–28, 49–50).

For one thing, over the course of the previous two years, much of the equipment hitherto at the disposal of newsreel makers, including some belonging originally to the Skobelev Committee, had evidently been pillaged, and the facilities at the disposal of the new All-Russia Film and Photo Division (VFKO) remained inadequate for a long time.

Cameraman Aleksandr Levitskij recounted how, in 1920, VFKO's nonfiction (still called "*khronika*") division was housed in a former film distribution office near the Moscow Soviet, whose only adornments were "an empty fireproof closet, a torn-up armchair . . . and a rickety table with a big teapot on it." All of these items, in addition to a corner of the office itself, were appropriated later that year as amenities and living quarters by Grigorij Boltianskij, who had been transferred (along with his wife Olga and their children) from Petrograd to Moscow to head up nonfiction filmmaking there.[96]

Although he continued to make films during this period, including *Battle for Tsaritsyn*, *History of the Civil War*, and two films about mobile agit-work,[97] Vertov was primarily occupied with administration of film shooting and exhibition on trains and other mobile units from the fall of 1919 through 1921. Initially involved with coordinating filming and perhaps exhibition for the military,[98] he moved on to work with the famous agitational trains established by the All-Russia Central Executive Committee (VTsIK)[99] at the beginning of 1920.

More than a few plumes of romantic leafage have grown around these early Soviet agit-trains, boats and other vehicles, despite—or perhaps, because of—the absence of anything like a full-scale historical treatment of them in any language.[100] One of the routes of the famous *October Revolution* train, on which

---

96 Levitskij, *Rasskazy o kinematografe*, 161, 169. Levitskij does not indicate the year of Boltianskij's move, but it seems that Lunacharsky ordered his transfer to Moscow in 1920 (RGALI f. 2639, op. 1, d. 63, ll. 9, 17). See also Listov, *Rossiia, revoliutsiia, kinematograf*, 109.

97 *The Red Star Literary-Instructional Agit-Steamer of the All-Russia Central Executive Committee* (1919; to be discussed in volume 2); *The Agit-Train of the All-Russia Central Executive Committee* (1921; no longer in existence). See *LR*, 406.

98 See certificate from the Moscow Military Commissariat releasing "Denis Arkad'evich Vertov" from military service (required to work on the military trains) from November 17, 1919 (RGALI f. 2091, op. 2, d. 384, l. 1); RGASPI f. 17, op. 125, d. 499, l. 43; and *SV*, 165. Special mobile cinemas for the Political Administration of the Revolutionary Military Soviet were established in mid-April 1919 (Flakserman, *V ogne zhizni i bor'by*, 142).

99 Abbreviation of "Vserossijskij Tsentral'nyj Ispolnitel'nyj Komitet."

100 A massive amount of archival material relating to early Soviet mobile agitation (mainly in GARF) has been preserved and still awaits detailed examination; I refer to it in a very limited way in what follows. Two activist accounts from the period—Ia. Burov, *Instruktorsko-agitatsionnye poezdki na poezdakh i parokhodakh VTsIK (tezisy Ia. Burova)* (Moscow: Otdel instruktorskikh-agitatsionnykh poezdov i parokhodov VTsIK, 1920); V. Karpinskij,

Vertov traveled and worked in early 1920, was ceremonially recreated in the Voronezh area in 1969 under the auspices of the local Communist Party committee (the train was renamed *Great October* for the occasion);[101] and many in the West first learned of Soviet "film-trains" through Chris Marker's now well-known film-essays on the topic—although Marker's films dealt principally with the later revival of train-based cinema agitation, in the form of Aleksandr Medvedkin's very different "kino-trains" of the early 1930s and, at least in the second redaction, took a far from naively reverential (if still melancholically romantic) attitude toward them.[102]

---

ed., *Agitparpoezda VTsIK* (Moscow: Gosudarstvennoe Izdatel'stvo, 1920)—and one Stalin-era collection of documents focusing on Mikhail Kalinin's involvement with the *October Revolution* train (B. Sergeev, "Agitpoezdki M. I. Kalinina v gody grazhdanskoj vojny," *Krasnyj Arkhiv* 86 [1938]: 93–163) are basic to any study of the agit-train phenomenon. The first major scholarly study of the agit-trains (L. V. Maksakova, *Agitpoezd "Oktiabr'skaia Revoliutsiia" (1919–1920)* [Moscow: Akademiia Nauk SSSR, 1956]) appeared in the immediate post-Stalin period, and remains an indispensable account; Aleksandr Lemberg's was among the earliest in a series of important memoirs of the agit-trains and boats (A. Lemberg, "Na agitparokhode 'Krasnaia Zvezda,'" *Iskusstvo Kino* 5 (1959): 107). Later studies include V. Listov, *Istoriia smotrit v ob'ektiv* (Moscow: Iskusstvo, 1973), 199–215; Richard Taylor, "A Medium for the Masses: Agitation in the Civil War," *Soviet Studies* 22, no. 4 (April 1971): 562–74, esp. 566–74, and *The Politics of the Soviet Cinema, 1917–1929* (Cambridge: Cambridge University Press, 1979), 52–63; Peter Kenez, *The Birth of the Propaganda State: Soviet Methods of Mass Mobilization, 1917–1929* (Cambridge: Cambridge University Press, 1985), 58–62; I. Bibikova, "Rospis' agitpoezdov i agitparokhodov," in *Agitatsionno-massovoe iskusstvo pervykh let Oktiabria: materialy i issledovaniia*, ed. E. A. Speranskaia et al. (Moscow: Iskusstvo, 1971), 166–98; and V. P. Tolstoj, ed., *Agitmassovoe iskusstvo Sovetskoj Rossii*. A recent article discusses the train on which Trotsky traveled, which was involved with extensive propaganda and publishing activity (N. S. Tarkhova, "Poezd Trotskogo — letuchij apparat upravleniia narkomvoena," in *Gosudarstvennyj apparat Rossii v gody Revoliutsii i Grazhdanskoj Vojny*, ed. T. G. Arkhipova (Moscow: RGGU, 1998), 128–40. A very recent study (Evgenij Anatol'evich Kozlov, "Agitatsionnye poezda i parokhody v Sovetskoj Rossii [1918–1922]: strategii kommunikatsii" [master's thesis, Russian State Humanities University, 2016]) came to my attention too late to be integrated here.

101 M. Gribanov et al., *Agitpoezd "Velikij Oktiabr'"* (Voronezh: Tsentral'no-chernozemnoe Knizhnoe Izdatel'stvo, 1969).

102 *Le train en marche* (1971); *Le Tombeau d'Alexandre* [*The Last Bolshevik*] (1993). On the contrast between "kino" and "agit-trains," see Thomas Tode, "Agit-trains, Agit-steamers, Cinema Trucks: Dziga Vertov and Travelling Cinema in the early 1920s in the Soviet Union," in *Travelling Cinema in Europe: Sources and Perspectives* [Kinotop Schriften 10], ed. Martin Loiperdinger (Frankfurt am Main: Stroemfeld Verlag, 2008), 153. On Medvedkin, see Emma Widdis, *Visions of a New Land: Soviet Film from the Revolution to the Second World War* (New Haven, CT: Yale University Press, 2003), 41–45; and *Alexander Medvedkin* (London: I. B. Tauris, 2005), 22–34. On the relation of the militant filmmaking group SLON (Société pour le Lancement des Oeuvres Nouvelles, founded 1967) and Marker to

Of course, there *is* something romantic about itinerant or mobile cinema: it suggests both the thrill of pioneering—bringing cinema to places it had never been, before its banalization as a fixture of everyday commodified existence—and an exploratory jettisoning of familiar norms of exhibition, by moving cinematic experience out of theaters and onto trains, boats, under the open sky—into "life," in short. Yet both the novelty and the liberating "experimentalism" of the Soviet trains are easy to exaggerate as well. We have already learned of Tsarist-era mobile film exhibition, and certainly the agit-trains can be seen as part of a much larger, indeed global history of mobile moving exhibitions associated with traveling fairs, lectures, educational projects and much else.[103] At the same time, mobile film has historically been promoted as an important step toward making certain kinds of administration (educational, commercial, state) permanent in areas where they hadn't existed before, and therefore as a colonizing and normalizing practice or, to use a phrase employed ad nauseum by Soviet agit-train activists, as a way of "linking the localities to the center."[104] The sense of novelty associated with traveling cinema is generated in part by that linking, which helps to concretize the difference between established center and soon-to-be-tamed localities.

Medvedkin and mobile cinema, see the interview conducted by Guy Hennebelle, "SLON: Working-class cinema in France."

103 See Loiperdinger, ed., *Travelling Cinema in Europe, passim,* especially Vanessa Toulmin, "'Within the Reach of All': Travelling Cinematograph Shows on British Fairgrounds 1896–1914" and Joseph Garncarz, "The Fairground Cinema—A European Institution," 19–33 and 78–90; Aldo Bernadini, *Gli Ambulanti: Cinema Italiano delle Origini* (Gemona del Friuli: La Cineteca del Friuli, 2001); Gregory A. Waller, "Richard Southard and the History of Traveling Film Exhibition," *Film Quarterly* 57, no. 2 (Winter 2003–4): 2–14.

104 Burov, *Instruktorsko-agitatsionnye poezdki*, 1. My thoughts on the agit-trains in this regard have been influenced by Brian Larkin's important study of the British-imperial mobile film units that operated in Northern Nigeria from the late '30s through the 1950s (called *majigi*: a derivation from "magic lantern") in his *Signal and Noise: Media, Infrastructure and Urban Culture in Nigeria* (Durham, NC: Duke University Press, 2008), 73–122. Larkin stresses the state- (as opposed to capital-) driven character of the majigi modernization project, in language that could be applied to the Soviet agitational efforts without much strain: "Majigi was a machine of the state traveling away from the political center and into the margins of the territory, pulling these margins into a state project. It was an institutional form of cinematic production that was, in essence, a bureaucratic instantiation of state power" (105–6). We should no doubt incorporate our contemporary proliferation of screens within previously screen-less public and private space into this history as well, given these screens' role in abetting the penetration of consumer capitalism and its bureaucracies into the very fiber of daily life, while enabling occasional resistance to these forces, and new kinds of sociability as well.

The building of links was also an assertion of the capacity of the Bolshevik regime to make its presence felt throughout the still contested territories of the war-torn and notoriously "undergoverned" country.[105] The first agit-train, the *V. I. Lenin Mobile Military Front Train*, sent to the Kazan' front in the early fall of 1918, did its work primarily among Red Army men, but later trains carried out propaganda work in all sections of the population.[106] Trotsky ordered five more of them to be outfitted at the end of 1919, and under the auspices of VTsIK, the trains traveled all over the country until around the fall of 1921, by which time Bolshevik victory was more or less complete, and administrative disorganization within Glavpolitprosvet (Main Political-Enlightenment Committee of the Republic, formed in November 1920), which brought the trains under its auspices, had badly undermined the efficiency of the mobile film units in any case.[107] (The White forces, incidentally, had set up their own mobile agitprop units in spring 1919, and also exhibited propaganda films, mainly newsreels and nonfiction shorts. Agit-train *Ataman Kaledin* and the *General Denikin* agit-barge began work that summer and made the rounds of White-controlled areas for about six months.)[108] Some of the names of the

---

105 The term is S. Frederick Starr's in *Decentralization and Self-Government in Russia, 1830–1870* (Princeton: Princeton University Press, 1972).

106 It is not clear exactly when the *Lenin* train departed Moscow for Kazan'. Some sources (e.g., Maksakova, *Agitpoezd "Oktiabr'skaia Revoliutsiia,"* 9) indicate a journey beginning in August; Viktor Listov gives a more precise and documented date of September 14, 1918 as the time of departure (*Istoriia smotrit v ob'ektiv*, 201). The first major VTsIK decrees on the trains, issued by the committee's chair (Iakov Sverdlov) and secretary (Abel Enukidze) date to January 11, 1919 (Russian S.F.S.R., *Dekrety sovetskoj vlasti*, vol. 4 [Moscow: Izdatel'stvo Politicheskoj Literatury, 1968], 289–91); the decrees called for the trains to be engaged in "organizational, instructional and informational work" among local institutions and representatives, both gathering information about those institutions and representatives, and acquainting them with the plans and projects of the central government and party (ibid.). Items two through four of *Kino-Nedelia* 29 (December 24, 1918) are devoted to the *Lenin* train (RGALI f. 2091, op. 2, d. 5, l. 9).

107 Taylor, *The Politics of the Soviet Cinema*, 53; Listov, *Rossiia, revoliutsiia, kinematograf*, 99. In a report of March 20, 1922, to Gosprokat head A. Anoshchenko (to be discussed again in volume 2), Vertov noted that mobile cinema work much declined in magnitude and effectiveness after the union with Glavpolitprosvet (which he had helped oversee), moving from six film train-wagons, three steamship film units, three film carts, one automobile-cinema, and a well-equipped photo lab at the end of 1920 to the loss of most of its equipment, staff, and films by the end of 1921. For a while, the film wagons became stationary, attached to *agitpunkty* (stationary propaganda outlets) to help disseminate propaganda about the terrible famine that began ravaging large parts of the country in 1921 (RGALI f. 2091, op. 2, d. 389, ll. 1–9; *LRK* 1, 346–47.).

108 *LRK* 1, 294, 297. See also L. A. Molchanov, "Deiatel'nost' informatsionnykh uchrezhdenii 'beloj' Rossii v gody grazhdanskoj vojny (1918–1920 gg.), in *Gosudarstvennyj apparat*

trains, and the remarkable murals that covered them (to be discussed below), reflected their itineraries and target audiences: *Red Cossack* (which passed through the Don region and the Kuban' and about which a now-lost film seems to have been made), *Red East* (to Turkestan and other Central Asian locales), *Soviet Caucasus, Red Railway Worker*, and so on.[109]

Initially housed in single compartments, the agitational units expanded quickly to occupy, first, a full wagon, and then an entire train. The agitators had "emergency [*pozharnaia*] assistance" as their goal, and were designed to get to places beyond the reach of the more sparsely distributed and stationary propaganda outlets (or *agitpunkty*: agitational points).[110] They also set out to organize agitation in accord with Taylorist models, in contrast to the supposedly "crude, primitive" methods involving single agitators attempting to influence the local population. Perhaps the most important agitational strategy on the trains involved arranging the appearance of major regime figures like Nadezhda Krupskaia, Viacheslav Molotov, Lunarcharsky, and Mikhail Kalinin at mass meetings all over the country. Indeed, as we will see, Kalinin was the primary public exhibit on the *October Revolution* train, with which Vertov was centrally involved.

Organizationally, the trains were comprised of a number of divisions and subdivisions, including an office that accepted complaints and petitions; an information division that prepared propaganda and agitational materials; the ROSTA division (*Rossijskoe telegrafnoe agenstvo* [Russian Telegraph Agency], devoted to both publishing and dissemination of publications and to broadcasting from the train's radio station); staff involved in the supervision and inspection of local bureaucracies (a function known in Russian as *kontrol'*); a shop and warehouse for printed materials; a section devoted to organizing special exhibitions; accounting, technical, and maintenance units that took care of budgets, repairing phones, maintaining sanitary facilities for those on board, and so on; and the cinema division, about which I will say more below.[111]

Rossii v gody Revoliutsii i Grazhdanskoj Vojny, ed. T. G. Arkhipova (Moscow: RGGU, 1998), 150–71, esp. 156. Some of these films were standard newsreel and actuality films, devoted to sports (e.g., *Khronika "Globus"* no. 2 from 1919 [RGAKFD 12029], on a kind of triathalon event involving boxing, jumping, and a race from Kharbin to Vladivostok) and other beloved newsreel themes.

109 See Tolstoj, ed., *Agitmassovoe Iskusstvo*, vol. 2 [tables and images], *passim*. On the *Red Cossack* film, see RGALI f. 2091, op. 2, d. 389, l. 5. According to Vertov, the other film made by the mobile film unit in 1920 was *The Work of the VTsIK Instructional-Agitational Trains* (ibid.).

110 Burov, *Instruktorsko-agitatsionnye poezdki*, 2.

111 V.M. Kleandrova, *Organizatsiia i formy deiatel'nosti VTsIK (1917–1924 g.g.)* (Moscow: Iuridicheskaia Literatura, 1968), 89–91. For data on the radio station onboard the *October*

Christ among the Herdsmen • CHAPTER 4   239

Vertov's time working on and for the agit-trains was an intense one, both professionally and personally. Although it is not clear when Vertov met his first partner, Estonian pianist Olga Toom (1895–1979), their acquaintance certainly did not postdate his involvement with the agit-trains. Toom, who had resided in Moscow since 1914 and worked as a nurse during World War I, headed up the film division onboard the *October Revolution* on its fifth and seventh journeys; like Vertov a few months later, she was mainly involved in film exhibition and oral commentary during and after screenings, although she also provided what was probably unusually fine piano accompaniment.[112] Vertov and Toom, possibly never officially married in any case, had broken up well before 1923 (when he married Svilova),[113] but they evidently kept in touch, and seem to have been involved at least through the fall of 1920, judging from Vertov's poetic tributes to Toom and her pianism (the first dated September 1920):

>   Tra-la-la flat
>   With a bow
>   Olga Toom
>   At a gallop[114]
>   Beat the keys of the brain
>   Hurl noise after noise
>   That God, or whoever rules up there
>   Might choke from a riot of thoughts[115]

Revolution train during its tenth journey, see GARF f. 2313, op. 2, d. 131, l. 4. On the importance and changing meanings of *kontrol'*, see Owen, "A Genealogy of *Kontrol'* in Russia," esp. 336.

112 GARF f. 1252, op. 1, d. 7, ll. 20–30; f. 1252, op. 1, d. 62, l. 165 (Toom's reports on daily screenings). Though the "head of cinema" (*zaveduiushchij kinematografom*), Toom often refers to herself on her daily screening reports as "*pianistka.*" The train's fifth (October 24 to November 19, 1919) and seventh (January 6–27, 1920) journeys took it to the Central Black Earth and central and southern regions (from Tula to Rostov-on-Don) respectively (GARF archival list for f. 1252, op. 1).

113 DVVS, 66.

114 RGALI f. 2091, op. 2, d. 228, ll. 20ob–21. The poem is titled "Olga Toom," and on the reverse side of one of the manuscript pages is the poem "Dziga Vertov," discussed earlier. "Bow" here means "a ribbon [or something similar] tied into a bow [*bant*]."

115 RGALI f. 2091, op. 2, d. 228, l. 10ob. The fragmentary shooting diary for *Kino-Eye* (1924) indicates that Mikhail Kaufman took some footage of Toom's sister Lidia smiling at the camera during that film's production, though it seems that this shot did not make it into the final cut (RGALI f. 2091, op. 2, d. 26, l. 22ob). Vertov also mentions Olga Toom in a long list of names and addresses of accomplished Soviet women he compiled in early 1937 in

These lines suggest that spectators onboard the *October Revolution*'s film-car must have been treated to some pretty wild piano playing—some of it Vertov's own, perhaps—alongside the pictures.

On the professional side, Vertov was occupied with the agit-trains, according to his own accounts, in 1920 and 1921, and the earliest documents we have concerning his work on the train date to January 1920, though there may have been some prior, tangential involvement.[116] We know that he was aboard the *October Revolution* during its eighth trip in March 1920, was involved with organizing and maintaining the cinema unit on the *Red East* in January 1920 (though he probably did not travel on that train), and continued to receive official mandates to lead film-related work on various agit-trains and boats through October 1920 and no doubt beyond.[117] He came into contact with numerous highly gifted people during his agit-train period, some of whom became well-known (like director Lev Kuleshov, who began to work for the Moscow Film Committee at the end of 1918 and headed up the Cultural-Enlightenment Section on the *Red East* in 1920),[118] and some who did not, like Olga Toom or the *October Revolution*'s implacably harsh Cheka representative, Ivan Ivanovich Skrameh (1893–1954), who also happened

---

preparation for making *Lullaby*, which suggests that he considered including her in the film in some way (RGALI f. 2091, op. 2, d. 254, l. 17). She should probably be counted as another of Vertov's important connections, to be sure. In the 1920s, Toom worked in the offices of *Pravda* with Lidia, and later as the secretary of Maria Ulianova (Lenin's sister) in the Petitions Bureau. She then worked in the libraries of the music conservatories in Moscow and Sverdlovsk, continued to play the piano, did occasional translations from Estonian, and raised a family. She was married to (though eventually divorced) the well-known musicologist Daniel' Zhitomirskij (1906–92), corresponded with the famous pianist and pedagogue Heinrich Neuhaus from 1943 to 1963, and was apparently well connected within the Soviet music world; see Daniel Shitomirski, *Blindheit als Schutz vor der Wahrheit*, trans. Ernst Kuhn, intro. Oksana Leontjewa (Berlin: Verlag Ernst Kuhn, 1996), 25; Laurel E. Fay, *Shostakovich: A Life* (Oxford: Oxford University Press, 2000), 315; and G. G. Nejgauz [Heinrich Neuhaus], *Pis'ma* (Moscow: Deka-VS, 2009). (Some of the information here comes from Professor Andrei Toom, Lidia Toom's grandson; my heartfelt thanks to María Soliña Barreiro González for providing me with it.)

116 RGASPI f. 17, op. 125, d. 499, l. 43 (an autobiographical chronology from 1947). In a document of March 2, 1922, Vertov indicates that he was enlisted by VTsIK to manage the trains' film and photo divisions in January 1920 (RGALI f. 2091, op. 2, d. 389, l. 1).

117 RGALI f. 2091, op. 2, d. 386, ll. 3–11. A mandate of October 21, 1920 indicates that Vertov may have been involved more generally in "literary-musical" work in the area of "agitation and artistic education of the broad masses of the population" (RGALI f. 2091, op. 2, d. 386, l. 11). See also Listov, *Istoriia smotrit v ob'ektiv*, 210.

118 L. V. Kuleshov, *Stat'i. Materialy*, ed. V. P. Mikhailov et al. (Moscow, Iskusstvo, 1970), 57; GARF f. 1252, op. 1, d. 162, l. 2.

to be, according to Aleksandr Levitskij, a remarkably talented violinist and declaimer of poetry.[119]

Although still a filmmaker, Vertov became more and more involved in the administration of mobile cinema through March 1922, until he received the assignment to begin the *Kino-Pravdas* sometime in the spring of 1922. By that time, Vertov was the head of VFKO's mobile cinema division with two assistants and a full staff, but was struggling to keep the units going; indeed, under the new, market-driven conditions of New Economic Policy (NEP), he was apparently moving toward converting the operation into a base for renting out projectors, prints, and technical help to theaters and workers' clubs, and might have gone fully into administration had the *Kino-Pravda* opportunity not appeared.[120] At any rate, as with newsreel production, much of the structure of train-based agitation had been established before Vertov came onboard, and it is difficult to know whether he contributed any specific innovations to the cinema part of the enterprise.

Throughout the history of their operation, the trains' primary immediate authority was the Political Division, which was divided into sections designated as "instructional" (devoted to more intensive on-site inspection and propaganda work with specific groups and institutions such as schools, hospitals, local party affiliates and so on) and "agitational-lecture" (focused on demonstrations, organizing public lectures, and other shorter-term efforts at mobilizing the population, including film screenings). This distinction—between more in-depth and pedagogical *propaganda* work and the more spectacular and punctual job of *agitation*—has been slighted or ignored in some of the historical literature on "Soviet propaganda," where "agitprop" tends to be seen as a diffuse cluster of practices of persuasion, political pedagogy and/or mind control.[121] For the

---

119 Levitskij, *Rasskazy o kinematografe*, 202; V. A. Goncharov and V. V. Nekhotin, "'Durylin soglasen dat' podpisku, chto on nikogda ne budet prikhodskim sviashchennikom': Iz materialov arkhivno-sledstvennogo dela po obvineniiu S.N. Durylina," *Vestnik PSTGU* II (2008): 131, 137. Like Toom, Skrameh was an Estonian; more on his agit-train activities below. Mayakovsky and El Lissitzky were involved in the trains as well, mainly as graphic artists and providing texts for ROSTA, although I have no evidence that they crossed paths with Vertov during this period (Taylor, *Politics of the Soviet Cinema*, 55).

120 RGALI f. 2091, op. 2, d. 389, ll. 6-9 (from report to Anoshchenko of March 20, 1922); RGALI f. 989, op. 1, d. 249, l. 4; GARF f. 2313, op. 1, d. 13, ll. 46–59, 61–61ob; Listov, "Molodost' mastera," *DVVS*, 98–104, esp. 100–101. For the later history of mobile cinema in early Soviet Russia, see Tode, "Agit-trains, Agit-steamers, Cinema Trucks," 149–53.

121 See, for instance, Kenez, *Birth of the Propaganda State*, 7–8; Taylor, *Politics of the Soviet Cinema*, 28. This is not to say that the distinction between the terms was always

close analysis of early Soviet media practice, however, the distinction is crucial, not least (as I will later argue) as it is reflected in Vertov's films.

1. AGITATION AND PROPAGANDA

In an important study of early Soviet journalistic practice, historian Matthew Lenoe offers a succinct account of the differences between "agit-" and "-prop" as articulated in social-democratic theory from the 1870s onward, and particularly by Lenin:

> According to Lenin, propaganda involved extended theoretical explanations of the socioeconomic processes that underlay surface phenomena such as unemployment. By appealing to audience members' reason, the propagandist aimed to cultivate in them a whole new worldview. Propaganda was a process of education that required a relatively sophisticated, informed audience. Agitation, on the other hand, motivated the audience to action by appealing to their emotions with short, stark stories. The agitator did not seek to change his listeners' worldview, but to mobilize them. Agitation was the tool of choice for unsophisticated, even ignorant audiences when quick action was required. Definitions from the first edition of *The Great Soviet Encyclopedia* link propaganda with education and agitation with organization/mobilization.[122]

As we will see, Vertov in his mature films (particularly in some of the *Kino-Pravdas* and in 1924's *Kino-Eye*, but in later works as well) directly thematizes the discursive contrast between agitation and propaganda. If the distinction is largely invisible to us today—if also clearly related to the now-familiar

---

rigorously maintained, but rather that there *was* a distinction that should be maintained, as we will see below.

122 Matthew Lenoe, *Closer to the Masses: Stalinist Culture, Social Revolution, and Soviet Newspapers* (Cambridge, MA: Harvard University Press, 2004), 28. To be sure, the Leninist formulation was preceded and anticipated by those of other social-democrats like Martov, Aksel'rod, and especially Plekhanov: see *Marxism in Russia: Key Documents 1879–1906*, ed. Neil Harding, trans. Richard Taylor (Cambridge: Cambridge University Press, 1983), 20–21, 59–67, 103–4, 114–16, 266–67. It is worth noting that the phrase "agitational-educational" (*agitatsionno-prosvetitel'noe*) was sometimes used in the 1920s to describe nonfictional, more-or-less politicized instructional films; see letter of April 25, 1922 from the "Rus'" studio to the Presidium of the Moscow Soviet in Listov and Khokhlova, eds., *Istoriia otechestvennogo kino*, 133.

opposition between a "cinema of attractions" and narrative cinema, or even "intellectual montage"[123]—it was fully in effect for the agit-train activists, and finds expression in a variety of ways.

The murals that adorned the sides of all the post-1918 agit-trains carried the initial agitational jolts that the trains delivered to audiences, and as such they provide an excellent occasion for examining how the agitation-propaganda distinction, which their forms both mobilized and allegorized, worked in practice.[124] Originally, the sides of the trains were plastered with posters that soon washed away, faded, or shredded in the wind.[125] Murals directly painted on the wagons proved to be the solution, and if much of their visual content borrowed heavily from the established iconographic repertoire of the revolutionary left, the form may have been more immediately inspired by circus or carnival caravans, and/or by commercial signage. One insightful observer referred to the atmosphere created by the trains as akin to that of an "artistic-political marketplace,"[126] and the murals, none of which have survived but which were quite

---

123 The contrast was established by Tom Gunning in a classic essay from 1985: "[T]he cinema of attractions directly solicits spectator attention, inciting visual curiosity, and supply pleasure through an exciting spectacle. . . Theatrical display dominates over narrative absorption, emphasizing the direct stimulation of shock or surprise at the expense of unfolding a story or creating a diegetic universe" (Tom Gunning, "The Cinema of Attractions: Early Film, its Spectator and the Avant-Garde," in Thomas Elsaesser, ed., *Early Cinema: Space, Frame, Narrative* [London: British Film Institute, 1990], 58–59). Gunning indicates that he derived the term "attraction" from the early writings of Eisenstein, of course; and although I cannot develop this line of inquiry here, the Eisensteinian pedigree strongly suggests the rootedness of "attraction," at least in its Soviet manifestations, in social democratic ideas about the agitation-propaganda distinction—recoded by Eisenstein as the contrast between "attraction" and "intellectual montage"—as much as in popular entertainments and fairground displays. Correspondingly, the association with agitation should make us dubious of any easy alignment of attractions with liberating free play, in contrast to the supposed authoritarianism of narrative. See my essay "Built on a Lie: Propaganda, Pedagogy and the Origins of the Kuleshov Effect," in *The Oxford Handbook of Propaganda*, ed. Jonathan Auerbach and Russ Castronuovo (Oxford: Oxford University Press, 2013), 219–36, from which parts of the current chapter derive.
124 Strictly speaking, the murals would have been seen as primarily "agitational" in function, but as I show below, their forms and rhetoric do help to illustrate "propaganda" functions as well (and thereby, perhaps, the porous divide between the two categories).
125 Karpinskij, ed., *Agitparpoezda VTsIK*, 1.
126 Ivan Ol'brakht, *Puteshestvie za poznaniem: Strana Sovetov;* quoted in Tolstoj, ed., *Agitmassovoe iskusstvo*, vol. 1, 64.

extensively photographed, clearly contributed to this bright and festive impression.[127]

At least initially, they also provoked disputes among agitators as to the kinds of representation best suited to propaganda within a "Soviet" context. In 1920, Iakov Burov, one of the founding organizers of the trains, complained of the earliest murals that they were

> ... extremely unsuccessful. The panels of the wagons were covered in Futurist-Symbolist pictures, depicting enormous monsters devouring the Revolution. The majority of these images were incomprehensible, and the local population frequently responded with perplexity. The [agit-train] organization had no experience in this matter, and artists were allowed nearly total freedom of action.
>
> Now, the panels ... are illustrated with pictures with *realistic content*; Futurism has been completely driven out.[128]

That the murals provided the occasion for early conflicts over realism versus modernism/formalism is not surprising: already during the Civil War, regime leaders, not all of them officials charged with fashioning cultural policy, expressed hostility to what was perceived as incomprehensible experimentation on public display.[129] Even though it is clear that both "realists" and (as in the case of Vertov) "Futurists" rode the trains, their opposition was in no way based on a straightforward contrast between utilitarian versus purist approaches. Burov asserts, for instance, that the successful realist murals also functioned as "art galleries" that "would [help] develop an understanding of art among working people."[130] The mural paintings indeed presented a diversity of representational approaches, sometimes offering flat, caricatural representations (often of various class antagonists: peasants and workers on

---

127 The best film record of the look of the agit-vehicles (in this case a steamship-plus-barge) is in *The Red Star Agitational-Educational Steamer* (1919–20), a remarkable film by Vertov to be discussed in volume 2.

128 Karpinskij, ed., *Agitparpoezda VTsIK*, 9. Emphasis in the original.

129 In Petrograd, the struggle against the incorporation of Futurist visual practices, involving such luminaries as Zinoviev and Lunacharsky, became exceptionally rancorous during these years, and we will return to it during our discussion of the *Kino-Pravdas* in volume 2; see Krusanov, *Russkij avangard*, vol. 2, part 1, esp. 67–68; and Robert Russell, "The Arts and the Russian Civil War," *Journal of European Studies* 20 (1990): 219–40.

130 Karpinskij, ed., *Agitparpoezda VTsIK*, 9.

one side, bourgeois and priests on the other), Soviet coats-of-arms, or other two-dimensional designs, but also incorporating elaborate perspective, offering "realistic" portrayals of bridges and railways receding into the distance, landscape panoramas, and so forth. In any event, it is clear that agitation-propaganda were common impulses among all artists working on the murals, regardless of painterly orientation.

Image 5: Mural by T. V. Gusev, painted on the *October Revolution* on the theme "Repair the bridges." Photograph dated 1920. Source: Tolstoj, *Agitmassovoe iskusstvo Sovetskoj Rossii* [Mass-agitational art of Soviet Russia], vol. 2, 80.

One typical mural on the *October Revolution* train (image 5) consisted of a tetraptych extending across the length of a single passenger wagon, depicting from left to right the narrative of a bridge destroyed during the Civil War and its reparation. Above the wagon's windows, on the first, third and fourth panels of the tetraptych, were painted two classically *agitational* slogans: "Repair the bridges!" and "Restore transportation links." The mural images proper, occupying the whole central section of the panels and composed artfully (and of necessity) around the wagon's windows, depicted (from left) a cantilever bridge with a collapsed central span; a large team of hammer-wielding uniformed workers constructing supports for a new span; the bridge under repair, with piles of makeshift supports holding the span; and, finally, in the fourth panel, a celebration in the foreground of the repaired bridge, depicted now from an angle shifted almost ninety degrees to the left, with a train making its way across the restored span and into the mural's perspectival depths.

Across the bottom of the wagon extend, in lettering about a third to half as large as that of the slogans, more detailed *propaganda* explanations of the content of the pictures: "White Guards blew up the bridge"; "The Labor Army[131] raises up the stricken proletariat"; "The bridge is reconstructed" and so on. To be sure, in terms of the ways that "propaganda" was employed during the Civil War, these small-font explanations were doubtless regarded as agitational in character; propaganda in the strict sense would have been a kind of instruction, involving detailed oral explanation of a given theme by an activist, followed by questions and answers. And indeed, activists would have sometimes engaged in oral propaganda explanations of the content of the murals (there is photographic evidence for this). On my reading, the smaller lettering, the explanatory character of the text, and the proximity and attention it requires, are best thought of as a kind of simulation of that instructional propaganda situation, an absorption of oral pedagogy into another (typographic) medium.

The separation and partial overlap of functions are thus made quite clear: the slogans emit sharp and clear messages—commands, to be precise, given an oral texture by their imperative mood and typographic boldness—surely visible even to those observing the train *en passant*. The smaller text along the mural's lower edge, much of it illegible in the existing photographs and no doubt requiring a more attentive scanning from passersby, offers historical explanations, rationales for policy, and names of the relevant protagonists. For their part, the mural's images provide both an attractive agitational spectacle and visual aids helping to concretize and elaborate the regime's message.[132]

As I have already indicated, Vertov made use of the rhetorical forms offered by the agit-train murals often in his mature work. I will discuss the famous "beef-to-bull" sequence of his *Kino-Eye* in their light in the next volume, but now need to mention three brief examples from *Stride, Soviet* (1925), in order to make what I have just described more cinematically concrete.[133] *Stride, Soviet* is a campaign film—specifically made to promote the reelection

---

131 *Trudovaia Armiia*: sections of the Red Army mobilized for labor and reparation purposes during the Civil War (specifically, from 1920–21).
132 To be sure, similar structures are apparent on other trains, including those that went to the Caucasus and Soviet Central Asia and included Georgian, Arabic and other scripts on their murals; see Tolstoj, ibid., 163 for an example from the *Red East* train.
133 *Stride, Soviet* will be discussed further in volume 2.

of the current members of the Moscow City Soviet—and as such can be seen as a sublimation-in-film of the agit-train's rhetorical tasks, insofar as it works to acquaint and connect the bulk of Moscow's population, extending out to the city's peripheries, with the activities of the "center." Indeed, that discursive labor of connection or "going to the people" is directly thematized in the film.

The before-after structure typical of agit-train murals is central to *Stride, Soviet*, which strings together rapid contrasts of decrepit Old with recuperating New like a long line of agit-wagons:

> From ruined buildings
> [Fade-in to single shot of ruined building]
> To new homes for workers
> [One shot of large new apartment building, panning downwards]
> And worker settlements
> [Two shots of a settlement under construction framing five other shots (a dog, children, a pig and so on) of life at a settlement]
> From overturned streetcars
> [Two shots of an overturned streetcar]
> To new streetcar lines
> [Four shots of men working on a new streetcar line just outside the Kremlin walls]
> On the outskirts of the city
> [Shot of streetcar rounding a corner on a village street; shot of someone buying something on a city street; shot of streetcar either heading to or returning from the village]
> From a quarter slice of bread
> [Six shots of a piece of bread being meticulously weighed]
> To...
> [Complex stop-action animation showing small slices of bread coming together into a full loaf, and a large pile of loaves rising around a lone loaf on a table]
> To a dietetic [i.e., nutritionally sound] cafeteria for workers
> [Four shots, including trick dissolves, of workers eating and being served in a cafeteria]
> From crippled plants and factories
> [Two shots, joined by a dissolve, of ruined factories]
> To an upsurge in industry

[Sixteen shots of factory work (iron smelting) framed at the beginning, middle and end by shots of industrial chimneys]
From an oil-lamp in the city center
[Three shots of a table with a small oil-lamp on it, next to a dreary meal of potatoes and smoked fish; the final shot depicts someone reading a newspaper to the lamp's faint light]
To the electrification of the city's outskirts
[Four shots of stringing electrical wires in a village, along with two inserted shots of a factory and its smoking chimneys]¹³⁴

Such a sequence essentially replicates a larger narrative-rhetorical shape typical, as we have seen, of the murals, even as it inserts effective agitational "attractions" in order to make its relatively simple points more striking and memorable (the pig, the children; the trick dissolves; and especially the animated multiplication of bread, a fanciful if precise allusion to the severe rationing that began in 1917).

"From overturned streetcars..."
"... to new streetcar lines."
"From a quarter slice of bread ... To ...": [Animation of a loaf forming out of quarter slices.]

At other points, however, the agitation-propaganda distinction becomes clearly perceptible, as though the film were suddenly alluding *to* the distinction itself, rather than simply organizing its discourse in accord with it. A few minutes earlier in the film, the following sequence of intertitles is offered, in an ensemble designed to articulate the struggle of workers, peasants, and soldiers with the social catastrophes brought about by the Civil War (I will withhold a detailed description of all the accompanying shots):

Workers
Peasants
Soldiers of the Red Army
Through ruin
Through cold
Through typhus

---

134   This sequence corresponds to intertitles 53 through 65.

Through hunger
Through cholera
Through death
Toward victory over cold
Toward victory over hunger[135]

The intertitles "through ruin" and "through cold" are followed by images of grim wreckage and bodies huddled in the cold, alternating with Red Army soldiers on guard or on the march. But a less predictable series of images succeeds the intertitle "through typhus": a single louse crawling across a piece of coarse cloth; two fingers apparently crushing the bug; a truly startling moving microphotographic image of (presumably) the typhus-causing *Rickettsia* bacteria; and back to the cloth, now home to two lice.

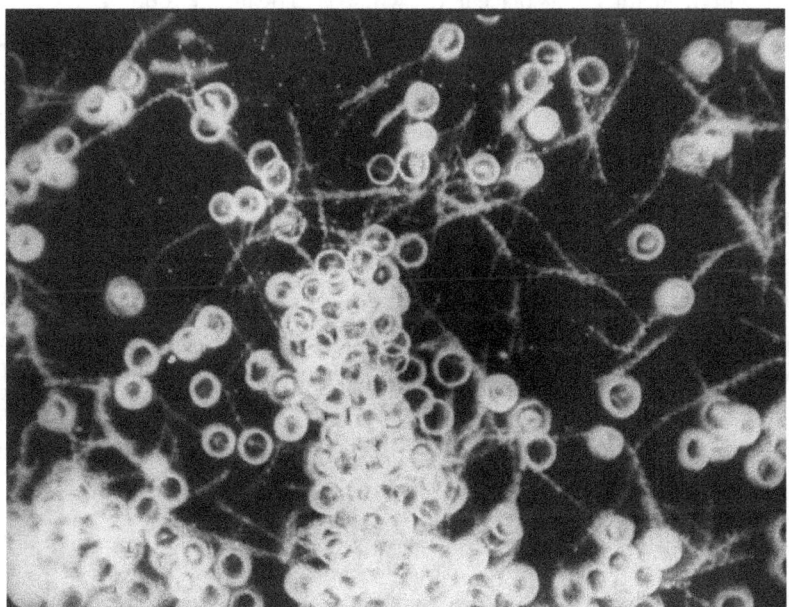

Image 6: "Through typhus . . . Through death": from *Stride, Soviet* (1926). Source: RGAKFD 10257.

Clearly, the point of the very brief sequence—or sub-sequence: almost an aside—is a terse revelation of the cause of the disease and its dissemination,

---

[135] The sequence comprises intertitles 25 through 33. No doubt due to inadequate information or archival notation, this sequence is unfortunately misidentified as belonging to Vertov's *History of the Civil War* (1921) in Seth Feldman, *Evolution of Style in the Early Work of Dziga Vertov*, 41–42.

rather than simply presenting its consequences (those appear soon enough, in the terrible images of heaped corpses that follow the intertitle "Through death"). Indeed, the sequence is so brief that it conveys less any explanation of typhus than the *idea* of explanation—of propaganda—as such. This impression might have been felt even more strongly by contemporary viewers, who would surely have been reminded, in watching this sequence, of innumerable lectures, pamphlets, exhibits, and newsreels about typhus and other diseases (and their prevention) heard and seen during the Civil War and earlier.[136] Vertov's strategy here can be thought of as a kind of absorption of oral narration, largely through visual allusion, into the image track—related to the ambiguous efforts elsewhere, especially Japan, to "purify" cinema of oral narrators in the silent period[137]—even as the sequence seems to allude *to* the lecture format as well, in part because its digressive compactness seems to require some imaginative "filling in the blanks" if its place in the whole is to be understood.

Finally, and as what I imagine to be a delayed and oblique critical response to the dismissal of Futurist influence upon agitprop practice by Burov and the like, Vertov incorporates one sequence toward the end of *Stride, Soviet* that manages to maintain the binary structure of the murals (now/then, good/bad) while experimentally complicating it to the verge of incomprehensibility. Following a no less remarkable sequence involving a "meeting of machines," a classically Vertovian false match links the motion of buses shot from a high angle to the forward movement through Moscow streets of a single bus captured through its windshield. Four shots of city commotion in winter follow—including two of a policeman directing traffic, a motif later taken up in *Man with a Movie Camera*—punctuated by the bold, quasi-vocalized intertitle query "where are you rushing off to?" A single undercranked overhead shot of a city square

---

136 On pre- and post-1917 medical hygiene propaganda in Russia, see Michael Zdenek David, "The White Plague in the Red Capital: The Control of Tuberculosis in Moscow, 1900-1940," (PhD diss., Yale University, 2001), 341–95. "The most severe typhus epidemic in the history of the world hobbled Russia and the Ukraine during 1918–20, infecting between seven and twenty-five million people and killing hundreds of thousands" (ibid., 57). Already in early 1918, the fledgling Narkompros Film Committee organized competitions for scripts for educational films about hygiene, cholera prevention and so on, and discussed using film to publicize the danger of typhus, although only one such film was apparently made (*LRK* 1, 278, 285). The last section of *Kino-Nedelia* 11 (August 13, 1918) was an educational film on "how to protect yourself from cholera" (RGALI f. 2091, op. 2, d. 2, l. 10).

137 For the best discussion of the controversies surrounding the famous *benshi* narrators and their complex relationship to the Japanese Pure Film Movement, see Aaron Gerow, *Visions of Japanese Modernity: Articulations of Cinema, Nation and Spectatorship, 1895–1925* (Berkeley: University of California Press, 2010), 133–73.

Christ among the Herdsmen • CHAPTER 4   251

(perhaps Sukharevka), now an emblem standing for "urban bustle," is succeeded by a series of catechistic questions contrasting "bad" and "good" kinds of activity, in accord with familiar propaganda conventions:

> To the church?
> [Four shots, including two of priests or monks walking leftwards through snow, and one of a church bell]
> Or to the evening school?
> [Two shots: a teacher at a blackboard; students in a classroom]
> To the [workers'] club?
> [Five shots, showing workers entering a doorway, and a game of chess being played]
> Or to the bar?
> [Four shots of evening carousing in a bar]
> To the evening clinic?
> [Four shots, including images of a shirtless man getting medical attention]
> Or to the Ermakovka [notorious Moscow flophouse]?[138]
> [Three shots: people entering the flophouse; a poor man in ragged clothes on a bed; a rightward pan across a lively group in the flophouse in medium close-up]

At this point appears the intertitle "The evening is full of contrasts," a text bearing lyrical-poetic (rather than oratorical) associations that unleashes an unusually complex and disorienting chain of images, one that pushes the tension between sheer juxtaposition and evaluation or judgment to the breaking point.

The sequence, to which I will return in volume 2, could be parsed in various ways, but it weaves approximately sixty-two mostly very short shots (for a total of about one minute and eighty-six seconds, 1.5 seconds per shot on average) into a twisting thematic skein that resolves, upon scrutiny, into motifs of *"communication/connection/traffic"* (shots 1–2 [telephone], 5 [buzzer], 22–25 [telegraph], 28–29 [traffic and newspaper], 33 and 35 [car and carriage respectively]); *"dance and (healthy) physical activity"* (shots 3 [depicting a group of women dancers standing in a row "fused" into a multiarmed being rather like the Hindu goddess Kali], 18–21, 26, 30, and 32 [dancing and ice skating]); *"poverty/homelessness"* (shots 4 and 46,

---

138 For more on the Ermakovka, see the discussion of *Kino-Eye* in volume 2.

Image 7: From *Stride, Soviet*: images from the "evening is full of contrasts" sequence. Source: RGAKFD 10257.

seemingly taken inside the Ermakovka);[139] *"bar and billiard hall"* (shots 6–9 [billiards], 16, 34, 36, 47, 51–52, 58–59 [bar]); *"shady dealings/crime"* (shots 10–15, depicting a gun being loaded); and *"foxtrot"* (shots 37–43, 45, 48–50, 60–62). When subdivided into "themes" in this way, the sequence fairly clearly breaks down, on the level of content, into a generalized contrast of what in Soviet terms would be "good" (healthy physical activity; probably connections/communication) versus "bad" (poverty, tavern, crime, the fox-trotting bourgeoisie). Spectators do not enjoy this kind of clarity as the sequence unfolds, however, and only in part because of the rapidity of the shot changes and absence of intertitles. Equally important is the intricately interwoven, syncopated relationship between the various thematic series, and the sense that formal matching of shots in relation to movements of hands and feet is what really pulls the sequence along, rather than thematic or narrative development.

---

139 No written record exists for shooting there, however; see RGALI f. 3081, op. 1, d. 297, esp. ll. 1–2ob.

Christ among the Herdsmen • CHAPTER 4   253

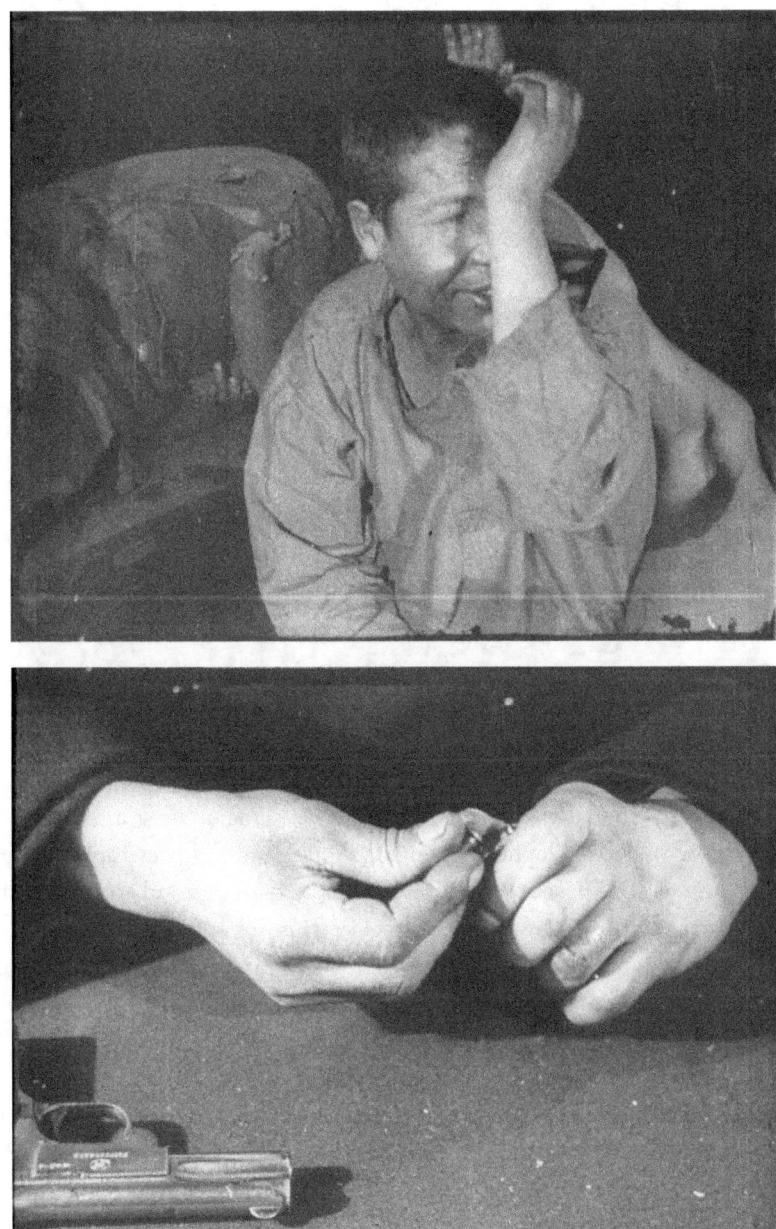

Image 8-9: From *Stride, Soviet*: images from the "evening is full of contrasts" sequence. Source: RGAKFD 10257.

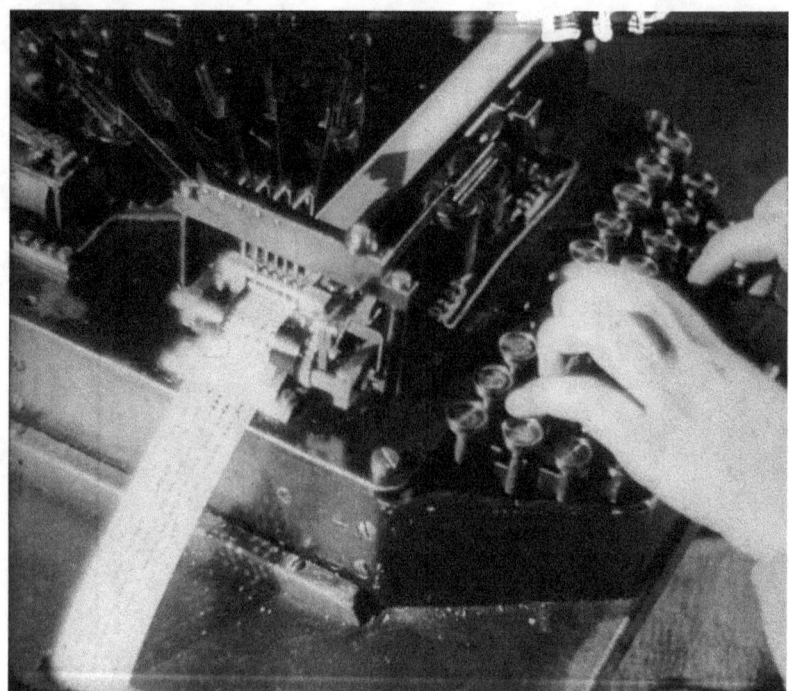

Image 10: From *Stride, Soviet*: images from the "evening is full of contrasts" sequence. Source: RGAKFD 10257.

As regards the latter, we might note the way the arching movement of the hand picking up a telephone receiver (shots 1 and 2) hypertrophies into a web of sinuous arms in shot 3, continues with the twisting hand and arm of the ragged Ermakovka-dweller wiping or shielding his or her face, before volatilizing into a whole array of other hand movements (typing, piano playing, loading a gun).[140] Indeed, it almost seems that the "goddess Kali" provides a repository of mobile hands and arms—not entirely unlike the "clusters" of hands in Vertov's early Scriabin poem, or like the categories ("databases") from which *Man with a Movie Camera* draws its material—that then circulate throughout the sequence. In terms of the interrelations between the series, consider how the shot of hands playing a piano (shot 17) seem to pertain *either* to the ("bad") tavern (shot 16) or to the ("good") gymnastic dancing (shot 18);[141] or

---

140 See also the draft plans for short films on the themes of "hands" and "legs," written between 1922 and 1924 and incorporating literally scores of different hand and leg positions in what seems like almost random order, in *DO*, 79–85.

141 Two split screen images of dancing-training-piano playing that appear later in the sequence (30 and 32) show a different instrument and pianist.

how the scenes of traffic apparently represent some general nighttime bustle, until the sub-sequence from shot 51 onward clearly links that traffic (or at least the horse-drawn carriage) with the life of the tavern. Indeed, the series "communication/connection/traffic" might be read as a figuration of Vertov's own cinematic practice here, inasmuch as that practice is but another work of interconnection, a reflection on the uncertain direction of, and the intervals between, messages and movements. In the end, the sequence generates a didactic meaning only by suddenly arresting the contrasts (with the introduction of the cliché of fox-trotters in shot 37), condensing into a single-themed blast of images legible in terms of "decadence and waste," and hammering the point home with an intertitle (shot 44) that makes the shift from sheer "contrasts" to value-laden "oppositions" completely clear: "In a fight to the death with a rotten, outmoded way of life."[142]

On some level, it would seem, the sequence also allegorizes what Vertov must have meant by a "Communist decoding of the world":[143] cinema, confronted with the chaos of social reality, plunges into it only to emerge with a vision of order, a useful paradigm for organizing that reality, in line with a technocratic notion of documentary practice that would become familiar in the English-speaking world through the work of John Grierson.[144] Nothing is in fact decoded here, of course; indeed, we might just as easily argue that Vertov *recodes* the footage in terms of early Soviet value hierarchies. If any lesson emerges from the sequence, of which Vertov seems to have been quite proud,[145] it concerns the basic theoretical and practical question of how to keep moving from one distinct theme, shot, or movement to another—that is, to incorporate the full mass of worldly detail—while generating some kind of satisfying, useable, or just comprehensible closure. What on the agit-train murals were static panels devoted to oppositions of good/bad and past/present become, at this point in *Stride, Soviet*, a well-nigh Whitmanian magma of images susceptible to articulation only through abrupt narrative arrest ("a fight to the death . . ."). Seen from the other direction, it turns out that the primitive binaries used on the murals could be deployed to generate sequences of remarkable complexity, even as, when rigorously applied to the units of which films are composed, they could shake the expectation that sheer "transitions

---

142 The next sequence shows how "the [Moscow] Soviet promotes physical education."
143 *KE*, 42.
144 See Rosen, *Change Mummified*, 247–63.
145 See his remarks in the 1947 "Artistic Calling Card" in Tode and Wurm, *Dziga Vertov*, 107.

from one movement to another" (Vertov's definition of the "interval") would terminate in a decoding of any kind.[146]

2. AN ENORMOUS FRONT OF DESTRUCTION

The murals were but one aspect of agit-train activism, of course, and their effects on Vertov's thinking about film become discernable only years after the trains themselves had come to a halt, and the murals painted over or discarded. It will not be possible here to provide a detailed survey of all the activities associated with the agit-trains once the murals, activists, and local organizers had pulled in the crowds, but some general outline of the physical, social, and discursive environment in which the trains operated needs to be sketched before moving on to agit-cinema specifically.

A remarkable account written sometime after mid-March 1919 by L. K. Likhterman, who headed up the early *Lenin* agit-train, offers one of the few first-person testimonies—not uninflected by euphemism, as we will see—that indicate what on-the-ground agitation was like:

> Work on the train never stopped during the day, and even continued on into the night during nocturnal stops at small stations. [The agitators] took advantage of even the shortest occasional stop, and when the train went past some platform or temporary stop, from the windows they threw leaflets, telegrams, and newspapers, all of which were eagerly picked up or grabbed in the air by chance passersby.
>
> After the arrival of the train, the remotest and most desolate stations became unrecognizable. Within minutes, all the buildings, signposts, and cars of trains headed the other direction were plastered with posters and appeals. An orderly row of buyers appeared at [the train's] store; literature . . . was distributed to various organizations; the movie screening began; and an open-air meeting was organized, attended by peasants, Red Army men and local young people, all of whom ran up to look at the "weird" train, attracted by its unusual appearance.

---

146 *KE*, 8. Liliana Mal'kova usefully summarizes the dialectic at work here when she notes that "the development of film documentary's own expressive and visual capabilities [in the service of developing more effective propaganda] meant its growing independence, enabling it in some cases to wrest itself from the general propaganda context" (*Sovremennost' kak istoriia*, 21). This may also be one way of defining what Soviet aesthetic dogma meant, from the 1930s onward, by the term "formalism."

These improvised meetings were lively and successful; the speakers were posed various kinds of questions (about land, about the new order, about communes and so on), to which they replied with full and exhaustive answers... At every station one of the agitators got out and explained the goals of the train, and the meaning of its murals, to those gathered around...

The peasantry met the train with great interest and amity; such was the general impression of everyone who participated in the first journey [of the *Lenin* train]... But the main spectators were children, who everywhere were the first to meet the train, and the last to follow along when it was departing. A special screening for children took place at almost every stop; they were given booklets, postcards, and writing accessories.

In larger centers where they had been informed about the train's imminent arrival by telegrams sent from nearby stations, the local party committees and executive committee greeted the train (sometimes this was an organized and highly festive affair, as for instance in Rezhitsa,[147] where Red Army soldiers came out to the train with music and torches); there, they held meetings together with the train's [propaganda] instructors, where they'd develop a work plan, figure out the length of time the train would remain in the city, and so on....[148]

Thus, upon their arrival, the trains became the immediate vortices of an immense amount of activity, ranging from agitation (pasting up posters), propaganda (explaining the murals and "the goals of the train"), organizing and supervising meetings and demonstrations, distributing printed material and (extremely scarce) writing utensils, and so on. They were displays of power as well as sources of diversion and information, and provided occasions for local party and Army authorities both to appear before the local citizenry and to assert their connection to the "center," as represented by the agit-train and its emissaries.

On the *October Revolution*, the most important emissary was certainly Mikhail Kalinin (1875–1946), former peasant, Old Bolshevik, chairman of VTsIK from 1919 to 1938, and a core member of what Sheila Fitzpatrick has called "Stalin's team" from 1926 until his death.[149] Although (as we will see) the

---

147 Today, Rezekne: a city in eastern Latvia.
148 In Tolstoj, ed., *Agitmassovoe iskusstvo*, vol. 1, 50–51. The report was written no earlier than March 11, 1919.
149 Sheila Fitzpatrick, *On Stalin's Team: The Years of Living Dangerously in Soviet Politics* (Princeton, NJ: Princeton University Press, 2015), 15–17, 28–36, 51–56, 84–85, 129–34, 154–61.

film screenings might have pulled in more spectators than any other agit-train events, Kalinin's speeches were certainly the main attractions from the agitators' point of view. Those speeches, sometimes transcribed on the spot (along with responses from auditors), provide a remarkable glimpse not only into the agit-train meetings and the topics that dominated them, but into the rhetorical strategies the Bolsheviks used to bring people in the war-stricken areas over to their side as well. They were certainly part of Vertov's ideological training, and we will make reference to them below.[150]

Four of the *October Revolution*'s sixteen journeys were made to southern Russia and Ukraine, and during 1920 the train's activists spent much of March, August, October, and part of May and June in that large and devastated area, especially in the neighborhood of the city of Kharkov and the far eastern provinces that make up the Donbas (short for Donets Basin) coal mining and industrial region.[151] The train's eighth journey (March 1–26, 1920) took Kalinin, Vertov, Levitskij, and their colleagues from Moscow through the Russian cities of Kursk and Belgorod and on into Ukraine (Kharkov, Slaviansk, Gorlovka), deeper into southern Russia (Taganrog, Rostov-on-Don, and Novocherkassk), then back north through the Donbas towns of Debal'tsevo and Kupiansk to Belgorod and the capital.[152] This borderland, dominated topographically by the Donets and Don Rivers and (underground) by enormous coal deposits, was at the physical epicenter of the Civil War: during the turmoil, at least twenty different political regimes were established in the Donbas prior to the Red victory. Indeed, when Vertov arrived in the region at the beginning of March, the Red Army had taken Novocherkassk, the headquarters of the White counterrevolutionary forces in the South, just a little over a month and a half before.[153]

The economically crucial Donbas region, whose very large working class was notoriously volatile and unpredictable in its political commitments, had been occupied by the end of October 1917 by counterrevolutionary forces that subjected pro-Soviet workers to appalling repression, later to be

---

150 Kenez, in his excellent summary of agit-train propaganda, refers to B. Sergeev's 1938 collection of transcripts of Kalinin's speeches on the train (*Birth of the Propaganda State*, 61). As I show below using material from GARF, Sergeev's selections were evidently distilled to make the meetings, and the interactions between activists and audiences, seem more harmonious than they really were.
151 Maksakova, *Agitpoezd "Oktiabr'skaia Revoliutsiia,"* 31–34. The area has become internationally well known recently due to the unrest in eastern Ukraine, alas.
152 GARF f. 1252, op. 1, d. 63, l. 81; Maksakova, *Agitpoezd "Oktiabr'skaia Revoliutsiia,"* 32.
153 Mawdsley, *Russian Civil War*, 221. Both Rostov and Novocherkassk were taken on January 7.

answered by Red reprisals more than equivalent in brutality and mindlessness. The independent Soviet republic briefly formed in the Donbas and adjoining Ukrainian and Russian industrial areas in February 1918 was swept away by German and Austrian troops, who occupied much of the territory in consort with the new and short-lived Skoropadskyi regime in Kiev from April until the German surrender that fall. Workers sympathetic to the Soviets and peasants who had seized landlords' property were terrorized by this new regime, most notoriously by means of savage corporal punishment (lethal floggings, beatings with ramrods and so on). The same pattern continued after the fall of Skoropadskyi in November 1918, during the frenzied fighting between Reds, Whites and other groups between December 1918 and May 1919, and later during the White occupation (May–December 1919). Cameraman Alexander Levitskij recalled how he and Vertov directly encountered victims of the violence as late as March 1920, when the agit-train was making its way south from Kharkov:

> While the train was loading up with water, Vertov and I stepped off to stretch our legs. Stepping over piles of railroad ties, broken stone and rails, we noticed a cargo train on the siding. We were taken aback by the strong smell emanating from the wagons; forcing open one of the doors, we recoiled in horror. Out reeked a sepulchral chill and stench. Judging from the bits of clothing that partially covered them, these were the corpses of Red Army soldiers. The traces of machine-gun bursts were evident on the naked bodies; some were horribly disfigured by saber blows.
>
> We moved away from that frightful train and spontaneously removed our caps.[154]

The area had also been the site of anti-Jewish brutality perpetrated by every combatant force, including the Whites, Reds, the Petliura Directorate (which replaced Skoropadskyi), and various armed bands. The majority of the pogroms, however—in the most savage anti-Jewish violence prior to the Holocaust, involving 1,500 pogroms in 1,300 settlements, 50,000 to 60,000 killed, 200,000 crippled and wounded, thousands of women raped, and around 300,000 children orphaned—occurred slightly further to the south and west in the Ukrainian heartland.[155] We know nothing of Vertov's direct response

---

154 Levitskij, *Rasskazy o kinematografe*, 213.
155 Budnitskij, *Rossijskie evrei*, 275–76. A number of powerful, now rarely seen films were made about the pogroms, including *Les pogroms juifs en Ucraine 1919–1920* (1920 [RGAKFD

to these atrocities, but do know that people in his circle were outraged by the frequent and detailed reports they received about them.[156]

Although Donbas workers and peasants were by no means uniformly sympathetic to the Bolsheviks—the at-gunpoint grain requisitioning and forced mobilization practiced by the Reds, not to mention their violent anticlericalism and their unforgotten "revolutionary defeatism" during the war against the Germans, stirred strong opposition from many working-class patriots—it seems clear that the Whites, with their ferocious antagonism toward worker autonomy, and desire to restore some version of the pre-February order, were regarded as a non-option by the majority.[157] Nonetheless, the victorious Bolsheviks regarded Donbas workers with suspicion after January 1920, not only because of their well-known independence and unpredictability but also because they had lived under "old regime" occupation during the Civil War, a misfortune that evidently called into question both their loyalty and their political maturity.[158] Civil servants were suspect as much or more, of course: an activist who inspected schools in towns visited by the *October Revolution* in

---

13964-I]), made by the Berlin-based "Historic Archive of Ukrainian Jews"; *The Jewish Pogroms in Ukraina 1919–1920* (1920 [RGAKFD 13964-II]; *Evrejskie pogromy* (1920 [RGAKFD 13964-III]). I know nothing about their distribution, but evidently they were made for French- and English-language audiences as well as Russian. The films are largely comprised of horrifying still photographs, among the earliest examples I know of still-photography-based documentary. On violence and anti-Semitism in the Kharkov-Donbas area, primarily in reference to the period June–October 1919, see Budnitskij, *Rossijskie evrei*, 325–27; and L. B. Miliakova, ed., *Kniga pogromov: pogromy na Ukraine, v Belorussii i evropejskoj chasti Rossii v period Grazhdanskoj Vojny 1918–1922 gg.* (Moscow: Rosspen, 2007), 177–92, 261–65, 776–84; and on pogroms committed later in 1920 in the area by Red forces (Budyonny's army, specifically), 423–24. Although only one-fifth of the total number of pogroms were carried out by White forces—first place was taken by the Directorate (40%), followed by various rebel bands (25%), the Whites (17%), the Reds (9%), and the "Grigor'ev" rebels (4%)—White anti-Jewish violence was concentrated in just a few months, during which time they "broke all records" for pogromist savagery (quoting Budnitskij, *Rossijskie evrei*, 276, 279). On pogroms committed by the Reds, see *Rossijskie evrei*, 118–34; on White anti-Semitic ideology and propaganda, 221–49.

156 For just one example, see Olga Boltianskaia's diary notes about "Black Hundred and White Guard" atrocities in a Jewish village in Ukraine in 1919 (RGALI f. 2057, op. 2, d. 26, ll. 575–76). Descriptions of White and Petliurist atrocities were also a staple of Bolshevik propaganda materials during the war: for an example, see V. A. Karpinskij's *S kem zhe vy, krest'iane? S kem idete? Komu pomogaete?* (Moscow: VTsIK, 1918).

157 My account here relies on Hiroaki Kuromiya, *Freedom and Terror in the Donbas: A Ukrainian-Russian Borderland, 1870s-1990s* (Cambridge: Cambridge University Press, 1998), 71–117.

158 Ibid., 115–17.

March 1920 growled that the teaching staff at the few functioning schools he discovered were tainted by a "Menshevik tendency."[159]

Certainly, the daily on-the-ground work of all the agit-train divisions took place in an environment wracked through and through by the war's effects. The following description by Levitskij of the situation in and around the main train station in Kharkov, where the *October Revolution* was parked from March 8–10, 1920, gives a good sense of the conditions in which the agit-train activists did their work:

> A train was near the station, its firebox smoking, apparently ready for departure to Moscow. It had a few passenger cars, with freight cars making up the rest.
>
> It was a kind of human anthill, comprised of bags and people. They hung from and clutched to the roofs, the carriage platforms and the buffers... Endless crowds of bag-people, shouting and swearing, climbed through the open doors of the cargo cars; they were forced back, shoved away, struck over the head, while they in turn would grab those standing in the cars by the legs and try to pull them off.
>
> Red Army men from the food procurement squads [*prodotriady*] wandered through the crowds, dragging people off the buffers. Dozens of others streamed in to take their place. A woman cried out in a heart-rending voice; her two children followed suit, clinging to her sleeveless, ragged coat.
>
> The train began to move, emitting whistles of warning. This did not frighten the crowd, but rather intensified the commotion. Shouts, noise, swearing, the whistling of the train all combined in a wild cacophony. Several people were struck off the buffers and the roof of the train, a few falling directly under the train. This didn't stop the crowd, and many ran behind the train as it was gathering speed, dragging their sacks behind them.
>
> I stood on the tracks, looking at the departing train, and for a long time could hear the sounds of voices mingling with the wheels as they rumbled and the train as it whistled.
>
> When I finally got to the station, I was struck by a revolting smell of carbolic acid, sweat, and who knows what else. The huge hall was filled with mist, the respiration of masses of people. It was damp, and the sun's bright rays barely penetrated the dirty windowpanes. Women with children and men, most wearing ragged overcoats and sheepskin jackets,

---

159 GARF f. 1252, op. 1, d. 64, l. 113. Most of the reports focused on the terrible conditions at the schools and of the students: hunger, filth, and lack of clothing (l. 109).

> sat and lay on benches and on the floor. Some, having taken off their outerwear and wrapped it around their shoulders, were beating their shirts to rid themselves of bugs. On the filthy floor, in the heat, people sick with typhus tossed back and forth. One man, clutching a bag containing his belongings, cast his lifeless gaze at the ceiling. Beside him several people had settled down on their sacks, calmly drinking hot water from cups and mess tins and lustily eating bread and lard. The weeping of children, someone sobbing and keening, incoherent mumbling and the sounds of an accordion, drunken shouting and a brawl somewhere on the far side of the hall....
>
> It occurred to me that the horrors of Dante's Hell were less terrifying than the reality of the Kharkov train station.[160]

Later the same day, very probably March 8, 1920, Levitskij encountered Vertov in the city, and they ended up walking back to the agit-train together, making a "wide berth" so as to avoid passing through the station.[161]

Vertov went off to show films to a group of children, probably in one of the local theaters. "A roar of children's voices, explosions of laughter," especially while watching the 1913 animated adaptation of Pushkin's *Tale of the Fisherman and the Little Fish*, was the response Vertov recorded.[162] It seems that on that day, and on many days, the agit-screenings functioned in part as straightforward distraction from the surrounding horrors, as Vertov suggested in a later report on the train's eighth journey:

> Almost every screening was accompanied by a general improvement in the mood of adults and children; the exchange of approving or hostile exclamations; exhaustion dispelled, excitement, noise; the laughter of a crowd that had been dead with melancholy only a moment before.[163]

Levitskij, when not fulfilling orders from Vertov or from one of the train's political commissars to shoot specific footage, was mainly an observer, not an

---

160 Levitskij, *Rasskazy o kinematografe*, 205–6. Levitskij reports going with Vertov later that day into downtown Kharkov and finding mainly closed shops filled to bursting with produce which the Soviet authorities soon began requisitioning (206–7). This is not a claim that can be taken at face value, however.
161 Ibid., 206–7.
162 GARF f. 1252, op. 1, d. 64, l. 149.
163 RGALI f. 2091, op. 2, d. 386, l. 19ob. The addressee of the report was Grigorij Lemberg, Aleksandr's father, then Vertov's superior in the film section of the agit-train administration.

activist engaged in direct propaganda, *kontrol'*, or inspection.[164] Those who were involved in those activities filled out report after report describing terrible conditions and utter material deprivation. At a meeting in Gorlovka on March 12, 1920, for instance, teachers bitterly complained that they "had not received a single dime from Soviet power." When filling out his inspection reports on local hospitals and clinics, the *October Revolution*'s medical commissar often simply wrote, "complete absence of everything, even the basic necessities." And a railroad commissar onboard the train in March indicated in his report that the situation was so bad that, apart from giving a few urgent directives, he was more engaged with photographing local conditions in order to convey to the relevant commissariats a concrete sense of the magnitude of what needed to be done.[165]

The crowds that gathered around the *October Revolution* in March 1920 were, of course, all too aware of all of this. The disasters—destruction, disease, poverty, ongoing violence, requisitioning—would have been palpable to anyone in the immediate environs of the train, and Kalinin did not flinch from discussing them:

> We are carrying out a whole series of exactions that are very hard on the peasantry. We are taking from the peasant all extra grain; we will confiscate butter and chickens . . . and in essence, we are giving nothing in return.[166]
>
> Comrades, our situation is outstanding militarily speaking. Victory is almost complete. But before us lies an enormous front of destruction and [the task] of restoring [destroyed] transportation lines. There is not a single building that has not been contaminated; not one city where the garbage [lying around in the streets] measures less than in the hundreds of wagon loads; not one city or region where the stores are stocked with goods. Almost no factories are operating anywhere in Russia. The northern part of Russia is starving . . . and there are regions . . . where

---

164 On the *October Revolution*, the orders sometimes came from the Bolshevik bosses traveling on the trains, such as Grigorij Petrovskij, who ordered the filming of blown-up bridges (GARF f. 1252, op. 1, d. 7, ll. 8–15). Vertov's involvement in filming during the period of his agit-train work is poorly documented, but see GARF f. 1252, op. 1, d. 64, ll. 162–63; RGALI f. 2091, op. 2, d. 386, l. 19.
165 GARF f. 1252, op. 1, d. 64, ll. 81–81ob, 94, 115. I have not seen any surviving photographs taken during this or other journeys of the *October Revolution*, apart from those devoted to documenting the agit-trains themselves.
166 GARF f. 1252, op. 1, d. 64, l. 73; from an address to soldiers in Iuzovka (later Stalino, today Donetsk, Ukraine) on March 14, 1920.

almost everyone has been felled by illness. Before us stretches an enormous task, work on an incomprehensible [scale].[167]

Indeed, the transcripts—extraordinary records of direct interactions between a member of the Bolshevik hierarchy and ordinary citizens—indicate that auditors, uniformly stricken by manifold calamities, confronted Kalinin regularly with complaints and petitions during the agit-train meetings. I would like to dwell on them for a page or two, primarily because they give a concrete sense of the discursive atmosphere into Vertov had been plunged (vastly different from anything he'd encountered before 1918, except perhaps among politicized students), to which he had to adapt, and within which (at times, at least) he would thrive.

Sometimes these petitions gave Kalinin the opportunity to appear magnanimous, as at a meeting in the Taganrog area when he promised to restore land to a peasant woman, single with a small child, after another villager had allegedly stolen her family property. Other requests were harder to satisfy. Peasants pointed to the problems brought about by the draft, and urged (for instance) that tailors and shoemakers be exempt from mobilization: "without them, it's difficult to live [in the village]." They bombarded Kalinin with questions about stolen horses, complaining that both the Reds and the Whites had taken so many that they had none left with which to farm:

> Kalinin: We have to solve this problem somehow. We need to get tractors [to the farms]; and the peasants with horses should plow communally on Sundays for those without.
> Peasant: And will any more horses be requisitioned?

When a local Communist official interjected that there would not be, the peasant immediately contradicted him, and insisted that horses were still being seized.[168]

These simmering animosities generated an atmosphere of high tension around the agit-train meetings and presentations, and the possibility of violence accompanied them like a background hum. According to Levitskij, the *October*

---

167 GARF f. 1252, op. 1, d. 64, l. 77ob; from an address to 2,500 people (mainly railway workers) in the Ukrainian city of Slaviansk on March 11, 1920.
168 These examples are from a meeting of March 16, 1920 at the Nikolaevka slobodka in the Taganrog region (GARF f. 1252, op. 1, d. 64, ll. 20–21). Much effort was expended on generating propaganda justifying Red food requisitioning: see, for example, Karpinskij's *S kem zhe vy, krest'iane?*

Revolution's highly strung Cheka head Skrameh wandered through the crowds with his hand on his Mauser, and Levitskij certainly had no doubts about his willingness to use it. When one of their colleagues—an overzealous orator who openly threatened peasants in one Ukrainian village with armed violence if they did not submit to the food requisitions—sparked a near-riot, Skrameh came very close to shooting him at point-blank range in the chest, were he not prevented (again, according to Levitskij) by Kalinin's direct and fatherly intercession.[169]

Given these problems, it is not surprising that Kalinin's most rhetorically effective arguments seem to have involved generalities and prophecy, rather than specifics. He spoke at length and in a progressive spirit about a range of policy-related topics, including equal rights for women and nationalities, gender relations in households, and ridding schools and government of the influence of religion. His concrete suggestions for a future rationalized peasant economy, however, seem to have been met with open skepticism:

> Kalinin: We consider that, for instance, if one day of labor is expended on the manufacture of one arshin [71 cm] of chintz, then [the equivalent] for the peasant should be the amount of grain he produces in a day. Keeping in mind, of course, an eight-hour workday for both peasants and workers.
>
> Peasant: Yes, but if you work by the hour [on the land], you'll end up not producing anything.
>
> Kalinin: We haven't set anything up yet, but in the future we must anticipate a time when we produce the same amount in a day that we used to put out in a week [due to the organization of production].[170]

The majority of his speeches, by contrast, mobilized an array of more general and emotional appeals, from inflaming national and class animosities to visions of a bright secular future. The charge of treachery was a common theme of White anti-Bolshevik propaganda, and Kalinin did his utmost to reverse this charge, arguing that the aristocracy loved Russia as long it sustained their "drunkenness and debauchery" and remained in servitude to "the American and English bourgeoisie."[171] This was a rhetoric that identified the Russian

---

169 Levitskij, *Rasskazy o kinematografe*, 231. Contrary to what Levitskij thought (ibid., 203–4), Skrameh left the Cheka/GPU in 1926, after suffering heart trouble and a nervous breakdown (Goncharov and Nekhotin, "'Durylin soglasen dat' podpisku," 137).
170 GARF f. 1252, op. 1, d. 64, l. 18.
171 GARF f. 1252, op. 1, d. 64, ll. 4–5. See also Sergeev, "Agitpoezdki M. I. Kalinina," 137.

people as a nation with the Russian people as the working masses and, conversely, associated the upper classes with class enemies abroad, making them the real "traitors" (*predateli*) of Russia: a "social patriotism" that deftly reversed that Bolshevik "revolutionary defeatism" so notorious during the Great War, and which eventually ossified into a figurative equation of "foreign" (or "Western-foreign") with "bourgeois" often visible in the films (fiction or nonfiction) of the 1920s and later.[172]

Even the appalling suffering then endured by Soviet citizens could be converted, by dint of a figurative machinery of redemption, sacrifice, and the like, into a source of future greatness that would be acknowledged by humankind at large:

> The English and the French come visit us now and see poverty, famine, and cold. But comrades, not all great ideas appeared in stone palaces: the idea of Christian doctrine occurred to Jesus Christ himself when he was among herdsmen. And all great ideas emerge out of suffering. I am certain that all the great ideas that have appeared as the result of great sacrifices will [eventually] earn the honor they deserve from future humanity.[173]

In speaking to Red Army soldiers—many of whom were of peasant origin, of course, and would have had relatives living and suffering in the villages—Kalinin made a point of linking the action of the army itself to the eventual alleviation of rural plight through industrialization:

> We see that our Red Army, which has . . . defeated the enemy, is now coming again to the Donets Basin to commence its military campaign,[174] so that the paralyzed Donets Basin can be turned into a place of creativity, a place for an enormous extension of [the powers of] human labor, so that coal and iron might flow thence like a river, to make it possible to start up the factories and plants.

---

172 See, for example, the typically satirical portraits of foreign (in this case Argentine) visitors to the USSR ("curious bourgeois") in *Sovkinozhurnal* 32/51 (1926 [RGAKFD 826]); similar portrayals in *Torzhestvo otkrytiia Vsesoiuznoj Sel'sko-khoziajstvennoj Vystavki (Otkrytie Sel'sko-khoziajstvennoj Vystavki v Moskve 1923* [Celebrating the opening of the All-Union Agricultural Exhibition (*Opening of the Agricultural Exhibition in Moscow 1923*); RGAKFD 706]); or Vertov's *One Sixth of the World*.
173 GARF f. 1252, op. 1, d. 64, l. 65; at a congress of teachers in Maloarkhangel'sk, probably on March 5, 1920.
174 This apparently refers to the military actions in and around the Donbas starting in February 1920.

This, Kalinin promised, is when the peasant will feel relief, and "all sacrifices will be justified."[175]

Most intriguingly, Kalinin sometimes appealed not to immediately collectivist sentiments, whether class or nationality-based, but rather to notions of *individual* wellbeing and happiness, albeit linked to a wider social struggle:

> I believe that victory is good not only in the results brought about by that victory, but that individual participation in the process of struggle leads to the greatest happiness for each person. Then, there will be no room for whining and boredom; life will become so broad and deep, that a person living at that time could over the course of a year, or half a year, experience far more than one could in 70 years today.
>
> And I believe that each person ... who wants to forge his own happiness will find it in this work. He will, without fail, find complete satisfaction for his own "I" [*polnoe udovletvorenie sobstvennomu Ia*] (applause).[176]

To be sure, all or most of Kalinin's rhetorical devices derive from familiar tropes and values of the Russian (and especially, revolutionary) intelligentsia, the ethos of sacrifice above all. They faithfully reflect the discursive arsenal of the agit-train activists, and would come to permeate the rhetoric of Vertov's films as well, from an early date.

Perhaps the most remarkable example from this time is Vertov's autobiographically inflected script for an elaborate and unproduced agitational fiction film—yes, a fiction film!—written in May 1920, just after his journey to the Donbas on the *October Revolution*, known as "Draft of a Scenario Intended to be Filmed During a Journey by the Agit-Train, The *Soviet Caucasus*."[177] It tells the story of Boris Ogarev, a film director from the Caucasian city of Grozny (then especially famous as one of the centers of the Russian oil industry) but working in Moscow during the Civil War, and his

---

175 GARF f. 1252, op. 1, d. 64, l. 73.
176 GARF f. 1252, op. 1, d. 64, l. 66 (at the Maloarkhangel'sk congress of teachers). To be sure, appeals to the *kollektiv* over the individual appear as well, though not as consistently or unambiguously as might be assumed; see Sergeev, "Agitpoezdki M.I. Kalinina," 148. See also Oleg Kharkhordin's discussion (building on research by N. A. Mel'nikova) of the ideology of Kalinin's speeches in terms of the individual-collective dialectic, in *The Collective and the Individual in Russia: A Study of Practices* (Berkeley, Los Angeles: University of California Press, 1999), 198.
177 *KE*, 275–78. The version in *SDZ* upon which this translation is based was significantly altered, as in many instances; here I employ both the *KE* translation and the full version ("Proekt stsenariia, prednaznachennogo k s'emke vo vremia poezdki agitpoezda 'Sovetskij Kavkaz'"; dated May 2, 1920) in *DO*, 44–47, 482, noting important differences below.

brother Mikhail, who along with their parents has been separated from Boris by the conflict. Mikhail, it turns out, has become "Red Misha," a Bolshevik activist organizing underground action (with the help of local "Greens," armed peasant groups who in reality were hostile to both Reds and Whites) in White-occupied Grozny. Arrested and tortured, Mikhail escapes with Green assistance and begins to organize another underground action upon learning of an imminent Red advance upon the city. Someone betrays the conspirators, however, and Mikhail and most of the Communists are again arrested and sentenced to death by White forces who shoot them, stab them, and beat their heads in with rifle butts. Mikhail miraculously survives a pistol shot to the head, and lives not only to give counsel to the advancing Reds and muster support from the Greens, but also to become the commissar in charge of oil production in Grozny and a legend among workers there, who call him the "arisen" or "resurrected one" (*voskresshij*).[178]

Meanwhile Boris, who has fallen for an agit-train worker named Nadia Morozova, both learns of Mikhail's heroic exploits through the Bolshevik press and gets the chance to go to Grozny (with Nadia) as head of the cinema division on the *Soviet Caucasus* train.[179] Boris and Mikhail meet on the oil fields, where Boris is heading up a photo shoot of the wells, and there he learns of the death of their parents at the hands of the Whites. Sitting to one side during a meeting of workers, commissars, and agitators at the oil plant, Nadia listens to Mikhail's story of war and suffering and evidently falls in love almost immediately (she "looks at him as though hypnotized," and eventually "with exaltation"), much to Boris's disappointment. "I try to forget all I've lived through," the now pale and serious Mikhail concludes, "through unceasing work, until I lose all strength."

Urged with mass cries of "the arisen one" to speak from the tribune, Mikhail delivers the film's moral, interspersed (according to the script) with images of oil workers repairing their equipment, a peasant in the field, a proletarian hammering, and "other workers at their labor posts":

> We take revenge on the old world, on behalf of our murdered sisters, brothers and parents, by engaging in stubborn and joyous labor for our own sakes.
> ... With millions of hands lifting the hammer of labor, we confidently forge our earthly happiness.

---

178 *DO*, 46. The version translated in *KE* softens the passages on White violence, and eliminates entirely the superstitious-sounding "resurrection" idea.
179 Along the way, Boris and Nadia help clean up a filthy and probably pestilent train station "with shovels and brooms," exactly in the spirit of the agit-train murals (*KE*, 276; *DO*, 45).

The script concludes—in one of the earliest clear indications of Vertov's mature manner and preferred iconography—with an "APOTHEOSIS: POETRY OF LABOR AND MOVEMENT," a machinery-montage in close-up of (among many other things) a hammer pounding on red-hot iron, saws wildly slicing up "black, wet" branches, the rotating axis of a locomotive, a train heading toward the camera, and the movement of mechanized city traffic. At film's end,

> The smoking stacks of factories and plants [extending] to the very horizon, as far as the eye can see. Strongly lit, one after another pass the "arisen one," Nadia, Boris, and—as though made of steel—the mighty workers across the screen, moving with a firm, devastating stride through factories and plants, carrying hammers and shovels.[180]

Together with its obvious but hard-to-decode personal-confessional signals—that the brothers are named Mikhail and Boris is especially curious—the *Soviet Caucasus* script seems to condense much of Vertov's Civil War experience into legible form, while presaging cinematic apotheoses to come: a kind of repository of the stories he had heard, the sights he had seen, the fears and hopes he had felt, and the rhetoric he had absorbed.

It was a rhetoric he would continue to deploy, whether in affirmations of the need for military readiness on the part of the whole population to "defend the gains of the Revolution" (in *The Eleventh Year*), in celebrations of industry as "extensions of human labor" (in *Enthusiasm*), in careful fusing of the iconographies of nation, class, and individual subjectivity (in the 1930s, and above all in *Three Songs of Lenin*), or, more complexly and consistently, by foregrounding women as builders of the new society. Vertov would retain the haunted backdrop of catastrophe as well, often alluded to through archival images, especially in some of the *Kino-Pravdas*, *Stride, Soviet*, and *Three Songs of Lenin*. Indeed, I believe this backdrop kept hanging there, in the back of Vertov's mind, for the rest of his life.

---

180 *KE*, 278; translation altered here in accord with *DO*, 46–47. Along with the "resurrection" theme, the source of the *KE* translation (*SDZ*, 271–74) completely removes the "love triangle" theme as well as the obviously traumatized Mikhail's remark about trying to forget the past by burying himself in work. On the trope of the "striding giant" proletarian in early Soviet culture, see Steinberg, *Proletarian Imagination*, 112–13.

3. A LURE TO GATHER ANY KIND OF MEETING

> *If we really want to understand the effect the motion picture has on the viewer, then we must first settle two things:*
> *1. which viewer?*
> *2. What effect on the viewer are we talking about?*[181]

More important than these tropes and commemorations, however, would be the oratorical or *meeting* context as such, as a *dispositif* for communication that Vertov would counterpoise to that of cinema. Vertov, as we will see in a moment, was intensively involved in film exhibition on the *October Revolution*, not least as a *bonimenteur* giving direct oral explanations during and after the projections. I will argue here that the frequency with which Vertov incorporates explicit figures for the film-going audience into his mature films, from *Stride, Soviet* through *Lullaby*, can be productively thought about in terms of his work as a film presenter on the agit-trains. Whether through second-person address (as in *One Sixth of the World*), the inclusion of audiences "inside" the films (*One Sixth, Stride, Soviet, Enthusiasm*, preeminently *Man with a Movie Camera*), or a more intent focus on the experience of specific viewers (especially in *Three Songs of Lenin*), Vertov's attention to spectators seems at once to force an awareness of the mediated character of cinematic experience, and (paradoxically) aspires to simulate a well-nigh immediate copresence of audience with film. This concern emerged, I believe, on the trains, although spending time in Abel Kaufman's bookstore-library-reading room might have preconditioned it, to be sure.

In two famous essays published in 1924 and 1925—the second of which, at least, was responding to a rather brusque provocation from Vertov[182]— Sergej Eisenstein both identified the audience as the basic "material" of film practice, and distinguished his own work upon audience from that of Vertov and the kinocs:

> If we regard cinema as a factor for exercising emotional influence over the masses (and even [Vertov's kinocs], who want to remove cinema from the ranks of the arts at all costs, are convinced that it is), we must secure its

---

181 *KE*, 62.
182 See *LR*, 125–26, and the discussion in volume 2.

place in this category and, in our search for ways of building cinema up, we must make widespread use of the experience and the latest achievements in the sphere of those arts that set themselves similar tasks. The first of these is, of course, theater, which is linked to cinema by a common (identical) *basic* material—the *audience*—and by a common purpose—*influencing the audience in the desired direction* through a series of calculated pressures on its psyche.[183]

... the important element—*the direction (the organization of the audience through organized material)* is, in this particular instance of cinema, possible, and not just through the *material* organization of the effective phenomena that are filmed but *optically*, through the actual shooting. Whereas in *theater* the director, in his treatment, recarves the *potential dynamics* (statics) of the dramatist, the actor and the rest into a *socially effective construction*, here in *cinema, by selective treatment*, he recarves *reality* and real phenomena through montage *in the same direction*. This is still *direction* and it has nothing in common with the *passionless representation* of the [kinocs], with the fixing of phenomena that goes no further than *fixing the audience's attention.*

The *[kino-eye]* is not just a symbol *of vision*: it is also a symbol *of contemplation*. But we need *not contemplation but action.*

It is not a *["kino-eye"] that we need but a ["kino-fist"]*.[184]

Eisenstein's criticism of Vertov—one that presages in intriguing ways the pro-realist, anti-montage/collage arguments that Georg Lukács would make in the 1930s[185]—takes the position that Vertov's rejection of art (acting, organized mise-en-scène, and so on) limits the resources that should be available to filmmakers if they are to "influence the audience in a desired direction." Passively relying on unstaged images of "real" things, naively assuming that "unspoiled" spectators (like peasants) react far more forcefully to nonfiction

---

183 Sergej Eisenstein, "The Montage of Film Attractions" [1924], in *The Eisenstein Reader*, ed. Richard Taylor (London: British Film Institute, 1998), 35.
184 "The Problem of the Materialist Approach to Form" [1925], ibid., 53–59; here 57–59.
185 The affinity centers on the question of the supposed inertness and passivity of merely juxtaposed documents, in contrast to carefully fashioned and internally coherent artistic narratives. The key text is "Realism in the Balance," in *Aesthetics and Politics*, ed. Ronald Taylor, trans. Rodney Livingstone, afterword Fredric Jameson (London: Verso, 1997), 28–59. We should not absolutize this distinction between Eisenstein and Vertov, however: as Shklovsky noted, both of them shared a radically negative attitude toward the "art institution" in the early 1920s (*DVVS*, 175, citing *LEF* 3 [1923]: 70).

newsreel than to "the sugary actors of a film-drama,"[186] Vertov precludes from the outset much of what enables cinema to exert "calculated pressures."

Indeed, there can be little doubt that Vertov, judging from his writings and particularly when compared to Eisenstein, spent relatively little time thinking in precise ways about the *cognitive* effects his films would have upon spectators.[187] As we will see, affirmations of the need to (for instance) "['carry'] the film viewer's eyes . . . in the most advantageous sequence . . . into an orderly montage study"[188] are actually very unusual in Vertov's written corpus, are often derivative (in this case, of Kuleshov) and even perfunctory. Where Eisenstein would refer, in his quest to understand and manipulate spectator response, to a host of psychophysiologists from Pavlov and Klages to Bekhterev—the latter scientist was never mentioned, incidentally, by Vertov in any of his writings[189]—Vertov hardly ever draws upon such science and pseudoscience.[190] In 1948, he provided an intriguing gloss to his now well-known line from the early poem "Start," where he announces his wish to

> Give people eyes
> To see a dog
> With
> > Pavlov's
> > > Eye.[191]

This means, writes Vertov, "to see what the ordinary eye doesn't see . . . to penetrate into the mysteries of conditioned reflexes, into the mysteries

---

186 *KE*, 61.
187 This distinction, to which we will return in the next volume, has been a critical motif at least since the late 1960s for those concerned with the two filmmaker-theorists. An early discussion can be found in Gianni Toti, "La 'produttività dei materiali in Ejzenstejn e Dziga Vertov," *Cinema & Film* 3 (Summer 1967): 281–87.
188 *KE*, 16.
189 We should also note that Vertov never began higher medical-scientific training at the Psychoneurological Institute prior to being drafted; nor had Bekhterev's often wildly reductive "collective reflexology" been fully conceptualized in any case. There are, in other words, few grounds for assuming any direct "reflexological" influence on Vertov's work. For a study that dissents from this view, however, and applies Bekhterev to Vertov in remarkably interesting ways, see Ute Holl, *Cinema, Trance and Cybernetics*, trans. Daniel Hendrickson (Amsterdam: Amsterdam University Press, 2017).
190 See David Bordwell, *The Cinema of Eisenstein* (Cambridge, MA: Harvard University Press, 1993), 115–27.
191 "Start (1917)," in *LR*, 35.

of the brain . . . to see the law of gravity in Newton's falling apple."[192] In other words, it refers not to any application of Pavlovian conditioning to film practice, but (yet again) to cinema's scientific vocation, its capacity to give us new knowledge about the world, rather than endlessly propagate reality-clouding narrative fictions.

Yet it seems indisputable that Vertov and Eisenstein agree on a fundamental (if apparently obvious) point: namely, that cinema cannot be thought without taking audiences into account. In Vertov's case, this conviction is far more easily detectable in his films (and in his working notes, as we will see) than in his theoretical writings. As I mentioned in the introduction, it is a minor scandal that, as concerns the two features most often associated with Vertovian filmmaking and film-thinking—the politicized defense of nonfiction against fiction film on the one hand, and a radical demand for self-reflexivity, on the levels of filming, editing, exhibition, and reception, on the other—the latter finds no effective theorization anywhere in his writings (with the partial and feeble exception of his mythologies about the kino-eye's perceptual powers). In no way does this mean, as some crude nominalist historical empiricism might have it, that the problematic of self-reflexivity is therefore irrelevant to Vertov's work; rather, it needs to be pursued largely through the films themselves. My own sense—writing here somewhat preemptively and cursorily about the Vertov-Eisenstein conflict, but also as a way of introducing Vertov's agit-train film work—is that the two filmmakers have different though not unrelated theoretical preoccupations, and assumptions, about audiences. In each case, those assumptions had a crucial double aspect, which we will be able to elaborate in full only in later chapters.

Eisenstein, it seems, maintained throughout his career that audiences were at once bundles of psychophysical resistances *and* endowed with the capacity, if properly stimulated, to dialectically or "ecstatically" transcend those resistances.[193] Think, for instance, of how he conceptualized planes, volumes, and lines as discrete units which, placed in dynamic juxtaposition (or "conflict") with contrastingly oriented planes, volumes, or lines, could generate *through those juxtapositions* powerful cognitive responses (due to the analogy between that formal patterning and "human psychological expression").[194] Eisenstein thought about audiences within the framework of an evolving and increasingly

---

192 *SV*, 451.
193 Bordwell, *The Cinema of Eisenstein*, 190–95.
194 "The Dramaturgy of Film Form" [1929], in *The Eisenstein Reader*, 98.

complex *cognitive-formalist rhetoric* of filmmaking, an effort to understand the relationship between artistic form and cognitive effect.

For his part, Vertov seems to have regarded spectators on the one hand as *objects of perception and knowledge*—that is, as entities to be scrutinized and categorized, not least in class terms, both by the "kino-eye" and by audiences themselves—and on the other as *capacities* or *powers of perceiving and knowing*, always thought of differentially, in relation to the various media-instruments at their disposal (voice, text, cinema, agit-train, "unarmed" human perception, and so on). Again, this binary is thematized above all in the films themselves, not in a theoretical methodology exterior to the films: in all those representations of human subjects (and sometimes non-human objects)—identifiable in terms of class, ethnicity, gender and so on—*being identified*, and identifying in turn; and on the other hand but inseparably, in all those representations and allegories of *looking and being looked at, addressing and being addressed,* through eye, ear, speaker, loudspeaker, earphones, intertitle, newspaper, camera lens, or screen, across varying ratios of time and space.

To be sure, the representations and allegories would be the crucial matter, not the instruments out of which they were built: as we will see, Vertov wanted to make specific films and kinds of films and wanted to be known for those films. More than anything else, this investment in the creation of discrete *works* (not networks) would bind him to the practice of "art," regardless of any later (and temporary) denials. But it is equally clear that Vertov's works-on-film are marked by an unusually acute awareness of the relationship of those works to their physical, social, institutional, and technological conditions of possibility, something that accounts in large part for the attractions he has exerted on media theorists, starting with Soviet writers on television.[195]

Considered on this level, Vertov's practice is also a kind of rhetoric, I believe, but (even) more idiosyncratic than Eisenstein's, and more difficult to name. My awkward and provisional descriptor would be: a *social-technological rhetoric* focused on *media practice*. ("Media practice" is not his term, obviously: my reasons for adopting this anachronism will, I hope, become clear soon enough.) Where Eisenstein takes the salient "resistances"—on which his artistic practice would exert calculated pressure—to be ultimately psychophysical, Vertov finds his various inert givens primarily in the realm of social "reality"

---

195 For but one of numerous examples, see S. Bezklubenko, "V predchustvii televideniia," *Iskusstvo Kino* 12 (December 1970): 86–100.

itself: in discrete representations of identity (class, ethnic, gender, local, etc.) to be sure, but also in dominant practices of social representation, that of mainstream fictional cinema above all. Resistances—that is, those existing conditions in relationship to and against which the revolutionary filmmaker must work—are largely the consequence of social development, and can be undone with the instruments at society's disposal.

If Eisenstein promises to "dialectically" go beyond cognitive resistance through careful work on the visual and aural form taken by the diegesis, Vertov believes that media technology itself, properly deployed, could undo that social inertia and generate the New: by connecting, on an experiential and intellectual level, subjects normally dispersed and alienated; perhaps by altering the circuitry of human perception as such, by finding ways to bring to it the (for Vertov) superhuman perceptual powers of the mediating technology, and specifically of cinema; and most importantly, by exposing the contingent and limited character of fictional conventions relative to what technologies of representation are capable of. Plainly enough, the viewpoints of both filmmakers are subtended by some ideology of progress or transcendence (and of technocracy)—even if, at least in Eisenstein's case, that progress often seems to unfold in immensely slow-moving, Hegelian spirals; Vertov, runner of "cinema races" (*kino-probegi*), is more impatient—and as such must be read not only as rhetorics, but as *allegories* of the revolutionary situation in which they hope to intervene, as we will see later on.

We will return, on somewhat different terms, to the Eisenstein-Vertov debate in the next volume. My point in introducing it here is simply to provide a broader conceptual framework for thinking about Vertov's work with spectators on the agit-train, work that, I hope to show, exerted a powerful and not-unproblematic influence on his later ideas about audience. Most important was the imperative to *categorize* audiences—in terms of the representational schemata of state activists, and derivative of older notions of class, gender, and ethnos—and conversely, the direct encounter with spectators as subjects endowed with their own powers of discernment, and with the cinematic medium's powers of attraction and revelation.

Because relatively little work has been done (in English, at least) on the non-film-related divisions of the agit-trains, it is easy to be led into thinking that film exhibition was what the trains were all about. Judging from the available documents, the Narkompros officials who oversaw the trains were much more concerned with the conditions of local schools than with showing films, and specifically cinema-related papers take up a very small proportion of the agit-train archives.[196] Yet if the trains' Cinema Divisions were not, from what I can tell, ranked among the most important, they were clearly crucial in drawing audiences, often of colossal size, to the trains and their environs. According to one source, an astonishing 2,216,000 people attended 1,962 agit-train screenings over the course of around 659 days in 1919–20.[197] The *October Revolution* alone had shown films to more than 620,000 spectators by the end of 1920,[198] and agit-train reports indicate that individual outdoor screenings often attracted extraordinarily large crowds: two screenings in Ranenburg on June 13, 1919, that attracted a total of 5,300 people, for instance, or another on August 3 in Tambov that drew an incredible 13,000 spectators.[199] Vertov reported that 63,520 people attended the *October Revolution*'s screenings during the eighth journey alone: that is, over a mere twenty-five days (at most: screenings did not take place every day), and organized by just one train.[200] Taking

---

196 Reports by the main political commissars on the *October Revolution* barely mention film; see GARF f. 1252, op. 1, d. 62, ll. 30–34; d. 64, ll. 81–137. Agit-cinema was under the auspices of both VTsIK and the cinema side of Narkompros's Cinema and Photo Division (or *VFKO: Vserossijskij Foto-Kino Otdel*). VFKO at this time was divided into four subsections dealing with filming (of *agitki* and *khronika*), production, distribution-exhibition, and supply (of positive and negative film, equipment, films for distribution, chemicals for developing and so on). The production subsection was comprised of the lab (involved in both editing and the developing and printing of completed films) and filmmaking workshops. Interestingly, the three main forms of mobile cinema—agit-trains and barges, film-carts, and automobiles equipped with film projection equipment [*avto-kino*]—were apparently associated with the production workshops rather than directly with the distribution unit, at least around 1921–22 (RGALI f. 2091, op. 2, f. 386, l. 39). This was possibly because the mobile cinema units usually had cameramen associated with them as well, and thus were considered arms of production rather than (or at least as much as) distribution and exhibition. Although it is sometimes rumored that there were mobile film labs on the agit-trains, I have not found any documentary evidence that this was the case. Photo labs, yes (see RGALI f. 2091, op. 2, d. 386, l. 20), but motion picture film was evidently sent to larger labs in the cities. Nor have I seen proof that the film presenters exhibited any film that had been freshly shot by agit-train cameramen during the course of a given journey.
197 Karpinskij, ed., *Agitparpoezda VTsIK*, 18.
198 Taylor, *Politics of the Soviet Cinema*, 58.
199 GARF f. 1252, op. 1, d. 47, ll. 2, 8.
200 RGALI f. 2091, op. 2, d. 386, l. 19ob. Many more examples could be provided, to be sure; the cinema agitator in charge of statistics for the *October Revolution* indicated that 102,142 people attended 87 screenings between June 13, and August 3, 1919 (GARF f. 1252, op. 1, d. 47, l. 46ob).

into account the likelihood of sheer statistical exaggeration—although it may also be that the cinema activists included as "spectators" all those who momentarily passed by the outdoor cinema shows on their way to some other meeting or spectacle (the *plein air* "seating arrangements" were not the rationalized and countable ones of contemporary movie theaters, of course)—it remains clear that the numbers of people encountering the screenings were enormous.

Other evidence of a more qualitative character testifies to the appeal of the agit-screenings as well, if not to their long-term effects. In a report of March 3, 1920, Vertov wrote of the "astonishment" experienced by a group of 100 mainly peasant children of five to ten years of age "who found themselves in the cinema for the first time" (the biggest hit was, as usual, Starevich's *The Grasshopper and the Ant* [1911]).[201] His report on the *October Revolution*'s eighth journey strongly affirmed the superiority of film as an agitational tool:

> The films shown, in spite of their wretchedness, had a more vivid and convincing impact upon the broad masses than the speeches of orators. . . . An illuminated screen, set up outside the train, is a lure around which one can get any kind of meeting to gather.[202]

Mobile cinema was evidently so popular that groups with access to equipment and films sometimes (though no doubt rarely) established their own units. In September 1921, the party cell of the Iakov Sverdlov Armored Car Detachment requested that the detachment's projector and other film-related items be returned to it, after having been requisitioned, apparently without sanction, by Glavpolitprosvet (the Central Committee of the Republic for Political Education: Narkompros's main agitation-propaganda section from 1920 to 1930) and passed on to the *October Revolution*'s cinema unit. It turns out that the detachment had created its own agit-train, complete with film exhibition capability, which was sent to the Donbas area on orders of the Revolutionary Military Soviet to work among soldiers; the detachment wanted that equipment back now that space had been set aside in the larger battalion quarters for "exhibition of films," where "the battalion's Cinema Club will be set up."[203]

---

201 GARF f. 1252, op. 1, d. 64, l. 145.
202 RGALI f. 2091, op. 2, d. 386, l. 19ob.
203 GARF f. 2313, op. 2, d. 151, l. 94; letter of September 12, 1921 to the film section of PUR RVSR. *Kino-Nedelia* 23 depicts a Red Army unit in Gzhatsk with its own film theater

Image 11: Exterior of the cinema car of the *October Revolution*. The legend above the entrance reads "THEATER OF THE PEOPLE." The texts on either side of the door read (on the left) "Before, the doors of the theater were closed to the people," and (on the right) "The sun of the Soviet Republic illuminates the path to truth, knowledge and justice [*pravda*]. The one with knowledge will be victorious." Source: Tolstoj, ed., *Agitmassovoe iskusstvo Sovetskoj Rossii*, 122.

The screenings themselves took place either onboard the train's cinema-wagon, which could hold around 250 people; outdoors if weather permitted; or in local theaters. The larger audiences were certainly those at outdoor séances or in the theaters, although Vertov, already fluent in Sovietese, noted that theater owners resented having their establishments used for free screenings, "having become accustomed, under [General] Denikin [i.e., under White occupation], to making a fortune with bourgeois film programs."[204] Inside the *October Revolution*'s cinema car and in theaters, films were generally projected

---

(*Dawn*), showing what looks to be a most unrevolutionary film called *The Mother-in-Law*. Jurisdiction over the army's cinema units had passed over to Narkompros on January 11, 1921 (*LRK* 1, 332.).

204 RGALI f. 2091, op. 2, d. 386, l. 19; from the report to Grigorij Lemberg, which dates to around April 1920. Vertov indicates that they showed film in local theaters in Kursk, Belgorod, Gorlivka, and Rostov during March 1920 (GARF f. 1252, op. 1, d. 64, ll. 146–149, 152, 154, 157). Theaters, especially those outside the "center," had by no means been nationalized by this point, and it is not clear that the VTsIK trains requisitioned theaters with armed force, or indeed were capable of doing so; perhaps some kind of nominal fee was given to the theater owners for renting their premises, although given the

with accompaniment from either a piano or a gramophone record player; outdoors, they were shown without music, although Vertov considered organizing "contests of potential [local] musicians" to provide outdoors accompaniment as well.[205] The gramophones were also used during intermissions to play the speeches of Lenin and Trotsky and recitations of the verses of Demian Bednyj and others, recordings which "became tiresome to listeners when played one after another," according to Vertov, who requested a better selection of records.

The film presenters were to offer oral explanations and commentary, though it is far from clear that all of them did so, or at what point during the screening (before, during, after, all three) the commentary was provided, or that film presenters were given any sort of script to follow (as they were later on, for instance, during the First Five-Year Plan period when conducting film agitation among Young Pioneers or collectivized peasants).[206] Judging from the extant daily film registers that I have seen, Vertov was more loquacious than the average presenter during the screenings, and took pride in his role as on-site explicator:

> I had to provide explanations of the films for nearly every audience. Most of the films were made crudely and carelessly, and an average viewer seeing them for the first time cannot understand them completely. Solving the riddles with my glosses made the films understandable even to the nearly illiterate.[207]

Of the four major (and interconnected) reasons for providing oral explanations of the films—the need to control message, the unfamiliarity of at least many of the spectators with cinema, deficiencies in the construction of the films themselves, and technical issues—it is not clear which would have been the most important at a given screening, although control of message was certainly the rationale for the explanations in the first place. When Vertov writes of the films' "wretchedness" (*ubogost'*), it is hard to tell if he is referring to their badness *as* films or to the quality of the prints; and although Vertov put in requests not only for "more agit-films" but for projector and curtain repair, permanent screens, and coating the interior of the cinema car with dark paint,[208] the *October*

---

context, the possibility of coercion was surely always on the horizon. Theaters were used for meetings without film exhibition as well (GARF f. 1252 op. 1, d. 64, l. 352).
205 RGALI f. 2091, op. 2, d. 386, l. 20.
206 See *Kino v pionerskom lagere* (Moscow: Soiuzkino, 1931); *Kino — v pomoshch' vesennemu sevu* (Moscow: Soiuzkino, 1931), esp. 30–40; *Kino v pomoshch' vypolneniiu programmy tret'ego goda Piatiletki* (Moscow: Soiuzkino, 1930), esp. 34ff.
207 RGALI f. 2091, op. 2, d. 386, l. 19ob (from report to Grigorij Lemberg).
208 RGALI f. 2091, op. 2, d. 386, l. 20 (request of April 9, 1920).

Revolution's cinema section does not seem to have been plagued by technical issues the way other mobile cinemas were:

> A film projector was sent to a village in Ingushetia [in the North Caucasus]. Gathered there were not only all the men young and old, but all the women of the village, in a huge break with tradition... the women stood there, touchingly, for five hours, never dropping their eyes from the white screen, across which spots were swimming murkily. You couldn't make anything out...[209]

In any case, it was the situation (or mise-en-scène, if you will) of oral narration-plus-cinema that would remain important for Vertov, as he went on to speculate, on paper and in film, about the relationship between verbal and visual "messages," the extent to which cinema required verbal supplements, and (conversely) the capacity of cinema to replicate the intensity and immediacy of the agit-train setting.

As far as the films themselves go—a small number of them have survived—the film presenters divided them into three categories: Soviet themes (*Their Eyes were Opened, Glory to the Strong, Deserters* [all short fictional agitation films, or *agitkas*],[210] *The Victory of May, Holiday of Communist Youth, Labor Commune, The Exposure of the Relics of Tikhon of Zadonsk, The Brain of Soviet Russia, Anniversary of the Revolution*, installments of *Kino-Nedelia*); children's films (especially, as I have mentioned, the famous Starevich animation *The Grasshopper and the Ant*); and scientific-educational films (*Birds' Nests, Life in Canada, A Dairy Farm in the Alps, On the Bottom of the Sea*). A small number of agitational films (one entitled *For the Red Banner*, for instance) were occasionally shown to children as well as adults, and Narkompros ordered that at least one "revolutionary" film be shown to each adult audience.[211] Vertov had about twenty films at his disposal on the

---

209 GARF f. 2313, op. 2, d. 131, l. 6; from a report on agit-cinema from mid-1920. A version of this report appeared in *Pravda* as well (A. Serafimovich, "Milliony v prorvu," *Pravda* 191 [August 31, 1920]: 1).

210 On the *agitka* productions, see Taylor, *Politics of the Soviet Cinema*, 48–58; Listov, *Rossiia, revoliutsiia, kinematograf*, 113–18.

211 RGALI f. 2091, op. 2, f. 386, l. 26 (which explicitly distinguishes the three categories, though without naming them); GARF f. 1252, op. 1, d. 7, ll. 20–30; d. 62, ll. 145–62; RGALI f. 2091, op. 2, f. 386, l. 19. I give the titles of only some of the films here. Levitskij mentions showing *Brain of Soviet Russia* on the trains (*Rasskazy o kinematografe*, 204).

October Revolution in March—including five in whose making he had participated (*Kino-Nedelias* 40 through 42, *Brain of Soviet Russia*, and *Anniversary of the Revolution*)—and presumably this was a typical size for an agit-train film arsenal.

These film categories corresponded in rough to categorizations of audience that film presenters included on each of their daily reports, particularly the distinction between children and adults, and between the most "revolutionary" elements (especially soldiers) and the rest:

October Revolution train, journey no. ____

Cinema questionnaire no. ____

[Date] 1920

Daily register

1. Place where train stopped
2. Where did the screenings take place
3. How many screenings
4. Which films were shown at each screening
5. Approximately how many spectators attended each screening
6. Make-up [*sostav*] of the audience
7. Who provided explanations of the films
8. What impression did the films make on the spectators, and how was it expressed
9. Which film or films did the audience like the most
    Cinema Head:[signature][212]

It is clear that determining the "make-up of the audience" was one of the cinema unit's most urgent tasks, although they were presumably aided in this by other activists and by local Communist organizers. In his report on film exhibition during the eighth journey, Vertov began not with what was shown or with attendance figures, but with a list of the various categories of spectator to whom films were exhibited: specifically, passing echelons of Red Army soldiers, railroad workers, workers in nearby factories, peasants from the area, children who were invited onboard the cinema car after discussion with the "local organizations," and local Communist workers.[213]

---

212 GARF f. 1252, op. 1, d. 63, ll. 145–60. The forms filled out by Olga Toom (GARF f. 1252, op. 1, d. 47, ll. 20–30) were only slightly different.
213 RGALI f. 2091, op. 2, d. 386, l. 19.

His reports on audience reaction, therefore, need to be considered in light of *who* (in the estimation of Vertov and other activists) is reacting, or which specific mix of constituencies:

> Kursk, March 4, 1920, Red Army soldiers: "Clearly expressed understanding of the films shown; witty and precise commentary by spectators."
>
> Belgorod, March 6, 1920, Red Army soldiers, local residents, peasants, children: "General interest in the films, conflicting remarks directed toward Soviet Power during the screening of *Brain of Soviet Russia, Glory to the Strong* and *The Day of Communist Youth*."
>
> Slaviansk, March 11, 1920, audience of railroad workers, students in the railway school, Red Army soldiers: "Ardent thanks, lengthy shouting of 'hurray!' and singing 'The International.'"
>
> Nikitovka, March 12, 1920, audience of children: "I note the orderliness and good organization of the children's groups...."[214]

What Vertov is engaged with here is certainly *surveillance* as historian Peter Holquist has conceptualized the term: not merely "the collection of information," but "an instrumental endeavor, aimed at reshaping society and transforming every individual in it."[215] In the case of the agit-trains, it would seem that the fundamental tool of "transformation" is the act of categorizing as such, the determination of a given audience's (or polity's) salient units. We will see that Vertov later carried out a good deal of preproduction surveillance of his own subjects as well, most notably of the various women who appear so prominently in *Man with a Movie Camera*.

However, as regards the important question of whether these categorizations were interestingly reflected in different programming for different audiences—especially for adult peasant audiences—at this early date in the history of Soviet cinema, I lack sufficient data to provide an answer. Children, of course, watched mainly "children's films," adults more serious and "revolutionary" works, although grownups sometimes got to see the Starevich animations as well; but these differentiations are too obvious to be interesting.

---

214 Quoted from GARF f. 1252, op. 1, d. 64, ll. 146, 148, 150, 151.
215 Peter Holquist, "'Information is the Alpha and Omega of Our Work': Bolshevik Surveillance in its Pan-European Context," *Journal of Modern History* 69, no. 3 (September 1997): 448–49. Holquist's superb essay discusses primarily the 1914–21 period, while considering the later persistence of and rationale behind surveillance practices in the Soviet Union and elsewhere.

The small number of prints carried on the agit-trains would have limited programming variety, to be sure, although the Soviet drive to socially engineer the population did lead to more specific targeting of segments of the film-going population: by 1926, no less important a body than the party's Central Committee was formulating parameters for "films for the village," stipulating that they should be (among other things) "short, with uncomplicated montage and an uncomplicated narrative."[216]

It is worth noting, however, that Vertov's summary report about the journey as a whole (probably dating from April 1920) offers a distillation of what were clearly more diverse descriptions of audience make-up set down in the daily registers. The latter included groupings like "peasant children," "local residents," "peasants," "students in the railway school," "children from zemstvo schools," "workers," "children of workers," and "peasant children from the ages of five to 10 with their teachers."[217] The varied metrics used to categorize audiences—age, occupation, educational status, party membership ("Communist workers"), age-and-class ("children of workers"), simple locality ("local residents"), and categories hovering between "class" and older "estate" identities ("peasant")—suggest that the process of discerning the make-up of audiences involved an initial perceptual and ideological grappling with a mass whose internal differentiations were not apparent: rather like the "editing during observation" that Vertov would later incorporate into kino-eye methodology. Categorization, the imposition of order, implies initial uncertainty, even disorientation, and it could not have been immediately clear to Vertov and other activists *who* was coming to see the films, or what their seeing amounted to.

Most strikingly, Vertov's daily registers contain far more detailed comments on audience reaction than any others that I have seen. Indeed, many film presenters wrote nothing about reactions at all, although audience "make-up" was always indicated. Even if Vertov's summaries concern mood ("noisy excitement," "general elation," "continuous cheering") more than critical, verbal response (e.g., "conflicting remarks directed toward Soviet Power"), and stress positive mood at that, his unusual preoccupation with response, and sheer intensity of response, stands out among the mass of other reports and registers.

---

216   RGALI f. 2091, op. 2, d. 271, l. 132. This statement evidently appeared in the journal *Sovetskij Ekran* on April 26, 1926.
217   GARF f. 1252, op. 1, d. 64, ll. 145–61.

As is well known, Vertov eventually applied what he called his "observations" of audience response on the agit-trains[218] to his larger defense of nonfiction film practice:

> 1920.
> I'm in charge of a cinema-train car. We're showing films at a remote station.
> There's a film-drama on the screen. The Whites and the Reds. The Whites drink, dance, kiss half-naked women; during the interludes they shoot Red prisoners. The Reds underground. The Reds at the front. The Reds fighting. The Reds win and put all the drunken Whites and their women in prison.[219]
> The content's good, but why should anyone want to show film-dramas based on the same old cliché used five years ago?
> The viewers—illiterate and uneducated peasants—don't read the titles. They can't grasp the plot. They examine individual details, like the drawings on the decorated train.[220]
> Coolness and distrust....
> A real tractor, which these viewers know of only from hearsay, has plowed over a few acres in a matter of minutes, before their very eyes. Conversations, shouts, questions. There's no question of actors. On the screen are their own kind, real people. There isn't a single false, theatrical movement to unmask the screen, to shake the peasants' confidence.
> This sharp division between the perception of film-drama and newsreel has been noted every place where film has been shown for the first, second, or third time—every place where the poison had not yet penetrated, where the addiction to the toxic sweetness of artistic drama and its kisses, sighs and murders had not yet set in.[221]

Vertov's insistence on the "sharp division between the perception of film-drama and newsreel" among unspoiled spectators can be regarded as largely

---

218 "To the Kinocs of the South" (1925), in KE, 51.
219 A reference to an *agitka*, whose title I have not been able to determine. It may well be a composite of several: see SV, 498.
220 Earlier in the passage, Vertov discusses the peasants' amusement at the ill-shodden horses represented in the agit-train murals, and claimed that the peasants referred to them as "actors" (dialectally inflected as "akhtery" in the original Russian [SV, 70]).
221 "Kino-Eye" (1926) in KE, 61. The essay was clearly composed at least in part of bits and pieces written earlier than 1926 (SV, 498).

ideological and certainly as unsubstantiated, even by his own daily agit-train reports. Anyone familiar with Russian reflections on art and education will immediately note the affinities between Vertov's remarks here and Leo Tolstoy's well-known pronouncements on peasant intolerance of artificiality and pretension, and the well-nigh natural capacity of untutored country folk to discern the authentic, the healthy and the lasting in works of art; Vertov's ideas, in this respect, are far more Tolstoyan than Leninist.[222] This cinematic Tolstoyism, if we can call it that, seems to share a certain amount with the doctrines and attitudes of the Constructivist-factographic avant-garde, surprisingly enough: in particular an intolerance of representational cliché and convention; a certain utilitarianism; a realism paradoxically charged with suspicions regarding mimesis; and a focus on "individual detail," on the material and on the *construction* of the image. (The enthusiasm for tractors is less Tolstoyan.)

Moving photography emerges as a kind of fulfillment of humankind's primordial perceptual capacities, rather than their replacement or supersession; indeed, we might take the passage as evidence of what Balibar has called the "extreme tension" in "the ideology of Soviet Communism" between antimodernity and "ultra-modernity," antitheses that often and strangely coexist, as we will see.[223] What is crucial in relation to the agit-train experience, however, is Vertov's ascription—however ideological its motivations may be—of discernment rather than limitation to peasant viewers. It is an acknowledgement of their power as spectators, rather than of the way they lag behind more "modern"

---

222 See, among many other texts, Tolstoy's 1862 essay "Who Should Teach Whom to Write, We the Peasant Children or the Peasant Children Us?"; and the 1896 *What Is Art?* I briefly suggested in chapter 1 that the vegetarian and teetotaler Abel Kaufman might have been a Tolstoyan; a deeper Tolstoy-Vertov linkage (on the level of thought about audience and representation) would be worth pursuing, though it will not be developed in these pages. A recent film that I have yet to see, scripted by Viktor Listov, does explore the connection (*Lev Tolstoj i Dziga Vertov: dvojnoj portret v inter'ere epokhi* [2016], directed by Galina and Anna Evtushenko) and sounds fascinating based on the descriptions I have read. For evidence regarding Tolstoy's enthusiasm for film, see Feldman, *Evolution of Style*, 16–17.

223 "The most interesting thing [in regard to 'the ideology of Soviet Communism and "real socialism"'] would be to analyze the extreme tension running through this ideology (which to a large degree doubtless explains its attraction), between a project of resistance to capitalist modernization (if not indeed of a *return* to the communal modes of life that modernization destroys), and a project of *ultra-modernity*, or of the supersession of modernity by a 'leap forward' into the future of humanity (not just 'electrification plus soviets,' as Lenin's slogan of 1920 had it, but the utopia of the 'new man' and the exploration of the cosmos)" (Balibar, *The Philosophy of Marx*, 87).

subjects, even if, dialectically, it ends up categorizing them in another manner: that is, as well-nigh "naturally" repulsed by fictions, and accordingly drawn to "unplayed" film.

The other significant perceptual capacity at play during the agit-train screenings—that of cinema itself—is most clearly revealed in a kind of film shown on the trains that seems to thematize cinema's powers of revelation more or less directly. I have in mind the propaganda subgenre of "exposure-of-saints'-relics" films that were made during the Civil War period, depicting how the remains of saints—which were not subject to decay, according to Orthodox lore[224]—were removed from the arks containing them and exposed, as fully decayed, to surrounding spectators and to the movie camera. At least sixty-five such exposures occurred between October 23, 1918, and December 1, 1920, and at least three of them were filmed.[225] The one "exposure" film that was definitely shown frequently on the agit-trains was the earliest, *Exposure of the Relics of Tikhon of Zadonsk* (filmed by Petr Novitskij on January 28, 1919),[226] much of which consists of one shot depicting the chairman of the Zadonsk Cheka, watched by (according to an intertitle) "members of the Cheka, the

---

224 On the Orthodox deification of the remains of deceased saints—a more complex matter than the Bolsheviks imagined—see Scott M. Kenworthy, *The Heart of Russia: Trinity-Sergius, Monasticism, and Society after 1825* (New York: Oxford University Press, 2010), 196.

225 *Exposure of the Relics of Tikhon of Zadonsk* (1919; RGAKFD 416); *Exposure of the Relics of Sergius of Radonezh* (1919; RGAKFD 423); and the lost *Exposure of the Relics of Mikhail of Tver'*. (In an undated document, probably from the first half of May 1919, Vertov indicates that ninety-three meters on the theme "Exposure of the Relics of Mikhail of Tver'" were shot but not used [RGALI f. 2091, op. 2, d. 381, l. 9]; they seem to have been released at some later point.) Although *Exposure of the Relics of Aleksandr Nevskij* (RGAKFD 12717) and *Exposure of Relics in the Aleksandr-Nevskij Lavra* (RGAKFD 26) evidently date from 1921, they make reference to an earlier opening of Nevskij's elaborate silver ark on July 24, 1917, when clergy at the monastery decided that it might be best, during that time of military and political crisis, to move the ark elsewhere and transfer the relics to a wooden container. The 1921 films propose to verify the results of that 1917 exposure, carried out by churchmen, and are thus perhaps better termed "re-exposure" films. A few more were made during the antireligious campaigns of 1929–30. My historical information on the exposures comes from Jennifer Jean Wynot, *Keeping the Faith: Russian Orthodox Monasticism in the Soviet Union, 1917–1939* (College Station, TX: Texas A&M University Press, 2004); 47; Robert H. Greene, *Bodies Like Bright Stars: Saints and Relics in Orthodox Russia* (De Kalb: Northern Illinois University Press, 2010), 122–59; Kenworthy, *The Heart of Russia*; Listov, *Istoriia smotrit v ob'ektiv*, 188–99; Listov, *Rossiia, revoliutsiia, kinematograf*, 105–6.

226 Greene, *Bodies Like Bright Stars*, 153. This film was also shown with great success in Budapest on June 19, 1919, during the Bela Kun period (*LRK* 1, 295).

[local] Executive Committee, doctors . . . Archimandrite Aleksandr, Father Innokentij, the brotherhood of monks, parishioners and Red Army soldiers of Zadonsk," as he unwraps Tikhon's remains and demonstrates the findings to those assembled and to the camera. The discoveries are recounted in a series of intertitles that preserve a dispassionate tone:

> Let us go on to expose what was beneath the clothing... The bones of the chest cavity and backbone had been replaced by an iron carcass, beneath which, in a pile of wadding and rags, they found a handful of decayed bones.
>
> In the wadding were discovered fragments of shinbone which had disintegrated into powder.
>
> Through what was no more than an opening cut into a glove, devotees had been kissing [wadding] wrapped in flesh-colored cardboard.

The version I have seen concludes with an ironic citation from the Holy Synod's *Anniversary Collection on Tikhon of Zadonsk*—

> "The body of St. Tikhon, notwithstanding its 78-year stay in the ground, was preserved without decaying thanks to the benefaction of God."

—and adds that this quote appeared in the *Collection*'s twentieth edition, "published by the Most Holy Synod in 1911 ... on page 27," thus contributing to the "scientific" demeanor of the entire presentation.[227]

The film incorporates a couple of shots of crowds gathered in the monastery square, presumably during or in anticipation of the exposure. They are filmed with backs turned to the camera, imparting a sense of the intensity with which those witnesses were awaiting the results of the procedure. A penultimate image of a skull, with eye, nose and mouth cavities stuffed with cotton wadding, is matched by a final image of a largely expressionless

---

[227] The film I have seen is somewhat illogically arranged, with material introducing the city of Zadonsk and the main protagonists appearing at the film's midpoint; there is, however, no original montage list with which to compare it. *Exposure of the Relics of Aleksandr Nevskij* (RGAKFD 12717) strongly emphasizes the presence of experts (medical, cultural, religious, juridical, historical) at the exposure, and incorporates still more documentary citation, including an image of a handwritten official church statement about the relics, apparently from 1917.

crowd, apparently reacting in some hard-to-read way to the exposure. In fact, "general," uninvited audiences were almost certainly not present at the exposure, though they did file past the unsealed remains, usually kept inside a church or chapel, in the days following. It is difficult not to take these images of audience as figures for those watching and responding to the *Tikhon of Zadonsk* film itself, and specifically to the way that moving photography corroborates, preserves, and propagates the exposure's anti-theatrical lesson: what were thought to be timeless remains are revealed by cinema to be but clothed wadding, carapace, and "flesh-colored cardboard" on top of bones.

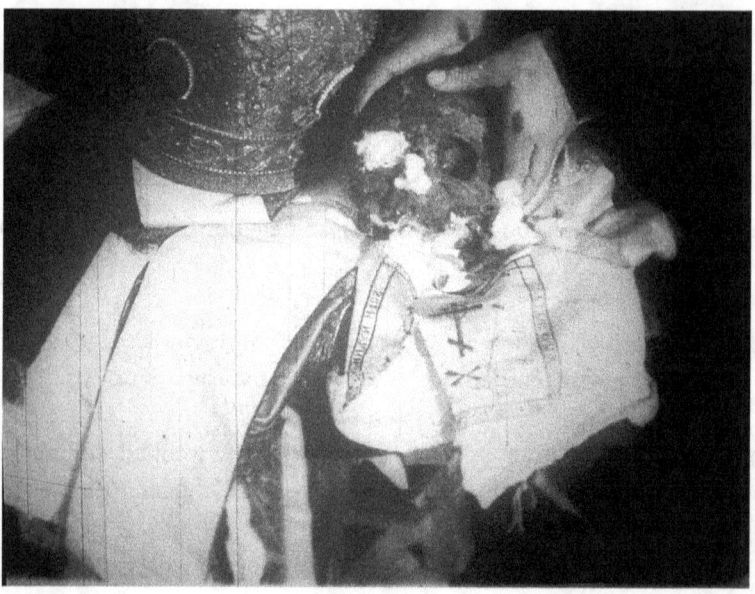

Image 12: From *Exposure of the Relics of Tikhon of Zadonsk*. Source: RGAKFD 416.

The Exposure of the Relics of Sergius of Radonezh—in whose production Vertov was controversially involved, as we will see in a moment—presents an unsealing carried out on April 11, 1919, at the Trinity-Sergius Lavra, most famous of all Russian Orthodox monasteries, and adopts a more tendentious manner from the outset. After providing a view of the town of Sergiev (later Zagorsk, today Sergiev Posad)—"built on a lie," an intertitle informs us—and of stock footage of a religious procession, the film depicts a huge crowd outside the Trinity Cathedral, waiting to see the results of the exposure. After members of the local Executive Committee and other representatives arrive,

Archimandrite Ioann is shown, filmed from the top or head-end of the coffin, meticulously unwrapping the body of the saint, until "Doctor Popov" steps in to examine the entirely unsealed remains. The film concludes more polemically than does *Tikhon*:

> Swindling the wretched, poor and ignorant people out of their last hard-earned cent, for five hundred years the priests and monks nasally intoned: "And here as the sun rose, your good remains were found to be imperishable..."—above this heap of decayed rags, dirt, dead moths and traces of bone.[228]

Throughout the brief film, shots of the exposure are intercut with images of the crowd outside the church—again, presumably "looking on" but in fact not actually observing the procedure.[229] The film's image track culminates with a view of Sergius's exposed skull, followed by a "reaction shot" of the crowd of mostly female faces, gazing in uniformly frontal if oddly varied directions, and a final image of the "decayed rags... traces of bone" and so on referred to in the intertitle.

The films and photographs of the exposures were shown widely and free of charge in cities and towns in Central Russia, and (on the agit-trains) beyond as well, especially from 1919–21. The *Sergius* film was readied in time for an Easter week screening in Moscow in 1919, as requested by Lenin, and "souvenir postcards with pictures of the exhumed saint" were sold in theater lobbies.[230]

Fundamentally, of course, these films are displays of power—specifically, of the capacity and willingness of the regime to carry out the desecrations, and of cinema's ability to capture and disseminate "truth"—and of powerlessness, insofar as the theatrics of religion prove incapable of preserving anything. (We can only wonder, too, what *personal* resonances the exposure films had for Vertov, familiar as he surely was with the anti-Semitic cult of Gavriil's imperishable relics back in Bialystok.)[231] It is worth recalling, in this connection, the popular

---

228 Similar denunciations of clerical deception appear in a couple of places in *Exposure of the Relics of Aleksandr Nevskij* (RGAKFD 12717).
229 The authorities brought in a few clergy and some local peasants (who had not been informed of what was about to take place) to witness the actual exposure (Kenworthy, *The Heart of Russia*, 315).
230 Greene, *Bodies Like Bright Stars*, 154. Antireligious museums continued to display the films and photos of the exposures after the Civil War had ended.
231 See chapter 1. It should be noted that even some Bolshevik agencies expressed opposition to the exposures. The Narkompros Department of Museum of Affairs protested the unsealing of Sergius's remains, complaining that "the impending opening of Saint

Images 13–14: From *Exposure of the Relics of Sergius of Radonezh* (1919). Source: RGAKFD 423.

atheistic pamphlet published right around this time (1920) by Mikhail Rejsner, Bekhterev's old colleague at the Psychoneurological Institute—entitled *Must we believe in God?*—and its optimistic arguments about film as both a cancellation and fulfillment of religion:

> If one compares what we achieve today with the help of science and technology with the miracles [wrought by] some old gods or other, then it turns out that we have long since surpassed all these creators and makers and their powers. The briefest overview of our achievements will provide sufficient proof to show who is stronger now, the new human being, or the old God. . . . And if it's necessary, to prove the power of humanity, to call up the dead from their graves—to make them speak and to display them to our sight as though alive—then that, too, has been achieved. On the gramophone record, human speech is recorded for an eternity. A reflection of our lives is laid upon cinematic film. And it is only a matter of placing the images of those long silent and forgotten into an electrical machine, and they will rise before us as though alive, speaking to us again in their authentic voice and language. It's not necessary now to turn to the prophetess or the sorcerer; there's no need to pray to God. We ourselves resurrect the dead for our eyes and ears.[232]

Rejsner's rhetoric was not unique: a Glavpolitprosvet project for setting up an agitational steamboat in the Volga region in 1921 underscored the need to maintain a photographic lab on the boat in order to demonstrate "the miracle of photography" in a struggle against those "other miracles" that commanded the faith of people in "the most backwards areas." Photos, the project suggested, would show peasants the ability of image technology to capture large swathes of the past, including images of the village, of village families, speeches by orators, and the boat's own journeys.[233]

Sergius's relics caused such anxiety in Sergiev Posad that it was interfering with the work of the Commission for the Preservation of the Lavra in restoration and study" (Kenworthy, *The Heart of Russia*, 314).

232 M. Rejsner, *Nuzhno li nam verit'v Boga*, 77–79.
233 GARF f. 2313, op. 2, d. 130, l. 2. Nor were such notions exclusively Russian by any means: see Joseph Landau's "Mechanized Immortality" (1912) in Kaes et al., eds., "The Cinematographic Archive," *October* 148 (Spring 2014): 33–35.

At the same time, the great effort taken to arrange, carry out, and film the unsealings, at considerable expense and during a time of war, suggests that *anxiety* about the power of religious-theatrical deception also motivated the exposure wave: would these disguises, which had retained their hold over the popular imagination for so long, not continue to do so? The test, of course, would be the actual response of audiences to the exposures; but how was that to be measured, and (still more importantly for us) registered silently on film? Not surprisingly, perhaps, the exposures seem to have generated ambiguous effects, beyond the unrest that accompanied many of the actual procedures (at Trinity-Sergius, for example).[234] Sources indicate responses ranging from "instantaneous conversion" to atheism to a "religious upsurge," although the absence of disinterested reportage on the events makes evaluation almost impossible.[235] Cinema's value as a token of humankind's superior "strength," to use Rejsner's vocabulary, nevertheless needed to be underwritten by spectators: thus, the careful suturing-together in the *Sergius* film of evidence of the saint's bodily decay with the crowd's response of . . . dismay? Sadness? Shock? Perplexity? Fear? (Even boredom?) Of course, that penultimate image of the crowd is no document of immediate "response" to the sight of the relics in any case, but rather a constructed "reaction shot" taken from material filmed that day and incorporated into a rhetorical structure: indeed, the image might well register response to the camera, rather than to the exposure.

It becomes important to recall, at this point, that both Vertov and Lev Kuleshov claimed to have made the *Sergius* film. Clearly, both were involved in some way with its making, although the exact proportions of their respective contributions will probably never be known.[236] It was around this time

---

234 Wynot, *Keeping the Faith*, 46. Sovnarkom acknowledged that numerous priests and monks were killed during the exposure wave (ibid., 47).
235 Greene, *Bodies Like Bright Stars*, 159; Kenworthy, *The Heart of Russia*, 318.
236 My own conjecture is that Vertov was primarily involved with the film in a supervisory capacity, with Kuleshov mainly handling the shooting and the montage. Vladimir Gardin gave Vertov authority over the shooting in Trinity-Sergius on April 10, 1919, assigning Kuleshov and cameramen Eduard Tisse and Sergej Petrovich Zabazlaev among others to work with him (Listov, *Istoriia smotrit v ob'ektiv*, 194; "Molodost' mastera," in *DVVS*, 92). Kuleshov later claimed, however, that several of the assigned cameramen feared violence and did not show up, something confirmed by Gardin in his memoirs (V. R. Gardin, *Vospominaniia*, vol. 1 [Moscow: Goskinoizdat, 1949], 173–74), although Gardin indicates that Grigorij Giber was the reluctant operator. In the end, according to Kuleshov, Zabazlaev shot the film under Kuleshov's direction (Gardin claimed that it was Petr Novitskij). Kuleshov explicitly denied that Vertov—at that very

(probably in 1920–21) that Kuleshov conducted his famous experiments with associative montage—which demonstrated how a single, emotionally neutral shot of the face of actor Ivan Mozzhukhin was interpreted by spectators as expressing grief, sexual desire, or hunger when juxtaposed with (respectively) a shot of a corpse, a woman, or a bowl of soup—and it is hard to avoid reading the intercutting of that crowd at Trinity-Sergius with the relics as another, unsung (but perhaps the earliest?) instance of the "Kuleshov Effect," regardless of whether Kuleshov or Vertov was responsible for it.[237] Not a single face, but a multitude of faces, whose juxtaposition with the relics seems to fuse their expressions into a single attitude of stunned disappointment: or does it?

Why was the shot of the crowd included in any case? To begin with, it affirms quite simply that the exposed relics were *seen*, then and there (or then- and thereabouts). Exposure for the "camera eye" alone would be insufficient, insofar as the real event sought out—or staged—by the authorities was not mere unwrapping of dust and rags, but an analogous reduction of religious belief to dust and rags, predicated on the notion that the sight of

---

moment engaged in the restoration of *Kino-Nedelia*, as we know—was involved with the filming or editing of *Sergius*, although he was under the false impression that Vertov might have incorporated some part of the film into one of his compilation works. In the mid-1960s, an independent participant in the exposure, one Robin, confirmed the presence of Kuleshov at the event (Kuleshov, *Stat'i. Materialy*, 57–59; E. Gromov, *Lev Vladimirovich Kuleshov* [Moscow: Iskusstvo, 1984], 68–70; Listov, *Istoriia smotrit v ob'ektiv*, 193–96). For his part, Vertov indicates in a list of films under production (dating from early May 1919) that 232 meters of *Sergius* had been printed and were now "being edited" (RGALI f. 2091, op. 2, d. 381, l. 9). He mentions *Sergius* on numerous occasions as one of his early works (*SV*, 218, 242, 267, 375, 421, 455, 460, 463), though never in detail; interestingly, he does not mention it in his 1947 "Artistic Calling Card," his long, detailed though problematic chronology of his career (in Tode and Wurm, *Dziga Vertov*, 81–158). Most Russian film scholars, including Listov and Kuleshov specialist E. Gromov, have maintained that both men were involved in making the film. A fictionalized version of this and some other episodes from Vertov's life appear in Irina Polianskaia's docu-fiction *Chitaiushchaia voda* (Moscow: Grant, 2001), esp. 132–43.

237 For one of the better-known accounts of the experiment, see Vsevolod Pudovkin, "The *Naturshchik* instead of the Actor" [1929], in *Vsevolod Pudovkin: Selected Essays*, ed. Richard Taylor, trans. Richard Taylor and Evgeni Filippov (London: Seagull Books, 2006), 160. For important documents on other early versions of the experiment (dating to 1921), see Yuri Tsivian et al., "The Rediscovery of a Kuleshov Experiment: A Dossier," *Film History* 8, no. 3 (1996): 357–67. Seth Feldman speculates on the Vertov-Kuleshov relationship and on possible uses of the "Effect" in *Kino-Nedelia* in *Evolution of Style*, 34–35, 44.

the saint's intact body had been the material support for that belief. Indeed, the event of *exposure* would not be complete, as the referent of the film, without an audience's regard, even a "constructed" one.

If we go on to assume that the film audience, or at least part of it, was perfectly aware of the construction—given that the exposure itself was clearly filmed in the dark interior of a church, while the crowd is seen outside in the Lavra's square—an intriguing identification effect may have been created here by confronting the film audience with another audience, also temporally (though not geographically) out of sync with the actual exposure, but positioned as "responding" to it within the rhetoric of the film. If we postulate that the audience in the film was *anticipating* the exposure, then it appears that Kuleshov-Vertov are generating a peculiar kind of Hitchcockian suspense-effect as well: the onscreen crowd, filmed in the (then) recent past, would be "reacting" to a sight that they *will* see but which we have *already* seen in the film. Though physically located in Sergiev, and thus tied "indexically" to the day's events, that onscreen audience is also a displaced—that is, cinematic—observer of the exposure.[238]

What this means, additionally, is that both audiences, onscreen and off, are linked by virtue of seeing—entirely figuratively in one case, less so in the other—through the implacable, "objective" gaze of the movie camera. It is far from clear that this can be called an *identification* with the camera. The results of the camera's gaze are presented confrontationally, as a challenge, as though human powers of sight had suddenly and jarringly been supplanted by other, greater ones that made those earlier powers seem like blindness. Importantly, the audience depicted in the film is primarily made up of women—that is, one of the groups most susceptible to the blandishments of mere image, according to age-old iconoclastic prejudice, and whose vision, therefore, is least trustworthy.[239] That this audience literally confronts the

---

238 The narrative of the *Exposure of the Relics of Aleksandr Nevskij* (RGAKFD 12717) mobilizes strategies of suspense more explicitly and ironically: prior to the actual exposure, an intertitle reads, "The last seals and bolts are removed"; we see a shot of the ark, followed by the title "The ark's been opened! / Where are the relics?"; and a shot of the empty ark. Ellipsis marks at the end of intertitle phrases also generate that sense of "what's next."

239 Art historian David Freedberg, discussing the iconoclasm of second–third century Christian author Tertullian, notes how women and the illiterate are regarded by this theology as those most susceptible to idols: "[The glory of material images] is worldly, and they seduce. They attract, directly, like the cruel spectacles of the arena and the

camera rather than the relics can stand as another figure, not for revelation, but for revelation of the power to reveal.

None of this makes any difference unless the audience's "response" is the correct one, of course; and we might well feel reluctant to read a response out of that crowd of faces, although we are certainly prompted (or being trained!) to do so associatively, in order to formulate and affirm our own response. It would seem (though it is not certain) that the crowd is gazing intently, even curiously, and most of the faces bear an expression we might call "anxious concentration," though we might have trouble getting more precise than that, or extracting any sense of their positive or negative evaluation of what is/has been/will be seen. The task of the Kuleshov Effect is to narrow those interpretive choices, by taking inchoate, latent features of the image and activating them in specific ways through carefully chosen juxtapositions: thus, "anxious concentration" on *these* (local women's) faces is to be read as *causally* (and not merely rhetorically) linked to what they now can see—or rather, to what the film audience has seen—and as part of a longer causal chain of observation and reaction that would lead, according to those organizing the exposures, to skepticism.[240]

Applying the skeptical lesson in reverse, we might be tempted to say that Kuleshov-Vertov are *staging* a response, through the as-yet-to-be-named "Effect," in much the same way that the clerics staged Sergius's bodily persistence: one falsifying "montage" replaces another. And I believe that they are indeed doing this, guided by the assumption that 1) audiences like the one depicted in *Sergius* are deeply bound by religious particularity

---

common and cheap appeals of the theater. Their attractiveness, in short, is like that of women—with respect to whom Tertullian naturally proceeds to advise moderation and caution. But who are the people who are seduced by the obviousness of colors and materiality? Not, of course, those for whom God is the Word, not the intellectuals who live in—or aspire to—so spiritual a realm that they do not need the crutch of the senses or material sensuality in general. Rather, it is women themselves, and the large body of ignorant people—the illiterate above all" (David Freedberg, *The Power of Images: Studies in the History and Theory of Response* [Chicago: University of Chicago Press, 1989], 398).

240 Kuleshov evidently felt that this was indeed the response elicited by the unsealings: see Listov, *Istoriia smotrit v ob'ektiv*, 195–96. My reading of the Kuleshov Effect is much influenced by Naum Kleiman's exegesis, summarized in my essay "Montage under Suspicion: Bazin's Russo-Soviet Reception," in *Opening Bazin: Postwar Film Theory and Its Afterlife*, ed. Dudley Andrew and Hervé Jourbert-Laurencin (Oxford: Oxford University Press, 2011), 291–301; esp. 296–97.

(i.e., superstition); and 2) that the representational powers of cinema have the capacity of undoing that inertia even (or perhaps especially) in "simple" spectators like these ones. They are, in other words, staging their own desire, *what they want cinema to be able to do to people they assume to be a certain way.*

However, it is crucial to recall that the Kuleshov Effect, vulgar exegeses of it notwithstanding, in no way posits a human cognition that mechanically links A to B to C to produce the required interpretation, as though tied to a leash. On the contrary, it presupposes a spectator *actively seeking out meaning* within texts that are held, at least provisionally, to be coherent.[241] (No meaning in Mozzhukhin's face would be sought at all, if spectators were not concerned to discover significance using the clues provided within that array of visual signs to which the "face" belongs.) Because the crowd's expression(s) remain unreadable, I would argue that it is with an impression of that *activity*, rather than *any* articulated expression, that we are left with when looking at those faces in *Sergius*. Indeed, the *capacity to perceive* is thematized—for us, if not for Kuleshov-Vertov—at least as much through an exposure of the *limits* of cinema's ability to discern and affix meaning, as it is demonstrated through any confident filmic presentation of "objective evidence," or by artfully linking and articulating disparate images. The crowd is *looking*, like the audience watching *Sergius*, like the camera and cameraman; and all of these looks remain heterogeneous powers, even as they seek to assign a meaning and identity to the looks that surround them.[242] (They would have to possess such powers, needless to say, if they were to construct a new society: a society neither bourgeois nor proletarian, but Communist.)

---

241 See, among other affirmations of this point, Pudovkin, "Proletarskij kinematograf."
242 Cf. Jacques Rancière, *The Ignorant Schoolmaster: Five Lessons in Intellectual Emancipation*, trans. and introduction by Kristin Ross (Stanford: Stanford University Press, 1991), esp. 45–73. For a recent and excellent historical exploration of the "considerable ambiguity" in early Soviet ideology and disciplinary practice concerning "categorical belonging and the agentic autonomy of individuals," see James Ryan, "'They Know Not What They Do?' Bolshevik Understandings of the Agency of Perpetrators, 1918–1930," *Historical Research* 90, no. 247 (February 2017): 151–71.

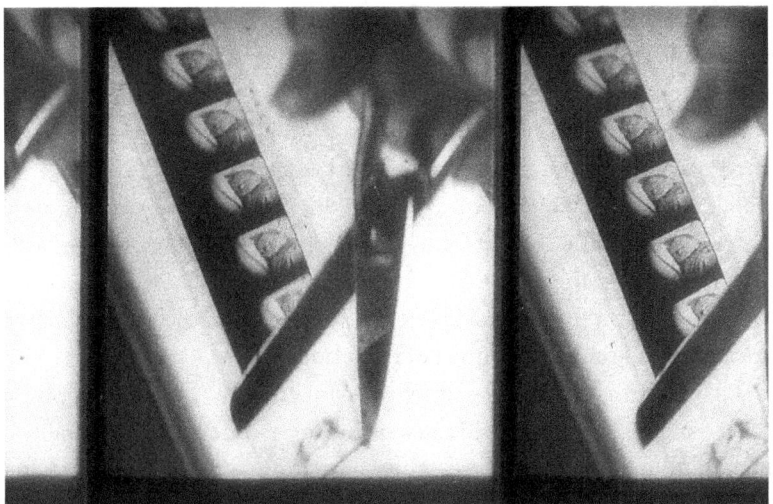

Image 15: Photograms from *Man with a Movie Camera* (1929). Source: Yale University Film Archive.

These motifs will be taken up, over and over again, in Vertov's films and writings, in all that counterpoising of "revelatory" non-acted cinema to the artifice of theater, fiction film, and even the theatricalization of everyday life; in the plentiful demonstrations of the capacity of editing to direct interpretation; and (in *Man with a Movie Camera* above all) in a meticulously dialectical unsealing of the ultimate fetish objects, cinematic images themselves. Just as importantly, Vertov will incorporate countless figurations of individual and collective spectators, as they perceive through the mediation of cameras and projectors, recording and playback devices, newspapers, photographs, or naked eyes and ears. (It may seem strange to designate "naked eyes and ears" as instruments of *mediated* perception, but we will see how Vertovian logic leads to that designation: in the wake of the emergence of technological media, and especially after cinema, no perception can be understood as unmediated. Corneas and cochleas themselves are machines of perception—inadequate ones, as it turns out!)

From the magic show in *Kino-Eye* and the simulated meetings of *Stride, Soviet* to the internalized memorial spectacles of *Three Songs of Lenin* and even the photograph linking the married couple at the center of *To You, Front* (1943), the *idea* (and the trope) of audience with all its affiliated terms—reception, enunciation, response, concentration, and so on—is central to all of Vertov's work (this list of examples could be greatly lengthened). Indeed, sometimes Vertov seems to remake the *Sergius* film, and replicate its ideology, in fairly transparent fashion, as in the scene of the Saami people listening to the phonographic and enlightening "voice of the living Lenin"—once again, a listening created by montage—in *One Sixth of the World*. The persistence of audiences-encountering-otherness in his work may also bear witness to some nostalgia for the immediacy of the agit-train viewing situation, and indeed (as we will speculate in the next volume) to a fear that cinema, by eliminating the possibility of direct interaction between the viewer and the viewed, might be inimical to a truly collective mode of reception.

But what, finally (and as a brief pendant to both this long chapter and the first volume) of the specific juxtaposition of cinema with religion—or rather, of film viewing with religious adoration—in the exposure films? Mikhail Rejsner claimed that cinema was capable of resurrection, implying that the desire for eternal life was a fully legitimate one that Communism would need to fulfill, rather than dismiss with a "secular" pooh-pooh. And although Vertov famously spoke of film as an instrument to be put at the disposal of a demystifying consciousness—

> Stupefaction and suggestion—the art-drama's basic means of influence—relate to that of a religion and enable it for a time to maintain a [person] in an excited unconscious state....
>
> Only consciousness can fight the sway of magic in all its forms.[243]

—he also (on occasion) attributed to it a creative power that might be called demiurgic:

> I am kino-eye. I create a [person] more perfect than Adam...[244]

Six years after Vertov traveled on the *October Revolution*, the witty Aleksandr Kurs would note of Vertov's pet emblem,

> *Kino-Eye* is a little terrifying, and for some reason it reminds you of either a Masonic or a theosophical symbol.[245]

---

243 *KE*, 63, 66.
244 Ibid., 17.
245 Kurs, "Who Will Make Film Newsreel?" [1926], in *LR*, 257.

Surely, the exposure films propose a new authority, and new authoritative images, to replace the old, though whether or not the authority (film plus Communism) and those images are themselves "religious" in some sense depends on what meaning attaches to that adjective. That the authority seems to derive from human praxis rather than anything beyond it—"*We ourselves resurrect the dead for our eyes and ears*"—might seem a distinguishing feature, although we will have the chance later to reflect on the salience of religion more deeply, when we look at Vertov's Lenin iconographies. We might suggest, again preemptively, that Vertov will create not a religion, but a *myth* of cinema, now in philosopher Hans Blumenberg's sense: a device for managing, and even incorporating all those often brutally recalcitrant differences—of geography, of culture, of language, of class, and so on—into a single representational frame that will articulate them all ("a visual bond between the workers of the whole world").[246]

In the meantime, to be sure, the tropes of religion—transcendence and sacrifice above all—will enter Vertov's discourse as they did Kalinin's, and indeed that of early Soviet culture as a whole, partially as a reaction to the hurling-together of disaster with revolutionary triumph that characterized the period.[247] I conclude with this cryptic verse dated October 1, 1921, written by Vertov in the midst of the devastating famine that had begun in the spring of that year, would ultimately take five million lives, and on which Vertov would report in his first *Kino-Pravda* about nine months later:

> Whistle.
> A *khronika* of death.
> Wan
> With leaves.
> A two-step of events.
> Funerals of centuries,
> Primers with yats,[248]

---

246 *KE*, 52. For Blumenberg's conception of myth as a struggle, on the level of representation, with the "absolutism of reality," see his great *Work on Myth*, trans. Robert M. Wallace (Cambridge, MA: MIT Press, 1990), esp. 268–69 (on philosophical Idealism as myth).

247 On sacred language in the early Soviet period, see Steinberg, *Proletarian Imagination*, esp. 224–81.

248 Here, "primers" refers to school textbooks (e.g., primers in poetry, social science, etc.); "yat'" refers to a Russian letter that was replaced by "e" in the first Soviet spelling reform of 1918.

Tsarist civil servants with whips,
Archbishops with crosses,
Alleluia in an eight-voiced canon
And through
German measles with their intestinal
Worms,
. . . .
and through
the dim honeycombs of sadness,
Christ the mechanic gazes
Intently,
With an electric eyelid.
"Enter!"[249]

---

[249] RGALI f. 2091, op. 2, d. 228, ll. 23ob–24.

Acknowledgments

Writing about Dziga Vertov is both very difficult and a lot of fun: a fatal combination, if you want to finish the work quickly.

Many years have passed since I first began to study Vertov, during which time I have received all sorts of help and support from many different people. It is my pleasure to give thanks for that assistance here, in its various forms (some names appear more than once).

My family has often wondered when the book about the guy with the weird name would finally appear. Through all the puzzlement, (in Canada) Jack, Betty, Pam, Peter, Stephanie, Alexandra, Aidan, Nicholas, Ian, and Adison; and (in Argentina) Raúl, Anamaria, Erich, Sonia, Cecilia, Camila, Ivan, Agustín, and Vera, have held up quite well, and helped me to hold up, too.

My deep gratitude to everyone at Academic Studies Press—above all Oleh Kotsyuba, Elena and Alexander Prokhorov, Faith Wilson Stein, Eileen Wolfberg, Kira Nemirovsky, and the editorial board and production staff—for working to bring this unwieldy project to fruition. Thanks, too, to my anonymous readers, to Rebekah Slonim for her excellent copyediting, and to Jane Friedman for her terrific work on the index.

I could not have undertaken any of the research informing this book without receiving an immense amount of support from Yale University, in particular from the Whitney Humanities Center, the MacMillan Center, and the Provost's Office. Special thanks to Emily Bakemeier, Rahima Chaudhury, Inessa Laskova, the late María Rosa Menocal, Ian Shapiro, Susan Stout, and Gary Tomlinson for their help.

Many people along the way offered concrete help with that research, much of it unexpected and revelatory of new aspects of the Vertov story. For that, I thank Peter Bagrov, Katerina Clark, Monika Dac, Olga Dereviankina, Aleksandr Deriabin, Judith Devlin, Rossen Djagalov, Bernard Eisenschitz, Viktor Fradkin, David Fresko, María Soliña Barreiro González, Mark Halpern, Naum Kleiman, David Litofsky, Jonas Mekas, Mihaela Mihailova, Maxim Pozdorovkin, Agata Pyzik, Joanne Rudof, Natalie Ryabchikova, Raisa Sidenova, Joshua Sperling, Barbara Wurm, Timothy Young, and Patricia Zimmermann.

For enabling the more scheduled research I performed, my great thanks to the wonderful staff at the Library of the Bialystok Historical Museum; Columbia University Library; the National Library of Poland in Warsaw; the National Library of Russia in St. Petersburg; Princeton University Library; the Russian State Library in Moscow; the Library of the University of Warsaw; and (for book-and-document-finding efforts bordering on heroism) Yale University Library.

The writing of the present volume was heavily dependent on work done in several archives. Many thanks to all the extraordinarily knowledgeable and helpful people at Anthology Film Archives; the Beinecke Library (Yale University); the Central State Historical Archive of St. Petersburg; Gosfilmofond (in Belye Stolby and Moscow); the National Historical Archive of Belarus (Grodno); the Russian State Archive of Film and Photo Documents (Krasnogorsk, especially Elena Kolikova); the Russian State Archive of Literature and Art, the Russian State Archive of Contemporary History, the Russian State Archive of Social-Political History, the Russian State Military-Historical Archive (all in Moscow); the State Archive in Bialystok (Poland); the State Archive of the Russian Federation (Moscow); the Swedish Film Institute (Stockholm); the Tamiment Library and Robert F. Wagner Labor Archive (New York University); the Yad Vashem Archives (Jerusalem); and the Yale University Film Archive.

One archive and its staff require special mention, however. My readers will notice the letters "RGALI" very frequently in the notes: that abbreviation references the treasure trove known as the Russian State Archive of Literature and Art, where the greater part of my archival research was done. For making it possible, and making my days at RGALI such a pleasure, my warmest thanks to Tatiana Goriaeva, Galina Zlobina, Dmitry Neustroev and, first and foremost, my dear friend Elena Tchougounova-Paulson.

For helping to bring some of my previous writing on Vertov to publication, my thanks to Liubov' Arkus, Jonathan Auerbach, Birgit Beumers, Russ Castronuovo, Alessia Cervini, Michael Hardt, Richard Koszarski, Sandro Mezzadra, Annette Michelson, Charles Musser, Karen Redrobe, Yuri Tsivian, and Malcolm Turvey. A note of particular gratitude to Vladimir Padunov, who was the first to publish my Vertov work, in very special circumstances.

My great thanks to Seth Feldman, Hannan Hever, Michael Kunichika, Elizabeth Papazian, Karen Pearlman, Natalie Ryabchikova, Erica Schild, Inna Shtakser, and Maria Sidorkina for reading and so helpfully commenting on drafts of this and volumes to come.

Audiences at conferences of the Association for Slavic, East European and Eurasian Studies; the Austrian Film Museum; Bard College; the Blinken Open

Society Archive (Budapest); Cambridge University; Centro de Cooperación (Buenos Aires); the Clark Institute; Colgate University; the College of William & Mary; Columbia University; Concordia University; Duke University; Emory University; the Gino Germani Institute (Buenos Aires); Harvard University; the Jewish Museum; Light Industry; Macquarrie University; Miami University; the Museum of Modern Art; New York University; Penn State University; the Philadelphia Jewish Film Festival; Princeton University; various meetings of the Society for Cinema and Media Studies; the Strelka Institute for Media, Architecture and Design (Moscow); SUNY Stony Brook; Tel Aviv University; Tufts University; Union Docs; the University of Basel; the University of Buenos Aires; the University of Chicago; the University of Iowa; the University of Pennsylvania; the University of Pittsburgh; the University of São Paulo; the University of Sydney; the University of Vienna; Visible Evidence; various departments, colleges and schools at Yale (Architecture, Branford College, Comparative Literature, Ezra Stiles College, Film and Media Studies, History of Art, Slavic); the Yale University Women's Organization; and York University have listened to and generously responded to versions of the work presented here. Many thanks to all of them, and to those who invited me to present my work.

Along the way, I have had scores of conversations and exchanges, even very brief ones, which helped me figure out what I was doing. For those, my immense gratitude to M. A. Akimenko, Evgenij Akkuratov, the members of the Alloy Orchestra, Liubov' Arkus, Richard James Allen, the late Robert Arrow, Thomas Beard, Maria Belodubrovskaya, Robert Bird, Rosalind Polly Blakesley, David Bordwell, Eliot Borenstein, Luca Caminati, Robert Cargni Mitchell, Michael Chaiken, Ciara Chambers, Jem Cohen, Nancy Condee, Michael Cowan, Piroska Csuri, Nathaniel Dorsky, Nataša Ďurovičová, Noam Elcott, Thomas Elsaesser, Laura Engelstein, Sheila Fitzpatrick, Jonathan Flatley, Natalia Fortuny, Jane Gaines, Cora Gamarnik, Ernie Gehr, Maria Gough, Ed Halter, Ken and Flo Jacobs, Mats Jönsson, Iza Kalinowska, William Kentridge, John Knecht, Rebecca Kobrin, Victor Kossakovsky, Oleg Kovalov, Clara Kriger, the late Richard Leacock, Jane Levin, Stuart Liebman, Anne Lounsbery, Sergei Loznitsa, Marcos Mariño, the late Chris Marker, the late Albert Maysles, Mariano Mestman, Daniel Morgan, Simon Morrison, Laura Mulvey, Bohdan Nebesio, Alice Nemirovsky, Stephen Norris, Kevin O'Brien, John Ochoa, Karla Oeler, Serguei Oushakine, Kevin Platt, Karen Redrobe, David Robinson, David Rodowick, Kristin Romberg, Stephanie Sandler, Felisa Santos, Mónica Saviron, Martin Scorsese, Jane Sharp, Andrej Shcherbenok, Joshua Siegel, Carolina Spataro, Przemyslaw Strozek, John Sutton, Irina Tcherneva, Justin Weir, Emma

Widdis, Susan Willis, Brian Winston, and Frederick Wiseman. Special thanks to Etienne Balibar, Fredric Jameson, and Philip Rosen for writing and conversation that influenced the making of this book profoundly.

To Ira, Lyosha and Liuda: thanks for all the friendship and support stretching back so many years. To Anya, Marina Evgenievna, Sonya, Stasya, Sergei, and Tim: my enormous gratitude for all the wonderful discussions, laughter, visits to the theater and the dacha, on top of feeding and housing me for all those great weeks and months in Moscow. Por toda la ayuda con mis charlas en Buenos Aires y por la amistad, míl gracias a Sofía Böhmer, Guillermo Romero von Zeschau, y Fabiana Spiridigliozzi. ¡Salud!

My extraordinary colleagues past and present in Yale's Department of Slavic Languages and Literatures and the Film and Media Studies Program have long been my key interlocutors and inspirations, to whom I owe far more than I can summarize here. My deepest thanks to (in Slavic) Vladimir Alexandrov, Edyta Bojanowska, Marijeta Bozovic, Molly Brunson, Katerina Clark, Irina Dolgova, Nancy Genga, Harvey Goldblatt, Vladimir Golstein, Bella Grigoryan, Kate Holland, Halyna Hryn, Krystyna Illakowicz, Robert Jackson, Hilary Kawall, Ilya Kliger, Carol McNish, Cheryl Morrison, Constantine Muravnik, Alexander Schenker, the late Edward Stankiewicz, Julia Titus, Tomas Venclova, and Karen von Kunes; and (in Film and Media Studies) Dudley Andrew, Jon Andrews, Francesco Casetti, Katerina Clark, J. D. Connor, Terri Francis, Katherine Germano-Kowalczyk, Aaron Gerow, Ronald Gregg, Susan Hart, Thomas Kavanagh, Marc Lapadula, Sandra Luckow, Millicent Marcus, Charles Musser, John Peters, Brigitte Peucker, Noa Steimatsky, Katie Trumpener, John Williams, and Laura Wexler. Special thanks to Katy Clark, who has been a support and inspiration for so long. My gratitude as well to all the folks in the Film Study Center (Michael Kerbel, Brian Meacham, Archer Neilson) and in ITS, and especially and above all to Tony Sudol.

To all my students at Yale, for the good fortune of having you in my classes, I will always be grateful: many of the ideas expressed in this study emerged out of those gatherings. Particular thanks to Rea Amit, Nicholas Avedisian-Cohen, Michael Cramer, Rossen Djagalov, Jason Douglass, Daniel Fairfax, Joshua Glick, Nora Gortcheva, Tatiana Grigorenko, Seung-hoon Jeong, Nicholas Kupensky, Jamicia Lackey, Dominick Lawton, Alice Lovejoy, Jeremy Melius, David Phelps, Patrick Reagan, Maria Sidorkina, Richard Suchenski, Jeremi Szaniawski, Takuya Tsunoda, Sarah Wolf, and Naoki Yamamoto. A special nod to Mihaela Mihailova and Raisa Sidenova, and above all to Masha Salazkina, who has been there from the beginning.

Also at Yale, I must thank Anya Bokov, Hazel Carby, Michael Denning, Paul Fry, the late Benjamin Harshav, David Quint, Michael Warner, and all the comrades in the Working Group in Marxism and Cultural Theory at the Whitney Humanities Center, especially Sumanth Gopinath.

Teaching a course on modern Russian culture for nearly two decades with Paul Bushkovitch has had an immense effect on every dimension of this study: I thank Paul for his guidance and inspiration.

To the host of Vertov specialists I have encountered around the world, all so different from one another and from whom I have learned so much, my heartiest thanks: Julia Alekseyeva, Stavros Alifragkis, Wolfgang Beilenhoff, Simon Cook, Natascha Drubek-Meyer, Devin Fore, Rasmus Gerlach, Klemens Gruber, Adelheid Heftberger, Jeremy Hicks, Svetlana Ishevskaia, Lilya Kaganovsky, Vera Kropf, Daria Kruzhkova, Peter Kubelka, Luis Felipe Labaki, Viktor Listov, Lev Manovich, Karen Pearlman, Valérie Pozner, Martin Stollery, Thomas Tode, Malcolm Turvey, Cristina Vatulescu and Emma Widdis. To those with whom I have traveled longest along those bumpy Vertovian paths—Aleksandr Deriabin, Michael Kunichika, Michael Nyman, Elizabeth Papazian, Maxim Pozdorovkin, Oksana Sarkisova and Barbara Wurm—I raise a special toast.

As with all Vertovians, my debt to Seth Feldman, Annette Michelson and Yuri Tsivian is incalculable, as the pages that follow will show. I thank all three of you for your enormous intellectual and personal support.

An unfortunately belated thanks to two true kinocs, Semiramida Pumpyanskaia and Lev Roshal', both no longer with us, who agreed to speak to me at length about Dziga Vertov and Elizaveta Svilova. And now, alas, to a third as well: my friend and former student, the extraordinary Hannah Frank, who died unexpectedly while this book was in the final stages of production.

To Andre and Angela Kaufman, for their extraordinary generosity and kindness, I offer my gratitude: it has been a privilege to meet and get to know you.

For laughter, support, companionship, mountains of ideas, compliments for my cooking and piano playing, toleration of my messiness, incredible patience, more incredible love: for all this and far more, I thank and embrace Moira Fradinger.

Finally, my two dedicatees. I first watched and read Vertov as a teaching assistant in Charlie Musser's Introduction to Film lecture course at Yale, back in 1993 (my first teaching assignment in graduate school). It was a pretty dark 16mm print of *Man with a Movie Camera*, without music, and I can still recall staggering out of the screening with both a throbbing headache and an inchoate sense of elation. Charlie quickly infected me with his enthusiasm—a

Vertovian affect if there ever was one—for Vertov, and has been my main support all along the way as mentor, exemplum, and friend. I have kept his writings on early cinema and documentary by my side while writing this book, constant and inspiring reminders of just how great film scholarship can be. For all that and much more, thank you, Charlie.

My dissertation advisor, Geoffrey Hartman (1929–2016), did not live to see this volume published, unfortunately. The topic would seem very far from Geoffrey's main interests; I know nonetheless that his influence and example course through every line.

Writing acknowledgments is difficult, and also a lot of fun; I hope I did not miss anyone. If I did, Academic Studies Press has generously given me two more opportunities to get it right.

Archives Consulted

In the footnotes and (when necessary) here, I offer the archival references to materials from Russian archives using the standard abbreviations ("f." (*fond*, archive), "op." (*opis'*, list), "d." (*delo*, file), "l." or "ll." (*list/listy*, page/pages).

FILM ARCHIVES*

1. Gosfil'mofond Rossii (State Film Archive of Russia). Belye Stolby, Russia.
2. RGAKFD (Rossijskij Gosudarstvennyj Arkhiv Kino-Foto Dokumentov [Russian State Archive of Film and Photo Documents]). Krasnogorsk, Russia.
3. Svenska Filminstitutet (Swedish Film Institute). Stockholm, Sweden.
4. Yale University Film Archive. New Haven, Connecticut, USA.

PAPER ARCHIVES

1. Anthology Film Archives. New York, New York, USA.
   Dziga Vertov file
2. Archiwum Państwowe w Białymstoku (State Archive in Bialystok). Bialystok, Poland.
   Fund 155 (Jewish marriage registry for Bialystok, 1894)
   Jewish birth registries for Bialystok (1896, 1897, 1899, 1902, 1903)
3. Beinecke Library, Yale University, New Haven, Connecticut, USA.
   GEN MSS 562 (Boris Kaufman)
4. Gosfil'mofond Rossii (State Film Archive of Russia). Belye Stolby, Russia.
   Dziga Vertov file
5. GARF (Gosudarstvennyi Arkhiv Rossiiskoi Federatsii [State Archive of the Russian Federation]). Moscow, Russia.
   f. 2313 (Glavpolitprosvet)

---

* see filmography for individual titles

f. 1252 (Agitatsionno-instruktorskie poezda i parokhody Vserossiiskogo Tsentral'nogo Ispolnitel'nogo Komiteta [Agitational-instructional trains and steamships of the All-Russian Central Executive Committee])

5. NIAB (Natsional'nyi Istoricheskii Arkhiv Belarusi [National Historical Archive of Belarus]). Grodno, Belarus.

    f. 1 (Kantseliariia Grodnenskogo gubernatora [Chancellery of the Governor of Grodno province])

    f. 8 (Stroitel'noe otdelenie Grodnenskogo gubernskogo pravleniia [Construction division of the administration of Grodno province])

    f. 15 (Grodnenskoi gubernskii prikaz obshchestvennogo prizreniia [Bureau of public welfare, Grodno province])

    f. 103 (Grodnenskoe gubernskoe po delam ob obshchestvakh i soiuzakh prisutstvie [Board for the affairs of societies and unions of Grodno province])

6. RGALI (Rossiiskii Gosudarstvennyi Arkhiv Literatury i Iskusstva [Russian State Archive of Literature and Art]). Moscow, Russia.

    f. 28 (Nikolai Aseev [poet])

    f. 989 (Goskino [1922-1926])

    f. 1951 (Stepan Kolesnikov [painter])

    f. 2057 (Grigorij Boltianskij)

    f. 2091 (Dziga Vertov)

    f. 2515 (Aleksandr Rozovskij [writer])

    f. 2563 (Boris Korneev [translator])

    f. 2639 (S. S. Ginzburg [film scholar])

    f. 2912 (*Iskusstvo Kino* [*Art of Cinema*])

    f. 2986 (Mikhail Kaufman)

    f. 3081 (Ilya Kopalin)

7. RGANI (Rossiiskii Gosudarstvennyi Arkhiv Noveishei Istorii [Russian State Archive of Contemporary History]). Moscow, Russia.

    f. 5, op. 67 (Otdely KPSS, 1974 [Sections of the Communist Party of the Soviet Union, 1974])

8. RGASPI (Rossiiskii Gosudarstvennyi Arkhiv Sotsial'no-Politicheskoi Istorii [Russian State Archive of Social-Political History]). Moscow, Russia.

    f. 17, op. 125 (Upravlenie propagandy i agitatsii TsK VKP(b) [Propaganda and agitation administration of the Central Committee of the All-Union Communist (Bolshevik) Party]).

9. RGVIA (Rossiiskii Gosudarstvennyi Voenno-istoricheskii Arkhiv [Russian State Military-Historical Archive]). Moscow, Russia.
    f. 860, op. 1, dd. 1-2 (Chuguev Military School, 1915-1916)
10. Tamiment Library and Robert F. Wagner Labor Archive, New York University. New York New York, USA.
    Jay Leyda Papers, series I, subseries B, box 8, folder 34 (correspondence between Leyda and Glauco Viazzi, 1955-1956)
11. TsGIASPb (Tsentral'nyi Gosudarstvennyi Istoricheskii Arkhiv Sankt-Peterburga [Central State Historical Archive of St. Petersburg]). St. Petersburg, Russia.
    f. 115 (Psikho-nevrologicheskii Institut, Petrograd, 1908-1917 [Psychoneurological Institute, Petrograd, 1908-1917])
    f. 436 (Petrogradskii Zhenskii Meditsinskii Institut, 1897-1917 [Petrograd Women's Medical Institute, 1897-1917])
12. Yad Vashem Archives. Jerusalem, Israel.
    Central Database of Shoah Victims' Names (http://yvng.yadvashem.org/)

Filmography

The following chronologically arranged filmography includes only extant films both referenced in the text of the present volume and consulted during its writing. It in no way pretends to be either a comprehensive Dziga Vertov filmography (forthcoming in volume 3) or a full listing of all the films watched as part of the research for this study, much less an accounting of the condition and completeness of the films themselves. Thus, it has a provisional character. I limit the information provided on the films to title, year, and (in the most important instances) primary author(s) and production company; square brackets indicate uncertain information. Country of origin other than Soviet Russia/USSR or (before November 1917 and after 1991) Russia is also noted. All entries to which archival locations or numbers are attached were watched on 35mm celluloid or (in a couple of instances) nitrate film.

[1906]

Pervoe zasedanie Gosudarstvennoj Dumy 1906 god (*First session of the State Duma, 1906*). Accessed July 2, 2017, https://www.youtube.com/watch?v=Kxe0gFgnjiY. The footage is of uncertain archival provenance, but may be taken from *Otdel'nye kinosiuzhety* (*1904–1906*) (*Particular film items* [*1904–1906*]). RGAKFD 2001.

1910

Torzhestvennye pokhorony Sergeia Andreevicha Muromtseva v Moskve (*State funeral of Sergej Andreevich Muromtsev in Moscow*). Produced by Pathé. RGAKFD 12083.

1913

Iubilejnye torzhestva (*Anniversary celebrations*). Produced by Pathé and Khanzhonkov. Filmed by A.K. Iangel'skij. RGAKFD 12867.

1914

Galitsiia (*Galicia*). [Produced by the Skobelev Committee.] RGAKFD 810.

1915

Padenie Peremyshlia (*Fall of Przemysl*). Produced by the Skobelev Committee. RGAKFD 11504.

Shturm i vziatie Erzeruma (*Storm and Taking of Erzurum*). Produced by the Skobelev Committee. RGAKFD 13076.

1916

Padenie Trapezunda (*Fall of Trebizond*). [Produced by the Military-Historical Division of the Caucasus Military District.] Filmed by S. S. Esadze. RGAKFD 11535.

[1914–16]

Pate-zhurnal (*Pathé Journal*). Produced by Pathé. RGAKFD 12240.

1917

Demonstratsiia v Petrograde za Uchreditel'noe Sobranie (*Demonstration in Petrograd in support of the Constituent Assembly*). RGAKFD 578.

K moskovskim noiabr'skim sobytiiam (*On the events in Moscow in November*). RGAKFD 11905.

[*K otkrytiiu*] *Uchreditel'nogo Sobraniia* ([*Toward the Opening of*] *the Constituent Assembly*). Produced by the Skobelev Committee. RGAKFD 11502.

Oktiabr'skij perevorot (*October Revolution*). Episode 3. Produced by the Skobelev Committee. RGAKFD 12530.

Oktiabr'skaia sotsialisticheskaia revoliutsiia v Moskve i Petrograde (*October Socialist Revolution in Moscow and Petrograd*). RGAKFD 628.

Pozhar kontory kinolenty (*Fire in the film bureau*). RGAKFD 472.

Svobodnaia Rossiia (*Free Russia*). Produced by the Skobelev Committee.

  Khronika "Svobodnaia Rossiia" (*"Free Russia" newsreel*). RGAKFD 541.

  Khronika "Svobodnaia Rossiia" (*"Free Russia" newsreel*). RGAKFD 733.

  S'ezd chlenov Gosudarstvennoj Dumy (*Congress of the members of the State Duma* [drawn from *Svobodnaia Rossiia*]). RGAKFD 12415.

  Svobodnaia Rossiia (*Free Russia*). RGAKFD 12655.

  Svobodnaia Rossiia no. 5 (*Free Russia 5*). RGAKFD 12377.

  Svobodnaia Rossiia no. 11 (*Free Russia 11*). RGAKFD 12741.

Vybory v Uchreditel'noe Sobranie (*Elections to the Constituent Assembly*). Produced by the Skobelev Committee. RGAKFD 12214. Online version at https://www.youtube.com/watch?v=i03h2l1azZo (accessed July 2, 2017).

[1917]

Letopis' vojny (*Chronicle of the war*). Produced by Pathé. RGAKFD 11796.

1918

Katastrofa v Kieve (*Catastrophe in Kiev*). RGAKFD 12724.

Mozg Sovetskoj Rossii (*Brain of Soviet Russia*). Produced by VFKO. Edited by Dziga Vertov and A. Savel'ev.

Mozg Sovetskoj Rossii (*Brain of Soviet Russia* [fragments]). RGAKFD 12913.

Otkrytie i likvidatsiia Uchreditel'nogo Sobraniia (*Opening and Dissolution of the Constituent Assembly*). Produced by the Skobelev Committee. RGAKFD 12521.

Sovetskoe pravitel'stvo [*Mozg Sovetskoj Rossii*] (*Soviet government* [*Brain of Soviet Russia*]). RGAKFD 12893.

1918–19

Kino-Nedelia (*Film-Week*). Forty-three installments between May 1918 and June 1919. Produced by VFKO. Edited by Dziga Vertov and others. Many of the issues are fragmentary; some discrete issues in RGAKFD are conjoined on the same reels.

At RGAKFD (issue numbers indicated):

2 (RGAKFD 949)

3 (RGAKFD 553)

5 (RGAKFD 549)

6 (RGAKFD 439)

7 (RGAKFD 550)

8 (RGAKFD 552)

10 (RGAKFD 551)

12 (RGAKFD 907)

14 (RGAKFD 313)

15 (RGAKFD 932)

17 (RGAKFD 435)

18 (RGAKFD 486)

20 (RGAKFD 12690)

21 (RGAKFD 13028)

22 (RGAKFD 12235)

23 (RGAKFD 12019)

24 (RGAKFD 12624)

25 (RGAKFD 458)

27 (RGAKFD 12644)

28 (RGAKFD 11556)

29 (RGAKFD 1912)

30 (RGAKFD 462)

31 (RGAKFD 950)

32 (RGAKFD 896)

33 (RGAKFD 12045)

34 (RGAKFD 12558)

35 (RGAKFD 1099)

36 (RGAKFD 442)

37 (RGAKFD 2022)

38 (RGAKFD 450)

39 (RGAKFD 12929)

40 (RGAKFD 11994)

41 (RGAKFD 11909)

42 (RGAKFD 11968)

43 (RGAKFD 1390)

At the Swedish Film Institute:

Issues 1, 3–5, 21–26, 31–35

1919

Khronika "Globus" no. 2 ("Globe" newsreel no. 2). RGAKFD 12029.

Literaturno-instruktorskij parokhod VTsIK "Krasnaia Zvezda" (*The "Red Star" Literary-Instructional Agit-Steamer of the All-Russia Central Executive Committee*). Produced by VFKO. [Edited by Dziga Vertov.] Filmed by Petr Ermolov. RGAKFD 11594.

Na Tsaritsynskom fronte (*On the Tsaritsyn front*). RGAKFD 12399.

[*Protsess*] *Mironova* (*The Trial of Mironov*). Edited by Dziga Vertov. RGAKFD 384.

Ukrainskaia Khronika (*Ukrainian Newsreel*). RGAKFD 10695.

Vskrytie moshchej Sergiia Radonezhskogo v Troitse-Sergievoj Lavre (*Exposure of the Relics of Sergius of Radonezh in the Trinity-Sergius Lavra*). Produced by the Film Division of Narkompros. [Directed and edited by Lev Kuleshov and Dziga Vertov.] [Filmed by Sergej Zabazlaev.] RGAKFD 423.

Vskrytie moshchej Tikhona Zadonskogo (*Exposure of the Relics of Tikhon of Zadonsk*). [Produced by the Moscow Film Committee.] Filmed by Petr Novitskij. RGAKFD 416.

Vziatie goroda Poltavy vojskami Generala Maj-Majevskogo 18 iiulia 1919 g. (*The taking of the city of Poltava by General Maj-Majevskij's forces on 18 July 1919*). RGAKFD 12374.

1920

Evrejskie pogromy na Ukraine v 1919-1920 godakh (*Jewish pogroms in Ukraine in 1919–1920*). RGAKFD 13964-III.

The Jewish Pogroms in Ukraina [sic] *1919–1920*. RGAKFD 13964-II.

Les pogroms juifs en Ucraine 1919–1920 (*Jewish pogroms in Ukraine 1919–1920*). Produced by the Historic Archive of Ukrainian Jews (Berlin). RGAKFD 13964-I.

1919–20

Khronika Grazhdanskoj Vojny 1919-1920 (*Khronika of the Civil War 1919–20*). RGAKFD 1145.

1921

Istoriia Grazhdanskoj Vojny (*History of the Civil War*). Produced by VFKO. Edited by Dziga Vertov. RGAKFD 13078.

Vskrytie moshchej Aleksandra Nevskogo v Petrograde (*Exposure of the Relics of Aleksandr Nevskij in Petrograd*). RGAKFD 12717 (indicated as dating to 1917).

Vskrytie moshchej v Aleksandro-Nevskoj lavre (*Exposure of Relics in the Aleksandr-Nevskij Lavra*). Filmed by N. Grigor. RGAKFD 26.

1922

Kino-Pravda. [Compilation of scenes from early (1922) issues of the *Kino-Pravda* newsreel series (1922–25), made by the Museum of Modern Art, New York.] Directed by Dziga Vertov.

1923

Torzhestvo otkrytiia Vsesoiuznoj Sel'sko-khoziajstvennoj Vystavki [*Otkrytie Sel'sko-khoziajstvennoj Vystavki v Moskve*] (*Official opening of the All-Union Agricultural Exhibition* [*Opening of the Agricultural Exhibition in Moscow*]). RGAKFD 706.

1924

Kino-Glaz: Zhizn' Vrasplokh (*Kino-Eye: Life Caught Unawares*). Produced by Goskino. Directed by Dziga Vertov. Filmed by Mikhail Kaufman. Edited by Dziga Vertov and Elizaveta Svilova. RGAKFD 12875.

1925

Bronenosets Potemkin (*Battleship Potemkin*). Produced by Goskino. Directed by Sergej Eisenstein. Filmed by Eduard Tisse.

Goskinokalendar' 46 (*Goskino Calendar 46*). Produced by Goskino. Filmed and edited by Grigorij Lemberg. RGAKFD 228.

Kino-Pravda 21 ("*Leninskaia*"). Produced by Kul'tkino. Directed by Dziga Vertov. Filmed by Mikhail Kaufman and others. Edited by Dziga Vertov and Elizaveta Svilova. RGAKFD 5232.

1926

Dagestan. Filmed by Petr Zotov and Iakov Tolchan. Edited by Sergei Liamin. RGAKFD 22016.

Shagaj Soviet (*Stride, Soviet*). Produced by Goskino. Directed by Dziga Vertov. Filmed by Ivan Beliakov. Film-scouting by Ilya Kopalin. Edited by Dziga Vertov and Elizaveta Svilova. Gosfilmofond; RGAKFD 10257; Yale University Film Archive.

Shestaia Chast' Mira (*One Sixth of the World*). Produced by Goskino. Directed by Dziga Vertov. Filmed by Samuil Benderskij, Nikolaj Bykov, Mikhail Kaufman, Nikolaj Konstantinov, Nikolaj Lebedev, Aleksandr Lemberg, Nikolaj Strukhov, Yakov Tolchan, and Petr Zotov. Edited by Dziga Vertov and Elizaveta Svilova. Gosfilmofond; Yale University Film Archive.

Sovkinozhurnal 32/51. Produced by Sovkino. RGAKFD 826.

1927

Les Halles Centrales (France). Directed and filmed by Boris Kaufman and André Galitzine.

Padenie dinastii Romanovykh (*Fall of the Romanov Dynasty*). Directed and edited by Esfir Shub.

Tret'ia Meshchanskaia (*Bed and Sofa*). Directed by Abram Room. Written by Viktor Shklovsky.

1928

Kruzheva (*Lace*). Directed by Sergej Iutkevich.

Odinnadtsatyj (*The Eleventh Year*). Produced by VUFKU (All-Ukrainian Film and Photo Administration). Directed by Dziga Vertov. Filmed by Mikhail Kaufman, Konstantin Kuliaev and Boris Tsejtlin. Edited by Dziga Vertov and Elizaveta Svilova. Gosfilmofond; Yale University Film Archive.

1929

Chelovek s kinoapparatom (*Man with a Movie Camera*). Produced by VUFKU. Directed by Dziga Vertov. Filmed by Mikhail Kaufman, Georgij Khimchenko, Konstantin Kuliaev, and Boris Tsejtlin. Edited by Dziga Vertov and Elizaveta Svilova. Gosfilmofond; Yale University Film Archive.

Turksib. Produced by Vostokkino. Directed by Viktor Turin.

1930

Entuziazm: Simfoniia Donbassa (*Enthusiasm: Symphony of the Donbass*). Produced by VUFKU. Directed by Dziga Vertov. Filmed by Boris Tsejtlin. Sound by Petr Shtro. Edited by Dziga Vertov and Elizaveta Svilova. Gosfilmofond; Yale University Film Archive.

Sol' Svanetii (*Salt for Svanetia*). Directed by Mikhail Kalatozov.

1931

Taris, roi de l'eau (*Jean Taris, Swimming Champion*) (France). Directed by Jean Vigo. Filmed by Boris Kaufman.

1934

Tri pesni o Lenine (*Three Songs of Lenin*). Produced by Mezrabpomfil'm. Directed by Dziga Vertov. Filmed by Boris Monastyrskij, Mark Magidson, and Dmitrij Surenskij. Sound by Petr Shtro. Music by Yurij Shaporin. Edited by Dziga Vertov and Elizaveta Svilova. Reedited in 1938 and 1970; 1934 version no longer extant. Gosfilmofond; Yale University Film Archive.

1937

Kolybel'naia (*Lullaby*). Produced by Soiuzkinokhronika/Moscow Film *Khronika* Studio. Directed by Dziga Vertov and Elizaveta Svilova. Sound by I. Renkov. Music by Daniil and Dmitrij Pokrass. Lyrics by V. Lebedev-Kumach. RGAKFD 4078.

1938

Prigovor suda — prigovor naroda (*The verdict of the court is the verdict of the people*). Produced by the Moscow Film *Khronika* Studio. Directed by Ilya Kopalin. Filmed by Ivan Beliakov and Boris Makaseev. RGAKFD 4140.

1949–50

Padenie Berlina (*The Fall of Berlin*). Produced by Mosfilm. Directed by Mikhail Chiaureli.

1954

Das Lied der Ströme (*The Song of the Rivers*) (East Germany). Produced by DEFA. Directed by Joris Ivens, Joop Huiskens, and Robert Menegoz. Narration by Paul Robeson. Music by Dmitrij Shostakovich. Lyrics by Bertolt Brecht.

1956

On the Bowery (USA). Directed by Lionel Rogosin.

1957

The Hunters (USA). Directed and narrated by John Marshall.

1958

S. Ejzenshtejn (*S. Eisenstein*). Produced by TsSDF (Central Documentary Film Studio). Directed by V. Katanian. RGAKFD 15954.

1959

Shadows (USA). Directed by John Cassavetes. Music by Charles Mingus and Shafi Hadi.

We Are the Lambeth Boys (UK). Directed by Karel Reisz.

1960

Primary (USA). Produced by Robert Drew. Filmed by Richard Leacock and Albert Maysles. Edited by D. A. Pennebaker.

1961

Chronique d'un été (*Chronicle of a Summer*) (France). Directed by Edgar Morin and Jean Rouch.

The Connection (USA). Directed by Shirley Clarke.

1963

Le Joli Mai (France). Directed by Chris Marker and Pierre Lhomme.

1964

Brat'ia Vasil'evy (*The Vasiliev Brothers*). Produced by Ekran. Directed by D. Spirkan. RGAKFD 33044.

1965

Film (USA). Written by Samuel Beckett. Directed by Alan Schneider. Performed by Buster Keaton. Filmed by Boris Kaufman.

[1965]

V kvartire kinorezhissera D. Vertova (*In the apartment of film director D. Vertov*). Filmed by G. Epifanov. RGAKFD 22578.

1966

Mir bez igry (*World Without Play*). Produced by TsSDF. Directed by Leonid Makhnach. Filmed by Z. Gromova, L. Kotliarenko, and A. Kochetov. Written by Sergej Drobashenko. Script consultation by Elizaveta Svilova-Vertova. Music by Vitalij Geviksman. RGAKFD 21650.

1968

Un film comme les autres (*A Film Like Any Other*) (France). Directed by Jean-Luc Godard.

1969

British Sounds (France/UK). Directed by Jean-Luc Godard and Jean-Henri Roger.

Tom, Tom, the Piper's Son (USA). Directed by Ken Jacobs.

Lotte in Italia (*Struggle in Italy*) (France/Italy). Directed by Jean-Luc Godard and Jean-Pierre Gorin. Released 1971.

Pravda (France/Czechoslovakia). Directed by Jean-Luc Godard, Jean-Pierre Gorin, and Jean-Henri Roger. Released in 1970.

1970

Vent d'Est (*Wind from the East*) (France). Directed by Jean-Luc Godard and Jean-Pierre Gorin.

1971

Le train en marche (*The Train Rolls On*) (France/USSR). Directed by Chris Marker.

Vladimir et Rosa (France/USA). Directed by Jean-Luc Godard and Jean-Pierre Gorin.

1972

Letter to Jane (France). Directed by Jean-Luc Godard and Jean-Pierre Gorin.

Tout va bien (France). Directed by Jean-Luc Godard and Jean-Pierre Gorin.

Ways of Seeing (UK). Written and narrated by John Berger. BBC television series in four episodes.

1976

Ici et Ailleurs (*Here and Elsewhere*) (France). Directed by Jean-Luc Godard and Anne-Marie Miéville.

1980

Sauve qui peut (la vie) (*Every Man For Himself*) (France). Directed by Jean-Luc Godard.

1993

Le Tombeau d'Alexandre (*The Last Bolshevik*) (France/Russia). Directed by Chris Marker.

1997

The Maelstrom: A Family Chronicle (Hungary/Netherlands). Directed by Péter Forgács.

2002

Dziga i ego brat'ia (*Dziga and His Brothers*). Directed by Evgeny Tsymbal.

Bibliography

A. P. "Kalendar' istorii kino." *Iskusstvo Kino* 12 (December 1956): 117–18.
Abel, Richard, ed. and introduction. *Encyclopedia of Early Cinema*. New York: Routledge, 2010.
———. *French Film Theory and Criticism. Volume I: 1907–1929*. Princeton, NJ: Princeton University Press, 1988.
Abramov, Al. "Rabolepstvuiushchie kosmopolity." *Iskusstvo Kino* 1 (February 1949): 17–19.
———. "Vspomnim o vidovoj." *Sovetskoe Kino* 4–5 (1926): 10–11.
Abramov, Nikolaj. *Dziga Vertov*. Moscow: Akademiia Nauk, 1962.
———. *Dziga Vertov*. Translated by Claudio Masetti. Introduction by Mario Verdone. Rome: Bianco e Nero, 1963.
———. [N. P. Abramov]. *Dziga Vertov*. Lyon: SERDOC, 1965.
———. "Dziga Vertov i iskusstvo dokumental'nogo fil'ma." *Voprosy kinoiskusstva* 4 (1960): 276–308.
———. "Siurealizm i abstraktsionizm v amerikanskom kino." *Voprosy kinoiskusstva* 5 (1961): 279–306.
Abramowicz, Zofia. *Imiona chrzestne białostoczan w aspeksie socjolingwistycznym (lata 1885–1985)*. Bialystok: Uniwersytet Warszawski Filia w Białymstoku, 1993.
Agapov, Boris. "Poezdka v Briussel'." *Novyj Mir* 1 (1959): n.p.
Aitken, Ian, ed. *Encyclopedia of the Documentary Film*. Vol. 1. London: Routledge, 2013.
Akimenko, M. A. "Vladimir Mikhailovich Bekhterev." *Journal of the History of the Neurosciences* 16, no. 1 (2007): 100–109.
Albera, François. "Le detour par Le Gray (en passant par Moussinac et Sadoul)." *1895* 58 (October 2009): 137–43.
Aleksandr, G. M. *Posle suda Beilisa*. Odessa: S. M. Tencher, 1913.
Alexander, Georg, and Wilfried Reichardt. "Jean-Luc Godard, Mitglied der Gruppe 'Dsiga Wertow.'" *Süddeutsche Zeitung* 80, no. 3 (April 4, 1971): 4 [unpaginated supplement].
Alifragkis, Stavros. "The Power of Musical Montage: Michael Nyman's soundtrack for Vertov's *Man with a Movie Camera*." *Scroope* 19 (June 2009): 160–63.
Allard, Pierre. "Godard: A Select Bibliography." *Take One* 2, no. 11 (June 1971): 10.
Althusser, Louis. "Contradiction and Overdetermination." *New Left Review* I/41 (January–February 1967): 15–35.
Althusser, Louis, and Étienne Balibar. *Reading Capital*. Translated by Ben Brewster. London: Verso, 1997.
Anderson, Benedict. *Imagined Communities: Reflections on the Origins and Spread of Nationalism*. 2nd ed. New York: Verso, 1991.

Anderson, Perry. "Modernity and Revolution." *New Left Review* I/144 (March–April 1984): 96–113.

Andrew, Dudley. "Ontology of the Photographic Image." In *The Routledge Encyclopedia of Film Theory*, 333–39. Edited by Edward Branigan and Warren Buckland. London: Routledge, 2015.

Angel'skij, V. *Kratkie istoricheskie svedeniia o Belostokskom Real'nom Uchilishche*. Bialystok: Sh. M. Volobrinskij, 1902.

———. *Otchet o sostoianii Belostokskago Real'nago Uchilishcha za 1901–2 uchebnyj god*. Bialystok: Sh. M. Volobrinskij, 1902.

Anonymous. "Benjamin Freeman, Tailor for Nixon and Eisenhower." *New York Times*, February 21, 1973, 46.

———. "Bor'ba s p'ianstvom." *Vestnik Kinematografii* 92/12 (June 21, 1914): 32.

———. "Canada through the Camera's Eye." *American Amateur Photographer* 4 (1892): 135–41.

———. *Delo Bejlisa: stenograficheskij otchet*. 3 vols. Kiev: Kievskaia Mysl', 1913.

———. *Delo o pogrome v Belostoke 1–3 iiunia 1906 goda*. 2nd ed. St. Petersburg: Trud, 1909.

———. *Evrei — nashi vragi! Tak li eto? Russkomu narodu na urazumenie i Soiuzu Russkago Naroda otvet*. Warsaw: Leppert and Co., 1907.

———. "Fil'my, kotorye vy ne videli." *Vecherniaia Moskva* 182 (August 4, 1959): n.p.

———. "Fil'my 4-x kontinentov." *Vecherniaia Moskva* 180 (August 1, 1959): n.p.

———. "Govoriashchiia kinematograficheskie lenty." *Vestnik Znaniia* 3 (March 1915): 204.

———. "Istoriia kinovedcheskogo otdeleniia." Accessed 24 June 2017, http://www.vgik.info/teaching/scenario/Kinoved/history.php.

———. "Jews of Russian city are being massacred." *New York Times*, June 15, 1906, 1.

———. *Katalog knizhnago magazina i biblioteki tovarishchestva "Obshchestvennaia Pol'za."* St. Petersburg: Obshchestvennaia Pol'za, 1905.

———. "Kinematografirovanie podvodnykh glubin." *Vestnik Znaniia* 3 (March 1915): 127–29.

———. "Kinematograf i shkola." *Vestnik Kinematografii* 89/9 (May 7, 1914): 36.

———. "Kinematograf i shkola." *Vestnik Kinematografii* 91/11 (June 7, 1914): 27.

———. "Kinematograf i shkola." *Vestnik Kinematografii* 92/12 (June 21, 1914): 26.

———. "Kinematograf na sluzhbe khirurgii." *Vestnik Kinematografii* 91/11 (June 7, 1914): 26.

———. *Kino v pionerskom lagere*. Moscow: Soiuzkino, 1931.

———. *Kino — v pomoshch' vesennemu sevu*. Moscow: Soiuzkino, 1931.

———. *Kino v pomoshch' vypolneniiu programmy tret'ego goda Piatiletki*. Moscow: Soiuzkino, 1930.

———. "Kto on dlia nas?" *Iskusstvo Kino* 2 (February 1971): 104–12.

———. *Mnemonik oder praktische Gedächtnisskunst zum Selbstunterricht nach den Vorlesungen des Herrn von Feinaigle*. Frankfurt am Main: Varrentrapp und Sohn, 1811.

———. "Moscow Today [Man with a Movie Camera] Hailed: Film Guild Cinema Audience Applauds Sovkino Scenic." *New York Times*, May 13, 1929, 32.

———. "Novoe izdaniie 'Istorii kinoiskusstva' Zhorzha Sadulia." *Sovetskaia Kul'tura* 29 (March 8, 1958): 4.

———. "O reaktsionnykh kontseptsiiakh sovremennoj burzhuaznoj estetiki kino." *Iskusstvo Kino* 8 (August 1963): 120–28.

———. *Obzor Grodnenskoj gubernii za 1908 god.* Grodno: Gubernskaia Tipografiia, 1909.

———. *Obzor Grodnenskoj gubernii za 1913 god.* Grodno: Gubernskaia Tipografiia, 1914.

———. *Opisanie prazdnovaniia 100-letniago iubileia Belostokskago Real'nago Uchilishcha.* Vilna: A. G. Syrkin, 1903.

———. *Otchet popetchitel'stva o evrejskoj detskoj kolonii v Druskenikakh (otdeleniia Vilensk[ogo] O[bshchest]va Evrejskikh Detsk[ikh] Kolonii) za 1910 god.* Bialystok: Dubner and El'ian, 1911.

———. "Pamiati Dzigi Vertova." *Moskovskaia Pravda* (March 29, 1959): n.p.

———. *Pamiatnaia knizhka Grodnenskoj gubernii na 1896 god.* Grodno: Grodnenskij Gubernskij Statisticheskij Komitet, 1895.

———. *Pamiatnaia knizhka Grodnenskoj gubernii na 1897 god.* Grodno: Grodnenskij Gubernskij Statisticheskij Komitet, 1896.

———. *Pamiatnaia knizhka Grodnenskoj gubernii na 1898 god.* Grodno: Grodnenskij Gubernskij Statisticheskij Komitet, 1897.

———. *Pamiatnaia knizhka Grodnenskoj gubernii na 1910 god.* Grodno: Grodnenskij Gubernskij Statisticheskij Komitet, 1909.

———. "Pamiatnik frantsuzskomu uchonomu Zhiuliu Marej — pervomu izobretateliu kinematografa." *Vestnik Kinematografii* 92/12 (June 21, 1914): 13.

———. "Parokhod-muzej." *Vestnik Kinematografii* 91/11 (June 7, 1914): 33.

———. "Past Films Screened." Accessed June 24, 2017, http://flahertyseminar.org/the-flaherty-seminar/films-screened/.

———. *Pervyj vsesoiuznyj s'ezd sovetskikh pisatelej 1934: stenograficheskij otchet.* Moscow: Sovetskij Pisatel', 1990.

———. "Po gorodam (otdel Belostok)." *Kino* [Riga] 3–4 (1915): 4.

———. "Russian Blood Bath." *Poverty Bay Herald* [Gisborne, New Zealand] XXXIII:10763 (August 4, 1906): 4.

———. "Shkol'nyia zadachi i kinematograf. Razumnyj kinematograf." *Vestnik Kinematografii* 113/13–14 (July 1, 1915): 26–30.

———. "Spisok kinematograficheskikh kartin, kotorye dopushcheny k publichnomu demonstrirovaniiu." *Vestnik Kinematografii* 87/7 (April 1, 1914): 51.

———. "Tribune de F.F.C.C.: le debat est ouvert sur 'L'Homme à la Caméra.'" *Cahiers du Cinéma* IV, no. 22 (April 1953): 36–40.

———. "Vecher, posviashchennyj tvorchestvu Dzigi Vertova." *Soiuz Rabotnikov Kinematografii SSSR* [*SRK*] 8 (1959): n.p.

———. "Vita del C. S. C. [Centro Sperimentale di Cinema]." *Bianco e Nero* XXV, no. 1 (January 1964): III.

———. *Zhitia sviatykh zemli rossijskoj: letopis' istorii otechestva X–XX vv.* St. Petersburg: Pokrovskij Dar, 2004 [based on an 1875 edition].

Aristarco, Guido. "Le fonti culturali de 'due novatori,' Dziga Vertov e Lev Kuleshov." *Cinema Nuovo* 8, no. 37 (1959): 31–37.

———. *Storia delle storiche del film.* Turin: Giulio Einaudi, 1951.

Aristotle. *The Politics*. Translated and introduction by Carnes Lord. Chicago: University of Chicago Press, 1984.
Arkhipova, T. G., ed. *Gosudarstvennyj apparat Rossii v gody Revoliutsii i Grazhdanskoj Vojny*. Moscow: RGGU, 1998.
Arkina, N. "Mozhet li takoe ustaret'!" In *Dziga Vertov v vospominaniiakh sovremennikov*, 232–34. Edited by E. I. Vertova-Svilova and A. L. Vinogradova. Moscow: Iskusstvo, 1976.
Arkus, Liubov' et al. "Zhivoj zhurnal." *Seans* (August 13, 2009). Accessed October 20, 2016, http://seance.ru/blog/zhivoy-zhurnal/.
Aronowitz, Stanley. "Film: The Art Form of Late Capitalism." *Social Text* 1 (Winter 1979): 110–29.
Arrighi, Giovanni. "Marxist Century, American Century: The Making and Remaking of the World Labor Movement." *New Left Review* I/179 (January–February 1990): 29–63.
Arthur, Paul S. "A Retrospective of Anthropological Film." *Artforum* (September 1973): 69–73.
Arvatov, B. "Language Creation (On 'Transrational' Poetry)." In *Words in Revolution: Russian Futurist Manifestoes 1912–1928*, 217–31. Translated and edited by Anna Lawton and Herbert Eagle. Washington, DC: New Academic Publishing, 2004.
———. "Rechetvorchestvo." *LEF* 2 (1923): 79–91.
Ascher, Abraham. *The Revolution of 1905: A Short History*. Palo Alto, CA: Stanford University Press, 2004.
Autera, Leonardo. "Retaggio teatrale e 'realismo socialista' del cinema sovietico (1924–1939)." *Bianco e Nero* XXIV, nos. 9–10 (September–October 1963): 55–81.
Avrich, Paul. *The Russian Anarchists*. Princeton, NJ: Princeton University Press, 1967.
Awramoff, Dobri. "Arbeit und Rhythmus: Der Einfluß des Rhythmus auf die Quantität und Qualität geistiger und körperlicher Arbeit, mit besonderer Berücksichtigung des rhythmischen Schreibens." *Philosophische Studien*. Vol. 18. Edited by Wilhelm Wundt. Leipzig: Wilhelm Engelmann, 1903.
Baecque, Antoine de. *La cinéphilie: invention de un regard, histoire de un culture 1944–1968*. Paris: Fayard, 2003.
———. *Godard: biographie*. Paris: Grasset & Fasquelle, 2010.
Baj, Jeannine, and Sabine Lenk. "'Le Premier Journal Vivant de l'Univers!' Le *Pathé Journal*, 1909–1913." In *La Firme Pathé Frères 1896–1917*, 263–72. Edited by Michel Marie and Laurent Le Forestier. Paris: AFRHC, 2004.
Bakhrushin, S. et al. *Bezhentsy i vyselentsy: otdel'nye ottiski iz no. 17 Izvestij Vserossijskago Soiuza Gorodov*. Moscow: Moskovskaia Gorodskaia Tipografiia, 1915.
Balázs, Béla. *Der sichtbare Mensch oder die Kultur des Films*. Edited and afterword by Helmut H. Diederichs. Frankfurt am Main: Suhrkamp, 2001.
Balibar, Étienne. *Masses, Classes, Ideas: Studies on Politics and Philosophy before and after Marx*. Translated by James Swenson. New York: Routledge, 1994.
———. *The Philosophy of Marx*. Translated by Chris Turner. London: Verso, 2007.
Bal'mont, Konstantin. *Svetozvuk v prirode i svetovaia simfoniia Skriabina*. Moscow: Rossijskoje Muzykal'noe Izdatel'stvo, 1917.

Bardèche, Maurice, and Robert Brasillach. *The History of Motion Pictures*. Translated and edited by Iris Barry. New York: W. W. Norton and Museum of Modern Art, 1938.

Barish, Jonas A. *The Anti-Theatrical Prejudice*. Berkeley: University of California Press, 1985.

Barnouw, Erik. *Documentary: A History of the Non-Fiction Film*. 2nd rev. ed. Oxford: Oxford University Press, 1993.

———. *Media Lost and Found*. Introduction by Dean Duncan. New York: Fordham University Press, 2001.

Baron, Nick, and Peter Gatrell. "Population Displacement, State-Building, and Social Identity in the Lands of the Former Russian Empire, 1917–23." *Kritika: Explorations in Russian and Eurasian History* 4, no. 1 (Winter 2003): 51–100.

Basin, V. "Ob'ektivnost'?" *Iskusstvo Kino* 2 (February 1964): 97–98.

Batalin, D. "Iz opyta RGAKFD po vosstanovleniiu kinematograficheskikh raritetov." Unpublished paper, accessed 15 October 2016, ekovideofilm.ru/doccenter/doc/D_Batalin.doc.

Batalin, V. N. *Kinokhronika v Rossii 1896-1916 gg.: opis' kinos'emok khraniashchikhsia v RGAKFD*. Moscow: OLMA-PRESS, 2002.

Baudry, Jean-Louis. "Cinéma: effets idéologiques produits par le appareil du base." *Cinéthique* 7–8 (1970): 1–8.

———. "Ideological Effects of the Basic Cinematographic Apparatus." Translated by Alan Williams. *Film Quarterly* 28, no. 2 (Winter 1974–75): 39–47.

Beard, Thomas, introduction and ed. *The Unfinished Film*. New York: Gladstone Gallery, 2011.

Beilis, Mendel. *The Story of My Sufferings*. Translated by Harrison Goldberg. Introduction by Herman Bernstein and Arnold D. Margolin. New York: Mendel Beilis Publishing, 1926.

Bekhterev, V. M. "Bessmertie chelovecheskoj lichnosti kak nauchnaia problema." *Vestnik Znaniia*. Otdel'nyj ottisk 2 (1916): 1–23.

———. *Collective Reflexology: The Complete Edition*. Edited by Lloyd H. Strickland. Translated by Eugenia Lockwood and Alisa Lockwood. New Brunswick, NJ: Transaction Publishers, 2001.

———. [W. v. Bechterew]. *Die Energie des lebenden Organismus*. Number 16 in the series *Grenzfragen des Nerven-und Seelenlebens*. Edited by L. Loewenfeld and H. Kurella. Wiesbaden: J. F. Bergmann, 1902.

———. "Kinematograf i nauka." *Kinematograf* 3 (1916): 1.

———. "Moral'nye itogi Velikoj Mirovoj Vojny." *Vestnik Znaniia* 10–11 (October–November 1915): 657–71.

———. *Psikhika i zhizn': izbrannye trudy po psikhologii lichnosti v dvukh tomakh*. Edited by G. S. Nikiforov and L. A. Korostyleva. St. Petersburg: Aleteiia, 1999.

———. *Ubijstvo Iushchinskogo i psikhiatro-psikhologicheskaia ekspertiza*. St. Petersburg: Prakticheskaia Meditstina, 1913.

———. *Voprosy nervno-psikhicheskago zdorov'ia v russkom naselenii*. St. Petersburg: Tipografiia Pervoj Sankt-Peterburgskoj Trudovoj Arteli, 1910.

Bekhterev, V. et al., eds. *Voprosy organizatsii truda: sbornik statej*. Petrograd: Gosudarstvennoe Izdatel'stvo, 1922.

Beliaev, H. Z., B. E. Efimov, and M. B. Efimov, eds. *Mikhail Kol'tsov, kakim on byl*. Moscow: Sovetskij Pisatel', 1989.

Beller, Jonathan L. *The Cinematic Mode of Production: Attention Economy and the Society of the Spectacle*. Lebanon, NH: Dartmouth College Press, 2006.

———. "Dziga Vertov and the Film of Money." *boundary 2* 26, no. 3 (1999): 151–99.

Benjamin, Walter. *Charles Baudelaire: A Lyric Poet in the Era of High Capitalism*. Translated by Harry Zohn. London: Verso, 1983.

Benoit-Lévy, Jean. *Les Grandes Missions du Cinéma*. Montréal: Lucien Parizeau, 1944.

Benvenuti, Francesco. "Armageddon not Averted: Russia's War, 1914–21." *Kritika: Explorations in Russian and Eurasian History* 6, no. 3 (Summer 2005): 535–56.

Berghaus, Günter, ed. *Futurism and the Technological Imagination*. Amsterdam: Rodopi, 2009.

Bergson, Henri. *Time and Free Will*. Translated by F. L. Pogson. London: Macmillan, 1910.

Berman, Marshall. *All That Is Solid Melts into Air: The Experience of Modernity*. London: Verso, 1988.

Bernadini, Aldo. *Gli Ambulanti: Cinema Italiano delle Origini*. Gemona del Friuli: La Cineteca del Friuli, 2001.

Bertetto, Paolo, ed. *Ejzenstejn, FEKS, Vertov: teoria del cinema del cinema rivoluzionario gli anni Venti in URSS*. Milan: Feltrinelli, 1975.

Bertieri, Claudio. "Taccuino della XXIV Mostra di Venezia." *Bianco e Nero* XXIV, nos. 9–10 (September–October 1963): I–VI.

Bertini, Antonio, ed. *Tecnica e ideologia*. Rome: Bulzoni, 1980.

Bezklubenko, S. "V predchustvii televideniia." *Iskusstvo Kino* 12 (December 1970): 86–100.

Bibikova, I. "Rospis' agitpoezdov i agitparokhodov." In *Agitatsionno-massovoe iskusstvo pervykh let Oktiabria: materialy i issledovaniia*, 166–98. Edited by E. A. Speranskaia et al. Moscow: Iskusstvo, 1971.

Binet, Alfred. "La problème de l'audition colorée." *Revue des Deux Mondes* 113 (October 1892): 586–614.

———. *Vopros o tsvetnom slukhe*. Translated by D. N. Moscow: I. N. Kushnerev, 1894.

Blejman, M. "Istoriia odnoj mechty (vmesto predisloviia)." In *Dziga Vertov v vospominaniiakh sovremennikov*, 49–64. Edited by E. I. Vertova-Svilova and A. L. Vinogradova. Moscow: Iskusstvo, 1976.

Blumenberg, Hans. *Work on Myth*. Translated by Robert M. Wallace. Cambridge, MA: MIT Press, 1990.

Blümlinger, Christa. "Mémoire du travail et travail de memoire: Vertov/Farocki (À propos de l'installation *Contre-chant*)." *Intermédialités* 11 (2008): 53–68.

Bobrovskij, N., ed. *Materialy dlia geografii i statistiki Rossii, sobrannye ofitserami general'nogo shtaba, 49-64. Grodnenskaia guberniia. Chast' pervaia*. St. Petersburg: General'naia Shtaba, 1863.

Boltianskij, G. "Fotografiia zvuka: po dokladu S. Ia. Lifshitsa v obshchem sobranii Russkogo Fotograficheskogo Obshchestva v Moskve 25 fevralia 1910 g." *Vestnik Fotografii* 4 (April 1910): 97.

———— ["Gam-Beta"]. "Kinematograf i proletariat." *Novaia Rabochaia Gazeta* 91 (26/XI:1913): 2.
————. *Kino-khronika i kak ee snimat'*. Moscow: Kinopechat', 1926.
Bonch-Bruevich, Vladimir. *Znamenie vremeni: ubijstvo Andreiia Iushchinskogo i delo Beilisa*. St. Petersburg: Zhizn' i Znanie, 1914.
Bonitzer, Pascal. "Hors-Champ (un espace en défaut)." *Cahiers du Cinéma* 234–35 (December 1971/January–February 1972): 15–26.
————. "Off-Screen Space." In *Cahiers du Cinéma, Volume 3: 1969–1972. The Politics of Representation*, 291–305. Edited and introduction by Nick Browne. Translated by Lindley Hanlon. London: Routledge, 1990.
Bordwell, David. *The Cinema of Eisenstein*. Cambridge, MA: Harvard University Press, 1993.
————. "Dziga Vertov: An Introduction." *Film Comment* 8, no. 1 (Spring 1972): 38–45.
————. *Figures Traced in Light: On Cinematic Staging*. Berkeley: University of California Press, 2005.
Borovkov, V. *Dziga Vertov: kratkaia letopis' tvorcheskoj zhizni Dzigi Vertova: Fakty. Zamysli. Fil'my. Publikatsii (k tsiklu prosmotrov v kinoteatre Gosfil'mofonda)*. Moscow: Iskusstvo, 1967.
Borrero, Mauricio. *Hungry Moscow: Scarcity and Urban Society in the Russian Civil War 1917–1921*. New York: Peter Lang, 2003.
Bowlt, John, ed. and trans. *Russian Art of the Avant-Garde 1902–1934*. New York: Viking Press, 1976.
Branigan, Edward, and Warren Buckland. *The Routledge Encyclopedia of Film Theory*. London: Routledge, 2015.
Braslavskij, L. "Istoriia odnogo zhurnala." In *Dziga Vertov v vospominaniiakh sovremennikov*, 234–37. Edited by E. I. Vertova-Svilova and A. L. Vinogradova. Moscow: Iskusstvo, 1976.
Brenez, Nicole et al., eds. *Jean-Luc Godard: Documents*. Paris: Centre Pompidou, 2006.
Breschand, Jean. *Le documentaire: l'autre face du cinéma*. Paris: Cahiers du Cinéma/SCÉRÉN-CNDP, 2002.
Brody, Richard. *Everything Is Cinema: The Working Life of Jean-Luc Godard*. New York: Henry Holt, 2008.
Browne, Nick, ed. and intro. *Cahiers du Cinéma, Volume 3: 1969–1972. The Politics of Representation*. London: Routledge, 1990.
Browning, Christopher R., and Lewis H. Siegelbaum. "Frameworks for Social Engineering: Stalinist Schema of Identification and the Nazi Volksgemeinschaft." In *Beyond Totalitarianism: Stalinism and Nazism Compared*, 231–65. Edited by Michael Geyer and Sheila Fitzpatrick. Cambridge: Cambridge University Press, 2009.
Brunius, J. Bernard. "Le Ciné-Art et le Ciné-Oeil." *La Revue du Cinéma* 4 (October 15, 1929): 75–76.
Brutskus, B. D. *Statistika evrejskago naseleniia*. Vyp. III. St. Petersburg: Sever, 1909.
Bücher, Karl. *Arbeit und Rhythmus*. Leipzig: Hirzel, 1896.
————. *Industrial Evolution*. Translated by S. Morley Wickett. New York: B. Franklin, 1967.
———— [Biukher]. *Rabota i ritm: rabochiia pesni, ikh proiskhozhdenie, esteticheskoe i ekonomicheskoe znachenie*. Edited by D. A. Koropchevskij. Translated by I. Ivanov. St. Petersburg: O. N. Popova, 1899.
———— [Biukher]. *Rabota i ritm*. Trans. S. S. Zaiaitskij. Moscow: Novaia Moskva, 1923.

———. *Trabajo y ritmo*. Madrid: Daniel Jorro, 1914.

———. *Unsere Sache und die Tagespresse*. Tübingen: J. C. B. Mohr, 1915.

Bücher, K., J. Schumpeter, and Freiherr von Wieser [Friedrich], ed. *Wirtschaft und Wirtschaftswissenschaft*. Tübingen: J. C. B. Mohr, 1914.

Buck-Morss, Susan. *Dreamworld and Catastrophe: The Passing of Mass Utopia in East and West*. Cambridge, MA: MIT Press, 2000.

Budnitskij, O. V. *Rossijskie evrei mezhdu krasnymi i belymi (1917–1920)*. Moscow: Rosspen, 2005.

Bukharev, I., ed. *Zhitiia vsekh vviatykh prazdnuemykh pravoslavnoiu greko-rossijskoiu tserkoviiu*. Moscow: I. D. Sytin, 1896.

Burbank, Jane. *Intelligentsia and Revolution: Russian Views of Bolshevism 1917–1922*. New York: Oxford University Press, 1986.

Burch, Noël. "Film's Institutional Mode of Representation and the Soviet Response." *October* 11 (Winter 1979): 77–96.

Burch, Noël, and Jorge Dana. "Propositions." Translated by Diana Matias and Christopher King. *Afterimage* 5 (Spring 1974): 41–66.

Burke, Kenneth. *A Grammar of Motives*. New York: Prentice-Hall, 1945.

Burov, Ia. *Instruktorsko-agitatsionnye poezdki na poezdakh i parokhodakh VTsIK (tezisy Ia. Burova)*. Moscow: Otdel instruktorskikh–agitatsionnykh poezdov i parokhodov VTsIK, 1920.

Carroll, Kent E. "Film and Revolution: An Interview with Jean-Luc Godard." *Evergreen* 14, no. 83 (October 1970): 47–50, 66–68.

Carroll, Noël. "Causation, the Ampliation of Movement and Avant-Garde Film." In Noël Carroll, *Theorizing the Moving Image*. Cambridge: Cambridge University Press, 1996. 169–86.

Casetti, Francesco. *Theories of Cinema 1945–1995*. Austin: University of Texas Press, 1999.

Chaadaev, Peter. *The Major Works of Peter Chaadaev*. Translated by Raymond T. McNally. Introduction by Richard Pipes. Notre Dame, IN: University of Notre Dame Press, 1969.

Chołodowski, Maciej. "Radni PiS: Wiertow zaangażowany w komunistyczne zbrodnie. Zniknie tablica filmowca?" *Wyborcza* (December 28, 2016). Accessed May 30, 2017, http://bialystok.wyborcza.pl/bialystok/1,35241,21174230,radni-pis-wiertow-zaangazowany-w-komunistyczne-zbrodnie-zniknie.html?disableRedirects=true.

Christophersen, Jens. *The Meaning of "Democracy" as Used in European Ideologies from the French to the Russian Revolution*. Oslo: Universitets-forlaget, 1966.

Clark, Katerina. "'Wait for Me and I Shall Return': The Early Thaw as a Reprise of Late Thirties Culture?" In *The Thaw: Soviet Culture and Society during the 1950s and 1960s*, 85–108. Edited by Denis Kozlov and Eleonory Gilburd. Toronto: University of Toronto Press, 2013.

Clark, Katerina, and Galin Tihanov. "Soviet Literary Theory in the 1930s: Battles over Genre and the Boundaries of Modernity." In *A History of Russian Literary Theory and Criticism: The Soviet Era and Beyond*, 109–43. Edited by Galin Tihanov and Evgeny Dobrenko. Pittsburgh, PA: University of Pittsburgh Press, 2011.

Clements, Barbara Evans. *Bolshevik Feminist: The Life of Aleksandra Kollontai*. Bloomington: Indiana University Press, 1979.

Coffinier, Adeline, Victor Gresard, and Christian Lebrat, eds. *Film Culture Index*. Paris: Paris Expérimental, 2012.

Comolli, Jean-Louis. "L'avenir de l'homme? Autour de *L'Homme à la caméra*." *Trafic* 15 (1994): 31–49.

———. *Cinema Against Spectacle: Technique and Ideology Revisited*. Edited, introduced, and translated by Daniel Fairfax. Amsterdam: Amsterdam University Press, 2015.

Cornand, Jérôme. "Sur deux films de Dziga Vertov: *Kino Glaz* et *L'Homme à la Camera*." *La Revue du Cinéma: Image et Son* 297 bis (1975): 55–62.

Courtés, Joseph. *La sémiotique narrative et discursive: méthodologie et application*. Introduction by A. J. Greimas. Paris: Hachette, 1993.

Cowan, Michael. *Cult of the Will: Nervousness and German Modernity*. University Park: Pennsylvania State University Press, 2008.

Crofts, Stephen, and Olivia Rose. "An Essay Towards *Man with a Movie Camera*." *Screen* 18, no. 1 (Spring 1977): 9–60.

Dal', Vladimir. *Zapiska o ritual'nykh ubijstvakh*. Moscow: Vitiaz', 1995.

Danilov, V., and T. Shanin, eds. *Filipp Mironov: Tikhij Don v 1917–1921 gg*. Moscow: Fond "Demokratiia," 1997.

Danilychev, Iu., et al. "Sinerama." *Iskusstvo Kino* 5 (May 1978): 159.

Dardot, Pierre, and Christian Laval. *The New Way of the World: On Neo-Liberal Society*. Translated by Gregory Elliott. London: Verso, 2013.

David, Michael Zdenek. "The White Plague in the Red Capital: The Control of Tuberculosis in Moscow, 1900–1940." PhD diss., Yale University, 2001.

Davies, R. W., Mark Harrison, and S. G. Wheatcroft, eds. *The Economic Transformation of the Soviet Union, 1913–1945*. Cambridge: Cambridge University Press, 1994.

Davies, William. "The New Neoliberalism." *New Left Review* II/101 (September–October 2016): 121–34.

Davis, Douglas. "Video Obscura." *Artforum* (April 1972): 65–71.

Dawson, George. *Manual of Photography*. London: J & A Churchill, 1873.

Debord, Guy. *The Society of the Spectacle*. Detroit: Black & Red, 1970.

Dejch, E. "Nezabyvaemoe." In *Dziga Vertov v vospominaniiakh sovremennikov*, 237–44. Edited by E. I. Vertova-Svilova and A. L. Vinogradova. Moscow: Iskusstvo, 1976.

Delahaye, Michel. "La chasse à l'I." *Cahiers du Cinéma* XXV, no. 146 (August 1963): 5–17.

Deleuze, Gilles. *Cinema 1: The Movement-Image*. Translated by Hugh Tomlinson and Barbara Habberjam. Minneapolis: University of Minnesota Press, 1986.

De Man, Paul. *Blindness and Insight: Essays in the Rhetoric of Contemporary Criticism*. 2nd ed. Introduction by Wlad Godzich. Minneapolis: University of Minnesota Press, 2003.

Denning, Michael. *Culture in the Age of Three Worlds*. London: Verso, 2004.

Deriabin, Aleksandr. "Vremia sobirat': Otechestvennoe kino i sozdanie pervogo v mire kinoarkhiva." *Kinovedcheskie zapiski* 55 (2001). Accessed 15 October 2016, http://www.kinozapiski.ru/ru/article/sendvalues/542/.

Dickerman, Leah. "The Fact and the Photograph." *October* 118 (Fall 2006): 132–52.

Didier, Jules. *Traité Complet de Mnémonique*. Lille: Thomas Naudin, 1808.

Disser, Nicole. "Relive the Indie Film Forum That Brought Us *Heavy Metal Parking Lot* and *Penis Puppets*." *Bedford + Bowery* (June 24, 2016). Accessed on September 12, 2016, http://bedfordandbowery.com/2016/06/relive-the-indie-film-forum-that-brought-us-heavy-metal-parking-lot-and-penis-puppets/.

Djagalov, Rossen, and Masha Salazkina. "Tashkent '68: A Cinematic Contact Zone." *Slavic Review* 75, no. 2 (Summer 2016): 279–98.

Dobrenko, Evgeny. "Literary Criticism and the Transformations of the Literary Field during the Cultural Revolution, 1928–1932." In *A History of Russian Literary Theory and Criticism: The Soviet Era and Beyond*, 43–63. Edited by Galin Tihanov and Evgeny Dobrenko. Pittsburgh, PA: University of Pittsburgh Press, 2011.

Dobrenko, Evgeny and Kalinin, Ilya. "Literary Criticism During the Thaw." In *A History of Russian Literary Theory and Criticism: The Soviet Era and Beyond*, 184–206. Edited by Galin Tihanov and Evgeny Dobrenko. Pittsburgh, PA: University of Pittsburgh Press, 2011.

Dobronski, Adam. *Białystok: Historia Miasta*. 2nd ed. Bialystok: Zarzad Miasta Białegostoku, 2001.

Dos Passos, John. *42-ia parallel'*. Translated by V. Stenich. Leningrad and Moscow: Khudozhestvennaia Literatura, 1931.

Douglas, Charlotte. "Energetic Abstraction: Ostwald, Bogdanov, and Russian Post-Revolutionary Art." In *From Energy to Information: Representation in Science and Technology, Art, and Literature*, 76–94. Edited by Bruce Clarke and Linda Dalrymple Henderson. Stanford, CA: Stanford University Press, 2002.

Dovgan, Ulyana. "The First Annual Golden Dziga." *Odessa Review* (May 5, 2017). Accessed July 24, 2017, http://odessareview.com/first-annual-golden-dziga/.

Drobashenko, S. "Poet revoliutsionnogo kino: k 80-letiiu so dnia rozhdeniia Dzigi Vertova." *Sovetskaia Kul'tura* 44 (January 6, 1976): 5.

———, ed. *Pravda kino i "kinopravda": po stranitsam zarubezhnoj pressy*. Moscow: Iskusstvo, 1967.

———. "Teoreticheskoe nasledie Dzigi Vertova." *Iskusstvo Kino* 12 (December 1965): 74–83.

Dronin, Nikolai M., and Edward G. Bellinger. *Climate Dependence and Food Problems in Russia, 1900–1990: The Interaction of Climate and Agricultural Policy and Their Effect on Food Problems*. Budapest: Central European University Press, 2005.

Drubek-Meyer, Natascha, and Jurij Murashov, eds. *Apparatur und Rhapsodie: Zu den Filmen des Dziga Vertov*. Frankfurt am Main: Peter Lang, 2000.

Ďurovičová, Nataša. "A Life Caught Unawares: Dziga Vertov's Collected Writings." *Quarterly Review of Film Studies* 10, no. 4 (April 1989): 325–33.

Durteste, Pierre. "Faut-il oublier Georges Sadoul? Georges Sadoul, une jeunesse nancéienne." *1895* 44 (2004): 29–46.

Efimov, Boris. "Ocherki o mul'tiplikatsii." *Sovetskaia Kul'tura* (May 23, 1958): 3.

Eisenstein, Sergej. *The Eisenstein Reader*. Edited by Richard Taylor. London: British Film Institute, 1998.

Ejkhenbaum, B. M., ed. *Poetika kino*. Introduction by Kirill Shutko. Moscow: Kinopechat', 1927.

Eklof, Ben, John Bushnell, and Larissa Zakharova, eds. *Russia's Great Reforms, 1855–1881*. Bloomington: Indiana University Press, 1994.

Elwood, Ralph Carter. *Russian Social Democracy in the Underground: A Study of the RSDRP in the Ukraine, 1907–1914*. Assen: Van Gorcum, 1974.

Engelstein, Laura. *Russia in Flames: War, Revolution, Civil War 1914–1921*. Oxford: Oxford University Press, 2017.

Enzensberger, Masha. "Dziga Vertov." *Screen* 13, no. 4 (1972): 90–107.

Ermakov, V. D., and P. I. Talerov, eds. *Anarkhizm v istorii Rossii ot istokov k sovremennosti: bibliograficheskij slovar'-spravochnik*. St. Petersburg: Solart, 2007.

Esquenazi, Jean-Pierre, ed. *Vertov: L'Invention du Rèel: Actes du Colloque de Metz, 1996*. Paris: L'Harmattan, 1997.

Evans, Walker. "Out of Anger and Artistic Passion." *New York Times Book Review* (May 3, 1953): 3.

Evstaf'ev, Il'ia. "V Ukraine vypustili pochtovye marki v chest' kinofil'mov." *OKino* (February 20, 2013). Accessed 9 August 2017, http://www.okino.ua/news/world/v-ukraine-vyipustili-pochtovyie-marki-v-chest-kino-5656/.

Fargier, Jean-Paul, et al. "'Ne copiez pas sur les yeux,' disait Vertov." *Cinéthique* 15 (1973): 55–92.

Faroult, David. "Du *vertovisme* du Groupe Dziga Vertov." In *Jean-Luc Godard: Documents*, 134–38. Edited by Nicole Brenez et al. Paris: Centre Pompidou, 2006.

———. "Filmographie du Groupe Dziga Vertov." In *Jean-Luc Godard: Documents*, 132–33. Edited by Nicole Brenez et al. Paris: Centre Pompidou, 2006.

Fay, Laurel E. *Shostakovich: A Life*. Oxford: Oxford University Press, 2000.

Feldman, Seth R. *Dziga Vertov: A Guide to References and Resources*. Boston: G. K. Hall and Co., 1979.

———. *The Evolution of Style in the Early Work of Dziga Vertov*. New York: Arno Press, 1977.

———. "Vertov after Manovich." *Canadian Journal of Film Studies* 16, no. 1 (Spring 2007): 39–50.

Fevral'skij, A. "Dziga Vertov i Maiakovskij." *Iskusstvo Kino* 10 (October 1973): 113–24.

Fielding, Raymond. *The American Newsreel: A Complete History, 1911–1967*. Jefferson, NC: McFarland and Company, 2006.

Figes, Orlando. *The Whisperers: Private Life in Stalin's Russia*. New York: Metropolitan Books, 2007.

Finley, M. I. *Democracy Ancient and Modern*. New Brunswick, NJ: Rutgers University Press, 1985.

Fitzpatrick, Sheila. *The Cultural Front: Power and Culture in Revolutionary Russia*. Ithaca, NY: Cornell University Press, 1992.

———. *Education and Social Mobility in the Soviet Union, 1921–1934*. Cambridge: Cambridge University Press, 1979.

———. *On Stalin's Team: The Years of Living Dangerously in Soviet Politics*. Princeton, NJ: Princeton University Press, 2015.

———. *The Russian Revolution*. 2nd ed. Oxford: Oxford University Press, 1994.

———. *Tear Off the Masks! Identity and Imposture in Twentieth-Century Russia*. Princeton, NJ: Princeton University Press, 2005.

Flakserman, Iu. N. *V ogne zhizni i bor'by: vospominaniia starogo kommunista*. Moscow: Izdatel'stvo Politicheskoj Literatury, 1987.

Flammarion, Kamill'. *Populiarnye lektsii po astronomii*. Translated and edited by V. V. Bitner. St. Petersburg: Vestnik Znaniia, 1905.

———. *V nebesakh i na zemle*. Moscow: I. D. Sytin, 1908.

Fletcher, Angus. *Allegory: The Theory of a Symbolic Mode*. Ithaca, NY: Cornell University Press, 1964.

Fomin, V. et al., eds. *Letopis' Rossijskogo Kino 1863–1929*. Moscow: Materik, 2004.

Fox, Michael S. "Glavlit, Censorship and the Problem of Party Policy in Cultural Affairs, 1922–28." *Soviet Studies* 44, no. 6 (1992): 1045–68.

Fox Talbot, William Henry. *The Pencil of Nature*. Introduction by Beaumont Newhall. New York: Da Capo Press, 1969.

Fradkin, G. "Prav li Richard Likok?" *Iskusstvo Kino* 11 (November 1965): 24–25.

Fradkin, Viktor. "Novoe o Mikhaile Kol'tsove." *Lekhaim* 8: 100. Accessed June 22, 2017, www.lechaim.ru/ARHIV/100/fradkin.htm.

Freedberg, David. *The Power of Images: Studies in the History and Theory of Response*. Chicago: University of Chicago Press, 1989.

Fri-Dik. "Kinotrazhnia." *Kinematograf* 1 (1915): 12.

Frye, Northrop. *The Secular Scripture: A Study of the Structure of Romance*. Cambridge, MA: Harvard University Press, 1978.

Fuchs, Barbara. *Romance*. New York: Routledge, 2004.

Fussell, Paul. *The Great War and Modern Memory*. Oxford: Oxford University Press, 1975.

Gallinari, Pauline. "Les Semaines du cinéma de 1955. Nouveau enjeu culturel des relations franco-soviétiques." *Bulletin de l'Institut Pierre Renouvin* 24 (Fall 2006). Accessed October 27, 2016, https://www.univ-paris1.fr/autres-structures-de-recherche/ipr/les-revues/bulletin/tous-les-bulletins/bulletin-n-24-art-et-relations-internationales/pauline-gallinari-les-semaines-du-cinema-de-1955-nouvel-enjeu-culturel-des-relations-franco-sovietiques/.

Galushkin, A. Iu. et al., eds. *Literaturnaia zhizn' Rossii 1920-kh godov*. Vol. 1. Part 1. Moscow: IMLI RAN, 2005.

Gan, Aleksej. "Leninizm v iskusstve." *Zrelishcha* (January 27, 1925): 1.

Gardin, V. R. *Vospominaniia*. Vol. 1. Moscow: Goskinoizdat, 1949.

Garncarz, Joseph. "The Fairground Cinema—A European Institution." In *Travelling Cinema in Europe: Sources and Perspectives* [Kinotop Schriften 10], 78–90. Edited by Martin Loiperdinger. Frankfurt am Main: Stroemfeld Verlag, 2008.

Gatrell, Peter. "Refugees in the Russian Empire, 1914–1917: Population Displacement and Social Identity." In *Critical Companion to the Russian Revolution 1914–1921*, 554–64. Edited by Edward Acton et al. Bloomington: Indiana University Press, 1997.

———. *A Whole Empire Walking: Refugees in Russia during World War I*. Bloomington: Indiana University Press, 1999.

Geduld, Harry M., ed. *Film Makers on Film Making: Statements on Their Art by Thirty Directors*. Indianapolis: Indiana University Press, 1967.

Gelvin, James L. *The Israel-Palestine Conflict: One Hundred Years of War*. 2nd ed. Cambridge: Cambridge University Press, 2007.

Genkina, E. *Bor'ba za Tsaritsyn v 1918 godu*. Moscow: Politizdat pri TsK VKP(b), 1940.

Gerow, Aaron. *Visions of Japanese Modernity: Articulations of Cinema, Nation, and Spectatorship, 1895–1925*. Berkeley: University of California Press, 2010.

Gershgorin, Bela. "Chetyre izmereniia brat'ev Kaufman." *Russkij Bazar* 50/556 (December 14–20, 2006). Accessed June 22, 2017, http://www.russian-bazaar.com/ru/content/9852.htm.

Gerver, A. V. eds. *Otchet o deiatel'nosti Psikho-Nevrologicheskago Instituta za 1912-j god*. St. Petersburg: Gramotnost', 1914.

Geyer, Michael, and Sheila Fitzpatrick, eds. *Beyond Totalitarianism: Stalinism and Nazism Compared*. Cambridge: Cambridge University Press, 2009.

Gibbs, John. *The life of mise-en-scène: Visual style and British film criticism, 1946–1978*. Oxford: Oxford University Press, 2015.

Gidal, Peter. *Materialist Film*. London: Routledge, 1989.

Ginzburg, S. S. et al., eds. *Iz Istorii Kino 2*. Moscow: Akademii Nauk SSSR, 1959.

Ginzburg, S. *Kinematografiia dorevoliutsionnoi Rossii*. Moscow: Iskusstvo, 1963.

———. "'Kino-Pravda.'" *Iskusstvo Kino* 1 (February 1940): 87–88.

Glushakov, Iurij. *"Revoliutsiia umerla! Da zdravstvuet revoliutsiia!" Anarkhizm v Belarusi (1902–1927)*. Moscow: ShSS, 2015.

Goffenshefer, V. "Karl Biukher." Accessed June 22, 2017, http://feb-web.ru/FEB/LITENC/ENCYCLOP/le2/le2-0511.htm.

Goldovskaya, Marina. *Woman with a Movie Camera: My Life as a Russian Filmmaker*. Translated by Antonina W. Bouis. Introduction by Robert Rossen. Austin: University of Texas Press, 2006.

Golston, Michael. *Rhythm and Race in Modernist Poetry and Science*. New York: Columbia University Press, 2008.

Goncharov, V. A., and V. V. Nekhotin. "'Durylin soglasen dat' podpisku, chto on nikogda ne budet prikhodskim sviashchennikom': Iz materialov arkhivno-sledstvennogo dela po obvineniiu S. N. Durylina." *Vestnik PSTGU* II (2008): 126–39.

[Godard, Jean-Luc and Jean-Pierre Gorin]. "Dziga Vertov notebook." *Take One* 2, no. 11 (June 1971): 7–10.

Gough, Maria. *The Artist as Producer: Russian Constructivism in Revolution*. Berkeley: University of California Press, 2005.

Graff, Séverine. *Le cinéma-vérité: Films et controverses*. Introduction by François Albera. Rennes: Presses universitaires de Rennes, 2014.

———. "Réunions et désunions autour du 'cinéma-vérité': le MIPE-TV 1963 de Lyon." *1895* 64 (Fall 2011): 64–89.

Granich, Tom. "Cinema documentario sovietico." *Sequenze* 3 (November 1949): 24–26.

Granja, Vasco. *Dziga Vertov*. Lisbon: Livros Horizonte, 1981.

Grashchenkova, I. *Abram Room*. Moscow: Iskusstvo, 1977.

Greene, Robert H. *Bodies Like Bright Stars: Saints and Relics in Orthodox Russia*. DeKalb: Northern Illinois University Press, 2010.

Gregor, Ulrich, ed. *Dokumentation zum Seminar Künstlerische Avantgarde im Sowjetischen Stummfilm*. Berlin: Freunden der Deutschen Kinemathek, 1974.

Gribanov, M., et al. *Agitpoezd "Velikij Oktiabr."* Voronezh: Tsentral'no-chernozemnoe Knizhnoe Izdatel'stvo, 1969.

Grierson, John. *Grierson on Documentary*. Edited by Forsyth Hardy. New York: Praeger, 1971.

Grieveson, Lee. "The Work of Film in the Age of Fordist Mechanization." *Cinema Journal* 51, no. 3 (Spring 2012): 25–51.

Grigor'ev, Gr. "Pravda zhizni i fal'shivye teorii." *Iskusstvo Kino* 1 (February 1949): 22–24.

———. "Vidy zemli sovetskoj." *Iskusstvo Kino* 3 (June 1949): 32–34.

Griunberg, P. N. *Istoriia nachala gramzapisi v Rossii*. Moscow: Iazyki Slavianskoj Kul'tury, 2002.

Gromov, E. *Lev Vladimirovich Kuleshov*. Moscow: Iskusstvo, 1984.

Gruber, Klemens, Barbara Wurm, and Vera Kropf, eds. "Digital Formalism: Die kalkulierten Bilder des Dziga Vertov." *Maske und Kothurn* 55, no. 3 (2009).

Gruber, Klemens, ed. "Dziga Vertov zum 100. Geburtstag." *Maske und Kothurn* 42, no. 1 (1996).

Guido, Laurent. *L'âge du rythme: Cinéma, musicalité et culture du corps dans les theories françaises des années 1910-1930*. Lausanne: Editions Payot, 2007.

Gunning, Tom. "The Cinema of Attractions: Early Film, Its Spectator and the Avant Garde." In *Early Cinema: Space, Frame, Narrative*, 56–62. Edited by Thomas Elsaesser. London: British Film Institute, 1990.

———. "The Whole Town's Gawking: Early Cinema and the Visual Experience of Modernity." *Yale Journal of Criticism* 7, no. 2 (Fall 1994): 189–201.

Gunst, Evgenij. *A. N. Skriabin i ego tvorchestvo*. Moscow: Mysl', 1915.

Günther, Hans. "Soviet Literary Criticism and the Formulation of the Aesthetics of Socialist Realism, 1932–1940." In *A History of Russian Literary Theory and Criticism: The Soviet Era and Beyond*, 90–108. Edited by Galin Tihanov and Evgeny Dobrenko. Pittsburgh, PA: University of Pittsburgh Press, 2011.

H. I. K. "G. M. Boltianskij: desiatiletie kino-deiatel'nosti." *Zrelishcha* 46 (1923): 9.

Habermas, Jürgen. *The Structural Transformation of the Public Sphere: A Inquiry into a Category of Bourgeois Society*. Translated by Thomas Burger and Frederick Lawrence. Cambridge, MA: MIT Press, 1991.

Halperin, Miriam [Proginin] [Masha Gal'pern]. "The Work of OZE in the Minsk District in the Years 1916-1918." In *Minsk, 'ir va'em: korot, ma'asim, 'ishim, ha'vai*, 602–4. Edited by David Cohen and Shlomo Even-Shoshan. Tel-Aviv: Association of Immigrants from Minsk and Its Surroundings, 1975.

Hansen, Miriam Bratu. *Babel and Babylon: Spectatorship in American Silent Film*. Cambridge, MA: Harvard University Press, 1991.

———. "Early Cinema, Late Cinema: Permutations of the Public Sphere." *Screen* 34, no. 3 (Autumn 1993): 194–210.

———. "The Mass Production of the Senses: Classical Cinema as Vernacular Modernism." In *Reinventing Film Studies*, 332–50. Edited by Christine Gledhill and Linda Williams. London: Arnold, 2000.

Harding, Neil, ed. *Marxism in Russia: Key Documents 1879–1906*. Translated by Richard Taylor. Cambridge: Cambridge University Press, 1983.

Harshav, Benjamin. *Language in Time of Revolution*. Berkeley: University of California Press, 1993.

———. *Marc Chagall and His Times: A Documentary Narrative*. Stanford, CA: Stanford University Press, 2004.

Heftberger, Adelheid. *Kollision der Kader: Dziga Vertovs Filme, die Visualisierung ihrer Strukturen und die Digital Humanities*. Munich: text+kritik, 2016.

Hegel, G. W. F. *The Encyclopedia Logic*. Translated by T. F. Geraets, W. A. Suchting, and H. S. Harris. Indianapolis: Hackett Publishing, 1991.

Hendershot, Heather. *Saturday Morning Censors: Television Regulation before the V-Chip*. Durham, NC: Duke University Press, 1998.

Hennebelle, Guy. "Dziga Vertov." *Écran* 13 (1973): 45.

———. "SLON: Working Class Cinema in France." Translated by Catherine Ham and John Mathews. *Cinéaste* 5, no. 2 (Spring 1972): 15–17.

———, et al. "Pratique Artistique et Lutte Idéologique." *Cahiers du Cinéma* 248 (September 1973): 53–64.

Heusch, Luc de. *The Cinema and Social Science: A Survey of Ethnographic and Sociological Films*. Paris: UNESCO, 1962.

Hicks, Jeremy. *Dziga Vertov: Defining Documentary Film*. London: I. B. Tauris, 2007.

Hobsbawm, Eric. *The Age of Empire: 1875–1914*. New York: Pantheon Books, 1987.

Holl, Ute. *Cinema, Trance and Cybernetics*. Translated by Daniel Hendrickson. Amsterdam: Amsterdam University Press, 2017.

Hollier, Denis, and Jeffrey Mehlman, eds. *Literary Debate: Texts and Contexts*. New York: New Press, 2001.

Holquist, Peter. "'Information is the Alpha and Omega of Our Work': Bolshevik Surveillance in Its Pan-European Context." *Journal of Modern History* 69, no. 3 (September 1997): 415–50.

Hundert, Gershon David. *Jews in Poland-Lithuania in the Eighteenth Century: A Genealogy of Modernity*. Berkeley: University of California Press, 2004.

Hunt, Ronald. "The Constructivist Ethos, Part I." *Artforum* (September 1967): 23–30.

———. "The Constructivist Ethos, Part II." *Artforum* (October 1967): 26–32.

———. "*Icteric* and *Poetry must be made by all / Transform the World*: A note on a lost and suppressed avant-garde and exhibition." Accessed on November 20, 2016, http://www.artandeducation.net/paper/icteric-and-poetry-must-be-made-by-all-transform-the-world-a-note-on-a-lost-and-suppressed-avant-garde-and-exhibition/.

———. "Introduction." In *Poetry must be made by all! Transform the world!*, 5–10. Stockholm: Moderna Museet Stockholm, 1969.

Iegis, Iosif. "O 'misterii' Skriabina." *Zrelishcha* 36 (1923): 5.

Iurenev, R. "Dziga Vertov i kniga o nem." *Iskusstvo Kino* 9 (September 1963): 135–37.
———. "O Vertove." *Iskusstvo Kino* 6 (June 1967): 65–68.
———. "Zhizn' i ekran: zametki s florentijskogo kinofestivalia." *Sovetskaia Kul'tura* 22 (February 20, 1964): 4.
Iurtsev, B. "[Orkestr veshchej]." *Zrelishcha* 6 (1922): 22.
Iutkevich, Sergej. "Kinoiskusstvo Frantsii: zametki kinorezhissera." *Izvestiia* 249 (October 20, 1955): 3.
———. "Mirovoe znachenie 'Bronenostsa 'Potemkina.'" *Iskusstvo Kino* 1 (January 1956): 49–62.
———. "My s uvlecheniem nachali s'emki." *Iskusstvo Kino* 2 (February 1988): 94–108.
———. "Pervoprokhodets." In *Dziga Vertov v vospominaniiakh sovremennikov*, 265–73. Edited by E. I. Vertova-Svilova and A. L. Vinogradova. Moscow: Iskusstvo, 1976.
———. "Razmyshleniia o kinopravde i kinolzhi." *Iskusstvo Kino* 1 (January 1964): 68–80.
Ivanov, A. E. [Anatolij Evgen'evich]. *Evrejskoe studenchestvo v Rossijskoj Imperii nachala XX veka: kakim ono bylo?* Moscow: Novyj Khronograf, 2007.
———. "Rossijskoe evrejskoe studenchestvo v period Pervoj Mirovoj Vojny." In *Mirovoj krizis 1914–1920 godov i sud'ba vostochnoevropejskogo evrejstva*, 142–61. Edited by O. V. Budnitskij et al. Moscow: Rosspen, 2005.
———. *Studenchestvo Rossii kontsa XIX-nachala XX veka: sotsial'no-istoricheskaia sud'ba*. Moscow: Rosspen, 1999.
———. *Vysshaia shkola Rossii v kontse XIX-nachale XX veka*. Moscow: Akademiia Nauk, 1991.
Ivanov, V. V. et al., eds. *Mir Velimira Khebnikova: stat'i, issledovaniia 1911–1998*. Moscow: Iazyki Russkoj Kul'tury, 2000.
Jahiel, Edwin. "The New Theater: Paris 1962–63." *Symposium* 18, no. 4 (Winter 1964): 313–20.
Jahn, Hubertus F. *Patriotic Culture in Russia during World War I*. Ithaca, NY: Cornell University Press, 1995.
James, Nick, et al. "The Greatest Films of All Time 2012." Accessed June 24, 2017, http://www.bfi.org.uk/sight-sound-magazine/greatest-films-all-time-2012-homepage.
Jameson, Fredric. "Pleasure: A Political Issue." In *The Ideologies of Theory: Essays 1971–1986*, 61–74. Vol. 2. Minneapolis: University of Minnesota Press, 1988.
———. *The Political Unconscious: Narrative as a Socially Symbolic Act*. Ithaca, NY: Cornell University Press, 1981.
Jangfeldt, Bengt. *Majakovskij and Futurism: 1917–1921*. Stockholm: Almqvist & Wiksell International, 1976.
———. *Mayakovsky: A Biography*. Translated by Harry D. Watson. Chicago: University of Chicago Press, 2014.
Johnson, Lorenzo D. *Memoria Technica*. 3rd ed. Boston: Gould, Kendall and Lincoln, 1847.
Jones, Polly, ed. and introduction. *The Dilemmas of De-Stalinization*. London: Routledge, 2006.
Joravsky, David. *Russian Psychology: A Critical History*. Oxford: Basil Blackwell, 1989.
Jordana, Verónica. "Herz Frank." In *Encyclopedia of the Documentary Film*, 445–46. Edited by Ian Aitken. Vol. 1. London: Routledge, 2013.

Kadlec, David. "Early Soviet Cinema and American Poetry." *Modernism/modernity* 11, no. 2 (April 2004): 299–331.

Kaes, Anton, Nicholas Baer, and Michael Cowan, eds. "The Cinematographic Archive: Selections from Early German Film Theory." *October* 148 (Spring 2014): 27–38.

Kaganovich, B. S. *Evgenij Viktorovich Tarle i peterburgskaia shkola istorikov*. St. Petersburg: Dmitrii Bulanin, 1995.

Kagarlitskij, Vl. "Dramaturgiia v dokumental'nykh fil'makh." *Iskusstvo Kino* 1 (February 1949): 28–30.

Kahana, Jonathan, ed. *The Documentary Film Reader: History, Theory, Criticism*. Oxford: Oxford University Press, 2016.

Kaletskij, Iu., ed. *Otchet belostokskoj Talmud'-tory s remeslennym uchilishchem za 1901 i 1902 gg*. Bialystok: Ts. Mishondzink, 1903.

Kamp, Marianne. *The New Woman in Uzbekistan: Islam, Modernity and Unveiling under Communism*. Seattle: University of Washington Press, 2006.

Kapralov, G., and D. Zarapin. "Volnuiushchee nachalo smotra." *Pravda* 217 (August 5, 1959): 6.

Karaseva, M. "Nikolaj Lebedev." *Kinograf* 8 (2000): 77–89.

Karatygin, V. G. *Skriabin*. Petrograd: N. I. Butkovskaia, 1915.

Karpinskij, V., ed. *Agitparpoezda VTsIK*. Moscow: Gosudarstvennoe Izdatel'stvo, 1920.

Karpinskij, V. A. *S kem zhe vy, krest'iane? S kem idete? Komu pomogaete?* Moscow: VTsIK, 1918.

Kassow, Samuel D. *Students, Professors, and the State in Tsarist Russia*. Berkeley: University of California Press, 1989.

Katanian, V. *Maiakovskij: Literaturnaia khronika*. 3rd ed. Moscow: Khudozhestvennaia Literatura, 1956.

Katanian, Vasilij. *Prikosnovenie k idolam*. Moscow: Zakharov-Vagrius, 2004.

Katsman, R. "Khronika — obraznaia publitsistika." *Iskusstvo Kino* 5 (May 1940): 4–10.

Kaufman, A. K. *Dobavochnyj katalog russkikh knig biblioteki A.K. Kaufmana v g. Belostoke*. Bialystok: Oppengejm, 1909.

———. *Katalog russkikh knig biblioteki dlia chteniia (pri knizhnom magazine) A.K. Kaufmana v g. Belostoke*. 1st ed. Bialystok: Sh. Volobrinskij, 1895.

———. *Katalog russkikh knig i periodicheskikh izdanij biblioteki (pri knizhnom magazine) A. K. Kaufmana v g. Belostoke*. 2nd ed. Bialystok: Sh. M. Volobrinskij, 1900.

Kaufman, Mikhail. "An Interview with Mikhail Kaufman." *October* 11 (Winter 1979): 54–76.

———. "Poet neigrovogo." In *Dziga Vertov v vospominaniiakh sovremennikov*, 70–79. Edited by E. I. Vertova-Svilova and A. L. Vinogradova. Moscow: Iskusstvo, 1976.

Kejrim-Markus, M. B. *Gosudarstvennoe rukovodstvo kul'turoj: stroitel'stvo Narkomprosa noiabria 1917-seredina 1918 gg*. Moscow: Nauka, 1980.

Kenez, Peter. *The Birth of the Propaganda State: Soviet Methods of Mass Mobilization, 1917–1929*. Cambridge: Cambridge University Press, 1985.

———. "The Cultural Revolution in Cinema." *Slavic Review* 47, no. 3 (Autumn 1988): 414–33.

Kenworthy, Scott M. *The Heart of Russia: Trinity-Sergius, Monasticism, and Society after 1825*. New York: Oxford University Press, 2010.

Kepley, Jr., Vance. "Soviet Cinema and State Control: Lenin's Nationalization Decree Reconsidered." *Journal of Film and Video* 42, no. 2 (Summer 1990): 3–14.

Kerzhentsev, Platon. *Biblioteka kommunista.* 4th ed. Moscow: Gosudarstvennoe Izdatel'stvo, 1919.

———. *Revoliutsiia i teatr.* Moscow: Dennitsa, 1918.

Kharkevich, Ia. and Cherepitsa, V. N. "Gavriil." Accessed June 22, 2017, http://www.pravenc.ru/text/161257.html.

Kharkhordin, Oleg. *The Collective and the Individual in Russia: A Study of Practices.* Berkeley: University of California Press, 1999.

Khvol'son, O. D. *Znanie i vera v fizike.* Petrograd: F. R. Fetterlein, 1916.

Kirzhnits, A. D., and M. Rafes, eds. *1905: Evrejskoe rabochee dvizhenie.* Moscow: Gosudarstvennoe Izdatel'stvo, 1928.

Klaue, W., and M. Lichtenstein, eds. *Sowjetischer Dokumentarfilm.* East Berlin: Staatliches Film Archiv der DDR, 1967.

Kleandrova, V. M. *Organizatsiia i formy deiatel'nosti VTsIK (1917–1924 g.g.).* Moscow: Iuridicheskaia Literatura, 1968.

Klier, John Doyle. *Imperial Russia's Jewish Question, 1855–1881.* Cambridge: Cambridge University Press, 1995.

Kliuev, L. *Bor'ba za Tsaritsyn: 1918–1919.* Moscow: Gosudarstvennoe Izdatel'stvo, 1928.

Kobrin, Rebecca. *Jewish Bialystok and Its Diaspora.* Bloomington: Indiana University Press, 2010.

Koenker, Diane P., William G. Rosenberg, and Ronald Grigor Suny, eds. *Party, State and Society in the Russian Civil War: Explorations in Social History.* Bloomington: Indiana University Press, 1989.

Kolonitskij, Boris Ivanovich. "'Democracy' in the Political Consciousness of the February Revolution." *Slavic Review* 57, no. 1 (Spring 1998): 95–106.

Kopalin, I. P. "Blizhajshie zadachi sovetskogo dokumental'nogo kino." In *Vsesoiuznaia tvorcheskaia konferentsiia rabotnikov kinematografii: stenograficheskij otchet,* 317–34. Moscow: Iskusstvo, 1959.

———. "Dokumental'noe kino za 30 let." *Iskusstvo Kino* 7 (December 1947): 22–25.

———, et al. "O masterstve kinopublitsistiki." *Iskusstvo Kino* 4 (April 1957): 1–14.

———. "Sovershenstvovat' iskusstvo obraznoj publitsistiki." *Iskusstvo Kino* 6 (June 1955): 18–28.

———. *Sovetskaia dokumental'naia kinematografiia.* Moscow: Vsesoiuznoe obshchestvo po rasprostraneniiu politicheskikh i nauchnykh znanij, 1950.

———. "Sovetskaia dokumental'naia kinematografiia." *30 let sovetskoj kinematografii,* 98–117. Edited by D. Eremin. Moscow: Goskinoizdat, 1950.

———. "V sporakh o dokumental'nom fil'me." *Iskusstvo Kino* 5 (May 1940): 33–35.

Kopalina, G. I. "Poslednee interv'iu Mikhaila Kaufmana." *Novyj Mir* 1 (1994). Accessed June 22, 2017, http://magazines.russ.ru/novyi_mi/1994/1/kaufman01.html.

Koptiaev, A. P. *A. N. Skriabin.* Moscow: I. Iurgenson, 1916.

———. *Evterpe: vtoroj sbornik muzykal'no kriticheskikh statej.* St. Petersburg: Glavnoe Upravlenie Udelov, 1908.

Kornienko, G. S. *Ukraine'ske radians'ke kinomistetsvo 1917–1929.* Kiev: Vidavnitstvo Akademii Nauk Ukraines'koi RSR, 1959.

Korolenko, V. G. *Istoriia moego sovremennika*. Edited by A. V. Khrabrovitskij. Moscow: Khudozhestvennaia Literatura, 1965.

Korotkij, V. M. *Operatory i rezhissery russkogo igrovogo kino, 1897–1921. Biofil'mograficheskij spravochnik*. Moscow: NII kinoiskusstva, 2009.

Koss, Juliet. *Modernism after Wagner*. Minneapolis: University of Minnesota Press, 2010.

Kotkin, Stephen. *Stalin. Volume 1: Paradoxes of Power*. New York: Penguin, 2014.

Kozintsev, Grigorij. *Sobranie sochinenij v piati tomakh*. Leningrad: Iskusstvo, 1984.

Kozlov, Denis, and Eleonory Gilburd, eds. *The Thaw: Soviet Culture and Society during the 1950s and 1960s*. Toronto: University of Toronto Press, 2013.

Kozlov, Evgenij Anatol'evich. "Agitatsionnye poezda i parokhody v Sovetskoj Rossii (1918–1922): strategii kommunikatsii." Master's thesis, Russian State Humanities University, 2016.

Kraszna-Krausz, A. "The First Russian Sound Films." *Close Up* 8, no. 4 (December 1931): 300–303.

Krusanov, A. V. *Russkij avangard: 1907–1932*. Vol. 1. St. Petersburg: Novoe Literaturnoe Obozrenie, 1996.

———. *Russkij avangard*. Vol. 2. Book 1. Moscow: Novoe Literaturnoe Obozrenie, 2003.

Kuhn, Annette. *Cinema, Censorship, and Sexuality, 1909–1925*. New York: Routledge, 1988.

Kuleshov, L. V. *Stat'i. Materialy*. Edited by V. P. Mikhailov et al. Moscow, Iskusstvo, 1970.

Kurlansky, Mark. *1968: The Year that Rocked the World*. New York: Ballantine, 2004.

Kuromiya, Hiroaki. *Freedom and Terror in the Donbas: A Ukrainian-Russian Borderland, 1870s–1990s*. Cambridge: Cambridge University Press, 1998.

Kushnirov, M. "Akter i dokument." *Iskusstvo Kino* 8 (August 1967): 50–58.

Langlois, Henri. *Écrits de cinéma (1931–1977)*. Edited by Bernard Benoliel and Bernard Eisenschitz. Paris: Flammarion, 2014.

Lapshin, I. *Zavetnye dumy Skriabina*. Petrograd: Mysl', 1922.

Larkin, Brian. *Signal and Noise: Media, Infrastructure and Urban Culture in Nigeria*. Durham, NC: Duke University Press, 2008.

Larsen, Egon. *Spotlight on Films: A Primer for Film-lovers*. Introduction by Sir Michael Balcon. London: Max Parrish & Co., 1950.

Larsen, Ernest. "Kino Revolution." *The Independent* 9, no. 8 (October 1986): 12–14.

Latour, Bruno. *We Have Never Been Modern*. Translated by Catherine Porter. Cambridge, MA: Harvard University Press, 1993.

Launet, Edouard. "Rétabli." *Libération* (May 2010). Accessed November 20, 2016, http://next.liberation.fr/culture/2010/05/17/retabli_626472.

Lawton, Anna. "Rhythmic Montage in the Films of Dziga Vertov: A Poetic Use of the Language of Cinema." *Pacific Coast Philology* 13 (October 1978): 44–50.

———. "Russian and Italian Futurist Manifestoes." *Slavic and East European Journal* 20, no. 4 (Winter 1976): 405–20.

Lawton, Anna, and Herbert Eagle, trans. and eds. *Words in Revolution: Russian Futurist Manifestoes 1912–1928*. Washington, DC: New Academic Publishing, 2004.

Lazareva, N. V. "Gosudarstvennyj apparat Sovetskoj Rossii po evakuatsii naseleniia v 1918–1923 gg." In *Gosudarstvennyj apparat Rossii v gody Revoliutsii i Grazhdanskoj Vojny*, 171–81. Edited by T. G. Arkhipova. Moscow: RGGU, 1998.

Lebedev, Nikolaj [N. A.]. *Kino: ego kratkaia istoriia, ego vozmozhnosti, ego stroitel'stvo v sovetskom gosudarstve*. Moscow: Gosudarstvennoe Izdatel'stvo, 1924.

———. "Na podstupakh k 'Chapaevu.'" *Iskusstvo Kino* 2 (April 1951): 9–14.

———. *Ocherk istorii kino SSSR*. Vol. 1. Moscow: Goskinoizdat, 1947.

Lechowski, Andrzej. *Białystok: urok starych klisz*. Bialystok: Benkowski, 2005.

Lederhendler, Eli. *The Road to Modern Jewish Politics: Political Tradition and Political Reconstruction in the Jewish Community in Tsarist Russia*. New York: Oxford University Press, 1989.

Le Grice, Malcolm. *Abstract Film and Beyond*. Cambridge, MA: MIT Press, 1977.

Leikin, Anatole. *The Performing Style of Alexander Scriabin*. New York: Routledge, 2016.

Lemberg, A. "Druzhba, ispytannaia desiatiletiami." In *Dziga Vertov v vospominaniiakh sovremennikov*, 79–86. Edited by E. I. Vertova-Svilova and A. L. Vinogradova. Moscow: Iskusstvo, 1976.

———. "Dziga Vertov prikhodit v kino." *Iz Istorii Kino* 7 (1968): 39–50.

———. "Iz vospominanii starogo operatora." *Iz Istorii Kino* 2 (1959): 117–31.

———. "Na agitparokhode 'Krasnaia Zvezda.'" *Iskusstvo Kino* 5 (1959): 107.

Lenin, V. I. "Ekonomika i politika v epokhu diktatury proletariata [7 November 1919]." Accessed June 22, 2017, http://leninism.su/works/78-tom-39/1274-ekonomika-i-politika-v-epoxu-diktatury-proletariata.html.

———. "The State and Revolution." In *The Lenin Anthology*, 311–98. Edited by Robert C. Tucker. New York: Norton, 1975.

Lenoe, Matthew. *Closer to the Masses: Stalinist Culture, Social Revolution, and Soviet Newspapers*. Cambridge, MA: Harvard University Press, 2004.

Lerner, Vladimir, Jacob Margolin, and Eliezer Witztum. "Vladimir Bekhterev: His Life, His Work and the Mystery of His Death." *History of Psychiatry* 16, no. 2 (2005): 217–27.

Leskov, Nikolaj. "Iz odnogo dorozhnago dnevnika." *Severnaia Pchela* 338 (December 14, 1862): 1335.

Levitskij, A. *Rasskazy o kinematografe*. Moscow: Iskusstvo, 1964.

Leyda, Jay. "Dziga Vertov: A Guide to References and Resources." *Cinéaste* 12, no. 1 (1982): 40–41.

———. *Kino: A History of the Russian and Soviet Film*. London: George Allen & Unwin, 1960.

Likhachev, B. S. *Istoriia kino v Rossii*. Leningrad: Academia, 1927.

Lincoln, W. Bruce. *Passage Through Armageddon: The Russians in War and Revolution, 1914–1918*. New York: Simon and Schuster, 1986.

Lindgren, Ernest. *The Art of the Film*. London: George Allen and Unwin, 1948.

Linhart, Robert. *L'Établi*. Paris: Éditions de Minuit, 1978.

———. *Lénine, les Paysans, Taylor: Essai d'analyse matériel historique de la naissance du système productif soviétique*. Paris: Seuil, 1976.

Linhart, Virginie. *Le jour où mon père s'est tu*. Paris: Seuil, 2008.

Listov, V. S. "Dve 'Kinonedeli.'" *Iskusstvo Kino* 5 (May 1968): 93–100.

———. *Istoriia smotrit v ob'ektiv*. Moscow: Iskusstvo, 1973.

———. "Molodost' mastera." *Dziga Vertov v vospominaniiakh sovremennikov*, 86–104. Edited by E. I. Vertova-Svilova and A. L. Vinogradova. Moscow: Iskusstvo, 1976.

———. *Rossiia, revoliutsiia, kinematograf: k 100-letiiu mirovogo kino*. Moscow: Materik, 1995.

Listov, V. S., and E. S. Khokhlova. *Istoriia otechestvennogo kino: dokumenty, memuary, pis'ma*. Moscow: Materik, 1996.

Listov, V. S., et al. "'Pryzhok' Vertova." *Iskusstvo Kino* 11 (November 1992): 96–108.

Liubosh, S. B. *Russkij fashist Vladimir Purishkevich*. Leningrad: Byloe, 1925.

Lohr, Eric. *Nationalizing the Russian Empire: The Campaign against Enemy Aliens during World War I*. Cambridge, MA: Harvard University Press, 2003.

Loiperdinger, Martin, ed. *Travelling Cinema in Europe: Sources and Perspectives* [Kinotop Schriften 10]. Frankfurt am Main: Stroemfeld Verlag, 2008.

Loisette, Alphonse. *Physiological Memory: or, The instantaneous art of never forgetting; (which uses none of the "Localities," "Keys," "Pegs," "Links," "Tables" or "Associations" of "Mnemonics") by Prof. A. Loisette, sole originator, proprietor and teacher thereof*. 4th ed. New York: Alphonse Loisette, 1886.

Löwe, Heinz-Dietrich. *The Tsars and the Jews: Reform, Reaction and Anti-Semitism in Imperial Russia 1772–1917*. Chur, Switzerland: Harwood Academic Publishers, 1993.

Luchitskij, I. V., introduction. *Rechi po pogromnym delam*. Kiev: S. G. Sliusarevskij, 1908.

Luddy, Tom, Ron Green, and Susan Rice. "Dziga Vertov reviews." *Take One* 2, no. 11 (June 1971): 12–14.

Lukács, Georg. *Ästhetik* [*Georg Lukács Werke* 12–13]. Darmstadt and Neuwied: Luchterhand, 1962–63.

———. "Realism in the Balance." In *Aesthetics and Politics*, 28–59. Edited by Ronald Taylor. Translated by Rodney Livingstone. Afterword by Fredric Jameson. London: Verso, 1997.

Macdonald, Kevin, and Mark Cousins, eds. *Imagining Reality*. London: Faber & Faber, 2006.

MacDonald, Scott. "Péter Forgács: An Interview." In *Cinema's Alchemist: The Films of Péter Forgács*, 3–38. Edited by Bill Nichols and Michael Renov. Minneapolis: University of Minnesota Press, 2011.

MacFarlane, Steve. "Interview with Jem Cohen." *The White Review* (October 2014). Accessed November 21, 2016, http://www.thewhitereview.org/interviews/interview-with-jem-cohen/.

MacIntyre, Alasdair. *After Virtue: A Study in Moral Theory*. 2nd ed. Notre Dame, IN: University of Notre Dame Press, 1984.

MacKay, John. "Allegory and Accommodation: Vertov's *Three Songs of Lenin* (1934) as a Stalinist film." *Film History* 18 (2006): 376–91.

———. "Built on a Lie: Propaganda, Pedagogy and the Origins of the Kuleshov Effect." In *The Oxford Handbook of Propaganda*, 219–36. Edited by Jonathan Auerbach and Russ Castronuovo. Oxford: Oxford University Press, 2013.

———. "Film Energy: Process and Metanarrative in Dziga Vertov's *The Eleventh Year* (1928)." *October* 121 (Summer 2007): 41–78.

———. *Inscription and Modernity: From Wordsworth to Mandelstam*. Bloomington: Indiana University Press, 2006.

———. "Montage under Suspicion: Bazin's Russo-Soviet Reception." In *Opening Bazin: Postwar Film Theory and Its Afterlife*, 291–301. Edited by Dudley Andrew and Hervé Jourbert-Laurencin. Oxford: Oxford University Press, 2011.

———. "The Truth about Kino-Pravda, or Censorship as a Productive Force." *KinoKultura* 55 (2017). Accessed June 22, 2017, http://www.kinokultura.com/2017/55-mackay.shtml.

———. "Vertov before Vertov: Jewish Life in Bialystok." In *Dziga Vertov: The Vertov Collection at the Austrian Film Museum*, 9–12. Edited by Thomas Tode and Barbara Wurm. Vienna: Österreichisches Filmmuseum/SYNEMA, 2006.

MacKay, John, and Charles Musser. "*Shestaia Chast Mira* / [*La Sesta Parte del Mundo/A Sixth Part of the World*]." In *23rd Pordenone Silent Film Festival Catalogue*, 55–58. Pordenone: Giornate del Cinema Muto, 2004.

Madrid, Francisco. *Cincuenta Años de Cine: Cronica del Septimo Arte*. Buenos Aires: Ediciones del Tridente, 1946.

Magidov, V. M. "Itogi kinematograficheskoj i nauchnoj deiatel'nosti B. Matushevskogo v Rossii." *Kinovedcheskie Zapiski* 43 (1999). Accessed October 15, 2016, http://www.kinozapiski.ru/ru/article/sendvalues/1075/.

———. "Iz arkhiva Vertova." *Kinovedcheskie Zapiski* 18 (1993): 161–64.

———. *Kinofotodokumenty v kontekste istoricheskogo znaniia*. Moscow: RGGU, 2005.

———. "Moskinokomitet i natsionalizatsiia kinopromyshlennosti." *Vestnik Moskovskogo Universiteta*, 3–19. Seriia IX: Istoriia. Vol. 5. Moscow: Izdatel'stvo Moskovskogo Universiteta, 1972.

———. *Zrimaia pamiat' istorii*. Moscow: Sovetskaia Rossiia, 1984.

Maksakova, L. V. *Agitpoezd "Oktiabr'skaia Revoliutsiia" (1919–1920)*. Moscow: Akademiia Nauk SSSR, 1956.

Mal'kova, Liliana. *Sovremennost' kak istoriia: realizatsiia mifa v dokumental'nom kino*. Moscow: Materik, 2001.

Mannoni, Laurent. *Histoire de la Cinémathèque Française*. Paris: Gallimard, 2006.

Manovich, Lev. *The Language of New Media*. Cambridge, MA: MIT Press, 2001.

———. "Visualizing Vertov" (2013). Accessed November 21, 2016, http://softwarestudies.com/cultural_analytics/Manovich.Visualizing_Vertov.2013.pdf.

Maor, Eli. "Science and Yiddish Don't Mix: Really?" *Journal of Scholarly Publishing* 44, no. 4 (July 2013): 340–54.

Marcorelles, Louis [with Nicole Rouzet-Albagli]. *Living Cinema: New Directions in Contemporary Film-making*. Translated by Isabel Quigly. New York: Praeger, 1973.

Marey, Etienne-Jules. *Mekhanika zhivotnago organizma: peredvizhenie po zemle i po vozdukhu*. St. Petersburg: Znanie, 1875.

Marin, Louis. *On Representation*. Translated by Catherine Porter. Stanford, CA: Stanford University Press, 2001.

Marinetti, F. T. *Critical Writings*. Edited and introduction by Günter Berghaus. Translated by Doug Thompson. New York: Farrar, Straus and Giroux, 2006.

Markov, Vladimir. *Russian Futurism: A History*. Berkeley: University of California Press, 1968.

Martin, Marcel. "*En avant, Soviet.*" *Cinéma* 57 (June 1961): 55–65.

———. "Histoire du Cinéma en 120 Films." *Cinéma* 61 (November–December 1961): 33–43.

Marx, Karl. *Capital.* Vol. 1. Accessed June 24, 2017, https://www.marxists.org/archive/marx/works/download/pdf/Capital-Volume-I.pdf.

———. *A Contribution to the Critique of Hegel's Philosophy of Right ["Introduction"].* Accessed June 24, 2017, http://www.marxists.org/archive/marx/works/1843/critique-hpr/intro.htm.

———. *A Contribution to the Critique of Political Economy ["Preface"].* Accessed June 24, 2017, https://www.marxists.org/archive/marx/works/1859/critique-pol-economy/preface.htm.

———. *Early Writings.* Translated by Rodney Livingstone and Gregor Benton. Introduction by Lucio Colletti. London: Penguin, 1992.

———. *Later Political Writings.* Edited by Terrell Carver. Cambridge: Cambridge University Press, 1996.

Marx, Karl, and Friedrich Engels. *Manifesto of the Communist Party.* Accessed June 24, 2017, https://www.marxists.org/archive/marx/works/1848/communist-manifesto/.

Matuszewski, Boleslas. *Écrits cinématographiques.* Edited by Magdalena Mazaraki. Paris: Association française de recherché sur l'histoire du cinéma and La Cinémathèque Française, 2006.

——— [Boleslav Matushevskij]. "Zhivaia fotografiia: chem ona iavliaetsia, i chem ona dolzhna stat'." Translated by Grigorij Boltianskij. Edited by Svetlana Ishevskaia and Denis Viren. *Kinovedcheskie Zapiski* 83 (2007): 127–61.

Maurin, Evgenij. *Kinematograf v prakticheskoj zhizni.* Petrograd: N. Kuznetsov, 1916.

Mawdsley, Evan. *The Russian Civil War.* Edinburgh: Birlinn, 2000.

May, Renato. "Dal cinema al cinema-verità." *Bianco e Nero* XXV, nos. 4–5 (April–May 1964): 1–15.

Mayakovsky, Vladimir. *Prostoe kak mychanie.* Petrograd: Parus, 1916.

Mayne, Judith. *Kino and the Woman Question: Feminism and Soviet Silent Film.* Columbus: Ohio State University Press, 1989.

———. "Kino-Truth and Kino-Praxis: Vertov's *Man with a Movie Camera.*" *Cine-Tracts* 1, no. 2 (Summer 1977): 81–89.

Mekas, Jonas. "The Experimental Film in America." *Film Culture* 3 (May–June 1955): 15–18.

——— [Dzonas Mekas]. "Kinematografiia SShA Segodnia." *Iskusstvo Kino* 12 (December 1958): 136–40.

Mendelsohn, Ezra. *Class Struggle in the Pale: The Formative Years of the Jewish Workers' Movement in Tsarist Russia.* Cambridge: Cambridge University Press, 1970.

———. *The Jews of East Central Europe between the World Wars.* Bloomington: Indiana University Press, 1983.

———. "A Note on Jewish Assimilation in the Polish Lands." In *Jewish Assimilation in Modern Times,* 141–45. Edited by Bela Vago. Boulder, CO: Westview Press, 1981.

Mendelson, Lois, and Bill Simon. "*Tom, Tom, the Piper's Son.*" *Artforum* 10, no. 1 (September 1971): 46–52.

Merridale, Catherine. "War, Death, and Remembrance in Soviet Russia." In *War and Remembrance in the Twentieth Century*, 61–83. Edited by Jay Winter and Emmanuel Sivan. Cambridge: Cambridge University Press, 1999.

Metz, Christian. *L'énonciation impersonnelle, ou le site du film*. Paris: Méridiens Klincksieck, 1991.

Michelson, Annette. "Film and the Radical Aspiration." In *Film Culture Reader*, 404–21. Edited and introduction by P. Adams Sitney. New York: Cooper Square Press, 2000.

———. "*L'Homme à la Caméra*: de la magie à la epistémologie." *Revue de Esthétique* 26, no. 2–4 (1973): 295–310.

———. "*The Man with the Movie Camera*: From Magician to Epistemologist." *Artforum* 10, no. 7 (March 1972): 60–72.

Mihailova, Mihaela, and John MacKay. "Frame Shot: Vertov's Ideologies of Animation." In *Animating Film Theory*, 145–66. Edited by Karen Beckman. Durham, NC: Duke University Press, 2014.

Miliakova, L. B., ed. *Kniga pogromov: pogromy na Ukraine, v Belorussii i evropejskoj chasti Rossii v period Grazhdanskoj Vojny 1918–1922 gg*. Moscow: Rosspen, 2007.

Miller, Francis Trevelyan, ed. *Photographic History of the [American] Civil War in ten volumes*. New York: Review of Reviews, 1911.

———, ed. *Photographic History of the Great War*. New York: New York Tribune, 1914.

Mirskij, D. "Dos-Passos, sovetskaia literatura i zapad." *Literaturnyj Kritik* 1 (June 1933): 111–26.

Molchanov, L. A. "Deiatel'nost' informatsionnykh uchrezhdenij 'beloj' Rossii v gody grazhdanskoj vojny (1918–1920 gg.)." In *Gosudarstvennyj apparat Rossii v gody Revoliutsii i Grazhdanskoj Vojny*, 150–71. Edited by T. G. Arkhipova. Moscow: RGGU, 1998.

Morin, Edgar. *Le Cinéma ou l'Homme Imaginaire: Essai d'Anthropologie Sociologique*. Paris: Éditions de Minuit, 1956.

———. "For a New Cinéma Vérité." Translated by Steven Feld and Anny Ewing. *Visual Communication* 11, no. 1 (Winter 1985): 4–5.

———. "Pour un nouveau 'cinéma-vérité.'" *France Observateur* 506 (1960): 23.

———. *Les Stars*. Paris: Éditions de Seuil, 1957.

Moussinac, Léon. *Le Cinéma Soviétique*. Paris: Gallimard, 1928.

———. "Iz rechi L. Mussinaka." *Sovetskaia Kul'tura* 149 (December 4, 1955): 4.

Munsterberg, Hugo. *The Photoplay: A Psychological Study*. New York: D. Appleton and Company, 1916.

Muratov, S. "Pristrastnaia kamera." *Iskusstvo Kino* 6 (June 1966): 108–20.

Murray-Brown, Jeremy. "False Cinema: Dziga Vertov and Early Soviet Film." *New Criterion* 8, no. 3 (November 1989): 21–33.

Musser, Charles. *The Emergence of Cinema: The American Screen to 1907*. New York: Charles Scribner's Sons, 1990.

Nathans, Benjamin. *Beyond the Pale: The Jewish Encounter with Late Imperial Russia*. Berkeley: University of California Press, 2002.

Navrátil, Antonín. *Dziga Vertov, revolucionář dokumentárního filmu*. Prague: Český filmový ústav, 1973.

Nejgauz, G. G. [Heinrich Neuhaus]. *Pis'ma*. Moscow: Deka-VS, 2009.

Norris, Stephen M. *A War of Images: Russian Popular Prints, Wartime Culture, and National Identity 1812–1945*. DeKalb: Northern Illinois University Press, 2006.

Orlovsky, Daniel T. "The Provisional Government and Its Cultural Work." In *Bolshevik Culture: Experiment and Order in the Russian Revolution*, 39–56. Edited by Abbott Gleason, Peter Kenez, and Richard Stites. Bloomington: Indiana University Press, 1985.

———. "State Building in the Civil War Era: The Role of the Lower-Middle Strata." In *Party, State and Society in the Russian Civil War*, 180–209. Edited by Diane P. Koenker, William G. Rosenberg, and Ronald Grigor Suny. Bloomington: Indiana University Press, 1989.

Osborne, Peter. *How to Read Marx*. New York: W. W. Norton, 2006.

Ostwald, Wilhelm [V. Ostval'd]. *Energicheskij imperativ*. Translated by V. M. Pozner. Introduction by V. Verner. St. Petersburg: 1913 [supplement to the journal *Za 7 dnej*].

———. *Individuality and Immortality*. Boston: Houghton Mifflin, 1906.

——— [V. Ostval'd]. *Mel'nitsa zhizni*. Translated by R. Kh. Makstys. Moscow: Latizdat, 1925.

——— [V. Ostval'd]. *O mezhdunarodnom iazyke*. Moscow: Esperanto, 1908.

———. *Die Philosophie der Werte*. Leipzig: Alfred Kröner, 1913.

Otten, Nikolaj. "Krasivyj mir." *Iskusstvo Kino* 12 (December 1937): 36–38.

Owen, Catherine. "A Genealogy of *Kontrol'* in Russia: From Leninist to Neoliberal Governance." *Slavic Review* 75, no. 2 (Summer 2016): 331–53.

Paisova, Elena. "Armen Medvedev: 'Zhurnal ne daval sovetskomu kino rasslabit'sia.'" *Iskusstvo Kino* 4 (April 2011): 106–12.

Pantenburg, Volker. *Farocki/Godard: Film as Theory*. Translated by Michael Turnbull. Amsterdam: Amsterdam University Press, 2015.

Paris, Aimé. *Exposition et pratique des procédés de la Mnemotechnie*. Paris: Aimé Paris, C. Farcy, 1826.

Perry, Marvin and Schweitzer, Frederick M. *Antisemitism: Myth and Hate from Antiquity to the Present*. London: Palgrave Macmillan, 2005.

Pesce, Anita. *La Sirena nel solco: Origini della riproduzione sonora*. Naples: Guida, 2005.

Petric, Vlada. *Constructivism in Film: The Man with a Movie Camera, A Cinematic Analysis*. Cambridge: Cambridge University Press, 1987.

Petrone, Karen. *The Great War in Russian Memory*. Bloomington: Indiana University Press, 2011.

Plisetskaya, Maya. *I, Maya Plisetskaya*. Translated by Antonina W. Bouis. Introduction by Tim Scholl. New Haven, CT: Yale University Press, 2001.

Pogorelskin, Alexis. "The Messenger of Europe." In *Literary Journals in Imperial Russia*, 129–49. Edited by Deborah A. Martinsen. Cambridge: Cambridge University Press, 1997.

Pogozheva, Liudmila. "Sostoianie i zadachi kritiki i teorii sovetskogo kinoiskusstva." In *Vsesoiuznaia tvorcheskaia konferentsiia rabotnikov kinematografii: stenograficheskij otchet*, 353–62. Moscow: Iskusstvo, 1959.

Poliakov, Iu. A. and Drobashenko, S.V. *Sovetskaia kinokhronika 1918–1925 gg.: annotirovannyj katalog*. Part 1. Moscow: Glavnoe Arkhivnoe Upravlenie pri SM SSSR, 1965.

Polian, P. et al., eds. *Gorod i derevnia v evropejskoj Rossii: sto let peremen*. Moscow: OGI, 2001.

Polianskaia, Irina. *Chitaiushchaia voda*. Moscow: Grant, 2001.

Polonsky, Antony. *The Jews in Poland and Russia*. Vol. 2. Oxford: Littmann Library of Jewish Civilization, 2010.

Pozdorovkin, Maxim. "Khronika: Soviet newsreel at the dawn of the information age." PhD diss., Slavic Languages and Literatures, Harvard University, 2012.

Pozner, Valérie. "'Joué' versus 'non-joué': la notion de 'fait' dans les débats cinématographiques des années 20 en URSS." *Communications* 79 (2006): 91–104.

——. "Vertov before Vertov: Psychoneurology in Petrograd." In *Dziga Vertov: The Vertov Collection at the Austrian Film Museum*, 12–15. Edited by Thomas Tode and Barbara Wurm. Vienna: Österreichisches Filmmuseum/SYNEMA, 2006.

Privat, Edmond. *Vivo de Zamenhof*. Leipzig: Ferdinand Hirt & Sohn/Esperanto Fako, 1923.

Prizhiborovskaia, Galina. *Larisa Rejsner*. Molodaia Gvardiia: Moscow, 2008.

Prokof'ev, N. "V bor'be s tuberkulezom." *Vestnik Kinematografii* 89/9 (May 7, 1914): 14.

Pudovkin, Vsevolod. "Proletarskij kinematograf." *Kino-Gazeta* 6 (1925): 2.

——. *Selected Essays*. Edited by Richard Taylor. Translated by Richard Taylor and Evgeni Filippov. London: Seagull Books, 2006.

Purishkevich, Vladimir. *Soldatskie pesni*. Petrograd: K. A. Chetverikov, 1914.

Rabinbach, Anson. *The Human Motor: Energy, Fatigue, and the Origins of Modernity*. New York: Basic Books, 1990.

Rabinowitch, Alexander. *The Bolsheviks come to Power: The Revolution of 1917 in Petrograd*. New York: W. W. Norton, 1976.

——. *The Bolsheviks in Power: The First Year of Soviet Rule in Petrograd*. Bloomington: 2007.

Rancière, Jacques, and Davide Panagia. "Dissenting Words: A Conversation with Jacques Rancière." *Diacritics* 30, no. 2 (Summer 2000): 113–26.

Rancière, Jacques. *The Ignorant Schoolmaster: Five Lessons in Intellectual Emancipation*. Translated and introduction by Kristin Ross. Stanford, CA: Stanford University Press, 1991.

Reifenberg, Benno. "Für wen sieht das 'Kino-Auge'? Zur Diskussion um den russischen Filmregisseur Dziga Vertov (Frankfurt, den 25 Juli)." *Frankfurter Zeitung* (July 25, 1929): n.p.

Reinbeck, Georg. *Travels from St. Petersburgh through Moscow, Grodno, Warsaw, Breslaw &c to Germany in the Year 1805 in a Series of Letters*. London: Richard Phillips, 1807.

Rejsner, Larisa. *Izbrannoe*. Moscow: Khudozhestvennaia Literatura, 1980.

Rejsner, Mikhail. *Bog i birzha: sbornik revoliutsionnykh p'es*. Moscow: Gosudarstvennoe Izdatel'stvo, 1921.

——. *Chto takoe Sovetskaia Vlast'?* Moscow: Izdatel'stvo Narodnogo Komissariata Zemledeliia, 1918.

——. *Gosudarstvo*. 2 vols. Moscow: I. D. Sytin, 1911.

——. *Nuzhno li nam verit' v Boga?* 2nd ed. Kursk: Knigoizdatel'skoe tovarishchestvo pri Kurskom Gubkome RKP(b), 1922.

Rejtblat, A. I., ed. and intro. *Lubochnaia povest': antologiia*. Moscow: O. G. I., 2005.

——. *Ot Bovy k Bal'montu: ocherki po istorii chteniia v Rossii vo vtoroj polovine XIX veka*. Moscow: MPI, 1991.

Renan, Sheldon. *An Introduction to the American Underground Film*. New York: E. P. Dutton, 1967.
Renault, Emmanuel. "L'idéologie comme légitimation et comme description." *Actuel Marx* 1, no. 48 (2008): 80–95.
Richardson, Charl'z [Charles Richardson]. *Kak chitat' knigi, chtoby oni prinosili nam pol'zu?* Translated by A. P. Valueva-Munt. St. Petersburg: M. M. Lederle, 1893.
Richter, Erika. "Dsiga Wertow: Publizist und Poet des Documentarfilms." *Filmwissenschaftliche Mitteilungen* 1 (March 1961): 24–25.
Rivesman, M. "Rodina." *Evrejskij Golos* 5 (February 12, 1906): 141–42.
Roberts, Geoffrey. *Stalin's Wars: From World War to Cold War, 1939–1953*. New Haven, CT: Yale University Press, 2006.
Robin, Corey. "Reclaiming the Politics of Freedom." *The Nation* (April 25, 2011). Accessed June 24, 2017, http://www.thenation.com/article/159748/reclaiming-politics-freedom.
Rogdaev, N. I. "Kratkij ocherk anarkhicheskogo dvizheniia v Pol'she, Litve i Lifliandii." *Anarkhisty: dokumenty i materialy*. Vol. 1. Edited by V. V. Shelokhaev et al. Moscow: Rosspen, 1998.
Rogger, Hans. *Jewish Policies and Right-Wing Politics in Imperial Russia*. Houndmills and London: Macmillan, 1986.
Rogova, Valentina. "Dziga Vertov: zlodej ili genij? Ego predannost' vlastiam ne znala granits." *Vek* 38 (November 1, 2002): 10.
———. "Strannaia sud'ba Dzigi Vertova. VChK prosila vsevozmozhnoe sodejstvie." *Nezavisimaia Gazeta* 33 (February 18, 2005): 24.
Rohmer, Eric, and Louis Marcorelles. "Entretien avec Jean Rouch." *Cahiers du Cinéma* XXIV, no. 114 (June 1963): 1–22.
Romanov, A., et al. "Dzige Vertovu, khudozhniku revoliutsii." *Iskusstvo Kino* 10 (October 1967): 41–42.
Romero Brest, Jorge A. "El elemento ritmo en el cine y en el deporte." *Nosotros* 247 (December 1929): 352–67.
Rosen, Philip. *Change Mummified: Cinema, Historicity, Theory*. Minneapolis: University of Minnesota Press, 2001.
———. "Now and Then: Conceptual Problems in Historicizing Documentary Imaging." *Canadian Journal of Film Studies/Revue Canadienne d'Études Cinématographiques* 16, no. 1 (Spring 2007): 25–38.
Rosenberg, Justin. "Why Is There No International Historical Sociology?" *European Journal of International Relations* 12, no. 3 (2006): 307–40.
Roshal', L. M., ed. "*Chelovek s kinoapparatom*: muzykal'nyj konspekt." *Kinovedcheskie Zapiski* 21 (1994): 188–97.
———. *Dziga Vertov*. Moscow: Iskusstvo, 1984.
———. *Nachalo vsekh nachal: fakt na ekrane i kinomysl' "Serebrianogo Veka."* Moscow: Materik, 2002.
———, ed. "Protokol N 11 otkrytogo partijnogo sobraniia Tsentral'noj Studii Dokumental'nykh Fil'mov ot 14–15 marta 1949 goda." *Iskusstvo Kino* 12 (December 1997): 128–33.
———. "Protokol odnogo zasedaniia." *Iskusstvo Kino* 12 (December 1997): 124–27.
Rosolovskaia, V. *Russkaia kinematografiia v 1917 g.: materialy k istorii*. Moscow: Iskusstvo, 1937.

Ross, Kristin. *May '68 and its Afterlives*. Chicago: University of Chicago Press, 2002.

Rothman, William. *Documentary Film Classics*. Cambridge: Cambridge University Press, 1997.

Roudinesco, Elisabeth, and Henri Deluy. "Entretien avec Elisabeth Roudinesco: Dziga Vertov ou le regard interdit." *Action Poétique* 59 (1974): 308–16.

Rubashkin, A. *Mikhail Kol'tsov: kritiko-biograficheskij ocherk*. Leningrad: Khudozhestvennaia Literatura, 1971.

Ruspoli, Mario. *Le Groupe Synchrone Cinématographique Léger*. Paris: UNESCO, 1963.

Russell, Robert. "The Arts and the Russian Civil War." *Journal of European Studies* 20 (1990): 219–40.

Russian S. F. S. R. *Dekrety Sovetskoj Vlasti*. Vol. 4. Moscow: Izdatel'stvo Politicheskoj Literatury, 1968.

Ryan, James. "'They know not what they do?' Bolshevik understandings of the agency of perpetrators, 1918–1930." *Historical Research* 90, no. 247 (February 2017): 151–71.

Rymkevich, P. A. *Chudesa XX veka (trud i tekhnika)*. 3rd ed. Leningrad, Priboj, 1925.

Sadoul, Georges. "Actualité de Dziga Vertov." *Cahiers du Cinéma* XXIV, no. 144 (June 1963): 23–31.

———. "A Lyon les 'caméras vivantes' ont recontré le 'cinéma-vérité.'" *Les Lettres Françaises* 970 (March 14, 1963): 7.

———. "Bio-filmographie de Dziga Vertov." *Cahiers du Cinéma* XXV, no. 146 (August 1963): 5–17, 18–20, 21–29.

———. "Les Chevaux de Muybridge: *Chronique d'un été*, expérience de cinéma-vérité, par Jean Rouch." *Les Lettres Françaises* 898 (October 26, 1961): 6.

———. "Cinéma-vérité ou Théâtre-vérité? *The Connection*, film américain de Shirley Clarke." *Les Lettres Françaises* 912 (February 1, 1962): 6.

———. "Cinémois" *Cinéma* (May 1963): 8.

———. "Ciné-Oeil et Film-Témoin: *Shadows*, film new-yorkais de Cassavetes." *Les Lettres Françaises* 873 (May 4, 1961): 6.

———. "Cinéastes et téléastes." *Les Lettres Françaises* 896 (12 October 1961): 6.

———. "Dziga Vertov." *Artsept* 2 (April–June 1963): 18–19.

———. *Dziga Vertov*. Edited by Bernard Eisenschitz. Introduction by Jean Rouch. Paris: Éditions Champ Libre, 1971.

———. "Dziga Vertov: Poète du ciné oeil y prophète de la radio oreille." *Image et Son* 183 (April 1965): 8–18.

———. "Enfin le cinéma-oeil!" *Les Lettres Françaises* 919 (March 22, 1962): 6.

———. *Histoire d'un art: Le cinéma des origines a nos jours*. Paris: Flammarion, 1949.

———. *Les Merveilles du Cinéma*. Paris: Éditeurs Français Réunis, 1957.

——— [Zhorzh Sadul']. "Zhivaia istoriia kino." *Pravda* 223 (August 11, 1959): 4.

Sadoul, Georges, et al. "Notes sur la famille Sadoul." Accessed June 24, 2017, http://sadoul.free.fr/Site_papa/HISTOIRE%20DE%20LA%20FAMILLE%20SADOUL.htm#Georges_bio.

Safran, Gabriella, and Steven J. Zipperstein, eds. *The Worlds of S. An-sky: A Russian Jewish Intellectual at the Turn of the Century*. Stanford, CA: Stanford University Press, 2006.

Samuel, Maurice. *Blood Accusation: The Strange Story of the Beilis Case*. New York: Knopf, 1966.

Sarkisova, Oksana. *Screening Soviet Ethnicities: Kulturfilms from the Far North to Central Asia*. London: I. B. Tauris, 2016.

Sauzier, Bertrand. "An Interpretation of Man with the Movie Camera." *Visual Communication* 11, no. 4 (Fall 1985): 30–53.

Schiller, Friedrich. *On the Aesthetic Education of Man*. Edited by Elizabeth M. Wilkinson and L. A. Willoughby. Oxford: Oxford University Press, 1967.

Schnitzer, Luba and Jean. *Le Cinéma soviétique par ceux qui l'ont fait*. Paris: Éditeurs français réunis, 1966.

Schumpeter, Joseph A. *Capitalism, Socialism and Democracy*. 3rd ed. New York: Harper & Row, 1975.

Segal-Marshak, E. "To, chto sokhranilos' v pamiati." In *Dziga Vertov v vospominaniiakh sovremennikov*, 244–61. Edited by E. I. Vertova-Svilova and A. L. Vinogradova. Moscow: Iskusstvo, 1976.

Selezneva, T. F. "Nasledie Dzigi Vertova i iskaniia 'cinéma-vérité.'" In *Razmyshleniia u ekrana*, 337–67. Edited by E. S. Dobin. Leningrad: Iskusstvo, 1966.

Serafimovich, A. "Milliony v prorvu." *Pravda* 191 (August 31, 1920): 1.

Serge, Victor. *Memoirs of a Revolutionary*. Translated by Peter Sedgwick and George Paizis. Edited by Richard Greeman. Introduction by Adam Hochschild. New York: New York Review Books, 2012.

Sergeev, B. "Agitpoezdki M. I. Kalinina v gody grazhdanskoj vojny." *Krasnyj Arkhiv* 86 (1938): 93–163.

Shalashnikov, M. "Nedeli sovetskogo fil'ma vo Frantsii: vecher v Zale Plejel'." *Sovetskaia Kul'tura* 149 (December 4, 1955): 4.

Shcherbenok, Andrej. "Dziga Vertov: dialektika kinoveshchi." *Iskusstvo Kino* 1 (January 2012): 76–87.

Shcherbina, V. "O gruppe estetstvuiushchikh kosmopolitov v kino." *Iskusstvo Kino* 1 (February 1949): 14–16.

Shitomirski, Daniel. *Blindheit als Schutz vor der Wahrheit*. Translated by Ernst Kuhn. Introduction by Oksana Leontjewa. Berlin: Verlag Ernst Kuhn, 1996.

Shklovsky [Shklovskij], Viktor. "Ob iskusstve i revoliutsii." *Iskusstvo Kommuny* 17 (March 30, 1919): 2.

———. "O Dzige Vertove." In *Dziga Vertov v vospominaniiakh sovremennikov*, 171–83. Edited by E. I. Vertova-Svilova and A. L. Vinogradova. Moscow: Iskusstvo, 1976.

———. *Room: zhizn' i rabota*. Moscow: Tea-Kino-Pechat', 1929.

Shtokalo, I. Z. et al., eds. *Istoriia mekhaniki v Rossii*. Kiev: Naukova Dumka, 1987.

Shub, Esfir'. *Krupnym planom*. Moscow: Iskusstvo, 1959.

Shuster, S., et al. "Kalendar' istorii kino." *Iskusstvo Kino* 12 (December 1961): 142–43.

Shvarts, L. B. "Pozitsiia rezhissera: interv'iu s A. Iu. Germanom." In *Peterburgskoe "Novoe Kino": sbornik statej*, 123–41. Edited by M. L. Zhezhelenko. St. Petersburg: MOL, 1996.

Sidenova, Raisa. "From Pravda to Verité: Soviet Documentary Film and Television, 1950–1985." PhD diss., Department of Slavic Languages and Literatures and Film and Media Studies Program, Yale University, 2016.

Siegelbaum, Lewis H. *Soviet State and Society between Revolutions, 1918–1929*. Cambridge: Cambridge University Press, 1992.

Simon, Bill. "Jean Vigo's *Taris*." *Artforum* (September 1974): 50–53.

Simon, Elena Pinto. "The Films of Peter Kubelka." *Artforum* (April 1972): 33–39.

Sitney, P. Adams. *Modernist Montage: The Obscurity of Vision in Cinema and Literature*. New York: Columbia University Press, 1990.

Slezkine, Yuri. *The Jewish Century*. Princeton, NJ: Princeton University Press, 2006.

Slonimskij, L. Z. et al., eds. *XIX vek: illiustrirovannyj obzor minuvshago stoletiia*. Supplement to *Niva* 52 (1901).

Smele, Jon. *Civil War in Siberia: The Anti-Bolshevik government of Admiral Kolchak, 1918–1920*. Cambridge: Cambridge University Press, 1996.

Smirnov, Vas. "Sila sovetskoj pravdy." *Iskusstvo Kino* 3 (June 1949): 16–21.

Smith, Margaret Keiver. *Rhythmus und Arbeit*. Leipzig: Wilhelm Engelmann, 1900.

Smith, Steve. "Year One in Petrograd." *New Left Review* II/52 (July–August 2008): 151–60.

Smither, Roger, and Klaue, Wolfgang, eds. *Newsreels in Film Archives: A Survey Based on the FIAF Newsreel Symposium*. Wiltshire, UK: Flicks Books, 1996.

Sokolov, P. A. *Pedagogicheskaia Psikhologiia*. 5th ed. St. Petersburg: Ia. Bashmakov, 1913.

Sonnenberg, Ben. "From the Diary of a Movie Buff." *Raritan* 21, no. 2 (2001): 1–7.

Stam, Robert. *Reflexivity in Film and Literature: From Don Quixote to Jean-Luc Godard*. New York: Columbia University Press, 1992.

Stanislawski, Michael. "Russian Jewry, the Russian State, and the Dynamics of Jewish Emancipation." In *Paths of Emancipation: Jews, States, and Citizenship*, 262–83. Edited by Pierre Birnbaum and Ira Katznelson. Princeton, NJ: Princeton University Press, 1995.

———. *Tsar Nicholas I and the Jews: The Transformation of Jewish Society in Russia: 1825–1855*. Philadelphia: Jewish Publication Society of America, 1983.

Starr, S. Frederick. *Decentralization and Self-Government in Russia, 1830–1870*. Princeton, NJ: Princeton University Press, 1972.

Steffen, James. *The Cinema of Sergei Parajanov*. Madison: University of Wisconsin Press, 2013.

Steinberg, Mark D. *Proletarian Imagination: Self, Modernity, and the Sacred in Russia, 1910–1925*. Ithaca, NY: Cornell University Press, 2002.

Stites, Richard. *The Women's Liberation Movement in Russia: Feminism, Nihilism, and Bolshevism, 1860–1930*. Princeton, NJ: Princeton University Press, 1978.

Strauven, Wanda. "Futurist Poetics and the Cinematic Imagination: Marinetti's Cinema without Films." In *Futurism and the Technological Imagination*, 201–28. Edited by Günter Berghaus. Amsterdam: Rodopi, 2009.

Streeck, Wolfgang. "The Post-Capitalist Interregnum." *Juncture* 23, no. 2 (2016): 68–77.

Sukharebskij, L. M. *Obzor sanprosvetitel'nykh kinofil'm za 10 let proletarskoj revoliutsii (1917–1927)*. Moscow: Moszdravotdel, 1928.

Sukharebskij, L., and A. Ptushko, eds. *Spetsial'nye sposoby kinos'emki*. Moscow: Khudozhestvennaia Literatura, 1930.

Suny, Ronald Grigor. *The Soviet Experiment: Russia, the USSR, and the Successor States*. New York: Oxford University Press, 1998.

———. "Toward a Social History of the October Revolution." *American Historical Review* 88, no. 1 (February 1983): 31–52.

Superanskaia, A. V. *Imia — cherez veka i strany*. Moscow: Nauka, 1990.

Sutyrin, V. *Problemy sotsialisticheskoj rekonstrutsii sovetskoj kinopromyshlennosti*. Moscow: Khudozhestvennaia Literatura, 1932.

Syrtsov, Boris. "Chuguevskoe voennoe uchilishche, 1916–1917 gg." *Voennaia Byl'* 90 (1968): 36–38.

T. W. D. *Mnemonics: or, the New Science of Artificial Memory*. New York: James Mowatt and Co., 1844.

Tager, A. S. *The Decay of Czarism: The Beiliss Trial*. Philadelphia: Jewish Publication Society of America, 1935.

Tarkhova, N. S. "Poezd Trotskogo — letuchij apparat upravleniia narkomvoena." In *Gosudarstvennyj apparat Rossii v gody Revoliutsii i Grazhdanskoj Vojny*, 128–40. Edited by T. G. Arkhipova. Moscow: RGGU, 1998.

Taruskin, Richard. *Defining Russia Musically*. Princeton, NJ: Princeton University Press, 1997.

Taylor, Lucien. "A Conversation with Jean Rouch." *Visual Anthropology Review* 7, no. 1 (Spring 1991): 92–102.

Taylor, Richard. *Film Propaganda: Soviet Russia and Nazi Germany*. London: Croom Helm and Barnes and Noble, 1979.

———. "A Medium for the Masses: Agitation in the Civil War." *Soviet Studies* 22, no. 4 (April 1971): 562–74.

———. *The Politics of the Soviet Cinema, 1917–1918*. Cambridge: Cambridge University Press, 1979.

Taylor, Richard, and Ian Christie, eds. *The Film Factory: Russian and Soviet Cinema in Documents, 1896–1939*. London: Routledge, 1988.

Thompson, Capt. Donald C. *Blood Stained Russia*. New York: Leslie-Judge, 1918.

Tiagaj, D. N., ed. *Rechi po pogromnym delam*. Introduction by V. G. Korolenko. Kiev: S. G. Sliusarevskij, 1908.

Tihanov, Galin, and Evgeny Dobrenko, eds. *A History of Russian Literary Theory and Criticism: The Soviet Era and Beyond*. Pittsburgh, PA: University of Pittsburgh Press, 2011.

Tode, Thomas. "Agit-trains, Agit-steamers, Cinema Trucks: Dziga Vertov and Travelling Cinema in the early 1920s in the Soviet Union." In *Travelling Cinema in Europe: Sources and Perspectives* [Kinotop Schriften 10], 143–53. Edited by Martin Loiperdinger. Frankfurt am Main: Stroemfeld Verlag, 2008.

———. "Vertov und Wien/Vertov and Vienna." *Dziga Vertov: Die Vertov-Sammlung im Österreichischen Filmmuseum*, 33–50. Edited by Thomas Tode and Barbara Wurm. Österreichisches Filmmuseum/SYNEMA: Vienna, 2006.

Tode, Thomas, and Barbara Wurm, eds. *Dziga Vertov: Die Vertov-Sammlung im Österreichischen Filmmuseum*. Österreichisches Filmmuseum/SYNEMA: Vienna, 2006.

Todorov, T., ed. *Théorie de la littérature: Textes des formalistes russes*. Paris: Seuil, 1965.

Tolstoj, Aleksej. *Khleb: Oborona Tsaritsyna*. Moscow: OGIZ, 1937.

Tolstoj, V.P., ed. *Agitmassovoe iskusstvo Sovetskoj Rossij: materialy i dokumenty*. 2 vols. Moscow: Iskusstvo, 2002.

Toscano, Alberto. "Logistics and Opposition." In *Logistics, Circulation, Class Struggle and Communism*, 1–10. Accessed July 1, 2017, https://advancethestruggle.files.wordpress.com/2014/08/logisticsreaderfinal1.pdf.

Toti, Gianni. "La produttività dei materiali in Ejzenstejn e Dziga Vertov." *Cinema & Film* 3 (Summer 1967): 281–87.

Toulmin, Vanessa. "'Within the Reach of All': Travelling Cinematograph Shows on British Fairgrounds 1896–1914." *Travelling Cinema in Europe: Sources and Perspectives* [Kinotop Schriften 10], 19–33. Edited by Martin Loiperdinger. Frankfurt am Main: Stroemfeld Verlag, 2008.

Trajnin, I. P. *Kino na kul'turnom fronte*. Moscow: Teakinopechat', 1928.

Trotsky, Leon [L. Trotskij]. *Kul'tura i sotsializm*. Moscow: Gosudarstvennoe Izdatel'stvo, 1926.

———. *Voprosy kul'turnoj raboty*. Moscow: Gosudarstvennoe Izdatel'stvo, 1924.

Tsivian, Yuri. "Early Russian Cinema and its Public." Translated by Alan Bodger. *Historical Journal of Film, Radio and Television* 11, no. 2 (1991): 105–20.

——— [Youri Tsyviane]. "*L'Homme à la caméra* de Dziga Vertov en tant comme texte constructiviste." *La Revue du Cinéma/Image et Son* 351 (June 1980): 109–25.

———. *Istoricheskaia retseptsiia kino: Kinematograf v Rossii 1896–1930*. Riga: Zinatne, 1991.

———, ed. and intro. *Lines of Resistance: Dziga Vertov and the Twenties*. Sacile/Pordenone: Le Giornate del Cinema Muto, 2004.

———, et al. "The Rediscovery of a Kuleshov Experiment: A Dossier." *Film History* 8, no. 3 (1996): 357–67.

———. "Vertov's Silent Music: Cue Sheets and a Music Scenario for *The Man with the Movie Camera*." *Griffithiana* 54 (October 1995): 92–121.

Tumarkin, Nina. *Lenin Lives! The Lenin Cult in the Soviet Union*. 2nd ed. Cambridge, MA: Harvard University Press, 1997.

Turvey, Malcolm. "Can the Camera See? Mimesis in *Man with a Movie Camera*." *October* 89 (Summer 1999): 25–50.

Tyler, Parker. "Sidney Peterson." *Film Culture* 19 (1959): 38–43.

———. "Stan Brakhage." *Film Culture* 18 (April 1958): 23–24.

———. *Underground Film: A Critical History*. New York: Grove Press, 1969.

Vagner, V. A. "Kinematograf, kak orudie izsledovanij." *Fotograficheskie Novosti* 6 (1915): 90–92.

———. "Rol' kinematografa v sfere iavleniia dvizheniia." *Kinematograf* 2 (1915): 1–2.

———. "Rol' kinematografa v sfere iavleniia dvizheniia." *Vestnik Kinematografij* 111/9 (May 1, 1915): 10.

Vanechkina, I. L., and B. M. Galeev. *Poema ognia: kontseptsiia svetomuzykal'nogo sinteza A. N. Skriabina*. Kazan': Izdatel'stvo Kazanskogo Universiteta, 1981.

Vaughan, Dai. *"The Man with the Movie Camera."* *Films and Filming* (November 1960): 18–20, 43.

Verdone, Mario. "Dziga Vertov nell'avanguardia." In Nikolaj Abramov, *Dziga Vertov*, XXI–XXII. Rome: Bianco e Nero, 1963.

Verner, V. "Kinematograf i ego primenenie." *Kino* 2 (1915): n.p.

Versari, Maria Elena. "Futurist Machine Art, Constructivism and the Modernity of Mechanization." In *Futurism and the Technological Imagination*, 149–176. Edited by Günter Berghaus. Amsterdam and New York: Rodopi, 2009.

Vertov, Dziga. *Articles, journaux, projets*. Translated by Sylviane Mosse and Andrée Robel. Paris: Union générale de éditions/Cahiers du Cinéma, 1972.

———. *Articulos, Proyectos y Diarios de Trabajo*. Translated by Victor Goldstein. Introduction by H. Alsina Thevenet. Buenos Aires: Ediciones de la Flor, 1974.

——— [Dsiga Wertow]. *Aufsätze, Tagebücher, Skizzen*. Edited by and translated by Hermann Herlinghaus and Rolf Liebmann. East Berlin: Institut für Filmwissenschaft an der Deutschen Hochschule für Filmkunst, 1967.

———. *Aus den Tagebüchern*. Edited by Peter Konlechner and Peter Kubelka. Translated by Reinhard Urbach. Vienna: Österreichisches Filmmuseum, 1967.

———. *Cikkek, naplójegyzetek, gondolatok*. Translated by Veress József and Misley Pál. Budapest: M. Filmtud. Int. és Filmarchívum, 1973.

——— [Vertof]. "Ciné-Oeil." *La Critique Cinématographique* 12 (April 15, 1937): 6.

———. "Ciné-Oeil." In *Anthologie du Cinéma: Rétrospective par les textes de l'art muet qui devint parlant*, 207–9. Edited by Marcel Lapierre. Paris: La Nouvelle Édition, 1946.

———. *El cine-ojo*. Edited and translated by Francisco Llinás. Madrid: Fundamentos, 1974.

———. *Człowiek z kamerą: wybór pism*. Translated by Tadeusz Karpowski. Introduction by Nikolaj Abramov. Warsaw: Wydawnictwa Artystyczne i Filmowe, 1976.

———. *Dramaturgicheskie opyty*. Edited by A. S. Deriabin. Introduction by V. S. Listov. Moscow: Ejzenshtejn-tsentr, 2004.

——— [Dsiga Wertow]. *Dsiga Wertow: Publizist und Poet des Dokumentarfilms*. Edited by Hermann Herlinghaus. East Berlin: VEB Progress Film-Vertrieb, 1960.

———. "Dziga Vertov on Film Technique." Translated by Samuel Brody. *Filmfront* 3 (January 28, 1935): 7–9.

———. "From the Notebooks of Dziga Vertov." Translated by Marco Carynnyk. *Artforum* 10, no. 7 (March 1972): 73–83.

———. "Iz rabochikh tetradej Dzigi Vertova." *Iskusstvo Kino* 4 (April 1957): 112–26.

———. *Kino-Eye: The Writings of Dziga Vertov*. Edited and introduction by Annette Michelson. Translated by Kevin O'Brien. Berkeley: University of California Press, 1984.

———. "Kinoki. Perevorot." *LEF* 3 (June–July 1923): 135–43.

———. "Kinoks-Révolution." *Cahiers du Cinéma* XXIV, no. 114 (June 1963): 32–34.

———. "Kinoks-Révolution II." *Cahiers du Cinéma* XXV, no. 146 (August 1963): 18–20.

———. *L'occhio della rivoluzione: Scritti dal 1922 al 1942*. Edited by Pietro Montani. Milan: Mazzotta, 1975.

———. "O liubvi k zhivomu cheloveku." *Iskusstvo Kino* 6 (June 1958): 95–99.

———. "On i ia." *Kino-Fot* 2 (September 8–15, 1922): 9–10.

———. *Schriften zum Film*. Edited and afterword by Wolfgang Beilenhoff. Munich: Carl Hanser, 1973.

———. *Sine-Göz*. Translated by Ahmet Ergenc. Istanbul: Agora Kitapligi, 2007.

———. *Stat'i, dnevniki, zamysly*. Edited by S. Drobashenko. Moscow: Iskusstvo, 1966.

———. *Stat'i i vystupleniia*. Edited by D. V. Kruzhkova and S. M. Ishevskaia. Moscow: Ejzenshtejn-Tsentr, 2008.

———. *Tagebücher, Arbeitshefte*. Edited by Thomas Tode and Alexandra Gramatke. Translated by Alexandra Gramatke. Konstanz: UVK Medien, 2000.

——— [Dsiga Wertow]. "Das Vermächtnis Dsiga Wertows" and "Tagebuchaufzeichnungen." *Deutsche Filmkunst* 10 (1957): 292–95.

———. "The Vertov Papers." Translated by Marco Carynnyk. *Film Comment* 8, no. 1 (Spring 1972): 46–51.

———. "We: A Manifesto by Film Worker Dziga Vertov." *Evergreen* 14, no. 83 (October 1970): 50–51.

———. "The Writings of Dziga Vertov." *Film Culture* 25 (Summer 1962): 50–65.

———. "The Writings of Dziga Vertov." In *Film Makers on Film Making: Statements on Their Art by Thirty Directors*, 79–105. Edited by Harry M. Geduld. Indianapolis: Indiana University Press, 1967.

———. "The Writings of Dziga Vertov." In *Film Culture Reader*, 353–75. Edited by P. Adams Sitney. New York: Praeger, 1970.

Vertova-Svilova, E. I., and A. L. Vinogradova, eds. *Dziga Vertov v vospominaniiakh sovremennikov*. Moscow: Iskusstvo, 1976.

Vertova-Svilova, E. I. "Pamiat' o Vertove." In *Dziga Vertov v vospominaniiakh sovremennikov*, 65–70. Edited by E. I. Vertova-Svilova and A. L. Vinogradova. Moscow: Iskusstvo, 1976.

Viazzi, Glauco, ed. "Il cinema sovietico (I)." *Sequenze* 3 (November 1949).

———. "Dziga Vertov e la tendenza documentarista." *Ferrania* (August–September 1957): 8–9.

———. *Scritti di cinema, 1940–1958*. Milan: Longanesi, 1979.

Vinnichenko, Elena. "*Chelovek s kinoapparatom*." *Iskusstvo Kino* 12 (December 1989): 111–13.

Vitoux, Georges [Zhorzh Vitu]. "Usovershenstvovannyj kinematograf." *Vestnik Znaniia* 10 (October 1910): 1056–60.

Vladimirov V. *Ocherki sovremennykh kaznej*. Moscow: A. P. Poplavskij, 1906.

Voloshin, P. "Russkie voennye orkestry." *Voennaia Byl'* 56 (1962): 37–40.

Waller, Gregory A. "Richard Southard and the History of Traveling Film Exhibition." *Film Quarterly* 57, no. 2 (Winter 2003–4): 2–14.

Wallerstein, Immanuel. "New Revolts Against the System." *New Left Review* II/8 (November–December 2002): 29–39.

Warner, Michael. *Publics and Counterpublics*. New York: Zone Books, 2005.

Wartenweiler, David. *Civil Society and Academic Debate in Russia 1905–1914*. Oxford: Clarendon Press, 1999.

Weeks, Theodore R. *Nation and State in Late Imperial Russia: Nationalism and Russification on the Western Frontier, 1863–1914*. DeKalb: Northern Illinois University Press, 1996.

Weibel, Peter. "Eisenstein, Vertov and the Formal Film." In *Film as Film: Formal Experiment in Film 1910–1975*, 47–51. Edited by Phillip Drummond et al. London: Arts Council of Great Britain, 1979.

Weinberg, Herman J. "The Man with the Movie Camera." *Film Comment* 4, no. 1 (Fall 1966): 40–42.

Weinryb, Bernard D. *The Jews of Poland: A Social and Economic History of the Jewish Community from 1100 to 1800*. Philadelphia: Jewish Publication Society of America, 1973.

Wibom, Anna-Lena. "Der Fund der *Kinonedelja* in Schweden." *Maske und Kothurn* 50, no. 1 (2004): 73–76.

Widdis, Emma. *Alexander Medvedkin*. London: I. B. Tauris, 2005.

———. *Visions of a New Land: Soviet Film from the Revolution to the Second World War*. New Haven, CT: Yale University Press, 2003.

Wildman, Allan K. *The End of the Russian Imperial Army*. Vol. 1. Princeton, NJ: Princeton University Press, 1980.

Williams, Alan. "The Camera Eye and the Film: Notes on Vertov's 'Formalism.'" *Wide Angle* 3, no. 3 (1979): 12–17.

Williams, Raymond. *The Country and the City*. New York: Oxford University Press, 1973.

Winter, Jay. *Sites of Memory, Sites of Mourning: The Great War in European Cultural History*. Cambridge: Cambridge University Press, 1995.

Witt, Michael. "Godard dans la presse d'extrême gauche." In *Jean-Luc Godard: Documents*, 165–73. Edited by Nicole Brenez et al. Paris: Centre Pompidou, 2006.

———. *Jean-Luc Godard, Cinema Historian*. Bloomington: Indiana University Press, 2013.

———. "In Search of Godard's *Sauve la vie (qui peut)*." *NECSUS* (Spring 2015). Accessed November 20, 2016, http://www.necsus-ejms.org/in-search-of-godards-sauve-la-vie-qui-peut.

———. "On and Under Communication." In *A Companion to Jean-Luc Godard*, 318–50. Edited by Tom Conley and T. Jefferson Kline. New York: Wiley-Blackwell, 2014.

Woll, Josephine. *Real Images: Soviet Cinema and the Thaw*. London: I. B. Tauris, 2000.

Wood, Michael. *Film: A Very Short Introduction*. Oxford: Oxford University Press, 2012.

Wortman, Richard S. *Scenarios of Power: Myth and Ceremony in Russian Monarchy*. Vol. 2. Princeton: Princeton University Press, 2000.

Wurm, Barbara. "1960. Die erste Retrospektive." In *Bilder einer gespaltenen Welt: 50 Jahre Dokumentar-und Animationsfilmfestival Leipzig*, 17–20. Edited by Ralf Schenk. Berlin: Bertz + Fischer, 2007.

Wynot, Jennifer Jean. *Keeping the Faith: Russian Orthodox Monasticism in the Soviet Union, 1917–1939*. College Station: Texas A&M University Press, 2004.

Yates, Frances. *The Art of Memory*. Chicago: University of Chicago Press, 1966.

Zagorskij, Mikhail. "Golod i rabotniki iskusstv." *Vestnik Iskusstv* 1 (1922): 5.

Zak, A. M. ed. *Samoe vazhnoe iz vsekh iskusstv: Lenin o kino*. Moscow: Iskusstvo, 1973.

Zavadskij, N. G. *Ispytanie vojnoj: rossijskoe studenchestvo i politicheskie partii v 1914– fevral' 1917 gg*. St. Petersburg: Nestor, 1999.

Zhdanov, Andrej. "Soviet Literature—The Richest in Ideas, the Most Advanced Literature." In *Soviet Writers Congress 1934: The Debate on Socialist Realism and Modernism in the Soviet Union*, 15–26. Edited by Maxim Gorky et al. London: Lawrence & Wishart, 1977. Accessed November 6, 2016, https://www.marxists.org/subject/art/lit_crit/sovietwritercongress/zdhanov.htm.

Zhemchuzhnyj, V. "*Shestaia chast' mira*." *Novyj Zritel'* 42, no. 145 (October 19, 1926): 16.

Zhurov, G. "Pervye shagi sovetskogo kino na Ukraine." *Voprosy Kinoiskusstva* 7 (1963): 187–209.

Zimmermann, Patricia R. "Reconstructing Vertov: Soviet Film Theory and American Radical Documentary." *Journal of Film and Video* 44, no. 1–2 (Spring–Summer 1992): 80–90.

———. "Strange Bedfellows: The Legacy of Vertov and Flaherty." *Journal of Film and Video* 44, nos. 1–2 (Spring–Summer 1992): 4–8.

Zipperstein, Steven J. *The Jews of Odessa: A Cultural History, 1794–1881*. Stanford, CA: Stanford University Press, 1986.

Žižek, Slavoj. "How to Begin from the Beginning." *New Left Review* II/57 (May–June 2009): 43–55.

Index

Page numbers in italics indicate illustrations.

A

Abramov, Nikolaj, xxxvii, xlvii, liv, lxiiin144, lxviiin159
   essay on Vertov (1960), 221n72
   monograph on Vertov (1962), xxivn28, xl–xli, xliv, xlivn84, xlix, livn119
actuality film(s)/actualities, lv, 171n139, 200, 204n29, 205, 205n30, 209n44, 212–13, 214, 216
   Kino-Nedelia and, 212, 212n53, 213, 213–14n55, 217, 223, 226n84
   newsreel and, 200–201, 205, 209n44, 212–13, 212n53, 220n69, 226n84, 229, 238n108
Agapov, Boris, lxv, lxvn150
agitation, 19n50, 42n124, 43, 142, 171, 171n138, 190, 201, 213
   khronika as means of, 200
   in *Kino-Nedelia*, 219, 220–21, 223
   propaganda vs., 242–43, 242n122, 243n123, 245, 248
   Vertov and, xcv–xcvi, 221, 240n117, 267
   See also agit-train(s)
agit-cinema, 256, 276n196
agitprop, 200, 237, 241, 241–42n121, 250
agit-train(s), xciv, 100, 193, 213, 234, 234–35n100, 235–37, 236, 236n104, 243, 275–76
   film screenings, 276–81, 278–79n204, 280n211, 283, 286–87, 289, 298
   murals on, 243–45, 243n124, 246, 247, 255–56, 268n179, 284n220
   October Revolution, 211, 234–35, 258–63
      film screenings, 276–82, 276n200, 278
      Kalinin and, 211, 238, 257–58, 263–67
      mural, 245–46, *245*
      Vertov and, 144, 211, 233, 235; 239–41, 262, 262n160, 262n163, 263n164, 267, 270, 276–77, 279–84, 298

Red East, 238, 240
Soviet Caucasus, 238, 267–69
   V. I. Lenin Mobile Military Front Train, 237, 237n106, 256, 257
   Vertov and, xcv–xcvi, 69, 83, 126, 128, 234, 239, 240–41, 240n116, 246, 247–48, 255, 270, 273, 274, 275, 280, 282, 284–86
Alexander I, 6
Alexander II, 16, 48
All-Russia Central Executive Committee (VTsIK), 257, 276n196
   agit-trains and, 234, 237, 237n106, 240n116, 276n196, 278n204
All-Russia Film and Photo Division (VFKO), 195, 233n95, 234, 241, 276n196
Althusser, Louis, 3n3, 4n6, lxxiiin173
anarchism, 51, 142, 159–60, 160n107
   Vertov and, 159–60, 159n105, 160n107
Anderson, Benedict, 219, 219n66
Anniversary of the Revolution (Vertov), 195, 197, 232, 280, *281*
   found footage in, 188, 195, 195n5, 223–24n75, 227, 227n85
An-sky, S., 56–57
Anthology Film Archives, lxxi
anti-cosmopolitan campaign, xxiii, xxxv, xxxvn56, xlviii, xciv, 49, 54
anti-Semitism/anti-Semitic, xxiii, 47, 48–49, 53, 56, 156
   in Bialystok, 47, 49–50, 49n149
   Gavriil cult, 49–50, 50n152, 289
   of Nicholas II, 52, 52n162
   politicians, 42n123, 55, 57
   of the Russian Army, 70, 70n3
   state-sponsored, xxiii, 82n48, 84
   See also anti-cosmopolitan campaign; Black Hundreds; blood libel; *numerus clausus*; Pale of Settlement; pogrom(s); Union of Russian People

Apollinaire, Guillaume, lxix, lviin125
Aragon, Louis, li
Artforum, lxx, lxx–lxxin164
Articles, Diaries, Projects (Vertov), xxxi, xl, lxii–lxiii, lxvii
Art of Cinema (Iskusstvo Kino), xxiv, xxivn28, xxxviii, xlii, xliin75, xliii–xlivn81, lxxn153, 64n189
 "From the Working Notebooks of Dziga Vertov" (Vertov), xliii, lxii
Art of the Commune, 150n76, 153
Arvatov, Boris, 112, 151
Aseev, Nikolai, 88
Association of Revolutionary Cinema Workers (ARRK), lxvn151
Astruc, Alexandre, lviin125
Austrian Film Museum, Vienna, xxxin47, xlix, lxxi, 196n7
avant-garde, xxxii, lviin125, lxiv, 152, 173
 cinematic/film, lxxii, lxxiiin169
 contemporary/postwar, lxx, lxxn163, lxxi, lxxin167, lxxiiin169, lxxiii, lxxiii–lxxivn173, lxxviiin180, lxxxn184, lxxxiii
 historical, lxxi, lxxiiin173, lxxxvii
 Russian/Soviet, lxixn160, lxxxiiin193, xcii, 153, 285
 US, lxix, lxxi
 Vertov and, lxix–lxxi, lxxinn166–67, lxxii, lxxxiii, lxxiiin173, lxxxvii, xcii, xcvi, 69, 144, 153

B
Babel', Isaak, 88
Bakhrushin, Sergej, 77–78, 78n32
Balibar, Étienne, 173, 175, 181, 182, 182–83n165, 285, 285n223
Barnet, Boris, 162, xxivn30
Battle for Tsaritsyn, The (Vertov), 89, 221–22, 222–23n74, 222n73, 234
Baudry, Jean-Louis, "Ideological Effects of the Basic Cinematographic Apparatus," lxxv–lxxvi
 Bonitzer's response to, lxxvi–lxxviii, lxxviin177
Beckett, Samuel, xxvii
Bed and Sofa (Room), xv, 90–91
Bednyj, Demian, 209n44, 279
Beilis, Menahem Mendel, trial of, 56–58, 56n177, 74
Bekhterev, Vladimir, 72, 75–76, 75–76n23, 76n24, 107, 107n121, 108n123, 272
 Beilis trial and, 58

"Cinema and Science," 105
collective reflexology, 107n122, 272n189
"Immortality of the Human Subject as a Scientific Problem, The," 108–11, 108–9n125, 109n128, 111n132
portrait of, 73
"Psyche and Life, The," 107–8, 108n123
Psychoneurological Institute and, 58, 72, 74–76, 74n18, 98, 107, 107n122, 291
Benjamin, Walter, 65–66n193, 122, lxxiiin173
Berger, John, lxxxviin198
Bergson, Henri, 112n136, 115n143, 138
Berman, Marshall, 4–5n7
Bialystok, 6, 6nn11–12
 Alexandrovskaia Street, 38, 51
 anti-Semitism in, 47, 49–50, 49n149
 as a border town/"frontier" location, 7–8, 26, 46
 circulating libraries in, 30, 30nn90–92
 Gavriil cult in, 49–50, 50n152, 289
 Haskalah in, 21, 21–22n60, 27
 Jews in, 6–7
 labor movement in, 43–44, 43n126
 Leskov on, 25, 25–26n71
 Modern School, 33, 36–40, 38nn111–12, 39nn113–14, 39nn116–17, 44, 46, 56, 59, 70, 137n40
 movie theaters in, 28, 29–30
 Music School, 3, 38, 141
 Nikolaevskaia Street, 8, 9, 30, 30n90, 33, 51
 pogrom (1906), 32n97, 42n123, 47, 50–52, 51–52n159, 53, 54, 62, 80
 population of, 6, 6n13
 textile industry/factories in, 25n71, 26, 27, 27nn76–78, 44
 Yiddish in, 13, 13n31, 32
"Birth of Kino-Eye, The" (Vertov), lxii–lxiv, lxiiin146, lxvi, lxvii, 3, 3n4
Black Hundreds (*Chernaia sotnia*), 42, 42n123, 57, 260n156
blood libel, 23, 50
 Beilis trial, 56–58, 56n177, 74
Blum, Albrecht Viktor, 231, 232
Blumenberg, Hans, 299
Bogdanov, Aleksandr, 112
Bogdanov, Nikolaj, lxv, lxvn150
Bolsheviks/Bolshevik Party
 Boltianskij and, 92n67, 165, 165n122
 dissolution of Constituent Assembly, 178, 187, 188–89, 189n181
 Donbas workers and, 260

insurrection/takeover/monopolization of power, 88, 141, 159n102, 162n115, 171, 187
Social Democratic Party and, 44n131, 84, 84n53, 165
Vertov's cooperation with, 124–25, 160
Boltianskij, Grigorij, 91–93, 91n65, 92, 98, 158n101, 196n7, 234, 234n96
Bolshevik Party and, 92n67, 165, 165n122
"Cinema and the Proletariat," 95–96, 95n77, 95n79, 96nn80–82
democracy (*demokratiia*) and, 168, 170, 172, 178–79
efforts to avoid the draft, 93, 93n69
History of the Civil War and, 228n87
Kino-khronika, 194, 200–202, 201n20, 203
Menshevism and, 92, 92n67
"Otkliki," 94–95, 94n76
"Photographing Sound," 93–94, 93n73, 94n74
proletarian/workers' cinema and, 96–97, 97–98n86, 97n84
Psychoneurological Institute and, 90, 91, 93, 163
Skobelev Committee and, 97, 157, 163, 164, 165, 165n125, 184, 185n175, 225–26, 225n81
Born out of Chaos, 184, 184n170
Elections to the Constituent Assembly, 171–72, 171n139
policy proposal (1917), 166–68, 170, 170n136, 178, 181, 211
Toward the Opening of the Constituent Assembly, 170–71, 186
Social Democratic Party and, 92–93, 163, 165
Vertov and, 90, 91, 96, 96n83, 97, 98, 105, 163, 228n87
Bonitzer, Pascal, lxxvi–lxxviii, lxxviin177
bookstore-libraries/circulating libraries, 8n20, 10, 10n24, 10n26, 22, 22n61, 23–24, 23n63, 30–32, 31–32n96, 32n98
Abel Kaufman's, 8–9, 9, 10n26, *11*, 12–15, 12n28, 13n29, 13n32, 16, 22–25, 23n62, 24n66, 30–33, 32n98, 34, 34n104, 43, 51, 62, 102, 161, 270
in Bialystok, 30, 30nn90–92
Born out of Chaos (Skobelev Committee), 184, 184n170

Brain of Soviet Russia (Vertov and Savel'ev), 105n5, 160n107, 209n44, 223n75, 225n80
footage from *Kino-Nedelia* in, 195, 210, 226–27, 227n85
showing of, on agit-trains, 280, 280n211, 281, 282
Brakhage, Stan, lxx, lxxn163
Braslavskij, Leonid, xxn22
Brault, Michel, lx
Brik, Lilya, lii, lxix, liin111
Brik, Osip, 153, xlvn88
Brunius, Jacques, lxxxviii
Bücher, Karl Wilhelm, 114–15, 114n140
Arbeit und Rhythmus, 115–18, 115n143, 118n153, 119–20, 127
Buchholtz, Adolf, 39
Burch, Noël, xviii
Burliuk, David, 141, 143
Burov, Iakov, 234–35n100, 244, 250

C

Cahiers du Cinéma, xix, xixn19, lix, lixn130, lxxi, lxxiin170, lxxivn173
"camera eye," lviin125, 119, 293–94
cameraman/cameramen, lv, lviin125, xc, 49, 97, 101, 224n75, 225
agit-train, 233, 276n196
celebration of, 214
Kino-Nedelia, 97, 140, 165–66, 166n125, 195, 211, 212n51, 213n55, 214, 217
in *Man with a Move Camera*, xv, xvi, lxxvi, 214
Skobelev Committee, 164n119, 165–66, 165n125, 185n175, 195, 211–12, 211n50
See also Dored, Ianis; Ermolov, Petr; Kaufman, Mikhail; Lemberg, Aleksandr; Levitskij, Aleksandr; Novitskij, Petr; Tisse, Eduard
Cassavetes, John, lviii
censorship, xcii, 16, 45n133, 66, 95n79, 208, 229, 230–31, 232
archives as censors, 232
"as a productive force," lxvii, 231
of circulating libraries, 31, 31–32n96
of *Kino-Nedelia*, 196n7, 210, 210–11n48, 224–25
of *Three Songs of Lenin*, 231
Central Documentary Film Studio (TsSDF), xxviin38, xxxv, xxxix, xlvin92
Boltianskij and, 91n65, 226

Central House of Cinema, xlvi
Chaadaev, Petr, 15
Cheka, 160, 187, 209n45, 286
  Skrameh and, 240, 265, 265n169
Chicherin, Georgij, 86, 157
Chuguev Military School, 71, 71n9, 125–27, 126n10, 127n13, 135
cinema/film(s)/filmmaking
  agit-cinema, 256, 276n196
  authored, 229, 231–32
  direct, liii, lvi, lviiin127, xc
  educational-scientific/scientific, xcv, 69, 93, 96–101, 103–5, 139
  exposure of relics, 213, 286, 289–91n231, 289–92, 292n234
  mobile, 100, 234n98, 236, 237n107, 241, 276n196, 277, 280
  nationalization of, lxxxin146, 190, 190n185, 233, 233n95
  "non-acted"/"unplayed"/"unstaged," 139, 163, 181, 204, 229, 286, 297
  scenic (*vidovaia*), 101, 200–204, 202n24, 202n26, 204n29
  silent, xxx, xxxvii, l
  sound, 90, 94n74
  "trial film," 209–10
  See also documentary film; fiction film; nonfiction film
cinéma-vérité, lx lxvii
  Morin and, lvi–lvii, lviiin125, lviii, lviiin126
  Sadoul and, lii–liii, lvi, lviii–lx, lviiin126, lxi–lxii, lxviii
  as a term, lviii, lix
  Vertovian legacy and, xxxiii, xlixn100, lii, lii–liii, lviiin127, lx, lxi, lxiii, lxvi, lxviii, lxxii, lxxiv, lxxxiii, xc
Civil War/Civil War era, 142n56, 158, 194, 197, 225, 232, 246n131, 248–49, 258, 258n153, 260
  anti-Jewish violence of, 259, 260n155
  disease/typhus, 248–49, 250, 250n136
  Red forces, 211, 217, 258, 259, 260, 260n155, 264, 268, 284
  Russian/Soviet casualties of, 122, 158, 158n100
  Vertov and, 58, 68, 162n116, 194, 197
  film script set amid, 267–69, 268nn178–79, 269n180
  White forces, 179n155, 209n45, 237, 246, 258, 259, 260, 260n155, 264, 268, 268n178, 284

See also agit-train(s); *Battle for Tsaristyn, The* (Vertov); *History of the Civil War* (Vertov); relics, exposure of
Clarke, Shirley, lviii
Cold War, xlviii, xc, xciv, 4n7
Comolli, Jean-Louis, xvi–xviin14
Constitutional Democratic (Kadet) Party, 185, 187–88, 189, 208
Constructivism, lxxixn182, 123, 129, 130n22, 153, 153n81
  response of, to famine, 83–84
  Vertov and, lxixn160, lxxin166, 153, 160, 285
Coutard, Raoul, lx
Crofts, Stephen, lxxixn182
cubism, lxix, 112n136, 145
Cultural Revolution (China), xxxiv, lxxxii
Cultural Revolution (Soviet Union), lxv, lxvn151, 78n32

D

Dejch, Aleksandr, 86
Deleuze, Gilles, lxxiiin173, 119–20, 120n157
Denikin, Anton, 209n45, 220n69, 237, 278
Deren, Maya, lxxn163, lxxi
détournement, 229, 230, 231–32
documentary film, xlvi, lvi, lvii, lviin125, lviiin127, 90, 91, 113
  Boltianskij and, 96n83
  cinéma-vérité and, lii, liii, lxiii, lxvi, lxxii, lxxiv
  Iurenev on, xlii, xliii, xliv
  khronika and, 163, 198, 204
  Kopalin on, xxxvi, xxxvii, xxxviin60, xxxviii–xxxix, xliv
  portraits, xxxixn68, xli, lxvii
  Shklovsky on, xliv–xlv
  Soviet, xxxvi, xlv, lxxi, lxxxix–xc
  Vertov and, xiv, xxxiv, xxvn32, xxxvn56, xxxvi, xxxvii, xxxviin60, xli, xlivn84, lii, liii, lix, lxiii, lxvi–lxvii, lxix, lxxii, lxxiv, lxxxvii, xc, xcii, 66, 138, 255
  "film-truth," lxvi, lxvii–lxviiin158
Donbas, 258–69, 258n151, 266n74, 277
  October Revolution (agit-train) in, 258, 266n74, 267
  See also *Enthusiasm* (Vertov)
Dored, Ianis, 165n125, 211
Dos Passos, John, xxii, xxii–xxiiin25
Dovzhenko, Aleksandr, ln105, xc, 117n50, 123
Drankov, Aleksandr, 101, 207

Drew, Richard, lx, lxn134
Drobashenko, Sergej, xxviiin40, liv, lxii, lxvi, lxvii, lxviii–lxixn159
trip to Europe with Svilova (1974), lxxxiii, lxxxiiin193
Drunkenness and Its Consequences (Khanzhonkov), 102, 102n102
Duchamp, Marcel, 112, 112n136
readymade, lxix, 230
Dulac, Germaine, lxxn162, lxxi
"Dziga Vertov" (poem by Vertov), 147–48

E

Efimov, Boris (Boris Fridliand), 25n69, 33–34, 39, 39n117, 40, 157, 157n98
Eisenschitz, Bernard, lii
Eisenstein, Sergej, ln105, lxxivn173, lxxixn182, lxxxi, xc, xci, 123, 153, 162, 211, 243n123
    Battleship Potemkin, 117n150, 179
    documentary on, xlin74, xxviin37
    Eisenstein-Vertov debate, 270–75
    as Vertov's rival, xxiii, xxivn30
Elections to the Constituent Assembly (Skobelev Committee), 171–72, 171n139
Eleventh Year, The (Vertov), xxxin47, xlixn100, ln105, 113, 204, 214, 269
    Brunius on, lxxxviii
    footage from, in *Shadow of Machines*, 231, 232
emancipation of the serfs, 16, 26
energeticism, 106–8, 107n121, 109n128, 111–14, 111n132, 111n134, 112n135
Engel, Morris, lx
Engels, Friedrich, 22, 32n98, 173, 180–81
Enthusiasm: Symphony of the Donbass (Vertov), xlixn199, lxxxv, 182, 214, 223, 269, 270
    availability/releases of, xxxin47
    denunciation of, xxxvn56
    restoration of, lxxin166
    soundtrack, 90, 119, 137, 151
Epstein, Jean, lxxi
Ermolov, Petr, 164n119, 165n125, 211, 213, 214, 214n57, 216n62
Exposure of the Relics of Alexander Nevskij, 286n225, 287n227, 289n228, 294n238
Exposure of the Relics of Sergius of Radonezh (Kuleshov and Vertov), 213, 286n225, 288–89, 290, 298
    Vertov and Kuleshov's involvement in, 288, 292–93, 292–93n236, 294–96

Vertov's revisiting of, 298
Exposure of the Relics of Tikhon of Zadonsk (Moscow Film Committee), 213, 280, 286–88, 286nn225–26, 287n227, 288, 289

F

Fall of the Romanov Dynasty (Shub), xlviin94, xlixn100, 208n41
Fall of Trebizond, 207n40
famine
    in Moscow, 157–58
    in Volga (1921–22), 83–84, 83n49, 122, 237n107, 299, 299n248
Farocki, Harun, lxxx, lxxxn187
February Revolution, 77, 86, 97, 140, 157, 162n115, 164, 165n124, 172
Festival dei Popoli, xlix, xlixn100, lvi
fiction film, xiv, xviiin17, xlv, liv, lvi–lviii, lix, lxvi, lxvin152, lxxxix, 34, 90, 99, 99n92, 140, 233, 266, 275
    agitkas, 280
    Boltianskij and, 97, 167, 172
    Kino-Nedelia and, 195
    Skobelev Committee and, 164, 167, 171, 172
    Vertov and
        battle against/opposition to, xiii, xiv, liv, 34, 147, 151, 273, 297
        script for, 267–69, 268nn178–79, 269n180
Film Culture, xxxi–xxxiin48, lxix–lxx, lxxn163
First Congress of Soviet Writers, lxiv–lxv
Fitzpatrick, Sheila, 162, 257
Flaherty, Robert, lvi, lviiin125
    Seminar, xlix–l, ln102
Flammarion, Camille, 22, 31, 102, 102–3n104
Forgács, Péter, xci–xcii
formalism, lxiv, lxix, lxxii, 244, 256n146
    accusations of, against Vertov, xxxvi–vii, xlvin92, lxv–vi, 139, 221
    in *Enthusiasm*, xxxvn56
    in *Man with a Movie Camera*, xxxvi
Formalism, Russian, lxxiii, lxxxn184
Freeman, Benjamin, 49
Fridliand, Boris. *See* Efimov, Boris
Fridliand, Mojsej. *See* Kol'tsov, Mikhail
"From the Working Notebooks of Dziga Vertov" (Vertov), xliii, liii, lxii, lxxx
Futurism/Futurist, Italian, lxixn161, 112n136, 150n77
Futurism/Futurist, Russian, 112, 123, 142, 151, 152, 244, 244n129, 250

poetry, xcv, 129, 142, 146, 153
Vertov and, xxi, lv, lxix, xcv, 129, 142–43, 145, 146, 148, 149–51, 150nn76–77, 152–54
"Vertov" as a Futurist neologism, 146, 154, 155
Vertov's Futurist-inspired poetry, 132, 147–48
See also Mayakovsky, Vladimir

G

Gal'pern, Chaya (Vertov's mother). See Kaufman, Chaya
Gal'pern, Masha (Miriam Halpern-Proginin) (Vertov's aunt), 9n22, 17–20, 62, 66, 67
Boris Kaufman and, 53, 82n48
emigration to Palestine, 53, 80, 82n48
Mikhail (Mojsej) Kaufman and, 18, 53, 60–61, 62n188
probable work with pogrom victims, 53, 53n163, 62
Society for the Protection of the Health of the Jews and, 53, 71, 80–83
Vertov and, xxiv, xxivn28, 18, 53, 60, 61, 62–63, 70, 82n48, 105, 156
poem dedicated to, 3, 61, 62n188
at the Women's Medical Institute, 18, 18n47, 52–53, 60, 61, 61n186, 62n188, 63, 66n195, 72, 80, 80n44
Gan, Aleksej, 123, 153
Gardin, Vladimir, 191n187, 195, 224, 292n236
Gatrell, Peter, 70n3, 77, 77n31, 79n39, 80, 80n43, 161
Gaumont, 97, 101, 165n125, 207
newsreels/news shorts, 29n89, 163, 164n120, 197, 205n33
German, Aleksej, Sr., lxxxix–xc
German Film and Television Academy, lxxx, lxxxn187
Gesamtkunstwerk, 131n28, 132
Giornate del Cinema Muto, xxxivn54, lxxxvin198
Godard, Jean-Luc, Groupe Dziga Vertov and, xlixn100, lxxxi–lxxxv, lxxixn183, lxxxin188, lxxxiin190, lxxxiiin193, lxxxivn194
Goldovskaya, Marina, xxv, xxviii, xxvn31
Goldovskij, Evsej, xxviii, xxviiin41, xxvn31
Gorin, Jean-Pierre, lxxxi
Gorky, Maksim, 22, 88

Gosfilmofond, xlvii, 196n7
Goskinokalendar', 199n14, 209, 233
Graff, Séverine, lii, liii, lviin125, lx, lxin137
Great Reforms, 10, 16–17, 19
Great Terror, lxxxix, 165, 197, 210
Greenaway, Peter, lxxi
Grierson, John, lxviii, lxxxviiin199, 255
Griffith, D. W., xv
Grinkrug, Lev, 88, 141–42
Grodno, 7–8, 7n16, 13n31, 25–26, 143, 143n61
as Abel Kaufman's birthplace, 7n16, 8, 9n22, 13n31, 21, 22
gymnasium, 40–43, 42nn122–24, 45, 45n135
School, 40, 41, 44, 47–48
Jews in, 8, 13n31, 21
main library in, 8n20
Grodno guberniia/province, 6, 6n12
factories/industry in, 27, 27n76
Jews in, 7, 7n17, 14, 14n34, 19, 19n51, 55
libraries in, 30, 31, 31–32n96
refugees in, 77n30, 78
"Groupe Dziga Vertov" (Dziga Vertov Group), xlixn100, lxxixn183, lxxxi–iv, lxxxin188, lxxxiin190
Gusev, T. V., 245

H

Haskalah (Jewish Enlightenment), 16, 18, 20–21, 20–21n57, 21–22n60, 24–25, 24–25n67
maskilim, 18, 21n57, 24–25n67, 25, 48
Between the Times (Weisbrem), 26–27, 26n75
"He and I" (Vertov), xx–xxii, xxiii, xxin24
Helmholtz, Hermann von, 106–7, 107n121, 108n123, 111, 112
Hendershot, Heather, lxvii, 231
Higher State Cinema Institute (VGIK), xxvn31, xxviii, xxxvn56, xlii, xliin75, xlvi
Hirsch, Storm de, lxx
History of the Civil War (Vertov), 228n87, 232, 234, 249n35
footage from *Kino-Nedelia* in, 197, 197n11, 217n63, 228, 228n87
intertitles, 220n69
Holocaust, xxiii, 8, 9, 9n22, 259
"How Kino-Eye was Born and Developed" (1935 lecture) (Vertov), lxiii, lxiiin145, 63–64, 64n189, 135, 137–38

I

"Ideological Effects of the Basic Cinematographic Apparatus" (Baudry), lxxv–lxxvi
  Bonitzer's response to, lxxvi–lxxviii, lxxviin177
Imaginists, 145, 145n64, 160
intertitles, 151, 166, 185n175, 221, 274
  absence of, in *Battle for Tsaritsyn*, 221
  in *Anniversary of the Revolution*, 188, 197
  in *Exposure of the Relics of Aleksandr Nevskij*, 294n238
  in *Exposure of the Relics of Sergius of Radonezh*, 288–89
  in *Exposure of the Relics of Tikhon of Zadonsk*, 286–87
  in *History of the Civil War*, 220n69
  in *Kino-Nedelia*, 195, 196n7, 197, 214, 215–16, 215nn58–59, 216n62, 217, 219–20, 221, 227–28n86
  in *Opening and Dissolution of the Constituent Assembly*, 188–89, 189n181
  in *Stride, Soviet*, 248–52, 248n134, 249n135, 255
  in *Svobodnaia Rossiia*, 206, 208, 210
In the Petrograd Proletariat's Children's Colony (Skobelev Committee), 185, 185nn173–74
In the Shadow of Machines (Blum), 231, 232
Ioganson, Karl, 84
Iurenev, Rostislav, xl–xlii, xlin74, xliin75, xliin77, xliv
Iutkevich, Sergej, lxxxii–lxxxiii, xlviin94
Ivens, Joris, xxxviii, xliii, lx, lviiin127
Izvestiia, 86, 89, 212, 220

J

Jacobs, Ken, lxx
Jameson, Fredric, 229n88
Jewry/Jews
  in Bialystok, 6–7
  Bund, 19n50, 32, 48n148, 54, 84n53
  emigration of, 13n31, 44, 48, 49, 54, 55, 82n48
  in Grodno, 8, 13n31, 21
  in Grodno guberniia, 7, 7n17, 14, 14n34, 19, 19n51, 55
  in Kiev, 7n17, 33n101
  Masha Gal'pern's relief work with, 53, 71, 80–83
  Recruitment Statute of the Jews, 18
  "Russian-Jewish intelligentsia," 24–25, 24–25n67
  See also anti-Semitism; blood libel; Haskalah; Pale of Settlement; pogrom(s)
Jost, Jon, lxxi

K

Kalinin, Mikhail, 211, 212, 238, 257–58, 263–67, 299
Kamenev, Lev, 185, 196n7, 210, 227–28n86
Kamenskij, Vasilij, 141, 141n54, 143
Karakhan, Lev, 165, 165n121
Karmen, Roman, xxvn31, 214
Kasso, L. A., 74–75, 75n21
Kassow, Samuel D., 44, 44n132, 46n137
Kastelin, Nikolaj, xxxix
Katanian, Vasilij (junior), xxviin37, liin112
Katanian, Vasilij (senior), xliin77, lii, liin111–12, lxix, *88*
Kaufman, Abel (Vertov's father), 7n16, 8–9, 8n18, 9n22, 21, 22, 36, 37, 49, 61–62, 71, 78
  bookstore-library, 8–9, *9*, 10n26, *11*, 12–15, 12n28, 13n29, 13n32, 16, 22–25, 23n62, 24n66, 30–33, 32n98, 34, 34n104, 43, 51, 62, 102, 161, 270
  orientation toward Russian, 13, 14, 14n37, 17, 22, 24–25
  as possible Tolstoyan, 13n33, 62, 285n222
  vegetarianism, 13n33, 60, 62
  Yiddish as first language of, 14
Kaufman, Boris (Vertov's brother), 9n22, 10, 37, 49, 78, 142
  as cinematographer, xxiv, xxvii, lxxn162, lxxxiii, 49, 217n64
  interviews with/recollections of, 98, 105, 126n10, 140n46, 142, 158
  Masha Gal'pern and, 53, 82n48
  Russian name of, 14n37, 156
  Vertov and, xxiv, xxivn28, lxxn162, lxxxiii–lxxxiv, lxxxiii–lxxxivn194, 269
Kaufman, Chaya (Vertov's mother), 9–10, 9n22, 10n23, 14n37, 18, 34, 37, 49, 50, 60, 63, 71, 78
  Abel's bookstore-library and, 12n28, 16, 36, 62
Kaufman, David. *See* Vertov, Dziga
Kaufman, Mikhail (Mojsej) (Vertov's brother), xix, 9n22, 10, 14n37, 33, 36, 37, 71, 71n6, 78n36, 140n46, 140n50

as cinematographer, xiv, xvii, l, xc, 62, 136, 162, 214, 239n115
interviews with/recollections of, xiv, 53n163, 59–63, 60n185, 62n188, 66, 71n9, 140, 155, 228n87
Masha Gal'pern and, 53, 60–61
Russian name of, 10, 71, 71n5, 156
Vertov and, xiv, xvii, xc, 59, 62, 136, 156, 214
Kaufman, Semyon (Vertov's brother), 14n37
death of, in infancy, 9n22, 10
Kejrim-Markus, M. B., 161, 161n113
Kerensky, Aleksandr, 86, 126n10
in *Svobodnaia Rossiia*, 185, 185n174
Khanzhonkov, Aleksandr, 101, 166n125, 207
Drunkenness and Its Consequences, 102, 102n102
Tuberculosis, 101–2
Kharkov, 17, 91, 100, 125n9, 126, 180
October Revolution (agit-train) in, 258, 259, 261–62, 262n160
Soviet, 127, 127n13
Khrushchev, Nikita, xxxiv
Kiev, 33, 56, 91, 95n77, 125n9, 180, 259
Jews in, 7n17, 33n101
Kol'tsov in, 86, 155, 157, 157n98, 194n2
pogroms in, 48, 49n149
"Kinocs: A Revolution" (Vertov), xxxiin48, lii, lixn130, lxxx, 111, 152
Kino-Eye: Life Caught Unawares (Vertov), xii–xiiin2, xxxvn56, xcvi, 148, 185n173, 239n115, 242, 297
availability/releases of, xxxin47
"beef to bull" sequence in, 66, 246
"Kino-Eye," liii, liv, lvn121, lvin123, lviin125, lxi, lxii, 105–6, 143–44, 149–50, 271, 273, 274, 283, 298
"cinema-vérité" and, lviii, lx
"Kino-Pravda" and, lv–lvi, lxii, lxv–lxvi
See also "Birth of Kino-Eye, The" (Vertov); "How Kino Eye was Born and Developed" (Vertov); "Kino-Eye" (Vertov)
"Kino-Eye" (Vertov), liv, livn120, lxv–lxvi, 284, 284n221
Kino-Fot, 153, 153n81
Kino-Nedelia (VFKO), 194–95, 196n7, 206nn34–35, 208–9, 211–19, 227–29, 233
agitation in, 219–21, 220nn69–70, 223
agit-trains and, 237n106, 280, 281
cameramen, 164n119, 165–66n125, 213n55, 214

disappearance of material/footage "missing" from, 210, 210–11n48, 227
footage from, in other films, 210, 223, 224n75
Anniversary of the Revolution, 223n75, 227, 227n85
Brain of Soviet Russia, 210, 223n75, 227, 227n85
History of the Civil War, 197, 197n11, 228, 228n87
Kino-Pravda, 197, 197n10
Stride, Soviet, 197, 197n10
Three Songs of Lenin, 197, 198
intertitles, 195, 196n7, 197, 214, 215–16, 215nn58–59, 216n62, 217, 219–20, 221, 227–28n86
issues of, sent to Norway, 196n7, 210, 226n84
Izvestiia/Pravda and, 212, 212n52
montage lists, 195n5, 196n7, 206n34, 210, 214, 215n58, 216, 216n62, 227, 227–28n86
poster (1918), 196n7, 227n86
restoration of, 224, 224n76, 226–28, 226n84, 227n85, 232, 293n236
Skobelev Committee and, 165, 198, 224n75
"slice of life" sequences, 217, 217nn64–65, *218*
Svobodnaia Rossiia and, 223, 223n75
topics in, 83n49, 212, 213
Vertov and, 1–2, 97, 125, 140, 164n119, 191n187, 194–96, 195n6, 197, 212, 212n51, 221, 227–28, 280–81
later dismissal of/ambivalence toward, 197, 198, 210
"Kino-Pravda," lxi, lxiii, lxvii
"cinéma-vérité" and, xxxiii, lviii, lx, lxi–lxii, lxvi
"Kino-Eye" and, lv, lxvi–lxvi
Kino-Pravda (Vertov), xx, xxi, xxxvi, lii, liii, lxvi, xcv, 83, 83n49, 123, 147, 197n10, 200, 201n20, 202, 203, 205, 209, 215, 231, 233, 241, 242, 269, 299
availability/releases of, xxxin47, ln102
footage from *Kino-Nedelia* in, 197, 197n10
Kino-Pravda 21 ("Lenin" *Kino-Pravda*), xxxvi, xlviii–xlix, xlixn100, 123
Pravda and, lv, lxi
screenings of, xlviii–xlix, xlixn100, ln102
Kirghizfilm, xliv
Kiselev, P. D., 19

Kleiman, Naum, xlvi, xlvin92, 295n240
Klier, John, 7–8n17, 24, 24–25n67
Kokoshkin, Fyodor, 189–90, 227n86
Kolchak, Aleksandr, 208, 217n63, 220, 220n69, 227n86
Kollontai, Aleksandra, 185, 196n7, 210, 226n84
Kolonitskij, Boris, 168–69, 169n131
Kol'tsov, Mikhail (Mojsej Fridliand), 33–34, 39–40, 86, 87, 88, 88, 91, 157
   All-Russian Cinema Committee and, 157, 157n98
   Moscow Film Committee and, 157, 194–95
   Psychoneurological Institute and, 33, 85, 85–86n56, 86, 93, 157
   Skobelev Committee and, 157, 190
   Vertov and, lxv, 33, 85, 86, 90, 97, 125, 155, 157, 161, 162, 197
Konlechner, Peter, xlix
Kopalin, Ilya, xxxvn56, xxxvi–xl, xxxvi-inn60–62, xxxviiin66, xlii, xliin75, xliin77, xliii, xliv
Kozhevnikov, Innokentij, 197n11, 214, 214n57, 216n62, 217n65
Kozintsev, Grigorij, xiii, xiiin6, xxivn30
Krupskaia, Nadezhda, 191, 238
Kubelka, Peter, xlix, lxx, lxxi, lxxin166
Kuleshov, Lev, xxivn30, xxvn32, xxviii, xlvn88, xci, 153, 222, 240, 272
   Exposure of the Relics of Sergius of Radonezh and, 292, 292–93n236, 294, 295n40
   Extraordinary Adventures of Mr. West in the Land of the Bolsheviks, xiii
   Kuleshov Effect, 293, 295–96
Kupferberg, Tuli, lxx
Kurs, Aleksandr, 298

L

labor/workers' movements, lxxii, 25, 43, 44, 46n137, 66, 96n80
Langlois, Henri, l–li, linn106–8, lxxxiiin193
Latvian Film Studio, xliv
Lavinskij, Anton, *88*
Lawton, Anna, lxxxvii
Leacock, Richard, lx, lxn134, xc, xcn210
Lebedev, Nikolaj, xxxvn56, xlvi, 200, 201
LEF (group), xiii, 153, lxixn160, lxxin166, xiiin4
LEF (journal), 152–53, 153n81
   "Kinocs: A Revolution" (Vertov), lii, lxxx, 152

Lemberg, Aleksandr, xxxixn68, 140, 140n50, 211, 212, 214, 235n100
   collaborations with Vertov, 140, 141n53, 222n73
   family apartment of, 125n9, 141n51, 142, 145
   Perskij and, 140, 141n52, 165n125
Lemberg, Grigorij, 140, 209, 262n163
Lenin, Vladimir
   decree of August 27, 1919 (nationalization of cinema), lxiiin146, 233, 233n95
   decree of March 30, 1918, 192
   "electrification plus soviets," 285n223
   at the Finland Station, 157
   iconographies/myth, 231, 299
   Kino-Pravda 21 ("Lenin" *Kino-Pravda*), xxxvi, xlviii–xlix, 123, 197, 197n10
   Kino-Pravda 22, xxxvi
   State and Revolution, The, 175–76
   in *Zrelishcha* (1925), 123, 123n4
   See also *Three Songs of Lenin* (Vertov); *V. I. Lenin Mobile Military Front Train* (agit-train)
Lenoe, Matthew, 242
Leskov, Nikolaj, 25, 25–26n71
Levin, A., 88
Levitskij, Aleksandr, 97, 144–45, 160, 165n125, 233, 234n96, 241
   October Revolution (agit-train) and, 144–45, 211, 233, 258, 259, 261–63, 264–65, 280n211
Leyda, Jay, lxixn161, xxivn30
Linhart, Robert, lxxxixn183, lxxxiv–lxxxv, lxxxvn196–97
Lissitzky, El, 241n119
Listov, Viktor, lxxxix, 25n69, 29n89, 185n175, 189n181, 190, 191, 195n4, 213n55, 225n81, 237n106, 285n222, 293n236
Łodz, 25, 25n70, 27n78, 39, 44n130
Lukács, Georg, 118, 271
Lullaby (Vertov), xxiii, xxvii, xl–xli, *lxxxvi*, lxxxix, 240n115, 270
   screenings of, xlvi, xlvin93, lxxxix
   sync-sound interviews in, xxxixn68, lxxvi–lxxvii
Lumière Brothers, lxxii, 29n85, 205n30, 225
Lunacharsky, Anatoly, 88, 185, 244n129
   Kol'tsov and, 86, 157, 234n96
   resistance of, to cinema nationalization, 190, 190n185, 192n191

M

MacDonald, Scott, xci–xcii
Magidov, Vladimir, 128, 157n93, 195n4
Makhnach, Leonid, xxviii
    World Without Play, *xviii*, xxvii–xxviii,
        xxviinn37–39, xxviiin40, xli, lixn130
Makhnach, Vladimir, xxviii, xxviiinn41–42
Malevich, Kazimir, 112, 143
Malkin, B., *88*
Mandelstam, Osip, 88
Man with a Movie Camera (Vertov), xv–xvi,
    xxi, xxxiii, *xl*, *xlviii*, liii, lvin124, *lxviii*, lxx,
    lxxiv, lxxxiiin193, lxxxv, lxxxviii–lxxx-
    ixn206, xci, xciin216, 63, 102, 113, 119,
    150, 155, 179, 181, 222, 232, 250, 254,
    270, 282, 297, *297*
    availability/releases of, xxx, xxxn44,
        xxxn47, xxxi, l–li, lin106, lin108
    Baudry on, lxxvi, lxxvi–lxxvii
    Bonitzer on, lxxvi–lxxvii, lxxviin177
    charges of Vertov's "formalism" and,
        xxxvi, xlvin92
    Comolli on, xvi–xviiin14
    as critical/popular favorite, xxix, xxixn43
    Crofts and Rose on, lxxixn182
    Michelson on, lxxixn181, lxxn164
    Mikhail Kaufman in, xc, 214
    montage in, liii, lxxvii
    "morning" sequence, 90
    musical scores for, xxx, xxxn45
    production/socialist construction in,
        182, 204
    references to, in film classes/textbooks,
        xxx, xxx–xxxin46
    screenings of, xlvin92, xlviii, xlix,
        xlixnn99–100
        Cinémathèque Française (1953),
            xix, xxiii, xxiiin27
    self-referentiality/critique of representa-
        tion in, lxx, lxxiv–lxxvi, lxxvii–lxxviii,
        lxxviin177, lxxviii–lxxx, xc, 204, 214
    Stam on, lxxviiin180
    view of Vertov as a disorderly filmmaker
        and, lxxxvii, lxxxviin199
    Weibel on, lxxviiin180
Mao Tse-tung, xxxiv, lxxi, lxxxii
Marey, Étienne-Jules, 99–100, 112, 112n136
Marker, Chris, ln104, lviiin127, lxxxix, 235
Markopoulos, Gregory, lxxi
Marx, Karl, xvii, xxivn30, 3n3, 114n139, 117,
    173, 176n150, 182–83n165, 219
    Capital, 32n98

Manifesto of the Communist Party, 173,
    175, 180
Marxism, lxixn161, lxxiii, 160, 173, 178n153,
    182, 182–83n165
Matuszewski, Boleslas, 225–26
May 1968, lxxii–lxxiii, lxxiiin171–72, lxxx,
    45n136
Mayakovsky, Vladimir, xiiin4, lii, 88, *88*, 141,
    142, 143, 143n61, 153, 241n119
    "From Street to Street," 146–47
    Kino-Fot and, 153, 153n81
    lecture (1914), 149, 150
    LEF/Novyj LEF and, xlv, lii, 152, 153
    poetry of, xxvi, 141, 146, 153
    suicide of, xxvi, 153
    Vertov and, xxvi, 123, 141, 142, 143–44,
        144n63, 146, 147–58
        memorial lecture (1935), 143n61,
            144n63
Maysles, Albert, liii, lx
Medvedkin, Aleksandr, xxvn31, lxxxix, 235
Mekas, Jonas, xxxi–xxxiin48, lxx, lxxn163
Mekhonoshin, Konstantin, 212, 212n53
Mendelsohn, Ezra, 43, 43n126
Mensheviks/Menshevik Party, 165,
    169nn131–32, 186, 187, 261
    Boltianskij and, 92, 92n67, 96n82, 165,
        165n22
    Social Democratic Party and, 44n131,
        84n53, 92, 165
    Tsereteli and, 185, 227n86
Michelson, Annette, xxxiiin49, 62n188
    "Film and the Radical Aspiration," xcvi
    "*Man with a Movie Camera*: From
        Magician to Epistemologist, The,"
        lxxn164, lxxviiin–lxixn181, lxxx-
        vin198
Miéville, Anne-Marie, lxxxiv, lxxxivn194,
    lxxxv
Minsk guberniia, 7, 7n17, 26, 27n76, 33,
    77n30
    Masha Gal'pern's relief work in, 71,
        80–82
MIPE-TV conference, lx–lix, lxnn134–35
Mironov, Filipp. See *Trial of [Colonel Filipp]*
    Mironov (Vertov)
mnemonics, 64, 64–65n190, 119, 135, 138,
    151–52, 152n80
modernization, xciii, 4–5n7, 20, 27, 83–84,
    236n104
    capitalist, 4, 4–5n7, 285n223
Molotov, Viacheslav, 179n155, 238

montage
　Dos Passos and, xxiin25
　Eisenstein and, 271
　"intellectual montage," 243, 243n123
　khronika, 203, 204
　Kuleshov and, 292n236, 293, 295–96
　lists for Kino-Nedelia, 195n5, 196n7, 206n34, 210, 214, 215n58, 216, 216n62, 227, 227–28n86
　Vertov and, xxvi, lxi, lvin123, lxvi, lxxii, lxxxiin190, lxxxiv, lxxxvii, 66, 99–100, 141n53, 182, 272
　　in Battle for Tsaritsyn, 221
　　in Man with a Movie Camera, xvin14, lii, lxxvii–lxxviii, lxxixnn181–82, 113
　　in One Sixth of the World, 298
　　of sound, 128, 135n35
　　sound/image, lxxxn184
　　stenographic, 135–36
　　of words, 135, 135n35
　　See also semiotic rectangle
Morin, Edgar, lx
　"For a new cinema-vérité," lvi–lviii, lvin124, lviin125, lix
　Sadoul and, lviii, lix, lviiin126
Moscow, xcv, 16, 100, 127, 157–59, 158n100, 159n102, 160, 188n179
　Bol'shaia Polianka Street 28, xxv, *xxix*
　Briansk station, 215
　Butyrskaia Gate, 215, 215n59
　City Soviet, 186, 197, 234, 242n122, 247, 255n142
　famine/food shortage in, 157–58, 159, 216n61
　Kaufmans in, 71, 71n6, 139–40, 140n46, 142
　Kozitskij Lane, 141, 141n51
　Kursk station, 220n69, 228n87
　Novodevichy Cemetery, xlvii, xlviin97
　poetry cafés in, 141, 142n56
　as Vertov's home base, 125–26, 125n9, 132, 135, 141, 141n51, 157–58
Moscow Film Committee, 222n73, 224–25, 225n81
　Kuleshov's employment with, 240
　Vertov's employment with, 157, 160, 188, 190, 194
Moscow International Film Festival (MIFF), xlvii, xlviin94, lii, liin113
Moussinac, Léon, livn120, ln105, lvin123

music, Vertov and, livn120, xcv, 38, 64, 69, 118, 119, 125, 127–28, 128n16, 136, 139, 240n117
　"etudes," 132–35, *134*, 254
　musical scores for Man with a Movie Camera, xxx, xxxn45
　See also Bialystok, Music School; Bücher, Karl Wilhelm; Chuguev Military School; Scriabin, Aleksandr; sound

N

Narkompros (Commissariat of Enlightenment), 157, 224, 275
　All-Russian Cinema Committee/Cinema and Photo Division/Film Committee/Photo and Film Division /VFKO, 157, 162n116, 195, 233n95, 234, 241, 250n136, 276n196, 278n203, 280
　Cinema Subsection, 191
　Department of Museum Affairs, 289–91n231
　Glavpolitprosvet, 237, 237n107, 277, 291
　IZO (Visual Arts Section), 226
　Skobolev Committee's absorption into, 190–91, 190n185, 192, 192n190
Nathans, Benjamin, 16–17, 17n46, 24
Nevskij, Aleksandr. *See Exposure of the Relics of Alexander Nevskij*
New Economic Policy (NEP), 113, 113n138, 241
newsreel(s)/news shorts
　actualities and, 200–201, 205, 209n44, 212–13, 212n53, 220n69, 226n84, 229, 238n108
　"film-journal" as designator for, 198, 199, 200, 205, 212, 226n84
　Gaumont, 29n89, 163, 164n120, 197, 205n33
　khronika and, xxxviii, 96n83, 167, 199, 199n13, 201, 201n20, 204, 204n29
　Pathé, 29, 29n89, 163, 164n120, 197, 205–7, 207n37, 208, 212
　See also Kino-Nedelia (VFKO); Kino-Pravda (Vertov); Skobolev Committee
New Wave, lvi, lix
Nicholas I, anti-Semitic attitudes/policies of, 19–20, 21n57, 24n67, 70n3
Nicholas II
　anti-Semitic attitudes/policies of, 52, 52n162, 56

caricature of, 40, *41*
See also Tsar Nicholas II, Autocrat of All Russia (Skobelev Committee)
noise, lxix, 3, 135n35, 137–38, 151, 155
  "indeterminate noises," 116, 120
  "noise music," lxix, 119
nonfiction film(s), xxvn31, xxviin39, xxviii, xxxvi, xcv, 99n92, 101, 139, 163, 192, 200–201, 233, 266, 271–72
  actualities/single-themed nonfiction film and, 200, 205, 212, 213
  Boltianskij and, 91, 96, 97, 163, 167, 234
  Flaherty and, lvi, lxi, lxviii
  khronika and, 198–99, 199nn13–14, 200, 201, 203, 204, 234
  Kol'tsov and, 157, 157n98
  Morin on, lvi–lvii
  as "poetic," xliii, xliv
  as "publicistic," xxxvii–xxxix, xlii, xliii, xliv
  Sadoul on, lviii, lviiin127, lxviii
  "scenic" (*vidovaia*), 202, 202n26
  Shklovsky on, xlv, xlvi
  shorts, 208n42, 212, 213, 237
  Vertov and, xiv, xv, xvii, xxix, xxxiv, xxxix, xlv, liv–lvn120, lx–lxin135, lxvi–lxvii, xciii, xcv, xcvi, 69, 85, 96, 138, 141, 179, 194
    defense of, liv, 273, 284
    earliest script for, 214
    legacy of, xxii, xliv, lvi, lviii, lxviii, xcv
  See also Kino-Nedelia (VFKO); newsreel(s); Skobelev Committee
Novikov, G. P., 195
Novitskij, Petr, 211, 224n75
  exposure films and, 286, 292n236
  Kino-Nedelia and, 97, 164n119, 166
  Skobelev Committee and, 97, 157, 164n119, 165n125, 166, 170–71
Novodumskij, S., 139, 139n45
Novyj LEF, xlv, 152, 153
numerus clausus, 17, 17n46, 22, 79, 79n40

O

October Revolution, xvii–xviii, lxxii, xciv, 4, 76, 112n135, 142, 157, 263n164, 276, 276n200
October Revolution (agit-train), 211, 234–35, 258–63
  film screenings, 276–82, 276n200, 278
  Kalinin and, 211, 238, 257–58, 263–67
  murals, 245–46, *245*
  Vertov and, 144, 211, 233, 235, 239–41, 262, 262n160, 262n163, 263n164, 267, 270, 276–77, 279–84, 298
October Revolution (film; Skobelev Committee), 158–59n102, 180
October Turning Point (Skobelev Committee), 185n175
Odessa, 17n45, 26, 47–48, 91, 100, 179, 212, 213
  pogroms/massacres of Jews in, 47, 48
Okladskij, Ivan, 209, 209n45
One Sixth of the World (Vertov), xxxvi, xlvii, 113, 113n138, 140, 181–82, 204, 214, 298
  availability/releases of, xxxin47
  foreign bourgeois in, 181, 266n172
  screenings of, xlvii, xlviii, li
  second-person address in, 182, 270
  Zhemchuzhnyj on, 202–3
Otsep, Fyodor, 200, 201

P

Pale of Settlement, 7, 7–8n17, 14n35, 16, 17n46, 19, 21n57, 32n96, 33n101, 47, 48n148, 49, 53, 53n163, 55, 79
  end of, 53, 79, 79n39
  May Laws, 49
  state-run schools in, 20–21
Palestine, 49, 53, 54, 82, 82n48
Paris, postwar screenings/reception of Vertov in, xix, l–li, ln104
Pathé, 99n92, 101, 136, 165n125
  newsreels/news shorts, 29, 29n89, 163, 164n120, 197, 205–7, 207n37, 208, 212
  Pathé Journal, 198, 205, 205n31, 206
  "ultramicroscopic films," 101
peasants
  agit-trains' encounters with, 256, 257, 261–66, 277, 281–84, 284n220, 285
  coercive measures against/brutal treatment of, 159n104, 209n45, 259, 263, 264, 264n168, 266–67
Perskij, Robert, 140, 141n52, 165n125
Petric, Vlada, lxxxvii
Petrograd
  Duma, 171, 186n175
  Finland station, 157
  food shortage in, 158n101, 159
  Kaufmans in, 71, 78, 98
  "slice of life" sequence in *Kino-Nedelia*, 217n65, 223n75

Soviet, 97, 164, 165, 171, 184, 191n188, 208
Taurida Palace, 171, 187, 188–89, 189n181, 224n75
See also Psychoneurological Institute
Philipe, Gérard, li–lii
Plekhanov, Georgij, 114n139, 129, 168, 227n86, 242n122
"poetic," as descriptor, lv
 applied by/to Vertov, xliii–xliv, xlivn84, xlv, xcii, 62, livn120
poetry
 cafés, 141, 142n56
 Futurist, xcv, 129, 142, 146, 153
 Mayakovsky's, xxvi, 141, 146, 153
 Vertov and, xxvi, lxix, xcv, xcvi, 3, 59–60, 106, 118, 125, 129, 132, 140–46, 150, 152, 153
  "Dziga Vertov," 147–48, 148n71, 239n114
  epigram dedicated to Purishkevich, 3, 57–58, 58n183, 61
  "etudes," 132–35, *134*, 254
  "Masha," 3, 61, 62n188
  "Olga Toom," 239–40, 239n114
  "Start," 272–73
pogrom(s), 17n46, 42n123, 48n148, 49n149, 259–60, 260n155
 Bialystok (1906), 32n97, 42n123, 47, 50–52, 51–52n159, 53, 54, 62, 80
 films about, 259–60n155
 Masha Gal'pern's assistance to victims of, 53, 62
 Nicholas II's approval/defense of, 52, 52n162
 wave, 47–48, 47n142, 53, 53n163, 63
 See also Black Hundreds
Poland
 Congress, 7–8n17, 8, 26
 independent, 53, 55
 Kingdom of, 27n76
 See also Bialystok
portraits
 documentary, xxxixn68
 film-portraits, lxvii, 195, 208–9, 209n44
Pravda, xlvii, lxi, 179n156, 212, 212n52, 220, 240n115, 280n209
Preobrazhenskij, Nikolaj, 225n79, 225n81, 227n85
Proletkult, 112, 119n155, 150n76
propaganda. *See* agitation; agit-train(s)
Protazanov, Iakov, xxivn30

Provisional Government, 126, 170n136, 171, 185n175, 188, 190, 224n75
 Boltianskij and, 97, 165
 leaders of, 86, 208
 Svobodnaia Rossiia and, 165, 208
Prussia, 6, 26, 46
Psychoneurological Institute, xcv, 58, 72–75, 72n11, 74n19, 75nn20–21, 77, 78–79, 78n36, 80, 84, 106–7
 Bekhterev and, 58, 72, 74–77, 74n18, 107, 107n22, 108–11, 291
 Boltianskij and, 90, 91, 91n65, 92–93, 163
 Bücher's influence at, 114–18, 118n152
 cinema/scientific films at, 98–99, 103–4, 105
 demonstrations at, 84n52, 85
 Kol'tsov and, 33, 85, 85–86n56, 86, 93, 157
 military hospital at, 78–79, 109
 Vertov and, xcv, 33, 58, 69–70, 71–72, 78, 85, 88–91, 98, 105, 106, 107n22, 126n10, 141, 143, 157, 272n189
"publicistic," as descriptor, xxxvii–xxxviii, xxxviinn61–62, xxxviiin66, xl, xliii
 applied to Vertov, xxxviin60, xxxvii–xxxix, xli, xlii, xliii–xlv, lvi, lxviiin159
Pudovkin, Vsevolod, xiv, lxxxi, xc, 123, 179n157, ln105, xxivn30
 documentary on, xxviin37, xlin74
Pumpyanskaya, Semiramida (Seda), xxiv, xxv, xlvin93
Purishkevich, Vladimir, 57, 63, 208, 224n75
 Vertov epigram dedicated to, 3, 57–58, 58n183, 61

R

Rabinbach, Anson, 106, 107n121, 109n128, 112n136, 113n137
Rabinowitch, Alexander, 186–87
Rainer, Yvonne, lxxi
Rappaport, Mark, lxxi
Raskol'nikov, Fyodor, 89–90, 89n61, 210, 223n75, 228n87
Red Army, 90, 142, 162, 181, 185n175, 214, 217n63, 227n86, 258, 259, 277–78n203
 Lenin agit-train and, 237, 256, 257
 October Revolution agit-train and, 261, 266, 281, 282
 in *Stride, Soviet*, 248, 249
Red Star Literary-Instructional Agit-Steamer of the All-Russia Central Executive Committee (Vertov), 185n173, 234n97

refugee(s), 79, 80n43, 90, 109, 161, 216n63
    crisis, 77–78, 77nn30–31, 80, 80n43,
        82–83, 122
    Kaufmans as, 70–71, 78, 98, 142
    Masha Gal'pern's work on behalf of,
        80–82
    Vertov as, xcv, 69, 98, 157, 161
Reifenberg, Benno, 65
Rejsner, Larisa, 74, 76n26, 88–90, 89, 89n61,
    97, 228n87
Rejsner, Mikhail, 74, 76, 76n26, 291,
    291n233, 292, 298
Rejtblat, A. I., 10, 22n61, 23, 30–31, 32,
    32n98
relics
    exposure of/exposure films, 213, 286,
        289–91n231, 289–92, 292n234
    of Gavriil, 49–50, 50n152, 289
Rice, Ron, lxx
Richter, Rolf, lxxxix
Rodchenko, Aleksandr, 84, 88, 153, 153n81
Room, Abram, xxivn30, ln105, 90, 91, 97
    Bed and Sofa, xv, 90–91
Rose, Olivia, lxxixn182
Rosen, Philip, 1–2, 203
Roshal', Lev, 126n10
Rouch, Jean, lvi, lviiin125, lviiin127,
    lixn130, lx, lxn134, lxvii, lxxii,
    lxxxiiin193
    Chronicle of a Summer, lviiin126, lix
Rozier, Jacques, lx
Ruspoli, Mario, lviin125
Russian Army, xcv, 18, 26, 42
    anti-Semitic policies of, 70, 70n3
Russian Association of Revolutionary Writers
    (RAPP), lxvn151
Russian Empire, xciv, xcv, 4, 6, 17n45,
    180, 183
    western, 7, 16, 25, 25n70, 27, 43, 44
    World War I casualties, 122
    See also Pale of Settlement
Russian Revolution (1905–7), 36, 47,
    lxxiiin171
Russian Telegraph Agency (ROSTA), 238,
    241n119
Russo-Japanese War, 42n124, 164
Ruttmann, Walter, li, lxxn162

S
Sadoul, Georges
    French Communist Party and, li, lviii,
        lxviii, liin111

*History of an Art: Cinema from Its Origins
    to Our Time*, li, lin109, liv–lv, lvn121,
        lviii, lxi
    Morin and, lviii, lviiin126
    as Stalin apologist, lviii, lviiin126
    Vertov revival and, xlvii, li–lii, liin113,
        livn120, lix–lxii, lixn129, lixn131,
        lxvii–lxix, lxviiin159, lxixn160
    Cahiers du Cinema, lviiin127, lix,
        lxxx
    cinéma-vérité, lii–liii, lv–lvi, lvn121,
        lviin125, lviii–lix, lviiinn126–27,
        lxvi, lxviii
Sauzier, Bertrand, lxxxvii
Savel'ev, A. *See Brain of Soviet Russia* (Vertov
    and Savel'ev)
Schiller, Friedrich, 5–6n10, 22, 117
Schlemmer, Edith, lxxin166
Schneider, Alan, xxvii
Scriabin, Aleksandr, 128–29, 130–31n25,
    130n22, 135n34
    Koptiaev on, 129–30, 129n20
    Vertov and, 128–32
    etudes, 132–35, 133n31, *134*, 134n32, 254
semiotic rectangle, 229, 229–33, 229n88
Serge, Victor, 86, 86n57, 227n86
Shcherbenok, Andrej, xxiv, xxivn30
Sheremetev, S. D., 47
Shingarev, Aleksandr, 189–90
Shklovsky, Viktor, xiv, lxxiiin173, 88, *88*,
    150n76, 271n185
"Where is Dziga Vertov Striding," xliv–xlvi,
    xlivn85, xlvn88
Shnejder, M., 195
Shub, Esfir', xiv, xxivn30, xxxvi, 153
    Fall of the Romanov Dynasty, xlviin94,
        xlixn100, 208n41
Sidenova, Raisa, xxxix, xliv
Sight and Sound, xxix
Simon, Bill, lxx
Sine-Fono, 94, 94n76, 99
Skobelev Committee, 97, 163–66, 164n119,
    165–66n125, 170, 184, 186, 188n179,
    189–90, 197, 198, 207–8, 208n42, 234
    Boltianskij and, 97, 157, 163, 164–65,
        184, 186, 225, 225n81
    demokratiia and, 184, 188
    Kino-Nedelia and, 164n119, 165,
        223–24n75
    nationalization of/absorption of, into
        Narkompros, 190–92, 190n185,
        191n188, 192n190

Skobelev Committee, films
   Born out of Chaos, 184, 184n170
   Elections to the Constituent Assembly, 171–72, 171n139
   In the Petrograd Proletariat's Children's Colony, 185, 185nn173–74
   October Revolution, 158–59n102, 180
   October Turning Point, 185n175
   Svobodnaia Rossiia, 165, 165n124, 171n138, 180, 180n160, 185, 185–86n175, 198, 206, 206n34, 208–10, 209n44, 224n76, 225n81
      Anniversary of the Revolution and, 195n5, 197
      few surviving issues of, 185n174, 206n34, 208n42
      Kino-Nedelia and, 223, 223n75
   Toward the Government of the People, 171n139, 190
   Toward the Opening of the Constituent Assembly, 170–71, 186–87, 187n177, 224n75
   Tsar Nicholas, Autocrat of All of Russia, 165n124, 180
Skrameh, Ivan, 240–41, 241n119, 265, 265n169
Smolianinov, N., 133, 133n31
Social Democratic Party, 32, 41, 44, 44n131, 76, 84, 84n53, 183n168
   on agitation vs. propaganda, 242, 242n122, 243n123
   Boltianskij and, 92, 163, 165, 184
socialist construction, 182, 204
socialist realism, xxxvii, lxiv
   Vertov and, xxxvi, lxv–lxvii, lxvn150, lxvin152, 153, lxxin168
Sonnenberg, Ben, xix
sound, lvi, lxvi, lxxxiin190, xcv, 65, 115, 118, 127, 137, 138n44, 148
   collage, 3
   of "Dziga," 155
   image and, lxxxn184, 151, 230, 232
   "laboratory of hearing," 69, 128, 135, 135n35
   organization of, 38, 64, 139
   recording of, 3, 64, 136–37, 136n39, 138n44
   "sounds of a sawmill," 64, 136, 136n39, 137
   soundtrack for *Enthusiasm*, 90, 119, 137, 151
   sync-sound interviews, xxxixn68, lxvi–lxvii

   See also Boltianskij, Grigorij; "Photographing Sound"; music; noise; Scriabin, Aleksandr
Sovkino, xlv
St. Petersburg, xcv, 16, 17n46, 26, 26n71, 100, 127
   "Bloody Sunday," 36
Stalin, Joseph, xxviii, xxxiv, xxxivn54, xl, liiin13, lxxiii, xcii, 65n191, 76n24, 153–54, 257
   death of, xix, 107n122
   era, xxiv, xxv, xxviii, xxxv, xxxvi, xxxviii, xxxix, xliii, lix, 77, 210, 235n100
   anti-cosmopolitan campaign, xxiii, xxxv
   First Congress of Soviet Writers, lxiv–lxv
   "varnishing" of reality, liii
   vydvizhentsy, 161–62
   Khrushchev's/Thaw era's denunciations of, xxxiv, xl
   role of, in the battle for Tsaritsyn, 222–23n74
   Sadoul as apologist for, lviii, lviiin126, lix
   Vertov's praise of, xcii, xciii
   Lullaby as Stalin panegyric, xl–xli, lxxxix
Stam, Robert, lxxviiin180
Stanislawski, Michael, 15n38, 18, 20, 20–21n57, 24
Starevich, Ladislas, 101, 102, 165n125, 184, 282
   Grasshopper and the Ant, The, 277, 280
Stepanova, Varvara, 84, 153, 153n81
Stride, Soviet (Vertov), xlivn85, lviiin127, 228n87, 246–47, 249, 269, 270, 297–98
   agit-train murals and, 246–51, 255–56
   availability/release of, xxxin47
   "evening is full of contrasts" sequence, 150, 251–55, *252*, *253*, *254*
   footage from *Kino-Nedelia* in, 197, 197n10
   screenings of, xlviii, xlixn100
Svilova, Elizaveta, xix, xxiv, *xxix*, xxxiv, xxxvi, xxviiin40, xlvi, xlvin93, xlix, xlixn99, lxvi, lxviii, 63, 233
   Articles, Diaries, Projects and, xl, xln72
   Film Culture's consultation with, lxxn163, xxxiin48
   memoir, xxv–xxvi, 222n73
   Sadoul's consultation with, lii, lix, lxi, lxviiin159
   Skobelev Committee and, 191n189, 222n73

trip to Europe (1974), lxxin166, lxxxiii, lxxxiiin193
as Vertov's wife/collaborator, xvii, xxv, xciv, 125n9, 141n51, 156, 222, 222n73, 239
Svobodnaia Rossiia (Skobelev Committee), 165, 165n124, 171n138, 180, 180n160, 185, 185–86n175, 198, 206, 206n34, 208–10, 209n44, 224n76, 225n81
Anniversary of the Revolution and, 195n5, 197
few surviving issues of, 185n174, 206n34, 208n42
Kino-Nedelia and, 223, 223n75

T

Tarle, Evgenij, 76, 76n27
Tasin, Georgij, 90, 91, 97
Tatlin, Vladimir, 143
Taylorism, lxxxiv–lxxxv, 117, 238
Vertov and, lxxixn183, lxxxiv–lxxxv, lxxxvn196, lxxxviii
Thaw, xxxvii, xxxviii, xlii, xliiin78, xliii–xlivn81, lxiv
call for truth telling, liii
denunciations of Stalin, xxxiv, xl
Third International Leipzig Documentary and Short Film Week, xlviii, xlviii–xlvixn99
Three Heroines (Vertov), lxvii
Three Songs of Lenin (Vertov), xxiii, xxvi, xxxvi, l, lviiin127, lxiii, 123, 269, 270, 298–99
Agapov on, lxv, lxvn150
availability/releases, xxxin47, lxvn150, xlviin97
Bogdanov on, lxv, lxvn150
censorship in, 231
folk influences in, 117, 154, *154*
footage from *Kino-Nedelia* in, 197, 197n10, *198*
Kopalin on, xxxvi, xxxviii–xxxix
Lebedev on, xxxvn56
screenings of, xlvi, xlvin93, xlviii, xlixn100, lin106, lin108, lxvn150
sync-sound interviews, lxvi, xxxixn68
Tisse, Eduard, 89n61, 165–66n125, 197n11, 211, 214n57, 292n236
Tolstoy, Leo, 15, 31–32n96, 117
Abel Kaufman and, 13n33, 31, 61–62, 285n222
Vertov and, 285, 285n222, xivn7

Toom, Olga, 128, 239–40, 239–40n115, 241n119, 281n212
Toti, Gianni, lxxxix
Toward the Government of the People (Skobelev Comittee), 171n139, 190
Toward the Opening of the Constituent Assembly (Skobelev Committee), 170–71, 186–87, 187n177, 224n75
To You, Front! (Vertov), xxvii, 297
Trajnin, Ilya, xlv, xlvn87
Trial of [Colonel Filipp] Mironov (Vertov), 209
Triolet, Elsa, li–lii
Trotsky, Leon, 89, 178n155, 179n156, 183n167, 185, 209n45, 220n69, 222n74
agit-trains and, 235n100, 237, 279
in *Kino-Nedelia*, 196n7, 210
Tsar Nicholas II, Autocrat of All of Russia (Skobelev Committee), 165n124, 180
Tsejtlin, Boris, 214
Tsivian, Yuri, xxxn44, lxxxvii, 134–35, 145
Tuberculosis (Khanzhonkov), 102–2
typhus, 90, 248–50, 249, 250n136, 262

U

Ukraine, 26, 91, 92, 93, 126, 186n175, 213, 250n136, 258, 258n151, 265
anti-Jewish violence in, 49n149, 260n156
Civil War in, 158, 179n155, 194, 211 214n57, 259
newsreels from, 194n2, 201
Vertov in, 71, 91, 125n9, 126n10, 140n46
Vertov's current eminence in, xxxiii, xxxiiin52
Ukrainian
dziga as a Ukrainian word, 155
holdings in Abel Kaufman's library, 13n32, 22
Union of the Archangel Michael, 42n123, 57
Union of the Russian People, 42n123, 52n162

V

Vagner, Vladimir, 74, 103–5, 104n109
VanDerBeek, Stan, lxx, lxxn163
Vaughan, Dai, lxxiv–lxxv, lxxvn174
Verdone, Mario, xlix
Vertov, Dziga (David Kaufman), 35, 37, 67, 233
Boltianskij and, 90, 91, 96, 96n83, 97, 98, 105, 163, 228n87
death of, xxiv, xxv, xxxiii, xxxiv, xxxv, xlvin93, 233

documentaries on, xxvii–xxviii, xxviinn38–39, xxviiin40, 25n69
kinocs, xv, xxxixn68, lxxxi, 85, 192, 209, 270–71
Kol'tsov and, lxv, 33, 85, 86, 90, 97, 125, 155, 157, 161, 162, 197
last years of, xxiii–xxv, xxivn28, xxviin38
Masha Gal'pern and, xxiv, xxiv28, 18, 53, 60, 61, 62–63, 70, 82n48, 105, 156
Mayakovsky and, xxvi, 123, 141, 142, 143–44, 143n61, 144n63, 146, 147–58
name change of, 140, 154–56, 155n88
recovery/revival, xxxiii–xxxv, xlvii
Vertov, Dziga (David Kaufman), films
 Anniversary of the Revolution, 195, 197, 232, 280, 281
  found footage in, 188, 195, 195n5, 223–24n75, 227, 227n85
 Battle for Tsaritsyn, The, 89, 221–22, 222–23n74, 222n73, 234
 Brain of Soviet Russia (with Savel'ev), 105n5, 160n107, 209n44, 223n75, 225n80
  footage from *Kino-Nedelia* in, 195, 210, 226–27, 227n85
  showing of, on agit-trains, 280, 280n211, 281, 282
 Eleventh Year, The, xxxin47, xlixn100, ln105, 113, 204, 214, 269
  Brunius on, lxxxviii
  footage from, in *Shadow of Machines*, 231, 232
 Enthusiasm: Symphony of the Donbass, xlixn199, lxxxv, 182, 214, 223, 269, 270
  availability/releases of, xxxin47
  denunciation of, xxxvn56
  restoration of, lxxin166
  soundtrack, 90, 119, 137, 151
 History of the Civil War, 228n87, 232, 234, 249n35
  footage from *Kino-Nedelia* in, 197, 197n11, 217n63, 228, 228n87
  intertitles, 220n69
 Kino-Eye: Life Caught Unawares, xii–xiiin2, xxxvn56, xcvi, 148, 185n173, 239n115, 242, 297
  availability/releases of, xxxin47
  "beef to bull" sequence in, 66, 246
  Kino-Pravda, xx, xxi, xxxvi, lii, liii, lxvi, xcv, 83, 83n49, 123, 147, 197n10, 200, 201n20, 202, 203, 205, 209, 215, 231, 233, 241, 242, 269, 299

   availability/releases of, ln102, xxxin47
   footage from *Kino-Nedelia* in, 197, 197n10
  Kino-Pravda 21 ("Lenin" *Kino-Pravda*), xxxvi, xlviii–xlix, xlixn100, 123
  Pravda and, lv, lxi
  screenings of, xlviii–xlix, xlixn100, ln102
 Lullaby, xxiii, xxvii, xl–xli, *lxxxvi*, lxxxix, 240n115, 270
  screenings of, xlvi, xlvin93, lxxxix
  sound-sync interviews in, xxxixn68, lxxvi–lxxvii
 Man with a Movie Camera, xv–xvi, xxi, xxxiii, xl, *xlviii*, liii, lvin124, *lxviii*, lxx, lxxiv, , lxxxiiin193, lxxxv, lxxxviii–lxxxixn206, xci, xciin216, 63, 102, 113, 119, 150, 155, 179, 181, 222, 232, 250, 254, 270, 282, 297, 297
  availability/releases of, xxx, xxxn44, xxxin47, xxxi, l–li, lin106, lin108
  Baudry on, lxxvi, lxxvi–lxxvii
  Bonitzer on, lxxvi–lxxvii, lxxviin177
  Comolli on, xvi–xviin14
  as critical/popular favorite, xxix, xxixn43
  Crofts and Rose on, lxxixn182
  as inspiring view of Vertov as a disorderly filmmaker, lxxxvii, lxxxviin199
  Michelson on, lxxxixn181, lxxn164
  Mikhail Kaufman in, xc, 214
  montage in, liii, lxxvii
  "morning" sequence, 90
  musical scores for, xxx, xxxn45
  production/socialist construction in, 182, 204
  screenings of, xix, xxiii, xxiiin27, xlviii, xlvin92, xlix, xlixnn99–100
  self-referentiality/critique of representation in, lxx, lxxiv–lxxvi, lxxvii–lxxviii, lxxviin177, lxxviii–lxxx, xc, 204, 214
  Stam on, lxxviiin180
  Weibel on, lxxviiin180
 Man with a Movie Camera (Vertov)
  charges of Vertov's "formalism" and, xxxvi, xlvin92
  references to, in film classes/textbooks, xxx, xxx–xxxiin46
 One Sixth of the World, xxxvi, xlvii, 113, 113n138, 140, 181–82, 204, 214, 298
  availability/releases of, xxxin47

foreign/bourgeois visitors in, 181, 266n172
screenings of, xlvii, xlviii, li
second-person address in, 182, 270
Zhemchuzhnyj on, 202
Red Star Literary-Instructional Agit-Steamer of the All-Russia Central Executive Committee, 185n173, 234n97
Soviet Caucasus, The, script for film about the agit-train, 267–69, 268nn178–79, 269n180
Stride, Soviet, xlivn85, lviiin127, 228n87, 246–47, 249, 269, 270, 297–98
    agit-train murals and, 246–51, 255–56
    availability/release of, xxxin47
    "evening is full of contrasts" sequence, 150, 251–55, *252, 253, 254*
    footage from *Kino-Nedelia* in, 197, 197n10
    screenings of, xlviii, xlixn100
Three Heroines, lxvii
Three Songs of Lenin, xxiii, xxvi, xxxvi, l, lviiin127, lxiii, 123, 269, 270, 298–99
    Agapov on, lxv, lxvn150
    availability/releases, lxvn150, xlviiin97, xxxin47
    Bogdanov on, lxv, lxvn150
    censorship in, 231
    folk influences in, 117, 154, *154*
    footage from *Kino-Nedelia* in, 197, 197n10, *198*
    Kopalin on, xxxvi, xxxviii–xxxix
    Lebedev on, xxxvn56
    screenings of, xlvi, xlvin93, xlviii, xlixn100, lin106, lin108, lxvn150
    sound-sync interviews in, lxvi, xxxixn68
Trial of [Colonel Filipp] Mironov, 209
To You, Front!, xxvii, 297
See also Kino-Nedelia (VFKO)
Vertov, Dziga (David Kaufman), writings/poems
    Articles, Diaries, Projects, xxxi, xl, lxii–lxiii, lxvii
    "Birth of Kino-Eye, The," lxii–lxiv, lxiiin146, lxvi, lxvii, 3, 3n4
    "Dziga Vertov," 147–48
    "From the Working Notebooks of Dziga Vertov," xliii, liii, lxii, lxxx
    "He and I," xx–xxii, xxin24, xxiii

"How Kino-Eye was Born and Developed" (1935 lecture), lxiii, lxiiin145, 63–64, 64n189, 135, 137–38
"Kinocs: A Revolution," xxxiin48, lii, lixn130, lxxx, 111, 152
"Kino-Eye," liv, livn120, lxv–lxvi, 284, 284n221
"We: Variant of a Manifesto," lxxxin189, 111
VGIK. *See* Higher State Cinema Institute (VGIK)
Viazzi, Glauco, lxixn161
Vigo, Jean, lxx
Vinkler, A., 97, 211n50
Volga (region), 83, 291
Volga (river), 89n61, 211, 217n65
Voznesenskij, Aleksandr, 86, 191

W

"We: Variant of a Manifesto" (Vertov), lxxxin189, 111
Weibel, Peter, lxxviiin180
Weisbrem, Israel, 26, 26n75
Whitman, Walt, x, xi, 1, 68, 121, 182, 193, 255
Winter, Jay, 121–22, 122n1, 123, 124, 124n8
World War I, 53, 68, 75n23, 76n26, 83, 90, 140n46, 239
    beginning of, 36, 54
    Vertov's drafting into Russian Army, xcv, 69, 71, 85, 125, 126, 160, 272n189
    See also refugee(s)
World Without Play (Makhnach), *xviii*, xxvii–xxviii, xxviinn37–39, xxviiin40, xli, lixn130

Y

Yiddish, 13n32, 14, 14n34, 14–15n37, 15–16n40
    holdings in Abel Kaufman's library, 13n32, 22, 30
    predominance of, in Bialystok, 13, 13n31, 32
Young Pioneers, lxxxvi, 192, 279

Z

Zabazlaev, Sergej, 292n236
Zamenhof, Ludwik, 32, 32n97
Zhdanov, Andrej, lxiv
Zhemchuzhnyj, Vitalij, 202–3
Zinoviev, Grigorij, 196n7, 210, 244n129
Zorkaia, Neia, lxxxix
Zrelishcha, 123, 130n22, 153n81

www.ingramcontent.com/pod-product-compliance
Lightning Source LLC
Chambersburg PA
CBHW051107230426
43667CB00014B/2469